Microsoft®
Excel
Version 2002
INSIDE OUT

The CD that helps you put your software to work!

Dig in—for the work-ready tools and resources that help you go way beyond just using Excel. You'll conquer it! Just like the INSIDE OUT book, we've designed your INSIDE OUT CD to be both comprehensive and supremely easy to use. All the tools, utilities, and add-ins have been tested against final Excel 2002 code—not beta. The sample chapters from other INSIDE OUT books help take your Office XP learning experience even deeper. You get essential links to online software updates, product support, and more—direct from the Microsoft Office team. And with the CD's intuitive HTML interface, you'll always know exactly where you are and what else you can do!

Your Inside Out CD features:

- Microsoft and Third-Party Add-ins—productivity-enhancing tools, utilities, demos, and trial software

- Office Tools on the Web—complete descriptions and links to official Microsoft Office resources on line

- Author Extras—handy templates, sample workbooks, databases, and financial tools

- More INSIDE OUT Books—sample chapters from INSIDE OUT books for other Office XP applications

- Complete Microsoft Press® eBook—the entire MICROSOFT EXCEL VERSION 2002 INSIDE OUT book in easy-search electronic format

- Step by Step Interactive Tutorials—trial version of official Microsoft interactive training for Office XP

Want to learn more? Read on for full details, including System Requirements (last page of this section).

Microsoft Add-Ins

Get Microsoft add-ins and tools for Excel—straight from the source.

Includes:

- ■ **MSN® MoneyCentral™ Stock Quotes Add-In**—get refreshable stock quotes right in Excel.

- ■ **Microsoft Office Visual Keyboard**—type in multiple languages on the same computer by using an on-screen keyboard for other languages.

- ■ **Microsoft Office Internet Free/Busy Service Wizard**—publish the blocks of time when you are free and when you are busy to a shared Internet location, so people who don't normally have access to your Microsoft Outlook® Calendar can check your schedule on the Web.

- ■ **Microsoft Visio® Auto-Demos**—use these customizable auto-demos to see how to put Visio diagramming software to work on your next project.

- ■ **Step by Step Interactive Tutorials**—try official Microsoft interactive training for Office XP, and teach yourself common tasks and key features and functions.

- ■ **Microsoft Office Sounds**—hear fun audio cues when you use toolbars, scroll bars, and dialog boxes, zoom in or out, or when you send mail.

Plus, Microsoft Excel Templates

Existing templates help you kick start your own projects. Use the sample templates included on this CD to learn more about Excel and get your work done more quickly.

- ■ **Currency Rates and Calculator**—this template uses a Web query to import today's world currency rates from MSN MoneyCentral. The built in calculator allows you to choose which currencies you want to convert to and from.

Microsoft Excel Templates *(continued)*

■ **Loan Calculator with extra payments**—once you enter your loan amount, annual interest rate, loan period, and optional extra payments, the template will display your payment schedule, principal, interest and ending balance for the life of the loan.

■ **Major Stock Indices**—this template uses a Web query to import the data for major U.S. stock market indices and shows the last price, previous close, high, low, volume, change, and more.

■ **Stock Quote Spreadsheet**—enter your stock symbols in cell B7. The Web query will automatically refresh and import stock data from MSN MoneyCentral. Build on this template to keep track of your own portfolio's performance.

Third-Party Utilities, Demos, and Trials

All the third-party add-ins on this CD have been tested for use with Excel 2002. In this section, you'll find all the details you need about each tool—including a full description, application size, system requirements, and installation instructions.

■ **MacroSystems Spreadsheet Assistant**—use this tool to knock off time-consuming tasks, such as selecting cells without scrolling or performing arithmetic functions on an entire range.

■ **ConvertAll Ltd. ConvertAll**—as unobtrusive as "Find & Replace" and works with the same ease and efficiency! Every conversion from $ to €, km to miles, lbs to kilos is executed quickly and effortlessly.

■ **HiSoftware's metaPackager**™—encapsulate your files in pure XML so they're easy to index and manage.

■ **Analycorp XLSim**™—perform risk-modeling and financial analyses with this easy-to-use Monte Carlo simulator for Microsoft Excel.

■ **ModernSoft's Financial Genome**™—develop fully integrated income statements, balance sheets, cash flow statements, ratio statements, and more.

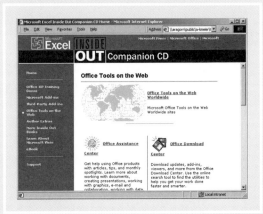

Office Tools on the Web

Here you'll find ready links to the most helpful and informative online resources for Office XP, direct from Microsoft. Find out exactly how each site can help you get your work done—then click and go!

Office Assistance Center

Get help using Office products with articles, tips, and monthly spotlights. Learn more about working with documents, data, and graphics; using e-mail and collaboration features; creating presentations and Web pages; and using everyday time-savers.

Office eServices

Use these Web services to get the most from Office. Learn how to store and share files on the Web; build and host Web sites; find communication services, language translation, learning and reference, and online postage resources; tune up your computer; and much more!

Office Product Updates

Obtain recommended and critical updates to enhance your Office XP experience.

Office Download Center

Download updates, add-ins, viewers, and more from the Office Download Center. Use the online search tool to find the utilities to help you work faster and smarter.

Design Gallery Live

Pick out clip art or photos for your Office project from this huge royalty-free selection. New items are constantly added to meet your needs. The advanced search facility makes finding the right artwork quick and easy.

Microsoft Office Template Gallery

Instead of starting from scratch, download a template from the Template Gallery. From calendars to business cards, marketing material, and legal documents, Template Gallery offers hundreds of professionally authored and formatted documents for Microsoft Office.

Online Troubleshooters

Microsoft has developed Office XP online troubleshooters to help you solve problems on the fly. Access them using the links on the CD—and get the diagnostic and problem-solving information you need.

Microsoft Excel
Version 2002
INSIDE OUT

Author Extras

Here's where your Inside Out author went the extra mile: more than 70 great sample files, ready for you to take apart and study! It's an excellent way to make the examples used inside the book come to life on your PC.

Includes:

- Ready-to-use templates
- Sample workbooks
- Sample databases
- Financial tools
- Examples of statistical analysis

More Inside Out Books

The Inside Out series from Microsoft Press delivers comprehensive reference on the Office XP suite of applications. On this CD, you'll find sample chapters from the companion titles listed below, along with details about the entire line of books:

- Microsoft FrontPage® Version 2002 Inside Out
- Microsoft Office XP Inside Out
- Microsoft Outlook Version 2002 Inside Out
- Microsoft Word Version 2002 Inside Out

Microsoft Excel
Version 2002
INSIDE OUT

Complete Microsoft Press eBook

You get the entire MICROSOFT EXCEL VERSION 2002 INSIDE OUT book on CD—along with sample chapters from other INSIDE OUT books—as searchable electronic books. These Microsoft Press eBooks install quickly and easily on your computer (see System Requirements for details) and enable rapid full-text search.

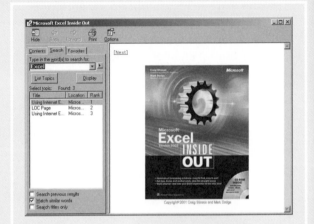

Features:

- Super-fast HTML full-text search
- Full-size graphics and screen shots
- Copy, paste, and *print* functions
- Bookmarking capabilities
- A saved history of every file viewed during a session

CD Minimum System Requirements

- Microsoft Windows® 95 or later operating system (including Windows 98, Windows Millennium Edition, Windows NT® 4.0 with Service Pack 3, Windows 2000, or Windows XP)
- 266-MHz or higher Pentium-compatible CPU
- 64 megabytes (MB) RAM
- 8X CD-ROM drive or faster
- 46 MB of free hard disk space (to install the eBook and interactive tutorials)
- 800 x 600 with high color (16-bit) display settings
- Microsoft Windows compatible sound card and speakers
- Microsoft Internet Explorer 4.01 or higher
- Microsoft Mouse or compatible pointing device

NOTE
System Requirements may be higher for the add-ins available on the CD. Individual add-in system requirements are specified on the CD. An Internet connection is necessary to access the hyperlinks in the Office Tools on the Web section. Connect time charges may apply.

Craig Stinson
Contributing Editor, PC Magazine

Mark Dodge
Microsoft Excel expert

Microsoft

Microsoft®
Excel
Version 2002

INSIDE
OUT

- **Hundreds of timesaving solutions—easy to find, easy to use!**
- **Get tips, tricks, and workarounds, plus the straight scoop**
- **Work smarter—and take your Excel experience to the next level**

PUBLISHED BY
Microsoft Press
A Division of Microsoft Corporation
One Microsoft Way
Redmond, Washington 98052-6399

Library of Congress Cataloging-in-Publication Data
Dodge, Mark.
    Microsoft Excel Version 2002 Inside Out / Mark Dodge, Craig Stinson.
        p. cm.
    Includes index.
    ISBN 0-7356-1281-1
    1. Microsoft Excel for Windows.   2. Business--Computer programs.   3. Electronic
spreadsheets. I. Stinson, Craig, 1943- II. Title.

    HF5548.4.M523 D627   2001
    005.369--dc21   2001030327

Printed and bound in the United States of America.

3 4 5 6 7 8 9   QWT   7 6 5 4 3

Distributed in Canada by H.B. Fenn and Company Ltd.

A CIP catalogue record for this book is available from the British Library.

Microsoft Press books are available through booksellers and distributors worldwide. For further information about international editions, contact your local Microsoft Corporation office or contact Microsoft Press International directly at fax (425) 936-7329. Visit our Web site at microsoft.com/mspress. Send comments to *mspinput@microsoft.com*.

Acquisitions Editor: Kong Cheung
Project Editor: Kristen Weatherby
Series Editor: Sandra Haynes

Body Part No. X08-03792

Contents At A Glance

Contents At A Glance

Table of Contents

Chapter 3
Custom-Tailoring the Excel Workspace 65

newfeature!

newfeature!

newfeature!

newfeature!

Chapter 8

Worksheet Formatting Techniques 199

Part 4
Adding Graphics and Printing   285

Chapter 10
Creating Spiffy Graphics   287

Chapter 11
Printing and Presenting   335

Chapter 17
Functions for Analyzing Statistics 471

Chapter 18
Performing What-If Analysis 499

Chapter 26

Working with Chart Data 671

Chapter 27
Advanced Charting Techniques   687

Part 9
Managing Databases and Lists   703

Chapter 28
Managing Information in Lists   705

Chapter 29
Working with External Data   749

Chapter 30
Analyzing Data with
PivotTable Reports   789

newfeature!

Part 10
Working with Visual Basic and Macros

831

Chapter 34
Debugging Macros and Custom Functions   887

Part 11
Appendixes   901

Appendix A
Installing Microsoft Excel   903

Appendix B
Using Speech and Handwriting Recognition   911

newfeature!

Acknowledgments

Many thanks to the acquisitions and production teams at Microsoft Press—Casey Doyle, Kong Cheung, Kristen Weatherby, and Bill Teel—for your unfailing professionalism and support, and to Jimmie Young and his group at Prolmage (Shan Young, Jim McCarter, Michelle Roudebush, Nancy Albright, Christy Parrish, and Susan Pink) for raising this baby up from manuscript to pages. And, as always, a huge thank you to my own group at home—Jean, Russell, and Miranda.

—Craig Stinson

As writers, we're the ones that have to do most of the sweating at the beginning, pumping chapters into the editorial pipeline at a torrid pace. But we usually miss the fun of the publishing endgame, where editorial and production schedules collide with reality, and where people have to take up the slack. My hat's off to everyone involved, including Kristen Weatherby, Kong Cheung, Jimmie Young, Jim McCarter, Allen Wyatt, Michelle Roudebush, Nancy Albright, Christy Parrish, Susan Pink, Bill Teel, Jim Kramer. Thanks for doing such a great job from inside (and outside) the ol' Microsoft Press-sure cooker. Musical thanks to melody-master Mark Knopfler for introducing us to Charlie Mason and Jeremiah Dixon, who "did America" and drew the line.

—Mark Dodge

We'd Like to Hear from You!

Our goal at Microsoft Press is to create books that help you find the information you need to get the most out of your software.

The INSIDE OUT series was created with you in mind. As part of an effort to ensure that we're creating the best, most useful books we can, we talked to our customers and asked them to tell us what they need from a Microsoft Press series. Help us continue to help you. Let us know what you like about this book and what we can do to make it better. When you write, please include the title and author of this book in your e-mail, as well as your name and contact information. We look forward to hearing from you.

How to Reach Us

E-mail:	nsideout@microsoft.com
Mail:	Inside Out Series Editor
	Microsoft Press
	One Microsoft Way
	Redmond, WA 98052

Note: Unfortunately, we can't provide support for any software problems you might experience. Please go to http://support.microsoft.com *for help with any software issues.*

Conventions and Features Used in This Book

This book uses special text and design conventions to make it easier for you to find the information you need.

Text Conventions

Convention	Meaning
Abbreviated menu commands	For your convenience, this book uses abbreviated menu commands. For example, "Choose Tools, Track Changes, Highlight Changes" means that you should click the Tools menu, point to Track Changes, and select the Highlight Changes command.
Boldface type	**Boldface** type is used to indicate text that you enter or type.
Initial Capital Letters	The first letters of the names of menus, dialog boxes, dialog box elements, and commands are capitalized. Example: the Save As dialog box.
Italicized type	*Italicized* type is used to indicate new terms.
Plus sign (+) in text	Keyboard shortcuts are indicated by a plus sign (+) separating two key names. For example, Ctrl+Alt+Delete means that you press the Ctrl, Alt, and Delete keys at the same time.

Design Conventions

newfeature!

This text identifies a new or significantly updated feature in this version of the software.

InsideOut

These are the book's signature tips. In these tips, you'll find get the straight scoop on what's going on with the software—inside information on why a feature works the way it does. You'll also find handy workarounds to deal with some of these software problems.

tip Tips provide helpful hints, timesaving tricks, or alternative procedures related to the task being discussed.

Troubleshooting

Look for these sidebars to find solutions to common problems you might encounter. Troubleshooting sidebars appear next to related information in the chapters. You can also use the Troubleshooting Topics index at the back of the book to look up problems by topic.

Cross-references point you to other locations in the book that offer additional information on the topic being discussed.

 This icon indicates sample files or text found on the companion CD.

caution Cautions identify potential problems that you should look out for when you're completing a task or problems that you must address before you can complete a task.

note Notes offer additional information related to the task being discussed.

Sidebar

The sidebars sprinkled throughout these chapters provide ancillary information on the topic being discussed. Go to sidebars to learn more about the technology or a feature.

Part 1

Examining the Excel Environment

What's New in Microsoft Excel 2002

Sometimes new versions of software just don't seem compelling enough for you to take the upgrade plunge. You wonder how many more big leaps can really be made in usability and functionality. Microsoft Excel has certainly evolved into a "mature" program. Nonetheless, this release is much more than cosmetic. Microsoft Excel 2002 includes lots of improvements to existing features and a few major new features that will have a positive impact on the way you work. Because most of us use more than one Microsoft Office program, many of the new features involve interoperability and consistency between Office applications, making your work easier and more intuitive. Here's an overview of the exciting new features you'll find in Microsoft Excel 2002 and Microsoft Office XP, including cross-references to the full discussions of each feature elsewhere in this book.

New Microsoft Office Features

With each new version, Microsoft improves the integration between the various Office applications and finds new ways to make each application more efficient. Numerous improvements have been made to each of the applications that comprise the various configurations of Microsoft Office, as well as many Office-wide *shared features,* which perform tasks that are common to all Office applications (such as opening and searching for files).

Before we enumerate the major new and improved features, we'll highlight a couple of the most visible and significant enhancements to the Microsoft Office experience: the *task pane* and *smart tags.*

3

The Task Pane

The task pane is the first new feature you'll notice, as you can see in Figure 1-1. It's hard to miss, and it radically repackages a few existing features and helps make them smarter, more responsive, and less intrusive than dialog boxes.

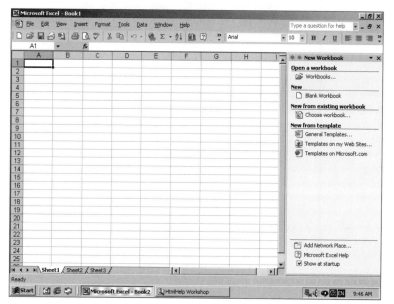

Figure 1-1.   The task pane appears on the right side of the workspace when you start Excel.

The task pane now is the primary entry point for creating new files, accessing templates, opening recently used files, searching for files, copying multiple items, inserting clip art, and more. The beauty of the task pane is its ability to cohabit with other workspace elements, unlike the dialog boxes it replaces. A dialog box is always in the way, demands your attention before you can do anything else, and hides its options and settings from you until you choose to display it. Conversely, the task pane remains available, stays out of your way, and makes its options visible at all times. Of course, it's easy to hide if you need the elbow room.

Because the task pane is so widely used, it is discussed in several places in this book. See "Using Template Files to Store Formatting" on page 253, "More AutoShapes" on page 298, "Using Clip Art and Other Media" on page 313, "Recovering from Crashes" on page 16, and "Creating and Opening Workbooks" on page 32.

Smart Tags

Smart tags give you instant access to commands and actions that are relevant to the task at hand. Many editing actions, such as copying and pasting cells, invoke a smart tag that appears adjacent to the last cell edited. If you click the tag, a *smart tag action menu* offers retroactive editing options, as shown in Figure 1-2.

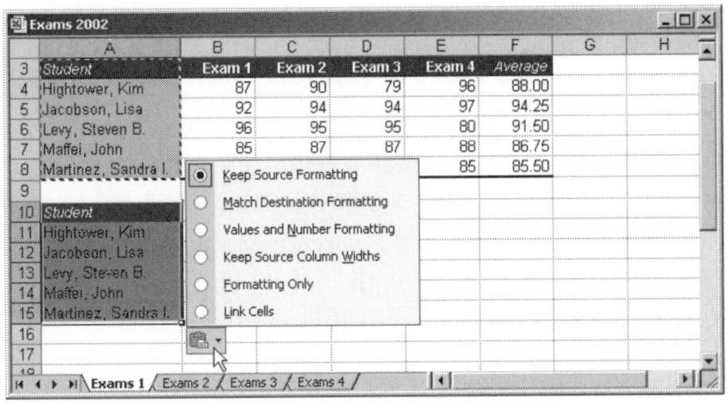

Figure 1-2. Click a smart tag to display the smart tag action menu.

Smart tags are *extensible*. That means that third-party developers can create custom smart tags that can be individually used for specific tasks. There are two custom smart tags included with Excel—one that recognizes your personal e-mail addresses and one that recognizes standard financial symbols. Additional custom smart tags will be made available on the Microsoft Office Update Web site.

Smart tags pop up in many situations, so you can read about them in several places in this book. For examples of smart tag use, see Chapter 7, "Worksheet Editing Techniques", "Understanding Numeric Text Entries" on page 113, "Tracing Errors" on page 264, "Copying Formulas and Pasting Only Their Resulting Values" on page 383, and "Entering a Series of Dates" on page 442.

Office Improvements

Besides the task pane, the most visible changes in Microsoft Office XP applications are the improvements that have been made to the user interface. All Office applications have a new "flatter" look that was designed for higher-resolution displays, and that renders the interface less obtrusive, allowing highlighted elements such as commands and toolbar buttons to really stand out. Here are some more specific interface improvements:

- **Opening and saving files.** The Open and Save As dialog boxes have been redesigned, allowing you to resize them by dragging the resize handle in the lower right corner of the dialog box. For more information, see "Saving Files" on page 37 and "Opening Files" on page 44.

- **Accessing FTP Sites.** If you regularly save files to or retrieve them from a particular FTP site, you can add that site to the My Places bar. The My Places bar is a navigational panel that appears at the left edge of Excel's Open and Save As dialog boxes. See "Adding a Site to Your My Places Bar" on page 555.

● **Searching for files.** The Search feature has a new interface and a new Basic Text Search option. In addition, you can selectively search for files in network locations, and even within Microsoft Outlook. See "Searching for Files" on page 49.

● **Getting help.** The Ask A Question box in the menu bar is now the primary entry point for the online Help system, and accepts plain-language queries to help you get unstuck. When you display a help topic, the Help window now includes the AutoTile button, which arranges the Excel program window and the Help window together on the screen. Many of you might be excited to learn that you can now dismiss the Office Assistant character permanently. See "Online Help Works—Really!" on page 54.

● **Copying multiple items.** The newly redesigned Collect And Copy feature lets you post twice as many items (24) to the Office Clipboard and uses the new Clipboard task pane. See "Collecting Multiple Items on the Clipboard" on page 148.

● **Using clip art.** The Insert Clip Art button now displays the Insert Clip Art task pane, which allows better interactivity and increased flexibility when working with art. The new Media Gallery represents a major overhaul of the old Clip Gallery, and allows you to easily organize and extend your media library. See "Using Clip Art and Other Media" on page 313.

New Office Features

These new features represent major enhancements to the Office family that significantly expand the horizons of all Office programs:

● **Voice recognition.** It is now possible to use your own voice to issue commands, navigate, and dictate text into Excel and other Office programs. You "train" the voice recognition feature to recognize the unique qualities of your voice and pronunciation tendencies for increased accuracy; the more you train, the better it works. See Appendix B, "Using Speech and Handwriting Recognition."

● **Handwriting input.** If you have a drawing pad and stylus (and even if you don't) you can now enter text directly into Excel and other Office programs using your own handwriting. See Appendix B, "Using Speech and Handwriting Recognition."

● **Full-featured diagrams.** No longer must you build the most widely used diagrams from scratch using rudimentary tools on the Drawing toolbar. You can now add full-featured, editable organizational charts, Venn diagrams, and other diagram types into your documents. See "Inserting Organization Charts" on page 319 and "Inserting Diagrams" on page 320.

- **Crash recovery.** If an Office program encounters a problem, it attempts to save any files that were open at the time the problem occurred and makes them available when you restart. If an Office program fails to start, the new Office Safe Mode feature helps preserve settings, and offers troubleshooting assistance the next time you start Windows. See "Recovering from Crashes" on page 16.

New Microsoft Excel Features

Most of the improvements made to Microsoft Excel 2002, beyond the Office-wide enhancements described in the previous section, are focused on usability, reliability, and collaboration. This version also includes several important enhancements to Excel's already formidable arsenal of data analysis tools.

What's Missing?

Most of the time, software upgrades provide features beyond what was previously available. But as we've come to realize over the years, upgrades also usually mean some features seem to disappear. Most of the time they don't really go away, they are just absorbed into another feature, or are renamed for one reason or another.

Among the things you will no longer see in Excel are Data Mapping (the Map button), Sound Notes, and XLM Macros. These are gone; no equivalent functionality exists in Microsoft Excel 2002. The Report Manager is no longer available as a "shipped" add-in, but you can still find it on the Office Update Web site (*officeupdate.microsoft.com*).

The New dialog box is gone forever, ably replaced by the New Workbook task pane. The New command still exists on the File menu, but instead of displaying a dialog box, it displays the task pane.

Usability Features

New and improved features don't always increase a program's usability—sometimes it's quite the opposite. The following sections introduce some that do help make Excel more usable.

Formatting

A well-formatted worksheet can illustrate the difference between data and information, taking hard-to-interpret data and making it easier to understand. Excel includes several new and improved features that assist you in this quest for greater understanding:

- **Cell formatting.** These new options are in the Format Cells dialog box:

  - The Number tab offers Locale options for the Special category, with over 120 worldwide formats for phone numbers and postal codes. See "Using the Special Formats" on page 214.

  - The Alignment tab allows text to be displayed right-to-left under certain conditions. This tab also features a Right Indent option and Distributed options; you can use the latter to evenly distribute individual fragments of text within a cell. See "Aligning Data in Cells" on page 223.

- **Border drawing.** A pencil-shaped tool can drag borders wherever you want them. See "Drawing Borders" on page 234.

- **Merge And Center.** This button is now a toggle; unmerge cells by clicking the Merge And Center button again. See "Selecting Alignment Using Toolbars" on page 229.

- **Picture formatting.** The new Washout option creates images similar to watermarks; the new Compress option reduces the amount of disk space used by images. See "Formatting Pictures" on page 322.

- **AutoShape rotation.** To make rotational manipulation of graphic objects more accessible, all two-dimensional objects now display a handle you can drag to rotate the object. These work so well that they even took the Rotate button off the Drawing toolbar. See "Working with AutoShapes" on page 296.

Printing

Printing has always been one of the trickier tasks in Excel, because unlike word-processing programs, spreadsheets are not confined to a paper-sized workspace. The new version of Excel resolves a few thorny printing issues and also adds a few helpful new features. (For more information on the following features, see Chapter 11, "Printing and Presenting.")

- Use the Find Printer button in the Print dialog box to search for any printer available on your network.

- Eliminate blank pages that might exist within the print range, because Excel now looks at the content of the current worksheet before sending it to the printer.

- Add graphics to Headers and Footers.

- Print pages set to A4 paper size on printers loaded with standard Letter size paper (and vice versa), and Excel adjusts the page setup.

- Suppress the printing of error values that appear on your worksheet.

Editing and Organizing

You strive to make sure that your workbooks speak the truth, and do so loud and strong, with clarity and structure. The faster and easier it is to accomplish these goals, the better. These features will help:

- **Error Checking.** This command quickly finds error values in the current worksheet. This is an invaluable aid when working with large worksheet models where tracking down error values can be an eye-straining experience. See "Checking for Errors" on page 257.

- **Color-coding sheet tabs.** Sheet tabs can be colored, offering more organizational flexibility in your workbooks. See "Coloring Sheet Tabs" on page 119.

- **Finding and replacing.** Excel now makes it possible to find and replace formatting and search the entire workbook, not just the current sheet. See "Finding and Replacing Stuff" on page 182.

- **Editing hyperlinks.** Hyperlinks used to be tricky to edit. You can now click a hyperlink and hold the mouse button, and after a second the cell is selected; then you can edit, format, or delete the link. See the tip "Edit hyperlinks easily" on page 580.

- **Inserting symbols.** Excel now provides access to the complete character set of all fonts installed on your computer, allowing you to enter characters with diacritical marks, symbols, and other "hidden" characters beyond those visible on the keyboard. See "Entering Symbols" on page 114.

Data Analysis Features

Analyzing data and crunching numbers are the principal functions of a spreadsheet program. As mature as these features already seem in Excel, there is always room for improvement:

- **AutoSum.** No longer is the AutoSum button a one-trick pony. Now it is possible to enter other popular functions, including Average, Count, Max, or Min instead of the SUM function. See "Using the AutoSum Button" on page 365.

- **The Function Wizard.** The functionality of the relocated Insert Function button has been completely overhauled. This is a major step forward in usability and includes a function search feature that allows you to find the right function by entering a plain language description of what you're trying to do. See "Inserting Functions" on page 366

● **Function ScreenTips.** Most of us use certain functions infrequently, but often enough that we know generally what the arguments are all about, but not necessarily the order in which they must appear. Now when you enter or edit a function, Excel displays a pop-up box showing the function syntax, so you don't have to spend time consulting online Help or the Function Wizard. See "Using Excel's Built-In Function Reference" on 389.

● **The Evaluate Formula command.** Editing and debugging long, complex formulas can be a major headache. The Evaluate Formula command helps debug complex formulas by stepping you through each calculation and showing you the results. See "Auditing and Documenting Worksheets" on page 256.

● **The Formula Watch Window.** If you need to keep an eye on remote cells as you make changes to other parts of a worksheet, the Formula Watch Window provides remote viewing of multiple cells on any open worksheet and provides dynamic data about each formula, including its location, its resulting value, and more. See "Watching Formulas" on page 260.

● **Text To Speech.** When you are faced with the task of hand-entering a lot of data, it is always prudent to double-check your entries for typing errors. Excel can now "read" the contents of cells to you as you visually check the original document, making auditing and proofreading chores a little easier. See "Having Excel Read Cells to You" on page 271.

● **The Trace Error button.** Because they are essentially "invisible" on a worksheet, incorrectly entered formulas can produce problems that aren't obvious until you do a careful audit. To make this less of an issue, Excel detects anomalies after editing a formula and displays a smart tag with a menu of pertinent actions. See "Tracing Errors" on page 264.

● **Improvements to PivotTable Reports.** PivotTables have been a boon as well as a bane to number-crunchers the world over. The following enhancements help make working with PivotTables a lot easier. (For details about PivotTables and PivotCharts, see Chapter 30, "Analyzing Data with PivotTable Reports.")

    ▨ **The PivotTable toolbar.** This has been redesigned so that it no longer includes the names of fields in the current table. These now appear in a separate PivotTable Field List window that can be toggled in and out of view. As a result of this change, your screen is less cluttered with user-interface paraphernalia, and you get to see more of your table.

    ▨ **PivotTable data reference.** Referring to data contained in PivotTables is now easier and more reliable. Any time you point to a PivotTable cell while building a formula outside the table, Excel creates the GETPIVOTDATA function for you. You don't have to concern yourself with the syntax of this function, and the reference stays in sync with the table, no matter how you pivot.

■ **PivotTable properties.** Users who build PivotTables from Online Analytical Processing (OLAP) data sources can take advantage of a new
feature that allows annotation of PivotTable data with item properties.

Collaboration and Connectivity Features

Excel is more connected—and connectable—than ever, thanks to several new and
improved features that make collaboration and file sharing easier:

● **Password-protected cell ranges.** These ranges provide access to specific
areas of a protected worksheet and even specify individual permissions. See
"Allowing Password Access to Specific Cell Ranges" on page 130.

● **My Places.** Add any folder or FTP site to your My Places bar—the navigation panel on the left in the Save As and Open dialog boxes. See "Adding a
Site to Your My Places Bar" on page 555.

● **Workbook Review.** A new command on the File, Send To menu provides
an easy way to circulate workbooks for comments and edits by other members of your workgroup. The e-mail message this command generates
includes a hyperlink to the current workbook and gives you the option of
embedding a copy of the document as well. See "Sending a Workbook for
Review" on page 544.

● **Web archives.** In previous versions of Excel, saving an entire workbook to
HTML generated a single HTM file plus (typically) a large folder full of
supporting documents. The current version introduces an optional Web
Archive format that encapsulates everything into a single file. It's cleaner,
more compact, less confusing, and less susceptible to mishap. You can set
Excel to continue using the older format for existing Web documents
but use Web Archive for new ones. See "Web Page or Web Archive?" on
page 562.

● **AutoRepublish.** A new AutoRepublish option makes it easier than ever to
keep Web pages up to date with Excel material. If you use this option, Excel
updates an HTML copy of your file every time you save changes to the
original. See "To Save or To Publish?" on page 562.

● **Microsoft SharePoint Team Services.** This is an Internet-based technology
for team communications and collaboration. SharePoint team Web site
requires a Web server equipped with Microsoft FrontPage Server Extensions 2002 and Microsoft Office Server Extensions. If you access a
SharePoint team Web site, you can carry on threaded discussions with your
colleagues, share a common document repository, announce (or read
about) events of common interest, share a team contact list, and more. See
"Using a SharePoint Team Services Site" on page 545.

- **Web queries.** You can now create queries to retrieve data from Web sites, without knowing anything about HTML or how those Web sites are constructed. You use a simple graphical interface to point to the information you want. Excel builds the Web query for you. With Web queries, your Excel workbooks can fetch current stock-price information, sports scores, or other Internet-based information. See "Using Web Queries to Return Internet Data" on page 781.

- **Support for Extensible Markup Language (XML).** You can now open and save Excel documents in XML and create queries to XML source data. The new XML support allows users to view, update, and review their data in Excel as an intermediate step in the context of a larger business process. See "Opening and Saving Files in XML" on page 565.

Reliability Features

Excel has taken a quantum leap forward in making a safe home for your precious data, with several new features that make it harder than ever for your computer to "eat your homework."

- **Crash recovery.** If Excel encounters a problem, it attempts to save any files that were open at the time the problem occurred and makes them available when you restart Excel. See "Recovering from Crashes" on page 16.

- **AutoRecover.** This feature saves recovery information at specified intervals, making the new Office-wide crash recovery feature more effective. When you restart Excel after a crash, the crash recovery feature attempts to recover any files that were open at the time. The AutoRecover feature helps ensure that the most recent version of these files is made available. See "Using AutoRecover" on page 17.

- **Open And Repair.** This command can either repair a corrupted file, or extract the data from it, offering a powerful recovery feature and a little extra peace of mind. See "Recovering Corrupted Files" on page 48.

- **Error Checking.** This command quickly finds error values in the current worksheet. See "Checking for Errors" on page 257.

Onward...

Taken together, the improvements made in Microsoft Office XP and Microsoft Excel 2002 represent a major leap forward in usability and integration with other applications, adding more depth and breadth to the Office experience than ever before. If your work involves using the Internet, or sharing and distributing data with other members of your workgroup, this might just be the upgrade you have been hoping for. Read on!

Running Excel

Before you can get the feel of the controls, you need to know where they are. This chapter tells you where to find Microsoft Excel's tools and accessories.

What Happens After You Install Excel?

OK, this is really basic, but we have a moral obligation to briefly mention it anyway. There are two principal ways to start Excel:

- Click the Windows Start button, point to Programs, and then click Microsoft Excel.

- In Windows Explorer, double-click any Excel file.

Registering Excel

When you start Excel for the first time, you will be asked to register the program. The easiest way to do this is by allowing Excel to register online, assuming your computer is connected to the Internet. Online registration is fast and painless and lots easier than taking a postcard to the mailbox. It is also highly recommended.

You may have qualms about any kind of owner registration, but in the case of software, it's really a good idea, trust us. When you register, you'll automatically be in the loop for bug fixes (there will certainly be a Service Release available within a year or so), updates, and "special offers". Maybe registering a garden tool, for example, is not worth the annoyance of "special offers," but if you essentially got a new tool for free in a few months, you just might go for it. You won't see too many upgrades for weed whackers, of course, but with software you can rely on getting an upgrade at some point.

Subscribing to Excel

They say that this is the future of software—something lovingly referred to as "the subscription model." It's a way of purchasing software that has been offered to big companies for years, but only now is the idea being floated to the general public.

A major software application is a living thing—the moment one version is completed, teams of developers begin working on the next version, while other teams work on bug fixes for the version they just shipped. When you buy a box of software off the shelf, it's not so much a finished product as a work in progress. If you update your software semi-regularly, it becomes more like a magazine subscription than a weed whacker you buy once and throw away when it dies. So, the idea is, why not make it just like a subscription? You make smaller, more regular payments, and you get automatic, periodic updates. Subscription might make excellent sense for frequent updaters, depending, of course, on the fee.

The Activate Product command on the Help menu starts the Microsoft Office Activation Wizard, shown in Figure 2-1. The Activate Product command also appears when you click the Windows Start button, point to Programs, and click Microsoft Office Tools.

The way you purchase Excel determines the way this works for you. If you purchased a standard shrink-wrapped retail version of Office or Excel, your product doesn't "expire" at all. But you can still purchase a subscription, which will transform yours into a subscription installation. Once you subscribe, you can always buy more time, just like you can with magazine subscriptions. Helpfully, The Microsoft Office Activation Wizard will remind you within 60 days of expiration that it's time to renew your subscription.

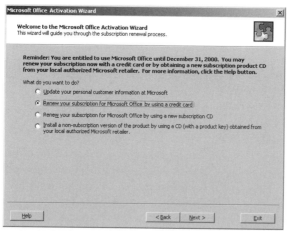

Figure 2-1. The Microsoft Activation Wizard helps you update or subscribe to Excel.

As you can see in Figure 2-1, you can use an option offered by the Microsoft Office Activation Wizard to update your personal customer information stored at Microsoft, which was recorded automatically if you registered online (and presumably is keyed in by Microsoft if you register by phone or mail). This is not necessarily very comforting to many of us, but it may be notable as the first time ever that you, the user, actually have the power to modify your own registration information online.

Why Are There So Many Bugs?

First of all, probably not as many bugs as you think actually affect your daily work. Such bugs are called "showstoppers." Software almost never actually ships with showstoppers anymore; rigorous Beta-testing generally takes care of the big, obvious problems. That being said, all companies routinely ship software that is riddled with bugs—it's the way of the software marketing world. Microsoft and every other software company are equally guilty. But why?

As the battle for market share raged among application developers in the 1980s and 1990s, the mantra among developers was "ship, ship, ship!" They raced to see how fast they could release the next version of the product for two main reasons.

First all the other companies were moving at the same torrid pace, and everybody had to keep up. Applications lived or died because of feature checklists published in major computer magazines. If your product was in any way ill-represented in the published feature comparisons, your product was simply going to lose market share. If the new version of your program didn't make it into, for example, the "Big Spreadsheet Showdown Issue," you and your development group were in deep doo-doo.

Second releasing an upgrade—that is, a new version of an existing program offered for sale rather than being free—represents a large infusion of income to software companies. This is where most of the money comes from on "mature" software products like Excel. Thus, the marketing folks would love to ship a new version every year, or even every six months!

But not only did their customers have a hard time justifying the purchase of upgrades every year or less, software development groups themselves had a hard time keeping that kind of pace. It takes time to develop ideas for new features, write the software code, integrate the new code with the existing code and make sure it doesn't introduce major problems, and then to document, design, manufacture, market, and distribute the product. Plus, the more "mature" a program becomes, the more complex and unpredictable it becomes. Chaos theory starts to rear its ugly head. (Remember *Jurassic Park*?)

One final but very important problem—technology may evolve, but these complex, bloated programs nonetheless had to remain compatible with "legacy" systems. This means not only that programs had to be able to recognize their own files even if they were created several versions ago, but also that commands and features that may have been rendered essentially obsolete had to be reconciled with new features. In some cases, this required continued support for old but often-used commands and keystroke shortcuts.

To completely debug a program as complex as Excel could take years. Some think that it is impossible to absolutely eliminate all potential malfunctions in any program. Just as the FDA certifies that it's OK for a certain small percentage of rat droppings to appear in hot dogs, software companies had to devise an acceptable threshold and severity of bugs that were acceptable to ship in a "finished" product. The good news is that generally these leftover bugs are so esoteric that most folks will never have to deal with them.

Chapter 2

Getting Updates

Microsoft releases free updates called *Service Releases* (SRs), which begin to appear a year or so after the most recent version of Office is released. There will probably always be at least one Service Release, at least until automatic Web updates become feasible. SRs comprise snippets of software code that replace bad bits, circumvent errors, or otherwise intercept known problems. They are commonly called *patches,* a euphemism borrowed from the colorful lexicon of emergency tire repair. Service Releases might even activate new features that were "hidden" because of being only partially implemented when the software finally had to ship.

Service Releases are always free, but they are not very well advertised. The Office Update Web site (*officeupdate.microsoft.com,* as shown in Figure 2-2 as it looked way back in November 2000) was created to provide a sort of central clearinghouse for Service Releases as well as templates, general assistance, news, and lesser patches that might be available for individual programs. You should definitely check it out—you'll find a lot more than just bug fixes. The easiest way to get there is to choose the Office On The Web command on the Help menu.

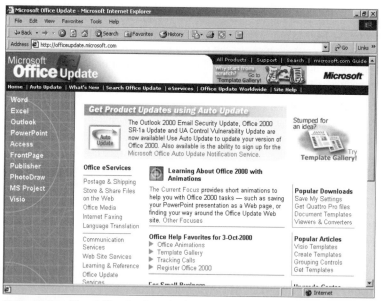

Figure 2-2. The Office Update Web site has a lot of interesting content beyond bug fixes.

newfeature!
Recovering from Crashes

In the past, "crash recovery" largely involved an initial flurry of expletives, followed by a brisk walk around the office and perhaps a couple of aspirin. Excel 2002 finally provides something beyond comfort and sympathy for digital mishaps—an

Chapter 2: Running Excel

actual mechanism that attempts to tuck away open files before the program comes screeching to a halt. And it works pretty well. If Excel encounters a problem, it attempts to save any files that were open at the time the problem occurred, before bad things happen to them when the program crashes and burns. When you restart Excel, these files are then listed in the Document Recovery task pane that appears on the left side of the screen, as shown in Figure 2-3. If the file listed in the Document pane is marked "[Recovered]," Excel had some success in saving the file.

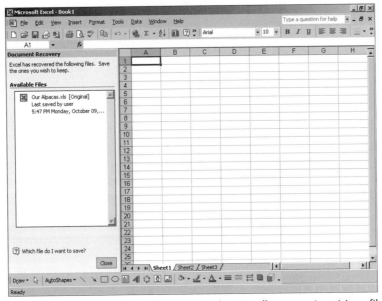

Figure 2-3. The Document Recovery task pane allows you to retrieve files you were working on when Excel crashed.

If the file listed in the Document Recovery pane is marked "[Original]," Excel determined that the file was open when the problem occurred, and opened the last-saved version of the file. The recovery procedure was either unnecessary, because the file had not been edited since the last save, or recovery was not possible. In the case of the file listed in the Document Recovery pane in Figure 2-3, a systemwide crash (induced on purpose by the author) made it impossible for Excel to recover the edited yet unsaved portion of the file, so only the original file is listed in the Document Recovery pane.

If a file listed in the Document Recovery task pane is listed twice, once as "[Recovered]" and once as "[Original]," you can view the recovered file, compare it with the original, and decide which one to save.

Using AutoRecover

Although Excel has greatly improved its ability to recover lost work after a crash, you should take advantage of the additional insurance provided by the AutoRecover feature, as shown in Figure 2-4 on the next page.

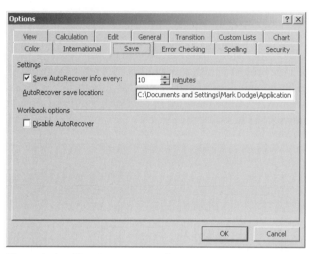

Figure 2-4. The AutoRecover feature gives you extra insurance against data loss.

AutoRecover is turned on by default. To turn it off, choose Tools, Options, and then click the Save tab and clear the Save AutoRecover Info Every check box. The AutoRecover Save Location is set to a subdirectory of the Windows\Application Data directory—this is OK, since you'll want to save the real files elsewhere rather than clutter up your working directories with recovery files. If you wish, you can easily change the location.

Heroic Measures

Excel does its best to recover any unsaved files after a crash, and it is pretty effective. While it is not always possible to restore lost work, there are a few additional tricks you can try if problems persist.

If Excel hangs up on you and refuses to close, call for MOAR help—Microsoft Office Application Recovery, that is. You'll find this command by clicking the Windows Start button and pointing to Programs and clicking Microsoft Office Tools. The Microsoft Office Application Recovery dialog box appears, as shown in Figure 2-5.

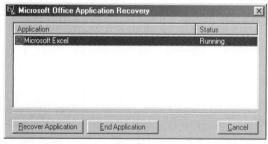

Figure 2-5. The Microsoft Office Application Recovery dialog box gives you a chance to save lost work if a crash paralyzes Excel.

If Excel is still open but not responding, you can click the Recover Application button to try to recover the files that you were working on. If you just want to shut down the program, click the End Application button.

Examining the Excel Workspace

This section will take you on a tour of not only the dashboard of Excel, but also the trunk and the glove compartment. We might even slip on some gloves and take a peek under the floor mats.

Facts About Worksheets

Here are a few random tidbits of interesting information about the grid we call the worksheet.

- Column letters range from A through IV. (After column Z comes column AA, after AZ comes BA, and so on, up to IV.) Row numbers range from 1 through 65,536.

- The currently selected cell is referred to as the *active cell*. When you select a range of cells, only the cell in the upper-left corner is considered the active cell. The reference of the active cell appears at the left end of the Formula Bar in the Name box.

- The headings for the columns and rows containing selected cells are highlighted, making it easier to identify the location of selected cells.

- With 256 columns and 65,536 rows, your worksheet contains more than 16 million individual cells. Before you try to unravel the mysteries of the universe on a single worksheet, however, remember that the number of cells you can use at any one time is limited by the amount of memory your computer has. Although Excel allocates memory only to cells containing data, you might have trouble actually using *all* the cells in one worksheet, no matter how much memory you have.

The Porthole Window

The workbook window is like a porthole through which you can see only a portion of the worksheet. To illustrate, suppose you were to cut a small, square hole in a piece of cardboard and place the cardboard over this page. At any given time, you could see only a portion of the page through the hole. By moving the cardboard around on the page, however, you could eventually read the entire page through the window in your piece of cardboard. Viewing worksheets in Excel is much the same. You can also open another window to view different sections of the same worksheet simultaneously.

Using the Workbook Window

A new workbook, shown *floating* (that is, neither maximized nor minimized) in Figure 2-6, originally consists of three individual worksheets.

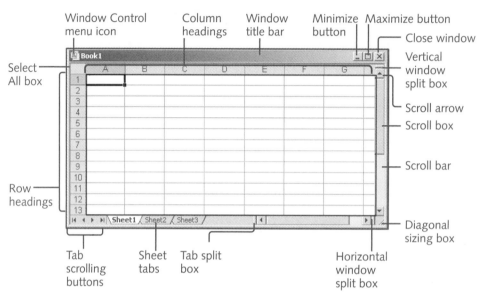

Figure 2-6. Workbooks initially comprise three worksheets.

For more information about using workbooks, see Chapter 6, "How to Work a Workbook."

Workbooks are great organizational tools. For example, you can keep together in the same workbook all the documents that relate to a specific project, department, or individual. Workbooks can eliminate a considerable amount of clutter on your hard drive. The more documents you have to manage, the more valuable workbooks become. You can use workbooks as a multiuser management tool. For example, you can organize worksheets in groups for individual tasks or individual users. You can also share a workbook so that more than one person can work on it at the same time. See "Sharing Files Using a Network" on page 531.

If you routinely create folders on your hard drive to contain groups of related files, you can think of workbooks as "folders" where you can keep all related spreadsheets.

The Title Bar

At the top of the Excel workspace is the title bar, which displays the application name along with the name of the workbook in which you are currently working. If the window is floating, as shown in Figure 2-6, the workbook name appears at the top of

the window instead of at the top of the Excel workspace. (For more information
about maximizing and minimizing your Excel workbook, see "Resizing the Window,"
on page 23.

Getting Around in the Workbook

At the bottom of the workbook window are controls you can use to move from sheet
to sheet in a workbook. Figure 2-7 shows these navigational controls.

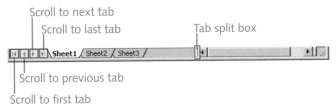

Figure 2-7. Use the workbook navigational controls to move among
undisplayed worksheets.

The tab scrolling buttons shown in Figure 2-7 are needed only when your workbook
contains more sheet tabs than can be displayed at once.

If You Have an IntelliMouse

You can use the wheel on your IntelliMouse to scroll through your worksheet. Turn
the wheel toward you to scroll down or away from you to scroll up. To scroll the
worksheet left to right, press the wheel button down and drag the mouse in the direction you want to move. (This is alternatively referred to as *panning*.) When you press
the wheel button, a gray directional device appears, which is anchored to the spot
where you first pressed the wheel button. The speed of panning depends on how far
you drag away from the anchored directional device. As you hold the button down
and drag, a black arrow appears, pointing in the direction you drag, as shown here.

	A	B	C	D	E
1					
2		◀·	✛		
3					
4					

You can change the default behavior of the wheel from scrolling to zooming. To do
so, choose Tools, Options and, on the General tab, select the Zoom On Roll With
IntelliMouse option.

For more information, see "Zooming Worksheets" on page 125.

Workbook Navigation Tips

There are many features and controls that help you navigate through the rows, columns, and sheets in a workbook. Here are the highlights:

- Use the tab scrolling buttons to view all the sheet tabs in your workbook; click a tab to view the contents of that sheet.

- Drag the tab split bar to the right if you want to see more sheet tabs at the expense of horizontal scroll bar width. To reset to the normal tab display, double-click the tab split bar.

- Press Ctrl+Page Down to activate the next sheet in the workbook; press Ctrl+Page Up to activate the previous sheet.

- Right-click any scroll bar to display a shortcut menu dedicated to scrolling actions, as shown in Figure 2-8.

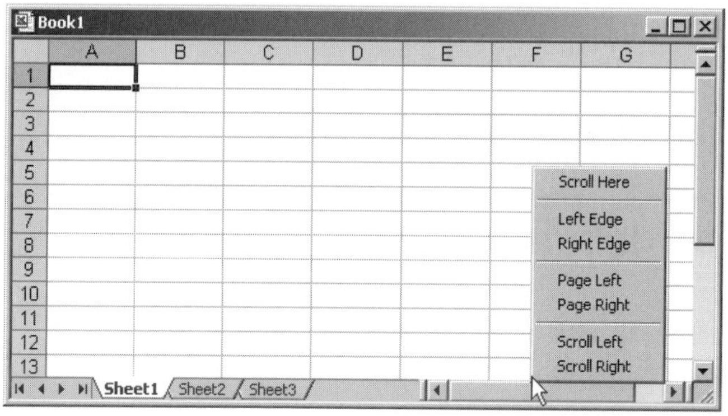

Figure 2-8. Right-click a scroll bar to display a shortcut menu of navigational commands. Only the *active* workbook window has scroll bars.

- Drag the scroll box (also known as the scroll thumb)to move around the worksheet. Click in the scroll bar anywhere outside the scroll box to move one screen in that direction.

- The size of the scroll box changes depending on the size of the scrollable area. For example, the scroll boxes shown in Figure 2-8 are more than half as large as the scroll bars themselves, indicating that there is little more to see in the active area of the workbook—nothing, in fact, because this is a blank workbook. As you add data to more columns and rows than can be displayed on a single screen, the scroll boxes get proportionally smaller, giving you immediate feedback about the size of the worksheet.

- The scroll arrows at either end of the scroll bars enable you to move through the worksheet one column or row at a time. Clicking the up or down arrow in the vertical scroll bar scrolls the sheet up or down one row at a time. Similarly, clicking the right or left arrow in the horizontal scroll bar scrolls the worksheet to the right or left one column at a time.

- The Name box at the left end of the Formula Bar always displays the active cell reference, regardless of where you scroll the window.

- As you scroll the worksheet, you might lose sight of the active cell. To quickly bring the active cell back into view, press Ctrl+Backspace. Alternatively, you can press one of the arrow keys to simultaneously move to an adjacent cell and bring the active cell into view.

- In very large worksheets, you can quickly scroll distant columns or rows into view by pressing Shift while you drag the scroll box. For example, by holding down Shift and dragging to the right end of the horizontal scroll bar, you can bring the last column of the worksheet—column IV—into view. Similarly, holding down Shift and dragging to the bottom of the vertical scroll bar allows you to bring row 65,536 into view.

- To scroll the worksheet without changing the active cell, press Scroll Lock. For example, to scroll to the right one full screen without moving the active cell, press Scroll Lock and then press Ctrl+Right Arrow.

What Is the Active Worksheet Area?

The *active area* of a worksheet is simply the rectangular area that encompasses all of the data the worksheet contains. So if you have just three rows and columns of actual data in the top-left corner of the sheet, the active area would be A1:C3. If a stray character (even a space) happens to be in cell AB1299, the active area would be A1:AB1299. In a new blank worksheet, however, Excel considers the default active area as roughly what you can see on the screen, even before you enter any data.

Resizing the Window

At the right end of the workbook window's title bar are the Minimize, Maximize/Restore, and Close buttons. When your workbook window is maximized, the active window is displayed at full size in the Excel workspace.

After you maximize the window, a button with two small boxes—the Restore button—takes the place of the Maximize button. When you click the Restore button, the active window changes to a floating window.

23

When you click the Minimize button (the one with a small line at the bottom), the workbook collapses to what looks like a small title bar.

Minimizing workbooks is a handy way to reduce workspace clutter when you have several workbooks open at the same time. Click the Restore button on the menu bar to redisplay the workbook at its former floating size, or click the Maximize button and the workbook fills the Excel workspace.

You can also drag the borders of a floating window to control its size. The smaller the window, the less you see of the worksheet; however, because you can open multiple windows for the same workbook, you might find it more convenient to view different parts of the workbook, or even of an individual worksheet, side by side in two small windows rather than switch between sheets or scroll back and forth in one large window.

---

tip **See more rows on your screen**

The Windows taskbar at the bottom of the screen can be set to automatically hide itself when not in use. Click the Start button, point to Settings, and click Taskbar & Start Menu. On the General tab, click Auto Hide, and then click OK. Now the taskbar stays hidden and pops up only when you move the mouse pointer to the bottom of the screen.

Microsoft and the SDI

No, we're not talking about the Strategic Defense Initiative (a.k.a. Star Wars). It's the *Single Document Interface* initiative that Microsoft implemented in the last two versions of Office. The way that Office applications now handle multiple open documents is a bit confusing. It used to be that regardless of the number of documents you had open, only the applications were visible and available for task-switching by using Alt+Tab or by using the Windows taskbar. If you had three Excel worksheets open, you only saw one instance of Excel.

Today, however, Microsoft's SDI initiative dictates that each document now generates its own separate window, which becomes a separate item in the taskbar. Open three Excel worksheets, and you'll see three items in the taskbar. This is arguably a more realistic way to handle documents, which is why Microsoft did it in the first place. The confusion comes from the way this was implemented in each application.

In Excel, each workbook has its own Minimize, Maximize/Restore, and Close buttons, just like all windows do in Windows. In addition, the Excel application has its own trio of buttons. If you minimize Excel, all the open workbooks minimize along with it (although they still appear as separate items in the taskbar). In Word, however, there is only one button—the Close button—in each document, while the application still has all three. When you minimize Word, you're actually only minimizing that document; the other Word documents remain full-screen size.

Exploring Menus and Dialog Boxes

After you get the raw data into Excel by whatever means, you'll be spending a lot of time using menus and dialog boxes to massage and beautify your data. Here are some fun facts and essential information about them.

Morphing Menus

When you first display a menu in Excel, the menu appears with a limited number of commands. After a few seconds, the menu automatically grows to include more commands, as shown in Figure 2-9. This feature is meant to help simplify the ever-increasing complement of commands Excel provides—by hiding some of them, at least for a while. When you first start Excel, the commands immediately visible are the ones that are historically the most often used, but as you work with Excel, the additional commands you choose will also appear on the shorter menus. This is referred to as the Recently Used Commands feature, which keeps track of your command-usage habits.

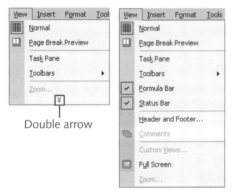

Double arrow

Figure 2-9. The shorter menu on the left shows its most recently used commands. The full menu on the right shows all its commands.

If you find yourself distracted by the delayed unfurling of menus, you have a couple of options. First you can simply double-click the menu name. Second you can click the double arrow at the bottom of the menu. The permanent solution is to choose Tools, Customize and then to click the Options tab in the Customize dialog box, shown in Figure 2-10 on the next page. Select the Always Show Full Menus option to eliminate the problem for good. If you clear the Show Full Menus After A Short Delay option, short menus will stay short unless you double-click the menu name or click the double arrow at the bottom of the menus.

The Recently Used Commands feature records your usage habits and adds commands that you use to shortened menus. When you click Reset My Usage Data in the Customize dialog box, all menus revert to their original state. The data collected about the commands you have used is discarded, and collection begins anew.

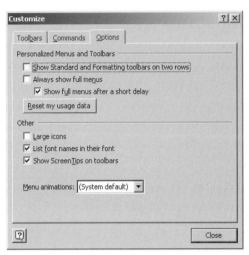

Figure 2-10.   On this tab, you can choose to always display full menus or clear the delayed-display option.

To suit your work style, you can rearrange Excel's menus and commands and create your own menus. For more information, see "Customizing Toolbars and Menus" on page 65.

tip   **Use shortcut keys**

Some commands on Excel's menus are followed by their keyboard equivalents. These key combinations allow you to choose a command without first displaying an Excel menu.

Accessing Menus with the Keyboard

Press the Alt key and the underlined letter of the menu name to activate a menu using the keyboard. When you press Alt, Excel activates the menu bar. Pressing either the Down Arrow key, the F key, or Enter displays the File menu. Then you can press the Right Arrow and Left Arrow keys to activate other menus, and the Up Arrow and Down Arrow keys to highlight commands in a menu. Once you highlight a command using the arrow keys, press Enter to choose it.

The underlined letter in each of the menu and command names designates the letter key you can press to display that particular menu, as an alternative to using the arrow keys. For example, after you press the Alt key to activate the menu bar, you can press the T key to display the Tools menu. Then, to choose a particular command such as Options, press the O key—the underlined letter in "Options"—to display the Options dialog box. So, instead of reaching for the mouse, simply pressing Alt, T, O gets you there. This makes for extremely fast command access once you've learned the right keys for things you do often.

Chapter 2: Running Excel

> **tip** **Menu-activating options**
>
> The slash (/) key can be used just like the Alt key to activate menus. But you can alter-
> natively set a different key to activate menus. Click Tools, Options, click the Transition
> tab, and type a different character in the Microsoft Excel Menu Or Help Key box.

Dialog Boxes and Tabs

Some menu commands have an ellipsis (…) after them, indicating that you must
supply more information before Excel can carry out the command. You supply this
information in a dialog box. For example, Figure 2-11 shows the dialog box that
appears when you choose the Delete command from the Edit menu.

Figure 2-11.   Menu commands followed by an ellipsis (…)
display a dialog box (such as this) to prompt you for more information.

Some commands actually encompass a myriad of settings and options. For these commands, Excel provides *tab dialog boxes,* which present several categorized sets of
options and settings for the same command. Figure 2-12 on the next page shows the tab
dialog box that appears when you choose the Options command from the Tools menu.

> ## The Options Dialog Box
>
> The tab dialog box that appears when you choose Tools, Options is probably the most
> important of all. As you can see in Figure 2-12, the Options dialog box contains tabs
> that control nearly every aspect of Excel, including general settings such as how many
> worksheets appear in a default workbook and the name and point size of the default
> font. The Options dialog box also provides special settings for saving Excel files as
> Web pages, for Lotus 1-2-3 transition assistance, and for many other hard-to-classify
> options. If you take a moment to click each tab and look through the options available
> in this dialog box, you'll get an idea of the scope of the program as well as the degree
> of control you have over your workspace. If you're unsure about what a particular
> setting or option does, simply click the Help button (the question mark) in the title bar
> of the dialog box, and then click the setting or option to display information about it.

Chapter 2

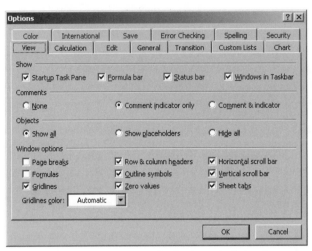

Figure 2-12. Some commands display tab dialog boxes, which provide multiple sets of options.

You can change settings on any and all tabs without dismissing the dialog box, and when you are done click OK to apply all settings on all tabs at once.

The Joy of Shortcut Menus

Shortcut menus contain only those commands that apply to the item indicated by the position of the mouse pointer when you activate the menu. Shortcut menus provide a handy way to access the commands most likely to be useful at the pointer's current location and help minimize mouse movements (which are hard on wrists!).

To access a shortcut menu, right-click. The menu pops up adjacent to the mouse pointer, as shown in Figure 2-13.

Figure 2-13. Right-clicking displays a shortcut menu.

Shortcut menus can contain many combinations of commands, depending on the position of the pointer and the type of worksheet. For example, if you display a short-cut menu when the pointer is over a cell rather than a column heading, some of the commands change to ones specific to cells rather than columns.

---

tip   **Use the toolbar buttons**

Many menu commands have corresponding toolbar buttons—an alternative, possibly easier, way to achieve the same result. An image that appears to the left of a menu command, such as the one next to the Copy command in Figure 2-13, indicates the toolbar button for that command. (Notice that the same image appears on the Standard toolbar as the Copy button.) If one of these images is not currently visible on a toolbar, it is either located on a toolbar that is not displayed or is an optional button you can use in creating or modifying your own toolbars.

For more information about using, modifying, and creating toolbars, see "Customizing Toolbars and Menus" on page 65.

Understanding the Formula Bar

Worksheet cells are Excel's building blocks. They store and display the information you enter in an Excel worksheet and allow you to perform worksheet calculations. You can enter information directly in a cell, or you can enter information through the Formula Bar, as shown in Figure 2-14.

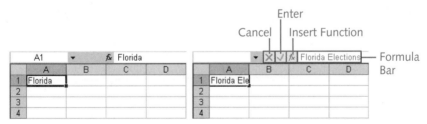

Figure 2-14.   The Formula Bar displays the contents of the active cell.

The contents of the active cell appear in the Formula Bar, and the active cell address is displayed in the Name box at the left end of the Formula Bar. The Insert Function button is always available, as shown on the left in Figure 2-14, but the other two formula-editing buttons appear only while you are entering or editing data in a cell, as shown on the right. Clicking the Cancel button cancels the current action in the cell and is the same as pressing the Esc key. Clicking the Enter button enters the current action into the cell and is the same as pressing the Enter key (except that pressing the Enter key also normally activates the cell directly below the active cell). Clicking the Insert Function button displays a dialog box that helps you construct formulas. For information about names, creating formulas, and using the Formula Palette, see Chapter 12, "Building Formulas."

---

tip   **Hide the formula bar**

By default, Excel displays the Formula Bar in your workspace. If you prefer to hide the Formula Bar, you can choose Formula Bar from the View menu. To redisplay the Formula Bar, simply repeat this process.

About the Status Bar

The status bar displays information about what's happening in your workspace. For example, most of the time, Excel displays the word Ready at the left end of the status bar, meaning the worksheet is ready to accept new information. As you type new information, Excel displays the word Enter in the status bar. When you activate the Formula Bar or double-click a cell that already contains data, Excel displays the word Edit in the status bar.

The boxes at the right end of the status bar display various keyboard modes that you can turn on or off. For example, CAPS appears in this area of the status bar when you press the Caps Lock key. When you press the Num Lock key to activate the numeric keypad (to use it for numeric entry rather than navigation), NUM appears in this area of the status bar.

For more information about keyboard modes, see "Keyboard Mode Codes" on page 103.

Quick Totals in the Status Bar

When two or more cells are selected and at least one of them contains a value, Excel displays the total of the values in the status bar, as shown in the following graphic. This is called the AutoCalculate feature. The AutoCalculate area of the status bar normally displays the sum of the selected values, but if you right-click the area, a menu appears from which you can choose other options. You can choose to get an average of the selected values, a count of the number of nonblank cells, a count of selected cells that contain only numbers, or the minimum or maximum values in the selection, or you can click None to turn the AutoCalculate display off.

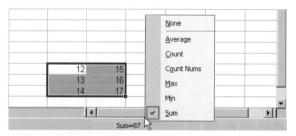

Click the AutoCalculate box in the status bar with the right mouse button to display the AutoCalculate shortcut menu. Then select a function from the menu to display its result in the status bar.

> **tip**   **Hide the status bar**
>
> Excel displays the status bar by default. If you want to hide it, choose View, Status Bar. To redisplay the status bar, simply repeat this.

Pointers About Pointers

In Excel, the pointer serves different functions in different areas of the worksheet.

- In the worksheet grid, the pointer's shape is a big, fat plus sign.

- In the menu bar, the pointer looks like the familiar Windows slanted selection arrow.

- In the Formula Bar, the pointer's shape changes to an I-beam insertion point, as in Microsoft Word. Click to place the insertion point where you want to edit or enter information.

- In the row and column headers, the cursor is in the shape of a horizontal or vertical arrow, hinting that you can select the entire row or column by clicking there.

You'll see the pointer take on other shapes as you begin using it to manipulate the worksheet, its window, and any objects you might add.

Introducing Toolbars

When you first start Excel, two toolbars are visible on the screen: the Standard and the Formatting toolbars, shown in Figure 2-15. These toolbars contain a lot of helpful buttons, but they are only the tip of the iceberg. Excel has many more toolbars, and you can place a staggering number of additional buttons on them.

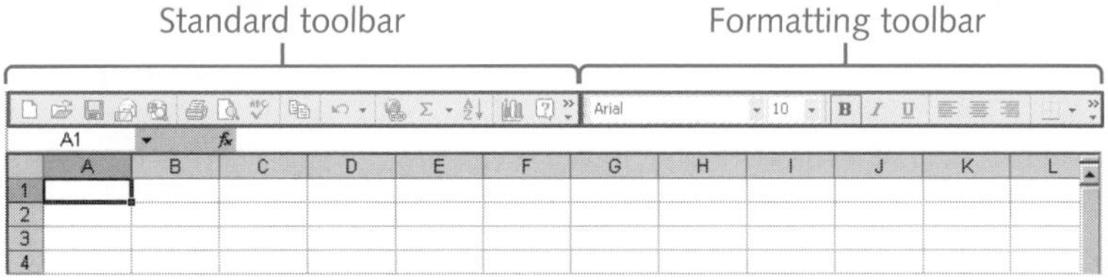

Figure 2-15.   Two toolbars are normally displayed when you start Excel.

Excel offers a smorgasbord of toolbars filled with buttons designed to simplify repetitive operations. You can build your own toolbars, choosing from over 500 predefined buttons, palettes, and drop-down list boxes, or using buttons that you create yourself. Even the Excel menu bar is a toolbar of sorts that you can customize and reposition on the screen.

Excel includes a number of built-in toolbars that provide handy shortcuts for many common actions. Some of the other toolbars are displayed automatically when you need them. For example, Excel displays the Chart toolbar automatically when you are working on a chart.

For more information about toolbars, see "Customizing Toolbars and Menus" on page 65.

File Management Fundamentals

One of the advantages of working with computers is the convenience of electronic files. In this section we describe both the usual and unusual ways you can create, open, save, and find your Excel files.

Creating and Opening Workbooks

To open existing workbooks, click the Open button (the second button on the Standard toolbar). The Open dialog box appears, as shown in Figure 2-16.

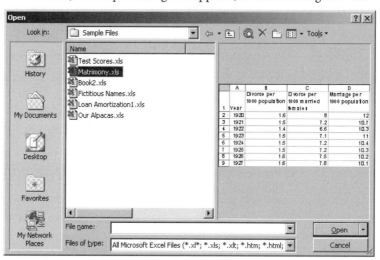

Figure 2-16. You can also choose File, Open to display the Open dialog box.

To create a new workbook, click the New button (the first button on the Standard toolbar). A fresh, blank worksheet appears. Each new workbook created in the current Excel session is numbered sequentially: Book1, Book2, and so on.

Choose File, New and instead of creating a new workbook, the New Workbook *task pane* appears on the right side of the screen, as shown in Figure 2-17.

Chapter 2: Running Excel

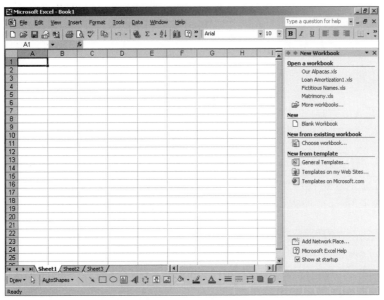

Figure 2-17.   Choose File, New to display the New Workbook task pane on the right.

The New Workbook task pane allows you to perform many of Excel's most often-used
file management actions, as evidenced by the headings in the task pane:

- **Open A Workbook.** The last four files you worked on are listed here. Click
  one to open it.

- **New.** Clicking the Blank Workbook icon creates just that—a new blank
  workbook, as if you had clicked the New toolbar button.

- **New From Existing Workbook.** Clicking Choose Workbook displays the
  dialog box shown in Figure 2-18 on the next page. This dialog box is
  almost identical to the Open dialog box, except that it opens any existing
  Excel file as a template. This means that two things happen differently than
  with the Open dialog box: First instead of opening the actual workbook, it
  opens a copy of it. Second when you save the workbook, it appends a number to the end of the file name and displays the Save As dialog box, making
  it virtually impossible to overwrite the original file.

- **New From Template.** Excel comes with a few installed templates, which are
  listed here. These templates are useful and are also helpful examples for a
  handful of Excel's zillions of formatting and layout possibilities. Clicking
  General Templates displays the dialog box shown in Figure 2-19 on the
  next page. Click the Spreadsheet Solutions tab for a few installed templates.

Figure 2-18. The New From Existing Workbook dialog box opens files as templates.

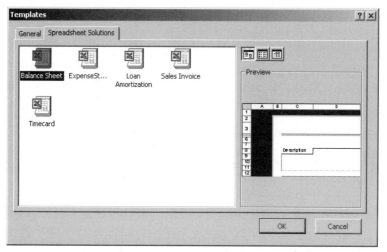

Figure 2-19. The Templates dialog box displays any installed templates.

Notice that the icons in the Templates dialog box look like little pads of paper. These pad icons indicate files that have been specifically saved in template format (see "File Formats" on page 39).

Installing Your Own Templates

This is a great thing to do with sheets you use a lot. Yes, there is a template format (see page 35). OK, you can use the task pane's New From Existing Workbook link to open any workbook as a template. Better yet, you can put any workbook into the following folder and it automatically becomes an *installed* Template:

● C:\Windows\Application Data\Microsoft\Templates (in Windows 9x)

● C:\Documents and Settings\<your name>\Application
Data\Microsoft\Templates (in Windows 2000)

Anything you put in this folder will appear on the General tab of the Templates dialog
box (shown in Figure 2-20), right next to the Workbook icon (which, as you know,
shows up when you click General Templates in the New Workbook task pane). Great
trick. Better still, you can copy subfolders full of workbooks into the aforementioned
folder, thereby creating new tabs in the dialog box that use the folder name as the
tab title.

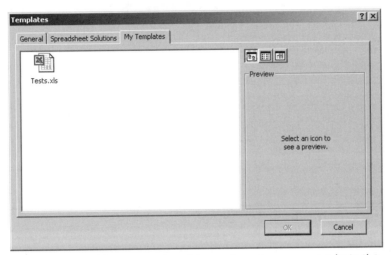

Figure 2-20.   Add your own templates and create your own tabs in the
Templates dialog box.

Use Your Own Folders for Templates

The Templates dialog box derives its contents from a special folder installed by
Microsoft Office. You can change this to a different folder, or you can specify an additional folder as a source for template files. There's just one catch—you have to display
the Office Shortcut Bar to do it. You may find this annoying because it takes up screen
space. But it's easy to turn off. Click the Windows Start button, point to Programs, click
Microsoft Office Tools, and then click Microsoft Office Shortcut Bar.

Right-click any part of the background of the Office Shortcut Bar, and click Customize
on the shortcut menu. On the Settings tab, you can specify two different folders for
your templates, as shown in Figure 2-21 on the next page. This means you can have
two folders full of workbooks essentially "feeding" the same Templates dialog box!

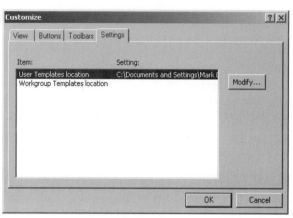

Figure 2-21. You can specify two separate locations for templates using the Office Shortcut Bar's Customize dialog box.

> **caution** When you specify folders for templates in the Office Shortcut Bar's Customize dialog box, you are not only changing the location for Excel, but for all Office applications. For this reason, we recommend that if you want to have access to any installed templates, leave the User Templates location alone and use the Workgroup Templates location to specify a folder where you can deposit your own workbooks.

Changing the Default Book and Sheet

Want to design your own "blank" workbook? You can create two templates to do this—one that determines the format and content of all new workbooks (Book.xlt), and one that determines the format and content of all individual sheets you insert using the Insert, Worksheet command (Sheet.xlt). These are special files that you create yourself and save in a special place:

C:\Program Files\Microsoft Office\Office\XLStart

You save an .XLT file by choosing Save As from the File menu and selecting Template in the Save As Type drop-down list at the bottom of the Save As dialog box.

> **note** Any workbook that you place in the XLStart folder is opened automatically each time you start Excel (except workbooks named Book.xls or Sheet.xls).

These files override the standard appearance and content of new workbooks and new worksheets. Even the default *Book1* that appears every time you start Excel takes on the characteristics you supply in Book.xlt. If you want to revert to the original, simply remove the files from the XLStart folder.

Note that by using these files you can change not only the formatting, but you can also include text, graphics, formulas, custom toolbars, macros, and certain window and calculation options. You can also determine the number and type of default sheets present in both new workbooks and inserted worksheets. That's right, you can actually save the workbook Sheet.xlt with four worksheets. Then when you choose Insert, Worksheet you will actually be inserting four worksheets instead of just one. If you don't want this to happen, simply delete additional sheets before saving Sheet.xlt.

For more information about custom toolbars, see the following sections in Chapter 3: "Creating New Toolbars" on page 77, and "Attaching Custom Toolbars to Workbooks" on page 78.

Saving Files

For more information about saving workbooks as Web pages, see "Saving and Publishing Excel Files in HTML" in Chapter 20.

Arguably the most important yet boring function of any computer application is preservation of data. In Excel, there are seven ways that your files can be saved, including the Save, Save As, Save As Web Page, Save Workspace, Close, and Exit commands, and the easiest way to save—clicking the Save button on the Standard toolbar.

One other command that saves your workbooks is the Share Workbook command on the Tools menu. When you choose this command, your workbook is saved in shared mode. Besides saving the file, this command makes the workbook available to others on a network, who may open it and make changes of their own.

For more information, see "Sharing Workbooks on a Network" on page 532.

tip   **Specify a default folder**

If you use the same folder most of the time, you can specify that folder as the default location that the Open, Save, and Save As dialog boxes use when you first open them. Choose Tools, Options, and then on the General tab, type the full path and filename for the folder you want to use in the Default File Location box.

Chapter 2

The first time you save a file, the Save As dialog box appears, shown in Figure 2-22.

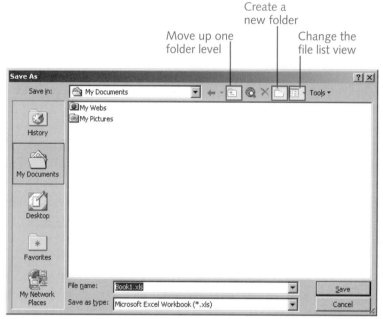

Figure 2-22. The Save As dialog box appears when you save a file for the first time.

How Much Disk Space Do You Need?

To ensure that a new copy of a file is properly saved before the original is deleted, Excel makes a temporary file when it saves, and then deletes the original and renames the temporary file to the original name. This prevents loss of both the original and the version being saved if something goes wrong in mid-save. Because of this you can never open, make changes to, and then save a file that is bigger than half the amount of available space on the disk being used. For example, if you have a 1.44 megabyte (MB) floppy disk, you cannot open, make changes to, and then save a file larger than approximately 720 kilobytes (KB) from within Excel (which is a pretty big file). In this case, you would need to make all your changes in a copy of the workbook located on your hard drive, and then save it to the floppy disk when you're finished.

Rules for File Naming

File names in Excel can have up to 218 characters. They can include any combination of alphanumeric characters, spaces, and the special characters, with the exception of the forward slash (/), backslash (\), greater-than sign (>), less-than sign (<), asterisk (*), question mark (?), quotation mark ("), pipe symbol (|), colon (:), and semicolon (;). Although you can use any combination of uppercase and lowercase letters, keep in mind that Excel does not distinguish case in file names. For example, the names "MYFILE," "MyFile," and "myfile" are identical to Excel.

The familiar MS-DOS three-character file extension helps identify your Excel files, and it is added automatically when you save a file. Note, however, that file extensions may not appear with Windows file names, depending on your settings. The following table lists some of Excel's default extensions.

Document Type	Extension
Add-in	.XLA
Backup	.XLK
Template	.XLT
Workbook	.XLS
Workspace	.XLW

File Formats

In addition to providing the file name and location, you can specify a different file format in the Save As dialog box. Click the arrow to the right of the Save As Type drop-down list box. The list expands to reveal all the formats in which you can save your files.

For more information about Excel's export formats, see "Importing and Exporting Files" on page 51.

The default format is Microsoft Excel Workbook, and you'll almost always use this option. If you want to export an Excel file to another program, however, you can use one of the other options to convert the file to a format that is readable by that program.

Document Types in Previous Versions of Excel   In Microsoft Excel versions 5.0 through 2002, worksheets, chart sheets, Excel 5.0 dialog sheets, and Excel 4.0 macro sheets are all contained in workbooks. In previous versions of Excel, worksheets, chart sheets, and macro sheets were saved separately. When you open one of these earlier sheet types in Excel 2002, it is automatically converted to an Excel 2002 workbook, which you can then choose to save in the current Excel format or keep in its original format. You can also combine sheets from a previous version of Excel in a single Excel 2000 workbook.

Excel 5.0 workbooks were compatible with Excel 95 and vice versa. This meant you could save a workbook in Excel 95, and then open it in Excel 5.0 without problems. the last three versions of Excel share a somewhat different file format than the one shared by Excel 95 and Excel 5.0. To accommodate situations where you must share files with others using different versions of Excel, The Files Of Type list in the Save As dialog box includes the special formats Microsoft Excel 5.0/95 Workbook and Microsoft Excel 97-2002 & 5.0/95 Workbook, the latter of which saves workbooks in these two formats simultaneously. Users of any of these versions of Excel can open a file saved in this format, but if someone using Excel 95 or Excel 5.0 saves changes to it, any features from Excel Versions 2000 or 2002 and formatting are lost.

Chapter 2

Specifying the Default File Format

Normally when you save a new workbook, it is saved in the Microsoft Excel Workbook format. You can specify a different format as the default for saving files. This might be helpful, for example, if you share files regularly with users of Excel 95. To do so, choose Tools, Options and click the Transition tab, shown in Figure 2-23.

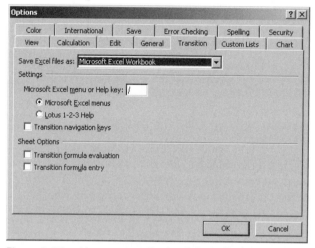

Figure 2-23. You can specify the default format to use when saving.

The Save Excel Files As list contains all the same file formats as the Save As Type list in the Save As dialog box.

Creating Automatic Backup Files

You can have Excel create a duplicate copy of your file on the same disk and in the same directory as the original, every time you save. Choose File, Save As, click the Tools button at the top of the Save As dialog box, and click General Options to display the Save Options dialog box shown in Figure 2-24. Then select the Always Create Backup option.

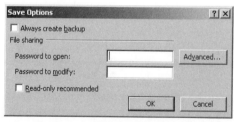

Figure 2-24. To display the Save Options dialog box, choose File, Save As, then click Tools, General Options.

The backup file is a duplicate file that carries the same name as your original, but the name is preceded by "Backup of" and has the file extension XLK.

InsideOut

Don't duplicate file names

Keep in mind that Excel always uses an XLK extension when creating backup files, regardless of the file type. Suppose you work with a workbook named Myfile.XLS as well as a template file on disk named Myfile.XLT, and you select the Always Create Backup option for both. Because only one Myfile.XLK can exist, the most recently saved file is saved as the XLK file, and Excel overwrites the other file's backup if one exists.

Protecting Files

You can password-protect your files by using options in the Save Options dialog box shown in Figure 2-24 on the previous page. Choose from two types of passwords: Password To Open and Password To Modify. Passwords can have up to 15 characters and capitalization matters. Thus, if you assign the password *Secret* to a file, you can't reopen that file by typing *SECRET* or *secret*. For added security, Excel does not display passwords on the screen when you type them to open a protected file.

- When you assign a Password To Open to a file and then you close it, Excel prompts you to supply that password before reopening the file.

- When you assign a Password To Modify, anyone can open the file, but they cannot save the file if they haven't opened it using the password.

- A third protection option, the Read-Only Recommended option, augments the security provided by passwords. If less stringent security meets your needs, this option gently suggests that the user open the file as read-only.

tip **Create a better password**

Although Excel's under-the-hood security measures have been tightened over the years, there are always people who delight in finding new and better ways to crack passwords. You can help by simply using better passwords. Make sure that your password is eight or more characters long—the longer the better—and try to use a healthy mix of capital and lowercase characters as well as numeric characters.

Adding Summary Information to Files

When you choose File, Properties, Excel displays a Properties dialog box that you use to record general information about the active workbook. The Properties dialog box is shown in Figure 2-25 on the next page.

Chapter 2

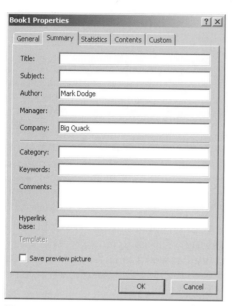

Figure 2-25. To examine a file's properties from the
Open dialog box, click the Views icon and choose Properties.

One thing you can do with properties, besides recording multiple categories of information in a special place in the workbook, is to use these properties while you are looking for a specific file. This is easy to do by using the Open dialog box shown in Figure 2-26.

In the Open dialog box, click the Views button, and click Properties to display a panel of information on the right side of the dialog box. All the property values available in the selected file appear here. Property values are also looked at whenever you use the Windows Search command to locate files on your computer.

Of course, you have to first add values to the Properties dialog box before it becomes useful, but reviewing the properties is a good habit to get into when you have to manage a lot of files.

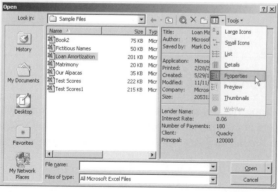

Figure 2-26. View properties about any file before you open it.

Linking Custom Properties to Cells

You can link a custom property in the Properties dialog box to a named cell in your worksheet. When you do, the value of the custom property becomes whatever the named cell contains and changes whenever the value in the cell changes. First you must name a cell (see "Rules for Naming" on page 373), which makes available the Link To Content check box on the Custom tab in the Properties dialog box. When the Link To Content box is selected, the workbook's defined names appear in the Value drop-down list (whose name changes to Source when linking content), as shown in Figure 2-27.

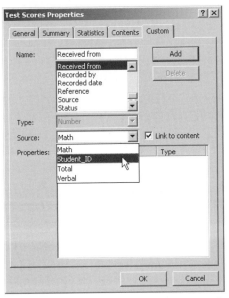

Figure 2-27. Use named cells to create dynamic properties based on worksheet cells.

Select or create a name for the custom property in the Name box. (The Type box becomes unavailable when you're linking to content.) When you've specified a Source (the named cell to which you want to link), click the Add button and the custom property appears in the Properties list box.

If the link is broken (the defined name is deleted, for example), the Properties dialog box stores the last value recorded for that property.

If the name defines a range of cells, only the value in the cell in the upper-left corner of the range is displayed as the property value.

Saving the Entire Workspace

Choose File, Save Workspace to save a snapshot of your current Excel environment. When you choose the Save Workspace command, the dialog box in Figure 2-28 appears on the next page.

43

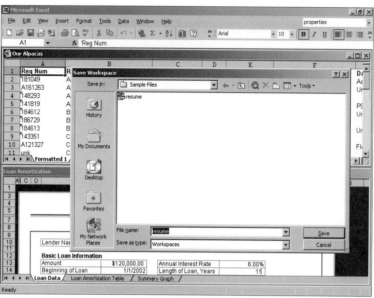

Figure 2-28. Save a snapshot of your Excel workspace with the Save Workspace command.

When you save a workspace, Excel notes the locations of all the workbooks that are currently open, as well as many of the workspace settings, so that you can retrieve your files and settings in the same configuration they were in when you saved. Settings that are saved with workspaces include many of the display and calculation settings available in the tab dialog box that appears when you choose Tools, Options. The default filename suggested for a workspace file is "Resume.xlw," but you can use a different name as long as you follow the file naming rules.

Opening Files

Only slightly less basic than saving files, is opening them. Choose File, Open, or click the Open button on the Standard toolbar to display the Open dialog box, shown in Figure 2-16 on page 32.

The icons on the left side of the dialog box are navigational controls that control the lists of files displayed in the main window of the dialog box. The My Documents icon is normally selected and displays the contents of the My Documents folder when you open the dialog box, unless you have changed the Default File Location (by choosing Tools, Options and click the General tab).

- The History icon displays a list of files you have opened and folders you have navigated to, in chronological order with the latest first. This view actually displays the contents of an Application Data folder named Recent, which is populated automatically with shortcuts to the files and folders you use in the Open or Save As dialog boxes.

Chapter 2: Running Excel

- The Desktop icon brings you to the very top level of your computer's file system so you can click your way down through the hierarchy.

- The Favorites icon displays the contents of the Favorites folder. When any folder other than Favorites is active in the Open or Save As dialog boxes, you can click the Tools button and choose the Add To Favorites command to create a shortcut to the currently selected file or folder and place it in the Favorites folder.

- The My Network Places icon opens files in any available locations on your network or on the World Wide Web.

- The Files Of Type list box near the bottom of the Open dialog box determines which files are available for selection. The default option is All Microsoft Excel Files, which displays file names whose three-character extensions begin with "XL." You can display specific file types or All Files by clicking the arrow button to the right of the list box.

> **tip**　To open several files at once, press the Ctrl key and click each file name that you want
> to open.

- The Views button selects a different way to display files in the dialog box. Notice that in Details view, headings appear over each section of file information. When you click one of these headings, the files are sorted in order, based on that heading. For example, if you click the Modified heading, the files are sorted in date order. You can also change the width of the columns displayed in Details view by dragging the lines between headings, similar to the way you can drag to change column width in a worksheet.

- The Tools button displays a drop-down menu (shown in Figure 2-29) that contains additional commands you can use on selected files.

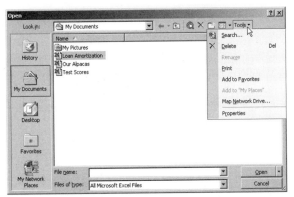

Figure 2-29. Click the Tools button to display additional useful commands.

Part 1: Examining the Excel Environment

> **tip** **Use the shortcut menu**
>
> You can right-click most files listed in the Open, New, or Save As dialog boxes to display a shortcut menu that contains commands you can use on the selected file. For example, you can delete a file displayed in the Open dialog box by using this shortcut menu.

Special Ways to Open Files

To the right of the Open button at the bottom of the Open dialog box is a small downward-pointing arrow. Clicking this arrow displays the menu shown in Figure 2-30.

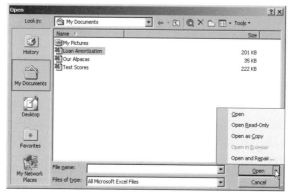

Figure 2-30. The arrow next to the Open button gives you more control when opening documents.

The opitons on this menu are as follows:

- **Open Read-Only** opens the file so that you cannot save any changes made to it without renaming it.

- **Open As Copy** creates a duplicate of the selected file, adds the words "Copy of" to the file name, and leaves the original unmolested.

- **Open In Browser** applies only to HTML documents and opens the selected file in your default Web browser.

- **Open And Repair** is a powerful feature that you can use to try opening corrupted files. For more information, see "Recovering Corrupted Files" on page 48.

Opening Files When You Start Excel

If you have files you need to work on every day, you can store them in a special folder called XLStart. Every time you start Excel, any files in the XLStart folder are automatically opened.

tip   Save the workspace

You can save workspace files in the XLStart folder so that the files, and the workspace setup are automatically loaded each time you start Excel. For more information about workspace files, see "Saving the Entire Workspace" on page 43.

The XLStart folder was created when you installed Excel, and is located in one of the following places:

C:\Program Files\Microsoft Office\Office10\XLStart

C:\Documents and Settings\<your name>\Application Data\
Microsoft\Excel\XLStart

You can create special files (and save them in the XLStart folder) that control the appearance and content of the default workbook and new worksheet. For more information, see "Changing the Default Book and Sheet" on page 36.

If you want to start Excel and simultaneously open files that are in a folder other than the XLStart folder, you can specify an alternate startup folder. Choose Tools, Options, click the General tab, and type the full path of the folder you want in the box labeled At Startup, Open All Files In, as shown in Figure 2-31.

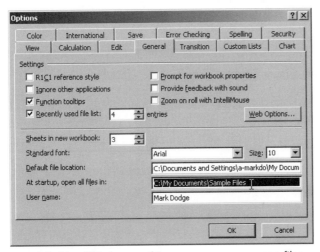

Figure 2-31.   This is one of two ways you can open files automatically at startup.

This feature is particularly useful if your computer is connected to a network and you want to open files from a shared folder.

newfeature!

Recovering Corrupted Files

Figure 2-30 on page 46 shows the Open Options menu, where you'll see the Open And Repair command. This command gives you a fighting chance at either repairing a corrupted file or extracting the data from it if it doesn't respond to a repair attempt. When you select a file and choose the Open And Repair command, the dialog box in Figure 2-32 appears.

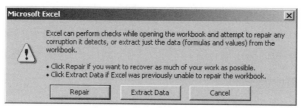

Figure 2-32. The Open And Repair command gives you a ray of hope for recovering lost data.

Try the Repair button first, and if Excel still has no luck opening the file, go back and try the Extract Data button, which displays the dialog box shown in Figure 2-33.

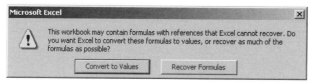

Figure 2-33. The Extract Data button offers two ways to recover your data.

You'll have to make a judgment call here—if you think your formulas will be OK after extraction, click the Recover Formulas button; otherwise choose Convert To Values. Recovering formulas will probably work unless the formulas include references to cells that were lost in corruption. Whatever you choose, the Open And Repair feature will extract all the data in your workbook, including all sheets and tabs, in the same order they appeared in the original file. Unfortunately, the recovery process ignores all formatting, charts, and other objects—only the actual cell contents (the important stuff) can be recovered.

Note that unless part of the file that became corrupted was the part storing passwords, you probably won't be able to use this technique to retrieve data from a password-protected file.

For more information about document recovery, see "Recovering from Crashes" on page 16. For more information about passwords, see "Hiding and Protecting Workbooks" on page 141.

Recover Data with Change Source

There is another trick you can use to recover data that you thought was lost from a corrupted workbook. It is essentially the same trick used by Excel's Open And Repair command, but it still might be worth a try if Open And Repair fails.

First open two new workbooks. Select cell A1 in one of the workbooks, and then press Ctrl+C to copy. Activate the second workbook and right-click cell A1. Choose Paste Special on the shortcut menu, and then click Paste Link. Next choose Edit, Links, click Change Source, and locate the corrupted workbook.

If luck is with you, data from cell A1 in the lost workbook appears in cell A1, thanks to the linking formula. If so, press F2 to activate Edit mode and press F4 three times to change the absolute reference $A$1 to its relative form, A1. Finally, copy the formula down and across until you can see all of the data you need to retrieve. Repeat for each sheet in the workbook.

This technique may even work when you need to bypass a password-protection problem. If after clicking the Change Source button you are prompted for a password, just click Cancel and see what happens in the cell. No guarantees, of course.

Searching for Files

You can use the file-finding features in the Open dialog box to search any place available to your computer. In the Open dialog box, click the Tools button and choose Search to display the dialog box shown in Figure 2-34 on the next page.

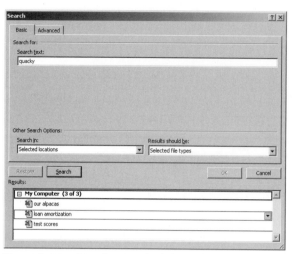

Figure 2-34. Use the Search dialog box to search for files in any location connected to your computer.

For more information about network issues, see "Sharing Files Using a Network" on page 531.

You can simply type something into the Search Text box and then click the Search button to start your search. However, we recommend that you first use the Other Search Options drop-down lists to narrow the search to certain locations and file types if you don't have a lot of time to wait while every file on your hard drive is inspected. A list of links to found files appears at the bottom of the dialog box. Click OK, or double-click a link to close the Search dialog box and insert the file location into the File Name box in the Open dialog box.

Click the Advanced tab in the Search dialog box to add more criteria to narrow your search. Create one criterion at a time using the Search For options at the top of the dialog box, and add as many criteria as you want. Once you have specified Property, Condition, and Value, click the Add button to add your criteria to the list below. You can add as many criteria as you need.

- The Property list includes most of the properties available in the Properties dialog box.

For more on the Properties dialog box, see "Adding Summary Information to Files" on page 41.

- The contents of the Condition box change depending on what you select in the Property box. For example, if you choose the Creation Date property, the list of conditions includes "on or after," "today," "last month," and so on.

- You make entries in the Value box that are appropriate for the specified con-dition. For example, you'd enter a date in the Value box if the selected condition is Creation Date.

- Use the And and Or buttons to specify whether each criterion you add is "in addition to" or "instead of" the previous criterion. Some property types allow only one "And." For example, if you attempt to add another Files Of Type criterion with the And button selected, a dialog box informs you that a file type already appears in the criteria list and asks if you want to change it to an Or criteria.

- Remove any selected criteria by clicking the Remove button, or click Remove All to clear the criteria list.

- Click Search to begin; click Restore to clear the search results but leave the criteria intact.

- When you find the file you're looking for, click OK to insert the location of the selected file into the File Name box in the Open dialog box.

- The next time you use the Search dialog box, the last search criteria you used is retained in case you want to use it again.

---

tip   **Set a properties reminder**

To help get into the habit of entering properties to identify groups of files, you can have the Properties dialog box appear automatically each time you save a file for the first time. Choose Tools, Options, and click the General tab, and click the Prompt For Workbook Properties option.

Importing and Exporting Files

Microsoft Excel gracefully accepts proprietary data created in many other applications. Excel also makes it easy to import data from text files and helps you parse it into worksheet columns.

---

note   There are mountains of very specific, sleep-inducing technical details available about importing and exporting files. If you need such detail for conversion issues like trans-ferring hundreds of macro-driven Lotus files into Excel, you should consult the *Microsoft Office Resource Kit,* available from Microsoft Press.

Using the Open and Save As
Commands to Import and Export Files

To *import* a file from another application or from an earlier version of Excel, choose File,
Open (or click the Open button on the Standard toolbar), and select the file you want to
import from the list of files in the Open dialog box. Use the Files Of Type drop-down list
at the bottom of the Open dialog box, shown in Figure 2-35. When you choose a file
type, the Open dialog box displays only that type of file in its list. Keep in mind that it is
not necessary to include a file name extension when you import a file, because Excel
determines the format of the file by examining the file's contents, not its name.

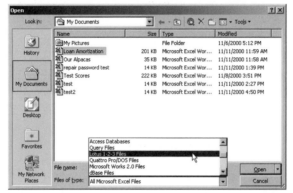

Figure 2-35. Use the Files Of Type list to specify files created by a particular application.

To *export* an Excel file to another application or to an earlier version of Excel, choose
File, Save As. Then select the application you're exporting to in the Save As Type drop-
down list box, which is similar to the Files Of Type list shown in Figure 2-35, except
that there are many more specific file formats that you can choose to save in. For
example, while "Lotus 1-2-3 Files" is the only Lotus format listed in the Open dialog
box, you can save an Excel file in many different Lotus 1-2-3 formats, including WKS,
WK1, WK3, FM3, and WK4.

What Is XML?

One of the file types listed in both the Open and Save As file type lists is XML (Extensible Markup Language). XML was created as a way for what we call "structured data"
to be interpreted and is primarily intended for use on the Web. If you intend to publish
the contents of worksheets on the Web or on your local intranet, you might want to
explore XML further—a subject well beyond the scope of this book. For some additional informatin about XML, see "Opening and Saving Files in XML" on page 565.

Importing and Exporting Text Files

To export an Excel file as a text file, choose File, Save As, and select one of the following eight text formats from the Save As Type list. In all of these formats, Excel saves only the current worksheet. Number formatting is preserved, but all other formatting is removed.

- **Formatted Text (Space delimited) (*.PRN).** This creates a file in which column alignment is preserved by means of space characters. You might want to use this kind of file when communicating via modem with a recipient who does not have Excel.

- **Text (Tab delimited) (*.TXT).** This separates the cells of each row with tab characters. Any cell in which a comma appears is surrounded by quotation marks.

- **Unicode Text (*.TXT).** This is a worldwide standard text format that stores each character as a unique number; Unicode defines a number for every character in every language and on any computer platform.

- **CSV (Comma delimited) (*.CSV).** This separates the cells of each row with commas. Comma-delimited text files are preferable to tab-delimited files for importing into database management programs. (Many database management programs can accept either form of text file, but some accept only .CSV files.) Also, many word processing applications can use .CSV files to store the information for form letters.

- **Text (Macintosh) (*.TXT).** The Macintosh options use the Macintosh character set, so select one of these options if you intend to transfer your file to a Macintosh application.

- **Text (MS-DOS) (*.TXT).** The normal Text and CSV options use the ANSI character set. You should select one of these options if you intend to import your text file into a Windows-based application, such as Microsoft Word for Windows.

- **CSV (Macintosh) (*.CSV).** The differences between the normal, Macintosh, and MS-DOS variants of each file type have to do only with characters that lie outside the normal 7-bit ASCII range.

- **CSV (MS-DOS) (*.CSV).** The MS-DOS options use the IBM PC extended character set—the same character set your computer uses when it's not running Windows. (The documentation for some Windows-based programs or for Windows itself might refer to this character set as OEM text.) Select one of these options if you intend to import your text file into a non–Windows-based application—such as XyWrite—or into an OS/2 application.

> **note** Excel 2002 shares a file format with its predecessors Excel 2000 and Excel 97 that is incompatible with previous Excel versions. You can use the Save As command, however, to export Excel 2002/2000/97 workbooks to any earlier version of Excel.
>
> If you regularly share files with colleagues who use Excel 5 or Excel 7, you might want to take advantage of the Microsoft Excel 97-2002 & 5.0/95 Workbook format. This saves your work in a format that can be read in any of these Excel formats.

Sharing Data with Excel for the Macintosh

Microsoft Excel 98 and 2001 for the Macintosh both use the same file format as Excel Version 2002, 2000, and Excel 97. You can share files with Macintosh users by simply transferring files from one computer to the other.

To save an Excel 2002 file to share with someone using the Macintosh version of Excel 5, use the File, Save As command and choose the Microsoft Excel 5.0/95 Workbook option.

Keep the following points in mind:

- To import Macintosh files to your PC, you first need to transfer the file to your PC via a cable, modem, disk, network, or utility program such as MacOpener. Simply choose File, Open and find the document you want.

- Exporting files from a Windows version of Excel to the Macintosh version is just as easy as importing Macintosh files. Transfer the file from the PC to Macintosh, and use the Open command to load the file just as you would load any other file.

Adjusting Date Values

Although the Windows and Macintosh versions of Excel share many characteristics and capabilities, they do not use the same date system. In the Windows version of Excel, the base date is January 1, 1900. In the Macintosh version, the base date is January 2, 1904. When you transfer files either to or from the Macintosh, Excel maintains the date type by selecting or clearing the 1904 Date System option on the Calculation tab of the Options dialog box. This technique is usually acceptable, but it can cause problems when a date from a Macintosh file is compared with a date from a Windows file. For this reason, we suggest that you use the same date setting on all your machines.

Online Help Works—Really!

Excel was a powerful program right out of the starting gate way back in 1985. Over the years, Excel has developed into an extremely complex and sophisticated application. So complex, in fact, that most people need to learn only 20 percent or so of its capabilities. Many people turn to books like this one to help them make sense of it all. But almost every Excel user turns to the online Help system at one time. And after a few years of working out the kinks, Microsoft has made the Help system in this version of Excel less obtrusive, more comprehensive, and much easier to use.

newfeature!

The Best Way to Use Help

The new Ask A Question box appears in the upper-right corner of the Excel workspace—it is actually part of the menu bar, as shown in Figure 2-36.

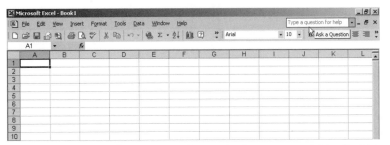

Figure 2-36. The Ask A Question box is the best entry point to the Help system.

All you have to do is type a question into the Ask A Question box and press Enter. Excel almost instantly displays a list of Help topics that are most likely to address your question, as shown in Figure 2-37. If the topic list doesn't address exactly what you're looking for, try rephrasing the question using a different word or two.

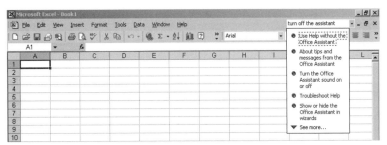

Figure 2-37. Type a question and get a list of possible answers.

If your question results in more than five topics, click the See More arrow at the bottom of the list to display additional topics. Not all questions you pose to the Assistant will return more than five topics, so the See More arrow might not always appear.

Click any of the questions in the list to invoke the Help window, which appears with the selected topic displayed, as shown in Figure 2-38 on the next page.

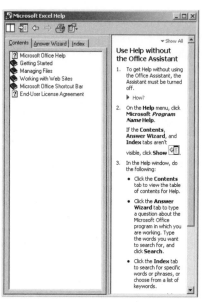

Figure 2-38. When the Help window appears, you can browse the entire Help system.

You can use the Microsoft Excel Help window to locate further information if necessary. Use the Contents tab to browse topic categories. The Answer Wizard tab offers the same functionality as the Ask A Question box. The Index tab allows you to enter keywords and find any topics that contain them.

The Wizard Behind the Curtain

The Ask A Question box is a deceptively simple-looking interface to a very sophisticated system. When you enter a question, Microsoft's Answer Wizard technology works very quickly and usually returns a short list of very relevant topics. The Ask A Question box (that is, the Answer Wizard) accepts questions in full or partial sentences, using natural language, just as if you were talking to the Excel guru down the hall. Then, based on key words, order of words, and verbs used, the Ask A Question box returns a list of topics that is generated by a sophisticated system of probabilities.

Managing the Assistant

In the last few versions of Excel, we have witnessed the birth and adolescence of the previously ubiquitous Office Assistant—whose most popular (and default) personality is known as Clippit. Previously the Assistant was impossible to ignore and impossible to get rid of. Even if you turned off the Assistant, it would pop up from time to time, depending

Chapter 2: Running Excel

on what you were doing. Our little friend has finally learned not to be heard and seen. For the first time, you can actually remove the Assistant completely. Good news for many of us (although we still enjoy making Rocky the dog do little dances occasionally).

You're Fired!

In Excel 2002, the Office Assistant is not as pushy as it was in its younger days. Nevertheless, it's still there and occasionally appears. If you would be happier if the Assistant never darkened your desktop again, choose Help, Show The Office Assistant (if it isn't already visible). Click the Assistant and then click the Options button at the bottom of the balloon. The Office Assistant dialog box, shown in shown in Figure 2-39, appears. On the Options tab, clear the Use The Office Assistant check box. When you do so, the rest of the options in the dialog box become unavailable.

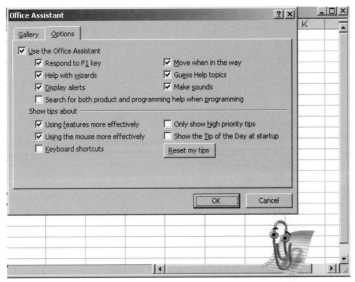

Figure 2-39. Click the Options tab to begin the "exit interview."

If you change your mind later, choose Help, Show The Office Assistant. This command changes to Hide the Office Assistant when the Assistant is visible, but does not fire it permanently. You still must use the Assistant Options dialog box if you want the Assistant to stay fired.

Chapter 2

You're History!

If firing the Assistant isn't enough for you (what, you're worried about retribution?), there is a more final solution—you can remove it completely from your hard drive. Your weapon of choice can be found by clicking the Windows Start menu, pointing to Settings, clicking Control Panel, and then double-clicking the Add/Remove Programs icon. You can then change your Microsoft Office installation by removing the Office Assistant, which is now available as its own installation item, separate from the Help system (which we suggest you keep).

Using the Assistant

Some of us like the Office Assistant, and I'm sure there are others who would like to give it a chance to prove itself. You don't need it, but you might like it.

The Assistant is more than happy to live in a corner of your screen, full time, ready to answer your every need. To give it this opportunity, choose Help, Show the Office Assistant to display Clippit, the default Assistant character. Click the Assistant to display its search balloon, which proffers an entry box and two buttons, as shown in Figure 2-40.

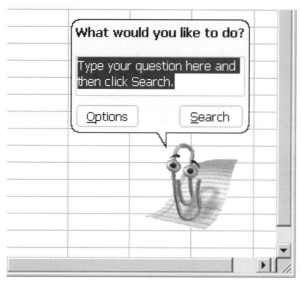

Figure 2-40. Click the Assistant to display the search balloon.

The entry box works the same way the Ask A Question box works (see "Here's the Best Way to Use Help," on page 55).

Selecting Office Assistant Options

When you click the Options button at the bottom of the Office Assistant search balloon, the Office Assistant dialog box appears. On the Gallery tab, shown in Figure 2-41, you can browse the characters available for the Office Assistant and select your favorite.

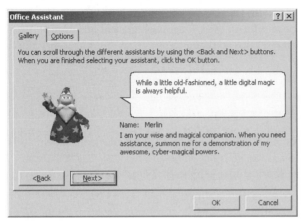

Figure 2-41. You can interview candidates for the Office Assistant position on your desktop.

You can control the many functions of the Office Assistant by using the Options tab.. Many of the options are self-explanatory, but here are a few facts about them.

- If you don't want the Assistant to appear when you press F1, clear the Respond To F1 Key option. If you do this, the Help window appears instead.

- With the Help With Wizards option selected, the Office Assistant appears automatically whenever you start any of Excel's wizards to help you work through it.

- With the Display Alerts option selected, the standard Excel alert messages warning you of impending problems are displayed by the Office Assistant rather than in a boring old alert box. For example, if you try to drag a cell over another cell that already contains data, an alert box warns, "Do you want to replace the contents of the destination cells?" With this option turned on, you not only get the message, but you're also treated to a dramatic little jig by the Office Assistant.

- With the Move When In The Way option turned on, the Office Assistant automatically moves when something like a dialog box appears on the screen in the same location.

- The Guess Help Topics option controls whether the Office Assistant supplies help topics based on what you're currently doing, as described in "Getting Answers to Unasked Questions" on page 61.

● Normally when you are working in the Visual Basic Editor or the Microsoft Script Editor, Help searches are limited to programming topics. With the Search for Both Product and Programming Help When Programming option selected, all Help topics are available for Help searches.

● The Show Tips About section lets you specify the kinds of tips you want to see. The Office Assistant keeps track of the tips it has already displayed. Once a tip has been offered, the Office Assistant will not display it again; however, you can reset tips so that all tips appear. To do so, click the Reset My Tips button.

The Animated Assistant

The Animate! command on the Office Assistant's shortcut menu, shown at the top of the following illustration, is like no other command in Excel. Call it the comic relief feature. (To display the shortcut menu, right-click the Assistant.)

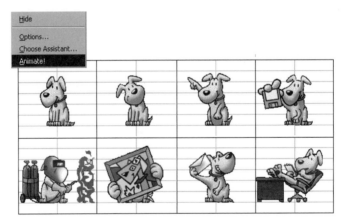

Each time you click the Animate! command, the Office Assistant performs a different quick cartoon-style vignette for you. The panels in the preceding illustration each show a moment from just a few of many different animation sequences for the "Rocky" assistant. Each character in the Office Assistant Gallery has its own unique, sometimes amusing routines. Take a break and tune in the Office Assistant show.

Getting Answers to Unasked Questions

The Office Assistant also makes educated guesses about what you might be trying to do at any given moment. For example, if you select a few cells, and then move them to a new location by clicking and dragging the border of the selection, a light bulb appears over the Assistant, as shown in Figure 2-42.

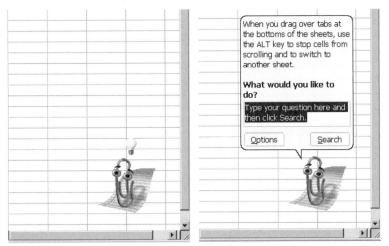

Figure 2-42. The light bulb tells you that the Assistant has a tip for you that applies to something you just did.

When you click the Assistant or the light bulb, a tip based on the action you just performed appears in the Search balloon, as shown on the right in Figure 2-42. As you work, the light bulb will keep popping up, indicating that another tip is available for you. After you click the Assistant to display the tip, click again to redisplay the search balloon if you want to ask another question.

Getting Information on the Spot

You can get instant information about a command, button, or just about anything else on the screen. Simply click Help, What's This? and use the question-mark pointer shown in Figure 2-43 on the next page to choose a command or click an object with which you want help. Excel then displays a pop-up Help topic that applies to the selected command or object.

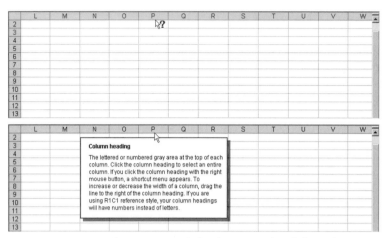

Figure 2-43. Get information on dialog box items by clicking the "?" button in the title bar and then clicking the item.

Getting Information on the Spot in Dialog Boxes

You can click the Question Mark button in most dialog boxes and tab dialog boxes to display a question-mark cursor similar to the one in Figure 2-43. Then click an option or area in the dialog box to display a tip for that item, as shown in Figure 2-44.

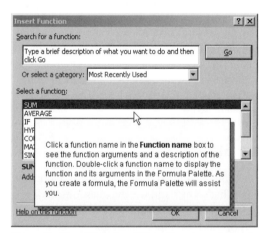

Figure 2-44. Click the "?" button in a dialog box title bar, and then click the item you want help on.

Identifying Toolbar Buttons

For those who have trouble remembering what all those toolbar buttons do, Excel provides ScreenTips. With ScreenTips activated, a descriptive label appears when you move the mouse pointer over a toolbar button, as shown below the Insert Hyperlink button in Figure 2-45.

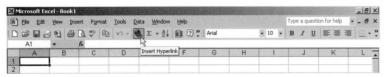

Figure 2-45. ScreenTips help you identify toolbar buttons.

ScreenTips are active by default. To deactivate them, choose View, Toolbars, Customize, and on the Options tab, clear the Show ScreenTips On Toolbars check box.

For more information about toolbars, see "Customizing Toolbars and Menus" on page 65.

What's on the Help Menu?

We've discussed the first three commands on the Help menu. The rest of the commands include the following:

- **Office On The Web** starts your Web browser and connects to the Microsoft Office Update site on the World Wide Web. It's a great place to look for more than just updates.

- **Activate Product** starts the Microsoft Office Activation Wizard, which enables you to do several things, including updating your customer information file at Microsoft and renewing subscriptions to Excel. For more information, see "Subscribing to Excel" on page 14.

- **About Microsoft Excel** displays information about the program and offers a couple of interesting services. For more information, see the sidebar "Before You Call Product Support" on page 64.

Two Help menu commands do not appear on shortened menus (double-click the Help menu to display them):

- **Lotus 1-2-3 Help** displays the Help for Lotus 1-2-3 Users dialog box. For more information, see "Help for Lotus 1-2-3 Users," below.

- **Detect And Repair** attempts to fix any errors that might have occurred in your Microsoft Office installation (not just Excel). This is similar to but not quite as drastic as rerunning the Office Setup program. One nice feature of Detect And Repair is that you can choose to retain or discard many of the customizations you have made to your Office programs.

For more information, see Chapter 3, "Custom-Tailoring the Excel Workspace." For more information about repairing your Excel installation, see "Heroic Measures" on page 18.

Help for Lotus 1-2-3 Users

The Lotus 1-2-3 Help command on the Help menu eases the transition of Lotus 1-2-3 users to Excel. When you choose this command, Excel displays a dialog box (shown in Figure 2-46) in which you can type the key sequence you would use to choose a particular command in Lotus 1-2-3.

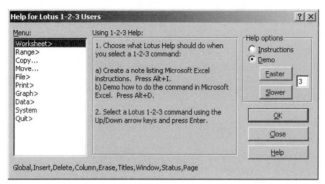

Figure 2-46. This dialog box helps you find the Excel commands that are closest to Lotus commands.

Before You Call Product Support

We encourage you to use Excel documentation, online Help, the Microsoft Excel Web site (*www.microsoft.com/excel*), and especially *this book* to find answers to your questions before you reach for the telephone. When you have exhausted these resources, it's time to call Microsoft Product Support. But before you do, choose Help, About Microsoft Excel, and click the System Info button. Doing so displays a dialog box that lists your current system configuration, the applications running, display information, and much more. If you want, you can print the information in a report or save it as a file on disk. Then you can click the Tech Support button in the About Microsoft Excel dialog box to display a Help topic you can use to find telephone numbers for Microsoft Product Support Services around the world. When you talk to Product Support, having the System Info report at your fingertips will assist the representative in diagnosing your problem and will save you both time. The other button in the About Microsoft Excel dialog box is Disabled Items. Clicking this button opens a dialog box that lists any items that somehow got in the way of an Office program's normal operation and were disabled. You can also try to start them up again by clicking the Enable button. If there is anything on this list, maybe that's your problem. Or maybe it's a symptom. In any case, the Disabled Items dialog box can provide good information to share with your Product Support representative.

Chapter 3

Custom-Tailoring the Excel Workspace

You needn't settle for the way Microsoft Excel's command and control systems are organized. There are a lot of ways to make them more comfortable for the way you work. This chapter tells you how to use Excel's metaphorical six-way power seats and adjustable steering column, and even where to stick that pesky hood release.

Customizing Toolbars and Menus

Don't you sometimes wish you could change the location of the speedometer or some hard-to-reach, dashboard-mounted item in your car? Excel's "dashboard" is completely modular, so you can dismantle and reassemble it any way you like.

Managing Buttons and Commands

When you first start Excel, the Standard and Formatting toolbars are displayed in what the Excel developers refer to as the *rafting* configuration. This means that both toolbars share the same row, as shown in Figure 3-1 on the next page.

You can change this so that each toolbar occupies its own row by choosing Customize from the Tools menu, and on the Options tab, selecting Show Standard And Formatting Toolbars On Two Rows. This way, your toolbars appear as shown in Figure 3-2 on the next page. You can also use the command Show Buttons On Two Rows on the Toolbar Options shortcut menu shown in Figure 3-3 on the page 67.

Toolbar options menu Move handle

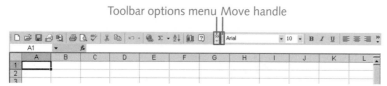

Figure 3-1. Add more buttons to a toolbar with the Toolbar Options menu; resize toolbars with the Move handle.

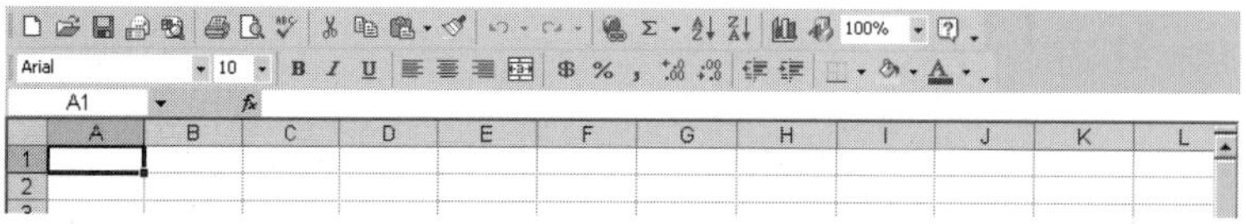

Figure 3-2. The complete Standard and Formatting toolbars are now displayed on separate rows.

Customizing Toolbars on the Fly

The advantage of having the Standard and Formatting toolbars occupy the same row is, of course, to make the greatest amount of screen space available to your worksheets. However, unless you have a very large monitor, some of the buttons in this configuration are hidden from immediate view. Still, you can get to the hidden buttons fairly easily by clicking the downward-pointing arrow—a.k.a. the Toolbar Options menu—at the right side of any toolbar, to display a drop-down menu similar to the one shown in Figure 3-3. Note that when toolbars are in their rafting configuration, there is also a double "fast forward" arrow (>>) above the Toolbar Options menu arrow. This lets you know at a glance that there are more buttons on this toolbar than can be displayed in its current configuration.

The first part of the menu in Figure 3-3 shows all the buttons included on that toolbar that are not currently displayed—the "overflow area." You can choose one of them from the menu, which is the same as clicking it on the toolbar. If you do so, Excel adds that button to the toolbar and removes one to make room. (The default precedence of buttons is preprogrammed, based on years of usage data collected by Microsoft.) It's hard to tell which button will be removed at any given time to make room, but eventually the toolbars should be populated with buttons that you actually use.

At the bottom of the menu in Figure 3-3 is the Add Or Remove Buttons command. You'll notice that the submenu offers yet another submenu, including button menus for both the Standard and Formatting toolbars. These two toolbars are special. In every other toolbar, there's only one button menu on the Toolbar Options menu. The check marks next to the button names in the Formatting submenu in Figure 3-3 indicate that those buttons are already on the toolbar (though perhaps not currently visible). Those names without check marks are prime candidates for addition to that particular

Chapter 3: Custom-Tailoring the Excel Workspace

toolbar. Each toolbar has different optional buttons available. You can click any button on the submenu to select it or to clear it. The changes are reflected immediately on the screen.

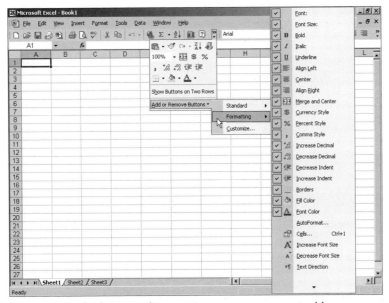

Figure 3-3. The button submenu stays open so you can add or remove as many buttons as you like.

---

tip   **Streamline your toolbars**

The Standard and Formatting toolbars (and others) probably include buttons you never use, so go ahead and remove a few of those important-sounding default buttons like Save and Open to make room for the ones you *really* use.

When you are done, just click anywhere outside the menu to collapse it. Play around all you want; you can always choose the Reset Toolbar command. This command is hidden at the bottom of the button submenu of each toolbar's Toolbar Options menu. On an 800 by 600 display, Reset Toolbar is probably off the screen, and if so, there's an arrow at the bottom to tell you that there's more, as shown in Figure 3-3.

---

note   The buttons that appear on toolbars are simply handy ways to issue commands. The commands that appear on menus are no different from buttons, and in fact, many commands display corresponding button images on the menu.

Chapter 3

Removing and Adding Buttons and Commands

Use the customize dialog box to add and remove buttons and commands from your menus and toolbars. You can find the Customize dialog box, shown in Figure 3-4, in any of the following places:

- On the Add Or Remove Buttons submenu of the Toolbar Options menu.

- At the bottom of the shortcut menu that appears when you click any toolbar or menu bar with the right mouse button.

- On the Toolbars submenu of the View menu.

- On the Tools menu.

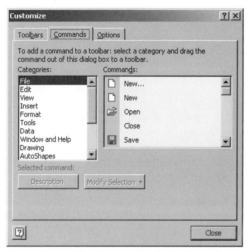

Figure 3-4. The Customize dialog box gives you total control over menus and toolbars.

Displaying the Customize dialog box is like flipping a switch that puts you into "modification mode," enabling you to add and remove commands and buttons, as well as move them among toolbars and menu bars. Though you might not need to use the dialog box, it must be open before you can make changes.

To remove commands or buttons, choose the Customize command. Then drag the button or menu command that you want to remove and drop it anywhere outside the bar or menu. Figure 3-5 shows the removal of the E-mail button.

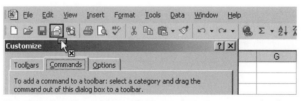

Figure 3-5. To remove a button, drag it away and release the mouse.

To add commands or buttons, click the Commands tab of the Customize dialog box and select one of the Categories. Then drag the button or menu command that you want to add to the desired toolbar or menu. A black I-beam insertion point appears, indicating where the button or command will go when you release the mouse button. Figure 3-6 shows the addition of the Save As Web Page button. Figure 3-7 shows the addition of the HTML source command to the View menu.

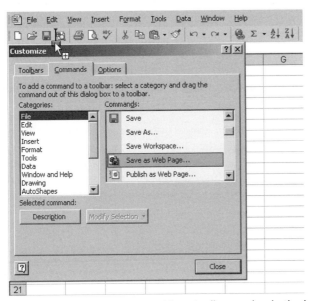

Figure 3-6. Drag a command to a toolbar, and only the button image appears.

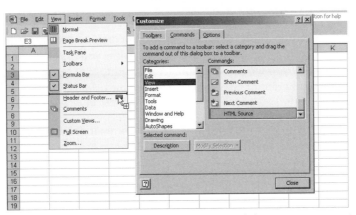

Figure 3-7. Drag a command to a menu, and the text appears automatically.

Chapter 3

69

> **tip** **Drag to copy, move, or delete**
>
> You can copy, move, or delete buttons from toolbars without opening the Customize dialog box. Hold down the Alt key and drag to remove buttons from toolbars or to relocate them to other toolbars. To copy a button to another toolbar, hold down both the Ctrl and Alt keys while dragging the button. This also works with menus such as File, Edit, and View, but not with menu commands.

Rearranging Buttons and Commands   Using the Toolbar Options menu, you can only add and remove buttons—their placement on toolbars is predetermined. With the Customize dialog box open, you can rearrange both buttons and menu commands by simply dragging buttons and commands to wherever you want them. You can even drag items from toolbars to menus and vice versa.

You can add or remove lines between groups of buttons on toolbars or between commands on menus. It takes a little practice, but the basic technique is simple. To add a line to the left of a button, drag the button to the right, releasing the mouse before the I-beam insertion point appears. To add a line above a menu command, drag the command down a couple of millimeters. Similarly, you can remove a line by dragging an adjacent button or command over the existing line until the button or command overlaps the line.

Another way to add and remove the lines between buttons and commands is to use the Modify Selection button on the Commands tab of the Customize dialog box. Selecting the Begin A Group command on the Modify Selection menu, shown in Figure 3-8, inserts a new line to the left of or above the selected button or command. To remove an existing line, select the button or command to the right of or below the line, and choose the Begin A Group command again to clear its check mark.

You can also copy buttons and commands between toolbars and menus. With the Customize dialog box open, hold down the Ctrl key while you drag the button or command you want to copy to the new location. (A small plus sign appears next to the mouse pointer.) The button or command remains in the original location, and a duplicate appears in the new location.

Controlling the Display of Button Faces   Many commands have associated buttons whose faces are normally displayed to the left of the commands on the menus. Many of the same button faces appear on toolbars and perform the same task as the equivalent menu command.

Chapter 3: Custom-Tailoring the Excel Workspace

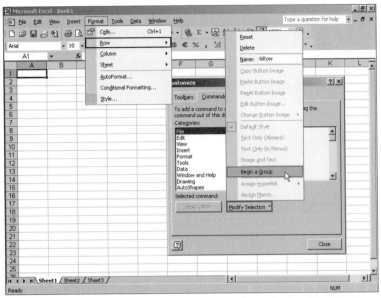

Figure 3-8. Use the Begin A Group command on the Modify Selection menu to add or remove lines.

You control the display of button faces by using commands on the Modify Selection menu shown in Figure 3-8. The Default Style command, the two Text Only commands, and the Image And Text command on the Modify Selection menu control the display of buttons. On toolbars, you can choose to show command names, button images, or both. If you choose the Text Only (In Menus) command, the button face disappears when the selected command is on a menu. If you then drag the command from a menu to a toolbar, the button face appears and the text disappears. If you choose the Text Only (Always) command, the button face does not appear in either location. The Image And Text command causes both the button face and the command text to appear in any location. The Default Style command restores the command to its normal appearance, which for most commands is image and text in menus, and image only on toolbars.

Giving Face to the Faceless   If a menu command does not have an associated button face, you can assign an existing button face or create one from scratch. Using the Customize dialog box, simply select the faceless command, click the Modify Selection button, and then click either Change Button Image or Edit Button Image. In Figure 3-9 on the next page, we added a happy face to the previously faceless Conditional Formatting command.

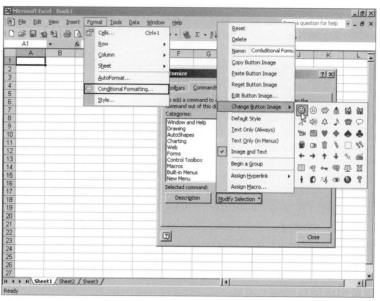

Figure 3-9. Add a face to a faceless command, or change an existing face.

You can also copy faces from other buttons (not necessarily the best idea, but it's possible), modify existing faces, and create brand-new button faces from scratch.

Rearranging Menus and Submenus You can customize your menus by using the same techniques employed when customizing toolbars and commands. An additional technique for customizing menus is to use Built-In Menus. Built-In Menus is a category on the Commands tab of the Customize dialog box that contains all the predefined menus and submenus available in Excel. As with any command or button, you can place items from the Built-In Menus list on any toolbar, menu, or menu bar. For example, you can drag the Toolbars menu from the Built-In Menus list to the menu bar to create a separate menu for toolbars, as shown in Figure 3-10. The Toolbars menu is normally a submenu of the View menu, so you could then drag Toolbars from the View menu to remove it.

Using the Customize dialog box, you can drag entire menus to other menus, transforming them into submenus. For example, you could drag the Help menu to the bottom of the View menu to transform the Help menu into a submenu. You can even add menus to toolbars and add toolbar buttons to menu bars.

Chapter 3: Custom-Tailoring the Excel Workspace

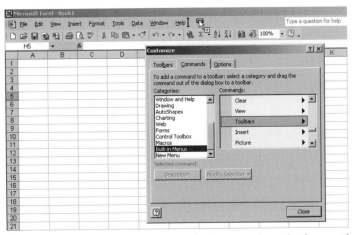

Figure 3-10. You can rearrange Built-In Menus to make frequently used commands more accessible.

Changing the Face of Buttons

There are several ways you can work with button faces. All of these methods start by displaying the Customize dialog box:

- Change a button face using the Change Button Image command.
- Change a button face using the Edit Button Image command.
- Create your own button face from scratch.
- Copy an existing button face.

Using the Customize dialog box, right-click on any toolbar button to display the short-cut menu. (Yes, this is the same as the Modify Selection menu.) As shown in Figure 3-9, the Change Button Image command displays a palette of faces that have not been used on any of Excel's built-in buttons.

If the selections on the Change Button Image palette don't float your boat, you can perform plastic surgery by selecting the Edit Button Image command, which displays the Button Editor, shown in Figure 3-11 on the next page.

Chapter 3

73

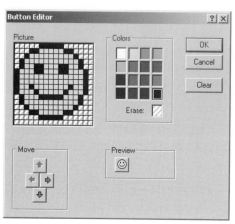

Figure 3-11. You can use the Button Editor to change the face of any toolbar button.

note If you want to create a button face where none currently exists, you'll first need to select the command to which you want to add a face. If the command isn't already on a menu or toolbar, you'll need to add it first.

How to Use the Button Editor

The small squares in the Picture section of the Button Editor dialog box correspond to *pixels,* which are the units of resolution on your computer screen. To erase some of the existing pixels, click the Erase square in the Colors area, and then click or drag through any pixels in the Picture area that you want to remove. The Preview box shows the button as it will appear in its actual size.

To create a new button face from scratch, first click Clear to erase the existing image. Then click a color square in the Colors section, and click or drag through the pixel squares in the Picture section, as if you were dipping your "brush" in paint and applying it to the canvas. When you create buttons with custom faces, those buttons are available on a toolbar or menu only. In other words, these buttons are not included in the Customize dialog box. If you're not satisfied with your custom button face, restore the original button face by using the Reset Button Image command on the button shortcut menu.

You can use the arrow buttons in the Move area to shift the image in the corresponding direction. This works only if there are blank pixels in the direction you want to shift. In Figure 3-11, for example, there is no room to shift the image to the left or up, but it can be shifted one pixel to the right or down.

Copying Button Faces

Here's how to copy a button face from one button to another. Using the Customize dialog box, right-click the button you want to copy, and choose Copy Button Image from

the shortcut menu. Then right-click the button you want to change, and choose Paste
Button Image from the shortcut menu.

Does Size Matter?

The default dimensions of Excel's toolbar buttons are 16 pixels wide by 16 pixels high.
These are also the dimensions of the pixel grid in the Picture section of the Button
Editor dialog box shown earlier in Figure 3-11. So what happens when you click the
Options tab in the Customize dialog box and then select the Large Icons option—one
of Excel's built-in accessibility features? The buttons appear larger, but their actual
pixel dimensions do not change. Instead, Excel displays a "zoomed-in" view of the
buttons. When editing or creating a button face, you can check it with the Large Icons
option to make sure it looks OK in this zoomed mode.

For more about accessibility in Excel and other Office programs, see "Enhancing Accessibility"
on page 89.

Managing Toolbars

You can display additional toolbars at any time, and you can have as many toolbars
active as you want—at the expense of your worksheet's window size, of course, as
shown in Figure 3-12. Activate toolbars by right-clicking a visible toolbar or menu bar,
and select the toolbar you wish to display.

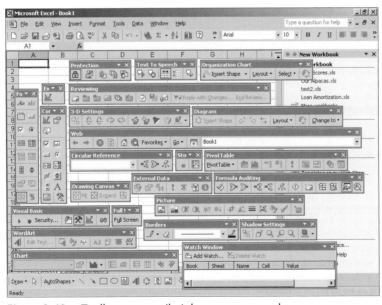

Figure 3-12. Toolbars can easily take over your workspace.

The most useful toolbars are listed on the toolbar shortcut menu, but there are more in the Customize dialog box. Some of these toolbars appear automatically only when needed.

Positioning Bars on Your Screen

When you first start Excel, the menu bar and the Standard and Formatting toolbars are *docked* at the top of the screen. You can *undock* a toolbar or menu bar by clicking its Move handle and dragging it to another location. The toolbars shown in Figure 3-12 are undocked; the toolbars shown in Figure 3-13 are docked.

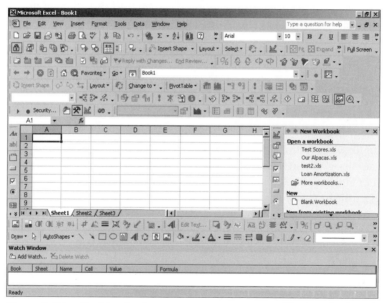

Figure 3-13. Docking toolbars saves screen space and looks a lot better, although you probably don't need this many toolbars visible.

When you undock a toolbar or menu bar, you can change its shape by dragging its borders, and Excel remembers the location and shape you choose. The next time you start Excel, the bar will appear just as it did when you quit the program.

You can dock an undocked bar by dragging it to any side of the screen, or by double-clicking the title bar of an undocked bar. You can dock a toolbar or menu bar on the side of your window, but some tools, such as drop-down lists, might not be visible if you do. (Oddly enough, you can safely dock the menu bar on the side of the screen if you so desire, and the menu names are rotated 90 degrees clockwise.) In addition, some of the buttons on a vertically docked toolbar might not be visible, depending on the type of display you have. With longer vertically docked toolbars, additional buttons might be shifted to the More Buttons menu.

note The downward-pointing arrow you click to display the Toolbar Options menu is displayed on the right side of docked toolbars. When a toolbar is undocked, the Toolbar Options arrow appears on the right side of the toolbar's title bar.

Creating New Toolbars and Menus

Rearranging and modifying buttons and menus is fine, but sometimes it makes more sense to start from scratch.

Creating New Toolbars

It's easy to create a new toolbar.

1 On the Toolbars tab of the Customize dialog box, click the New button.

2 Type a name for your new toolbar into the New Toolbar dialog box, shown in Figure 3-14. When you click OK, a small, empty, floating toolbar appears.

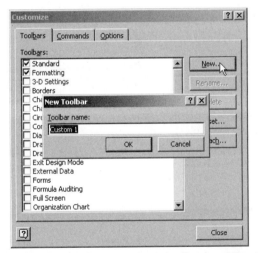

Figure 3-14. Start your new toolbar by giving it a concise name—hopefully one more descriptive than "Custom 1."

3 Add buttons to the empty toolbar by dragging buttons from the Commands tab of the Customize dialog box, or by copying or moving buttons from other toolbars.

After you define a custom toolbar and close the Customize dialog box, that toolbar's name appears in all the places that other toolbar names appear. You can display, hide, and dock custom toolbars just like any default toolbar.

Creating Custom Commands and Buttons

Note a special category—Macros—on the Commands tab of the Customize dialog box. Macros are sequences of commands you can create to help perform repetitive tasks. The Macros category contains two commands: Custom Menu Item and Custom Button. The only real difference between the two is that no button image is associated with the Custom Menu Item. But as we have seen, you could add one anyway, if you like. These two items are simply blank starting points you can use to create your own commands and buttons.

To use the Custom Menu Item or Custom Button command, drag either one of these items to a menu, menu bar, or toolbar, right-click the new command or button, and choose the Assign Macro command on the shortcut menu. All the macros available in the current workbook are listed in this dialog box. You can choose an existing macro and assign it to the selected command or button, or you can click the Record button to start recording a new macro.

> For more information about creating macros, commands, and buttons, see Chapter 31, "Recording Macros."

Attaching Custom Toolbars to Workbooks

Toolbar settings, including custom toolbars, are saved when you exit Microsoft Excel. When you start Excel the next time, those settings and toolbars are reactivated and ready for use. Excel also enables you to attach a custom toolbar to a workbook so that the toolbar is activated only when the corresponding workbook is opened. That way you can create toolbars for specific tasks in specific workbooks. You can even send copies of workbooks to coworkers, and the attached toolbars appear when they open the workbook.

To attach a custom toolbar to your workbook, open the Customize dialog box and click the Attach button to display the dialog box shown in Figure 3-15.

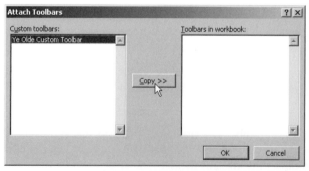

Figure 3-15. Attach custom toolbars to workbooks using the Attach Toolbars dialog box.

Select the toolbar you want to attach to your workbook from the Custom Toolbars list. (Only custom toolbars can be attached to workbooks.) Click the Copy button to add the toolbar to the Toolbars In Workbook list on the right.

---

tip   **Automatically activate a custom toolbar**

After you attach a custom toolbar to a workbook, you can delete the toolbar from the Customize dialog box. Simply select the toolbar on the Toolbars tab and click the Delete button. Then whenever you open the workbook, the custom toolbar is activated. When you close the workbook, the attached custom toolbar remains, allowing you to customize or remove it as needed.

To detach a custom toolbar from a workbook, you must use the Attach Toolbars dialog box again—except this time, select the toolbar in the Toolbars In Workbook list, and then click the Delete button. (The Copy button changes to Delete when you select an attached toolbar.) If you do not detach a toolbar in this way, it will reappear every time you open the workbook, even if you remove it from the Toolbars list.

Deleting Custom Toolbars

To remove a custom toolbar, display the Customize dialog box and on the Toolbars tab, select the name of the custom toobar and click the Delete button. Note the following:

● After you delete a toolbar, you cannot use the Undo command or button to restore it.

● You cannot remove any of Excel's built-in toolbars.

Creating New Menus

The Categories list on the Commands tab of the Customize dialog box contains a category called New Menu. This is a unique category that contains only one item: New Menu. When you drag the New Menu item to a menu bar, a menu, or a toolbar, a blank menu named, surprisingly enough, New Menu, appears. "New Menu" probably isn't a sufficiently descriptive name, so you can rename the new menu. Right-click New Menu and type a name in the Name box, as shown in Figure 3-16 on the next page. You can then populate the new menu with any commands, menus, or buttons you like. You can even put drop-down lists on menus.

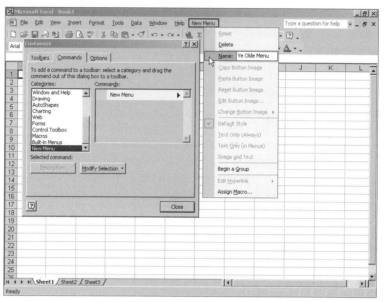

Figure 3-16. Create your own menus from scratch.

Resetting Menus

To remove custom menus and return relocated menus and commands to their original positions, click the Worksheet Menu Bar option (or Chart Menu Bar, if a chart is selected) on the Toolbars tab of the Customize dialog box. Then click Reset.

Preserving Toolbar and Menu Changes

When you exit Microsoft Excel, any predefined toolbars or menus you changed or any custom toolbars or menus you created are saved in the condition and position they were in when you quit. Each time you start Excel, your custom and modified toolbars and menus are ready for use. Excel saves your custom toolbar and menu settings in a special file named Excel.xlb. To create different combinations of toolbar or menu settings, you can save modified and custom toolbar and menu variations by creating custom .XLB files.

To save your current settings, exit Excel and in Windows Explorer, navigate to the following folder and change the name of the Excel.xlb file:

- Windows\Application Data\Microsoft\Excel (Win 9x)

- Documents and Settings\<your name>\Application Data\Microsoft\Excel (Win 2000)

Chapter 3: Custom-Tailoring the Excel Workspace

> **tip** **Recover file extensions**
>
> If you don't see file extensions in the Windows Explorer, choose Folder Options from
> the View menu (or the Tools menu in Windows 2000), and on the View tab, clear the
> Hide File Extensions For Known File Types check box.

The settings that were active when you exited Excel are saved under the new filename,
and any modifications you make during the next Excel session are saved in a fresh
Excel.xlb file. In this way, you can create any number of toolbar and menu configurations, which you can access by double-clicking the .XLB file. Or you can create a
shortcut for any .XLB file on the desktop, or even create a "Special Excel Configurations" folder in the Windows taskbar Start menu.

> **tip** To totally reset all menus and toolbars and discard all personalization data, simply exit
> Excel and delete the Excel.xlb file. Excel creates a new one the next time you start.

Restoring Toolbars and Menus

Now that you've thoroughly scrambled your menus and toolbars, perhaps you're
having a bit of remorse. Don't worry, it's easy to get things back to normal.

- **Restoring a toolbar.** In the Customize dialog box, select the name of the
  toolbar you want to restore from the Toolbars list, and then click the Reset
  button. Click OK to confirm the restoration.

- **Restoring a menu.** In the Customize dialog box, right-click the menu you
  want to restore, and then choose the Reset command from the shortcut
  menu that appears.

- **Restoring all menus.** This resets all menus, submenus, and commands at
  the same time. Click the Toolbars tab in the Customize dialog box, and
  select the Worksheet Menu Bar option (or the Chart Menu Bar option, if a
  chart is currently active). Then click the Reset button. Click OK to confirm
  the restoration. Click Close when you are finished.

Restoring Personalized Toolbars and Menus

The preceding procedures reset toolbars and menus in terms of their inventory of
commands and buttons, but they do not affect which commands and buttons are
visible when personalization options are turned on. The Personalized Menus And
Toolbars options are on the Options tab of the Customize dialog box.

Chapter 3

When the Show Standard And Formatting Toolbars On Two Rows option is *not* selected, the toolbar equivalent of the "recently used commands" option is activated. Your usage habits, which are recorded by Excel as you work, partially determine which buttons are visible on the Standard and Formatting toolbars (or on any rafting toolbar). To discard this usage data and return all menu commands and toolbar buttons to their original places, click the Reset My Usage Data button.

Other Toolbar and Menu Options

There just seems to be no end to the customization options you have at your command in Excel. Here are a few more that are quite helpful, and one that is kind of silly.

- If you want, you can enlarge all the toolbar buttons for easy selection and improved legibility. Simply select the Large Icons option on the Options tab of the Customize dialog box. Note, however, that magnifying the buttons reduces the number of buttons visible on a docked toolbar.

- When the Show ScreenTips On Toolbars option is selected, a small label appears when you move the mouse pointer over any toolbar button. (For more on ScreenTips, see "Show ScreenTips on the Toolbar" on page 89.)

- The Options tab in the Customize dialog box also contains a drop-down list labeled "Menu Animations." This is one of the so-called "visceral" elements in Excel, along with sound feedback and animated row-and-column insertion and deletion (both of which are controlled by the Tools, Options command). You can select one of the four options in the Menu Animations list: Random, Unfold, Slide, and Fade (the default). When you click menus when animations are turned on, instead of simply appearing, they appear with a flourish!

- You can click the Always Show Full Menus option to make all commands on all menus available at all times. This eliminates the need to either wait for menus to unfurl, or to click the arrow at the bottom of a shortened menu to display it in its entirety.

- The List Font Names In Their Font option does just what it says and only applies to the Font drop-down list.

For more information about fonts and formatting, see Chapter 8, "Worksheet Formatting Techniques."

Controlling Other Elements of the Excel Interface

There are three important tabs in the Options dialog box (shown in Figure 3-17): the View tab, the General tab and the Color tab. You can use these tabs to control the way your documents appear on screen.

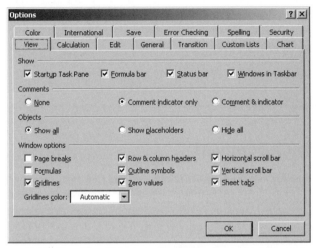

Figure 3-17. The View tab, the General tab, and the Color tab in the Options dialog box control the appearance of your workbook.

The View tab controls the display of the formula and status bars as well as the appearance of automatic page breaks, formulas, gridlines, column and row headings, outline symbols, zero values, and objects, among other things. The Color tab enables you to modify the set of 56 colors available for any given workbook. The General tab specifies the default font.

The options you select in the Window Options section on the View tab of the Options dialog box affect only the active workbook; they do not change the display of other workbooks.

If you clear the Row & Column Headers, Horizontal Scroll Bar, Vertical Scroll Bar, or Sheet Tabs options, those window elements disappear from view in the current workbook. You can use these options to polish your workbooks for display purposes. They do not affect the way the worksheets in the current workbook will look when you print them.

Displayed vs. Printed Gridlines

Typically, Excel displays a grid to mark the boundaries of each cell in the worksheet. Although this grid is usually helpful for selection and navigation, you might not want it displayed all the time. To suppress gridline display, clear the Gridlines check box on the View tab of the Options dialog box.

Clearing the Gridlines check box removes the gridlines from your screen and also suppresses them for printing. If you want gridlines printed but not displayed (or vice versa), choose File, Page Setup, click the Sheet tab, and then select or clear the Gridlines check box in the Print section.

For more on printing a document without gridlines, see Chapter 11, "Printing and Presenting."

Displaying Underlying Formulas

Normally when you enter a formula in a cell, you see the results of that formula, not the formula itself. Similarly when you format a number, you no longer see the underlying (unformatted) value displayed in the cell. You can normally see the underlying values and formulas only by selecting individual cells and looking at the formula bar.

The Formulas option on the View tab of the Options dialog box enables you to display all the underlying values and formulas in your worksheet. As you can see in Figure 3-18, the underlying contents of each cell appear, as in the sum formulas in row 6 of the bottom window, and all cells are left-aligned. (Excel ignores any alignment formatting when you select the Formulas option.) In addition, the width of each column in the worksheet approximately doubles to accommodate the underlying formulas, and the Formula Auditing toolbar appears. (The actual width of the columns remains unchanged; columns only appear wider on the screen.)

tip   Display and hide formulas

You can quickly display and hide formulas in your worksheet by pressing Ctrl+single opening quote ('), which is located on the tilde key on most keyboards. To redisplay values, press Ctrl+' again.

When you clear the Formulas option, Excel restores all columns to their former widths and closes the Formula Auditing toolbar.

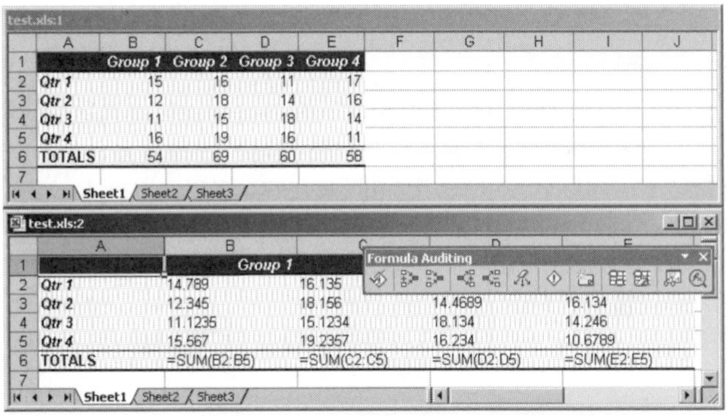

Figure 3-18. Display underlying values and formulas for easier auditing.

---

tip **Display each window differently**

If you use the New Window command on the Window menu to create two or more windows in which to view the same workbook, you can use different display options in each window. For example, you can display formulas in one window and see the results of those formulas (the normal view) in another window.

The Formulas option is particularly helpful when you need to edit a large worksheet. You can see your formulas without having to activate each cell and view its contents in the Formula Bar. You can also use the Formulas option to document your work: after you select Formulas, you can print your worksheet with the formulas displayed for archiving purposes.

Hiding Zeros

Normally zeros are displayed on your worksheet. Sometimes, especially for presentation purposes, it is helpful to eliminate the clutter of excessive zero values on a worksheet. To hide zeros, clear the Zero Values option on the View tab of the Options dialog box. Any cells containing only zeros, or any formulas that result in zero, appear as blank cells on the sheet. The underlying entries are unaffected, of course. If you edit an entry or if the result of a formula changes so that the cell no longer contains a zero value, the value immediately becomes visible. If the Formulas option on the View tab is selected, clearing the Zero Values option has no effect on the display.

---

caution If you hide zero values, be careful when editing your worksheet. What appears to be an empty cell might actually contain a formula.

Changing the Standard Font

The standard font is used not only for all text and numbers that you enter into a workbook, but it also determines the font used in row and column headings. In addition, the standard font is used as the font definition for the Normal style. You change the Standard Font option on the General tab of the Options dialog box, shown in Figure 3-19. The default standard font is 10-point Arial, but in Figure 3-19, the standard font was changed to 14-point Times New Roman, a good choice for high visibility, but a bad choice if you want to view many cells on the screen at one time.

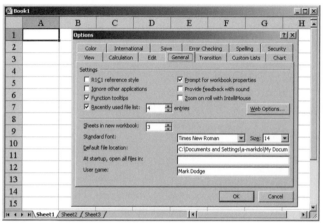

Figure 3-19. Choose Tools, Options and click the General tab to change the Standard Font used in new workbooks.

Maybe what you really want to do is change the font used only in the current workbook, rather than in all new workbooks. To do so, choose Format, Style, click the Modify button, and then on the Font tab, change the Font attributes you want. Changes to the Normal style affect only the current workbook—the standard font continues to determine the font used in all new workbooks.

After you select the font name and size you want from the corresponding drop-down lists on the General tab of the Options dialog box and click OK, a dialog box informs you that the new standard font will not become active until you quit and restart Excel. The next time you start Excel, all new workbooks you create are displayed with the new standard font. If you choose Style from the Format menu you'll see that the Normal style now includes the new standard font.

For more on other options in this dialog box, see "Managing Worksheets" on page 117 (for information about the number of worksheets in a workbook; and "Saving and Publishing Excel Files in HTML," in Chapter 20.

Changing the Color Palette

In a number of locations in Excel, you can set the colors of items like fonts, borders, patterns, gridlines, and so on. The available color options are determined by your default color palette, which consists of 56 colors. Choose the Tools, Options command, and using the Color tab shown in Figure 3-20, you can modify any color in the palette.

The Standard Colors area presents samples of each solid color in the current palette. The Chart Fills and Chart Lines areas reflect the default colors, as well as the order in which Excel colors chart elements.

To substitute a different color for one of the current colors, select the current color and then click Modify to display the Colors dialog box, also shown in Figure 3-20.

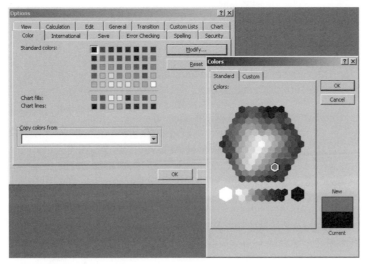

Figure 3-20. The Color tab in the Options dialog box controls the default color palette.

The Standard tab in the Colors dialog box displays a "color wheel" of sorts, with 127 colors and 15 shades of gray you can choose from. The New/Current box enables you to see the difference between the color you want to change (on the bottom) and the color you select (on the top). The Custom tab, shown in Figure 3-21 on the next page, gives you even more precise control over the color palette.

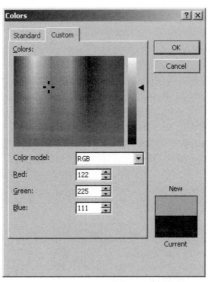

Figure 3-21.   The Custom tab in the Colors dialog box gives you extreme control of your colors.

Colors displayed on your screen are defined by three parameters—their red, green, and blue (RGB) values. An alternative system of specification uses three different parameters: hue, saturation, and luminescence (HSL). You can choose either of these systems by using the Color Model list, which changes the values used in the three spin boxes below. Type new values or click the arrows next to the spin boxes to define a new color.

Alternatively, the cross-hairs pointer in the large Colors box controls hue (left to right) and saturation (up and down), and the arrowhead pointer beside the vertical scale controls luminescence. By experimenting with these two pointers and looking at the samples that appear in the New/Current box, you can come up with new colors without having to know anything about the parameters that define them.

> **note**   If you define colors that are not among your system's repertoire of solids, Excel produces them by mixing dots from solid colors. Such blended colors, which are said to be *dithered,* work well for shading. But for text and lines, Excel always uses the nearest solid color in preference to a dithered color.

After you edit the color palette, click OK to save it. Your customized palette then becomes an attribute of the current workbook. Click the Reset button on the Color tab to revert to the original color palette.

Copying Palettes from Other Workbooks

To achieve a consistent look among workbooks, you can copy your custom palette. To do so, open both the source and destination workbooks, and make the destination workbook active. Choose Options from the Tools menu, click the Color tab, and click the arrow next to the Copy Colors From drop-down list to see a list of all other open workbooks. Select your source workbook and then click OK.

Enhancing Accessibility

Excel and all other Office XP programs now support the Microsoft Active Accessibility 2.0 specification. This makes various accessibility aids more effective, including screen readers and screen enlargers. For more information, visit the Microsoft Accessibility Web site at *http://www.microsoft.com/enable*.

Here is a list of built-in features that, either by design or by default, enhance Excel's accessibility:

- **Large Icons.** Increases the size of toolbar buttons. Click the option of the same name on the Options tab of the Customize dialog box (found by clicking Toolbars on the View menu). For more information, see "Other Toolbar and Menu Options" on page 82.

- **Show ScreenTips On Toolbars.** Displays the little yellow labels under toolbar buttons with the button name. Click the option of the same name on the Options tab of the Customize dialog box. For more information, see "Other Toolbar and Menu Options" on page 82.

- **Provide Feedback With Sound.** Provides audio cues for actions such as clicking and scrolling. Click the option of the same name on the General tab of the Options dialog box (found by clicking Options on the Tools menu).

- **Function ToolTips.** Displays yellow boxes with labels describing the syntax and arguments for functions entered or selected in the Formula bar or in cells. Click the option of the same name on the General tab of the Options dialog box. For more information, see Chapter 13, "Using Functions."

- **Provide Feedback With Animation.** Adds visual cues for actions including menu display, scrolling, and inserting/deleting. Click the option of the same name on the Edit tab of the Options dialog box. For more information, see "Other Toolbar and Menu Options" on page 82.

- **Enable AutoComplete For Cell Values.** When entering data in a column, automatically inserts existing entries in the same column that match the current entry. Saves keystrokes, for example, when repeatedly typing the same entry. Click the option of the same name on the General tab of the Options dialog box. For more information, see "Letting Excel Help with Typing Chores" on page 195.

newfeature!

- **Gridlines Color.** Changes the color of gridlines in your worksheet. Choose a color in the list box of the same name on the View tab of the Options dialog box.

newfeature!

- **Colored Sheet Tabs.** Makes it easier to find key sheets in a workbook, or color code to differentiate tabs. Choose Sheet on the Format menu and click Tab Color. For more information, see "Coloring Sheet Tabs" on page 119.

newfeature!

- **Text To Speech.** Reads the contents of cells to you. Point to Speech on the Tools menu, click Show Text To Speech Toolbar, and click the Speak Cells button. Or click the Speak On Enter button to have Excel vocalize what you just entered, to help increase accuracy. For more information, see "Having Excel Read Cells to You" on page 271.

- **Keyboard Shortcuts.** Gives you access to any command in Excel using the keyboard. For more information, see Appendix C, "Keyboard Shortcuts."

- **Scroll And Pan.** If you have a Microsoft Intellimouse, enables you to scroll through a worksheet by simply turning the wheel in the direction you want to scroll. If you press down on the wheel and drag the mouse, you can pan the worksheet in any direction.

- **Zoom In.** Enlarges the worksheet display up to 400% using the Zoom box on the Standard toolbar, or by holding down Ctrl and turning the wheel on a Microsoft Intellimouse.

Part 2

Building Worksheets

Worksheet Design Tips

There's nothing particularly mysterious about creating a worksheet—after all, it's just a bunch of rows and columns. And we certainly wouldn't want to stifle your creativity. Even after more than a decade of writing about spreadsheets, we continue to see stunning new uses for the ol' grid. But there are a few guidelines that make life a little easier and some gotchas that you need to watch out for. This chapter poses a number of questions you should ask yourself before you put on your digital hardhat and start worksheet construction.

Which Data Should Be in Rows, and Which in Columns?

Sometimes this is rather obvious, but generally speaking, you'll want the data that will be most abundant to fill rows rather than columns. Consider the readability of your data when you make this decision. For example, a month-oriented worksheet like the one in Figure 4-1 on the next page can work well with the month labels either across the top or down the left side of the worksheet. But in this case, having the month labels down the side makes it is easier to view the worksheet on-screen and easier to fit it on a printed page. The worksheet in Figure 4-1 contains only four columns of detail data, but if your worksheet has more categories of detail data than the number of months, you may want to run the months in columns instead.

Usually the detail you accumulate in a worksheet best fits into rows from top to bottom—relatively speaking, a deep and narrow worksheet. It is not unheard of to build a spreadsheet that is shallow and wide (only a few rows deep, with lots of columns), but you might regret it later. A shallow and wide sheet can be annoying to deal with if you must continually scroll to the right to find information and deal with odd column breaks when

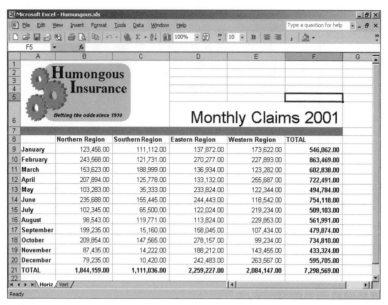

Figure 4-1. Monthly total worksheets are often oriented vertically, as shown here.

printing. And once you've got the worksheet filled with data, it's very time consuming to change it—especially when it could have been designed differently from the start.

You may also prefer the worksheet to be long rather than wide so you can use the Page Up and Page Down keys to navigate on-screen. When oriented horizontally, the worksheet shown in Figure 4-1 would still work, as shown in Figure 4-2, but you would have to scroll to the right to view all the data.

Will You Need to Print the Worksheet?

Before you start work on a worksheet, you also need to ask yourself if the worksheet will need to be printed. You may realize that you don't need to worry about printing at all, if, for example, the worksheet is to be used for information storage or reference purposes only.

If you will want to print the sheet, consider how your data will look and how the sheet will work on paper. This will make a huge difference to your overall worksheet design. For example, the worksheet in Figure 4-2 will require two pages to print, even if you orient it horizontally (using Landscape mode in the File, Page Setup dialog box). The second page of the printout will contain some of the monthly totals, but you won't see the names of the regions unless you use Microsoft Excel's Print Titles feature to repeat the headings on each page. For large worksheets in either horizontal or vertical orientation, using Print Titles is an absolute necessity for intelligible printouts.

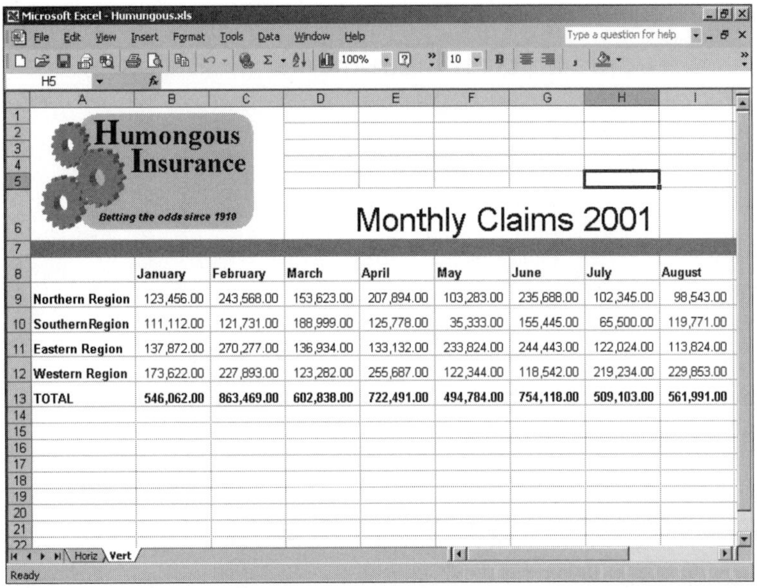

	January	February	March	April	May	June	July	August
Northern Region	123,456.00	243,568.00	153,623.00	207,894.00	103,283.00	235,688.00	102,345.00	98,543.00
Southern Region	111,112.00	121,731.00	188,999.00	125,778.00	35,333.00	155,445.00	65,500.00	119,771.00
Eastern Region	137,872.00	270,277.00	136,934.00	133,132.00	233,824.00	244,443.00	122,024.00	113,824.00
Western Region	173,622.00	227,893.00	123,282.00	255,687.00	122,344.00	118,542.00	219,234.00	229,853.00
TOTAL	546,062.00	863,469.00	602,838.00	722,491.00	494,784.00	754,118.00	509,103.00	561,991.00

Figure 4-2. Worksheets are often harder to view and print when oriented horizontally.

If you will want to print the sheet, consider how your data will look and how the sheet will work on paper. This will make a huge difference to your overall worksheet design. For example, the worksheet in Figure 4-2 will require two pages to print, even if you orient it horizontally (using Landscape mode in the File, Page Setup dialog box). The second page of the printout will contain some of the monthly totals, but you won't see the names of the regions unless you use Microsoft Excel's Print Titles feature to repeat the headings on each page. For large worksheets in either horizontal or vertical orientation, using Print Titles is an absolute necessity for intelligible printouts.

For more about page setup and print titles, see Chapter 11, "Printing and Presenting."

You also need to consider what the printout will be used for. If it's going to be used in a management report, you'll want to try getting the salient information to fit on one page. If it's for a presentation, you may need to distill it further, or create smaller, more digestible chunks of data that can be summarized in a small grid of a dozen cells or so, so it will fit onto a transparency or a slide. If you have massive amounts of data to start with, you can create summary pages for various purposes, as shown in Figure 4-3 on the following page, or use outlining to collapse the detail in large worksheets, showing only the totals, as shown in Figure 4-4 on the next page.

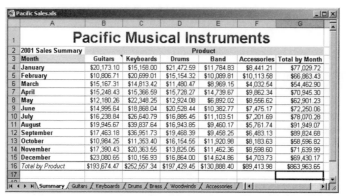

Figure 4-3. If showing all the detail data is too cumbersome, you can create summary sheets for reporting purposes.

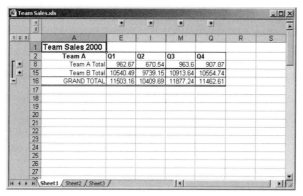

Figure 4-4. You can use outlining to hide the detail for summary purposes.

For information about outlining, see "Outlining Worksheets" on page 272.

If the worksheet is for auditing or reference purposes, you'll probably want to see everything. Orientation is a big issue here. You can print either in landscape (horizontal) or portrait (vertical) format, so design your worksheet accordingly. Sometimes using a landscape orientation helps if you have lots of columns. If you have an inordinate number of columns, you may want to try and segment your data into an overall system of worksheets—chunks that can be realistically printed without losing context or readability. For example, the sheet tabs at the bottom of the workbook shown in Figure 4-3 give evidence that the displayed summary sheet actually consolidates the data from six other sheets in the same workbook.

Who Is the Audience?

Are you building a worksheet for your own use, or will you be sharing it with others online or in printed form? In other words, does the worksheet need to look marvelous, or is fancy formatting optional? Do you need to create a big-picture summary or overview for others? It's definitely important to consider audience when deciding how your worksheet is going to look.

If you're close to the data in your worksheet—that is, this is your job—you probably think that the details are a lot more interesting than others might. You need to think like the people you will be presenting this information to, and tell them what they need to know—no more, and certainly no less. If your worksheet contains a lot of data that your audience doesn't really need to see, which is almost always the case, you can create a summary sheet (like the one shown in Figure 4-3) specifically for the purpose of mass consumption. If your worksheet will have more than one type of audience, create different summary sheets for each group, all using the same underlying data.

Would Your Worksheet Survive Without You?

If you are creating sheets that might at some point be used by others, make sure they are understandable and well documented. Most of us don't think about documentation, but every spreadsheet you create for business or personal use should be created with the possibility in mind that others will need to figure it out some day—possibly without your help. If you change jobs, you will be leaving a good legacy behind for the next person, which reflects well on you. A little documentation goes a long way, as shown in Figure 4-5. You can use Excel's Comment feature to add notes anywhere a little explanation is in order.

Figure 4-5. Make sure that critical worksheets are understandable and well documented.

> For information about documenting your worksheets, see "Adding Comments to Cells" on page 266.

You also need to prepare worksheets containing important personal records with survivability in mind. Not to sound too morbid, but if you were to unexpectedly shed this mortal coil, you wouldn't want to leave your family in the lurch because your financial worksheets are undecipherable.

Does the Worksheet Rely on Imported Data?

Many people work with data that is compiled elsewhere as the basis for their worksheet analyses. For example, a database located either on your computer or somewhere on a network is often the repository for specific information that you extract and analyze. If this is the case, try to make it easy on yourself. Often, we use the "ad hoc" approach to working—that is, we do it quickly, when it's needed, with no particular attention paid to repeatability. If you gather information from a database, you might be able to construct *queries* that you can execute again and again, on whatever schedule you need, rather than starting from scratch each time. This way, you can assure that the imported data will be structured in exactly the same way each time. Then you might use the structure of the imported data as the basis for your worksheet design. Or it might make sense to keep the imported data on a separate sheet that no one will see, and to construct nicely formatted sheets you can use to extract only the pertinent information. For example, Figure 4-6 shows just such a worksheet. You can see that the raw data is on a separate sheet behind the information sheet.

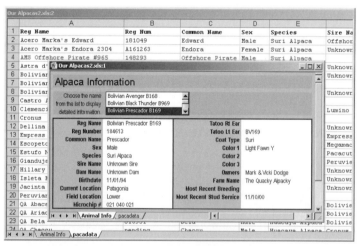

Figure 4-6. You can put raw imported data on its own sheet and use a formatted sheet to present the pertinent information.

For information about using information stored elsewhere, see Chapter 29, "Working with External Data," as well as the chapters in Part VI, "Collaboration and the Internet."

Databases, Fields, and Records

Sometimes when you say the word "database," you can watch people's eyes glaze over in anticipation of a barrage of incomprehensible terminology. While using a database program can be overwhelmingly complex, consider that many of the worksheets you'll create in Excel (such as the underlying sheet in Figure 4-6) are actually rudimentary databases. The telephone directory is an example of a database in printed form. In database terminology, each phone listing in the directory is a *record* of the database, while each item of information in a listing (first name, last name, address, and telephone number) is a *field* of the record.

Do You Need More than One Worksheet?

Spreadsheet programs began as a better way to store, present, and interpret information that previously had been kept on paper and calculated by hand, probably using a ten-key calculator. Often the first sheets we created when we were climbing the old Excel learning curve were little more than clean two-dimensional reproductions of what we used to do on paper. One way to step up from the old paper paradigm is to use *modular design*. Modular design is a sort of "structured programming" or "object oriented" approach, where you carve your data into logical chunks that make sense as stand-alone elements. (The other design approach is called *hierarchical*, which is organized for error identification and maximum readability.) Since there's usually no need to keep detail data in any kind of presentable format, why bother? Concentrate your worksheet beautification program on the summary sheets and charts that you will share with others. Design a *system* of worksheets rather than trying to get everything on a single worksheet. Figure 4-6 shows a rudimentary example of modular design—that is, there is one sheet for data and another for a specific type of analysis. In a complex modular system, you might have dozens of sheets, each dedicated to a specific task.

Have You Allowed Room to Insert New Rows and Columns?

It's critical to allow for expansion and editing after your worksheet is assembled. It's generally a good idea to add a few extra rows and columns to the detail area and to keep totals separated from the detail data by a row or column or two, if possible. One of the most common editing actions you'll perform is inserting new rows and columns. Excel has gotten a lot smarter about this over the years, making obsolete some of the rules of thumb that we old-timers have collected. But it's still possible to mess up.

There's a rather famous folkloric tale about an accounting person who inserted a row at the bottom of a range of cells but forgot to adjust the totals formulas and was fired because his numbers were $200,000 off. The moral: edit worksheets carefully and audit yourself ruthlessly, especially if your job is on the line.

99

How to Work a Worksheet

The worksheet is Microsoft Excel's playing field, where all your base hits, grand slams, errors, and wild pitches occur. This chapter discusses the "innings and outs" of using worksheets, including the quickest way to get from cell A1 to cell IV65536 (and anywhere between), the hidden methods of selecting, and the basics of editing.

You probably already know most of these techniques, but here we'll present alternative methods. You might find that there is a better, or faster, way to do something you do frequently. If there's one thing Excel has a lot of, it's alternatives.

Moving Around

You already know how to use scroll bars and the Page Up and Page Down keys. There are many other ways to get around, including some unique tricks you'll find only in Excel.

Navigating Regions

A *region* is a range of cell entries bounded by blank cells or column and row headings. In Figure 5-1, the range A3:E7 is a region, as are the ranges G3:H7, A9:E10, and G9:H10. (Strictly speaking, cell A1 is also a region because there are no adjoining cells containing entries.)

In Figure 5-1 on the next page, for example, cell E7 is within a region, even though it's empty. The *active area* is a rectangle that encompasses all regions—that is, all the filled cells in the active worksheet.

The techniques used to navigate regions are especially helpful if you typically work with large tables of data. Getting to the bottom row of a 500-row table is easier when you don't have to use the scroll bars. Read on to find out how.

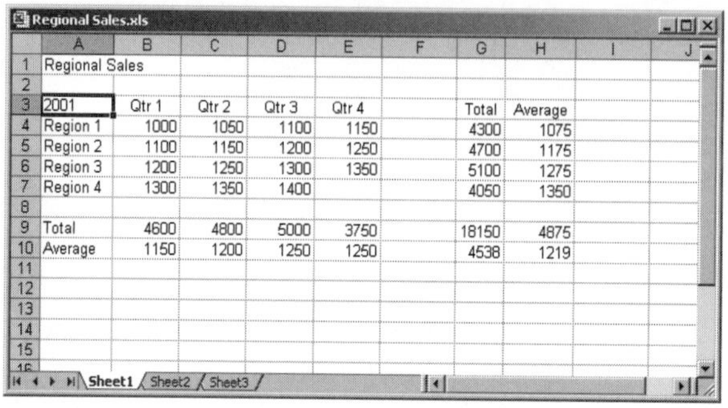

	A	B	C	D	E	F	G	H
1	Regional Sales							
2								
3	2001	Qtr 1	Qtr 2	Qtr 3	Qtr 4		Total	Average
4	Region 1	1000	1050	1100	1150		4300	1075
5	Region 2	1100	1150	1200	1250		4700	1175
6	Region 3	1200	1250	1300	1350		5100	1275
7	Region 4	1300	1350	1400			4050	1350
8								
9	Total	4600	4800	5000	3750		18150	4875
10	Average	1150	1200	1250	1250		4538	1219

Figure 5-1. The four blocks of cells on this worksheet are separate regions.

> **note** The small square in the lower right corner of the active cell is called the *Fill handle.* If the Fill handle isn't visible on your screen, it means that the Allow Cell Drag And Drop option, which is necessary for region navigation to work, isn't available. Choose Tools, Options, click the Edit tab, and select Allow Cell Drag And Drop.

Navigating Regions with the Keyboard

To move between the edges of regions, hold down the Ctrl key while pressing any of the arrow keys. For example, in Figure 5-1, cell A3 is the active cell; press Ctrl+Right Arrow to activate cell E3.

If a blank cell is active when you press Ctrl and an arrow key, Excel moves to the first filled cell in that direction or to the last available cell in the worksheet if there are no filled cells in that direction. In Figure 5-1, for example, suppose cell F3 is active; if you press Ctrl+Right Arrow, the selection moves to cell G3.

Navigating Regions with the Mouse

When you move the mouse pointer over the edge of the active cell's border, the pointer changes from a plus sign to an arrow. With the arrow pointer visible, you can double-click any edge of the border to change the active cell to the cell on the edge of the current region in that direction—it is the same as pressing Ctrl and an arrow key in that direction. For example, if you double-click the bottom edge of the active cell in Figure 5-1, Excel selects cell A7.

The right side of the status bar displays the indicators in Table 5-1 when the corresponding mode is active.

Table 5-1. Keyboard Mode Codes

Code	Description
EXT	**Extend mode.** Press F8 to turn on the Extend mode, which you can use to extend the current selection using the keyboard. (Make sure Scroll Lock is turned off.) This is a keyboard equivalent of selecting cells by dragging the mouse. Furthermore, unlike holding down the Shift key and pressing an arrow key, you can extend the range by pressing only one key at a time. Press F8 again to turn off Extend mode.
ADD	**Add mode.** Press Shift+F8 to add more cells to the current selection using the keyboard. The cells need not be adjacent; after pressing Shift+F8, click any cell or drag through any range to add it to the selection. This is the keyboard equivalent of holding down Ctrl and selecting additional cells with the mouse.
NUM	**Num Lock mode.** This mode is on by default and locks the keypad in numeric-entry mode. To turn off Num Lock mode, press the Num Lock key.
FIX	**Fixed Decimal mode.** Choose Tools, Options, click the Edit tab, and select Fixed Decimal to add a decimal point to the numeric entries in the current selection. Excel places the decimal point in the location you specify in the Places box. For example, if you turn on Fixed Decimal mode and specify two decimal places, a cell containing the number 12345 changes to 123.45. To turn off Fixed Decimal mode, return to the Edit tab of the Options dialog box and clear the Fixed Decimal option.
CAPS	**Caps Lock mode.** Press the Caps Lock key to enter typed text in capital letters. Number and symbol keys are not affected. To turn off Caps Lock mode, press the Caps Lock key again.
SCRL	**Scroll Lock mode.** Press Scroll Lock to use the Page Up, Page Down, and arrow keys to move the viewed portion of the window without moving the active cell. When Scroll Lock mode is off, the active cell moves one page at a time when you press Page Up or Page Down, or one cell at a time when you press one of the arrow keys. To turn off Scroll Lock mode, press the Scroll Lock key again.

(continued)

Chapter 5

Table 5-1. Keyboard Mode Codes *(continued)*

Code	Description
END	**End mode.** Press the End key and then press an arrow key to move the selection to the edge of the region in that direction, or to the last worksheet cell in that direction. This mode functions like holding down Ctrl and pressing an arrow key, except that you need to press only one key at a time. To turn off End mode, press the End key again. End mode is also turned off after you press one of the arrow keys. While End mode is active, the word END appears toward the right side of the status bar.
OVR	**Overwrite mode.** Click the formula bar or double-click a cell and press the Insert key to turn on Overwrite mode. Normally, new characters you type in the formula bar are inserted between existing characters. With Overwrite mode turned on, the characters you type replace any existing characters to the right of the insertion point. Overwrite mode turns off when you press Insert again or when you press Enter or one of the arrow keys.

Navigating with Special Keys

The following table shows how you can use the Home and End keys alone and in conjunction with other keys to make selections and to move around a worksheet.

Press	To
Home	Move to the first cell in the current row.
Ctrl+Home	Move to cell A1.
Ctrl+End	Move to the last cell in the last column in the active area. For example, in Figure 5-1, pressing Ctrl+End selects cell H10.
End	Start End mode. Then use an arrow key to move within cell regions.
Scroll Lock+Home	Move to the first cell within the current window.
Scroll Lock+End	Move to the last cell within the current window.

Selecting Stuff

Before you can work with a cell or range, you must *select* it, and when you do, it becomes active. The reference of the active cell appears in the Name box at the left end of the formula bar. Only one cell can be active at a time, but you can select *ranges* of cells. You can change the active cell in a selected range without changing your range selection.

Selecting with the Mouse

To select a range of cells, drag the mouse over the range. Alternatively, instead of dragging through all the cells you want to select, you can use a technique known as *extending* to indicate two diagonal corners of the range. For example, to extend the selection A1:B5 so that it becomes A1:C10, hold down the Shift key and click cell C10. When you need to select a large range, this technique is more efficient than dragging the mouse across the entire selection.

Selecting Beyond the Window Borders

It's impossible to see an entire workbook on the screen. Knowing that, what do you do if you need to select a gigantic range of cells? You can drag the mouse pointer past the window border and wait for the automatic scrolling to get you where you need to go, but this method can be frustrating if you have trouble managing the scrolling speed and keep overshooting the target.

A better method is to use the Zoom command to get a bird's-eye view of the worksheet, as shown in Figure 5-2. Choose View, Zoom, or use the Zoom box on the Standard toolbar, and select or type the zoom percentage you want. The Zoom feature is limited to a range from 10 through 400 percent. You still won't be able to see the whole worksheet, but it certainly helps.

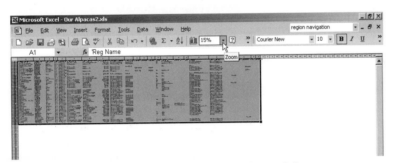

Figure 5-2. Use Zoom to select large areas of a worksheet.

Selecting Columns, Rows, and Multiple Areas

Multiple-area ranges (also known as nonadjacent or noncontiguous ranges) are cell ranges that do not encompass a single rectangular area, as shown in Figure 5-3. To select multiple-area ranges with the mouse, use the Ctrl key and drag through each range you want to select. The first cell you click in the last range you select becomes the active cell. As you can see in Figure 5-3, cell G9 is the active cell.

Chapter 5

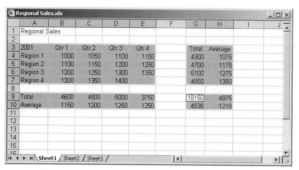

Figure 5-3. Hold down the Ctrl key to select multiple-area ranges with the mouse.

To select an entire column or row, click the column or row heading. In other words, to select cells B1 through B65536, click the heading for column B. The first visible cell in the column becomes the active cell. To select more than one adjacent column or row at a time, drag through the column or row headings, or click the heading at one end of the range, press Shift, and then click the heading at the other end. To select nonadjacent columns or rows, as shown in Figure 5-4, hold down Ctrl and click each heading you want to select.

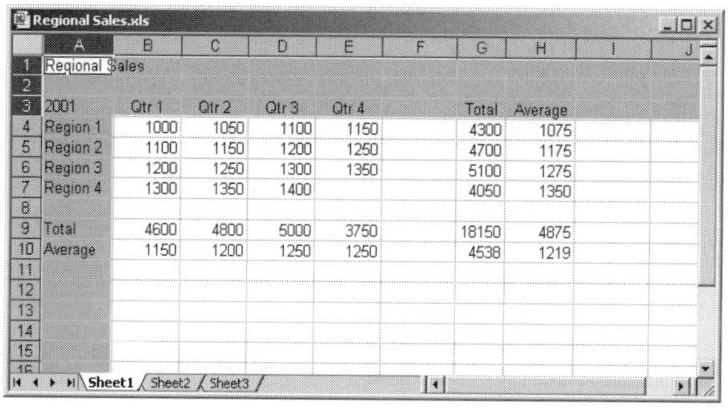

Figure 5-4. Select entire columns and rows by clicking their headings, or hold down the Ctrl key while clicking to select nonadjacent rows and columns.

> **tip** **Select everything with the mouse**
>
> At times, you will want to select all the cells in a worksheet to change the format for the entire worksheet or to copy the contents of one worksheet to another. To select the entire worksheet at once, click the Select All box located in the upper left corner of your workbook window (where the column and row headings intersect).

Use the following methods to select with the keyboard:

- To select an entire column with the keyboard, select any cell in the column and press Ctrl+Spacebar.

- To select an entire row with the keyboard, select any cell in the row and press Shift+Spacebar.

- To select several entire adjacent columns or rows with the keyboard, select any cell range that includes cells in each of the columns or rows and then press Ctrl+Spacebar or Shift+Spacebar, respectively. For example, to select columns B, C, and D, select B4:D4 (or any range that includes cells in these three columns) and then press Ctrl+Spacebar.

> **tip**   To select the entire worksheet with the keyboard, press Ctrl+Shift+Spacebar.

Selecting Regions

If you hold down the Shift key as you double-click the edge of an active cell's border, Excel selects all the cells from the current selection to the next edge of the region in that direction. The cell from which you start the selection process remains the active cell.

Selecting with the Go To Command

To quickly move to and select a cell or a range of cells, choose Edit, Go To to open the Go To dialog box (or press F5); then enter a cell reference, range reference, or defined range name in the Reference box, and press Enter. You can also use Go To to extend a selection. For example, to select A1:Z100, you could click A1, open the Go To dialog box, type **Z100**, and then hold down the Shift key while pressing Enter.

> For more information about defined range names and references, see "Naming Cells and Cell Ranges" on page 371 and "Using Cell References in Formulas" on page 356.

To move to another worksheet in the same workbook, open the Go To dialog box and type the name of the worksheet, followed by an exclamation point and a cell name or reference. For example, to go to cell D5 in a worksheet called Sheet2, type **Sheet2!D5**.

> **note**   You cannot use Go To to move across workbooks.

Excel keeps track of the last four locations from which you used the Go To command and lists them in the Go To dialog box. You can use this list to move among these locations in your worksheet. This is handy when you're working on a large worksheet or jumping around among multiple locations and sheets in a workbook. Figure 5-5 on the next page shows the Go To dialog box displaying four previous locations.

Figure 5-5. The Go To dialog box keeps track of the last four locations from which you used the Go To command.

---

tip **Beam back and forth**

When you use the Go To command, Excel lists in the Reference edit box the cell or range from which you just moved. This way, you can easily move back and forth between two locations by repeatedly pressing F5 and then Enter.

When you click the Special button in the Go To dialog box, the Go To Special dialog box opens, presenting a number of options you can choose from to go to places other than simple cell references. Figure 5-6 shows the Go To Special dialog box.

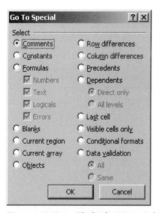

Figure 5-6. Click the Special button in the Go To dialog box to display the Go To Special dialog box.

Entering Stuff

Excel accepts two basic types of cell entries: *constants* and *formulas*. Constants fall into three main categories: numeric values, text values (also called labels or strings), and date/time values. Excel also recognizes two special types of constants called logical values and error values.

> For more on date values, see Chapter 15, "Formatting and Calculating Date and Time."

Making Entries in Cells and in the Formula Bar

To make an entry into a cell, just select the cell and start typing. As you type, the entry appears both in the formula bar and in the active cell. The flashing vertical bar in the active cell is called the *insertion point*.

After you finish typing, you must "lock in" the entry to store it permanently in the cell by pressing Enter. Pressing Enter normally causes the active cell to move down one row. You can change this so that when you press Enter, either the active cell doesn't change or it moves to an adjacent cell in another direction. Choose Tools, Options, click the Edit tab, and either clear the Move Selection After Enter option or change the selection in the Direction list. You can also lock in an entry when you move the selection to a different cell by pressing Tab, Shift+Tab, Shift+Enter, or an arrow key, among other methods, after you type the entry, as shown in the following table.

Press	To Open
Enter	The cell below the active cell, or whatever Direction is set for the Move Selection After Enter option on the Edit tab of the Options dialog box
Shift+Enter	The cell above the active cell, or the opposite of the Direction set for the Move Selection After Enter option on the Edit tab of the Options dialog box
Tab	The cell one column to the right of the active cell
Shift+Tab	The cell one column to the left of the active cell

When you begin typing an entry, three buttons appear on the formula bar: the Cancel button, the Enter button, and the Insert Function button. When typing a formula where the entry begins with an equal sign (=), a plus sign (+), or a minus sign (-), a drop-down list of frequently used functions is also displayed, as shown in Figure 5-7 on the next page.

> For more about editing formulas, see Chapter 12, "Building Formulas."

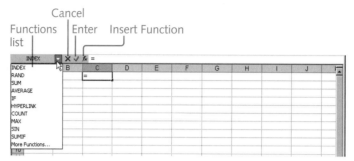

Figure 5-7. When you start entering a formula, the formula bar offers ways to help you finish it.

Entering Simple Numeric and Text Values

An entry that includes only numerals 0 through 9 and certain special characters, such as + - E e ( ) . , $ % and /, is a *numeric value*. An entry that includes almost any other character is a *text value*. The following table lists some examples of numeric and text values.

Numeric Values	Text Values
123	Sales
123.456	B-1
$1.98	Eleven
1%	123 Main Street
1.23E+12	No. 324

Using Special Characters

A number of characters have special effects in Excel. Here are some guidelines for using special characters:

- If you begin a numeric entry with a plus sign (+), Excel drops the plus sign.

- If you begin a numeric entry with a minus sign (-), Excel interprets the entry as a negative number and retains the sign.

- In a numeric entry, the characters E and e specify an *exponent* used in scientific notation. For example, it interprets 1E6 as 1,000,000 (1 times 10 to the sixth power).

- Excel interprets numeric constants enclosed in parentheses as negative numbers, which is a common accounting practice. For example, Excel interprets (100) as −100.

- You can use decimal points and commas as you normally would. When you enter numbers that include commas as separators, however, the commas

110

appear in the cell but not in the formula bar; this is the same as if you had applied one of Excel's built-in Number formats. For example, if you enter **1,234.56**, 1234.56 is displayed in the formula bar.

● If you begin a numeric entry with a dollar sign, Excel assigns a Currency format to the cell. For example, if you enter **$123456**, Excel displays $123,456 in the cell and 123456 in the formula bar. In this case, Excel adds the comma to the worksheet display because it's part of the Currency format.

● If you end a numeric entry with a percent sign (%), Excel assigns a Percentage format to the cell. For example, if you enter **23%**, Excel displays 23% in the formula bar and assigns a Percentage format to the cell, which also displays 23%.

● If you use a forward slash (/) in a numeric entry and the string cannot be interpreted as a date, Excel interprets the number as a fraction. For example, if you enter **11 5/8** (with a space between the number and the fraction), Excel assigns a Fraction format to the entry, meaning that the formula bar displays 11.625 and the cell displays 11 5/8.

---

tip   **Enter numbers as fractions**

To make sure Excel does not interpret a fraction as a date, precede the fraction with a zero and a space. For example, to prevent Excel from interpreting the fraction 1/2 as January 2, type **0 1/2**.

For more about Excel's built-in Number formats, see "Formatting in Cells" on page 204. For more information about date and time formats, see "How Autofill Handles Dates and Times" on page 176.

Understanding the Difference Between Displayed Values and Underlying Values

Although you can type more than 16,000 characters in a cell, a numeric cell entry can maintain precision to only a maximum of 15 digits. This means that you can enter numbers longer than 15 digits into a cell, but Excel converts any digits after the fifteenth to zeros. If you are working with figures over 999 trillion, or decimals smaller than trillionths, perhaps you need to look into alternative solutions, such as a Cray supercomputer.

If you enter a number that is too long to appear in a cell, Excel converts it to scientific notation in the cell, if no other formatting has been applied. Excel adjusts the precision of the scientific notation depending on the cell width. If you enter a very large or a very small number that is longer than the formula bar, Excel displays it in the formula bar using scientific notation. In Figure 5-8 on the next page, we entered the same number into both cells A1 and B1; however, because cell B1 is wider, Excel displays more of the number, but it is still displayed using scientific notation.

Chapter 5

111

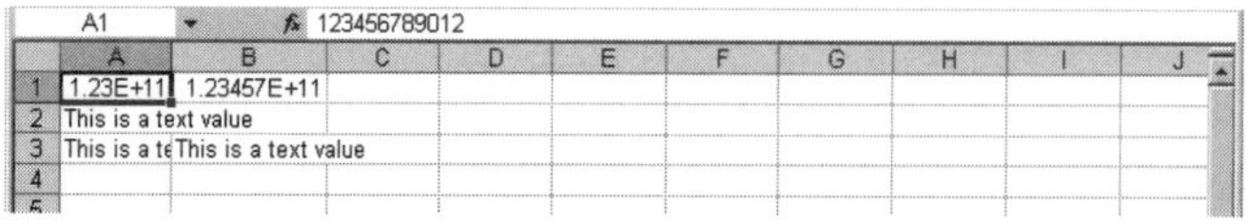

Figure 5-8. Because the number 123456789012 is too long to fit in either cell A1 or B1, Excel displays it in scientific notation.

> For more information about increasing the width of a cell, see "Changing Column Widths" on page 238.

The values that appear in formatted cells are called *displayed* values; the values that are stored in cells and that appear in the formula bar are called *underlying* values. The number of digits that appear in a cell—its displayed value—depends on the width of the column and any formatting that you have applied to the cell. If you reduce the width of a column that contains a long entry, Excel might display a rounded-off version of the number, a string of pound signs (#), or scientific notation, depending on the display format you're using.

tip **Shed those pounds**

If you see a series of pound signs (######) in a cell where you expect to see a number, simply increase the width of the cell to see the numbers again.

Troubleshooting

My Formulas Don't Add Numbers Correctly

Suppose, for example, you write a formula and Excel tells you that $2.23 plus $5.55 equals $7.79, when it should be $7.78. Check your underlying values. If you use currency formatting, numbers with more than three digits to the right of the decimal point are rounded to two decimal places. In your example, if the underlying vales are 2.234 and 5.552, the result is 7.786, which rounds out to 7.79. You can either change the decimal places, or you can use the Precision As Displayed option (Tools, Options, Calculation tab) to eliminate the problem. Be careful if you use Precision As Displayed, however, because it permanently changes all the underlying values in your worksheet to their displayed values.

Creating Long Text Values

If you enter text that is too long for Excel to display in a single cell, Excel overlaps the adjacent cells, but the text remains stored in the single cell. If you then type text in a cell that is overlapped by another cell, the overlapping text appears truncated, as shown in cell B3 in Figure 5-8.

> **tip** **Double-click and reveal**
>
> The easiest way to eliminate overlapping text is to widen the column by double-clicking the column border in the heading. For example, in Figure 5-8, when you double-click the line between the A and the B in the column heading, the width of column A adjusts to accommodate the longest entry in the column.

Using Word Wrapping

If you have long text entries, word wrapping can make them easier to read. Word wrapping allows you to type long strings of text that wrap onto two or more lines within the same cell rather than overlapping adjacent cells. Select the cells where you want to use word wrapping, choose Format, Cells, click the Alignment tab, and select the Wrap Text box. To accommodate the extra lines, Excel increases the height of the row.

For more about wrapping text in cells, see "Wrapping Text in Cells" on page 226.

Understanding Numeric Text Entries

Sometimes you might want to make an entry that contains special characters that Excel would not normally treat as plain text. For example, you might want +1 to appear in a cell. If you type +1, Excel interprets this as a numeric entry and drops the plus sign (as stated earlier). In addition, Excel normally ignores leading zeros in numbers, such as 01234. You can force Excel to accept special characters as text by using numeric text entries.

A numeric text entry can consist of text and numbers or all numbers. To enter a combination of text and numbers, such as G234, just type it. Because this entry includes nonnumeric characters, Excel interprets it as a text value. To create a text entry that consists entirely of numbers, you can precede the entry with a *text alignment prefix character,* such as an apostrophe. You can also enter it as a formula by typing an equal sign and enclosing the entry with quotation marks. For example, to enter the number 01234 as text so that the leading zero is displayed, type either **'01234** or **="01234"** into a cell. Whereas numeric entries are normally right-aligned, a numeric text entry is left-aligned in the cell just like regular text, as shown in Figure 5-9 on the next page.

Text-alignment prefix characters, like formula components, appear in the formula bar, but not in the cell. Table 5-2 lists all the text-alignment prefix characters.

Table 5-2. **Text-Alignment Characters**

Character	Action
' (apostrophe)	Left-aligns data in the cell
" (double quotation mark)	Right-aligns data in the cell
^ (caret)	Centers data in the cell
\ (backslash)	Repeats characters across the cell

Chapter 5

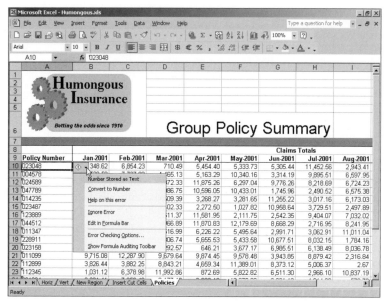

Figure 5-9. The policy numbers in column A were typed as text.

> **note** The alignment-prefix characters always work with numeric entries. With text entries, however, the ^ and " Characters work only if you choose Tools, Options, click the Transition tab, and then select the Transition Navigation Keys option.

When you create a numeric entry that starts with an alignment prefix character, a small flag appears in the upper left corner of the cell, indicating that there's a problem with that cell that you might need to address. When you select the cell, an error-type *smart tag* appears to the right. Clicking this smart tag displays a menu of specific commands (refer to Figure 5-9). Because the apostrophe was intentional, you can click Ignore Error.

> **tip** **Resolve a range of smart tags**
>
> If there is a range of cells that share the same problem, as in column A in Figure 5-9, you can select the entire cell range and use the smart tag menu to resolve the problem in all the cells at the same time. For more information about smart tags, see Chapter 1, "What's New in Microsoft Excel 2002."

newfeature!

Entering Symbols

If you ever wanted to use Wingdings in Excel, you're in luck. Choosing Insert, Symbol gives you access to the complete character set for every installed font on your computer. Figure 5-10 shows the Symbol dialog box.

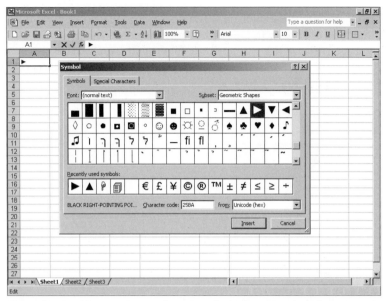

Figure 5-10. You can insert characters from the extended character sets of any installed font.

On the Symbols tab, select the font from the Font drop-down list, and the entire character set is displayed. You can jump to specific areas in the character set using the Subset drop-down list, which also indicates the area of the character set you are viewing if you are using the scroll bar to browse through the available characters. The Character Code box displays the code of the selected character. You can also highlight a character in the display area by typing in a character code number. You can select decimal or hexadecimal ASCII character encoding, or Unicode, using the From drop-down list. If you choose Unicode, you can select from a number of additional character subsets in the Subset drop-down list.

---

tip **Select special characters quickly**

The Special Characters tab in the Symbol dialog box gives you quick access to a number of commonly used characters, such as em dash, ellipsis, trademark, and copyright symbols.

Making Entries in Ranges

To make a number of entries in a range of adjacent cells, first select those cells. Then use Enter, Shift+Enter, Tab, and Shift+Tab to move the active cell within the range. For example, to fill in a range of selected cells, select the range and begin typing entries, as shown in Figure 5-11 on the next page. Each time you press Enter, the active cell moves to the next cell in the range. The active cell never leaves the selected range until you

115

specifically select another cell or range; in other words, when you reach the edge of the range, the active cell scrolls to the beginning of the next column or row. You can continue to make entries in this way until you fill the entire range. The advantage of this trick is that you don't need to take your hands off the keyboard to select cells with the mouse when making many entries at once.

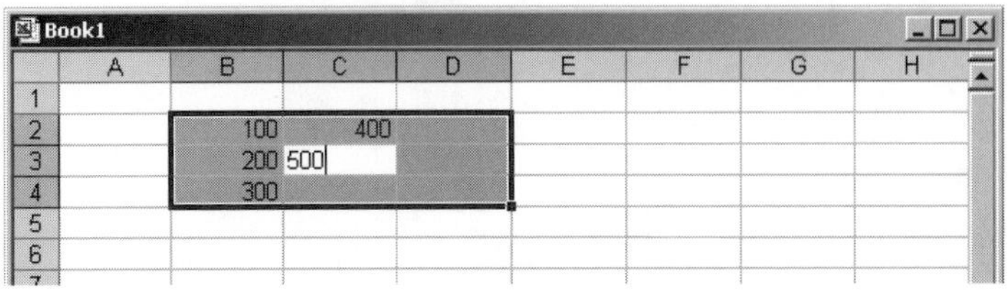

Figure 5-11. You can easily make entries in a range of cells by first selecting the entire range.

> **tip** **Make multiple entries**
>
> To enter the same value in all selected cells at once, type your entry and hold down Ctrl while you press Enter.

Editing and Undoing Entries

You can correct simple errors as you type, and before you press Enter to lock in the cell entry, by pressing Backspace, which erases the character to the left of the insertion point. However, to make changes to entries that you have already locked in, you first need to enter Edit mode. (The mode indicator at the lower left corner of the status bar has to change from Ready to Edit.) Use the following techniques to enter Edit mode:

- To edit a cell using the mouse, double-click the cell and position the insertion point at the location of the error.

- To edit a cell using the keyboard, select the cell and press F2. Use the arrow keys to position the insertion point in the cell.

By selecting several characters before you begin typing, you can replace several characters at once. To select several characters within a cell, enter Edit mode, place the insertion point just before or just after the characters you want to replace, hold down Shift, and press the Left or Right Arrow key to extend your selection.

> **tip** **Move one "word" at a time**
>
> If you don't want to take your hands off the keyboard to move from one end of a cell entry to the other, press Home or End while in Edit mode. To move through an entry one "word" at a time, hold down Ctrl and press the Left or Right Arrow key.

Chapter 5

116

If you need to erase the entire contents of the active cell, press Delete, or press Back-space and then press Enter. Pressing Enter acts as a confirmation of the deletion. If you press Backspace accidentally, click the Cancel button or press Esc to restore the contents of the cell before pressing Enter. You can also erase the entire contents of a cell by selecting the cell and typing the new contents to replace the old. Excel erases the previous entry as soon as you begin typing. To revert to the original entry, press Esc before you press Enter.

To restore an entry after you press Delete or after you have locked in a new entry, choose Edit, Undo or press Ctrl+Z. The Undo command remembers the last 16 actions you performed. If you press Ctrl+Z repeatedly, each of the last 16 actions is undone, one after the other, in reverse order. You can also click the small drop-down arrow to the right of the Undo button to display a list of remembered actions. Drag the mouse to select one or more actions, as shown in Figure 5-12. After you release the mouse button, all the selected actions are undone. The Redo button works the same way; you can quickly redo what you have just undone, if necessary.

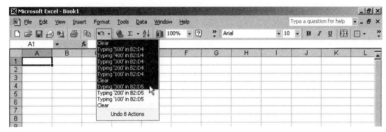

Figure 5-12.   Click the small arrow next to the Undo button to select any number of the last 16 actions to undo at once.

> **note**   It is important to remember that you can't undo individual actions in the middle of the list. If you select an action, all actions up to and including that action are undone.

Managing Worksheets

You can have as many as 255 sheets in a workbook; consequently, there's no need to try to fit everything onto one page. The following sections present the basics, as well as a few interesting features you can use to organize your worksheet world.

Inserting and Deleting Sheets

To insert a new sheet in an existing workbook, choose Insert, Worksheet. The new sheet tab appears in front of the active sheet tab. You can also quickly insert sheets by right-clicking a sheet tab to display the shortcut menu shown in Figure 5-13 on the next page. Choosing Insert opens the Insert dialog box containing a list of objects that you can insert, such as chart sheets and worksheets.

Chapter 5

117

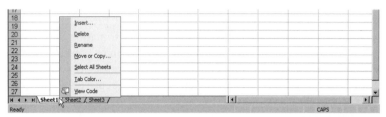

Figure 5-13.   Right-click any sheet tab to display a worksheet-focused shortcut menu.

In addition to providing a convenient method for inserting, deleting, renaming, moving, and copying sheets, this shortcut menu contains the Select All Sheets command. As its name indicates, you use this command to select all the sheets in a workbook, which you will need to do to perform certain functions, such as copying or formatting, on all the sheets at once. The View Code command on this shortcut menu launches the Microsoft Visual Basic Editor, showing the Code Window for the current worksheet.

> For more information about the Visual Basic Editor, see Chapter 31, "Recording Macros."

You can also add multiple sheets to a workbook at the same time. To do so, select a sheet tab, press Shift, and then click other sheet tabs to select a range of sheets—the same number that you want to insert—before selecting Insert Worksheet from the sheet tab shortcut menu. (Notice that Excel adds [Group] to the workbook title in the window title bar, indicating that you have selected a group of sheets for editing.) Excel inserts the same number of new sheets as you selected and places them in front of the first sheet in the selected range.

> For more information about group editing, see "Editing Multiple Worksheets" on page 187.

You cannot undo the insertion of a new worksheet. If you do need to delete a sheet, choose Edit, Delete Sheet. If you want to delete more than one sheet, you can hold down Shift to select a range of sheets, or you can hold down Ctrl and select nonadjacent sheets before you choose Delete from the sheet tab shortcut menu. Be careful! You cannot bring back a worksheet that you have deleted.

Naming and Renaming Sheets

Notice that Excel numbers the new sheets based on the number of sheets in the workbook. If your workbook contains three sheets, the first sheet you insert is Sheet4, the next is Sheet5, and so on. If you grow weary of seeing Sheet1, Sheet2, and so on, in your workbooks, you can give your sheets more imaginative and helpful names by double-clicking the tab and typing a new name. You can also choose Format, Sheet, Rename or right-click a tab to use the Rename command on the sheet tab shortcut menu.

You can use up to 31 characters in your sheet names. Nevertheless, you should remember that the name you use determines the width of the corresponding tab at the bottom of the workbook window, as shown in Figure 5-14. Therefore, you might still want to keep your sheet names concise so that you can see more than one or two tabs at a time.

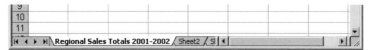

Figure 5-14. Double-click the sheet tab to type a new name.

---

tip **Change the size of tabs**

The only way to alter the size of sheet tabs and the size of the tab text is to alter the size of your scroll bars. You can do that by clicking the Display applet in Windows Control Panel, choosing the Appearance tab, clicking a scroll bar in the sample display, and then changing the Size value. As you expand or reduce the size of your scroll bars, Excel adjusts the width of its sheet tabs and modifies the font to fit.

---

newfeature!
Coloring Sheet Tabs

As you can see in the shortcut menu shown in Figure 5-13, the sheet tab shortcut menu also contains a Tab Color command. You can find the same command on the Format, Sheet submenu. When you choose the Tab Color command, the Format Tab Color dialog box, shown in Figure 5-15, is displayed.

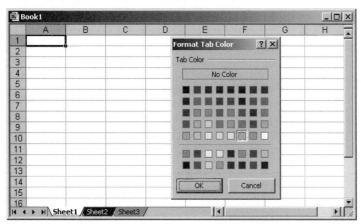

Figure 5-15. You can color-code your sheet tabs.

As you can see in Figure 5-15, the tab of the active sheet is white, except for a line of the selected color beneath the sheet name; the inactive sheet tabs are displayed in full color.

Chapter 5

Moving and Copying Sheets

As you might expect, Excel provides an easy way to move a sheet from one place to another in the same workbook. In fact, all you have to do is click a sheet tab to select it and then drag it to its new location. Figure 5-16 shows this process. When you drag a sheet, a small worksheet icon appears, and a tiny arrow indicates where the sheet will be inserted in the tab order.

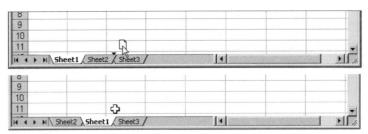

Figure 5-16. Click and drag sheet tabs to rearrange worksheets.

When you move sheets, remember these tips:

- If you want to move a sheet to a location that isn't currently visible on your screen, drag past the visible tabs in either direction. The sheet tabs scroll in the direction you drag.

- You can move several sheets at the same time. When you select several sheets and drag, the worksheet icon changes to look like a small stack of pages.

- You can copy sheets using similar mouse techniques. First, select the sheet or sheets you want to copy, and then hold down Ctrl while you drag the sheet or sheets to the new location. When you copy a sheet, an identical sheet appears in the new location. A number in parentheses is appended to the copy's name to distinguish it from the original sheet. For example, making a copy of Sheet1 results in a new sheet named Sheet1 (2).

- You can move or copy nonadjacent sheets at the same time by holding down Ctrl while you click to select the sheet tabs. Before dragging, release the Ctrl key to move the selected sheets or keep holding it down to create copies.

- You can choose Edit, Move Or Copy Sheet (also available on the sheet tab shortcut menu) to handle similar sheet-management functions, including moving and copying sheets between workbooks. The Move Or Copy dialog box is shown in Figure 5-17.

Figure 5-17. Use the Move Or Copy dialog box to manage sheets in the same workbook or between workbooks.

If you want to move or copy sheets to a different workbook, first make sure that workbook is open. Next open the Move Or Copy dialog box, and then select the workbook name in the To Book list, which also offers a New Book option if you prefer to start from scratch.

Dragging Sheets Between Workbooks

You can move and copy sheets between workbooks by dragging—which is one of the more interesting features of Excel. You use the same methods to move and copy that you use for worksheets in the same workbook. For example, suppose you have two workbooks arranged horizontally in the workspace and you want to move a sheet from one to the other. Drag it to the new location in the other workbook, as shown here.

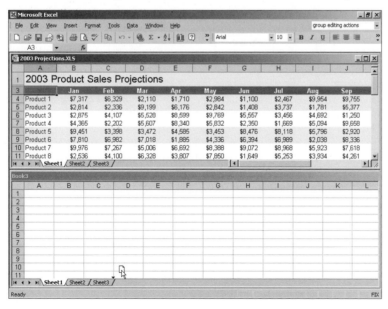

Chapter 5

Looking at Worksheets

Excel provides a few helpful features that you can use to change the way worksheets are displayed. You can set up your workspace for specific tasks, and then save the same view settings for the next time you need to perform the same task.

Splitting Sheets into Panes

Sheet *panes* allow you to view different areas of your worksheet simultaneously. You can split any sheet in a workbook vertically, horizontally, or both vertically and horizontally, with synchronized scrolling capability. In the worksheet shown in Figure 5-18, columns B through M and rows 4 through 37 contain data. Column N and row 38 contain the totals. In normal view, it's impossible to see the totals and the headings at the same time.

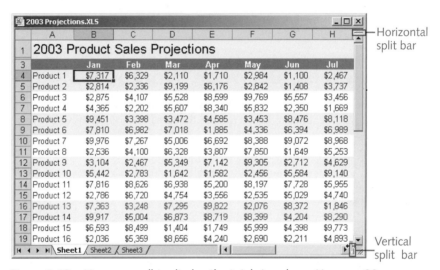

Figure 5-18. You can scroll to display the totals in column N or row 38, but the headings won't be visible.

It would be easier to navigate the worksheet in Figure 5-18 if it were split into panes. To do so, choose Window, Split; the window divides into both vertical and horizontal panes simultaneously. You can use the mouse to drag either split bar toward the middle of the sheet. If you double-click a split bar, the window is divided approximately in half. When your mouse pointer is over the vertical split bar, it changes to a double-headed arrow, as shown over the vertical split bar in Figure 5-18.

---

tip **Select before you split**

Before choosing Window, Split or double-clicking one of the split bars, select a cell in the sheet where you want the split to occur. The sheet is split immediately to the left or above the selected cell. If cell A1 is active, the split occurs in the center of the sheet. Figure 5-19 shows the worksheet after choosing Window, Split with cell B4 selected.

	A	I	J	K	L	M	N	O
1	2003 P							
3		Aug	Sep	Oct	Nov	Dec	Total	
24	Product 21	$2,214	$1,542	$9,343	$1,036	$2,694	$51,121	
25	Product 22	$2,956	$2,506	$1,542	$1,542	$9,371	$53,854	
26	Product 23	$2,603	$2,501	$8,753	$3,019	$7,839	$67,190	
27	Product 24	$5,130	$6,123	$6,827	$7,109	$5,770	$65,310	
28	Product 25	$9,523	$6,319	$1,250	$1,916	$7,698	$67,914	
29	Product 26	$8,783	$2,647	$4,293	$2,442	$8,692	$65,138	
30	Product 27	$4,425	$4,209	$7,456	$9,793	$5,571	$63,544	
31	Product 28	$1,727	$4,163	$1,542	$2,613	$4,497	$53,610	
32	Product 29	$9,111	$8,539	$4,208	$1,875	$3,885	$68,256	
33	Product 30	$6,720	$8,134	$5,653	$1,542	$1,542	$63,689	
34	Product 31	$7,052	$7,731	$2,375	$1,250	$3,381	$59,393	
35	Product 32	$4,782	$4,114	$2,463	$6,552	$9,818	$77,073	
36	Product 33	$9,873	$9,457	$7,250	$2,556	$8,959	$77,489	
37	Product 34	$6,991	$6,162	$7,318	$1,983	$3,002	$58,913	
38	**Total**	$163,779	$181,090	$179,051	$165,149	$174,081	$2,133,689	
39								

Figure 5-19. With the window split, you can scroll each pane independently.

With the window split into four panes, as shown in Figure 5-19, four scroll bars are visible—two for each direction. Now we can use the scroll bars to view columns A through N without losing sight of the Product headings in column A. In addition, when we scroll vertically between rows 1 and 38, we'll always see the corresponding headings in row 3.

After a window is split, you can reposition the split bars by dragging. If you are ready to return your screen to its normal appearance, choose Window, Remove Split (the command name changes automatically), which removes all split bars. You can also re-move an individual split by double-clicking the split bar or by dragging the split bar back to the top or right side of the window.

---

tip **Jump quickly from pane to pane**

To move from pane to pane using the keyboard, press F6. Each time you do, the active cell moves to the next pane in a clockwise direction, opening the upper right cell in each pane. If you select a cell in any pane, pressing F6 moves to the last cell you selected in that pane. Pressing Shift+F6 moves you to the next pane in a counter-clockwise direction.

Chapter 5

Freezing Panes

After you've split a window into panes, you can freeze the left panes, the top panes, or both by choosing Window, Freeze Panes. When you do so, the data in the left and top panes is "locked" into place. As you can see in Figure 5-20, the pane divider lines have changed from thick, three-dimensional lines into thin lines.

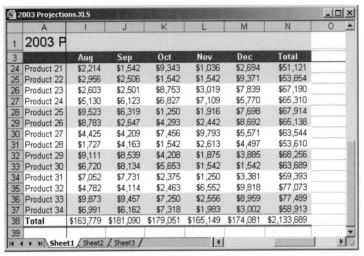

Figure 5-20. Freezing panes locks the top and left panes.

---

tip   **Split and freeze**

You can split and freeze panes simultaneously by choosing Window, Freeze Panes without first splitting the sheet into panes. If you use this method, you will simultaneously unfreeze and remove the panes when you choose Window, Unfreeze Panes. (The command name changes when panes are frozen.)

Notice also that in Figure 5-19, the sheet tabs are invisible because the horizontal scroll bar for the lower left pane is so small. After freezing the panes, as seen in Figure 5-20, the scroll bar returns to normal and the sheet tabs reappear.

---

tip   **Toggle between sheets**

To open another sheet in the workbook if the sheet tabs are not visible, press Ctrl+Page Up to open the previous sheet or Ctrl+Page Down to open the next sheet.

After you choose Freeze Panes, you cannot scroll to the upper left pane(s) in any direction. You can scroll only the columns in the upper right pane and only the rows in the lower left pane. You can scroll the lower right pane in either direction.

InsideOut

Make frozen panes easier to see

Generally speaking, all the things you do with panes work better when the windows are frozen. Unfortunately, it's harder to tell that the window is split when the panes are frozen because the thin frozen pane lines look just like cell borders. To make frozen panes easier to see, you can use a formatting clue that you will always recognize. For example, select all the heading rows and columns and fill them with a particular color—such as "ice" blue…

Zooming Worksheets

As mentioned previously, you can use the Zoom box on the Standard toolbar or choose View, Zoom to change the size of your worksheet display. The Zoom dialog box has one enlargement option, three reduction options, and a Fit Selection option that determines the necessary reduction or enlargement needed to display the currently selected cells. Use the Custom box to specify any zoom percentage from 10 through 400 percent.

tip   **Zoom multiple worksheets**

The Zoom command affects all selected sheets; therefore, if you group several sheets, Excel will display all of them at the selected Zoom percentage. For more about grouping sheets, see "Editing Multiple Worksheets" on page 187.

For example, to view the entire worksheet shown in Figure 5-18, you can try different zoom percentages until you get the results you want. Better still, select the entire active area of the worksheet, and select the Fit Selection option in the Zoom dialog box. Now the entire worksheet is displayed on the screen, as shown in Figure 5-21 on the next page.

Of course, reading the numbers might be a problem at this size, but you can select other reduction or enlargement sizes for that purpose. While your worksheet is zoomed, you can still select cells, format them, and enter formulas as you normally would. The Zoom option that is in effect when you save the worksheet is the displayed setting when you reopen the worksheet.

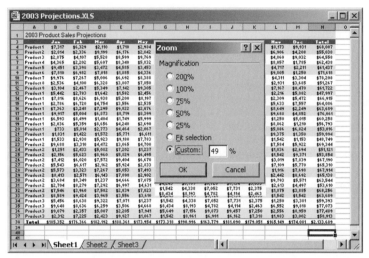

Figure 5-21. After using the Fit Selection option with the active area selected, open the Zoom dialog box to see the chosen percentage in the Custom box.

If You Have an IntelliMouse

The wheel on an IntelliMouse normally scrolls the worksheet. You can also use the wheel to zoom. Simply hold down the Ctrl key and turn the wheel backward (toward your hand) to zoom out, or turn the wheel forward (away from your hand) to zoom in. If you want, you can make zooming the default behavior of the wheel, making it unnecessary to press the Ctrl key. To do so, choose Tools, Options, click the General tab, and select Zoom On Roll With IntelliMouse.

Using Custom Views

Suppose you want your sheet to have particular display and print settings for one purpose, such as editing, but different display and print settings for another purpose, such as an on-screen presentation. By choosing View, Custom Views, you can assign names to specific view settings, which include column widths, row heights, display options, window size, position on the screen, pane settings, the cells that are selected at the time the view is created, and, optionally, the print and filter settings. You can then select your saved view settings whenever you need them, rather than manually changing the settings each time.

---

tip   **Create a normal custom view first**

Before you modify your view settings for a particular purpose, you should save the current view as a custom view, named Normal. This provides you with an easy way to return to the regular, unmodified view. Otherwise, you would have to retrace all your steps to return all the view settings to normal.

In the Custom Views dialog box, the Views list is empty until you click the Add button to save a custom view. Figure 5-22 shows the Custom Views dialog box with two views added, as well as the Add View dialog box that we used to add them.

Figure 5-22.   Click Add to name the current view and print settings in the Custom Views dialog box.

---

tip   **Use a better Custom Views option**

Custom Views is a useful feature that you can make even more useful by performing a bit of user interface (UI) surgery. You can add a Custom Views drop-down list to any toolbar or menu. If you plan to use this feature often, add the button to a toolbar. If you want to make the menu command more useful, replace the existing Custom Views with the one that includes the drop-down list. To make this change, choose View, Toolbars, Customize, and click the View category on the Commands tab. Then choose the View menu and drag the Custom Views command off the menu. Finally, drag the Custom Views command from the Customize dialog box to the View menu.

---

newfeature!
Protecting Worksheets

In addition to password protection for your files, Excel offers several features that allow you to protect your work—workbooks, workbook structures, individual cells, graphic objects, charts, scenarios, windows, and more—from access or modification by others. You can also choose to allow specific editing actions on protected sheets.

By default, Excel "locks" (protects) all cells and charts, but the protection is disabled until you choose Tools, Protection, Protect Sheet to access the Protect Sheet dialog box, shown in Figure 5-23. The protection status you specify applies to the current worksheet only.

After protection is enabled, you cannot change a locked item. If you try to change a locked item, Excel displays an error message. As you can see in the figure, the Allow All Users Of This Worksheet To list contains a list of specific editorial actions to occur even on protected sheets. In addition to the options visible in Figure 5-23, you can also allow users to sort, use AutoFilter and PivotTable reports, and edit objects or scenarios.

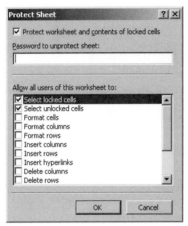

Figure 5-23. The Protect Sheet dialog box gives you pinpoint control over many common editing actions.

Unlocking Individual Cells

If you choose the Protect Sheet command without specifically unlocking individual cells, every cell in the worksheet is locked by default. Most of the time, however, you will not want to lock every cell. For example, you might want to protect the formulas and formatting but leave particular cells unlocked so that necessary data can be entered without unlocking the entire sheet. Before you protect a worksheet, select the cells you want to keep unlocked, choose Format, Cells, click the Protection tab, and then clear the Locked check box, as shown in Figure 5-24.

> For information about using Tools, Protection, Protect and Share Workbook, see "Sharing Files Using a Network" on page 531.

128

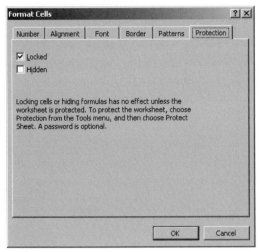

Figure 5-24. Use the Protection tab in the Format Cells dialog box to unlock specific cells for editing.

---

tip **Add visual clues**

Keep in mind that Excel does not provide any on-screen indication of the protection status for individual cells. To distinguish unlocked cells from the protected cells, apply a specific format, such as cell color or borders.

You can also choose Tools, Protection, Protect Workbook to prevent the alteration of a workbook's structure and to lock in the position of the workbook window itself. The Protect Workbook dialog box is shown in Figure 5-25.

Figure 5-25. Use the Protect Workbook dialog box to set the protection status for the entire workbook.

---

tip **Tab to the next unlocked cell**

You can easily move between unprotected cells on a locked sheet by pressing the Tab key.

Chapter 5

newfeature!
Allowing Password Access to Specific Cell Ranges

If you need to do more than protect workbooks or individual worksheets, choose
Tools, Protection, Allow Users To Edit Ranges. Use the Allow Users To Edit Ranges
dialog box, shown in Figure 5-26, to provide editorial access to specific areas of a protected worksheet. If you are using Windows 2000, you can even specify exactly who is
allowed to do the editing.

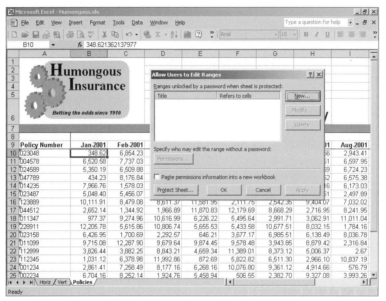

Figure 5-26. You can specify cells that can be edited, as well as the individuals who are
allowed to edit them, by using the Allow Users To Edit Ranges dialog box.

When you click the New button in the Allow Users To Edit Ranges dialog box to add a
cell range to the list, the New Range dialog box appears, as shown in Figure 5-27. Type
a title for the range of cells you want to allow users to edit. Type a cell range or range
name in the Refers To Cells box or click in the box and drag through the range you
want to specify, as shown in Figure 5-28.

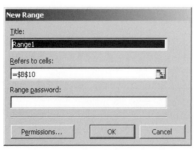

Figure 5-27. Specify ranges you want to allow users to edit using the New
Range dialog box.

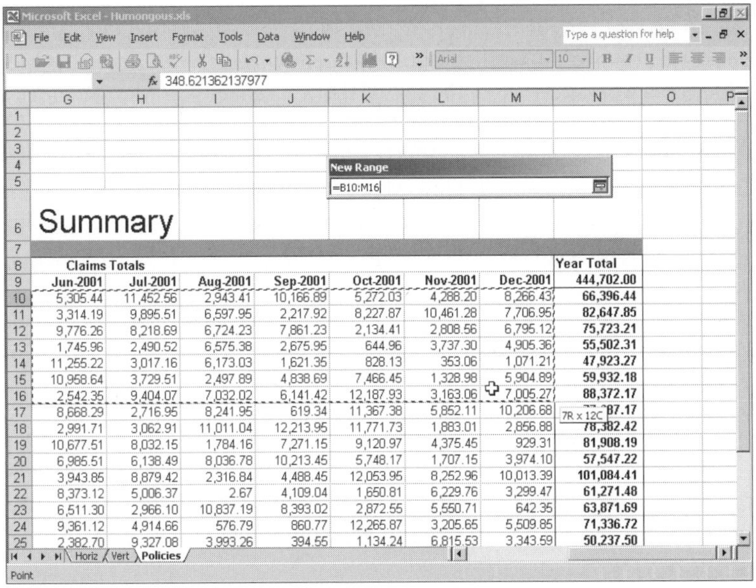

Figure 5-28. When you drag to select cell ranges, the dialog box collapses out of the way.

If you are not using Windows 2000, using the Allow Users To Edit Ranges command is the same as using the Protection tab in the Format Cells dialog box to unlock individual cells. If you are using Windows 2000, you can click the Permissions button to specify individuals who are allowed to edit each range. The Paste Permissions Information Into A New Workbook check box is a handy way to keep track of who and what you've specified in the Permissions list. Note that you can click the Protect Sheet button for quick access to the Protect Sheet dialog box shown in Figure 5-23.

For information about Excel and networks, see "Sharing Files Using a Network" on page 531.

Hiding Cells and Sheets

In a protected sheet, if you applied the Hidden protection format to a cell that contains a formula (using the Protection tab in the Format Cells dialog box shown in Figure 5-24), the formula remains hidden in the formula bar even when you select that cell. Formulas in these cells are still functional, of course; they are hidden from view. In any case, the result of the formula is still visible.

For more information about hiding numbers, see "The Hidden Number Format" on page 223.

You can also hide entire worksheets within a workbook. Any data or calculations in a hidden worksheet are still available through references; the worksheet is hidden from view. To hide a worksheet, click the tab of the worksheet you want to hide and choose Format, Sheet, Hide. Unlike hiding cells, hiding a sheet happens immediately. After a sheet is hidden, the Unhide command is added to the Format, Sheet menu, allowing you to restore the hidden sheet. However, if you hide a sheet and then choose Tools, Protection, Protect Workbook, the Unhide command is no longer available, which helps keep the hidden sheet even better protected.

> For more information about workbook protection, see "Hiding and Protecting Workbooks" on page 141.

Using Passwords

When you choose Protect Sheet, Protect Workbook, or Protect And Share Workbook, you can assign a password that must be used to disable the protection. You can use unique passwords for each worksheet or workbook that you protect.

> **caution** Password protection in Excel is serious business. After you assign a password, there is no way to unprotect the sheet or workbook without it. Don't forget your passwords! Remember, capitalization matters!

How to Work a Workbook

In early versions of Microsoft Excel, worksheets, charts, and macro sheets were stored as separate documents. Since Excel 5, however, all these types of data, and more, peacefully coexist in workbooks. You can keep as many sheets containing as many different types of data as you want in a workbook, you can have more than one workbook open at the same time, and you can have more than one window open for the same workbook. The only limitations to these capabilities are those imposed by your computer's memory and system resources.

Managing Multiple Workbooks

This chapter describes how to protect workbooks, how to use more than one workbook at a time, as well as how and why to split your view of a workbook into multiple windows. Generally, when you start Excel, a blank workbook opens with the provisional title Book1. The only exceptions occur when you start Excel by opening a workbook or when you have one or more Excel files stored in the XLStart directory so that they open automatically.

If you start Excel with Book1 visible and then open an existing Excel file, Book1 disappears unless you have edited it. You can open as many workbooks as you like until your computer runs out of memory.

For more on working with multiple windows, see "Opening Multiple Windows for the Same Workbook" on page 138. For more information about the XLStart directory, see "Opening Files When You Start Excel" on page 47.

Navigating Between Open Workbooks

If you have more than one workbook open, you can activate a particular workbook in any of the following three ways:

- Click its window, if you can see it.

- If you have all of your workbook windows maximized, you can shuffle through the "stack" of open workbooks by pressing Ctrl+Tab to activate each workbook in the order you opened them. Press Shift+Ctrl+Tab to activate them in reverse order.

- Choose a window name from the Window menu, which lists as many as nine open workbooks or, if you have more than nine, displays a More Workbooks command that presents a list dialog box.

Arranging Workbook Windows

To make all open workbooks visible at the same time, choose Window, Arrange. Excel displays the Arrange Windows dialog box, shown in Figure 6-1. Figure 6-1 also shows the workbooks arranged in the Tiled configuration, in which the screen is divided into a patchwork of open documents. Figure 6-2 shows the same workbooks in a Horizontal configuration.

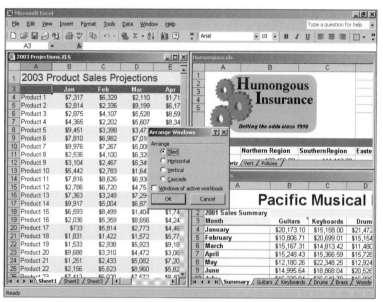

Figure 6-1. Selecting Window, Arrange opens the Arrange Windows dialog box, which gives you a choice of configurations.

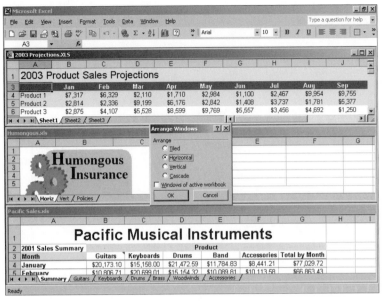

Figure 6-2. These windows are arranged in the Horizontal configuration.

Figure 6-3 on the next page shows the Vertical configuration of the Arrange Windows dialog box; Figure 6-4 on the next page shows the Cascade configuration. If you select the Windows Of Active Workbook option in the Arrange Windows dialog box, only the active window is affected by the configuration setting, and then only if more than one window is open for the active workbook. Excel arranges those windows according to the option set in the Arrange section of the dialog box. This is handy if you have several workbooks open but only want to arrange the active workbook's windows without closing the others.

For more information about working with multiple worksheets from one workbook, see "Opening Multiple Windows for the Same Workbook" on page 138.

tip   **If you like it, save it**

If you're working with several workbooks in a particular arrangement that is often useful, choose File, Save Workspace. This preserves the current settings and enables you to re-create the window arrangement simply by opening one file. For more information, see "Saving the Entire Workspace" on page 43.

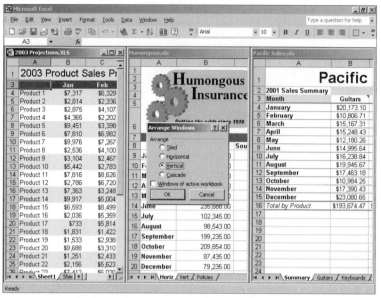

Figure 6-3. These windows are arranged in the Vertical configuration.

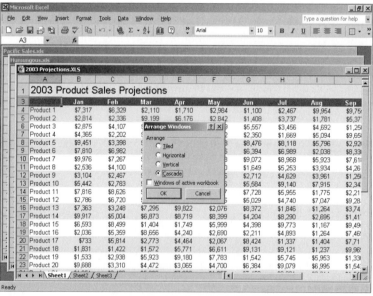

Figure 6-4. These windows are arranged in the Cascade configuration.

Chapter 6

Getting the Most out of Your Screen

You can maximize the workbook window if you need to see more of the active worksheet, but if that still isn't enough, you can try the Full Screen command on the View menu. When you do so, Excel removes the formula bar, status bar, toolbars, and title bars from your screen—everything except the menu bar, the Close Full Screen button, and the maximized workbook window—as shown in Figure 6-5.

For more on maximizing and minimizing windows, see "Resizing the Window" on page 23.

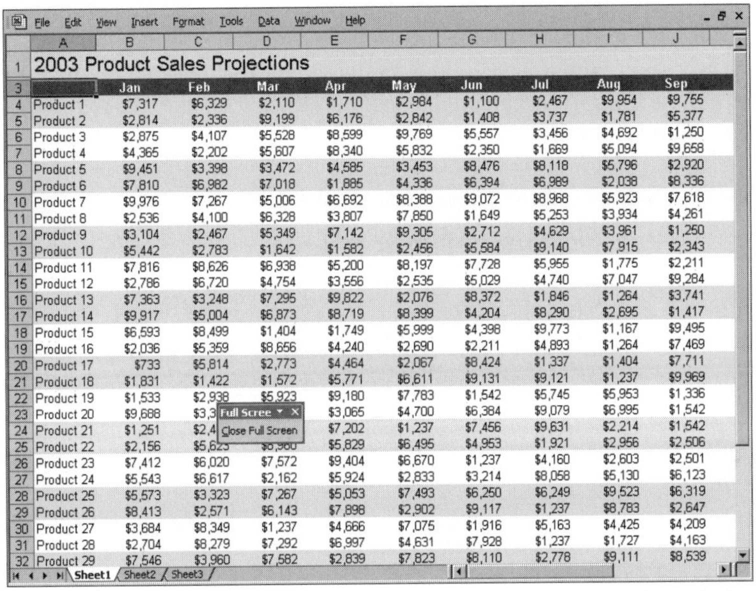

Figure 6-5. Choosing View, Full Screen hides the status bar, formula bar, and toolbars to maximize the screen space available for viewing your data.

note The Full Screen command provides a convenient way to display the most information on the screen without changing the magnification of the data. For more information about changing the magnification, see "Zooming Worksheets" on page 125.

To return the screen to its former configuration, click the Close Full Screen button or choose the Full Screen command again.

> **note** When you save a workbook, Excel also saves characteristics, such as the window's size, position on the screen, and display settings. The next time you open the workbook, the window looks the same as it did the last time you saved it. When you open it, Excel even selects the same cells that you selected when you saved the file.

Opening Multiple Windows for the Same Workbook

Suppose you've created a workbook like the one shown in Figure 6-6. You might want to monitor the cells on the Summary sheet while working on one of the other sheets in the workbook. On the other hand, if you have a very large worksheet, you might want to keep an eye on more than one area of the same worksheet at the same time. To do either of these things, you can open a second window for the workbook by choosing Window, New Window.

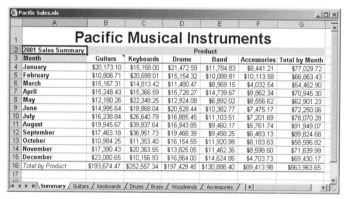

Figure 6-6. To view the Summary sheet while working on the Brass sheet, open a second window by choosing Window, New Window.

To view both windows together on your screen, choose Window, Arrange, and select any of the Arrange options except Cascade. If you choose the Cascade option (shown in figure 6-4 on page 136), you'll only be able to view the top sheet in the stack. If you select the Horizontal option, your screen looks similar to the one shown in Figure 6-7.

You might notice that Excel assigned the name Pacific Sales.xls:2 to the new workbook window. In addition, it changed the name of the original workbook window to Pacific Sales xls:1. Because it was the active window when the New window command was issued, Pacific Sales.xls:2 now becomes the active window, and as such, it's positioned on top, as indicated by the color of its title bar and the presence of scroll bars.

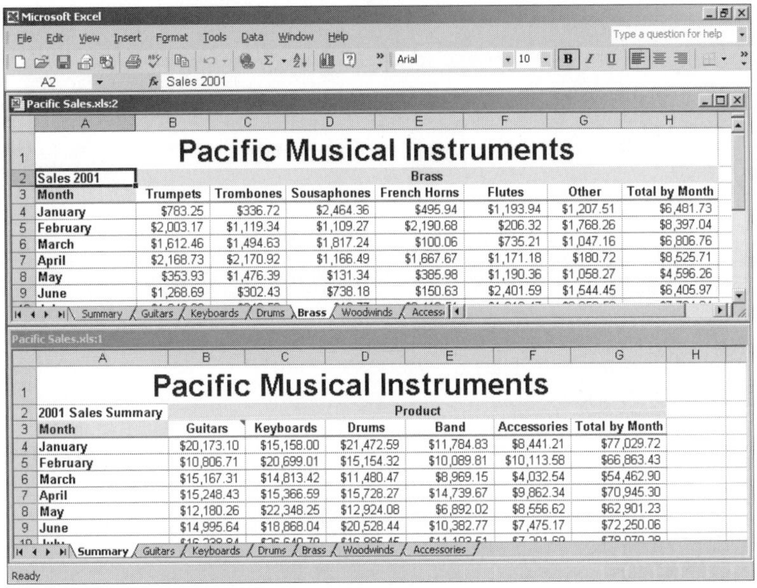

Figure 6-7. After using the New Window command to open a second window for the same workbook, use the Arrange command to fit both windows on the screen simultaneously.

---

tip   Don't arrange other workbook windows

If other workbooks are open but you want to view only the windows on the active workbook, select the Windows Of Active Workbook box in the Arrange Windows dialog box.

You can view any part of the workbook in any window associated with that workbook. In Figure 6-7, Pacific Sales.xls:2 originally displayed the Summary sheet when we first created it, because that was the active sheet when we issued the New Window command. Then we clicked the Brass tab, leaving the Summary sheet visible in Pacific Sales.xls:1.

Useful Inconsistencies of New Windows

When you create multiple windows of the same workbook, anything you do in one window happens in all windows—almost. New entries; formatting changes; inserted or deleted rows, columns, or sheets; and just about any other editing changes are reflected in all windows. Display characteristics—or views—are not. This enables you to zoom in or out and change anything on the View tab of the Tools, Options dialog box and almost anything on the View menu. View adjustments affect only the active window, as shown in Figure 6-8 on the next page.

Chapter 6

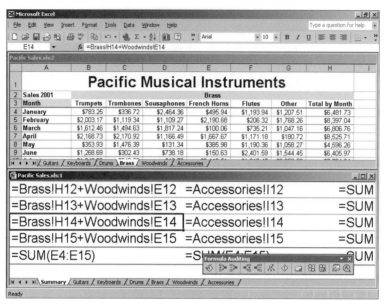

Figure 6-8. You can change the display characteristics of one window without affecting the other.

Figure 6-8 shows a somewhat exaggerated example of worksheet auditing. In Pacific Sales.xls:1, formulas are displayed, the sheet is zoomed in, and scroll bars, row and column headings, and gridlines are removed—all in an effort to review the formulas in the Summary sheet to make sure they refer to the proper cells. You can also use this technique to audit your worksheets.

If you create a view like Pacific Sales.xls:1 in Figure 6-8 and you want to be able to re-create it in the future, choose View, Custom View to save it. If you want to be able to re-create the entire workspace, including additional windows and their view settings, use the File, Save Workspace command.

For more information about custom views, see "Using Custom Views" on page 126. For more information about saving workspaces, see "Saving the Entire Workspace" on page 43. For more information about the auditing features in Excel, see "Auditing and Documenting Worksheets" on page 256. For more information about formulas, see Chapter 12, "Building Formulas."

Chapter 6

140

Close the Default Settings Window Last

When you have two windows open on the same workbook and then close one of them, the "number" of the open window isn't important, but the view settings are. In the example shown in Figure 6-8, if we finish our work and close Pacific Sales.xls:2, the modified view settings in Pacific Sales.xls:1 become the active view for the workbook. If we then save the workbook, we also save the modified view settings. Make sure that you close the windows with view settings you don't want to keep before you close the one whose settings you want to use as the default—don't worry about the window number.

Hiding and Protecting Workbooks

Sometimes you might want to keep certain information out of sight or simply protect it from inadvertent modification. You can conceal and protect your data by hiding windows, workbooks, or individual worksheets from view.

For information about protecting individual cells, see "Protecting Worksheets" on page 127.

Hiding Workbooks

At times, you might need to keep a workbook open so that you can access the information it contains, but you don't want it to be visible. When several open workbooks clutter your workspace, you can use the Hide command on the Window menu to conceal some of them. Excel can still work with the information in the hidden workbooks, but they don't take up space on your screen, nor do their file names appear on the Window menu.

To hide a workbook, simply activate it and choose Window, Hide. Excel removes the workbook from view, but the workbook remains open and available in the workspace. To bring the hidden workbook into view, choose Window, Unhide. This option is available only when you have a workbook hidden. A dialog box like the one shown in Figure 6-9 lists all hidden workbooks.

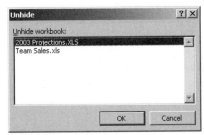

Figure 6-9. The Unhide dialog box lists all the workbooks that you currently have hidden.

> **note** The Hide command conceals any open window. However, if you have multiple windows open for the same workbook, choosing the Hide command hides only the active window. The entire workbook isn't hidden. For more information, see "Opening Multiple Windows for the Same Workbook" on page 138.

Troubleshooting

Nothing Happens when I Try to Open a Workbook

If, when you try to open a workbook, you don't see any error messages or dialog boxes, and the workbook doesn't appear to open, the window was probably hidden when it was last saved. The workbook is actually open, you just can't see it.

If, in a previous Excel session, you chose the Window, Hide command and then forgot about the hidden window when you exited Excel, you probably saw a message like "Do you want to save changes you made to Book1." This would have been the hidden file—the change that was made was the act of hiding it. The next time you open the file, it appears that nothing has happened, but if you look on the Window menu, you'll see the Unhide command, which only appears when a hidden window is open in the workspace. Choose this command and select the filename to make it visible once again, then save it before exiting Excel.

Protecting Workbooks

Protecting a workbook not only prevents changes to the complement of worksheets contained in the workbook, but also prevents any modifications to the way that the workbook windows are displayed. To protect a workbook, choose Tools, Protection, Protect Workbook to display the dialog box shown in Figure 6-10.

Figure 6-10. Choosing Tools, Protection, Protect Workbook helps insulate your workbooks from inadvertent modification.

Selecting the Structure option prevents any changes to the position, name, hidden, or unhidden status of the worksheets contained in the active workbook. When you select the Windows option, the workbook's windows cannot be closed, hidden, unhidden, resized, or moved—in fact, the minimize, maximize, and close buttons disappear. This does not mean that you cannot close the workbook itself; you can still choose the File, Close command. However, if you have more than one window open for the workbook, you cannot close any of them.

These settings take effect immediately. You can turn them off by choosing Tools, Protection, Unprotect Workbook (the Protect Workbook command changes when protection is activated). If you specified a password in the Protect Workbook dialog box, Excel will prompt you to supply that password before the worksheet protection turns off.

Saving Workbooks or Windows as Hidden

Sometimes you might want to hide a particular workbook, perhaps even to prevent others from opening and viewing its sensitive contents in your absence. If so, you can save the workbook as hidden. A hidden workbook is not visible when it's opened. You can save a workbook as hidden by following these steps:

1 Make sure the workbook you want to hide is active, and choose Window, Hide.

2 Hold down the Shift key, and choose File, Close All.

3 When a message appears asking whether you want to save changes to the workbook, click Yes.

The next time the workbook is open, its contents are hidden. To ensure that it cannot be unhidden by others, you might want to assign a password by choosing Tools, Protection, Protect Workbook before hiding and saving the workbook.

Also save a workbook with a hidden window. Simply create the new window, hide it by choosing Window, Hide, and then save the workbook.

Hiding Worksheets

If you want to hide a particular worksheet in a workbook, you can choose Format, Sheet, Hide. When you do so, the active worksheet no longer appears in the workbook. To unhide a hidden worksheet, choose Format, Sheet, Unhide. The Unhide dialog box for worksheets is almost identical to the Unhide dialog box for workbooks shown earlier in Figure 6-9.

Part 3

Formatting and Editing Worksheets

Chapter 7

Worksheet Editing Techniques

Cut and paste. Insert and delete. Undo and redo. It all seems elementary, but as always in Microsoft Excel, there are features hidden beneath the obvious approach to even the simplest task, as well as solutions to problems you probably never even thought of. We'll cover all the essential editing techniques, including multiple-sheet editing, checking spelling, selective pasting, and creating data series. This chapter dives deep into the pool of possibilities.

Copying, Cutting, and Pasting

When you copy an item, Excel saves it in memory, using a temporary storage area called the Clipboard. You capture the contents as well as the formatting and any attached comments or objects.

For more information about comments, see "Auditing and Documenting Worksheets" on page 256. For more information about objects, see Chapter 10, "Creating Spiffy Graphics."

When you copy or cut cells, a *marquee* appears around the cell. (We used to refer to this scrolling dotted line as "marching ants.") This marquee indicates the area copied or cut. You can even paste copied or cut cells to other worksheets or workbooks without losing the marquee.

We suggest that you learn and use the keyboard shortcuts for the quintessential editing commands listed in Table 7-1. You can use their command equivalents on the Edit menu, but really—if you never learn another keyboard shortcut, learn these.

Table 7-1. **The Essential Keyboard Shortcut Quick Reference**

Press	To
Ctrl+C	Copy
Ctrl+X	Cut
Ctrl+V	Paste
Ctrl+Z	Undo
Ctrl+Y	Redo

Copying and Pasting

When you copy, you can paste more than once. As long as the marquee is visible, you can continue to paste the information from the copied cells. You can copy this information to other worksheets or workbooks without losing your copy area marquee. The marquee persists until you press Escape or perform another editing action.

newfeature!

Collecting Multiple Items on the Clipboard

Using the newly redesigned and enhanced Collect And Copy feature, you can copy (or cut) up to 24 separate items and then paste them where you want them—one at a time or all at once. You do this by displaying the Clipboard task pane shown in Figure 7-1.

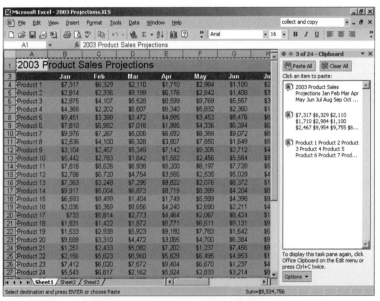

Figure 7-1. The Clipboard task pane stores multiple items that you copy or cut.

Normally when copying, you can work with only one item at a time. If you copy several items in a row, only the last item you copied is stored in the Clipboard. However, if you display the Clipboard task pane and copy or cut several items in succession, each item is stored in the task pane, as shown in Figure 7-1.

---

tip **Always collect**

You can change the normal collect and copy behavior so that Excel collects items every time you copy or cut, regardless of whether the Clipboard task pane is present. To do so, click the Options button at the bottom of the Clipboard task pane and choose Collect Without Showing Office Clipboard.

There are several ways to display the Clipboard task pane:

- Choose Edit, Office Clipboard.

- Press Ctrl+C twice, quickly, without changing the selection.

- If the task pane is already visible, click the small downward-pointing arrow in the task pane title bar and choose Clipboard from the menu.

Each time you copy or cut an item, a short representation of the item appears in the Clipboard task pane. Figure 7-1 shows three different items in the Clipboard task pane. You can paste any or all of the items wherever you choose. To paste an item from the Clipboard task pane, select the location where you want the item to go, and then click the item in the task pane. To empty the Clipboard task pane for a new collection, click the Clear All button.

---

tip **Assemble quick lists**

Although Collect And Copy is useful for editing tasks, it can also be a great tool for gathering information. Copy items such as names or addresses from various locations in the order you want them to appear. Then click the Paste All button on the Clipboard task pane to paste all the items you have collected, in the order collected, into a single column.

Pasting Multiples

After you copy, press Ctrl+V to paste whatever you copied. It's a no-brainer. However, did you know that if you select a range of cells before pasting, Excel fills every cell in that range when you paste? Figure 7-2 on the next page illustrates this.

Part 3: Formatting and Editing Worksheets

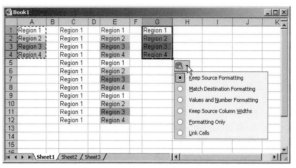

Figure 7-2. Before you paste, select more cells than you copied to create multiple copies of your information.

In Figure 7-2, we did the following:

- Copied cell A1, and then selected the range C1:C12 and pasted, resulting in Excel repeating the copied cell in each cell in the selected range.

- Copied Cells A1:A4, and then selected the range E1:E12 and pasted, resulting in Excel repeating the copied range within the range.

- Copied cells A1:A4, and then selected cell G1 and pasted, resulting in an exact duplicate of the copied range.

> **note** If the selected paste range contains more cells than the copied range, Excel repeats the copied cells until it fills the destination. However, if the paste range is smaller than the copied range, Excel pastes the entire copied range anyway.

newfeature!
Using The Paste Options Smart Tag

Notice in Figure 7-2 that we clicked the Paste Options smart tag action menu that appears near the lower left corner of the pasted range. This smart tag appears whenever and wherever you paste, offering action options applicable *after* pasting—a sort of "Smart Paste Special." The best part is that you can try each action in turn. Keep selecting Paste options until you like what you see, and then press Enter. The following describes each item on the Paste Options smart tag action menu:

> For more information about using smart tags, see "Smart Tags" on page 4.

- **Keep Source Formatting.** Retains formatting. This is the default action. If the other options don't work for you, you can always come back to this one before you press Enter.

- **Match Destination Formatting.** Copies formatted data into a differently formatted table without having to redo the formatting.

newfeature!

- **Values And Number Formatting.** Pastes values without losing number formats.

newfeature!

- **Keep Source Column Widths.** Retains column widths. This option is like choosing Keep Source Formatting with the added action of "pasting" the column width.

- **Formatting Only.** Leaves the contents of the cells alone and transfers the formatting. This works in the same way as the Format Painter button on the Standard toolbar.

- **Link Cells.** Instead of pasting the contents of the cut or copied cells, pastes a reference to the source cells, ignoring the source formatting.

Cutting and Pasting

When you cut rather than copy cells, subsequent pasting places one copy in the selected destination, removes the copied cells from the Clipboard, and removes the marquee. Select the range you want to move, and press Ctrl+X, which places the marquee around the cut cells. When you press Ctrl+V to paste, Excel moves the cut cells to their new location, and removes them from their original location.

When you cut and paste, the following rules apply:

- Excel clears both the contents and the formats of the cut range and transfers them to the cells in the paste range.

- Excel adjusts any formulas outside the cut area that refer to that cell.

- The area you select for cutting must be a single rectangular block of cells. If you try to select more than one range, you'll get an error message.

newfeature!

- Regardless of the size of the range you select before pasting, Excel pastes only the exact size and shape of the cut area. The upper left corner of the selected paste area becomes the upper left corner of the moved cells. In previous versions of Excel, you had to either select a single cell as the destination, or make sure the source and destination areas were exactly the same size and shape.

- Excel overwrites the contents and formats of any existing cells in the range where you paste. If you don't want to lose existing cell entries, be sure your worksheet has enough blank cells below and to the right of the cell you select as the upper left corner of the paste area to hold the entire cut area.

- You cannot use Paste Special after cutting. Furthermore, no smart tag menu appears when you paste after cutting.

newfeature!
Pasting Selectively Using Paste Special

Paste Special is quite possibly the most useful (and most used) power-editing feature of all. There are many ways to use this feature, but probably the most popular is copying the value in a cell without copying the formatting or the underlying formula. After you copy a cell or cells, choose Edit, Paste Special to display the dialog box shown in Figure 7-3. (You must choose Copy to use Paste Special. When you choose Cut, Paste Special is unavailable.)

> **tip**   **Choose Paste Special from the shortcut menu**
>
> Here's a quicker way to display the Paste Special dialog box. After you copy a cell or range, right-click the cell where you want to paste, and a shortcut menu appears containing Paste Special.

Figure 7-3.   Paste Special is probably the most popular power-editing feature.

Here's what the options in the Paste section of the Paste Special dialog box do:

- **All.** Predictably, pastes all aspects of the selected cell, which is the same as simply using the Paste command.

- **Formulas.** Transfers only the formulas from the cells in the copy range to the cells in the paste range, adjusting relative references.

- **Values.** Pastes static text, numeric values, or only the displayed values resulting from formulas.

- **Formats.** Transfers only the formats in the copy range to the paste range.

> **tip**   **Quickly duplicate multiple formats**
>
> You can quickly copy and paste formats from a single cell or from a range of cells using the Format Painter button on the Standard toolbar.

- **Comments.** Transfers only comments attached to selected cells.

- **Validation.** Pastes only the Data Validation settings that you have applied to the selected cells.

> For more information about data validation, see "Validating Data Entry" on page 710.

- **All Except Borders.** Transfers data without disturbing the border formats you spent so much time applying.

- **Column Widths.** Transfers only column widths, which is handy when trying to make a sheet look consistent for presentation.

- **Formulas And Number Formats.** Transfers only formulas and number formats, which is handy when copying formulas to previously formatted areas. Usually, you'll want the same number formats applied to formulas you copy, wherever they happen to go.

- **Values And Number Formats.** Transfers resulting values (but not the formulas) and number formats.

---

tip   **Use the smart tag menu**

You can apply a few common Paste Special options, including Values and Number Formatting, by clicking the smart tag action menu that appears after you paste, as shown in Figure 7-2.

Because the All option pastes the formulas, values, formats, and cell comments from the copy range into the paste range, it has the same effect as selecting Paste, making you wonder why Excel offers this option. That question brings us to our next topic— the Operation options.

Pasting Using Math Operators

You use the options in the Operation section of the Paste Special dialog box to mathematically combine the contents of the copy area with the contents of the paste area. When you select any option other than None, Excel does not overwrite the destination cell or range with the copied data. Instead, it uses the specified operator to combine the copy and paste ranges.

For example, say we want to get a quick total of the Northern and Eastern regions in Figure 7-4. First we copied the Northern Region totals to column G, and then we copied the Eastern Region totals in column D and chose Edit, Paste Special. We clicked the Values and Add options in the Paste Special dialog box, and after clicking OK, we saw the result shown at the bottom of Figure 7-4.

	D	E	F	G
	Eastern Region	Western Region	TOTAL	Northern Region
	137,872.00	173,622.00	546,062.00	123,456.00
	270,277.00	227,893.00	863,469.00	243,568.00
	136,934.00	123,282.00	602,838.00	153,623.00
	133,132.00	255,687.00	722,491.00	207,894.00
	233,824.00	122,344.00	494,784.00	103,283.00
	244,443.00	118,542.00	754,118.00	235,688.00
	122,024.00	219,234.00	509,103.00	102,345.00
	113,824.00	229,853.00	561,991.00	98,543.00
	158,045.00	107,434.00	479,874.00	199,235.00
	278,157.00	99,234.00	734,810.00	209,854.00
	188,212.00	143,455.00	433,324.00	87,435.00
	242,483.00	263,567.00	595,705.00	79,235.00
	2,259,227.00	2,084,147.00	5,054,856.00	

Paste Special dialog box: Paste — All, Formulas, Values (selected), Formats, Comments, Validation, All except borders, Column widths, Formulas and number formats, Values and number formats. Operation — None, Add (selected), Subtract, Multiply, Divide. Skip blanks, Transpose. Paste Link, OK, Cancel.

	A	B	C	D	E	F	G
8		Northern Region	Southern region	Eastern Region	Western Region	TOTAL	Northern Region
9	January	123,456.00	111,112.00	137,872.00	173,622.00	546,062.00	261,328.00
10	February	243,568.00	121,731.00	270,277.00	227,893.00	863,469.00	513,845.00
11	March	153,623.00	188,999.00	136,934.00	123,282.00	602,838.00	290,557.00
12	April	207,894.00	125,778.00	133,132.00	255,687.00	722,491.00	341,026.00
13	May	103,283.00	35,333.00	233,824.00	122,344.00	494,784.00	337,107.00
14	June	235,688.00	155,445.00	244,443.00	118,542.00	754,118.00	480,131.00
15	July	102,345.00	65,500.00	122,024.00	219,234.00	509,103.00	224,369.00
16	August	98,543.00	119,771.00	113,824.00	229,853.00	561,991.00	212,367.00
17	September	199,235.00	15,160.00	158,045.00	107,434.00	479,874.00	357,280.00
18	October	209,854.00	147,565.00	278,157.00	99,234.00	734,810.00	488,011.00
19	November	87,435.00	14,222.00	188,212.00	143,455.00	433,324.00	275,647.00
20	December	79,235.00	10,420.00	242,483.00	263,567.00	595,705.00	321,718.00
21	TOTAL	1,844,159.00	1,111,036.00	2,259,227.00	2,084,147.00	5,054,856.00	

Figure 7-4. We used the Values option of Paste Special to add the totals from column D to those in column G.

The other options in the Operation section of the Paste Special dialog box combine the contents of the copy and paste ranges using the appropriate operators. Just remember that the Subtract option subtracts the copy range from the paste range, and the Divide option divides the contents of the paste range by the contents of the copy range. Also note that if the copy range contains text entries and you use Paste Special with an Operation option (other than None), nothing happens.

Choose the Values option when you use any Operation option. As long as the entries in the copy range are numbers, you can use All, but if the copy range contains formulas, you'll get "interesting" results. As a rule, avoid using the Operation options if the paste range contains formulas.

note Excel assigns the value 0 to blank spaces in the copy and paste ranges, regardless of which Operation option you select.

Pasting Links

The Paste Link button in the Paste Special dialog box, shown in Figure 7-4, is a handy way to create references to cells or ranges. When you click the Paste link button, Excel enters an *absolute* reference to the copied cell in the new location. For example, if you copy cell A3, and then select cell B5, choose Edit, Paste Special, and click the Paste Link button, the following formula =$A$3 is entered into cell B5.

If you copy a range of cells, the Paste Link button enters a similar formula for each cell in the copied range to the same sized range in the new location.

Skipping Blank Cells

The Paste Special dialog box contains a Skip Blanks option that you use when you want Excel to ignore any blank cells in the copy range. Generally, if your copy range contains blank cells, Excel pastes those blank cells over the corresponding cells in the paste area. As a result, empty cells in the copy range overwrite the contents, formats, and comments in corresponding cells of the paste area. When you select Skip Blanks, however, the corresponding cells in the paste area are unaffected.

Transposing Entries

One of the often-overlooked but extremely useful Paste Special features is the Transpose option, which helps you to reorient the contents of the copied range when you paste—that is, entries in rows appear in columns, and entries in columns appear in rows. For example, in Figure 7-5 on the next page, we needed to use the column headings in Row 3 of the top sheet to create identical row headings in column A of the bottom sheet. Accomplishing this was as simple as copying cells B3:G3 in the top sheet, clicking cell A4 in the bottom sheet, and using Paste Special with Transpose selected.

---

tip   **Transpose formulas**

If you transpose cells containing formulas, Excel transposes the formulas and adjusts cell references. If you want the transposed formulas to continue to correctly refer to nontransposed cells, make sure the references in the formulas are absolute before you copy them. For more information on absolute cell references, see "Using Cell References in Formulas" on page 356.

Using Paste Special with Arrays

As with any other formula, you can convert the results of an array formula to a series of constant values by copying the entire array range and—without changing your selection—choosing Paste Special. If you select the Values option in the Paste Special dialog box, Excel overwrites the array formulas with their resulting constant values. Because the range now contains constant values rather than formulas, Excel no longer treats the selection as an array. For more information about arrays, see "Using Arrays" on page 387.

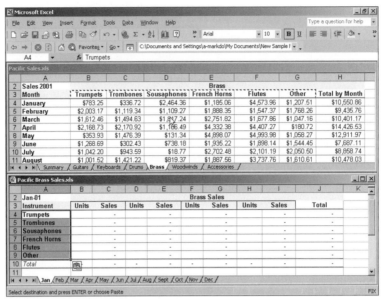

Figure 7-5. We copied the column headings in the top sheet and used the Paste Special Transpose option to create row headings in the bottom sheet.

Pasting Hyperlinks

The Paste As Hyperlink command has a specific purpose: to paste a hyperlink to the copied data in the location you specify. When you create a hyperlink, it's as if Excel draws an invisible box that acts like a button when you click it, and places it over the selected cell.

Hyperlinks in Excel are closely related to the links you see on Web sites that, when clicked, launch a different Web page. With a Web browser installed, you can add hyperlinks to locations on the World Wide Web to your workbooks, a handy way to make related information readily available. You can use hyperlinks to do similar things among your Excel worksheets, perhaps to provide an easy way to access other sheets or workbooks that contain additional information. You can even create hyperlinks to other Office documents, such as a report created in Microsoft Word or a Microsoft PowerPoint presentation.

Within Excel, you create a hyperlink by copying a cell or range, navigating to the location where you want the hyperlink (on the same sheet, a different sheet, or in a different workbook), and then choosing Edit, Paste As Hyperlink. When you move the mouse over the new hyperlink, the pointer changes to a little hand, indicating that something will happen when you click there. A ScreenTip appears, showing you the name and location of the document to which the hyperlink is connected, as shown in Figure 7-6.

> **newfeature!**
> **tip** You can select a cell containing a hyperlink without opening the hyperlink by holding down the mouse button until a plus pointer appears when you click the cell.

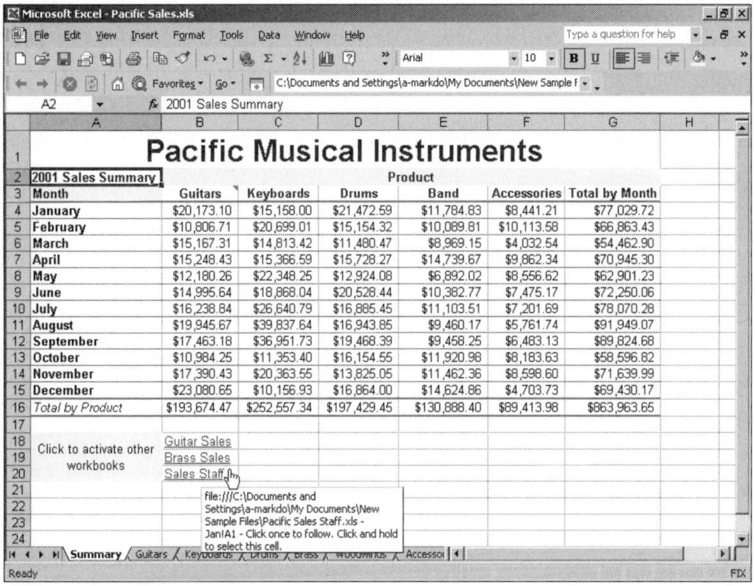

	A	B	C	D	E	F	G
1	Pacific Musical Instruments						
2	2001 Sales Summary	Product					
3	Month	Guitars	Keyboards	Drums	Band	Accessories	Total by Month
4	January	$20,173.10	$15,158.00	$21,472.59	$11,784.83	$8,441.21	$77,029.72
5	February	$10,806.71	$20,699.01	$15,154.32	$10,089.81	$10,113.58	$66,863.43
6	March	$15,167.31	$14,813.42	$11,480.47	$8,969.15	$4,032.54	$54,462.90
7	April	$15,248.43	$15,366.59	$15,728.27	$14,739.67	$9,862.34	$70,945.30
8	May	$12,180.26	$22,348.25	$12,924.08	$6,892.02	$8,556.62	$62,901.23
9	June	$14,995.64	$18,868.04	$20,528.44	$10,382.77	$7,475.17	$72,250.06
10	July	$16,238.84	$26,640.79	$16,885.45	$11,103.51	$7,201.69	$78,070.28
11	August	$19,945.67	$39,837.64	$16,943.85	$9,460.17	$5,761.74	$91,949.07
12	September	$17,463.18	$36,951.73	$19,468.39	$9,458.25	$6,483.13	$89,824.68
13	October	$10,984.25	$11,353.40	$16,154.55	$11,920.98	$8,183.63	$58,596.82
14	November	$17,390.43	$20,363.55	$13,825.05	$11,462.36	$8,598.60	$71,639.99
15	December	$23,080.65	$10,156.93	$16,864.00	$14,624.86	$4,703.73	$69,430.17
16	*Total by Product*	$193,674.47	$252,557.34	$197,429.45	$130,888.40	$89,413.98	$863,963.65
17							
18	Click to activate other workbooks	Guitar Sales					
19		Brass Sales					
20		Sales Staff					

Figure 7-6. We created hyperlinks to supporting workbooks at the bottom of this sheet.

When you click a hyperlink, the linked document opens. In addition, the Web toolbar appears when the link refers to an external document, as shown in Figure 7-6. You can use the Forward and Back buttons on the left side of the Web toolbar to move quickly back and forth between hyperlinked worksheets to which you have recently navigated. To edit or delete a hyperlink, right-click it, and then choose Edit Hyperlink or Remove Hyperlink from the shortcut menu.

For more information about hyperlinks, see Chapter 22 "Using Hyperlinks."

Moving and Copying with the Mouse

Also called Direct Cell Manipulation, this feature allows you to quickly move a cell or range to a new location. It's that simple. When you select a cell or range, move the mouse over the border of the selection until the arrow pointer appears, and then click the border and drag the selection to wherever you like. As you drag, an outline of the selected range appears, which you can use to help position the range correctly.

To copy a selection rather than move it, hold down the Ctrl key while dragging. The mouse pointer then appears with a small plus sign next to it, as shown in Figure 7-7, which indicates you are copying rather than moving the selection.

> **note** If direct cell manipulation doesn't seem to be working, choose Tools, Options, and on the Edit tab, make sure you have selected the Allow Cell Drag And Drop option.

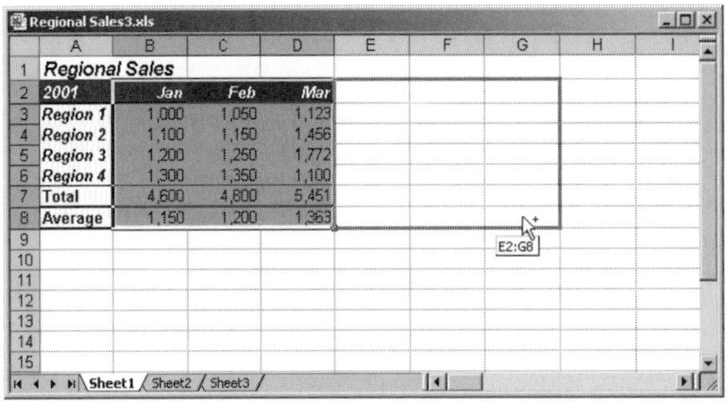

Figure 7-7. Before you finish dragging, press Ctrl to copy the selection. A plus sign and destination reference appear next to the pointer.

> For information on using the keyboard for this task, see "Inserting Copied or Cut Cells" on page 162.

You can also use direct cell manipulation to insert copied or cut cells in a new location. For example, on the left in Figure 7-8, we selected cells A3:D3 and then dragged the selection while holding down the Shift key. A gray I-beam indicates where Excel will insert the selected cells when you release the mouse button. The I-beam appears whenever the arrow pointer passes over a horizontal or vertical cell border. In this case, the I-beam indicates the vertical border between rows 5 and 6, but we could just as easily insert the cells horizontally. You'll see the I-beam insertion point flip between horizontal and vertical as you move the mouse around the worksheet. To insert the cells, release the mouse button while still pressing the Shift key. When you release the mouse button, the selected cells move to the new location, as shown on the right in Figure 7-8.

If you press Ctrl+Shift while dragging, the selected cells are copied and inserted instead of moved. Again, a small plus sign appears next to the arrow pointer, and Excel inserts a copy of the selected cells in the new location, leaving the original selected cells intact. You can also use these techniques to select entire columns or rows and then move or copy them to new locations.

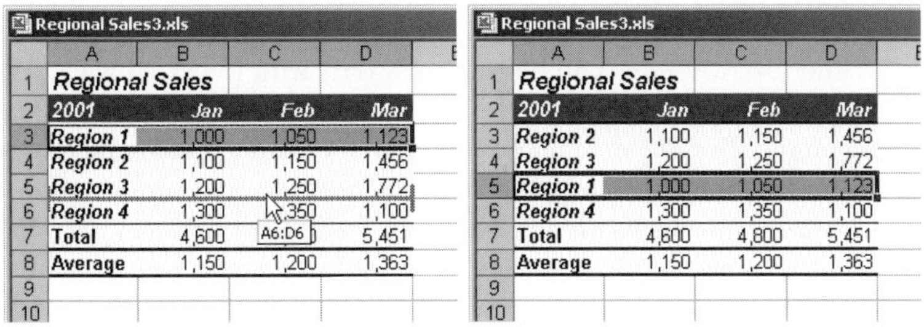

Figure 7-8. The I-beam indicates where Excel will insert the selected cells.

Inserting and Deleting

In the realm of spreadsheets, the complementary actions of inserting and deleting are collectively the second most-used editing techniques. There are nuances to inserting and deleting rows and columns of information that don't exist, for example, in the world of word-processing, but that must be taken into consideration.

Inserting Columns and Rows

You can choose options on the Insert menu to add cells, columns, and rows to a worksheet. However, when you insert, it's easiest to right-click the column or row heading, which simultaneously selects the row or column and displays the shortcut menu shown in Figure 7-9 on the next page. (You can also drag through several rows or columns, and then right-click the selection.) Then just choose Insert from the short-cut menu.

Issuing Commands with the Keyboard

Some of us are mouse fans; others are keyboard jockeys. If you're a good typist, you might prefer to keep your hands on the keys as much as possible. If so, this table of keyboard shortcuts for various Insert options is for you.

Press	To
Alt, I, R	Insert rows
Alt, I, C	Insert columns
Alt, E, D	Delete selected rows or columns
Ctrl+Spacebar	Select columns
Shift+Spacebar	Select rows

Part 3: Formatting and Editing Worksheets

Suppose you discover that you must add another region to the worksheet shown in Figure 7-9 and that you must combine the new data with the existing data. To insert space for the new region, right-click the column heading—column D in this case—and click Insert on the shortcut menu. The contents of column D move to column E, leaving the freshly inserted column D blank and ready for new information, as shown in Figure 7-10. The newly inserted cells take on the same formats as the cells in the column to the left, and Excel adjusts the formulas in cells G9:G21 to account for the expanded range.

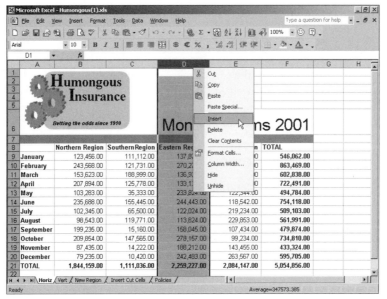

Figure 7-9. Right-click a row or column heading, and choose Insert.

A smart tag appears after you insert, which you can use to change the formatting of the inserted cells. Click the smart tag to display the smart tag action menu shown in Figure 7-10. If you want to extend a table by inserting a column on its right, for example, you might want to use either the Format Same As Right or Clear Formatting options. The default Format Same As Left option works for our example.

note When you insert a row, the smart tag options are Format Same As Above (the default), Format Same As Below, and Clear Formatting.

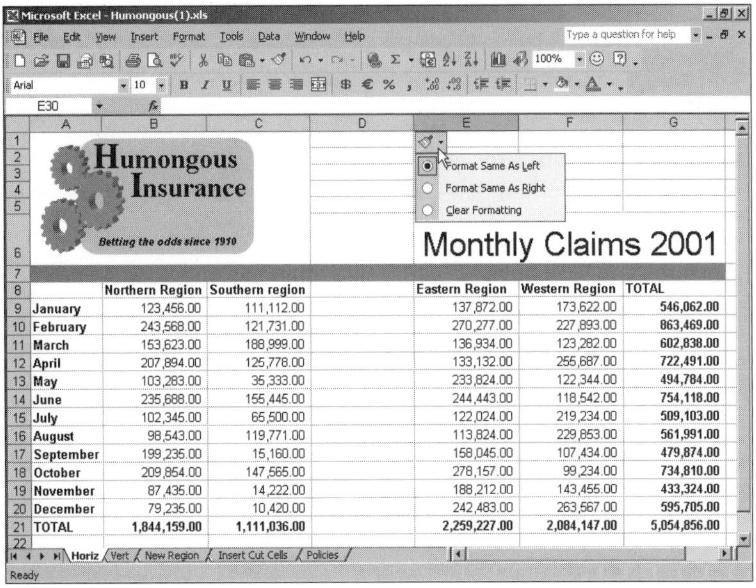

Figure 7-10. Click the smart tag after you insert, for post-insertion options.

Inserting Cells

You can insert cells rather than entire rows or columns by choosing Insert, Cells, which displays the dialog box shown in Figure 7-11. Instead of choosing Insert, Cells, you can right-click the selection and choose Insert Cells from the shortcut menu.

Figure 7-11. Use the Insert dialog box to choose the direction to move existing cells in your worksheet.

If you cut or copied some cells before right-clicking the selection, the words Cut Cells or Copied Cells replace Cells in the command name. You can use either of these options to simultaneously insert the necessary number of cells and paste the contents of the Clipboard into the new cells.

note You can insert multiple nonadjacent selections when you use the Insert command, except when inserting cut or copied cells.

Creating a Custom Insert and Delete Toolbar

Excel provides six buttons for inserting and deleting rows and columns. These buttons are not located on any toolbar, so to use them you must either create a custom toolbar or modify an existing toolbar. If you do a lot of inserting and deleting, you might want to create an Insert and Delete toolbar containing all six tools, like the one shown here.

The buttons are, from left to right: Insert Cells, Insert Rows, Insert Columns, Delete, Delete Rows, and Delete Columns. To create this toolbar, choose Tools, Customize, click the Toolbars tab, click the New button, and then type a name for the toolbar. Then click the Commands tab. The Insert buttons are in the Insert category, and the Delete buttons are in the Edit category. For information about how to create custom toolbars, see "Creating New Toolbars and Menus" on page 77.

When using this toolbar, you won't see any dialog boxes when you choose the Insert Cells or Delete buttons. Instead, Excel uses common-sense rules to determine the direction in which to shift the surrounding cells. Using the Insert Rows, Insert Columns, Delete Rows, and Delete Columns buttons is equivalent to selecting the Entire Row or Entire Column options in the Insert and Delete dialog boxes. You need not first select entire rows or columns to use these buttons.

Inserting Copied or Cut Cells

Often you need to copy or move existing data into the middle of another area of existing data, moving things out of the way in the process. You can do this the hard way, by inserting just the right amount of space in the destination area, and then copying or cutting cells and pasting them to the new location. However it's much easier to choose Insert, Copied Cells or Insert, Cut Cells, because they handle these actions for you. These commands appear on the Insert menu (or on the shortcut menu) only when you have copied or cut cells. If Excel needs more information about how to adjust the worksheet, it will present a dialog box similar to the one shown in Figure 7-11.

> You can also use the mouse to insert cut cells. For more information about mouse shortcuts, see "Moving and Copying with the Mouse" on page 157.

For example, you can use cutting and inserting to rearrange the names of the months shown on the left in Figure 7-10 so that they start with September and end with August to reflect the company's fiscal year. To do so, follow these steps:

1 Select A17:G20 and choose Edit, Cut.

2 Click cell A9.

3 Choose Insert, Cut Cells.

Excel puts the data from A17:G20 in cells A9:G12 and then moves the rest of the table down to accommodate the insertion, as shown in Figure 7-12.

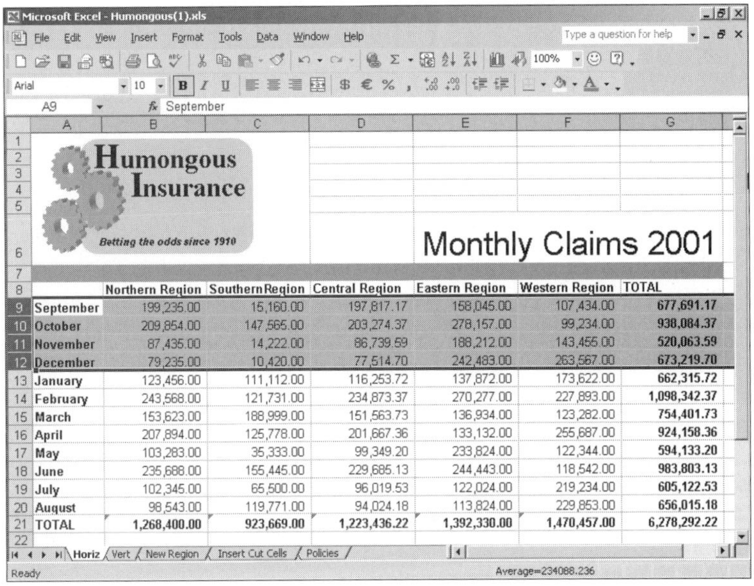

Figure 7-12. By choosing Edit, Cut and then Insert, Cut Cells, we moved the four months from the bottom of the table to the top.

Deleting Cells, Columns, and Rows

You can choose Edit, Delete to remove cells from your worksheet. Unlike Clear, which erases the formats, contents, or comments in a cell but leaves the cell in place, Delete removes the selected cell or range from the worksheet. In other words, Clear works like an eraser, and Delete works like a pair of scissors and shifts cells to fill the empty space you create. Here are some guidelines for using Delete:

- You can delete multiple nonadjacent rows by selecting the row heading before choosing Edit, Delete. Excel shifts everything below the deleted rows upward and adjusts any formulas accordingly.

- Delete entire columns by selecting the column heading before choosing Edit, Delete. Excel moves everything to the right of the deleted columns left and adjusts any formulas accordingly.

- Delete multiple nonadjacent selections in one operation as long as you delete either entire rows or entire columns. You cannot delete entire rows and columns at the same time, however, because they overlap.

- Delete partial rows and columns by selecting a cell or cells and pressing Edit, Delete. Excel displays the Delete dialog box shown in Figure 7-13. You can choose the direction you want to shift remaining cells to fill the gap, or you can choose to eliminate the entire rows or columns inhabited by the selected cells.

newfeature! Fixing Formula Problems

In Figure 7-12, notice that the formulas in row 21 have small triangular indicators in the upper left corner of each cell (they are green on your screen). This means that there is an error; in this case, we moved the cells, so the formulas no longer include the cells we moved. Notice in the figure below that the formula bar displays the formula =SUM(B13:B20), omitting cells B9:B12, which were among the cells that we cut and inserted in Figure 7-12. This problem occurs whenever you insert or move rows or columns at the edge of cell ranges referred to by formulas. Until now, you had to figure this out on your own, but Excel 2002 offers help. As shown here, not only do the little flags appear, but when you select one of the formula cells, a smart tag appears offering a Formula Omits Adjacent Cells menu containing pertinent options.

The Update Formula To Include Cells option works correctly in our example. This is a much easier solution than in past versions of Excel: editing each formula manually. For more information about formulas and cell references, see Chapter 12, "Building Formulas." For more information about smart tags, see "Smart Tags" on page 4.

Chapter 7: Worksheet Editing Techniques

Figure 7-13. Use the Delete dialog box to choose the direction to move cells.

When you delete partial rows or columns, it's easy to misalign data. For example, in Figure 7-14, we deleted cells B9:F12, with the default Shift Cells Up option selected. This eliminated the cells referred to by the formulas in column G, producing #REF errors. In addition, the column G totals in rows 13 through 20 now refer to the data in rows 9 through 12. This is a case where we might have simply wanted to clear the cell contents rather than delete the cells.

	A	B Northern Region	C Southern Region	D Central Region	E Eastern Region	F Western Region	G TOTAL
9	September	123,456.00	111,112.00	116,253.72	137,872.00	173,622.00	#REF!
10	October	243,568.00	121,731.00	234,873.37	270,277.00	227,893.00	#REF!
11	November	153,623.00	188,999.00	151,563.73	136,934.00	123,282.00	#REF!
12	December	207,894.00	125,778.00	201,667.36	133,132.00	255,687.00	#REF!
13	January	103,283.00	35,333.00	99,349.20	233,824.00	122,344.00	662,315.72
14	February	235,688.00	155,445.00	229,685.13	244,443.00	118,542.00	1,098,342.37
15	March	102,345.00	65,500.00	96,019.53	122,024.00	219,234.00	754,401.73
16	April	98,543.00	119,771.00	94,024.18	113,824.00	229,853.00	924,158.36
17	May	1,268,400.00	923,669.00	1,223,436.22	1,392,330.00	1,470,457.00	594,133.20
18	June						983,803.13
19	July						605,122.53
20	August						656,015.18
21	TOTAL						6,278,292.22

Figure 7-14. You can create errors when you delete the wrong cells.

caution Although you can generally use Undo to cancel a deletion, you should take heed of these important points. Before you delete an entire column or row, scroll through your worksheet to be sure you're not erasing important information that is not currently visible. Deleting cells that are referred to by formulas can be disastrous, as Figure 7-14 illustrates. Finally, when you delete a column or row referred to by an argument of a function, Excel modifies the argument, if possible, to account for the deletion. This adaptability is a compelling reason to use functions wherever possible. For more about using functions, see Chapter 13, "Using Functions."

Inserting, Deleting, and Clearing Cells with the Mouse

To perform the next group of operations, you use the fill handle, which appears in the lower right corner of the selection rectangle when you select a cell or range. If you select one or more entire rows or columns, the fill handle appears next to the heading.

When you select a single cell and drag the fill handle in any direction, Excel copies the contents of that cell to all the cells through which you drag (with exceptions, which you'll look at later). When you select more than one cell, Excel either copies the range or extends a data series in the direction you drag, depending on the cell contents, the shape of the selection, and whether you are holding down Ctrl.

In the worksheet on the left in Figure 7-15, we selected A6:D6 and dragged the fill handle one row down while pressing the Shift key. The mouse pointer became a double-headed arrow. The worksheet on the right in Figure 7-15 shows the newly inserted cells.

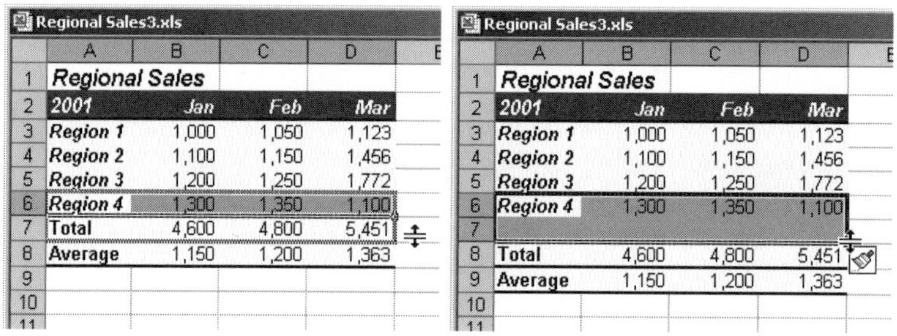

Figure 7-15. Drag the fill handle while pressing Shift to insert cells.

You use the same technique to insert entire rows or columns—just select the row or column headings, or press Shift and drag the fill handle, which appears adjacent to the row or column headings. You can just as easily delete cells, columns, or rows using a similar technique. To delete the cells we inserted in Figure 7-15, select A7:D7, hold down Shift, and then drag the fill handle back up one row. The area turns a medium shade of gray, and the mouse pointer changes to a similar double-headed arrow, with the arrows pointing inward this time. When you release the mouse button, Excel deletes the selection.

If you drag the fill handle back over selected cells (without pressing Shift), you clear the cell contents instead of deleting the cells. This is equivalent to choosing Edit, Clear, Contents, which clears formulas, text, and numbers only. If you hold down the Ctrl key while dragging back over a selection, you perform an operation that is equivalent to choosing Edit, Clear, All, which clears the entire contents of a cell, including formats and comments.

Fill Handles and Cell Selection Rectangles

The *cell selection rectangle* is the heavy black-bordered box that surrounds the currently selected cells. By default, the *fill handle* is visible in every cell selection rectangle, as shown here.

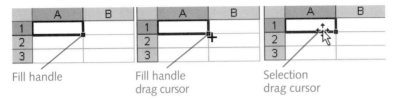

Fill handle Fill handle Selection
drag cursor drag cursor

Dragging the fill handle extends the selection and performs other feats of prowess, as described in this chapter. Dragging the selection rectangle moves or copies the selection, also as described in this chapter. If the fill handle is not visible, you need to choose Tools, Options, click the Edit tab, and select the Allow Cell Drag And Drop option.

Dragging with the Right Mouse Button

If you select cells and then drag the selection rectangle using the right mouse button, a shortcut menu appears when you release the button, as shown in Figure 7-16 on the next page. You can use the options on the shortcut menu to consummate your edit in a variety of ways. The options in the shortcut menu are as follows:

- **Move Here.** Moves the source cells to the selected destination.

- **Copy Here.** Copies the source cells to the selected destination.

- **Copy Here As Values Only.** Copies the values contained in the source cells to the selected destination cells but does not copy formulas.

- **Copy Here As Formats Only.** Copies the formats of the source cells to the destination cells, without affecting the contents.

- **Link Here.** Creates linking formulas at the destination that refer to the source cells.

- **Create Hyperlink Here.** Creates a Web-style "hot link" to the source cells in the selected destination.

● **The Shift options.** Allow you to copy or move the source cells to a location that contains existing data, shifting it out of the way in the selected direction.

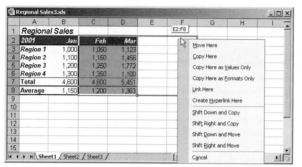

Figure 7-16. Drag the selection with the right mouse button to display a shortcut menu.

Undoing Previous Actions

The word undo was never very widely used until we started using computers; now it's a verb that we all wish we could apply to more things in life. In Excel, you can choose Edit, Undo or click the Undo button to recover from editing mistakes without having to reenter data or patch information back in place.

The Undo button on the Standard toolbar includes a drop-down list of up to the last 16 actions you performed. You can then select and simultaneously undo any number of these actions at once. You display the drop-down list by clicking the small downward-pointing arrow next to the Undo button, as shown in Figure 7-17.

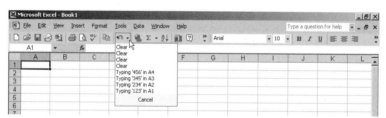

Figure 7-17. Click the arrow next to the Undo button to select and simultaneously undo up to the last 16 actions.

With the drop-down list visible, simply drag the mouse down the list and select the number of actions you want to undo. When you click the mouse, your worksheet reverts to the condition it was in before the selected actions.

Undo reverses the effect of most actions on the Edit menu and restores any entry in the formula bar. For example, if you accidentally delete a range of data, choose Undo to replace the entries. If you edit the contents of a cell and subsequently discover that your changes are incorrect, choose Undo to restore the original cell entry. In addition, you can use Undo to reverse formatting and many other types of actions.

Unfortunately, Excel has many actions that Undo can't reverse, such as Save and Delete Sheet. After you perform an un-undoable action, Can't Undo appears on the Edit menu in the place of Undo. Predictably, actions that you cannot undo will not appear in the Undo button's drop-down list.

Redoing What You've Undone

After you use Undo, you can then use Redo, which predictably reverses Undo. The Redo command on the Edit menu and the Redo button on the Standard toolbar operate in the same manner, allowing you to redo the last action by clicking the button itself or to redo up to the last 16 actions at once. When you undo a number of actions using the Undo drop-down list, Excel transfers these actions to the Redo button's drop-down list. If you then redo the same actions, Excel transfers them back to the Undo drop-down list.

You can take advantage of Undo and Redo to see the effects of an editing change in your worksheet. If you edit a cell that is referred to in several formulas, you can use Undo and Redo to get a "before and after" look at the results displayed by the formulas.

Repeating Your Last Action

Edit, Repeat and Edit, Redo share the same keyboard equivalent (Ctrl+Y), because you can do only one or the other at any given moment. Being able to repeat the last action is a great time-saver, and is particularly handy with repetitive formatting chores. The phrase last action is the key to understanding the difference between the two faces of this option. The option's name changes to reflect your most recent action. Redo is valid only if Undo was your last action. After you have redone all the "undos" (up to 16), you're back to the "true" last action—that is, the last thing you did before you used Undo. For example, press Delete to clear the contents of a cell. When you choose the Edit menu, both Undo Clear and Repeat Clear appear there. If you choose Undo Clear and then choose the Edit menu again, Redo Clear replaces Repeat Clear. If you choose Redo Clear and then choose the Edit menu, Repeat Clear reappears.

Unlike Undo, Repeat works with most actions. The only exceptions are those actions that you can't logically repeat. For example, if you save a file using File, Save, you can't repeat the action. Whatever the case, Repeat reflects the last repeatable action.

Editing Cell Contents

You can use the formula bar to edit the contents of a selected cell, or you can perform your editing "on location" in the cell itself. Excel also includes a few special features you can apply to tasks such as entering date sequences, which once used to involve editing each cell but are now semiautomatic, if you know where to find the "trigger."

Editing in the Formula Bar

You can also use Cut, Copy, Paste, and Clear to edit entries using the formula bar. Often, simply reentering a value or formula is easier, but the Edit menu options are convenient when you're working with a long, complex formula or label. These options work just as they do in a word-processing program such as Word when you're working in the formula bar. For example, you can copy all or part of a formula from one cell to another. For example, suppose cell A10 contains the formula **=IF(NPV(.15,A1:A9)>0,A11,A12)**, and you want to enter **=NPV(.15,A1:A9)** in cell B10.

To do so, select cell A10, and in the formula bar, select the characters you want to copy—in this case, NPV(.15,A1:A9)—and choose Edit, Copy. Select cell B10, type = to begin a formula, and choose Edit, Paste (or click the Paste button).

> **note**   Excel does not adjust cell references when you cut, copy, and paste in the formula bar. For information about adjustable references, see "How Copying Affects Cell References" on page 360.

Editing Directly in Cells

You can also edit the contents of cells without using the formula bar. By double-clicking a cell, you can perform any formula-bar editing procedure directly in the cell. The added advantage of editing formulas in the cell is that Excel gives you visual aids called *range finders* to help you audit, as shown in Figure 7-18.

> For more information about auditing, see "Auditing and Documenting Worksheets" on page 256.

> **note**   For in-cell editing, you must have Edit Directly In Cell enabled. If this option, which is on by default, has been turned off, you can restore it by choosing Tools, Options, clicking the Edit tab, and then selecting the Edit Directly In Cell option.

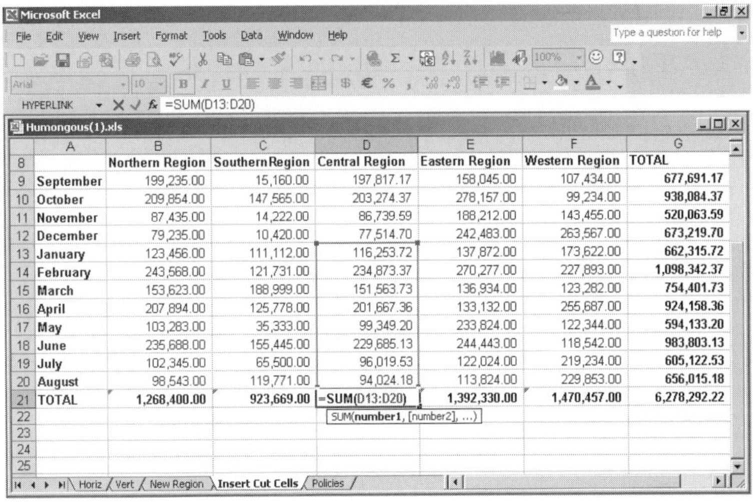

	A	B	C	D	E	F	G
8		Northern Region	SouthernRegion	Central Region	Eastern Region	Western Region	TOTAL
9	September	199,235.00	15,160.00	197,817.17	158,045.00	107,434.00	677,691.17
10	October	209,854.00	147,565.00	203,274.37	278,157.00	99,234.00	938,084.37
11	November	87,435.00	14,222.00	86,739.59	188,212.00	143,455.00	520,063.59
12	December	79,235.00	10,420.00	77,514.70	242,483.00	263,567.00	673,219.70
13	January	123,456.00	111,112.00	116,253.72	137,872.00	173,622.00	662,315.72
14	February	243,568.00	121,731.00	234,873.37	270,277.00	227,893.00	1,098,342.37
15	March	153,623.00	188,999.00	151,563.73	136,934.00	123,282.00	754,401.73
16	April	207,894.00	125,778.00	201,667.36	133,132.00	255,687.00	924,158.36
17	May	103,283.00	35,333.00	99,349.20	233,824.00	122,344.00	594,133.20
18	June	235,688.00	155,445.00	229,685.13	244,443.00	118,542.00	983,803.13
19	July	102,345.00	65,500.00	96,019.53	122,024.00	219,234.00	605,122.53
20	August	98,543.00	119,771.00	94,024.18	113,824.00	229,853.00	656,015.18
21	TOTAL	1,268,400.00	923,669.00	=SUM(D13:D20)	1,392,330.00	1,470,457.00	6,278,292.22
22							
23							
24							
25							

Figure 7-18. Double-click a cell containing a formula to edit it, and to display range finders.

Editing Options

The Edit tab in the Options dialog box (choose Tools, Options) contains an assortment of options that control editing-related workspace settings, as shown in Figure 7-19 on the next page. These options include the following:

- **Edit Directly In Cell.** Required for in-cell editing. See "Editing Directly in Cells" on page 170.
- **Allow Cell Drag And Drop.** Required for direct manipulation of cells using the mouse. See "Moving and Copying with the Mouse" on page 157.
- **Move Selection After Enter.** Locks in the entry and makes the cell below active. To change the direction of the selection after you press Enter, select the Direction drop-down list. When you clear this option, pressing Enter simply locks in the entry and leaves the same cell active.
- **Fixed Decimal.** Enters decimal points. Normally you enter numbers and decimal points manually. To have Excel enter decimal points for you, choose this option and select the number of decimal points you want. For example, when you enter **12345** with two fixed decimal places specified, Excel enters 123.45 into the cell. When you apply fixed decimals, FIX appears in the status bar. The Fixed Decimal option applies only to entries you make after you select the option, without altering existing data. It also applies only when you do not type a decimal point. If you type a number including a decimal point, the option has no effect.

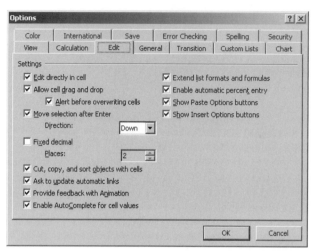

Figure 7-19. Choose Tools, Options and click the Edit tab to
display editing-related workspace settings.

Understanding Fixed and Floating Decimals

The Fixed Decimal option on the Edit tab of the Options dialog box is handy when
you need to enter long lists of numeric values. (It's equivalent to the floating decimal
feature available on most ten-key calculators.) For example, if you're performing a
lengthy data-entry task such as entering multiple dollar values into a worksheet, select
the Fixed Decimal option and choose 2 in the Places list box. Then just type numbers
and press Enter, saving you an extra keystroke for the decimal point in each entry. If
you're entering a thousand values, typing **295** instead of **2.95** eliminates 25 percent
of the keystrokes you would otherwise have to perform. However, you need to
be careful to enter trailing zeros or add a decimal point. For example, you would
normally type **5** to enter a 5.00 value, but with 2 fixed decimals turned on, the same
entry becomes 0.05, making it necessary to type either **500** or **5** to correctly locate the
decimal point.

- **Cut, Copy, And Sort Objects With Cells.** Required to "attach" graphic
  objects to cells. See "Tools to Help You Position Objects on the Worksheet"
  on page 308.

- **Ask To Update Automatic Links.** Displays a message before updating
  formulas that refer to cells in remote workbooks. See "Choosing Automatic
  or Manual Update" on page 577.

- **Provide Feedback With Animation.** Animates the action. With this option
  selected, using the arrows on the scroll bars or inserting and deleting rows
  or columns will appear animated on your screen. That is, the rows or columns appear to roll in the direction of the action.

- **Enable AutoComplete For Cell Values.** Allows Excel to suggest cell entries by comparing existing values it finds in your worksheet as you type. See "Letting Excel Help with Typing Chores" on page 195.

- **Extend List Formats And Formulas.** Allows Excel to apply formatting to new cells entered in a "list" or table, based on the formats of existing cells. See "Extending Existing Formatting" on page 182.

- **Enable Automatic Percent Entry.** Helps you enter values in cells with the Percentage format. With this option selected, all entries less than 1 are multiplied by 100. With this option clear, all entries—including those greater than 1—are multipled by 100.

- **Show Paste Options Buttons/Show Insert Options Buttons.** Shows the smart tag menu. Normally when you perform a paste or insert operation, a smart tag action menu appears, offering various specific actions you can perform after the fact. Clear this option to turn off these features.

Clearing Cell Contents and Formats

You can choose Edit, Clear to erase the contents of a cell or range, the format assigned to that cell or range, comments attached to a cell, or a chart. The Clear submenu offers the following four options:

- **All.** Erases the contents of the selected cells, any formats (other than column width and row height), and any comments attached to those cells.

- **Formats.** Removes the formats from the selected cells but leaves their contents and comments in place; the selected cells then revert to the General format and the Normal style.

- **Contents.** Removes the contents of the selected cells but leaves their formats and comments intact. This is the same as selecting cells and pressing the Delete key.

- **Comments.** Removes any comments from the selected cells but leaves their contents and formats in place. For information about cell comments, see "Adding Comments to Cells" on page 266.

> **note** The Delete key works differently if you're working in the formula bar or editing directly in a cell. In these cases, pressing the Delete key erases the selected characters or the character to the right of the insertion point; pressing Backspace erases the selected characters or the character to the left of the insertion point.

Filling and Creating Data Series

As described earlier in this chapter, the fill handle has many talents to make it simple to enter data into worksheets. Uses of the fill handle include quickly and easily filling cells and creating data series using the incredibly useful AutoFill feature.

Take a look at Figure 7-20. If you select cell A2 in this worksheet and drag the fill handle down to cell A5, Excel copies the contents of cell A2 to cells A3 through A5. However, if you click the smart tag action menu, you can select a different AutoFill action after you drag, as shown on the right in Figure 7-20.

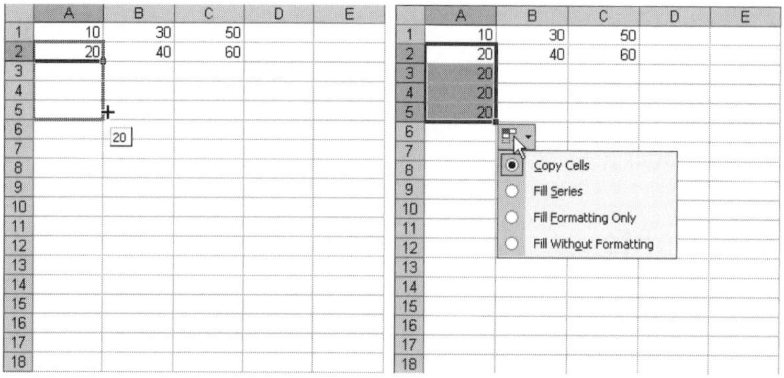

Figure 7-20. Copy the contents of a cell to adjacent cells by dragging the fill handle.

If you choose Fill Series on the smart tag action menu, Excel creates the simple series 21, 22, 23 instead of copying the contents of cell A2. If you select the range C1:C2 in Figure 7-20 and drag the fill handle down to cell A5, you create a series that is based on the interval between the two selected values, as shown in Figure 7-21.

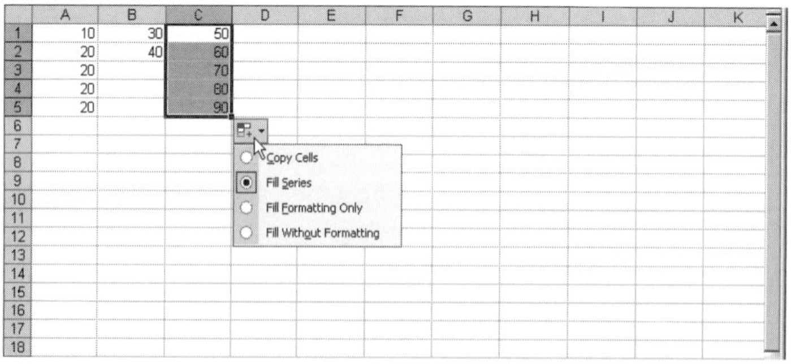

Figure 7-21. Create a data series by selecting a range of values and dragging the fill handle.

If you choose Copy Cells on the smart tag action menu in Figure 7-21, instead of extending the series, Excel copies the cells, repeating the pattern of selected cells as necessary to fill the range. Instead of filling C3:C5 with the values 70, 80, and 90, as shown in Figure 7-21, choosing Copy Cells results in copying the values 50, 60, and 50 into the same range instead.

---

tip   **Create decreasing series**

Generally, when you create a series, you drag the fill handle down or to the right, and the values increase accordingly. You can also create a series of decreasing values, however, by simply dragging the fill handle either up or to the left. Enter the starting values in the cells at the bottom or to the right of the range you want to fill and then drag the fill handle back to the beginning of the range.

If you select a text value and drag the fill handle, Excel copies the text to the cells where you drag. If, however, the selection contains both text and numeric values, the AutoFill feature takes over and extends the numeric component while copying the text component. You can also extend dates in this way, using a number of date formats, including Qtr 1, Qtr 2, and so on. If you enter text that describes dates, even without numbers (such as months or days of the week), Excel treats the text as a series.

Figure 7-22 shows some examples of simple data series created by selecting single cells containing values and dragging the fill handle. The values in column A were typed, and the values to the right of column A were extended using the fill handle. Figure 7-23 on the next page shows examples of creating data series using two selected values that, in effect, specify the interval to be used in creating the data series. We typed the values in columns A and B and extended the values to the right of column B using the fill handle. These two figures also show how AutoFill can create a series even when you mix text and numeric values in cells.

	A	B	C	D	E	F	G	H	I	J
1	Selected Value	Resulting Series								
2										
3	9:00	10:00	11:00	12:00	13:00	14:00	15:00			
4	1/1/2002	1/2/2002	1/3/2002	1/4/2002	1/5/2002	1/6/2002	1/7/2002			
5	Qtr 1	Qtr 2	Qtr 3	Qtr 4	Qtr 1	Qtr 2	Qtr 3			
6	Jan	Feb	Mar	Apr	May	Jun	Jul			
7	January	February	March	April	May	June	July			
8	Day 1	Day 2	Day 3	Day 4	Day 5	Day 6	Day 7			
9	Mon	Tue	Wed	Thu	Fri	Sat	Sun			
10	Product 1	Product 2	Product 3	Product 4	Product 5	Product 6	Product 7			
11										

Figure 7-22. Create simple data series by selecting a single value and dragging the fill handle.

---

tip   **Suppress AutoFill**

If you hold down Ctrl while dragging the fill handle, you suppress AutoFill and copy the selected values to the adjacent cells. Conversely, Excel normally copies a single selected value, such as 100, to adjacent cells when you drag the fill handle. However, if you hold down Ctrl while dragging, Excel extends the series 100, 101, 102, and so on.

	A	B	C	D	E	F	G	H	I	J
1	Selected Values		Resulting Series							
2										
3	9:00	10:00	11:00	12:00	13:00	14:00	15:00			
4	2001	2002	2003	2004	2005	2006	2007			
5	1/1/2002	2/1/2002	3/1/2002	4/1/2002	5/1/2002	6/1/2002	7/1/2002			
6	1/1/2002	3/1/2002	5/1/2002	7/1/2002	9/1/2002	11/1/2002	1/1/2003			
7	1-Jan	2-Jan	3-Jan	4-Jan	5-Jan	6-Jan	7-Jan			
8	Dec-02	Dec-03	Dec-04	Dec-05	Dec-06	Dec-07	Dec-08			
9	Dec-02	Dec-04	Dec-06	Dec-08	Dec-10	Dec-12	Dec-14			
10	Product 1	Product 2	Product 3	Product 4	Product 5	Product 6	Product 7			
11	1 1/2	2 3/4	4	5 1/4	6 1/2	7 3/4	9			
12										

Figure 7-23. Specify data series intervals by selecting a range of values and dragging the fill handle.

How AutoFill Handles Dates and Times

AutoFill normally increments recognizable date and time values when you drag the fill handle, even if you initially select only one cell. For example, if you select a cell that contains Qtr 1 or 1/1/02 and drag the fill handle, AutoFill extends the series as Qtr 2, Qtr 3, or 1/2/02, 1/3/02, and so on. If you click the smart tag action menu after you drag, you'll see that it contains special options if the original selection contains dates, or the names of days or months, as shown here.

	A	B	C	D	E	F
1	1/1/2002	1/2/2002	1/3/2002			
2						
3						
4				○ Copy Cells		
5				● Fill Series		
6				○ Fill Formatting Only		
7						
8				○ Fill Without Formatting		
9				○ Fill Days		
10				○ Fill Weekdays		
11						
12				○ Fill Months		
13				○ Fill Years		
14						

An interesting feature of this menu is Fill Weekdays, which not only increments a day or date series, but also skips weekend days. Depending on the original selection, you might see different options on the smart tag action menu.

Extending with AutoFill

Sometimes you can double-click the fill handle to extend a series from a selected range. AutoFill determines the size of the range by matching an adjacent range. For example, in Figure 7-24, we filled column A with a series of values. Then we filled column B by simply selecting the range B1:B2 and double-clicking the fill handle. The newly created series stops at cell B5 to match the adjacent cells in column A. When the selected cells contain something other than a series, such as simple text entries, double-clicking the fill handle copies the selected cells down to match the length of the adjacent range.

	A	B	C	D
1	10	30	50	
2	20	40	60	
3	30			
4	40			
5	50			
6				
7				

	A	B	C	D
1	10	30	50	
2	20	40	60	
3	30	50		
4	40	60		
5	50	70		
6				
7				

Figure 7-24. We extended a series into B3:B5 by selecting B1:B2 and double-clicking the fill handle.

Dragging the Fill Handle with the Right Mouse Button

When you use the right mouse button to fill a range or extend a series, a shortcut menu appears when you release the button, as shown in Figure 7-25. This menu differs somewhat from the smart tag action menu, and allows you to specify what you want to happen in advance, as opposed to the smart tag action menu's ability to change the action after the fact.

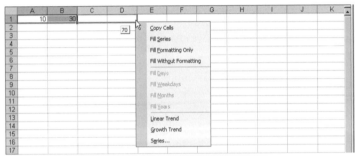

Figure 7-25. If you right-click and drag the fill handle, this shortcut menu appears when you release the mouse button.

The box that appears on the screen adjacent to the arrow pointer indicates what the last number of this sequence would be if we dragged the fill handle normally (with the left mouse button)—in this case, 70. If the source cells contain dates, Fill Days, Fill Weekdays, Fill Months, and Fill Years on the shortcut menu are available, allowing you to extend a series where only the corresponding component of the date is incremented.

Choose Linear Trend to create a simple linear series similar to that which you can create by dragging the fill handle with the left mouse button. Growth Trend creates a simple nonlinear growth series, using the selected cells to extrapolate points along an exponential growth curve. In Figure 7-26 on the next page, rows 4 through 6 in column A contain a series created using Linear Trend, and the same rows in column C contain a series created using Growth Trend, using the same starting values.

Chapter 7

	A	B	C	D	E	F	G	H	I	J
1	Linear Trend		Growth Trend							
2	10		10							
3	20		20							
4	30		40							
5	40		80							
6	50		160							
7										
8										

Figure 7-26. We created a linear trend series in column A and a growth trend series in column C.

When you choose Series on the shortcut menu, the Series dialog box appears, allowing you to create custom incremental series. For more information about using series, see "Filling Series" on page 180.

Creating Custom Lists

If you find yourself repeatedly entering a particular sequence in your worksheets, such as a list of names or products, you can use Excel's Custom Lists feature to make entering that sequence as easy as dragging the mouse. After you've created the sequence, you can enter it in any range of cells by simply typing any item from the sequence in a cell and then dragging the fill handle. For example, Figure 7-27 shows the single name we entered in cell A1 and the custom list we entered in cells A2:A11 by simply dragging the fill handle.

Figure 7-27. You can create custom lists that you can enter by dragging the fill handle.

To create a custom list, follow these steps:

1 Choose Tools, Options and click the Custom Lists tab.

2 With NEW LIST selected in the Custom Lists box, type the items you want to include in your list in the List Entries list box. Be sure to type the items in the order you want them to appear.

3 Click the Add button to add the list to the Custom Lists box.

4 Click OK to return to the worksheet.

Chapter 7

Importing Custom Lists

You can also create a custom list by importing the entries in an existing cell range. To import the entries shown in Figure 7-27, we first selected the range A4:A13 before opening the Tools, Options dialog box. Then we clicked the Import button on the Custom Lists tab to add the selected entries as a new list, as shown in Figure 7-28.

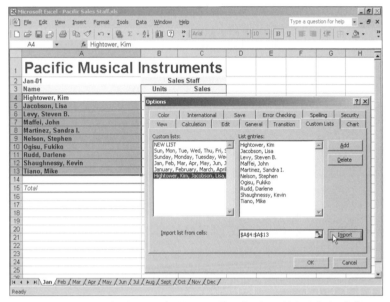

Figure 7-28. Use the Import button on the Custom Lists tab to define existing selected cell entries as custom lists.

Using Fill Options on the Edit Menu

Choosing Edit, Fill displays a submenu with several options that offer an alternative, menu-driven way to perform many of the mouse-driven copying and filling actions described in previous examples in this chapter. The following sections explore these options.

Filling Down, Right, Up, and Left   Use Down, Right, Up, and Left to copy selected cells to an adjacent range of cells. Before choosing these commands, select the range you want to fill, including the cell or cells containing the formulas, values, and formats that you want use to fill the selected range. (Comments are not included when you use these Fill commands.)

---

tip   You can also use keyboard shortcuts to duplicate Edit, Fill, Down (press Ctrl+D) and Edit, Fill, Right (press Ctrl+R).

Filling Across Worksheets   Choose Edit, Fill, Across Worksheets to copy cells from one worksheet to other worksheets in the same workbook. For more information about using the Across Worksheets feature, see "Filling a Group" on page 191.

Filling Series   You can choose Edit, Fill, Series to quickly create a series of numbers or dates. Select a cell containing a starting value, specify an interval with which to increment the series (step value), and, if you want, specify a maximum value for the series (stop value). There are a couple of advantages to using this option over the direct mouse manipulation techniques described earlier in this chapter. First, you do not need to select a range to fill, and second, you can specify increments (step values) without first selecting cells containing example incremented values. You can select example values and a fill range in advance, if you want, but it is not necessary.

Suppose cells A1 and A2 contain the values 10 and 20. If you select cells A1:A10 and choose Edit, Fill, Series, Excel displays a dialog box like the one in Figure 7-29.

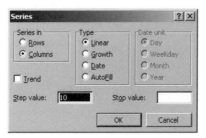

Figure 7-29.   Use the Series dialog box to create a regular series of numbers.

The Rows option tells Excel to use the first value in each row to fill the cells to the right. The Columns option tells Excel to use the first value in each column to fill the cells below. In this case, the selection is taller than it is wide, so Excel selects the Columns option. Excel uses the Type options in conjunction with the start values in selected cells and the value in the Step Value box to create your data series. If you select example cells first, the Step Value reflects the increment between the selected cells, as shown in Figure 7-29; otherwise, the Step Value is 1.

The Linear option adds the value specified in the Step Value box to the selected values in your worksheet to extend the series. The Growth option multiplies the last value in the selection by the step value, and extrapolates the rest of the values to create the series. If you select the Date option, you can specify the type of date series from the options in the Date Unit section. The AutoFill option works like using the fill handle to drag a series, extending the series using the interval between the selected values, determines the type of data, and attempts to "divine" your intention.

For more about AutoFill and the fill handle, see "Filling and Creating Data Series" on page 174. For more about entering dates, see "Entering a Series of Dates" on page 442.

Chapter 7: Worksheet Editing Techniques

Distributing Long Entries Using the Justify Command   Choosing Edit, Fill, Justify doesn't do what you might think it does. It splits a cell entry and distributes it into two or more adjacent rows. Unlike other Fill commands, Justify modifies the contents of the original cell.

> For information about the *other* justify—that is, justifying text in a single cell, see "Justifying Text in Cells" on page 226.

For example, in the worksheet on the left in Figure 7-30, cell A1 contains a long text entry. To divide this text into cell-sized parts, select cell A1 and choose Edit, Fill Justify. The result is shown on the right in Figure 7-30.

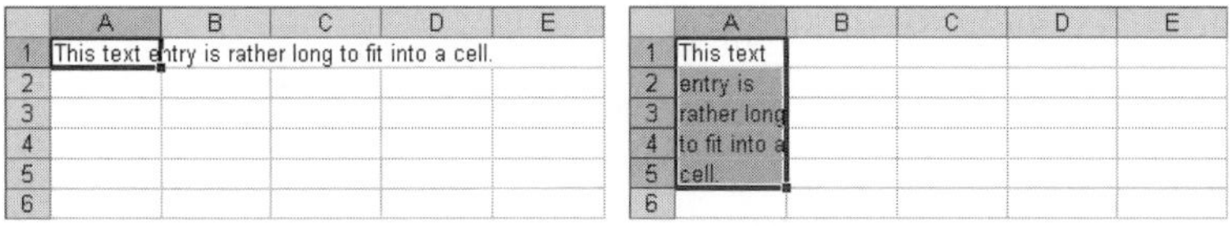

Figure 7-30.   Choosing Justify distributed the long label in cell A1 to cells A1:A5.

When you choose Justify, Excel displays this message: Text will extend below selected range. The message warns you that this command will use as many cells below the selection as necessary to distribute the contents. Excel overwrites any cells that are in the way in the following manner:

- If you select a multi-row range, Justify redistributes the text in all selected cells. For example, you can widen column A in Figure 7-30, select the filled range A1:A5, and choose Justify again to redistribute the contents using the new column widths.

- If you select a multi-column range, Justify redistributes only the entries in the leftmost column of the range, but uses the total width of the range you select as its guideline for determining the length of the justified labels. The cells in adjacent columns are not affected, although the justified text will appear truncated.

> **tip**   **Use horizontal distribution**
>
> You can choose Data, Text To Columns to distribute cell entries horizontally. The Text To Columns option is located on the Data menu because you use it most often when you import database information into Excel from other programs.

Chapter 7

Extending Existing Formatting

This feature allows you to add new columns of data to a previously constructed table without having to apply formatting to the new cells. For example, if you want to add another column to the existing table in Figure 7-31, simply select cell E2 and enter the column heading, and then continue entering numbers in cells E3–E6.

Regional Sales3.xls				
	A	B	C	D	E
1	Regional Sales				
2	2001	Jan	Feb	Mar	
3	Region 1	1,000	1,050	1,123	
4	Region 2	1,100	1,150	1,456	
5	Region 3	1,200	1,250	1,772	
6	Region 4	1,300	1,350	1,100	
7					
8	Total	4,600	4,800	5,451	
9	Average	1,150	1,200	1,363	

Regional Sales3.xls				
	A	B	C	D	E
1	Regional Sales				
2	2001	Jan	Feb	Mar	Apr
3	Region 1	1,000	1,050	1,123	1,050
4	Region 2	1,100	1,150	1,456	1,234
5	Region 3	1,200	1,250	1,772	1,110
6	Region 4	1,300	1,350	1,100	
7					
8	Total	4,600	4,800	5,451	
9	Average	1,150	1,200	1,363	

Figure 7-31. Automatic format extension adds data to an existing table without reformatting.

Excel correctly surmises that you want the new entries to use the same formatting as the adjacent cells in column D. You can turn this feature off by choosing Tools, Options, clearing on the Edit tab the Extend List Formats and Formulas option.

Finding and Replacing Stuff

Suppose you've built a large worksheet and you now need to find every occurrence of a specific string of text or values in that worksheet. (In computerese, a *string* is defined as any series of characters you can type in a cell—text, numbers, math operators, or punctuation symbols.) You can choose Edit, Find to locate any string, cell reference, or range name in cells or formulas on a worksheet. In addition to strings, you can now also find formatting, with or without strings attached. You can then choose Replace to overwrite the strings or formatting you locate with new strings or new formatting.

When you choose Edit, Find (or press Ctrl+F), a dialog box like the one in Figure 7-32 appears. (If yours looks different, click the Options button to expand the dialog box.) Use the options on the Find tab in the following ways:

- **Find What.** Type the string of characters you want to find.

- **Match Case.** Distinguish capital letters from lowercase letters, finding only those occurrences that exactly match the uppercase and lowercase characters of the Find What string. If you leave this box unselected, Excel disregards the differences between uppercase and lowercase letters.

- **Match Entire Cells Contents.** Find only complete and individual occurrences of the string. Normally Find searches for any occurrence of a string, even if it is part of another string.

- **Within.** Choose to search only the active Sheet or the entire Workbook.

- **Search.** Choose to search by rows or by columns. When you select the By Rows option, Excel looks through the worksheet horizontally, row by row, starting with the currently selected cell. Select this option if you think the string is located to the right of the selected cell. The By Columns option searches through the worksheet column by column, beginning with the selected cell. Select this option if you think the string is below the selected cell.

- **Look In.** Choose formulas, values, or comments. When you select Formulas, Excel searches only in formulas. When you select Values, Excel searches any constant values as well as the displayed results of formulas. When you select Comments, Excel examines only text attached as a comment to a cell.

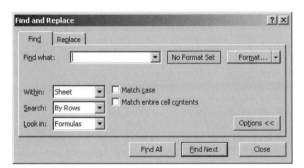

Figure 7-32. Use the Find tab to locate a character string.

> **tip** **Select a single cell**
>
> If you want to search the entire workbook or worksheet to locate a string of characters (depending on the selection you make in the Within box), select a single cell before choosing the Find command. Excel begins its search from that cell and travels through the entire worksheet or workbook. To search only a portion of a worksheet, select the appropriate range before choosing Find.

The nuances of the Formulas and Values Look In options can be confusing. Remember that the underlying contents of a cell and the displayed value of that cell are often not the same. When using these options, you should keep in mind the following:

- If a cell contains a formula, the displayed value of the cell is usually the result of that formula.

- If a cell contains a numeric value, the displayed value of the cell may or may not be the same as the cell's underlying value.

- If a cell has the General format, the displayed value of the cell and the cell's contents are usually the same.

- If a cell contains a number that has a format other than General, the contents of the cell and its displayed value may be different.

- The underlying and displayed values of a cell that contains a text entry are usually the same.

For example, if you type **1000** in the Find What box and select Values as the Look In option, Excel looks at what is displayed in each cell. If you have an unformatted cell with the value 1000 in it, Excel finds it. If another cell has the same value formatted as currency ($1,000), Excel does not find it because the displayed value does not precisely match the Find What string. Because you're searching through values and not formulas, Excel ignores the fact that the underlying content of the cell is the number 1000.

> **tip** **Use keyboard shortcuts to repeat a search**
>
> If you close the Find dialog box and want to search for the next occurrence of the Find What string in your worksheet, you can press F4, the keyboard shortcut for repeating the last action. You can also repeat your last search (even if you have done other things since that search) by pressing Shift+F4.

newfeature!
Finding Formatting

Excel now provides a way to find and replace cells based on formatting in conjunction with other criteria, and even to find and replace specifically formatted cells, regardless of their content. If you click the Format button in the Find And Replace dialog box shown in Figure 7-33, the dialog box shown in Figure 7-34 appears. This dialog box has two names—Find Format and Replace Format—depending on whether you clicked the Format button that is adjacent to the Find What box or the one adjacent to the Replace With box. Otherwise, the two dialog boxes are identical. You can select any number of options in this dialog box, and when you are finished, click OK to add them to your criteria.

If you click the arrow button next to the Format button to display the Format menu, you can select Choose Format From Cell, as shown in Figure 7-34. Choose Format From Cell is also available from within the Find Format and Replace Format dialog boxes.

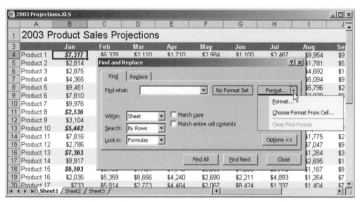

Figure 7-33. Select Choose Format From Cell to use the formatting of a selected cell as search criteria.

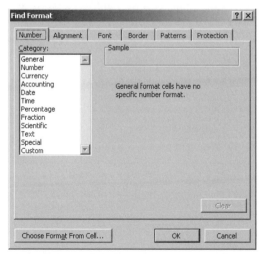

Figure 7-34. Click the Format button in the Find And Replace dialog box to display the Find Format dialog box.

When you click Choose Format From Cell, the dialog box disappears, and a small eye-dropper appears next to the cursor. Click a cell that is formatted the way you want and the dialog box reappears with a preview of the selected format in the box that otherwise displays the message No Format Set. After you set your formatting criteria, Excel will not find the character strings you search for unless the formatting criterion also matches. For example, if you search for the word Sales and specify bold as a formatting criterion, Excel finds any cells that contain the word Sales in boldface. A cell containing the words Sales Staff formatted in bold, italic, and underlined would be found because it contains both the word Sales and bold formatting, among other things. The more formatting options you set, the narrower the search. Select Clear Find Format to remove the formatting criteria.

Specifying Variables Using Wildcard Characters

You can use the wildcard characters ? and * to widen the scope of your searches. Wildcard characters are helpful when you're searching for a group of similar but not identical entries or when you're searching for an entry you don't quite remember. Use them as follows:

- The ? character takes the place of any single character in a Find What string. For example, the Find What string 100? matches the values 1000, 1001, 100A, 100B, and so on.

- The * character takes the place of zero or more characters in a Find What string. For example, the string 12* matches the entries 120, 125, 1200000, and even 123 Maple Street.

You can use the wildcard characters anywhere within a Find What string. For example, you can use the string *s to find all entries that end with s. Alternatively, you can use the string *es* to find each cell that contains the string sequence es anywhere in its formula or value.

To search for a string that contains either wildcard character (? or *), enter a tilde (~) preceding the character. For example, to find the string Who? including the question mark, enter **Who~?** as your Find What text.

Replacing What You Find

Replace works much like Find—in fact, they invoke the same dialog box. When you choose Edit, Replace (or press Ctrl+H), you see a dialog box like the one in Figure 7-35 (if yours looks different, click the Options button to expand the dialog box).

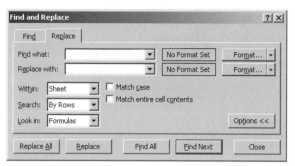

Figure 7-35. You can find and replace character strings and formats by choosing Edit, Replace.

For example, to replace each occurrence of the name Joan Smith with John Smith, type **Joan Smith** in the Find What box and **John Smith** in the Replace With box. You can also find and replace formats using the dual Format buttons. For example, you could search for every occurrence of 14-point bold italic Times Roman, and replace it with 12-point double-underlined Arial.

To replace every occurrence of a string or formatting, click the Replace All button. Instead of pausing at each occurrence to allow you to change or skip the current cell, Excel locates all the cells that contain the Find What string and replaces them.

note Although you can use wildcards in the Find What box to aid in your search, if you enter wildcard characters in the Replace With box, Excel uses a literal ? or * symbol when it replaces each occurrence of your Find What text.

Editing Multiple Worksheets

As long as you are editing one worksheet, why not edit a bunch of worksheets simultaneously? If the workbook you're creating will eventually contain a separate sheet for each month, division, product, or whatever, you can save a lot of time by creating them all at once using the techniques described in this section, and then tweak each sheet as needed.

For more information about formatting, see Chapter 8, "Worksheet Formatting Techniques."

Grouping Sheets for Editing

You can group any number of sheets in a workbook and then add, edit, or format data in all the sheets in the group at the same time. Use this feature when you're creating or modifying a set of worksheets that are similar in purpose and structure—a set of monthly reports or departmental budgets, for example.

You can select and group sheets using one of these methods:

● Click the sheet tab of the first sheet in a range of adjacent sheets you want to work on, hold down Shift, and click the tab of the last sheet in the range.

● Select the tab any one of the sheets you want to work on, hold down Ctrl, and click the tabs of each sheet you want to include in the group, whether or not the sheets are adjacent.

● Right-click the sheet tab and choose Select All Sheets from the shortcut menu.

Let's go through the procedure of creating a workbook containing a separate sheet for each month, starting with a blank workbook:

1 Click the Sheet1 tab, hold down Shift, and then click the Sheet3 tab. The sheets are now grouped, as shown in Figure 7-36. Notice that the title bar of the workbook displays the bracketed word [Group] after the worksheet name.

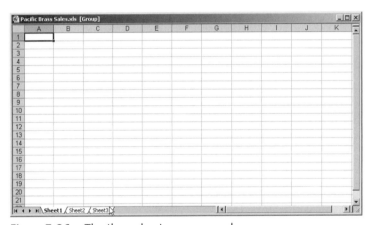

Figure 7-36. The three sheets are grouped.

2 Right-click any of the selected tabs and choose Move Or Copy from the shortcut menu. Select both Move To End and Create A Copy in the dialog box that appears and then click OK. Excel creates three new sheets, as shown in Figure 7-37.

Figure 7-37. Copying a group of sheets creates the same number of new sheets.

3 Group all six sheets and repeat step #2, to create 12 sheets.

4 Rename the sheets by double-clicking each tab and typing in a new name. We used the month abbreviations Jan through Dec.

5 Group all 12 sheets. Now, any entries or formatting changes you make in any one of the sheets is duplicated in all the sheets in the group

6 Enter and apply formats as shown in Figure 7-38.

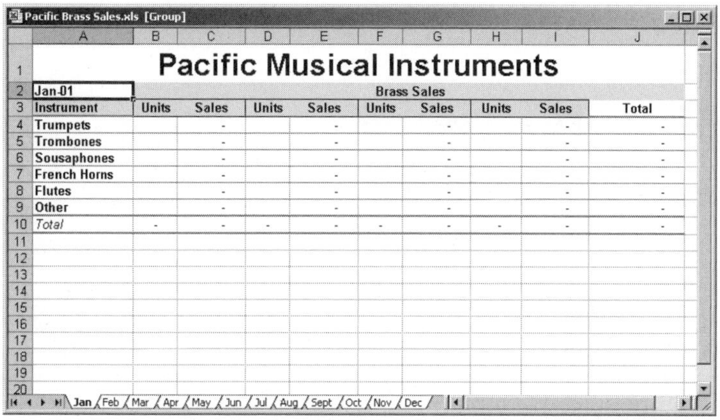

Figure 7-38. With group editing, Excel applies all edits and formats to all the sheets.

7 When all entries, common formulas, and formatting are finished, click any sheet to ungroup, and then make edits to individual sheets, such as adding each month name and entering units and sales data.

Getting Unstuck in Group-Editing Mode

When you group several sheets and then click one of the sheets in the group with the intention of editing it individually, you're still in group-editing mode, possibly making inadvertent changes to all your grouped sheets. Getting out of group-editing mode works differently, depending on how many sheets you have grouped.

If all sheets in a workbook are grouped, clicking any sheet tab except that of the active sheet exits group editing mode and removes the [Group] indicator from the title bar of the workbook. However, if you have not selected all the sheets in a workbook, as in your example, clicking any other grouped sheet tab makes that sheet active but does not exit group editing mode. Click any tab outside the group to exit group-editing mode.

You can add formatting, formulas, or any other data to the active worksheet in a group, and Excel modifies all member worksheets simultaneously. Excel transfers any changes you make to column width, row height, view options such as gridlines and scroll bars, and even to the currently active cell to the group.

Dragging Grouped Sheets

Besides using Move and Copy to rearrange and duplicate sheets in a workbook, you can also use the mouse to perform the same actions directly. Simply select a group and drag to move it to a different location.

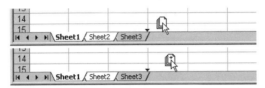

The cursor changes to include a little pad of paper, as shown above. To copy a group of sheets, drag the group and then press Ctrl before releasing the mouse button. The little pad of paper appears with a plus sign inside. You can also drag grouped sheets from one open workbook to another.

Editing by Group

Use Excel's group editing feature to perform the following actions on all member sheets simultaneously:

- **Entering Text.** Duplicates what you type in one sheet in all grouped sheets.

- **Printing.** Choosing Print, Print Preview, and Page Setup, located on the File menu, affects every sheet in your group at the same time.

- **View Menu.** Choosing Normal or Page Break Preview changes all selected sheets to that view.

- **Format Menu.** Applies any changes you make with the Format Cells dialog box to all group members at the same time. In group editing mode, changes to Row, Column, AutoFormat, Conditional Formatting, and Style options apply changes across worksheets. You can even choose Format, Sheet, Hide to hide all grouped sheets, unless every sheet in the workbook is in the group.

- **Edit Menu.** Applies all commands on the Edit menu including Find and Replace to the group.

- **Insert Menu.** Applies the Cells, Rows, Columns, Worksheet, Name, and Function commands to the group.

- **Tools Menu.** Applies Spelling and Track Changes to every sheet in the group, as do most of the options on the View tab of the Options dialog box (accessed by choosing Tools, Options).

Chapter 7: Worksheet Editing Techniques

Filling a Group

If you aren't starting from scratch, but want to duplicate existing data in one sheet to a number of other sheets in a workbook, you can choose Edit, Fill, Across Worksheets. This option is available only if you establish a group. Excel displays the Fill Across Worksheets dialog box shown in Figure 7-39.

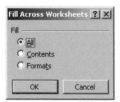

Figure 7-39. Use the Fill Across Worksheets dialog box to copy data to all the sheets in a group.

For example, if the worksheet shown in Figure 7-38 was an existing sheet and all the other sheets in the workbook were blank, we could select the range A1:J10 and then choose Across Worksheets. Excel duplicates the All option, all text, formulas, and formatting in every other sheet in the group. If you select the Contents option, Excel duplicates only text and values; the Formatting option predictably duplicates only the formats. As you might expect, filling across worksheets does not apply row height, column width, or view options.

Getting the Words Right

Worksheets are not all numbers, of course, so Excel includes several features to help make entering and editing text easier. AutoCorrect helps you fix common typing errors even before they become spelling problems. For the rest of the words in your worksheets, the Spelling Checker helps make sure you've entered your text according to Webster. Finally, you might be able to get AutoComplete to do some of the typing for you.

Fixing Errors as You Type

Perhaps you have to stop and think "i before e except after c" every time you type "receive." Perhaps you're a blazing typist that constantly hits the second letter of a capitalized word before the Shift key snaps back. Excel's AutoCorrect feature helps fix many common typing and spelling errors on the fly. Choose Tools, AutoCorrect Options to display the AutoCorrect dialog box shown in Figure 7-40 on the next page.

> **note** AutoCorrect works when entering text in cells, formulas, text boxes, on-sheet controls, and chart labels. AutoCorrect does not work when entering text in dialog boxes.

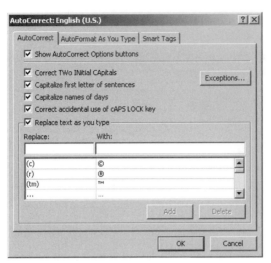

Figure 7-40. You can add your most common typing errors to the AutoCorrect dialog box.

The AutoCorrect dialog box contains the following options:

- **Show Auto Correct Options Buttons.** Controls the display of the smart tag action menu when Excel detects an error, listing actions you can perform on the affected cell.

- **Correct TWo INitial Capitals.** If a word contains both uppercase and low-ercase characters, checks that there's only one capital letter at the beginning of the word. If not, Excel changes subsequent uppercase characters to lower-case. If a word is all caps, Excel leaves it alone (assuming that this was intentional). Apparently due to their increasing usage, AutoCorrect does not attempt to modify "mid-cap" words such as AutoCorrect.

- **Capitalize First Letter Of Sentence.** Makes sure you use "sentence case" (even if your sentences aren't grammatically correct), based on the position of periods.

- **Capitalize Names Of Days.** Recognizes days and applies initial caps. Does not work on abbreviations like Sat.

- **Correct Accidental Use Of cAPS LOCK Key.** Scans for this kind of random Shift-key mistake.

- **Replace Text As You Type.** Opens the replacement list at the bottom of the dialog box, which lists a number of common replacement items.

In addition to correcting common typing errors such as replacing *adn* with *and*, AutoCorrect also provides a few useful shorthand shortcuts in its replacement list. For example, instead of searching for the right font and symbol to add a copyright mark, you can simply type (c) and AutoCorrect replaces it with ©.

Logic, not Magic

All these AutoCorrect options use very specific rules of order. For example, the TWo INitial CApitals option uses the following rules to determine likely candidates for autocorrection:

● Words that start with a capital letter

● Words in which the second letter of the word is also capitalized

● An entire word that is not capitalized

● Words that you have not indicated as exceptions

● Words that are more than two characters long

● Words containing at least one vowel

● Words that do not have more than two uppercase characters in a row

All the AutoCorrect features use similar, very logical, methods to determine your real meaning. There's a moral–don't assume that AutoCorrect (or spelling check) knows what you mean. Always proofread important work.

note If you have other Microsoft Office programs installed, anything you add to the AutoCorrect list will also appear in other Office programs' AutoCorrect lists.

Formatting As You Type

We like to refer to this feature as "AutoAutoFormat." The AutoFormat As You Type tab in the AutoCorrect dialog box offers a single Replace As You Type option—Internet and Network Paths With Hyperlinks. This converts a recognized URL or network path to a hyperlink as you finish typing it; you can click it immediately and go there.

Using Custom AutoCorrect Smart Tags

The Smart Tags tab in the AutoCorrect dialog box shown in Figure 7-41 on the next page is the repository for customized smart tags. Excel comes with a couple of them, and you can download additional smart tags as they become available on the Office Update Web site (*officeupdate.microsoft.com*).

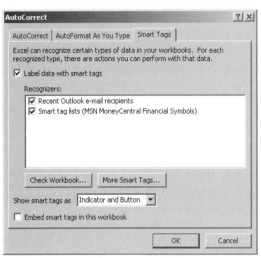

Figure 7-41. The new Smart Tags tab in the AutoCorrect
dialog box is the control center for all your Smart Tag needs.

The following smart tag options are available from the Office Update Web site:

● **Recognizers.** Describes the currently installed smart tags in terms of what
they look for as you type, and includes e-mail recipients and stock ticker
symbols, whose smart tag action menus are shown in Figure 7-42.

● **Check Workbook.** Applies the selected recognizers to existing data in your
workbook, allowing you to add smart tags to existing workbooks. If you
do, you need to select the Embed Smart Tags In This Workbook option.

● **More Smart Tags.** Adds custom recognizers found on the Office Update
Web site to the Recognizers list. You'll need to be connected to the Internet.

● **Show Smart Tags As.** Displays smart tags. Choose Indicator and Button
(the default), Button only, or None. Smart tags normally appear as a small
triangle in the lower right of the cell (the indicator), plus an icon that
appears when you hover the mouse over the cell (the button).

● **Embed Smart Tags In This Workbook.** Permanently attaches smart tags to
previously recognized data.

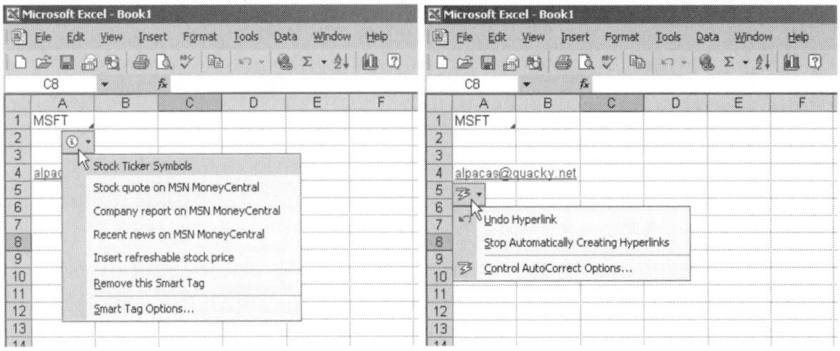

Figure 7-42. Excel includes built-in custom smart tag action menus for stock ticker symbols and recent email addresses.

Letting Excel Help with Typing Chores

Often, when entering a large amount data in one sitting, you end up typing the same things repeatedly. The AutoComplete feature cuts down the amount of typing you need to do. It also increases the accuracy of your entries by partially automating them. AutoComplete is on by default, but you can turn it off by choosing Tools, Options, clicking the Edit tab, and clearing the Enable AutoComplete For Cell Values option.

When you begin typing a cell entry, AutoComplete scans all the entries in the same column and, as each character is typed, determines whether there is a possible match in the column. (Note that this works only when you are typing in a cell adjacent to other entries.) For example, in Figure 7-43, as soon as we typed **Sh** into cell A14, AutoComplete finished the entry with the unique match found in the same column: Shaughnessy, Kevin. The text added by AutoComplete is highlighted, so you can either continue typing, if that wasn't your intended entry, or press Enter or an arrow key to accept the completion and move to another cell.

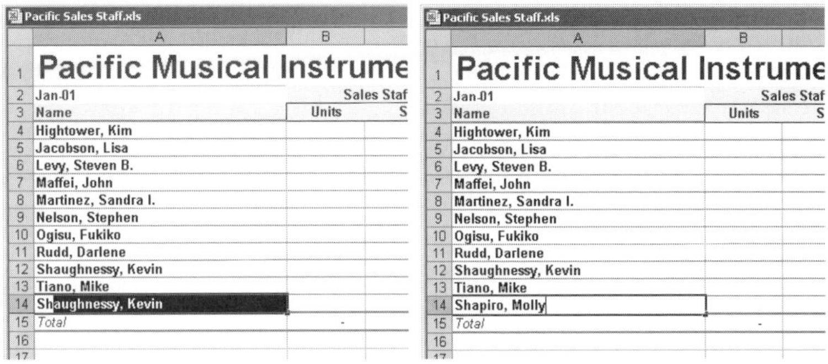

Figure 7-43. Type enough letters to match an existing entry, and AutoComplete finishes it for you. As shown on the right, simply keep typing to override AutoComplete.

195

AutoComplete matches only exact cell entries, not individual words in a cell. For example, if you begin typing **Kevin** in column A of the worksheet, AutoCorrect doesn't intervene, because it is not an exact match for any existing entry. Wisely, AutoComplete does not work when editing formulas.

Instead of typing, you can choose Pick From List on the shortcut menu to select an existing entry from the same column. To do so, right-click a cell and choose Pick From List from the shortcut menu, as shown in Figure 7-44. After Excel displays the pick list, click the entry you want, and Excel immediately enters it in the cell. Of course, you can't add new entries this way, as we did in Figure 7-43; only existing entries in the same column are available in the list.

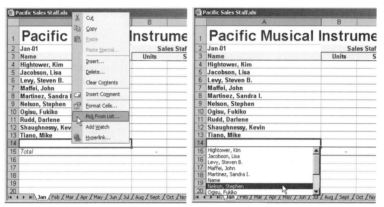

Figure 7-44. Right-click the cell directly below a list and choose Pick From List to display a list of unique entries in the column.

Creating Your Own Typing Shorthand

You can use AutoCorrect to add your own common typing errors and create your own shorthand typing shortcuts. Choose Tools, AutoCorrect Options dialog box and add your shorthand entries in the Replace Text As You Type area. Type the characters you want to use as the code into the Replace box, and then enter the characters with which you want to replace them into the With box and click the Add button. For example, you can type **MS** in the Replace box, and then type Microsoft Corporation into the With box. Thereafter, each time you type **MS**, Excel replaces it with the words Microsoft Corporation. Make sure you choose unique codes; otherwise, Excel might apply AutoCorrect to entries you don't want changed.

Cheking Yer Speling

You can choose Tools, Spelling to check for typing errors, or you can click the Spelling button on the Standard toolbar. Either way, you can check the spelling for an entire worksheet or any part of it. If Excel finds any suspect words, the dialog box shown in Figure 7-45 appears. Keep the following tips in mind when using the Spelling Checker:

- If you select a single cell, Excel checks the entire worksheet, including all cells, comments, Excel graphic objects, and page headers and footers.

- If you select more than one cell, Excel checks the selected cells only.

- If the formula bar is active, Excel checks only its contents.

- If you select words that are within the formula bar, Excel checks the selected words only.

- If the range you select for spelling check contains hidden or outlined cells that are not visible, Excel checks these as well.

- Cells that contain formulas are not checked.

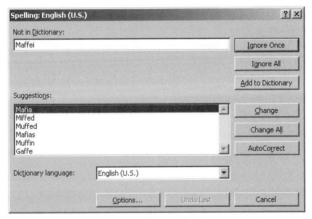

Figure 7-45. Use the Spelling dialog box to review your text and add often-used words to your dictionary.

> **tip** You can press F7 to instantly begin a spelling check.

Chapter 8

Worksheet Formatting Techniques

When creating a worksheet in Microsoft Excel, you probably don't ask yourself the question: Why use formats? But we'll answer it anyway. Compare Figure 8-1 to Figure 8-2 on the next page and we need say no more. Although the data is the same in both worksheets, the worksheet in Figure 8-2 takes advantage of the formatting features available in Excel and is therefore much easier to read and interpret. Proper use of formatting helps transform data into information; this chapter shows you how to do just that.

Formatting Fundamentals

Formatting worksheets in Excel is easy: just select the cell or range and choose the appropriate Format menu commands. The Format Cells command displays the dialog box shown in Figure 8-3 on the next page, which controls most of the formatting features you can apply to your worksheets. You'll examine the inner workings of the Format Cells dialog box throughout this chapter.

> **tip** To quickly access the Format Cells dialog box, press Ctrl+1.

When you select a category in the Category list, the formats and options available for that category type are displayed on the right side of the dialog box. The sample area at the top of the dialog box shows you how the selected format will affect the contents of the active cell.

	A	B	C	D	E	F	G
1	Pacific Musical Instruments						
2	2001 Sales Summary	Product					
3	Month	Guitars	Keyboards	Drums	Band	Accessories	Total by Month
4	January	7835.31	9901.837301	15292.36244	15853.9642	8441.206584	57324.68053
5	February	6118.82	14315.38813	11196.22402	11128.53466	10113.57889	52872.54571
6	March	7986.38	11789.55917	8264.235666	12563.56133	4032.538316	44636.27448
7	April	7241.7	5598.890897	6732.802139	20640.48118	9862.341053	50076.21527
8	May	10244.89	16649.41238	8669.958733	15207.73009	8556.620161	59328.61137
9	June	9492.45	10022.16078	14219.94604	11663.91485	7475.173287	52873.64496
10	July	6376.39	15729.99497	12884.34538	12178.20441	7201.685938	54370.6207
11	August	12944.92	23277.24849	8833.541499	12928.61605	5761.736402	63746.06244
12	September	9217.92	18845.94517	11392.41385	11667.4068	6483.13334	57606.81916
13	October	4375.62	2953.292188	8180.500544	16304.29072	8183.630589	39997.33405
14	November	10130.28	9936.858294	9585.571494	15522.44472	8598.604698	53773.75921
15	December	13467.24	7966.550997	12713.94051	20104.65364	4703.73497	58956.12012
16	Total by Product	105431.92	146987.1388	127965.8423	175763.8027	89413.98423	645562.688
17							
18							

Figure 8-1. All entries in this worksheet are displayed in their default formats.

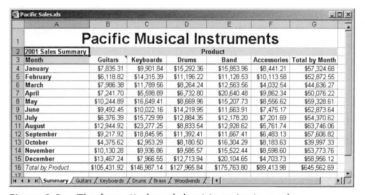

Figure 8-2. The formatted worksheet is easier to read.

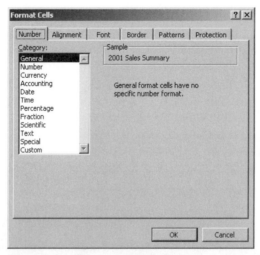

Figure 8-3. The Format Cells dialog box is your command
central for worksheet formatting.

The following are some of the fundamentals of using the Format Cells dialog box:

● A formatted cell remains formatted until you remove the format or apply a new format.

● When you overwrite or edit an entry, you need not reformat the cell.

● When you copy or cut a cell, the formats applied to that cell travel with it.

To remove all assigned formats, select the cell or range, and choose Edit, Clear, Formats. To also remove the values in cells, choose All from the Clear submenu. For more information about the Clear command, see "Clearing Cell Contents and Formats" on page 173.

---

tip   **Edit cells on multiple sheets**

To format (or remove all formats from) a common set of cells in two or more worksheets in the same workbook, you can use the group-editing feature. For more information about editing multiple sheets, see "Grouping Sheets for Editing" on page 187.

Painting Formats

Format
Painter

The Standard toolbar contains a single formatting button: Format Painter. This button copies formats from selected cells to other cells and worksheets in the current workbook and even in other workbooks.

---

note   If a button isn't visible on your screen, click the Toolbar Options button (the small downward-pointing arrow on the right end of a toolbar) on either the Standard or Formatting toolbars and select Show Buttons On Two Rows. By default, the buttons you use most often appear on toolbars.

Select the cell or range from which you want to copy formatting, and click the Format Painter button. (A small paintbrush icon appears next to the pointer.) Then select the cell or cells to which you want to copy the formatting. It's that simple.

InsideOut

Move the Format Painter

The Format Painter button—one of the more useful buttons—appears on the Standard toolbar rather than on the Formatting toolbar, where it belongs. If you want your toolbars to make just a little more sense, hold down the Alt key and drag the Format Painter button from the Standard toolbar to the Formatting toolbar.

If you copy formats from a range of cells and then select a single cell when you paste, the Format Painter pastes the format from the entire range—from the selected cell down and to the right. However, if you select a range of cells when you paste formats, the Format Painter follows the shape of the copied range. If the range you want to format is a different shape from the copied range, the pattern is repeated or truncated as necessary.

Troubleshooting

Buttons I Need Don't Appear on the Formatting Toolbar

Many of the most often used formatting options are available in button form on the Formatting toolbar shown here. Unfortunately, with the new default single-row toolbar configuration, some of these buttons might not be visible on your screen. But they are readily available nonetheless.

The Formatting toolbar buttons are, from left to right: Font, Font Size, Bold, Italic, Underline, Align Left, Center, Align Right, Merge And Center, Currency Style, Percent Style, Comma Style, Increase Decimal, Decrease Decimal, Decrease Indent, Increase Indent, Borders, Fill Color, and Font Color. You can find out the name of any button by hovering the mouse pointer over it. When you do so, a yellow box appears, containing the button name.

Normally, only a few of the Formatting toolbar buttons are visible. (We dragged the toolbar away from its docked position to display it as it looks in the previous figure). However, you can access any button by clicking the Toolbar Options button. Once you display a "hidden" button in this way, it is subsequently visible on the toolbar, while another seldom-used button is remanded to the Toolbar Options menu to make room.

Turbo Formatting with AutoFormat

The AutoFormat command provides a way to apply collections of complementary formats to cell regions on your worksheets quickly and easily. The AutoFormat dialog box, shown in Figure 8-4, applies predefined combinations of formatting criteria to your worksheets. You can change the number style, font, alignment, border, pattern, column width, and row height, all with just one click.

note If your dialog box doesn't look like the one in Figure 8-4, click the Options button.

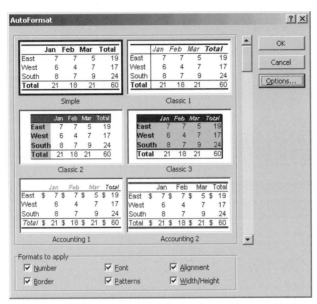

Figure 8-4. The AutoFormat dialog box offers a selection of predefined formats you can apply with one click.

AutoFormat can be applied to any region of cells, which AutoFormat calls a *table*. You simply click anywhere within the table, or region of cells, choose Format, AutoFormat, and then select one of the sample table formats in the AutoFormat dialog box. When you click OK, Excel selects the entire table and applies the selected table format to it. AutoFormat looks at the position of formulas, constants, and text to determine how to apply formatting. Although it does a good job with simple tables, you usually need to make a few adjustments afterward. For example, starting with the raw data shown in Figure 8-1, we applied the List 3 table format. The result is shown in Figure 8-5 on the next page.

Here are a few tips to keep in mind when using AutoFormat:

- If you don't like the way something looks, choose Edit, Undo AutoFormat.

- The boundaries of a table are defined by blank rows and columns, or the edges of the worksheet. Try adding blank columns or rows around your table, to effectively fence off areas you don't want AutoFormat to touch.

- Select more than one cell before issuing the command and AutoFormat affects only the selected cells. In fact, only by selecting first can you AutoFormat blank cells that are not within a table.

- In the Formats To Apply area at the bottom of the AutoFormat dialog box (click Options to display it), you can select or clear any format category, and the Sample window that dominates the dialog box adjusts accordingly.

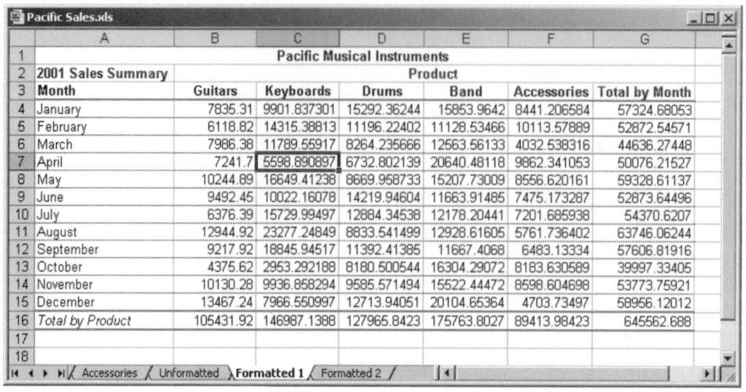

Pacific Sales.xls

	A	B	C	D	E	F	G
1	Pacific Musical Instruments						
2	2001 Sales Summary	Product					
3	Month	Guitars	Keyboards	Drums	Band	Accessories	Total by Month
4	January	7835.31	9901.837301	15292.36244	15853.9642	8441.206584	57324.68053
5	February	6118.82	14315.38813	11196.22402	11128.53466	10113.57889	52872.54571
6	March	7986.38	11789.55917	8264.235666	12563.56133	4032.538316	44636.27448
7	April	7241.7	5598.890897	6732.802139	20640.48118	9862.341053	50076.21527
8	May	10244.89	16649.41238	8669.958733	15207.73009	8556.620161	59328.61137
9	June	9492.45	10022.16078	14219.94604	11663.91485	7475.173287	52873.64496
10	July	6376.39	15729.99497	12884.34538	12178.20441	7201.685938	54370.6207
11	August	12944.92	23277.24849	8833.541499	12928.61605	5761.736402	63746.06244
12	September	9217.92	18845.94517	11392.41385	11667.4068	6483.13334	57606.81916
13	October	4375.62	2953.292188	8180.500544	16304.29072	8183.630589	39997.33405
14	November	10130.28	9936.858294	9585.571494	15522.44472	8598.604698	53773.75921
15	December	13467.24	7966.550997	12713.94051	20104.65364	4703.73497	58956.12012
16	*Total by Product*	105431.92	146987.1388	127965.8423	175763.8027	89413.98423	645562.688
17							
18							

Accessories / Unformatted / **Formatted 1** / Formatted 2

Figure 8-5. In seconds, you can use AutoFormat to transform a raw worksheet into something much more presentable.

tip **Don't rush to start formatting**

Build the worksheet first; apply formatting later. Sometimes, the *least* efficient thing you can do is use AutoFormat too soon and eventually waste time reformatting. Trust us, you'll be doing some reformatting no matter what. Give yourself extra time and the freedom to rearrange until the layout becomes clear for your purposes.

You can use the AutoFormat command's Colorful 2 option as a starting point for the worksheet shown in Figure 8-2, but afterward you need to perform the following minor enhancements, all of which were accomplished using the Formatting toolbar:

- Select cell A1, click the Bold button, and select 24 in the Font Size box.
- Select cells A3, B2:G2, click the Fill Color button, and select Yellow.
- Select B4:G16 and click the Currency Style button.

Formatting in Cells

The Format Cells command controls the display characteristics of numbers and text. It is important to keep in mind the difference between underlying and displayed worksheet values. Formats do not affect the underlying numeric or text values in cells. For example, if you type a number with six decimal places in a cell that is formatted with two decimal places, the number is displayed with only two decimal places. However, the underlying value isn't changed, and Excel uses the underlying value in calculations.

> **tip** **Format before you copy**
>
> When you copy a cell, you copy both its contents and its formatting. If you then paste this information into another cell, the formatting of the source cell replaces any pre-existing formatting. To take advantage of this time-saver, be sure to format your source cell before you choose the Copy and Paste commands or the Fill command. For more information about copying and pasting, see Chapter 7, "Worksheet Editing Techniques."

Formatting Individual Characters

If you select a cell and apply formats, the entire contents of the cell receive the formats. However, you can also apply formatting to the individual characters within cells (but not formulas). Select individual characters or words, and apply the attributes you want. When you are finished, press Enter to see the results shown in Figure 8-6 on the next page.

> For more examples of formatting individual characters, see "Using Fonts" on page 230.

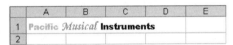

Figure 8-6.   You can format individual characters within a cell.

> **note** If you try to apply formats to the individual characters of a numeric entry, the formats disappear when you press Enter because they are overridden by the numeric format of the cell.

Formatting as You Type

You can include special formatting characters—such as dollar signs, percent signs, commas, or fractions—to format numbers as you enter them. When you type numeric-entry characters that represent a format Excel recognizes, Excel applies that format to the cell, on-the-fly. The following list describes some of the more common special formatting characters:

● If you type $45.00 into a cell, Excel interprets your entry as the value 45 formatted as currency with two decimal places. Only the value 45 appears in the formula bar after you press Enter, but the formatted value, $45.00, appears in the cell.

- If you type **1 3/8** (with a single space between the 1 and the 3), 1 3/8 appears in the cell and 1.375 appears in the formula bar. However, if you type **3/8**, 8-Mar appears in the cell, because date formats take precedence over fraction formats. Assuming you make the entry in the year 2002, 3/8/2002 appears in the formula bar. To display 3/8 in the cell as a fraction so that 0.375 appears in the formula bar, you must type **0 3/8** (with a space between the 0 and the 3). For information about entering dates and a complete listing of date and time formats, see "Entering Dates and Times" on page 440.

- If you type **23%** into a cell, the no-decimal percentage format appears in the cell, and 23% also appears in the formula bar. Nevertheless, Excel does use the 0.23 decimal value for calculations.

- If you type **123,456** into a cell, the comma format is applied without decimal places. If you type **123,456.00**, the cell is formatted with the comma format including two decimal places.

Build a Power Formatting Toolbar

The Formatting toolbar offers plenty of formatting power, but there are many other formatting buttons available. Everyone has their own favorite techniques, and making the techniques easier is always a good thing. For example, we created a Power Formatting toolbar, shown here, that contains a number of useful buttons, including some that are not available on any built-in toolbar.

To construct the Power Formatting toolbar, follow these steps:

1 Choose View, Toolbars, Customize.

2 On the Toolbars tab, click the New button, type **Power Formatting** in the Toolbar Name box, and click OK. A small empty bar appears next to the dialog box.

3 On the Commands tab, click the Format category and drag the following buttons to the toolbar: Style Box, Merge Cells, Unmerge Cells, Increase Font Size, Decrease Font Size, Vertical Text, Rotate Text Up, Rotate Text Down, Angle Clockwise, Angle Counterclockwise, Cycle Font Color, Dark Shading, Light Shading, and Auto Format.

4 Click Close when you finish adding buttons.

You can rearrange buttons on the toolbar as long as you keep the Customize dialog box open. For more information about customizing toolbars, see Chapter 3, "Custom-Tailoring Excel."

Using the General Format

The General format is the first category in the Format Cells dialog box. Unless you specifically change the format of a cell, Excel displays any text or numbers you enter in the General format. Except in the three cases listed next, the General format displays exactly what you type. For example, if you type **123.45**, the cell displays 123.45. Here are the three exceptions:

- The General format abbreviates numbers too long to display in a cell. For example, the number 12345678901234 (an integer) is displayed as 1.23457E+13 in a standard-width cell. Long decimal values are also rounded or displayed in scientific notation. Thus, if you type **123456.7812345** in a standard-width cell, the General format displays the number as 123456.7812. The actual entered values are preserved and used in all calculations, regardless of the display format.

- The General format does not display trailing zeros. For example, the number 123.0 is displayed as 123.

- A decimal fraction entered without a number to the left of the decimal point is displayed with a zero. For example, .123 is displayed as 0.123.

Formatting Numbers

The Number category in the Format Cells dialog box contains options for displaying numbers in integer, fixed-decimal, and punctuated formats, as shown in Figure 8-7. It is essentially the General format with additional control over displayed decimal places, thousand separators, and negative numbers. You can use this category to format any numbers that do not fall into any of the other categories.

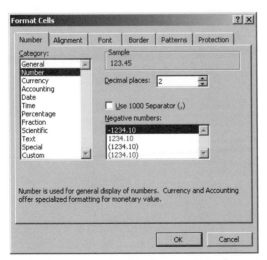

Figure 8-7. Use the Number category for general-purpose, noncurrency numeric formatting.

Use these guidelines when using the Number category:

● Select the number of decimal places to display (0 to 30) by typing or scroll-ing to the value in the Decimal Places box.

● Select the Use 1000 Separator (,) option to add commas between hundreds and thousands, and so on.

● Select the Negative Numbers option to display negative numbers preceded by a minus sign, in red, in parentheses, or in both red and parentheses.

> **tip** When formatting numbers, always select a cell containing a number before opening the Format Cells dialog box so that you can see the results in the Sample area. For information about creating numeric formats, see "Creating Custom Formats" on page 215.

Formatting Currency

The Currency formats are similar to the Number formats except that instead of select-ing the thousands separator (which accompanies all currency symbols by default), you can select which currency symbol, if any, precedes (or trails) the number. Select the currency symbol in the Symbol drop-down list, which includes more than 350 different currency symbols from around the world, some of which are shown in Figure 8-8.

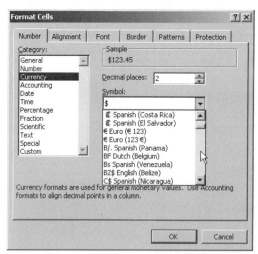

Figure 8-8. You can choose from a list of more than 350 worldwide currency symbols.

All of the Currency formats produce a blank space (the width of a parenthesis) on the right side of positive values, ensuring that decimal points align in a column of similarly formatted positive and negative numbers.

> **tip**   **Apply Currency formatting buttons**
>
> You apply a two-decimal Currency format when you click the Currency Style button on the Formatting toolbar. To apply a two-decimal Currency format without currency symbols, click the Comma Style button on the Formatting toolbar.

Using the Euro Currency Tools Add-in

Now that the European Union has implemented the Euro currency standard, you might find yourself using the ¤ symbol increasingly in your worksheets. Excel now includes the Euro Currency Tools add-in, which can make your life much simpler. To install this add-in, choose Tools, Add-Ins, click the Euro Currency Tools check box, and click OK. If the Euro Currency Tools check box does not appear in the Add-Ins dialog box, you need to run Setup again to install it. For more information about using Euro Currency Tools, see Appendix A, "Setting Up Microsoft Excel."

Euro

This add-in provides much more than just the Euro button on the Formatting toolbar. The add-in also provides the EuroValue toolbar shown in Figure 8-9, as well as the Euro Conversion command.

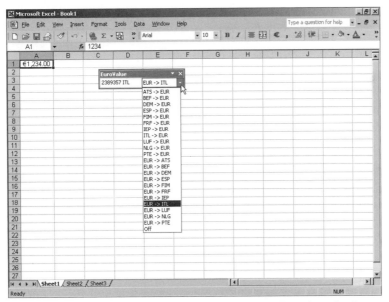

Figure 8-9.   Use the EuroValue toolbar to see what the selected value would be, if changed into any European Union member's currency.

Choose any conversion in the list on the EuroValue toolbar and see what the value in the selected cell would be if converted to the selected currency. The result, which you can also select and copy from the toolbar, is displayed to the left of the selected conversion option in the EuroValue toolbar, as shown in Figure 8-9.

209

Part 3: Formatting and Editing Worksheets

If you need to convert the values in a sheet full of cells (or just one cell) from one European Union member currency to another, use the Euro Conversion command on the Tools menu, which displays the dialog box shown on the left in Figure 8-10. Options in this dialog box work as follows:

- The Source Range box, when selected, allows you to drag the mouse to select the range you want to convert. In the Destination Range box, you only need to select one cell, which will become the upper left corner of the resulting range.

- The From and To boxes in the Currency Conversion area select the European Union member currency of the Source Range and Destination Range, respectively.

- The Output Format list pastes the resulting values in the corresponding currency format, in International Standardization Organization (ISO) format (which uses the appropriate ISO three-letter code instead of currency symbols), or None if you prefer unformatted numbers.

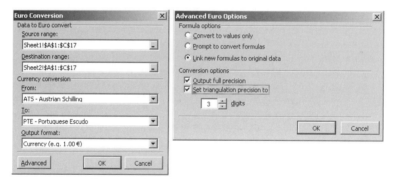

Figure 8-10. Choose Tools, Euro Conversion to convert all the values in a cell range from one Euro currency to another.

Clicking the Advanced button displays the Advanced Euro Options dialog box, shown on the right in Figure 8-10. The Formula Options control what happens to any formulas in your Source Range:

- **Convert To Values Only** converts all numbers and formulas in the Source Range to raw values, which is the default option.

- **Prompt To Convert Formulas** displays a dialog box during the conversion process in which you can specify conversion options for each formula, including three that are not available in the Advanced Options dialog box. You can copy the original formula instead of creating a conversion formula in the destination cell; you can choose to leave the cell blank; or you can edit each formula individually.

● **Link New Formulas To Original Data** pastes formulas instead of values in the Destination Range for any corresponding Source Range cells that contain formulas. These new formulas use the EUROCONVERT function with the same references used in the source formulas, creating dynamically updating conversion formulas.

> For more information about the EUROCONVERT function, see Appendix D, "Function Reference."

● **Output Full Precision** controls the rounding of numbers. Normally, based on European Union rules, converted currency values are calculated with a rounding factor that uses six significant digits of precision. To suppress this rounding factor, check the Output Full Precision box.

● **Set Triangulation Precision To** determines the number of significant digits of precision, from 3 through 15, to be used in the intermediate calculations when converting between two European Union member currencies, which are performed in Euros.

> **note** The membership of the European Union is subject to change; therefore, if a member country currency isn't available in any of the Euro Currency Tools, check the Microsoft Office Update Web site (officeupdate.microsoft.com) for the new information and a version of the add-in.

Using Accounting Formats

Excel provides special formats that address the needs of accounting professionals (and benefit the rest of us as well). When these formats are used with the accounting underline font formats, you can easily create profit and loss (P&L) statements, balance sheets, and other schedules that conform to generally accepted accounting principles (GAAP).

The Accounting formats correspond roughly to the Currency formats in appearance—you can display numbers with or without your choice of currency symbols, and specify the number of decimal places. However, there are some distinct differences between the two formats, which are described as follows:

● The Accounting format displays every currency symbol flush with the left side of the cell and numbers are flush with the right side, as shown in Figure 8-11 on the next page. The result is that all the currency symbols in the same column are vertically aligned, which looks much cleaner than Currency formats.

● Negative values are always displayed in black rather than in red, a common currency format portrayed in the saying "in the red."

● The Accounting format treats zero values as dashes. The spacing of the dashes depends on whether you select decimal places. If you include two decimal places, the dashes line up under the decimal point.

● Finally, the Accounting formats are the only built-in formats that include formatting criteria for text. They include spaces equivalent to the width of a parenthesis on each side of text so that it, too, lines up evenly with the numbers in a column.

	A	B	C	D
1	Accounting format		Currency format	
2	$ 12,345,678.00		$12,345,678.00	
3	$ (12,345,678.00)		-$12,345,678.00	
4				
5	Accounting underline		Regular underline	
6	$ (12,345,678.00)		-$12,345,678.00	
7				

Figure 8-11. The Accounting format aligns currency symbols to the left of a cell and numbers to the right.

Using Accounting Underlines The two Accounting underline formats on the Font tab of the Format Cells dialog box differ from their normal counterparts in two ways. First, accounting underlines are applied to the entire width of the cell, whereas regular underlines are applied only under the actual characters in a cell, as shown in Figure 8-11. If the cell contains a text entry that extends beyond the cell border, the accounting underlines stop at the cell border. Second, the Accounting underline formats appear near the bottom of cells, unlike normal underlines, which are applied much closer to the numbers or text in the cell, drawing annoying lines through the descenders of letters like g and p.

For information about font formats, see "Using Fonts" on page 230.

Formatting Percentages

The formats in the Percentage category of the Format Cells dialog box display numbers as percentages. The decimal point of the formatted number, in effect, moves two places to the right and a percent sign appears at the end of the number. For example, if you choose a percentage format without decimal places, the entry 0.1234 will be displayed as 12%; if you select two decimal places, 0.1234 will be displayed as 12.34%.

tip **Apply Percentage formatting quickly**

You can also apply a Percentage format without decimals by clicking the Percent Style button on the Formatting toolbar.

Formatting Fractions

The formats in the Fraction category, shown in Figure 8-12, display fractional numbers as actual fractions rather than as decimal values. As with all number formats, the underlying value does not change, despite the displayed value of the fraction.

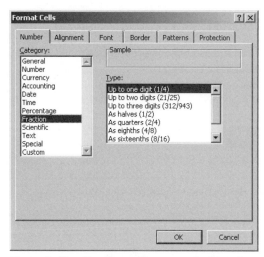

Figure 8-12. Excel provides many fraction-formatting options.

When formatting fractions, remember these guidelines:

- The single-digit fraction format displays 123.456 as 123 1/2, rounding the display to the nearest value that can be represented as a single-digit fraction.

- The double-digit fraction format uses the additional precision allowed by the format and displays 123.456 as 123 26/57.

- The triple-digit fraction format displays 123.456 as the even more precise 123 57/125.

- The remaining six fraction formats specify the exact denominator you want, displaying 123.456 using the As Sixteenths format as 123 7/16.

Formatting Scientific (Exponential) Values

The Scientific formats display numbers in exponential notation. For example, the two-decimal Scientific format displays the number 98765432198 as 9.88E+10. The number 9.88E+10 is 9.88 times 10 to the 10th power. The symbol E stands for the word exponent, a synonym here for 10 to the nth power. The expression *10 to the 10th power* means 10 times itself 10 times, or 10,000,000,000. Multiplying this value by 9.88 gives you 98,800,000,000, an approximation of 98,765,432,198. Increasing the decimal places increases the precision of the display, but at the possible cost of making the displayed number wider than the cell.

You can also use the Scientific format to display very small numbers. For example, this format displays 0.000000009 as 9.00E–09, which equates to 9 times 10 to the negative 9th power. The expression *10 to the negative 9th power* means 1 divided by 10 to the 9th power, 1 divided by 10 nine times, or 0.000000001. Multiplying this number by nine gives our original number, 0.000000009.

213

Understanding the Text Format

Applying the Text format to a cell indicates that the entry in the cell is to be treated as text, even if it's a number. For example, a numeric value is normally right aligned in its cell. If you apply the Text format to the cell, however, the value is left aligned as if it were a text entry.

For all practical purposes, a numeric constant formatted as text is still considered a number because Excel is capable of recognizing its numeric value. However, if you apply the Text format to a cell that contains a formula, the formula is considered text and is displayed as such in the cell. Any other formulas that refer to a formula that has been formatted as text return either the text value itself or the #VALUE error.

> **tip** **Create an intentional error**
>
> Formatting a formula as text is useful as a way of seeing the effects of removing a formula without deleting it. Format a formula as text so that it's visible on the worksheet and then locate the dependent formulas that produce error values. After you apply the Text format, however, you must click the formula bar and press Enter to recalculate the worksheet and change the formula to a displayed text value. To restore the formula to its original condition, apply the numeric format you want to the cell, click the formula bar again, and press Enter.

newfeature!
Using the Special Formats

The four Special formats shown in Figure 8-13 are a result of many requests from users. These generally noncalculated numbers include two ZIP Code formats, a phone number format (complete with the area code in parentheses), and a social security number format. Using each of these special formats, you can quickly type numbers without having to enter the punctuation characters.

The following are guidelines for using the Special formats:

- **Zip Code.** Leading zeros are retained to correctly display the code as 04321. In Normal format, if you type **04321**, Excel drops the zero and displays 4321.

- **Phone Number.** Excel applies parentheses around the area code and dashes between the digits, making it much easier to enter many numbers at the same time, because you don't have to move your hand from the keypad. Furthermore, the numbers you enter remain numbers instead of becoming text entries, which they would become if you entered parentheses or dashes in the cell.

- **Social Security Number.** Places dashes after the third and fifth numbers. For example, if you type **123456789**, it would appear as 123-45-6789.

newfeature!

● **Locale.** This list box allows you to select from more than 120 different locations with unique special formats. For example, if you select Vietnamese, there are two Special formats: Metro Phone Number and Suburb Phone Number.

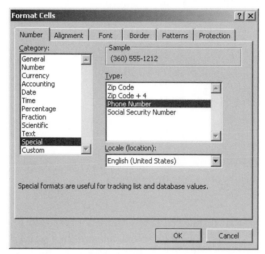

Figure 8-13. Excel provides several frequently requested formats in the Special category.

Creating Custom Formats

Use the Custom tab in the Format Cells dialog box, shown in Figure 8-14, to create custom number formats using special formatting codes. Excel adds new formats to the bottom of the list of formatting codes in the Type list, which also includes built-in formats. To delete a custom format, select the format in the Format Cells dialog box and click Delete. You cannot delete built-in formats.

Creating New Number Formats

The quickest way to start creating a custom format is to use one of the existing custom formats as a starting point for creating your own format. Here's an easy way to build on an existing format, as well as to see what the codes in the Type list mean:

1 Type a number and format it using the built-in format that most closely resembles the custom format you want to create. Leave this cell selected.

2 On the Number tab of the Format Cells dialog box, click the Custom category. The format you selected is highlighted in the Type list, representing the code equivalent of the format you want to modify.

3 Edit the contents of the Type box, using the codes listed in Table 8-1. The original format isn't affected, and the new format is added to the bottom of the Type list.

215

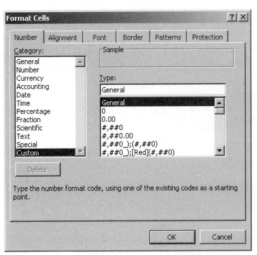

Figure 8-14. Use the Custom category to create new formats using special codes.

For example, to create a format that displays a date with the longest-available format for day, month, and year, start by entering a date into a cell and then select it. On the Custom category of the Format Cells dialog box, edit the format in the Type box to read *dddd, mmmm dd, yyyy* (including spaces and commas), and then click OK. The result is shown in Figure 8-15.

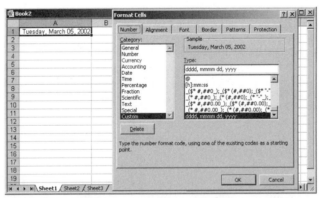

Figure 8-15. We created a custom date format by typing codes in the Type box.

---

tip   **Create traveling formats**

Saving your workbook saves new formats, but to carry special formats from one workbook to another, you must copy and paste a cell with the Custom format. For easy access to special formats, consider saving them in one workbook.

You can create any number format using the codes in Table 8-1.

Table 8-1. **Custom Format Symbols**

Symbol	Meaning
0	**Digit placeholder**. This symbol ensures that a specified number of digits appears on each side of the decimal point. For example, if the format is *0.000*, the value .987 is displayed as 0.987. If the format is *0.0000*, the value .987 is displayed as 0.9870. If a number has more digits to the right of the decimal point than the number 0s specified in the format, the number in the cell is rounded. For example, if the format is *0.00*, the value .987 is displayed as 0.99; if the format is *0.0*, .987 is rounded to 1.0.
?	**Digit placeholder**. This symbol follows the same rules as the 0 placeholder, except that space is left for insignificant zeros on either side of the decimal point. This placeholder aligns numbers on the decimal points. For example, 1.4 and 1.45 would line up on the decimal point if both were formatted as *0.??*.
#	**Digit placeholder**. This symbol works like 0, except that extra zeros do not appear if the number has fewer digits on either side of the decimal point than #s specified in the format. This symbol shows Excel where to display commas or other separating symbols. The format #,###, for example, tells Excel to display a comma after every third digit to the left of the decimal point.
.	**Decimal point**. This symbol determines how many digits (0 or #) appear to the right and left of the decimal point. If the format contains only #s to the left of this symbol, Excel begins numbers smaller than 1 with a decimal point. To avoid this, use 0 as the first digit placeholder to the left of the decimal point instead of #. If you want Excel to include commas and display at least one digit to the left of the decimal point in all cases, specify the format #,##0.
%	**Percentage indicator**. This symbol multiplies the entry by 100 and inserts the % character.
/	**Fraction format character**. This symbol displays the fractional part of a number in a nondecimal format. The number of digit placeholders that surround this character determines the accuracy of the display. For example, the decimal fraction 0.269 when formatted with # *?/?* is displayed as 1/4, but when formatted with # *???/???* is displayed as 46/171.

(continued)

Table 8-1. **Custom Format Symbols** *(continued)*

Symbol	Meaning
,	**Thousands separator**. If the format contains a comma surrounded by #s, 0s, or ?s, Excel uses commas to separate hundreds from thousands, thousands from millions, and so on. In addition, the comma acts as a rounding and scaling agent. Use one comma at the end of a format to tell Excel to round a number and display it in thousands; two commas tell Excel to round to the nearest million. For example, the format code #,###,###, would round 4567890 to 4,568, whereas the format code #,###,###,, would round it to 5.
E- E+ e- e+	**Scientific format characters**. If a format contains one 0 or # to the right of an E-, E+, e-, or e+, Excel displays the number in scientific notation and inserts E or e in the displayed value. The number of 0s or #s to the right of the E or e determines the minimum number of digits in the exponent. Use E- or e- to place a negative sign by negative exponents; use E+ or e+ to place a negative sign by negative exponents and a positive sign by positive exponents.
$ - + / ( ) space	**Standard formatting characters**. These symbols type these characters directly into your format.
\	**Literal demarcation character**. Precede each character you want to display in the cell (except for : $ - + / ( ) and space) with a backslash. (Excel does not display the backslash.) For example, the format code #,##0 \D;-#,##0 \C displays positive numbers followed by a space and a D, and negative numbers followed by a space and a C. To insert several characters, use the quotation-mark technique described in the "Text" table entry.
_	**Underscore**. This code leaves space equal to the width of the next character. For example, _) leaves a space equal to the width of the close parenthesis. Use this formatting character for alignment purposes.
"Text"	**Literal character string**. This formatting code works like the backslash technique except that all text can be included within one set of double quotation marks without using a separate demarcation character for each literal character.
*	**Repetition initiator**. Repeats the next character in the format enough times to fill the column width. Use only one asterisk in the format.
@	**Text placeholder**. If the cell contains text, this placeholder inserts that text in the format where the @ appears. For example, the format code "This is a" @ displays "This is a debit" in a cell containing the text "debit".

Table 8-2 lists the built-in formats and indicates how these codes relate to the other categories on the Number tab. (Note that this table does not list Date and Time codes, which are covered in Chapter 15, "Formatting and Calculating Date and Time.")

Table 8-2. **Built-In Custom Format Codes**

Category	Custom Format Codes
0	Digit
General	No specific format
Number	0 0.00 #,##0 #,##0.00 #,##0_);(#,##0) #,##0_);[Red](#,##0) #,##0.00_);(#,##0.00) #,##0.00_);[Red](#,##0.00)
Currency	$#,##0_);($#,##0) $#,##0_);[Red]($#,##0) $#,##0.00_);($#,##0.00) $#,##0.00_);[Red]($#,##0.00)
Percentage	0% 0.00%
Scientific	0.00E+00 ##0.0E+0
Fraction	# ?/? # ??/??
Date	(See Chapter 15)
Time	(See Chapter 15)
Text	@
Accounting	_($* #,##0_);_($* (#,##0);_($* "-"_);_(@_) _(* #,##0_);_(* (#,##0);_(* "-"_);_(@_) _($* #,##0.00_);_($* (#,##0.00);_($* "-"??_);_(@_) _(* #,##0.00_);_(* (#,##0.00);_(* "-"??_);_(@_)

Creating Four-Part Formats

Within each custom format definition, you can specify completely different formats for positive, negative, zero, and text values. You can create custom formats with as many as four parts, separating the portions by semicolons—*Positive Number; Negative Number; Zero; Text*—as shown in Figure 8-16 on the next page.

	B	C	D	E	F
2	Syntax:	*Positive Number;*	*Negative Number;*	*Zero;*	*Text*
3	*Accounting #3*	_($* #,##0.00_);	_($* (#,##0.00);	_($* "-"??_);	_(@_)
4	*Value*	123.45	-123.45	0	see note
5	*Displayed Value*	$ 123.45	$ (123.45)	$ -	see note
6	*Custom Billing*	Amount due: $#,##0.00_);	"Credit: "($#,##0.00);	"Let's call it even.";	"Please note: "@
7	*Value*	123.45	-123.45	0	
8	*Displayed Value*	Amount due: $123.45	Credit: ($123.45)	Let's call it even.	Please note: due 3/15
9	*Custom Part #*	"Part # "###-####			
10	*Value*	1234567			
11	*Displayed Value*	Part # 123-4567			
12					

Figure 8-16. You can create your own four-part formats.

Among the built-in formats, only the Accounting formats use all four parts, as shown in Figure 8-16, which shows the third Accounting format in Table 8-2 . The following are some guidelines for creating multipart formats:

- If your custom format includes only one part, Excel applies that format to positive, negative, and zero values.

- If your custom format includes two parts, the first part applies to positive and zero values; the second part applies only to negative values.

- If your custom format has three parts, the third part controls the display of zero values.

- The fourth and last element in a four-way format controls text-value formatting. Any formats with three or fewer elements have no effect on text entries.

---

tip   **Hide zeros**

You can suppress all zero values in a worksheet. Choose Tools, Options, and then click the View tab. Clear the Zero Values option in the Window Options area.

Adding Color to Formats

You can also use the Number formats to change the color of selected cell entries. For example, you might use color to distinguish categories of information or to make totals stand out. You can even create formats that assign different colors to specific numeric ranges so that, for example, all values greater than or less than a specified value appear in a different color.

Create Custom Billing and Part Number Formats

Suppose you create a billing statement and you want to format the totals in the Amount Due column so that they display differently, depending on the value in each cell. You might create the Custom Billing format shown in Figure 8-16, which was created using the following code:

```
"Amount due: "$#,##0.00_);"Credit: " ($#,##0.00); "Let's call it
even. ";"Please note: "@
```

Suppose you're creating an inventory worksheet and you want all the entries in a particular column to appear in the format *Part # XXX-XXXX*, shown as the *Custom Part #* format in Figure 8-16, which was created using the following code:

```
"Part # "###-####
```

---

tip   **Use built-in conditional formatting**

You can create codes that assign different colors based on the value in the cell, but there's an easier way to do it that's built into Excel: the Format, Conditional Formatting command. For more information, see "Applying Conditional Formats" on page 245.

To change the color of an entry, type the name of the new color, in brackets, in front of each segment of code. For example, if you want to apply blue Currency format with two decimal places, edit the *$#,##0.00_);($#,##0.00)* format as follows:

```
[Blue]$#,##0.00_);($#,##0.00)
```

When you apply this format to a worksheet, positive and zero values appear in blue; text and negative values appear as normal, in black. The following format displays positive values in blue, negative values in red, zero values in yellow, and text in green.

```
[Blue];[Red];[Yellow];[Green]
```

You can specify the following color names in your formats: Black, Blue, Cyan, Green, Magenta, Red, White, and Yellow. You can also specify a color as COLORn, where n is a number in the range 1 through 16. Excel selects the corresponding color from your worksheet's current 16-color palette. If that color is dithered (combines dots of two or more solid colors), Excel uses the nearest solid color.

For more information about using custom format codes, see "Creating New Number Formats" on page 215.

Troubleshooting

Decimal Points in My Currency Formats Don't Line Up

Sometimes when you use currency formats with trailing characters, such as the French Canadian dollar (23.45 $), you want to use the GAAP practice of using currency symbols only at the top and bottom of a column of numbers. The numbers between do not display any currency symbols, so how do you make all the decimal points line up properly?

You can create a custom format code to apply to the noncurrency format numbers in the middle of the column. An underscore character (_) in the format code tells Excel to leave a space that is equal in width to the character that follows it. For example, the code _$ leaves a space equal to the width of the dollar sign. Thus, the following code does the trick for you.

```
#,##0.00 _$;[Red]#,##0.00 _$
```

Make sure you add a space between the zeros and the underscores to properly line the numbers up with the built-in French Canadian dollar format.

Using Custom Format Condition Operators

You can create custom formats that are variable. To do so, you can add a condition operator to the first two parts of the standard four-part custom format. This, in effect, replaces the positive/negative formats with either/or formats. The third format becomes the default format for values that don't match the other two conditions, or the else format. You can use the conditional operators <, >, =, <=, >=, or <> with any number to define a format.

For example, suppose you are tracking accounts-receivable balances. To display accounts with a balance of more than $50,000 in blue, negative values in parentheses and in red, and all other values in the default color, create this format:

```
[Blue][>50000]$#,##0.00_);[Red][<0]($#,##0.00);$#,##0.00_)
```

Using these condition operators can also be a powerful aid if you need to scale numbers. For example, if your company produces a product that requires a few milliliters of a compound for each unit and you make thousands of units every day, you need to convert from milliliters to liters and kiloliters when you budget the use of this compound. Excel can make this conversion with the following numeric format:

```
[>999999]#,##0,,_m"kl";[>999]##,_k_m"L";#_k"ml"
```

The following table shows the effects of this format on various worksheet entries:

Entry	Display
72	72 ml
7286957	7 kl
7632	8 L

As you can see, using a combination of conditional formats, the thousands separator, and the proportional space indicator can improve both the readability and effectiveness of your worksheet, without increasing the number of formulas.

The Hidden Number Format

To hide values in a worksheet, assign a null format to them. To create a null format, enter only the semicolon separator for that portion of the format. For example, to hide negative and zero values only, use this format:

```
$#,##0.00;;
```

To hide all entries in a cell, use this format:

```
;;;
```

The null format hides the cell contents in the worksheet, but the entry is still visible in the formula bar and accessible via reference in formulas. To hide the cell contents so that they don't appear in the worksheet or the formula bar, use the protection features. For more information about the protection features in Excel, see "Protecting Worksheets" on page 127.

Aligning Data in Cells

The Alignment tab in the Format Cells dialog box, as shown in Figure 8-17 on the next page, positions text and numbers in cells. It also contains options you can use to create multiline text labels, repeat a series of characters within one or more cells, and orient text vertically or at any angle in cells. The Alignment tab includes the following options:

- **Horizontal.** These options control the right or left alignment within the cell. The General option, the default for Horizontal alignment, right aligns numeric values and left aligns text values.

- **Vertical.** These options control the top-to-bottom position of cell contents within cells.

- **Orientation.** These controls align text at virtually any angle within a cell.

- **Text Control.** These three options wrap text in cells, reduce cell contents until they fit in the current cell width, and merge cells into one.

- **Text Direction.** The options on this list format individual cells for right-to-left languages. This feature is used only if support is available for right-to-left languages using Microsoft Office Language Settings, which can be found by clicking the Windows Start button, pointing to Programs, and selecting the Microsoft Office Tools folder.

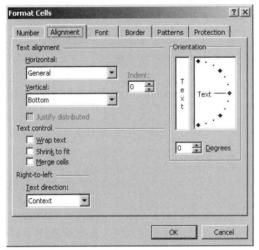

Figure 8-17. In Excel, alignment means a lot more than just right, left, or justified.

Aligning Text Horizontally

The Left (Indent), Center, and Right (Indent) options in the Horizontal drop-down list align the contents of the selected cells, overriding the default cell alignment. Figure 8-18 shows the horizontal alignment options in action.

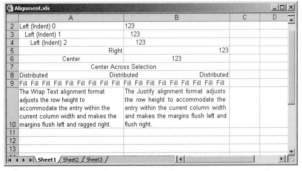

Figure 8-18. Use the Horizontal options to control placement of text from left to right.

Indenting Cell Contents

The Left (Indent) and Right (Indent) options are linked to the Indent control, located next to the Horizontal drop-down list shown in Figure 8-17. Normally, when you apply an Indent, the value in the box of this control is zero—the standard left-alignment setting. Each time you increase this value by one, the entry in the cell begins one character-width to the right. (One character-width is approximately the width of the capital X in the Normal style.) For example, in Figure 8-18, row 2 is formatted with no left indent, row 3 with a left indent of 1, and row 4 with a left indent of 2. The maximum indent value you can use is 15.

Distributing Cell Contents

A new feature in this version of Excel is the capability to distribute individual text fragments contained in a cell across the cell with equal spacing. For example, cells A8:B8 were first merged into one cell, and then the text Distributed was entered in the merged cell and the Distributed (Indent) horizontal alignment was applied. The result shows that the spaces between words were expanded in equal amounts to justify the contents within the cell.

Centering Text Across Columns

The Center Across Selection option in the Horizontal text alignment drop-down list centers text from one cell across all selected blank cells to the right or to the next cell in the selection that contains text. For example, in Figure 8-18, the Center Across Selection format was applied to cells A7:B7. The centered text is in cell A7.

---

tip   **Center without merging**

Although the results might look similar, the Center Across Selection alignment option uses a different process than the Merge And Center button on the Formatting toolbar. When you use the Merge And Center button, the cells you select are merged—that is, they are replaced with a single cell, whereas when you use Center Across Selection, the text from the leftmost cell remains in its cell but is displayed across the entire range. For more information about merging cells, see "Merging and Unmerging Cells" on page 241.

Filling Cells with Characters

The Fill option in the Horizontal alignment list repeats your cell entry to fill the width of the column. For example, in Figure 8-18, cells A9:B9 contain the single word Fill, with the Fill option applied. Note that only the first cell in the range needs to contain text. Excel repeats the text to fill the range. Like the other Format commands, the Fill option affects only the appearance, not the underlying contents, of the cell.

> **note** Because the Fill option affects numeric values, as well as text, it can cause a number to look like something it isn't. For example, if you apply the Fill option to a 10-character-wide cell that contains the number 3, the cell appears to contain the number 3333333333.

Wrapping Text in Cells

If you enter a label that's too wide for the active cell, Excel extends the label past the cell border and into adjacent cells—provided those cells are empty. If you select the Wrap Text option in the Text Control area of the Alignment tab, however, Excel displays your label entirely within the active cell. To accommodate the entire label, Excel increases the height of the row in which the cell is located and then wraps the text onto additional lines within the same cell. As shown in Figure 8-18, cell A10 contains a multiline label formatted with the Wrap Text option.

InsideOut

Adjust row height manually

You can select the Wrap Text option with any alignment option. However, if you wrap text formatted using the Orientation controls, the row height might not adjust to accommodate angled text in quite the way you expect. If you want to wrap angled text, it is best to adjust the row height manually to achieve the effect you want.

Justifying Text in Cells

The Alignment tab provides two Justify options—one in the Horizontal drop-down list and one in the Vertical drop-down list. The Horizontal Justify option wraps text in the active cell, adjusts the row height accordingly, and forces the text to align flush with the right margin, as shown in cell B10 in Figure 8-18.

> **note** Do not confuse the Horizontal Justify option with the Justify command on the Fill submenu of the Edit menu, which redistributes a text entry into as many cells as necessary below the initial entry, dividing the text into separate chunks. For more information about the Justify command on the Fill submenu, see "Distributing Long Entries Using the Justify Command" on page 181.

The Vertical Justify option does essentially the same thing as its Horizontal counterpart, except that it adjusts cell entries relative to the top and bottom of the cell rather than the sides, as shown in cell F3 of Figure 8-19.

Aligning Text Vertically

The Vertical drop-down list, on the Alignment tab of the Format Cells dialog box, includes five alignment options—Top, Center, Bottom, Justify, and Distributed—

which are similar to the corresponding Horizontal alignment options. Cells B3:D3 in Figure 8-19 show examples of the first three alignment options. As noted earlier, cell F3 shows the Justify option. Cell E3, containing the percent signs, was formatted using the Distributed option.

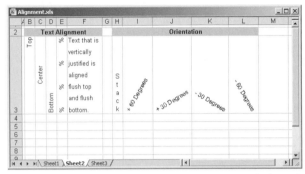

Figure 8-19. Use the Vertical options to control placement of text from top to bottom.

The options in the Vertical drop-down list create the following effects:

- **Top, Center, and Bottom.** These options force cell contents to align to each respective location within a cell.

- **Justify.** This option expands the space between words so that text entries align flush with the top and bottom of the cell.

- **Distributed.** This option spreads the contents of the cell evenly from top to bottom, making the spaces between words as close to equal as possible.

Controlling Text Orientation

The Orientation area of the Alignment tab in the Format Cells dialog box contains options to change the angle of cell contents to read horizontally (the default), vertically from top to bottom (stacked), or at any angle from 90 degrees counterclockwise to 90 degrees clockwise. Excel automatically adjusts the height of the row to accommodate vertical orientation unless you previously or subsequently set the row height.

Cell H3 in Figure 8-19 shows what happens when you click the tall, skinny Text button at the top left of the Orientation area. Although the button is labeled Text, you can also apply this stacking effect to numbers and formulas.

The angle controls allow you to rotate text to any point in a 180-degree arc. You can use either the Degrees box at the bottom (called a spinner) or the large dial above it to adjust text rotation. To use the dial, click and drag the Text pointer to the angle you want, and the number of degrees appears in the spinner below. You also can click the small up and down arrow buttons in the Degrees spinner to increment the angle one degree at a time from horizontal (zero), or highlight the number displayed in the spinner box and type a number from −90 through 90. Cells I3:L3 in Figure 8-19 show some examples of rotated text.

Chapter 8

227

A Cool Application of Angled Text

Many times the label at the top of a column is much wider than the data stored in it. You can use the Wrap Text option to make a multiple-word label narrower, but sometimes that's not enough. Vertical text is an option, but it can be difficult to read and takes a lot of vertical space. Try using rotated text and cell borders.

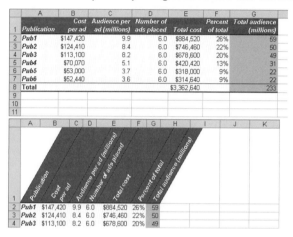

Here's how to do it:

1 Select the cells you want to format and choose Format, Cells.

2 On the Border tab, apply vertical borders to the left, right, and middle of the range.

3 On the Alignment tab, use the Orientation controls to select the angle you want. (It's usually best to select a positive angle between 30 and 60 degrees.)

4 In the Horizontal Text Alignment list, select Center, and then click OK. Excel rotates the left and right borders along with the text.

5 Drag down the bottom border of the Row 1 header to make it deep enough to accommodate the labels without wrapping.

6 Select all the columns; choose Format, Column, AutoFit Selection to shrink all the columns to their smallest possible width.

For more about cell borders, see "Customizing Borders" on page 231. For more about row heights, see "Changing Row Heights" on page 240.

Shrinking Text to Fit in Cells

The Shrink To Fit option on the Alignment tab of the Format Cells dialog box reduces the size of the font in the selected cell until the contents can be completely displayed in the cell. This is useful when you have a worksheet in which adjusting the column width to allow a particular cell entry to be visible has undesirable effects on the rest of the sheet, or where angled text, vertical text, and wrapped text aren't feasible solutions. In Figure 8-20, the same text was entered in cells A1 and A2, but the Shrink To Fit option was applied to cell A2.

	A	B	C	D
1	Shrink-to-Fit			
2	Shrink-to-Fit			
3				
4				

Figure 8-20. The Shrink To Fit alignment option reduces the font size until the cell contents fit within the cell.

The Shrink To Fit format is dynamic and readjusts if you change the column width, either increasing or decreasing the font size as needed. The assigned size of the font does not change in a cell with a Shrink To Fit-adjusted font size. The assigned font size is retained; therefore, no matter how wide you make the column, the contents expand only to the assigned size.

The Shrink To Fit option can be a good way to solve a problem, but keep in mind that this option reduces the font to as small a size as necessary. If the cell is narrow enough and the cell contents long enough, the result might be too small to read.

Selecting Alignment Using Toolbars

You can select Align Left, Center, Align Right, or Merge And Center by clicking the corresponding buttons on the Formatting toolbar. When you turn on one of the toolbar alignment options, its button appears as if it has been pressed to show that the option is selected. As a result, you can always glance at the toolbar to see whether one of these alignment options has been applied to the active cell. Use the following guidelines when working with the toolbar alignment options:

- To turn an alignment option off (and return the active cell to General alignment), click the button a second time.

Increase
Indent

- The Increase Indent button on the Standard toolbar applies the Left (Indent) format. However, this button does not turn the alignment option off when clicked a second time. Instead, each click increases the indent by another character width. To reduce indentation, use the adjacent Decrease Indent button.

newfeature!

Merge and
Center

- The Merge And Center button on the Formatting toolbar does two things: first, it merges the selected cells to form a single cell, and then it applies center alignment to the cell. In this version of Excel, this button is a toggle, removing center alignment and unmerging cells when clicked a second time. For more information about merged cells, see "Merging and Unmerging Cells" on page 241.

Using Fonts

The term font refers to a typeface (such as Arial), along with its attributes (such as point size and color). In Excel, you use the Font tab in the Format Cells dialog box to select fonts. Use fonts in a worksheet just as you do in printed text: to emphasize headings and to distinguish different kinds of information. To specify a font for a cell or for a range, select the cell or range; choose Format, Cells (or press Ctrl+1); and click the Font tab, shown in Figure 8-21.

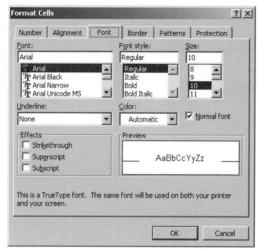

Figure 8-21. On the Font tab you can assign typefaces, character styles, sizes, colors, and effects to your cell entries.

The numbers in the Size list show the sizes at which Excel can optimally print the selected typeface, but you can enter any number—even fractional point sizes up to two decimal places. Unless you preset the row height, Excel adjusts the height as needed to accommodate the largest point size in the row. The available font styles vary, depending on the typeface you select in the Font list box. Most fonts offer italic, bold, and bold italic styles. To reset the selected cells to the font and size defined as the Normal style, select the Normal Font option.

For more information about using the Normal style, see "Formatting with Styles" on page 247.

Formatting Fonts with Toolbar Buttons

You can apply font format options using the following boxes and buttons on the Formatting toolbar: Font, Font Size, Bold, Italic, Underline, and Font Color.

U

Underline

The Underline button applies the single underline style. To apply other underline styles, use the Format, Cells command and click the Font tab. To remove a button-applied format from a cell or range, select the cell or range and then click the toolbar button again to switch off the format. When you click the arrow to the right of the Font Color button (or the Fill Color button), a palette of colors drops down, as shown in Figure 8-22. This button is a tear-off palette, which means that you can click the gray bar at the top of the palette and drag the palette away, so that it floats separately from the toolbar.

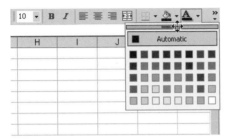

Figure 8-22.   Drag the gray bar at the top of a tear-off palette to keep it handy.

After you select a color in the palette, the color in the Font Color button changes so that you can apply the same color again by clicking the button itself, without needing to use the palette. To return the palette to the Formatting toolbar, click the Close button in the upper right corner of the floating palette.

In the Font drop-down list, font names are normally displayed using their own font so that you to see what each font looks like. However, you can switch off this feature by choosing Tools, Customize, clicking the Options tab, and clearing the List Font Names In Their Font option.

InsideOut

Automatic font color isn't Automatic

If you select Automatic (the default color option), Excel displays the contents of your cell in black. You might think that Automatic should select an appropriate color for text, based on the color you apply to the cell, but this isn't the case. If, for example, you apply a black background to a cell, you might think that the automatic font color would logically be white. Not so; Automatic is always black unless you have selected another Window Font color in the Display Properties dialog box (accessed from the Windows Control Panel). For more information about applying colors to cells, see "Applying Colors and Patterns" page 235.

Customizing Borders

Borders and shading can be effective devices for defining areas in your worksheet or for drawing attention to important cells. Figure 8-23 on the next page shows the Border tab in the Format Cells dialog box, as it appears when more than one cell is selected. If

231

you have more than one cell selected when you open the dialog box, the Border preview area includes tick marks in the middle and at the corners, as shown in Figure 8-23.

> **note** A solid gray line in the preview area means that the format applies to some, but not all, of the selected cells.

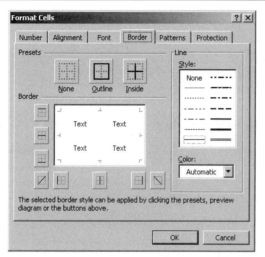

Figure 8-23. Using the Border tab, you can assign 13 styles of borders in 56 colors.

To apply borders, you can either click in the preview area where you want the border to appear or you can click the buttons located around the preview area. An additional preset button, Inside, becomes active and, when you have more than one cell selected, you can use it to apply borders to all sides of all the selected cells. If you click the Outline button, borders are applied only to the outside edge of the entire selection. The None preset removes all border formats from the selection.

> **tip** **Remove gridlines**
>
> Borders often make a greater visual impact when worksheet gridlines are removed. Choose Tools, Options, and click the View tab. Clear the Gridlines option to remove gridlines from your worksheet. For more information on gridlines, see "Displayed vs. Printed Gridlines" on page 84.

The default, or Automatic, color for borders is black. To select a line style, click the type of line you want to use in the Line area, and then click any of the buttons in the Border area to apply that style in the selected location. (The first finely dotted line in the Style area is a solid hairline when printed.) To change a border style, reselect the cell or range and then redisplay the Format Cells dialog box. To remove a border, click the corresponding button, or the line in the preview window, without selecting another style. Figure 8-24 shows some of the border styles that Excel is capable of creating.

Chapter 8: Worksheet Formatting Techniques

	2003 Budget Summary				
Cost Center	1st Qtr	2nd Qtr	3rd Qtr	4th Qtr	Total
100	7,951.00	7,861.00	9,052.00	6,798.00	31,762.00
110	7,893.00	8,086.00	1,969.00	8,820.00	26,878.00
120	8,330.00	5,838.00	1,773.00	9,601.00	25,662.00
130	9,949.00	8,361.00	3,069.00	2,589.00	24,098.00
140	6,135.00	1,503.00	894.00	7,308.00	15,980.00
150	7,859.00	4,686.00	965.00	7,523.00	21,183.00
160	8,979.00	4,669.00	4,849.00	6,673.00	25,330.00
170	2,595.00	7,396.00	5,282.00	4,377.00	19,820.00
180	4,320.00	6,805.00	3,553.00	3,933.00	18,791.00
Total	64,011.00	55,205.00	31,406.00	57,622.00	208,244.00

Figure 8-24. This worksheet makes (questionable) use of multiple border styles.

Applying Border Formats with Toolbar Buttons

You can apply many combinations of border formats using the Borders button on the Formatting toolbar. When you click the small arrow on the Borders button, Excel displays a tear-off palette from which you can select a border style. (Refer to Figure 8-22 for an example of a tear-off palette as it initially appears.) The options on the Borders palette show, in miniature, the border combinations available. The last border option that you selected appears on the face of the Borders button, which you can click to repeat the last format used, without requiring you to display the palette. To remove all border formats from a selected cell or range, click the first option in the Borders palette.

With the palette open, you can click the arrow and then click the gray bar at the top of the palette and drag; the Borders palette tears off the toolbar and floats independently of the toolbar, as shown in Figure 8-25. To return the Borders palette to the Formatting toolbar, click the Close button in the upper right corner of the palette.

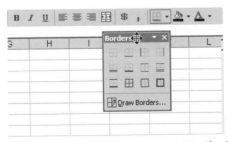

Figure 8-25. Click the arrow next to the Borders button, and then drag to tear off the palette

An Angled Border Trick

Sometimes you might want to use that pesky cell that generally remains empty in the upper left corner of a table. You can use an angled border to create dual-label corner cells like the one shown in the following example.

	A	B	C	D	E	F	G
1	First Quarter Exam Scores						
2							
3	Exam # / Student	1	2	3	4	Average	
4	Nelson	87	90	79	96	88.00	
5	Rudd	92	94	94	97	94.25	
6	Tiano	96	95	95	80	91.50	
7	Hightower	85	87	87	88	86.75	
8	Jacobson	81	88	88	85	85.50	
9							
10							

Here's how to do it:

1 Select the cell you want to format and type about ten space characters. You can adjust this later (there are 20 spaces before the Exam # label in the example).

2 Type the label you want to correspond to the column labels across the top of the table.

3 Hold down the Alt key and press Enter twice to create two line breaks in the cell.

4 Type the second label, which corresponds to the row labels down the left side of the table, and press Enter.

5 With the cell selected, choose Format, Cells, and click the Border tab.

6 Select a line style and click the upper left to lower right angled border button.

7 Click the Alignment tab, click the Wrap Text option, and then click OK.

You will probably need to fine-tune a bit by adjusting the column width and row height and by adding or removing space characters before the first label. In the example, we also selected cells B3:F3, and then selected the Top vertical alignment option on the Alignment tab so that all the labels line up across the top of the table. For more information about alignment, see "Aligning Data in Cells" on page 223. For more about entering line breaks and tabs in cells, see "Formula-Bar Formatting" on page 367.

newfeature!
Drawing Borders

The Borders palette on the Formatting toolbar includes the Draw Borders command. When you click this command, the cursor changes to a pencil, and you drag directly on the worksheet where you want your borders to go. The default or last-used border style is applied.

Chapter 8: Worksheet Formatting Techniques

Figure 8-26 shows the process of adding borders to the sheet shown in Figure 8-22. We tore off the Borders palette for easy access during the task. Notice also that because this particular sheet is displayed without gridlines, the Draw Borders feature adds dots in each cell corner to make the grid more visible. When gridlines are visible, these dots are not necessary.

> **note** When you click the Draw Borders command, the Borders toolbar might appear docked at the bottom or the top of the screen. To make the toolbar more apparent and easier to use, we dragged it away for easier viewing.

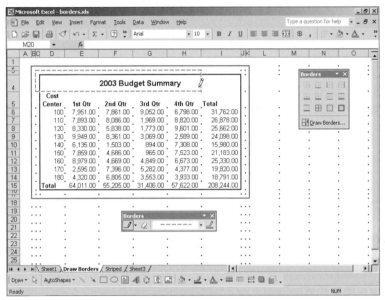

Figure 8-26. Use the Draw Borders command on the Borders palette to create borders directly on the worksheet by dragging.

Before you drag to draw a border, you can use the Borders toolbar to choose line style and color. You can click the Erase Border button on the Borders toolbar and drag over any portion of a border to erase it. To exit Border Drawing mode, you can click the Draw Borders command on the Borders palette or click the pencil button on the Borders toolbar.

Applying Colors and Patterns

The Patterns tab of the Format Cells dialog box offers colors and shading you can apply to selected cells. The main feature of the Patterns tab is a palette displaying the current standard palette, as specified on the Color tab of the Options dialog box. Another feature of the Patterns tab is the Pattern drop-down list, as shown in Figure 8-27 on the next page. You use this drop-down list to not only select different patterns for the cell, but also different colors that are applied to those patterns. (The colors at the top of the Patterns tab are for the cell contents, whereas those in the Pattern drop-down list are for any pattern you apply.)

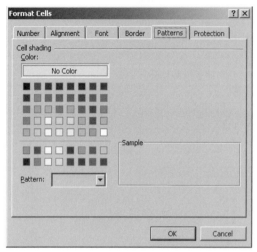

Figure 8-27. Using the Patterns tab, you can select colors and patterns for cell backgrounds.

Follow these guidelines when using the Patterns tab:

- The Color area controls the background of selected cells. When you choose a color and do not select any pattern, a solid colored background is applied.

- To return the background color to its default state, click No Color.

- If you pick a color and then select a pattern, the pattern is overlaid on the solid background. For example, if you select red from the Color area and then click one of the dot patterns, the result is a cell that has a red background and black dots.

- The color options in the Pattern list box, shown in Figure 8-28, control the color of the pattern itself. For example, if you leave the Color area set to No Color and select both red and the dot pattern in the Pattern drop-down list, the cell will have a white background with red dots.

---

tip **Color carefully**

When selecting colors for cell backgrounds, select one on which you can easily read the text and numbers that are formatted using the default color, black. For example, yellow is an excellent background color for black text. However, unless you have a color printer, you should print a sample worksheet to be sure the colors you select are acceptable when printed in black and white.

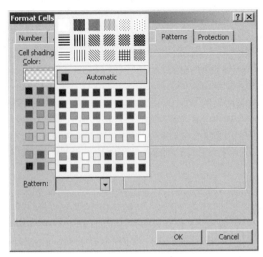

Figure 8-28. The Pattern list offers both patterns and colors for those patterns.

Adding Colors with Toolbars

Fill Color

You can use the Fill Color button on the Formatting toolbar to apply color to a cell or range. When you click the arrow on the Fill Color button, a tear-off palette appears from which you can select a color. (Refer to Figure 8-22 for an example of a tear-off palette.)

Adding Graphic Backgrounds to Worksheets

Adding background images to worksheets is easy in Excel. Simply choose Format, Sheet, Background, and Excel displays a dialog box from which you can open a graphic file stored on disk. The graphic image is then applied to the background of the active worksheet, as shown in Figure 8-29 on the next page.

Figure 8-29. Add a background graphic to any worksheet.

● The example in Figure 8-29 is a cover sheet for a large workbook; be careful when using backgrounds behind data. It could be difficult to read cell entries with the wrong background applied. You might want to turn off the display of gridlines, as shown here. To do so, choose Tools, Options, click the View tab, and clear the Gridlines option. If you don't like the way the background looks with your data, choose Format, Sheet, Delete Background to delete the background. Remember the following when working with background images: the graphic image is tiled in the background of your worksheet, which means that the image is repeated as necessary to fill the worksheet.

● Cells to which you have assigned a color or pattern override the graphic background. For example, you could apply a white or yellow solid color to cells containing data, allowing the text and numbers to stand out while the background pattern decorates the rest of the worksheet.

● Backgrounds are preserved when you save the workbook as a Web page.

> For more information about Web page backgrounds, see Chapter 20, "Transferring Files to and from Internet Sites."

Controlling the Size of Cells

The primary methods you use to control the size of cells are adjusting the row height or changing the column width. In addition, you can adjust the size of cells by merging several cells into one or by unmerging previously merged cells.

Changing Column Widths

The default column width for Excel is 8.43 characters; however, this does not mean that each cell in your worksheet can display 8.43 characters. Because Excel uses proportionally spaced fonts (such as Arial) as well as fixed-pitch fonts (such as Courier), different characters can take up different amounts of space. A default-width column, for example, can display about eight numerals in most 10-point fixed-pitch fonts.

If the standard column width isn't wide enough to display the complete contents of a cell, the following will occur:

● A label that is too long runs over into adjacent cells.

● Long labels are truncated at the border if the adjacent cell isn't empty.

● Long numbers appear in scientific notation by default (for example, 1.23E+12).

● A series of pound signs (#) appears if you assign a numeric format.

If any of these situations occurs, you probably want to change the width of the affected column or columns. Drag one of the lines between column headings. As you drag, the width of the column and the number of pixels are displayed in a ScreenTip, as shown in Figure 8-30. This figure also illustrates how to change the width of multiple columns at the same time: drag to select column headings, or hold down Ctrl and click headings to select nonadjacent columns. Then, when you drag a line between any selected column, all the selected column widths change simultaneously to the same width as the column whose heading you drag.

Figure 8-30.   The cursor looks like a double-headed arrow when adjusting column width or row height with the mouse.

Using Column Commands

Choose Format, Column to display a submenu that includes five commands: Width, AutoFit Selection, Hide, Unhide, and Standard Width. To assign a column width, select cells in each column you want to change (you need not select entire columns) and then choose the Width command. A number representing the width of the selected columns normally appears in the Column Width dialog box. If no width appears, more than one column of different widths is selected. In either case, you can type a number from 0 through 255.

To restore the default width of one or more columns, select any cells in those columns and choose Format, Column, Standard Width. To change the standard width for all default-width columns in the worksheet, type a new value in the Standard Column Width box. All columns adjust to the new setting, except those whose width you have changed manually.

Changing Row Heights

Excel adjusts the standard height of a row to accommodate the largest font used in that row. Thus, you don't usually need to worry about characters being too tall to fit in a row.

Adjusting row height is the same as adjusting column width—just drag one of the lines between row headings. See "Changing Column Widths" on page 238 for more about selecting and resizing columns using headings.

Using Row Commands

Choose Format, Row to display a submenu that includes four commands: Height, AutoFit, Hide, and Unhide. You can use the Height command to change the heights of several rows at the same time. Select at least one cell in each row you want to change and choose Format, Row, Height.

---

tip **Change all rows**

To change the heights of all the rows in the current worksheet, click one of the column headings at the top of the worksheet (or select any cell and press Ctrl+Spacebar), and then choose the Height command.

A number representing the height of the selected rows normally appears in the Row Height dialog box. If no height appears, more than one row of different heights is selected. In either case, you can type a number from **0** through **409**.

To restore the default height of one or more rows, select any cells in those rows and choose Format, Row, AutoFit. Unlike column width, you cannot define a standard row height. The AutoFit command serves the same function, returning empty rows to the standard height needed to accommodate the default font and fitting row heights to accommodate the tallest entry. When you create or edit a multiline text entry using the Wrap Text or the Justify options on the Alignment tab of the Format Cells dialog box, Excel automatically adjusts the row height to accommodate it.

For more information, see "Wrapping Text in Cells" on page 226 and "Justifying Text in Cells" on page 226.

Hiding a Column or Row

If you want to hide information within a worksheet, you can hide entire columns or rows. To hide a column, select any cell in the column you want to hide and choose Format, Column, Hide. Excel sets the width of the column to zero. You can also hide a column by dragging the line between the column headings to the left until you have narrowed the column to zero; or you can type **0** in the Column Width dialog box. When a column's width is set to 0, Excel skips over the column when you move the active cell, and the column's letter disappears from the top of the worksheet. For example, if you hide column C, the column heading line reads A, B, D, and so on.

To redisplay a column, drag to select the column headings on both sides of the hidden column and choose Format, Column, Unhide.

You can hide and redisplay rows in a similar manner, using the mouse or the equivalent Row submenu on the Format menu. Note that the Hidden option on the Protection tab of the Format Cells dialog box hides only formulas in the formula bar. For more information about protection options, see "Protecting Worksheets" on page 127.

Merging and Unmerging Cells

The spreadsheet grid is arguably the most versatile type of document. Still, it was occasionally necessary to play formatting tricks with the grid to arrive at the effect you wanted, especially when creating forms—that is, until *merged cells* became available.

Select the cells you want to merge and choose Format, Cells; then select Merge Cells on the Alignment tab and if you want, click the Wrap Text option. The spreadsheets shown in Figure 8-31 illustrate how merging cells can help you clean up a complex form.

caution   When you merge several cells that contain data, only the data in the uppermost, leftmost cell is preserved. Data in subsidiary cells is overwritten. Copy any data you need to another location before merging.

When you merge cells, you end up with a single cell that comprises the original cells. For example, in the top sheet in Figure 8-31, text in the range G1:J5 is unevenly spaced because of the different row heights needed to accommodate the text in cell C2. In the bottom sheet, merging the ranges A1:B3, C1:F3, and G1:J5 before entering the text eliminates this problem.

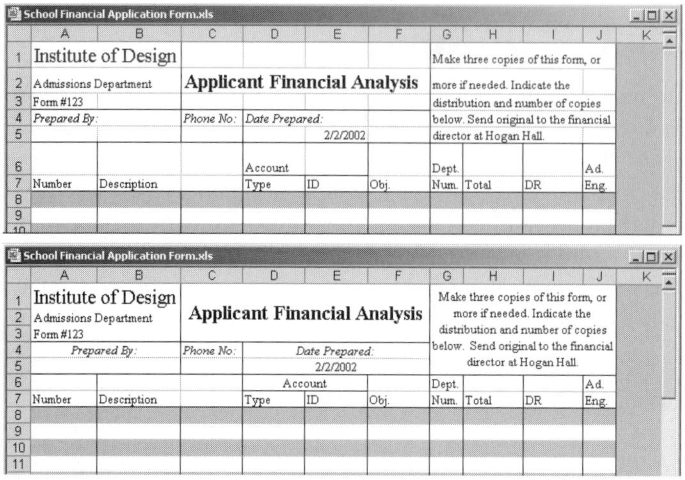

Figure 8-31. The sheet on the bottom uses merged cells to create a better-looking form.

---

tip Merge and center

The Merge And Center button on the Formatting toolbar applies a specialized version of merging to selected cells that is particularly useful for creating labels across multiple rows or columns. This button merges the selected cells and then centers the contents horizontally in the newly merged cells. Click again to restore the merged cell to individual cells.

When you merge cells, the new big cell uses the address of the cell in the upper left corner, as shown in Figure 8-32. Cell A1 is selected, as shown in the name box. The headings for rows 1, 2, and 3 and columns A and B are highlighted, which would normally indicate that the range A1:B3 is selected. For all practical purposes, however, cells A2:A3 and B1:B3 no longer exist. The other merged cells, or the subsidiary cells, are essentially nonexistent. A merged subsidiary cell acts like a blank cell when referred to in formulas and returns zero (or an error value, depending on the type of formula).

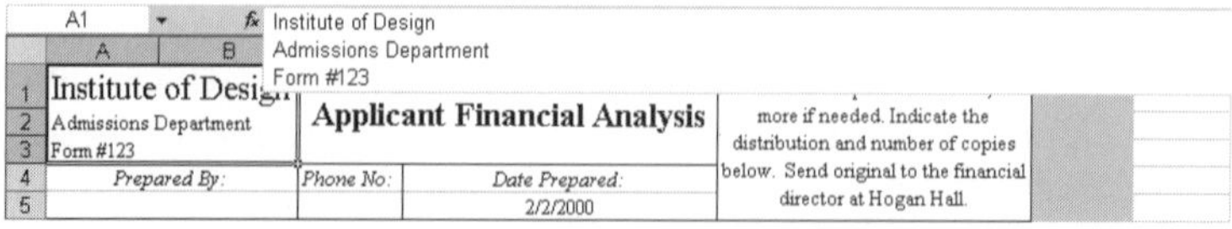

Figure 8-32. Cell A1 is a big cell created by merging cells A1:B3.

> **tip** **Enter line breaks**
>
> In Figure 8-32, the information in the formula bar is on three lines. To enter line breaks within a cell, press Alt+Enter. For more information, see "Formula-Bar Formatting" on page 367.

Merging cells obviously has interesting implications, considering that it seems to violate the grid—one of the defining attributes of spreadsheet design. That's not as bad as it sounds, but there are a few things to keep in mind:

- If you select a range to merge and any one cell contains text, a value, or a formula, the contents are relocated to the new big cell.

- If you select a range of cells to merge and more than one cell contains text or values, only the contents of the uppermost, leftmost cell are relocated to the new big cell. Contents of subsidiary cells are deleted; therefore, if you want to preserve data in subsidiary cells, make sure that you add it to the upper left cell or relocate it.

- Formulas adjust automatically. A formula that refers to a subsidiary cell in a merged range changes to refer to the address of the new big cell. If a merged range of cells contains a formula, relative references adjust. For more on references, see "Using Cell References in Formulas" on page 356.

- You can copy, delete, cut and paste, or click and drag big cells as you would any other cell. When you copy or move a big cell, it replaces the same number of cells at the destination. The original location of a cut or deleted big cell returns to individual cells.

- You can drag the Fill handle of a big cell as you can drag the Fill handle of regular cells. When you do so, the big cell is replicated, in both size and content, replacing all regular cells in its path. For more on using the Fill handle, see "Filling and Creating Data Series" on page 174.

- If you merge cells containing border formatting other than along any boundary of the selected range, border formats are erased.

- You can explode, or unmerge, a merged cell to return it to the original range of individual cells. To unmerge cells, select the big cell, choose Format, Cells, Alignment, and clear the Merge Cells option.

Chapter 8

243

Chapter 9

Advanced Formatting and Editing Techniques

This chapter introduces a number of features designed to assist you in turning your data into effective information. These techniques are more involved and more powerful than those discussed in Chapters 7, "Worksheet Editing Techniques," and 8, "Worksheet Formatting Techniques," and they might be among the most useful tools you'll use. In this chapter, we'll cover applying conditional formats, creating and using styles and templates, outlining your worksheets, and using Excel's built-in auditing features.

Applying Conditional Formats

Choosing Format, Conditional Formatting offers an easy way to apply formats that stay "asleep" until the values in the formatted cells achieve a specified state. We call this *trapping* a value. Sometimes tables with this sort of conditional formatting are referred to as *stoplight tables*, because they are often used to call attention to potential problem areas in a business model.

For example, you could apply conditional formatting to a range of cells that contain sales totals, specifying that if any of the totals drops below $10,000, the format of the cell changes to stand out from the other cells. To apply conditional formatting to cells, follow these steps:

1 Select the cells you want to format.

2 Choose Format, Conditional Formatting to display the Conditional Formatting dialog box, shown in Figure 9-1 on the next page.

245

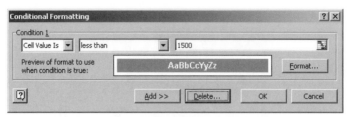

Figure 9-1. You can create formatting "alarms" in cells by choosing Format, Conditional Formatting.

3 Select from the following options:

■ Use the first drop-down list to either apply a condition based on the value in the selected cell, or to create a formula that uses other values to determine a condition. Normally you want to use the Cell Value Is option, which looks at the displayed value in the cell. Use the Formula Is option if you want to enter your own formula to determine the condition. For an example, see the sidebar "Creating Conditional Formatting Formulas" on page 248.

■ Choose an operator in the second condition drop-down list. Your choices are Between, Not Between, Equal To, Not Equal To, Greater Than, Less Than, Greater Than Or Equal To, or Less Than Or Equal To.

■ Enter the comparison values in the entry boxes. If you choose Between or Not Between in the second condition list, two entry boxes appear in which you provide an upper and a lower limit. Otherwise, only one box appears, as shown in Figure 9-1.

4 After you establish the condition you want to apply, click the Format button. An abbreviated version of the Format Cells dialog box appears, containing only Font, Border, and Patterns tabs. Specify any combination of formats to be applied when your condition or conditions are met.

Figure 9-2 shows an unformatted table and the same table formatted conditionally using the options shown in Figure 9-1. Formatting options were chosen so that if values are $1,500 or less, the cell background turns gray and the font turns white and bold.

You can add up to three conditional formats at a time to a cell or range. To do so, click the Add button in the Conditional Formatting dialog box to display another set of conditions you can apply to the same cell or range.

To remove conditional formatting, select the cell or range, choose Format, Conditional Formatting, and then click the Delete button. The Delete Conditional Format dialog box shown in Figure 9-3 appears. Even after the selected condition disappears from the Conditional Formatting dialog box, the condition is not removed until you click OK in the Conditional Formatting dialog box.

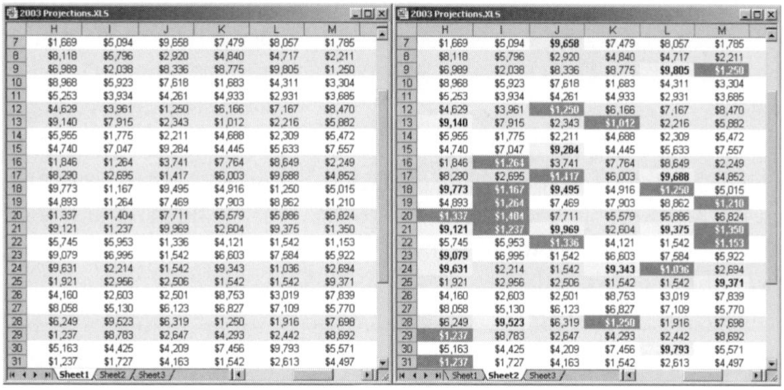

Figure 9-2. Conditional formatting makes it easier to find the values—and the trends—you need to notice.

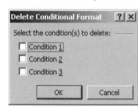

Figure 9-3. You can delete one or all of the conditions you applied.

Formatting with Styles

Microsoft Excel's style feature allows you to assign names to combinations of formatting attributes. You can then apply those attributes by selecting the name from a list, which eliminates a lot of time clicking buttons, opening dialog boxes, and choosing individual options. Styles help you achieve consistency in formatting, both within a worksheet and across worksheets and workbooks. Using styles, you can easily modify the formatting characteristics of many cells at once.

Every new workbook contains six predefined styles:

- **Comma.** Number formatting only, with thousand separators and two decimal places.

- **Comma [0].** Number formatting only, with thousand separators, rounded to the nearest integer.

- **Currency.** Number formatting only, Accounting format with currency signs, thousand separators, and two decimal places.

- **Currency [0].** Number formatting only, accounting format with currency signs and thousand separators, rounded to the nearest integer.

- **Normal.** Includes defaults for all formatting attributes. See Figure 9-4.

- **Percent.** Number formatting only, percentage format with no decimal places.

Chapter 9

247

> **note** If you have set up and used a hyperlink in your workbook, two other styles might already exist: Hyperlink and Followed Hyperlink. For information about hyperlinks, see Chapter 22, "Using Hyperlinks."

These predefined styles have the same characteristics on each worksheet in a workbook and in each new workbook you create, but you can change them for any workbook and you can add styles of your own. When you save a workbook, all its style definitions are saved with the rest of your data.

Creating Conditional Formatting Formulas

The first drop-down list in the Conditional Formatting dialog box shown in Figure 9-1 offers the Formula Is option, which you use when you want to enter your own conditional formatting formulas. You can create formulas to perform tasks such as identifying dates that fall on specific days of the week, specifying the smallest or largest value in a range, and highlighting specific text. For example, select a cell or range and choose Format, Conditional Formatting. Select the Formula Is option from the first condition list, and then type the following formula into the edit box on the right: **=MOD(ROW(),2)=0**.

Click the Format button, select a color on the Patterns tab, and then click OK twice to close the two dialog boxes and apply the format. The MOD formula applies your selected color to every other row, as shown here.

	A	B	C	D	E	F
1			**Pacific Musical Instruments**			
2	2001		Guitar Sales			
3	Month	Hanson	Deloria	Lakes	Used	Total by Month
4	January	3,788.32	1,316.15	1,336.59	1,394.25	$7,835.31
5	February	3,371.54	2,415.00	281.16	51.12	$6,118.82
6	March	4,021.66	1,638.99	1,336.59	989.14	$7,986.38
7	April	3,899.39	1,319.45	1,464.39	558.47	$7,241.70
8	May	5,557.57	2,383.30	1,796.67	507.35	$10,244.89
9	June	4,389.25	1,364.20	2,749.86	989.14	$9,492.45
10	July	3,253.18	1,801.79	383.40	938.02	$6,376.39
11	August	6,722.90	2,658.09	3,056.58	507.35	$12,944.92
12	September	5,001.62	1,492.00	2,724.30	-	$9,217.92
13	October	2,154.10	859.37	1,362.15	-	$4,375.62
14	November	5,638.47	2,293.88	1,285.47	912.46	$10,130.28
15	December	7,216.59	2,686.72	3,056.58	507.35	$13,467.24
16	Total by Product	$55,014.59	$22,228.94	$20,833.74	$7,354.65	$105,431.92
17						

When you use the Formula Is option, you can enter any formula that results in the logical values TRUE (1) or FALSE (0). For example, you could use a logical formula such as =N4>AVERAGE($N$4:$N$37), which combines relative and absolute references to apply formatting to a cell when the value it contains falls below the average of the specified range. When you use relative references in this situation, the formatting formulas adjust in each cell where you apply or copy them, as regular cell formulas do. For more information, see "Using Cell References in Formulas" on page 356; "Understanding Logical Functions" on page 424; Chapter 14, "Everyday Functions"; and "Calculating Date and Time" on page 448.

Chapter 9: Advanced Formatting and Editing Techniques

You define styles by choosing Format, Style. The Style dialog box in Figure 9-4 shows the attributes of the Normal style.

Figure 9-4. Excel's predefined Normal style includes defaults for all formatting attributes.

Styles can have a minimum of one and a maximum of six attributes. All the predefined styles except Normal have only one attribute—a number format. The predefined Currency style, for example, has the Accounting number format with two decimal places.

The predefined Normal style is applied to every cell in every new workbook. Thus, if you want a cell to have the standard set of formatting attributes, you don't need to do anything. If, however, you want to change the default attributes for all cells in a worksheet, you can redefine any or all attributes of the Normal style.

Applying a Style

To apply a style to a cell or range, select the cell or range and choose Format, Style. Then select any style from the Style Name list, as shown in Figure 9-5.

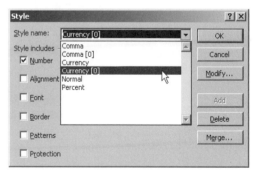

Figure 9-5. You can apply styles to cells or ranges in your workbook with the Style dialog box.

> **tip**   **Add the style list**
>
> If you find yourself using styles constantly, you can add the Style list to any toolbar. To do so, choose View, Toolbars, Customize, and on the Commands tab, click the Format category and drag the Style box (not the Style… command) to a toolbar. Besides being able to apply styles, you can also determine which style has been applied to a selected cell by checking the name that appears in the Style box.

Defining Styles

You can define a style in either of two ways: by providing an example of the style attributes you want or by choosing Format, Style and filling out the Style dialog box. After you define a new style, you can use it anywhere in the current workbook. You also can copy it to another workbook.

> For more on copying styles to other workbooks, see "Merging Styles from Different Workbooks" on page 252.

Defining Styles by Example

If you have already applied formatting attributes to a cell or a range that you would like to use often, you can use the style-by-example procedure to encapsulate those attributes in a new style. For example, suppose you format a cell with right alignment and 18-point Arial Black. To make this combination of attributes a new style, follow these steps:

1   Select the cell that contains the formatting you want (in this case, right alignment and 18-point Arial Black).

2   Choose Format, Style.

3   Type **MyStyle** in the Style Name edit box.

4   Clear the Number, Border, Patterns, and Protection options in the Style Includes section, and click OK. The name of the new style appears in the Style dialog box.

The safest way to create a style by example is to select only one cell—one that you know has all the attributes you want to assign to the new style. If you select two or more cells that are not formatted identically, the new style assumes only those attributes that all cells in the selection have in common.

Defining Styles from Scratch

To create a new style without first formatting a cell, use the following procedure:

1   Choose Format, Style, and in the Style Name edit box, type a name for the new style.

2 Click the Modify button. The Format Cells dialog box appears, as shown in Figure 9-6. All the changes you make in the Format Cells dialog box apply to your new style definition.

3 Select format options on the Number, Alignment, Font, Border, Patterns, and Protection tabs, and then click OK to return to the Style dialog box.

4 The Style Includes section of the dialog box reflects the formats you added. Clear the Style Includes options you don't want to include in your new style.

5 Click the Add button.

Your new style appears among all the others defined for the current workbook. You can apply it at any time from the Style Name list (or the Style box if you add it to a toolbar).

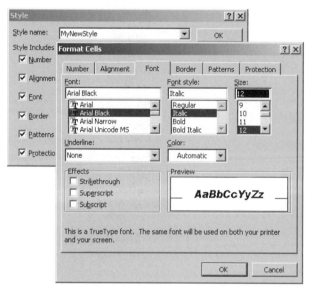

Figure 9-6. Click the Modify button in the Style dialog box to display the Format Cells dialog box. Excel applies changes made here to the current style.

---

tip **Define styles using the toolbar**

You can also easily define a style by example using the Style box, if you add it to a toolbar. Select a cell with the formats you want, click the Style box, type a name for the new style, and press Enter. The custom style is saved and appears in both the Style toolbar box and in the Style dialog box. (You can also redefine a style using this procedure. See the next section for more information on redefining styles).

Modifying a Style

The principal advantage of using styles is that if you change your mind about the appearance of a particular element in your workbook, you can revise every instance of that element at once by changing the style. For example, if you'd like the font in the MyStyle style—which is now 18-point Arial Black—to be italic as well as bold, you can redefine MyStyle.

To modify a style definition, follow these steps:

1 Choose Format, Style.

2 Select the style (in this case, MyStyle) from the Style Name list, and then click Modify to display the Format Cells dialog box.

3 Select the appropriate format options. (For this example, click the Font tab and select the Bold Italic option in the Font Style list.)

4 Click OK to return to the Style dialog box, and then click OK to confirm your changes.

Overriding a Style with Direct Formatting Changes

You can change the appearance of any cell or range in your worksheet, whether or not you have applied a style to that cell or range, by choosing Format, Cells. You also can change the appearance of cells and ranges by using buttons on the Formatting toolbar.

Merging Styles from Different Workbooks

To maintain formatting consistency across a group of worksheets, you can keep the worksheets in the same workbook. If this is impractical but you still want to maintain stylistic consistency, you can copy style definitions between workbooks.

To copy a style from one workbook to another, take the following steps:

1 Open both the source workbook (the one you're copying from) and the destination workbook (the one you're copying to).

2 Click the destination workbook to make it the active window.

3 Choose Format, Style and click the Merge button. Excel displays a list of all other open workbooks, as shown in Figure 9-7.

4 Select the name of the workbook you want to copy styles from, and click OK.

Chapter 9: Advanced Formatting and Editing Techniques

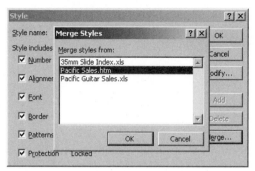

Figure 9-7. When you copy styles from one workbook to another,
Excel displays a list of all other open workbooks.

> **caution**   If a style in the source workbook has the same name as one already in your
> destination workbook, an alert box asks whether you want to merge styles that have
> the same name from the source workbook. You will receive this warning only once,
> however, no matter how many duplicate style names exist. If you choose Yes, the
> styles from the source workbook override those with the same names in the
> destination workbook.

Deleting a Style

To delete a style's definition, choose Format, Style, select the style in the Style Name
list, and then click Delete. Any cells that were formatted with the deleted style revert to
the Normal style. (You cannot delete the Normal style.) Any cell that was formatted
with a deleted style and was then also formatted directly, however, retains all the
direct formatting.

Using Template Files to Store Formatting

A *template file* is a model that can serve as the basis for new worksheets. A template can
include both data and formatting information. Template files are great time-savers.
They're also an ideal way to ensure a consistent look among reports, invoices, and other
documents you tend to create repeatedly. Figure 9-8 on the next page shows an example
of a template for an expense report. This worksheet would work well as a template
because expense reports are used repeatedly, but each time you'll want to start with a
fresh, clean copy.

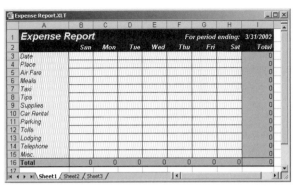

Figure 9-8. This template file serves as the basis for creating new expense reports.

The advantages to using templates are standardization and protection. It is difficult to save over the original accidentally, because when you save a new template-based workbook for the first time, you must supply a new name for it. This way you can repeatedly create new workbooks with the same appearance without worrying about overwriting the original.

To create a template file, follow these steps:

1 Open the workbook you want to use as a template.

2 Choose File, Save As, and supply a file name.

3 Choose Template from the Save As Type list, and click Save.

When you choose the Template format in the Save As dialog box, Excel switches to the Template folder so that your new template will be saved there. This is the location that ensures that your template will always be available when you choose File, New, and click General Templates in the task pane.

Any Excel workbook can be used as a template, even if it was not saved in template format. When you installed Excel, a folder named Templates was installed on your hard disk in one of the following locations:

C:\Windows\Application Data\Microsoft\Templates (Windows 9x)

C:\Documents and Settings\<your name>\Application Data\Microsoft\Templates (Windows 2000)

note In Windows 2000, the Application Data folder is normally hidden. When you choose the Template format in the Save As dialog box, you can save template files there, but you won't be able to see it in the Windows Explorer unless you change the view options. To do so, in the Windows Explorer choose Tools, Folder Options, and on the View tab, click Show Hidden Files And Folders.

Any workbook you move or copy to the Templates folder appears on the General tab of the Templates dialog box and behaves like a template file. When you open a workbook that appears in the Templates dialog box, the workbook does not open; a fresh copy of the workbook is created. The copy is given a temporary name made up of the original file name plus a number. If the template file is named Expenses, for example, the working copy is named Expenses1.

---

tip   Show file extensions

You can choose to display MS-DOS three-character extensions (such as XLT for template and XLS for regular workbook) so you can tell at a glance what format the file was saved in. To do so, open the Windows Explorer. On the Explorer's Tools menu, choose Folder Options and clear the Hide File Extensions For Known File Types option on the View tab.

InsideOut

The New Dialog box is dead, long live the task pane

When you choose File, New, the New dialog box is not displayed, as it has been since Excel 1.0. Now when you choose File, New, the New Workbook task pane appears on the right side of the workbook window, which is probably a step forward in usability. But it might confound you for a while until you get used to it. For example, if the New Workbook task pane is already open, choosing File, New seems to do nothing at all—especially if you're expecting a dialog box to appear. What used to be called the New dialog box is now called the Templates dialog box, and you open it by clicking General Templates in the task pane under New From Template.

Adding Templates to the XLStart Folder

Any Excel files that you place in the XLStart folder are opened every time you start Excel, except for templates. When you place templates (with the XLT extension) in the XLStart folder, they are not opened; they appear in the Templates dialog box when you click General Templates in the New Workbook task pane.

The XLStart folder was created when you installed Excel, and is located in one of the following locations:

C:\Program Files\Microsoft Office\Office10\XLStart

C:\Documents and Settings\<yourname>\ApplicationData\Microsoft\
Excel\XLStart

There are two files you can create that have unique properties when placed in the XLStart folder:

- If you place a workbook with the special name Book.xls in the XLStart folder, its format determines the default for new blank workbooks you create when you click Blank Workbook in the New Workbook task pane or the New button on the Standard toolbar. It is not opened on startup.

- If you place a workbook with the special name Sheet.xls in the XLStart folder, its format (the format of its first worksheet) determines the default for new worksheets you insert by choosing Insert, Worksheet. It is not opened on startup.

Spreadsheet Solutions Templates

The Spreadsheet Solutions tab of the Templates dialog box provides several handy predesigned templates. These templates include Sales Invoice, Expense Statement, Loan Amortization, Timecard, and Balance Sheet (this is not the kind of balance sheet you probably think it is). Additional templates are available on the Office Update Web site. Choose Help, Office on the Web to jump directly to the Office Update Web site. You can access the Spreadsheet Solutions tab and its templates by clicking General Templates in the New Workbook task pane.

Auditing and Documenting Worksheets

Excel has a number of powerful and flexible features that help you audit and debug your worksheets and document your work. In this section, you explore the following features: cell tracers, error checking, Formula Auditing mode, the Evaluate Formula dialog box, the Watch Window, Text To Speech, the Comment command, and Go To Special.

Most of Excel's auditing features can be accessed via the Formula Auditing toolbar, which is shown in Figure 9-9. You display the Formula Auditing toolbar by choosing Formula Auditing on the Tools menu and then clicking Show Formula Auditing Toolbar.

Figure 9-9. The Formula Auditing toolbar provides access to most of Excel's auditing features.

newfeature!
Checking for Errors

Choose Tools, Error Checking (or click the Error Checking button on the Formula Auditing toolbar) to quickly find any error values displayed on the current worksheet and display the Error Checking dialog box, as shown in Figure 9-10. The first erroneous cell in the worksheet is selected and its contents are displayed in the dialog box, along with a suggestion about the nature of the problem.

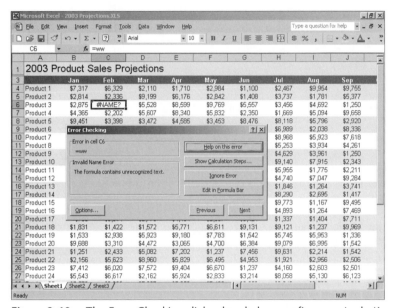

Figure 9-10. The Error Checking dialog box helps you figure out what's wrong with formulas that display error values.

When your problem appears in the dialog box, the following selections are available:

- Help On This Error displays a Help topic relating to the problem cell.

- Show Calculation Steps displays the Evaluate Formula dialog box. See "Evaluating and Auditing Formulas" on page 258.

- Ignore Error skips over the selected cell. To "un-ignore" errors, click the Options button and then click Reset Ignored Errors.

- Edit In Formula Bar opens the selected cell in the formula bar for editing. When you're finished, click Resume (the Help On This Error button changes to Resume).

Click the Previous and Next buttons to locate additional errors on the current worksheet. Click the Options button to display the Options dialog box shown in Figure 9-11 on the next page. Select or clear options in the dialog box to determine the

Chapter 9

kinds of problems you want to find when you choose Error Checking. Click the Reset Ignored Errors button if you want to recheck or if you clicked the Ignore error button by mistake.

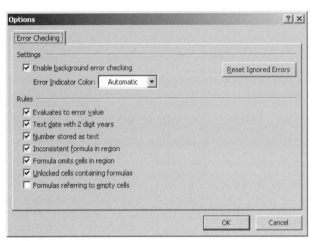

Figure 9-11. Click the Options button in the Error Checking dialog box to specify error-checking rules.

With the Options dialog box closed, you can continue checking errors. When you have addressed the last error, Excel displays an alert box informing you that the error check is complete for the entire sheet. Click OK to clear the alert box, and the Error Checking dialog box closes.

Evaluating and Auditing Formulas

Sometimes it's difficult to tell what's going on in a complex *nested* formula. A formula is nested when parts of it (called *arguments*) can be calculated separately. For example, in the formula =INDEX(pacadata!$A$2:$U$43,'Animal Info'!$B$5,5), the reference 'Animal Info'!$B$5 indicates a cell containing a number. To make this formula easier to read, you can substitute this reference with the number contained in the cell—for example, 7. The formula would then be =INDEX(pacadata!$A$2:$U$43,7,5).

When you choose Tools, Formula Auditing, Evaluate Formula, you can check complex formulas easily. Figure 9-12 shows the Evaluate Formula dialog box in action.

For more information about formulas and arguments, see Chapter 12, "Building Formulas."

Click Evaluate to replace calculable arguments with their resulting values. You can click Evaluate as many times as necessary if your formula contains many nested levels. For example, if you click Evaluate in Figure 9-12, the formula displayed in the Evaluation box replaces the aforementioned Animal Info reference with its value. Clicking Evaluate a second time calculates the next available level—which in this case is the end result, Suri Alpaca, as shown in Figure 9-13.

Chapter 9: Advanced Formatting and Editing Techniques

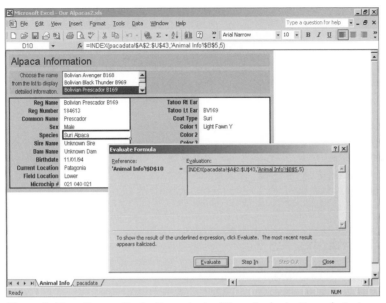

Figure 9-12. Choose Tools, Formula Auditing, Evaluate Formula to inspect nested formulas.

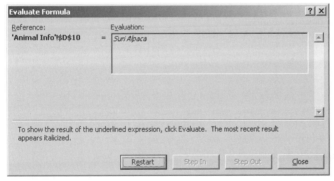

Figure 9-13. Each time you click the Evaluate button, another nested level in the selected formula is calculated.

Eventually, clicking the Evaluate button results in the formula's displayed value, and the Evaluate button changes to Restart, allowing you to go through the steps again. Click Step In to separate each calculable reference into separate boxes, making the hierarchy more apparent. In our example, the evaluated reference is to a constant, which cannot be further evaluated. If the reference were to a cell containing another formula, that would appear in the Evaluate Formula dialog box, as shown in Figure 9-14 on the next page. Where there are no more steps to be displayed, click the Step Out button to close the Step In box and replace the reference with the resulting value.

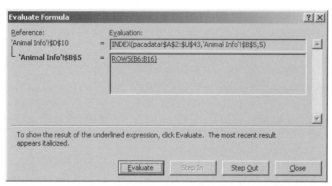

Figure 9-14. Use the Step In and Step Out buttons to display calculable arguments separately.

Watching Formulas

Sometimes you might want to keep an eye on a formula as you make changes to other parts of a worksheet, or even when working on other workbooks that supply information to a worksheet. Instead of constantly having to return to the formula's location to see the results of your ministrations, you can use the Watch Window, which provides remote viewing for any cell on any open worksheet.

Select a cell you want to keep an eye on and choose Tools, Formula Auditing, Show Watch Window. You click the Add Watch button in the Add Watch window as shown in Figure 9-15.

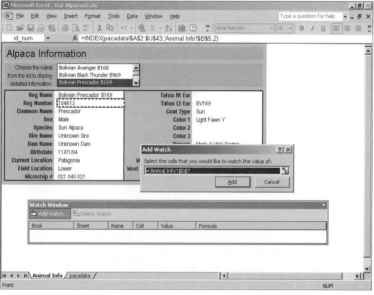

Figure 9-15. Select a cell and click Add Watch to keep an eye on it, no matter where you are currently working.

You can click a cell you want to watch either before or after you display the Add Watch
dialog box. Click the Add button to insert the cell information in the Watch Window.
The Watch Window can be docked, as shown in Figure 9-16, but it acts like a toolbar,
so you can change its size by dragging its borders or dragging it away from its
docked position.

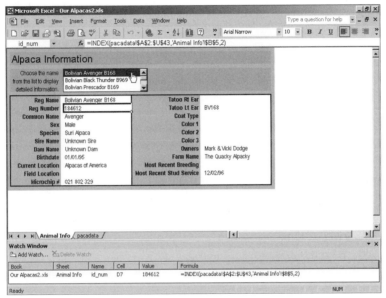

Figure 9-16. The Watch Window displays all the current information for the
watched formula.

---

note   To make room for more watched cells if the window is docked, drag the top border of
the Watch Window upward.

While your workbook is still open, you can select any item in the Watch Window list
and delete it by clicking Delete Watch. Close the Watch Window by choosing Tools,
Formula Auditing, Hide Watch Window; or click the close button (the X) at the top of
the Watch Window toolbar. When you close a workbook, any watched cells it contains
are removed from the Watch Window list.

Tracing Cell References

If you've ever looked at a large worksheet and wondered how you could get an idea of
the data flow—that is, how the formulas and values relate to one another—you'll
appreciate *cell tracers*. You can also use cell tracers to help find the source of those
pesky errors that occasionally appear in your worksheets.

The Formula Auditing toolbar (refer to Figure 9-9) contains six buttons that control different functions of the cell tracers: Trace Precedents, Remove Precedent Arrows, Trace Dependents, Remove Dependent Arrows, Remove All Arrows, and Trace Error. You can also choose Tools, Formula Auditing to control the cell tracers (and to display the Formula Auditing toolbar).

Understanding Precedents and Dependents

The terms precedent and dependent crop up quite often in this section. They refer to the relationships that cells containing formulas create with other cells. A lot of what a spreadsheet is all about is wrapped up in these concepts, so here's a brief description of each term:

- *Precedents* are cells whose values are used by the formula in the selected cell. A cell that has precedents always contains a formula.

- *Dependents* are cells that use the value in the selected cell. A cell that has dependents can contain either a formula or a constant value.

For example, if the formula =SUM(A1:A5) is in cell A6, cell A6 has precedents (A1:A5) but no apparent dependents. Cell A1 has a dependent (A6), but no apparent precedents. A cell can be both a precedent and a dependent if the cell contains a formula and is also referenced by another formula.

Tracing Dependent Cells

In the worksheet in Figure 9-17, we selected cell B2, which contains the hourly rate value. To find out which cells contain formulas that use this value, you can click the Trace Dependents button on the Formula Auditing toolbar. Although this worksheet is elementary, to make it easier to illustrate the cell tracers, consider the ramifications of using the cell tracers in a large and complex worksheet.

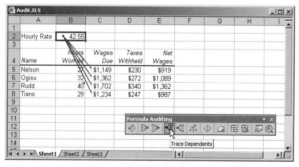

Figure 9-17. When you trace dependents, arrows point to formulas that directly refer to the selected cell.

The tracer arrows indicate that cell B2 is directly referred to by the formulas in cells C5, C6, C7, and C8. A dot appears in cell B2, indicating that it is has dependents. If you click Trace Dependents again, another set of arrows appears, indicating the next level of dependencies—or indirect dependents. Figure 9-18 shows the results.

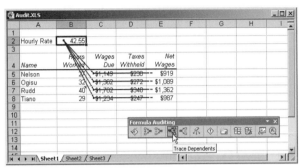

Figure 9-18. When you trace dependents again, arrows point to the next level of formulas, ones that indirectly refer to the selected cell.

You can click the Remove Dependent Arrows button (next to the Trace Dependents button) to go backward. Click once to remove the level of dependents you last displayed, and click again to remove the next level.

One handy feature of the tracer arrows is that you can use them to navigate, which can be a real advantage in a large worksheet. For example, in Figure 9-18 with cell B2 still selected, double-click the arrow pointing from cell B2 to cell C8. (When you move the mouse pointer over a tracer arrow, it becomes arrow-shaped.) The selection jumps to the other end of the arrow, and cell C8 becomes the active cell. Now if you double-click the arrow pointing from cell C8 to cell E8, the selection jumps to cell E8. If you double-click the same arrow again, the selection jumps back to cell C8 at the other end. If you double-click an arrow that extends beyond the screen, the window shifts to display the cell at the other end. You can use this feature to jump from cell to cell along a path of precedents and dependents.

Clearing Tracer Arrows

Each time you trace another cell's precedents or dependents, additional tracer arrows appear. You'll find, however, that your screen quickly becomes cluttered, making it difficult to discern the data flow for particular cells. It's a good idea to start fresh each time you want to trace cells. To remove all the tracer arrows from the screen, click the Remove All Arrows button on the Formula Auditing toolbar.

Tracing Precedent Cells

You can also trace in the opposite direction by starting from a cell that contains a formula and tracing the cells that are referred to in the formula. In Figure 9-19 on the next page, we selected cell E5, which contains one of the net wages formulas. To find out which cells this formula refers to, we clicked the Trace Precedents button.

263

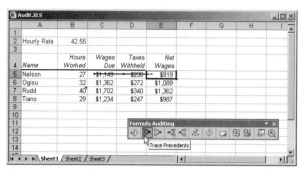

Figure 9-19. When you trace precedents, arrows point from all the cells that the formula in the selected cell directly refers to.

This time, an arrow appears with dots in cells C5 and D5. The dots identify these cells as precedents in the data flow. (The appearance of dots in both C5 and D5 indicates that both cells are equally precedent to the selected cell.) Notice that the arrow still points in the same direction—toward the formula and in the direction of the data flow—even though we started from the opposite end of the path. To continue the trace, click the Trace Precedents button again. Figure 9-20 shows the results.

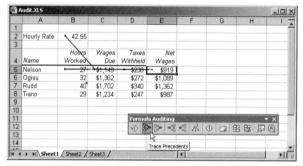

Figure 9-20. When you trace precedents again, arrows point from the next (indirect) level of cells that the formula in the selected cell refers to.

Tracing Errors

Suppose your worksheet displays error values, like the ones shown in Figure 9-21. To trace one of these errors back to its source, select a cell that contains an error.

Notice that the cells containing errors display smart tag indicators in the upper left corner of each cell, and when you select one of them, the smart tag actions menu appears, as shown in Figure 9-22. The smart tag actions menu displays applicable options, including Trace Error.

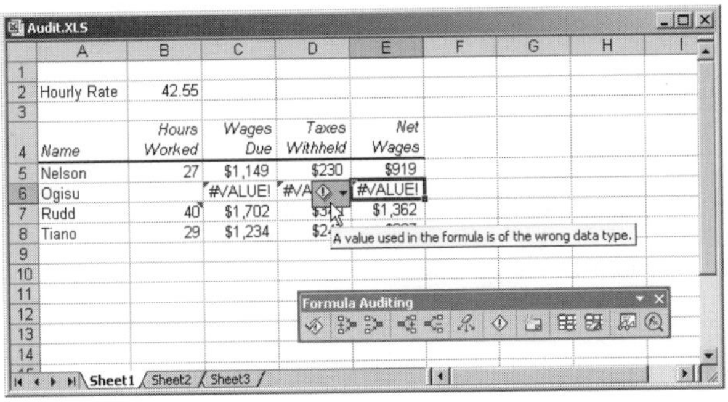

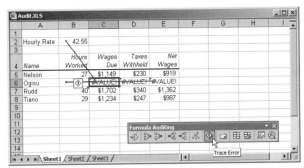

Figure 9-21. Cells with error values display smart tag action menus.

Figure 9-22. Select a cell that contains an error value and click the Trace Error button to display arrows that trace the error back to its source.

Excel selects the cell that contains the first formula in the error chain and draws arrows from that cell to the cell you selected. Excel draws arrows to the cell that contains the first erroneous formula from the values the formula uses. It's up to you to determine the reason for the error; Excel takes you to the source formula and shows you the precedents. In our example, the error is caused by a space character inadvertently entered in cell B6, replacing the hours-worked figure.

Tracing References to Other Worksheets

If a cell contains a reference to a different worksheet or to a worksheet in another workbook, a dashed tracer arrow appears with a small icon attached, as shown in Figure 9-23 on the next page. You cannot continue to trace precedents from the active cell when a dashed tracer arrow appears.

If you want, you can open the referenced worksheet or workbook and then start a new trace from the referenced cell. If you double-click a dashed tracer arrow, the Go To dialog box appears, with the reference displayed in the Go To list, as shown in Figure 9-24 on the next page.

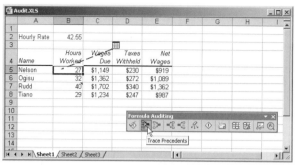

Figure 9-23. If you trace the precedents of a cell that contains a reference to another worksheet or workbook, a special tracer arrow appears.

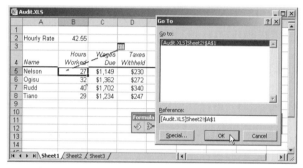

Figure 9-24. Double-clicking the external tracer arrow displays the Go To dialog box.

You can select the reference in the list and click OK to open the worksheet or workbook. However, if the reference is to another workbook that is not currently open, an error message appears.

The Circle Invalid Data button on the Auditing toolbar draws a red circle around cells containing values that violate the specific parameters of Data Validation. The Clear Validation Circles button, as you might expect, removes these circles from the worksheet.

For more on data validation, see "Validating Data Entry" on page 710.

Adding Comments to Cells

You can attach comments to cells to document your work, explain calculations and assumptions, or provide reminders. Select the cell you want to annotate and click the New Comment button on the Auditing toolbar. Then type your message in the comment box that appears, as shown in Figure 9-25.

Chapter 9: Advanced Formatting and Editing Techniques

Audit.XLS									
	A	B	C	D	E	F	G	H	I
1									
2	Hourly Rate	42.55							
3									
4	Name	Hours Worked	Wages Due	Taxes Withheld	Net Wages				
5	Nelson	27	$1,149	$230	$919				
6	Ogisu	32			$1,089				
7	Rudd	40			$1,362				
8	Tiano	29			$987				
9									
10									
11									
12									
13									
14									

Comment box in figure:
Mark Dodge: We can approve up to 50 hours per week for Darlene.

Figure 9-25. You can attach comments to cells to help document your worksheet.

When you add a comment to a cell, your name appears in bold at the top of the comment box. You can specify what appears here by choosing Tools, Options, clicking the General tab, and typing your name (or any other text) into the User Name edit box. The text you type here appears at the top of the comment box, followed by a colon.

Normally, a small red triangle appears in the upper right corner of a cell, indicating the presence of a comment. When you move the cursor over a cell displaying this comment indicator, the comment pops up. You can suppress the display of this indicator by choosing Tools, Options, clicking the View tab, and clicking the None option in the Comments group. You also can display all the comments all the time by clicking the Comment & Indicator option.

Although you can attach only one comment to a cell, you can make your comment as long as you like. If you want to begin a new paragraph in the comment box, press Enter. When you're finished, you can drag the handles to resize the comment box.

After you've added text to your comments, nothing is set in stone. You can edit a comment by selecting the cell containing the comment and clicking the Edit Comment button. (The New Comment button changes to Edit Comment when you select a cell containing a comment.) To delete a comment, click the hatched border of the comment after you open it for editing and press the Delete key.

You can work with comments a little more easily when you use the Reviewing toolbar shown in Figure 9-26. To display the Reviewing toolbar, choose View, Toolbars, and click Reviewing.

Reviewing toolbar buttons. Reply with Changes... End Review...

Figure 9-26. Use the Reviewing toolbar to work with comments.

The buttons you use to work with Comments on the Reviewing toolbar are as follows:

- **New Comment/Edit Comment.** Use this button to add a comment to the selected cell. If the selected cell already contains a comment, this button changes to Edit Comment, which opens the comment for editing.

267

● **Previous Comment and Next Comment.** Use these buttons to open each comment in the workbook for editing, one at a time. Even if your comments are located on several worksheets in the same workbook, these buttons allow you to jump directly to each one in succession without using the sheet tabs.

● **Show Comment.** Use this button to display (rather than open for editing) the comment in the selected cell. This button changes to Hide Comment if the comment is currently displayed.

● **Show All Comments.** Use this button like the Show Comment button, except that it displays all the comments on the worksheet at once.

● **Delete Comment.** Use this button to remove comments from all selected cells.

Printing Comments

To print comments, follow these steps:

1 Choose File, Page Setup.

2 Click the Sheet tab, and select one of the options in the Comments list,

■ At End Of Sheet prints all the comments in text form after the worksheet is printed.

■ As Displayed On Sheet prints comments as they appear as text boxes if you display all the comments at once on the worksheet. Be careful, however, because comments printed this way can obscure some contents of the worksheet itself, or if your comments are clustered together, they might overlap.

3 Click OK to close the Page Setup dialog box.

4 Click the Print button on the Standard toolbar.

For more information about printing, see Chapter 11, "Printing and Presenting."

Using Go To Special

Choosing Edit, Go To is familiar to most Excel users as a way to jump from place to place in your workspace. The Special button at the bottom of the Go To dialog box opens a dialog box called Go To Special, but you can think of it as "Select Special," because you can use it to quickly find and select cells that meet certain specifications. To access the Go To Special dialog box, shown in Figure 9-27, choose Edit, Go To (or press F5), and then click the Special button.

Chapter 9: Advanced Formatting and Editing Techniques

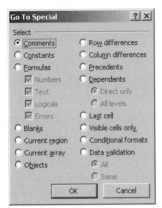

Figure 9-27. Choose Edit, Go To, and click the Special button to display the Go To Special dialog box—a handy auditing and debugging tool.

After you specify one of the Go To Special options and click OK, Excel highlights the cell or cells that match the criteria. With a few exceptions, if you select a range of cells before you open the Go To Special dialog box, Excel searches only the selected range; if the current selection is a single cell or one or more graphic objects, Excel searches the entire active worksheet.

---

tip **Navigate multiple selections**

Some of the Go To Special options—such as Comments, Precedents, and Dependents—might cause Excel to select multiple nonadjacent ranges. To navigate through these without losing the selection, press Enter to move down or to the right one selected cell at a time. Press Shift+Enter to move up or to the left one cell at a time.

The following are guidelines for using the Go To Special options:

- Current Region is handy when you're working in a large, complex worksheet and need to select blocks of cells. (Recall that a region is defined as a rectangular block of cells bounded by blank rows, blank columns, or worksheet borders.) You can press Ctrl+Shift+* to select the current region without using the Go To Special dialog box.

- If the selected cell is part of an array range, Current Array selects all the cells in that array. You can press Ctrl+/ to select the current array without using the Go To Special dialog box.

- Last Cell selects the cell in the lower right corner of the range that encompasses all cells that contain data, comments, or formats. When you select Last Cell, Excel finds the last cell in the active area of the worksheet, not the lower right corner of the current selection.

- Visible Cells Only excludes from the current selection any cells in hidden rows or columns. You can press Alt+; to select only the visible cells without using the Go To Special dialog box.

- Objects selects all graphic objects in your worksheet, regardless of the current selection.

- Conditional Formats selects only those cells that have conditional formatting applied.

- Data Validation selects all cells to which Data Validation has been applied.

> For more information about graphic objects, see Chapter 10, "Creating Spiffy Graphics."
> For more information about conditional formatting, see "Applying Conditional Formats" on page 245. For more information about data validation, see "Validating Data Entry" on page 710.

Selecting Precedents and Dependents

The Precedents and Dependents options in the Go To Special dialog box allow you to find cells that are used by a formula or cells on which a formula depends. To use the Precedents and Dependents options, first select the cell whose precedents or dependents you want to select. When searching for precedents or dependents, Excel always searches the entire worksheet. When you click the Precedents or Dependents option, Excel opens the Direct Only and All Levels options:

- Direct Only finds only those cells that directly refer to or that directly depend on the active cell.

- All Levels locates direct precedents and dependents plus those cells that are indirectly related to the active cell.

---

tip　**Select precedents and dependents quickly**

You can also use these keyboard shortcuts to quickly select precedents and dependents of the active cell:

Ctrl+[selects direct precedents.

Ctrl+Shift+{ selects all precedents.

Ctrl+] selects direct dependents.

Ctrl+Shift+} selects all dependents.

Selecting Row or Column Differences

The Row Differences and Column Differences options in the Go To Special dialog box compare the entries in a range of cells to spot potential inconsistencies. To use these

Chapter 9: Advanced Formatting and Editing Techniques

debugging options, select the range before displaying the Go To Special dialog box. The position of the active cell in your selection determines which cell or cells Excel uses to make its comparisons. When searching for row differences, Excel compares the cells in the selection with the cells in the same column as the active cell. When searching for column differences, Excel compares the cells in the selection with the cells in the same row as the active cell.

Among other things, the Row Differences and Column Differences options look for differences in your cell and range references and select those cells that don't conform to the comparison cell. They also verify that all the cells in the selected range contain the same type of entries. For example, if the comparison cell contains a SUM function, Excel flags any cells that contain a function, formula, or value other than SUM. If the comparison cell contains a constant text or numeric value, Excel flags any cells in the selected range that don't exactly match the comparison value. The options, however, are not case-sensitive.

---

tip   **Select column and row differences quickly**

You can also use keyboard shortcuts to select column differences or row differences. To search for column differences, select the range you want to search and press Ctrl+Shift+I. To search for row differences, select the range you want to search and press Ctrl+\.

---

newfeature!
Having Excel Read Cells to You

If you ever had the pleasure of comparing printed matter with data in a worksheet, you know how tedious and time-consuming it can be. For example, suppose you have a list of names on a sheet that you need to check with a printed list to make sure no one is missing. Assuming that your printed list is sorted in alphabetical order (or in some other order, such as customer number), you can sort your worksheet list and then have Excel read it to you while you scan the printed list to locate omissions. To do this, display the Text To Speech toolbar shown in Figure 9-28.

---

note   You must first have Speech Recognition installed to use this feature. For more information, see Appendix A, "Installing Microsoft Excel."

Figure 9-28.   The Text To Speech toolbar provides access to Excel's reading features.

Select the cells you want Excel to read and click the Speak Cells button, as shown in Figure 9-29 on the next page. Excel's "voice" then reads each item in the selection in order until it reaches the end of the selection.

271

Figure 9-29. You can listen to Excel read the contents of selected cells as you compare what you hear to a printed reference.

If you select a single cell instead of a range, Excel reads all cells in the current region. If the By Rows button is selected, Excel reads each cell in the row and then moves to the next row down. If you select the By Columns button, Excel reads all the entries in the first column and then moves to the next column to the right.

You can also have Excel read each cell back to you as you enter it, which is handy when entering lists of data. Hearing the result immediately after entry might alert you to a spelling error that you can correct before moving on. To do so, click the Speak On Enter button.

You have control over the type of voice Excel uses, the reading speed, the language used, and the location of the audio output. To change any of these settings, click the Windows Start menu, click Settings, Control Panel, and double-click the Speech icon.

For more about Excel's speech features, see Appendix C, "Keyboard Shortcuts."

Outlining Worksheets

Many typical spreadsheet models are built in a hierarchical fashion. For example, in a monthly budget worksheet, you might have a column for each month of the year, followed by a totals column. For each line item in your budget, the totals column adds the values in each month column. In this kind of structure, you can describe the month columns as subordinate to the totals column because their values contribute to the outcome of the totals column.

The line items also can be set up hierarchically, with groups of expense categories contributing to category totals. Excel can turn worksheets of this kind into outlines.

Figure 9-30 shows a table of sales figures before and after outlining. To accomplish this, we selected a cell in the table and chose Data, Group And Outline, AutoOutline. (To outline a specific range, select the area before choosing AutoOutline.) Figure 9-31 shows how you can change the level of detail displayed after you outline a worksheet.

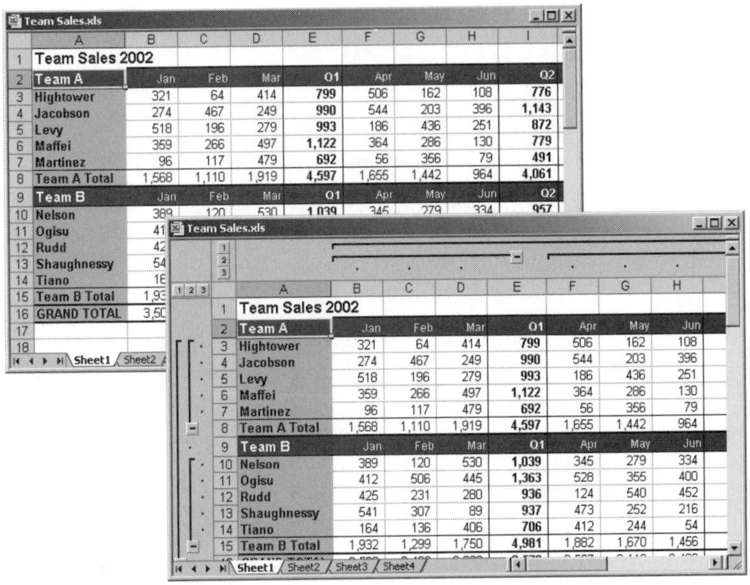

Figure 9-30. With Excel, you can outline a worksheet.

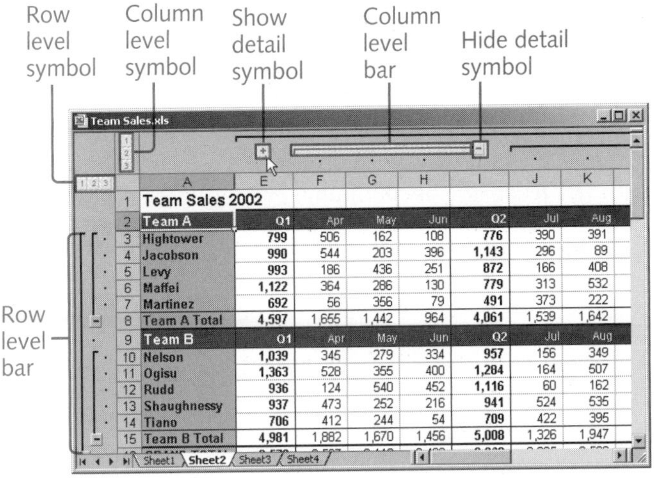

Figure 9-31. Two clicks of the mouse button transformed the outlined worksheet in Figure 9-30 into this quarterly overview.

The difference between the outlined worksheets in Figures 9-30 and 9-31 is that the columns and rows listing the months and individual team members are hidden in Figure 9-30. Without outlining, you would have to hide each group of columns and rows manually; with outlining, you can collapse the outline to change the level of detail instantly.

The outline in Figure 9-31 is a simple one. It uses three levels each for columns and rows. You can create much more complex outlines—Excel can handle a maximum of eight outline levels each for columns and rows.

Creating an Outlining Toolbar

The outlining buttons offer some shortcuts for working with an outline. Each corresponds to selections or dialog-box options available elsewhere, but the buttons help make fast work of this task. A custom toolbar containing the six outlining buttons is shown here.

To create this custom toolbar, choose View, Toolbars; then choose Customize and click the Toolbars tab. Click the New button, type **Outlining**, and click OK to create a new blank toolbar. Click the Commands tab, and select Data in the Categories list. From the Commands box, drag all the buttons shown to the new toolbar except Select Visible Cells (the button on the far right), which is in the Edit category. For more information about creating custom toolbars, see "Creating New Toolbars and Menus" on page 77.

Outlining a Worksheet with Nonstandard Layout

The standard outline settings reflect the most common worksheet layout. To change these settings, choose Data, Group And Outline, Settings to display the Settings dialog box shown in Figure 9-32. If your worksheet layout is not typical, such as a worksheet constructed with rows of SUM formulas (or other types of summarization formulas) in rows above the detail rows or with columns of formulas to the left of detail columns, clear the appropriate Direction option—Summary Rows Below Detail or Summary Columns To Right Of Detail—before outlining.

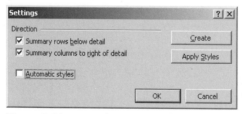

Figure 9-32.   Use the Settings dialog box to adjust for a nonstandard layout.

When you use nonstandard worksheet layouts, be sure that the area you want to outline is consistent to avoid unpredictable and possibly incorrect results; that is, be sure all summary formulas are located in the same direction relative to the detail data. After you select or clear one or both Direction options, click the Create button to create the outline.

Extending the Outline to New Worksheet Areas

At times, you might create an outline and then add more data to your worksheet. You might also want to re-create an outline if you change the organization of a specific worksheet area. To include new columns and rows in your outline, repeat the procedure you followed to create the outline in the first place: select a cell in the new area and then choose Data, Group And Outline, Auto Outline. Excel asks you to confirm that you want to modify the existing outline; click OK.

InsideOut

Apply formats manually

The Automatic Styles option and Apply Styles button apply formats to your outline that are meant to help distinguish different levels of data, such as totals and detail data. Unfortunately, the automatic styles used by Excel provide very little help in this regard. To ensure that the outline is formatted the way you want, you should plan to apply formats manually or select AutoFormat for the entire outline. For more information, see "Turbo Formatting with AutoFormat" on page 202.

Hiding or Clearing an Outline

When you outline a worksheet, Excel displays symbols above and to the left of the row and column headings (refer to Figure 9-31). These symbols take up screen space, so if you want to suppress them, you can click the Show Outline Symbols button if you created the custom Outlining toolbar. Alternatively, you can choose Tools, Options, click the View tab, and clear the Outline Symbols option. Click the button or select the option again to redisplay the outline symbols.

Remember, when you hide the outline symbols, the outline still exists; it's just hidden. To remove the outline completely, click Data, Group And Outline, Clear Outline.

You can also remove either the column or row levels (or both) from an outline by ungrouping all the outline's levels to the highest level. If your outline is many levels deep and your worksheet is large, this process can be laborious. Another way to make your worksheet behave as though it is not outlined is to display all the levels of detail (by clicking the highest numbered level button for both columns and rows) and then suppress the display of Excel's outline symbols. You can do this by clicking the Show Outline Symbols button on the custom Outlining toolbar or by choosing Tools, Options and clearing Outline Symbols on the View tab.

Collapsing and Expanding Outline Levels

When you create an outline, the areas above and to the left of your worksheet are marked by one or more brackets that terminate in hide detail symbols, which have minus signs on them. The brackets are called *level bars*. Each level bar indicates a range of cells that share a common outline level. The hide detail symbols appear above or to the left of each level's summary column or row.

To collapse an outline level so that only the summary cells show, click that level's hide detail symbol. For example, if you no longer need to see the sales numbers for January, February, and March in the outlined worksheet (refer to Figure 9-30), click the hide detail symbol above column E. The worksheet then looks like Figure 9-33.

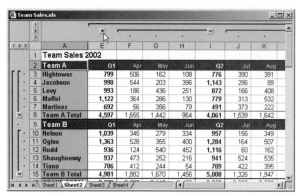

Figure 9-33. When you hide the details for January through March by clicking the hide detail symbol above Q1, Excel displays a show detail symbol above Q1.

A show detail symbol with a plus sign on it now replaces the hide detail symbol above the Q1 column (column E). To redisplay the hidden monthly details, click the show detail symbol.

Collapsing and Expanding with an Intellimouse

You can use the wheel on your IntelliMouse to manipulate an outline without using the detail symbols or level symbols. This is helpful if you prefer to suppress the display of outline symbols to see more of the worksheet on screen, yet you still want to be able to use the outlining feature.

Hold the mouse pointer over the summary row or column you want to expand or collapse; then hold down the Shift key and turn the wheel backward (toward your hand) to collapse the outline or forward (away from your hand) to expand it. For example, if you press Shift, hold the mouse pointer over cell E1 in Figure 9-33, and turn the wheel forward, the detail columns for Q1 reappear.

If you hold the pointer over a cell where a summary row and summary column intersect, the outline collapses or expands in both directions at once. For example, if you hold the pointer over cell I8 in Figure 9-33, hold down the Shift key, and turn the wheel backward, both the Team A detail rows and the Q2 detail columns collapse simultaneously.

276

Displaying a Specific Outline Level

To collapse each quarter so that only the quarterly totals and annual totals appear, you can click the hide detail symbols above Q1, Q2, Q3, and Q4. The level symbols—the squares with numerals at the upper left corner of the worksheet—provide an easier way, however. An outline usually has two sets of level symbols, one for columns and one for rows. The column level symbols appear above the worksheet, and the row level symbols appear to the left of the worksheet.

You can use the level symbols to set an entire worksheet to a specific level of detail. The outlined worksheet shown in Figure 9-30 has three levels each for both columns and rows. By clicking both of the number 2 level symbols in the upper left corner of the worksheet, you can transform the outline shown in Figure 9-30 to the one shown in Figure 9-31. By clicking the number 1 level symbols, you can further reduce the level of detail displayed by the worksheet so that only the grand total sales figure for the year, in cell R16, is shown.

Selecting Only Visible Cells

When you collapse part of an outline, Excel hides the columns or rows that you don't want to see. In Figure 9-33, for example, the detail columns are hidden for Q1. Normally, if you select a range that includes hidden cells, those hidden cells are included in the selection. Whatever you do with these cells also happens to the hidden cells, so if you want to copy only the displayed totals, using copy-and-paste gives you the entire table. By choosing Edit, Go To, clicking the Special button, and selecting the Visible Cells Only option, you can restrict the selection to only the visible cells within a range.

The Select Visible Cells option is ideal for copying, charting, or performing calculations on only those cells that occupy a particular level of your outline. Select Visible Cells works the same way in worksheets that have not been outlined; it excludes any cells in hidden columns or rows from the current selection.

Ungrouping and Grouping Columns and Rows

If the default automatic outline doesn't give you the structure you expect, you can adjust it by ungrouping or grouping particular columns or rows. You can easily change the hierarchy of outlined columns and rows by choosing Data, Group And Outline. Select the columns or rows you want to change and choose one of the options.

For example, you could select row 8 in the outlined worksheet shown in Figure 9-30 and choose Ungroup to change row 8 from level 2 to level 1. The outlining symbol to the left of the row moves to the left under the row level 1 button. To restore the row to its proper level, choose Group.

> **note** You cannot ungroup or group a nonadjacent selection, and you cannot ungroup a selection that's already at the highest hierarchical level. If you want to ungroup a top-level column or row to a higher level so it is displayed separately from the remainder of the outline, you have to group all the other levels of the outline instead.

Consolidating Worksheets

You can use the Consolidate dialog box (choose Data, Consolidate), shown in Figure 9-34, to combine the values from a set of worksheets in the same workbook or from different workbooks. The Consolidate command allows you to assemble information from as many as 255 supporting worksheets into a single master worksheet.

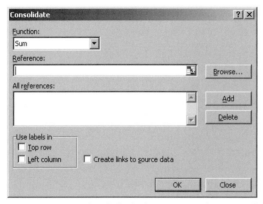

Figure 9-34. The default function in the Consolidate dialog box is Sum.

For example, if you have data for each month in separate worksheets or financial data for several divisions in separate workbooks, you can use the Consolidate command to create a master worksheet that comprises the totals for the corresponding items in each location. You can use the Consolidate command in a number of ways:

● Link the consolidated data to the supporting data so that subsequent changes in the supporting worksheets are reflected in the consolidation worksheet.

● Consolidate the source data on an ad hoc basis, without creating a link.

● Consolidate by position, where Excel gathers information from the same cell location in each supporting worksheet.

● Consolidate by category, where Excel uses column or row labels as the basis for associating worksheets. Consolidating by category gives you more flexibility in the way you set up your supporting worksheets. For example, if your January column is column B in one worksheet and column D in another, you can still gather the correct January numbers when you consolidate by category.

- Use any of the functions listed in the Function list in the Consolidate dialog box, including Count (which corresponds to the COUNTA function), Average, Max, Min, Product, Count Nums (which corresponds to the COUNT function), StdDev, StdDevp, Var, and Varp. As shown in Figure 9-34, the default function is Sum.

> For more information about functions, see Chapter 13, "Using Functions," and Chapter 14, "Everyday Functions."

- Consolidate worksheets in workbooks that are currently open or in workbooks that are stored on disk. The workbook containing the worksheet that receives the consolidated data must be open, but supporting workbooks can be closed—provided you give Excel the correct locations so it can find each workbook file. You must save all supporting workbooks before you begin consolidation.

tip You can also use PivotTable Reports to consolidate worksheets. For information, see "Using a PivotTable to Consolidate Ranges," on page 823.

Consolidating by Position

When you consolidate by position, Excel applies the consolidation function (Sum, Average, or whatever else you select) to the same cell references in each supporting worksheet. This is the simplest way to consolidate, but your supporting worksheets must have exactly the same layout.

Figure 9-35 shows a simple example of a workbook containing a master worksheet—Consolidated—that matches the layout of 12 supporting monthly worksheets. These worksheets can be consolidated by position because each contains identically structured data.

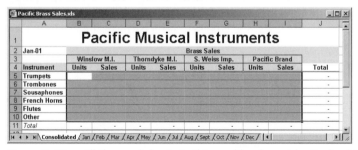

Figure 9-35. All the worksheets in this workbook are identical, which is necessary when consolidating by position.

To consolidate the monthly worksheets in Figure 9-35 into the sheet named Consolidated, follow these steps:

1 Open the consolidation worksheet and select the block of cells that will receive the consolidated data. In Figure 9-35, the destination area is the range B5:I10.

2 Choose Data, Consolidate.

3 Use the default Sum function in the Function list. Leave the options in the Use Labels In section and the Create Links To Source Data option unselected.

4 Select each source range with the mouse.

---

tip **Open supporting workbooks**

If you are consolidating data in more than one workbook, you have to type references to the data ranges you want to consolidate in any workbooks that are not currently open. For this reason, make sure all supporting workbooks are open. If you do have to type a reference, it must use the form [Filename]Sheetname! Reference. If the reference is in the same workbook, the file name (and its surrounding brackets) is unnecessary. If the source range has been assigned a name, you can use this name in place of Reference (highly recommended).

If you use the mouse to select your source ranges, click the button on the right end of the Reference box to collapse the Consolidate dialog box and get it out of the way. Open worksheets by clicking their tabs. If a workbook is open but obscured by other workbooks on the screen, you can get to it by choosing its name from the Window menu. All these window maneuvers can be performed while you make your selections in the Consolidate dialog box; the dialog box remains active until you close it.

5 Click the Add button in the Consolidate dialog box. Excel transfers the reference from the Reference edit box to the All References list. Figure 9-36 shows the completed dialog box. Repeat for each sheet you want to consolidate.

After you select the first range—$B$5:I$10 in the Jan sheet—Excel selects the same range in each sheet when you click its tab. Just click a sheet tab and then click the Add button to add references. Figure 9-37 shows the resulting consolidation.

---

tip **Preserve consolidation references**

After you perform a consolidation, the references you enter in the Consolidate dialog box are retained when you save the workbook. The next time you open the workbook and want to refresh the consolidated values, rather than entering the references again, choose Consolidate and click OK.

Chapter 9: Advanced Formatting and Editing Techniques

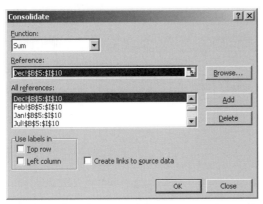

Figure 9-36. The Consolidate command uses the references in the All References box to create the consolidated totals.

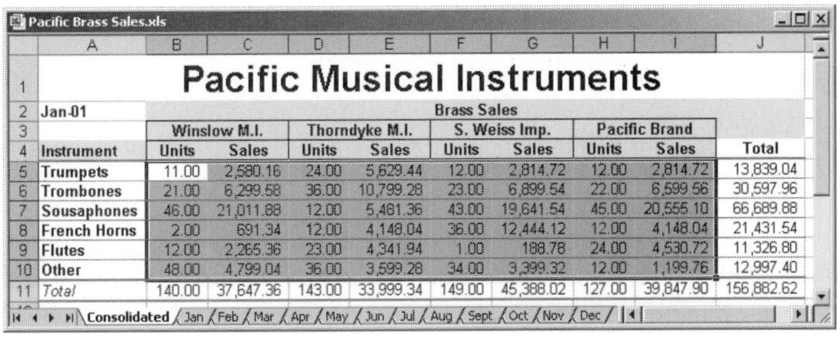

Instrument	Winslow M.I.		Thorndyke M.I.		S. Weiss Imp.		Pacific Brand		Total
	Units	Sales	Units	Sales	Units	Sales	Units	Sales	
Trumpets	11.00	2,580.16	24.00	5,629.44	12.00	2,814.72	12.00	2,814.72	13,839.04
Trombones	21.00	6,299.58	36.00	10,799.28	23.00	6,899.54	22.00	6,599.56	30,597.96
Sousaphones	46.00	21,011.88	12.00	5,481.36	43.00	19,641.54	45.00	20,555.10	66,689.88
French Horns	2.00	691.34	12.00	4,148.04	36.00	12,444.12	12.00	4,148.04	21,431.54
Flutes	12.00	2,265.36	23.00	4,341.94	1.00	188.78	24.00	4,530.72	11,326.80
Other	48.00	4,799.04	36.00	3,599.28	34.00	3,399.32	12.00	1,199.76	12,997.40
Total	140.00	37,647.36	143.00	33,999.34	149.00	45,388.02	127.00	39,847.90	156,882.62

Figure 9-37. Range B5:I10 in the Consolidated worksheet now contains totals of the corresponding cells in the 12 supporting worksheets.

Consolidating by Category

Now let's look at a more complex example. The Pacific Sales Staff workbook contains monthly sales totals for each salesman, but each monthly sheet has different salespeople and a different number of salespeople, as shown in Figure 9-38.

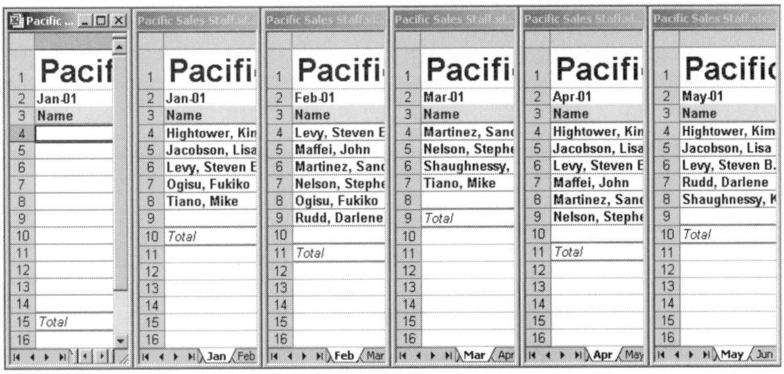

Figure 9-38. Use the categories in the left column of each source worksheet as the basis for this consolidation.

The consolidation worksheet has column headings for Units and Sales—each
worksheet is the same in this respect. However, the consolidation worksheet has no row
headings. You need to omit the row headings because they are not consistently
arranged in the source worksheets. As you'll see, the Consolidate command enters the
row headings for you.

To consolidate by category, follow these steps:

1 Select the destination area.

   This time the destination area must include the row headings—but how
   many rows? To answer that, you can look at each source worksheet and
   determine how many unique line items you have. An easier way, however, is
   to select cell A4 as the destination area. When you specify a single cell as
   your destination area, the Consolidate command fills in the area below and
   to the right of that cell as needed. In the example, to preserve the formatting, we inserted more than enough rows to accommodate the data.

2 Choose Data, Consolidate.

3 To consolidate by row categories in this example, select Left Column in the
   Use Labels In section. Use the default Sum function in the Function list.

4 The consolidation worksheet already has column labels, so you can omit
   them from the source worksheet references. Each source reference must
   include row headings, Units and Sales. Select these ranges on each monthly
   worksheet. For example, on the Jan sheet, we selected $A$4:$C$8. Unlike
   when consolidating by position, you have to manually select the ranges in
   each supporting sheet, because Excel selects the last range you added, which
   will not necessarily be what you want.

5 Click OK, and Excel fills out the Consolidated worksheet, as shown in
   Figure 9-39.

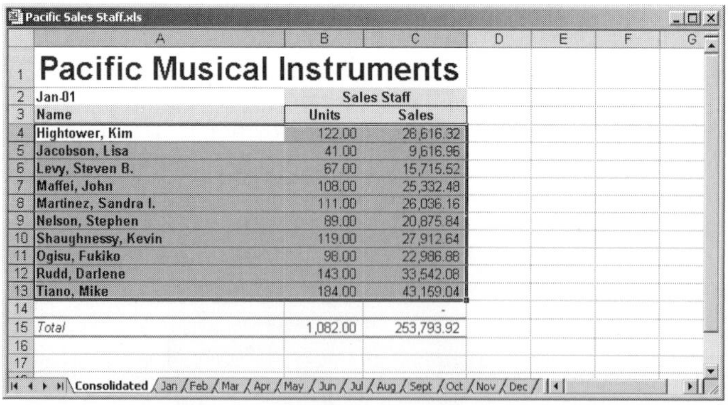

Figure 9-39. The Consolidate command created a separate line item in
the consolidation worksheet for each unique item in the source worksheets.

The consolidation worksheet now includes a category that corresponds to each unique line item in the source worksheets. If two or more worksheets have the same line item, the consolidation worksheet performs the selected mathematical operation on the corresponding figures for each column position.

> **note** It's important that your categories—in our example, the names of salespeople—are spelled identically on each supporting sheet. Otherwise, Excel will create a separate line and consolidation for each spelling variation.

Creating Links to the Source Worksheets

The previous examples consolidated numbers with the Sum function, resulting in a range of consolidated constants. Subsequent changes to the source worksheets will not affect the consolidation worksheet until you repeat the consolidation.

You can also use the Consolidate command to create links between the consolidation and source worksheets. To do so, select the Create Links To Source Data option in the Consolidate dialog box and then consolidate using the same techniques. When you consolidate with links, Excel creates an outline in the consolidation sheet, as shown in Figure 9-40. Each source item is linked separately to the consolidation worksheet, and Excel creates the appropriate summary items. Additional columns and rows are created as necessary for each category—one for each unique entry in each sheet, as shown in rows 35 to 41. The figure also shows, in the formula bar, the linking formula for the April units figure in cell C35.

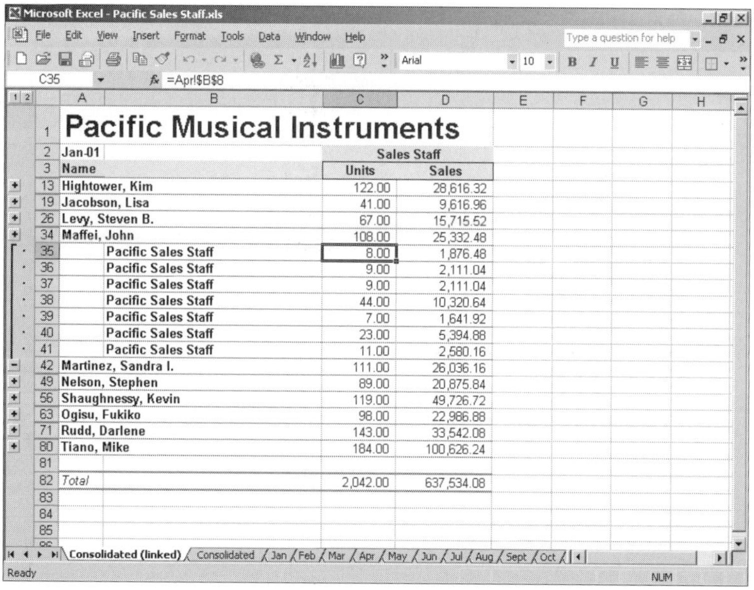

Figure 9-40. When you create links to the source worksheets, the consolidation sheet is outlined and linking formulas are created in subordinate outline levels.

Note that when you create links, any rows or columns you subsequently add to the source worksheets are not included in the consolidation. However, it is easy to modify the consolidation references. Open the Consolidate dialog box, select the reference you want to change and click the Delete button. Then select the modified range and click the Add button.

For more information about outlining worksheets, see "Outlining Worksheets" on page 272

Part 4

Adding Graphics and Printing

Creating Spiffy Graphics

Microsoft Excel gives you the tools to create a variety of graphic objects—boxes, lines, circles, ovals, arcs, freeform polygons, text boxes, buttons, and a wide assortment of complex, predefined objects called AutoShapes. You can specify font, pattern, color, and line formats, and you can position objects in relation to the worksheet or to other objects. You can also take pictures of your worksheets and use them in other Excel documents or in documents created in other applications. If you already have graphics created in other applications, Excel imports those graphics as well.

Throughout this chapter, we add graphics to worksheets, but you can also add many of the same kinds of graphics to chart sheets. In addition, you can apply the techniques discussed in this chapter to a variety of graphic objects called controls that you create using Microsoft Excel Visual Basic for Applications (VBA).

> For more information about Visual Basic for Applications, see Part 10, "Working with Visual Basic and Macros."

Using the Drawing Tools

Excel's drawing tool chest offers many of the powerful capabilities of dedicated illustration programs. You can use this tool chest to create smooth curves; linked objects using connectors; basic and not-so-basic shapes, such as three-dimensional boxes and lightning bolts; a variety of straight, curved, and multiheaded arrows; flow charts; stars, emblems, and banners; and callouts. You create these graphic objects using the buttons and menus on the Drawing toolbar shown in Figure 10-1 on the next page. The easiest way to display the Drawing toolbar is by right-clicking any displayed toolbar or the menu bar and choosing Drawing from the shortcut menu.

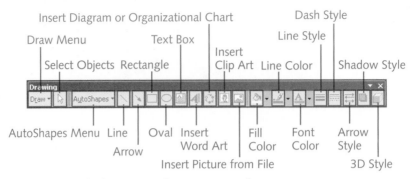

Figure 10-1. The buttons on the Drawing toolbar.

If you have ever used a drawing program, such as Microsoft Paint or CorelDRAW, you already know how to create lines, arrows, ovals, rectangles, and text boxes. In Excel, as in graphics programs, click the button you want on the Drawing toolbar and then drag the pointer to create the object. When you drag a simple box shape using the Rectangle button, for example, Excel displays Rectangle 1 in the Name box at the left end of the formula bar. Excel refers to new graphic objects by category and numbers them in the order in which you create them.

---

tip   **Lock the tool to draw multiple objects**

To draw several objects one after the other, double-click the button to lock Excel into Drawing mode. The button you double-click remains active until you cancel the drawing session or select another button. To cancel the drawing session, click the button again, or press Esc.

Objects that you create appear to float over the worksheet or chart in a separate layer. Objects are separate from the worksheet or chart and can be grouped and formatted as discrete items. Here are a few more important facts you should know about using the drawing tools:

● Excel leaves Drawing mode each time you finish drawing an object. You can cancel Drawing mode by clicking anywhere in the worksheet or chart without dragging.

● Formatting that you apply to underlying worksheet cells has no effect on objects.

● When you move the mouse pointer over an object, the pointer changes to the move arrow. You can then select the object or move it elsewhere by dragging.

● If you select an object, you can stretch and resize the object by dragging the handles that appear on its perimeter.

● If you drag a center handle, you change the object's height or width.

288

Drawing Constrained Objects

The word constrain has a somewhat negative connotation, but in computer lingo, a *constraint* is a good thing. If you apply a constraint to an object you draw, for example, you force the object to adhere to a specific angle or proportion. Using constraints is the easiest way to create perfect circles and squares. For example, you can hold down Shift (and sometimes Ctrl) while creating objects, to constrain them, as Figure 10-2 illustrates.

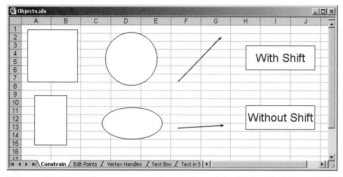

Figure 10-2. When you create or size objects, hold down Shift to constrain them.

The key you use to constrain your object depends on the type of constraint you want to cause. The following lists describe the types of constraints created using each method.

Holding down the Shift key causes the following constraints:

- The Line and Arrow buttons draw perfectly horizontal or vertical lines, or diagonal lines constrained to exact 15-degree increments (0°, 15°, 30°, 45°, 90°, and so on).

- The Rectangle button draws perfect squares.

- The Oval button draws perfect circles.

- AutoShapes are drawn to predefined, roughly symmetrical constraints. AutoShapes come in many different forms, so the effect of the Shift key varies considerably, depending on the shape.

Holding down the Ctrl key causes the following constraints:

- While dragging to create lines and arrows, the object is centered on the point at which you click the mouse button. As you drag away from the point where you clicked, lines are drawn simultaneously in both the direction you drag and the opposite direction.

● While dragging to create rectangles, ovals, text boxes, and AutoShapes, the object is centered on the point at which you click the mouse button. Objects grow out from the center point as you drag.

● When dragging a handle to resize a previously drawn object, the object remains centered on its original center point and resizes equally in all directions.

● When dragging an object to move it, holding down Ctrl creates a copy of the object, leaving the original in place.

Hold down the Alt key causes the following constraint:

● You can hold down Alt while creating objects to use the gridlines on a worksheet as a drawing grid. The edges of your objects are then forced to follow the gridlines. If you use Shift and Alt together to draw a square or a circle aligned to the grid, Excel does its best, but the result might not be perfect. This is because the default height and width of the cells on a worksheet might not provide an ideal grid for perfect squares or circles.

InsideOut

Enter "The Object Zone"

When you work with objects, it's almost as if there's another program with a transparent desktop that floats over the worksheet—as if the objects you draw are in another dimension. In a sense, they are. What goes on in the grid of Excel has little to do with what goes on in the drawing layer we'll call "The Object Zone," although you do have opportunities to create interaction between object and worksheet using macros and formulas.

When you are working normally in cells, you can click on any graphic object to select it, and then click in the worksheet to select cells. You can hop back and forth, no problem. However, when you click the Select Objects button (the arrow) on the Drawing toolbar, you enter "The Object Zone," where you cannot select a cell to save your life. This button is a toggle—you're in "The Object Zone" until you click it again. This essentially locks out the worksheet so that you can toil in that phantom program to your heart's content. This is handy when you are doing a lot of graphic work, because it makes it easier to select and work with objects without worrying about inadvertently clicking the sheet and exiting "The Object Zone." If you forget that you've clicked the Select Objects button, you might experience a moment of panic, wondering what happened, and worrying that perhaps Excel has crashed. Just look at the Select Object button, which stays highlighted. Click it again, to leave "The Object Zone."

Using Tear-off Palettes

Many of the submenus located on the Drawing toolbar are *tear-off palettes*. On the Draw menu, you can tear off the Order, Nudge, Align or Distribute, and Rotate or Flip commands. Each command on the AutoShapes menu (except the More AutoShapes command) is a tear-off palette—in fact, you can tear off the entire AutoShapes menu itself, as shown in Figure 10-3. Click the selection bar (the three horizontal lines at the top of the menu) and drag it away. You can do the same with any menu or submenu that is displayed as a selection bar.

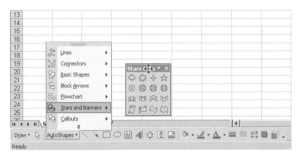

Figure 10-3.   Many of the submenus on the Drawing and AutoShapes menus are palettes you can tear off by dragging.

Creating Graphic Objects

Each of the various object types available in Excel has strengths, idiosyncrasies, and issues you need to be aware of. In this section, we discuss these issues and describe the various object types in detail.

Drawing Freehand Lines and Polygons

The Line and Arrow buttons on the Drawing toolbar are extremely easy to use. Just click a button on the toolbar, and then click and drag to create the object on the worksheet. But to draw lines other than simple straight lines and arrows, choose AutoShapes, Lines.

The tools on the Lines submenu are as follows:

- **The Line and Arrow buttons.** These buttons work identically to the ones on the Drawing toolbar. They draw straight lines and arrows.

- **The Double Arrow button.** Draws arrows just as the Arrow button does, with an extra arrowhead.

- **The Curve button.** Draws smoothly curved lines between clicked points.

- **The Freeform button.** Draws combined freehand lines and straight lines.

- **The Scribble button.** Draws unconstrained lines. (However, when you release the mouse button, the resulting line is smoothed somewhat.)

The Freeform and Curve buttons are different from the others in that when you release the mouse button, you're not done drawing. To finish drawing using either of these buttons, you must either click the starting point to close the loop and create a solid object or to create a line, double-click where you want the line to end. Figure 10-4 shows a few objects created using these buttons.

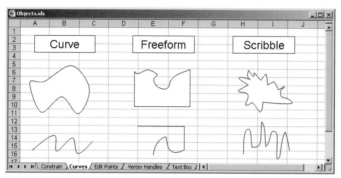

Figure 10-4. A sampling of objects created using the Curve, Freeform, and Scribble buttons.

For example, if you click the Freeform button and then click anywhere on the worksheet or chart to begin drawing, the line remains anchored to the point you clicked. If you release the mouse button, the line stretches from the anchor point to the cross-hair pointer like a rubber band. If you stretch the line and click again, you create a segment that is anchored between the first and second point. You can continue this as long as you want, creating additional segments with each new anchor point.

You can also hold down the mouse button while using the Freeform button to create a freehand line, or click points to create straight segments. By combining both of these methods, you can create a hybrid object with both straight and curved lines.

Adjusting Freehand Shapes with the Edit Points Command

Drawing an attractive freehand line or polygon shape with a mouse can be challenging. If you have difficulty dragging the shape you want, use the Edit Points command, which changes a line or polygon created with the Scribble, Curve, or Freeform buttons into a series of points you can drag to reshape the object.

To adjust a Scribble, Curve, or Freeform shape, right-click the object, and then choose Edit Points from the shortcut menu. (The Edit Points command also appears on the Draw menu.) A new set of handles appears, following the curves and corners of the object. You can then drag as many of the handles as necessary to new positions. For example, we used the Freeform button to create the shape on the left in Figure 10-5, and then we selected the shape. The shape on the right is the same freeform polygon after we chose Edit Points.

> **tip** **Add or delete Edit Points**
>
> After you choose Edit Points, you can add or delete any of the handles on an object. If you want to clean up your drawing by eliminating some of the end points, press the Ctrl key and click each handle you want to delete. If you want to add end points, press Ctrl and click anywhere on a line where you want a handle to appear.

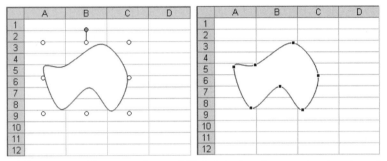

Figure 10-5. When you choose Edit Points, handles appear at each vertex, as in the image on the right.

Adding the Edit Points Button to a Toolbar

Edit Points is so useful for drawing freeform curves and polygons that you'll want to keep it handy. You might even want to add the Edit Points button to the existing Lines palette. Here's how:

1 Click AutoShapes on the Drawing toolbar, click Lines, and then drag the selection bar away from the menu to float the Lines palette.

2 Choose View, Toolbars, Customize.

3 Click the Drawing category and drag the Edit Points button from the Commands list to the floating Lines palette.

For more information on customizing toolbars, see "Customizing Toolbars and Menus" on page 65.

Working with Curves

When you edit the points in an object created using the Scribble, Curve, or Freeform buttons, you can fine-tune the curves even further, by using commands on the shortcut menu that appears when you right-click any edit point, as shown in Figure 10-6 on the next page.

Chapter 10

293

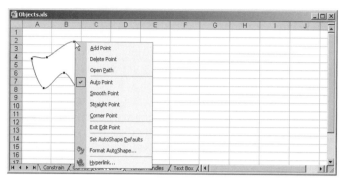

Figure 10-6. Change the type of a selected edit point by right-clicking it and using commands on the shortcut menu.

There are four types of points. Each type is available through a corresponding command on the shortcut menu:

- **Auto Point.** Auto Points are determined by the button used to create the line and the way it was drawn. The Curve button always creates Auto Points, which display no vertex handles.

- **Straight Point.** Lines flowing out from either side of a straight point are equally curved and display vertex handles of equal length when selected. Drag a vertex handle and the opposite handle moves equally in the opposite direction. You can select any existing point and make it a straight point.

- **Smooth Point.** Smooth points create gradual transitions between the lines flowing out from either side, which can be unequal, and display vertex handles when selected. You can drag vertex handles separately.

- **Corner Point.** Corner points create abrupt transitions between the lines flowing out from either side, and display vertex handles when selected, which can be dragged separately. The Scribble button always creates Corner Points.

All types of points except Auto Points provide vertex handles when selected. These handles, shown in Figure 10-7, allow two-way control over the shape of a curve. The longer the vertex handle, the flatter the curve in the direction you drag. These powerful controls can be tricky to master at first. As you know, practice makes perfect.

Working with Text Boxes

Use the Text Box button on the Drawing toolbar to add notes, headings, legends, and other text to your worksheets and charts to give more impact to or to clarify the data you're presenting.

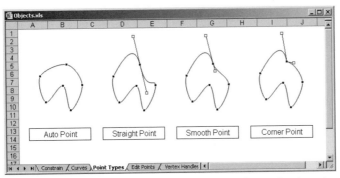

Figure 10-7. Change the shape of freeform objects by dragging the vertex handles that appear when you click any type of point except an Auto Point.

Click the Text Box button and a box appears. A blinking cursor appears in the box, indicating that you can begin typing. After you are finished, you can select and format text using the same commands you use for text in cells.

---

tip **Check the spelling of text in objects**

If you choose the Spelling command with a single cell selected, all the text in the current worksheet is checked, including text in text boxes. If you choose Spelling while a text box (or any object) is selected, only that text box (or object) is checked.

Adding Text to Other Shapes

The Text Box button is quick and easy to use, but if you want to add a graphic assistance to your message, you can add text to many of the shapes created by using the AutoShapes menu, including arrows, banners, boxes, and just about any shape except lines and connectors.

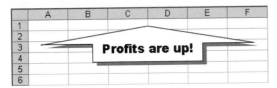

To do so, just draw the shape you want and then start typing. Resize the object as needed, and use Format, AutoShape to give the shape and its text the look you want.

---

tip   **Create linked objects**

You can create a link from a text box—or any other shape containing text—to a cell so that you can display that cell's contents in the text box. First draw a text box. With the text box selected, type an equal sign in the formula bar, and then type a cell reference or defined name. For example, suppose cell D3 contains a formula that returns the value $123.45. When you type **=$D$3** into the formula bar while a text box is selected, the value $123.45 appears in the text box. When you link a text box in this way, you cannot type additional text into it. To remove the link, select the text box and delete the reference formula in the formula bar.

Working with AutoShapes

The AutoShapes menu on the Drawing toolbar offers dozens of predrawn shapes you can use to add effective visual communication to your worksheets. Notice that most AutoShapes display a yellow, diamond-shaped handle somewhere on the perimeter. If you drag this handle, you can control a specific dimension of the shape, as Figure 10-8 illustrates.

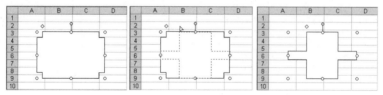

Figure 10-8.   Many AutoShapes have special diamond-shaped handles that you can drag to control a specific feature of the shape.

newfeature!

In addition to the diamond handle, all two-dimensional objects in Excel now display a panhandle that you drag to rotate the object as shown in Figure 10-9. This is a handy way to rotate objects, and makes the Free Rotate button less important, which is why it was removed from the default Drawing toolbar. (Free Rotate is still available as a command on the Draw, Rotate or Flip submenu.)

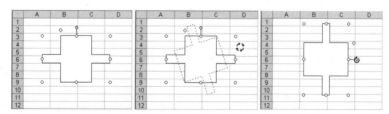

Figure 10-9.   Drag the panhandle of any two-dimensional object to rotate it.

Using Connectors and Callouts

Most AutoShapes are easy to use and somewhat self-explanatory. Connectors and Callouts, however, have some special qualities that bear mentioning. If you've ever spent time creating drawings using simple lines and boxes only to find that you need to reposition anything later, you know what a problem this can be. You usually end up spending as much time fine-tuning the drawing as you spent drawing it in the first place. Connectors can help. They are special kinds of lines that are "sticky" on both ends. You use them when you want to connect shapes using lines that remain attached and stretch, making it easier to reposition objects later with a minimum of tweaking.

After you click one of the buttons on the Connectors palette on the AutoShapes menu, special blue points appear when you hover the mouse pointer over any existing shape. These are *connection points*, and if you click one of them, the connector line attaches to that point. The second mouse click attaches the other end of the connector line to a blue point on another object and finishes the connector line. As Figure 10-10 shows, the resulting connector line stays attached to the two points, even when you move the shapes around. You don't have to attach connectors to anything. For example, you can connect one end to a shape and leave the other end free to create your own custom callout.

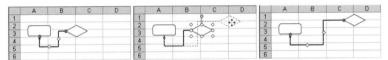

Figure 10-10. Connector lines remain attached to the points where you place them, even when you drag the shape to a new location.

> **tip** **Create easily modified flow charts**
>
> Connectors are particularly useful for creating flow charts. First, sketch out your rough ideas using the Flowchart And Connectors palettes on the AutoShapes menu. You can move flow chart symbols around as you work, and the connector lines reroute themselves as necessary.

Callouts are special text boxes with connector lines already attached. You can use them to add labels to important information or to describe important items. The most familiar type of callout is the kind you see in comics. Excel includes several of these balloon callout, shown in Figure 10-11 on the next page with additional formatting applied. Note that in this type of callouts, the tip of the balloon pointer is the sticky point.

Figure 10-11. Callouts help you describe important items or call attention to important messages.

After drawing a callout, you can immediately begin typing the text you want in the callout. Then drag the diamond-shaped handle to move the tip of the callout indicator to the location you want.

More AutoShapes

When you choose More AutoShapes on the Drawing toolbar's AutoShapes menu, a version of the Insert Clip Art task pane appears. Any clip art that can be used as an AutoShape, such as Windows Metafile (WMF) format images, is displayed in the task pane.

The clip art selected for use by More AutoShapes is somewhat rudimentary, but you can manipulate it like an AutoShape. To insert a shape, drag it from the task pane to the worksheet. For more information about clip art and the Microsoft Media Gallery, see "Using Clip Art and Other Media" on page 313.

Shape Shifting

If you're unhappy with one of your shape selections, you needn't delete it and draw a new one. Just use the Change AutoShape command on the Drawing toolbar's Draw menu. You can change most AutoShapes, with the exception of lines and connectors, regardless of whether the shape contains text. However, if the original shape did contain text, you might need to adjust alignment of the text within the new shape.

Creating WordArt

The Insert WordArt button on the Drawing toolbar opens a palette of fancy text styles that you can employ to create impressive logos and headings. After you select the effect you want, click OK. The Edit WordArt Text dialog box opens where you select the font and size and enter the text you want, as shown in Figure 10-12.

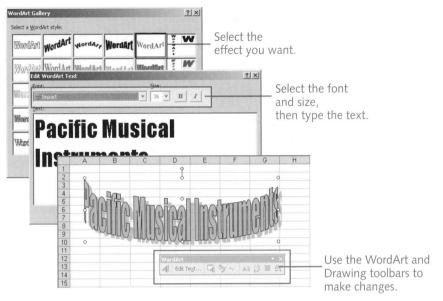

Select the
effect you want.

Select the font
and size,
then type the text.

Use the WordArt and
Drawing toolbars to
make changes.

Figure 10-12. Use the Insert WordArt button to create stunning logos and headings.

Notice that in Figure 10-12, selected WordArt objects display the same handles as AutoShapes, including the free rotate panhandle and the diamond-shaped handle that changes a specific characteristic of the selected shape.

After you create your WordArt, and anytime you select a WordArt object, the WordArt toolbar appears, shown in Figure 10-13 on the next page.

The buttons on the WordArt toolbar do the following:

- **WordArt Gallery.** Displays a selection of different effects in the WordArt Gallery dialog box.

- **Format AutoShape.** Opens the dialog box of the same name, where you can adjust fill and line styles, size, protection, and positioning properties.

- **WordArt Shape.** Displays a palette of additional shapes you can apply to an existing WordArt object.

- **WordArt Same Letter Heights.** Offers an interesting effect by making all letters fit into the same amount of vertical space. Lowercase letters are enlarged as necessary to be the same height as uppercase letters, and any letters with descenders (parts of letters that extend below the baseline, such as the tail on a y) are moved up and fit into the same space.

Chapter 10

299

● **WordArt Vertical Text.** Switches the orientation of the selected WordArt object to vertical so that the letters are stacked on top of one another.

● **WordArt Alignment.** Changes the alignment of WordArt objects (where alignment is applicable). In addition to the familiar alignment options, you'll see three Justify options. Word Justify behaves like normal justification; it forces text to align to both the left and right margins. Letter Justify adds the space between letters as well as words. Moreover, Stretch Justify adds no space at all—instead it just stretches the letters to fit.

● **WordArt Character Spacing.** Displays a palette of commands you can use to control the amount of space between characters, sometimes called tracking, as well as the spacing of letter pairs, also known as kerning. However, the WordArt implementation of tracking isn't what you might expect. Instead of adding or removing space between characters, it makes the letters themselves wider or smaller, leaving the actual length of each word the same. Kern Character Pairs is either on or off, and it affects only pairs of letters that represent perennial spacing problems, such as AV.

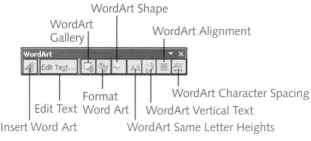

Figure 10-13. Create and edit WordArt objects with the WordArt toolbar.

Working with Graphic Objects

After you create graphic objects on your worksheet, you'll need to move them around and format them. You can also control their protection attributes, and specify the way objects respond to changes in the position of underlying cells. This section discusses the many ways that you can use Excel to help you accomplish these tasks.

Selecting and Grouping Objects

Sometimes you'll find it convenient to move, resize, or even reformat more than one object at a time. If you create a logo using multiple objects, for example, you will want to move all objects as a single unit, preserving their positions relative to one another. For these purposes, Excel includes the Select Objects button on the Drawing toolbar, as well as the Group, Ungroup, and Regroup commands on the Drawing toolbar's Draw menu. Keep in mind the following when you work with the Select Objects button:

- When you click the Select Objects button, you can select only objects, not cells; Excel remains in Selection mode until you click the button again. For more information about Selection mode, see "Enter The Object Zone" on page 290.

- If an object has a macro assigned to it and the macro is normally activated when the object is clicked, you can use the Select Objects arrow to select it without activating the macro.

- You can use the Select Objects arrow to select a group of objects by dragging a rectangle around them, as shown in Figure 10-14.

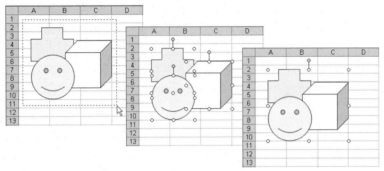

Figure 10-14. Click the Select Objects button and drag a rectangle around the objects you want to select, and then choose Draw, Group to lock them together.

---

tip **Alternative object selection methods**

You can also select objects by clicking individual objects while holding down Shift. You can select all the objects on the current worksheet or chart by choosing Edit, Go To, clicking the Special button, and then selecting the Objects option.

After you select a group of objects, you can lock them together using Group on the Drawing toolbar's Draw menu. The sets of handles around each selected object are then replaced by a single set of handles for the entire group, as shown in Figure 10-14. After the objects are grouped, you can manipulate the set of objects as a single object. You can resize, move, and apply formatting to them as a group. When you apply formatting, however, the separate objects might behave differently, especially if you have grouped different kinds of objects with different formats. It's best to apply formatting before you group objects together, unless the objects are similar.

To ungroup a set of objects, select the group and then click Draw, Ungroup. You can also apply Regroup to the objects you most-recently ungrouped. For example, this is handy if you ungrouped a set of objects to make changes to one or more of them. Rather than selecting them again and choosing Group, just choose Regroup.

301

Selecting Objects That Contain Text

Unlike other objects, when you click an object containing text, a gray border appears around it to indicate that it's selected. You can then manipulate and format the box as you would any other object. When you double-click an object containing text, a flashing insertion point appears in the text area, giving you the opportunity to edit the text inside. If you want to move an object containing text while its text area is active, you must drag the gray border.

Formatting Objects

You can apply patterns, colors, and shading to objects using the command that appears at the top of the Format menu when an object is selected. The actual command name differs, depending upon the type of object selected. For example, the command can be AutoShape, Text Box, or Picture, when the corresponding object type is selected. If you choose any form of this command, or if you double-click the object (or the gray border of an object containing text), a dialog box similar to the one shown in Figure 10-15 appears.

> **note** The name of the first command on the Format menu varies depending on which object you have selected. Similarly, the name of the associated dialog box changes as well. For example, if a chart's legend is selected, the command on the Format menu appears as Selected Legend and opens the Format Legend dialog box.

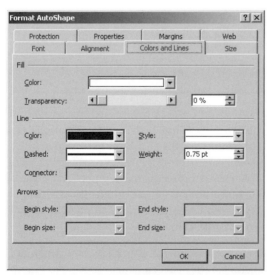

Figure 10-15. This dialog box changes, depending on the type of object selected.

> **note** If an object is selected that doesn't contain text, the Font, Alignment, and Margins tabs do not appear in this dialog box.

The Colors And Lines tab of this dialog box gives you control over the style, color, and weight of the object's border, as well its fill color and pattern. Generally, the options available on this tab are self-explanatory, but here are a few facts that aren't obvious:

● The Dashed drop-down list offers different dashed line styles; the default line style is not dashed. (The Line Style and Dash Style buttons on the Drawing toolbar make the corresponding formats more readily available.)

● The Weight list seems to offer many of the same line options as the Style list, except that you have the additional option of typing in any point size.

● The Color options include the 56 colors on the Color tab of the Options dialog box.

● The Fill Effects option in the Color drop-down list displays the Fill Effects dialog box, which you can use to add patterns, gradient fills, pictures, or textures, such as wood, marble, canvas, and even a paper bag effect, to your objects.

● If you apply a pattern using the Pattern tab in the Fill Effects dialog box, the color you select for the foreground is assigned to the pattern itself, and is reflected in the sample pattern thumbnails displayed in the dialog box. The color you select for the background is assigned to the white areas of the pattern.

Changing Colors in the Palette

The palette of colors available for use with objects is determined by the Color tab of the Options dialog box. To modify the palette, click the Color tab, select a color, click the Modify Color button, and pick a different color.

Adding Transparency

When you use the Transparency slider in either the Format Object or the Fill Effects dialog box, the worksheet and anything else that falls underneath the selected object shows through in the percentage you select. This option essentially turns off alternative fill color pixels, partially revealing whatever is behind it. Figure 10-16 on the next page shows two identical objects, but 50 percent transparency was applied to the one on the right.

Chapter 10

newfeature!
Why the Web Tab?

In Figure 10-15, notice that the dialog box contains a Web tab. If you click it, you'll see that the only option is to add Alternative Text—what is known in Web parlance as Alt Text—as shown in the following figure.

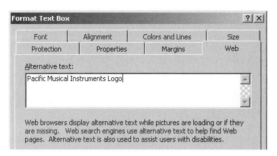

When you save an Excel document as a Web page, graphics are converted to their Web-based equivalents. In HTML, the language of the Web, alternative text is added to images for three reasons. First, Alt Text appears in the browser while an image is loading, which is particularly helpful for large images. Second, when you hover the mouse over an image containing Alt Text, the text appears in a pop-up box in your browser. Finally, Alt Text is used by text-reading software commonly used by the blind, allowing them to hear a description of the image. If you're planning to save your workbook in HTML format, you should consider adding alternative text to all your graphics. For more info on Excel and the Web, see Chapter 22, "Using Hyperlinks."

Figure 10-16. The Transparency setting allows whatever is behind the object to show through.

Formatting Lines and Arrows

If you double-click a line or an arrow, the Arrows options on the Colors And Lines tab become available. In addition to the Line options, you can change the style of each end of the selected line to include different types of arrowheads, or none. You can change a line to an arrow, and vice versa. You can add arrowheads at either end or both ends of a line. The Arrow Style button on the Drawing toolbar offers a selection of commonly used arrow styles, including More Arrows, which displays the Format AutoShape dialog box.

304

Applying Shadows

You can use the Shadow button on the Drawing toolbar to add depth to any graphic object. In Figure 10-17, we created an object using the Explosion 1 button from the Stars And Banners palette on the AutoShapes menu. Then we applied effects using the Shadow button. Shadow Settings on the Shadow palette displays the Shadow Settings toolbar.

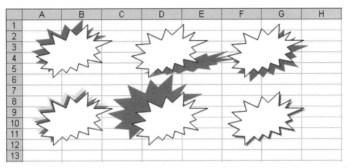

Figure 10-17. You can create a variety of shadow effects using the Shadow button on the Drawing toolbar.

The Shadow Settings toolbar, seen in Figure 10-18, includes the Shadow Color button that displays a familiar color palette and offers the interesting Semitransparent Shadow command, which makes an applied shadow effect work more like an actual shadow. Fine-tune the positioning of the shadow using the four Nudge buttons.

Shadow On/Off
Nudge Shadow Up
Nudge Shadow Down

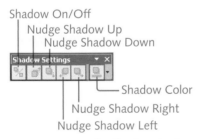

Shadow Color
Nudge Shadow Right
Nudge Shadow Left

Figure 10-18. The Shadow Settings toolbar.

Applying 3-D Effects

Click the 3D Style button on the Drawing toolbar to display a palette of predefined three-dimensional effects. You can apply three-dimensional effects to any object, including lines, arrows, and WordArt objects. If you apply one of these effects, several special formats are applied to the selected object: horizontal tilt, vertical tilt, depth, direction, lighting position, surface type, and color of the extruded area. In Figure 10-19 on the next page, we started with three copies of the same object and applied effects using buttons on the 3D Style palette. The object on the left has no effect applied, 3D Style 1 was applied to the object in the middle, and 3D Style 4 was applied to the object on the right.

Chapter 10

305

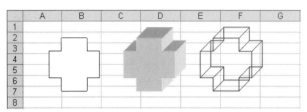

Figure 10-19. Start with a basic shape and give it depth using the 3D button on the Drawing toolbar.

After you apply an effect, click the 3D Style button and select 3D Settings to display the toolbar shown in Figure 10-20. The buttons on the 3D Setting toolbar are:

- **3-D On/Off.** This button, predictably, turns the 3D effect on and off.

- **Tilt.** These four buttons adjust the position of the selected object in three-dimensional space.

- **Depth.** This button displays a palette you use to change the depth of the selected object in points, from zero to infinity.

- **Direction.** This button displays a palette that controls the trajectory of the extruded portion of the selected object. Use the Perspective and Parallel options in the Direction palette to determine whether the sides of the extruded portion exhibit perspective—that is, appear to fade off into the distance.

- **Lighting.** This button displays a palette that controls the brightness and direction of the imaginary light source. The palette displays a small sample object surrounded by lamp buttons. Click a lamp button and the shading of the selected object changes, as if a light were shining on the object from that direction.

- **Surface.** This button displays a palette that you can use to select the type of surface treatment: Matte, Plastic, Metal, or Wire Frame.

- **3D Color.** This button displays a palette that controls the color of the extruded area of the selected object.

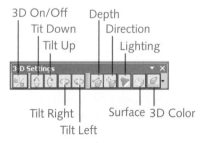

Figure 10-20. The 3D Settings toolbar.

Formatting Objects that Contain Text

There are two ways to select objects containing text: you select either the text area or the entire object. You can tell the difference by looking at the border, as Figure 10-21 shows. Usually, if you first click an existing text object, the border is a gray dot pattern, indicating that the entire object is selected. Double-click the object and the border changes to a hatched-line pattern, indicating that only the text area is selected.

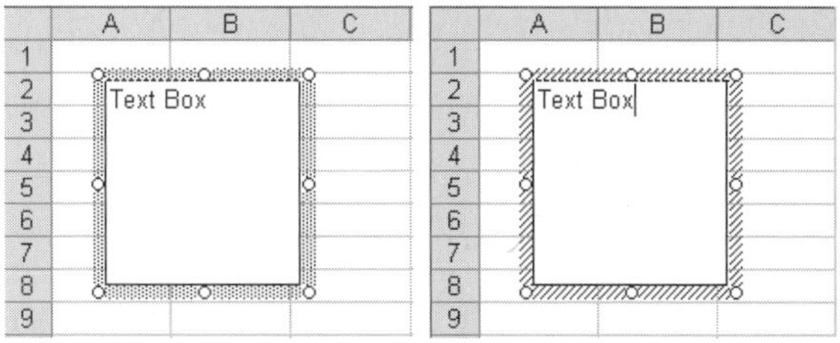

Figure 10-21. The dotted border on the left indicates that the object is selected; the hatched-line border on the right indicates that only the text area is selected.

If you select an object containing text and choose Format, Text Box, the tabs that appear in the dialog box differ depending on the way in which the object was selected. If only the text area is selected, only the Font tab appears; if the entire object is selected, all eight tabs appear, as shown in Figure 10-15.

The options on the Alignment tab of the Format Text Box dialog box control the alignment of text within the object. For example, we formatted the text boxes in Figure 10-22 with various alignment and orientation options. In addition, we selected the Automatic Size option on the Alignment tab for the two boxes containing the Center label. The Automatic Size option adjusts the size of the text box to fit the text it contains.

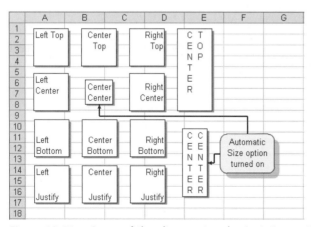

Figure 10-22. Some of the alignment and orientation options are available on the Alignment tab.

307

For more on alignment, see "Aligning Data in Cells" on page 223. For more on fonts, see "Using Fonts" on page 230. For more on Web options, see Chapter 22, "Using Hyperlinks."

Setting the Default Format for Objects

If you find that you keep applying the same formatting options to objects you create, you can easily make these hard-earned formats the default for all new objects you create. Select any object formatted the way you like, and then choose Draw, Set AutoShape Defaults. The formats affected include fills, line styles, and even shadow and 3-D settings.

Positioning Objects

Think of the objects on a worksheet as stacked on top of each other. Each new object you draw is placed on top of the stack. You can adjust the position of objects in the stack by choosing Draw, Order, which displays a tear-off palette containing the Bring To Front, Send To Back, Bring Forward, and Send Backward commands.

Figure 10-23 shows two identical sets of ungrouped objects along with the torn-off Order palette. In the set on the right, we positioned the banner in front of the other objects in the stack using the Bring To Front button, and, in the set on the left, we positioned the banner behind the other objects using the Send To Back button.

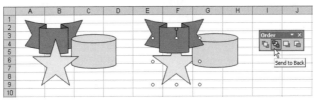

Figure 10-23.   You can reposition objects in relation to each other using the Order palette.

The Bring Forward and Send Backward buttons work in a similar manner, except that instead of moving the selected object all the way to the front or back of the stack, they move the object just one layer at a time though the stack.

You can change the way objects behave in relation to changes in the worksheet using the options on the Properties tab of the Format AutoShape dialog box. The default Object Positioning option is Move And Size With Cells, meaning that if you do anything to change the size or shape of the underlying cells, the object adjusts accordingly. An underlying cell is any cell whose right or bottom border is between the upper left corner and the lower right corner of the object. Here are some things you need to know about the Object Positioning options:

- If you insert columns or rows to the left of an object formatted with the Move And Size With Cells option, the object moves accordingly.

● If you insert columns or rows between the first and last cells underlying an object formatted with the Move And Size With Cells option, the object stretches to accommodate the insertion.

● If you select the Move But Don't Size With Cells option and then insert or delete columns or rows, the object moves but retains its shape and proportion.

● If you select the Don't Move Or Size With Cells option, the object floats above the worksheet and isn't affected by any changes you make to the underlying cells.

● The Print Object option is normally turned on. If you turn it off, the selected object isn't printed when you print the worksheet.

---

tip   **Cut, copy, and sort objects with cells**

In addition to moving and sizing objects with cells, Excel allows you to control what happens when you cut, copy, or sort cells to which objects are attached. Choose Tools, Options, click the Edit tab, and then select or clear the Cut, Copy, And Sort Objects With Cells option.

Tools to Help You Position Objects on the Worksheet

It's great to be able to create cool graphics with Excel, but the free-floating nature of graphic objects sometimes makes it hard to maintain a semblance of order on your worksheet. The Draw menu contains several menus and tear-off palettes you can use to straighten things up. Here are some key points to remember about using these object positioning commands:

● To Grid, on the Snap submenu, uses the columns and rows of the worksheet to align objects. Pre-existing Objects don't line up with the grid when you choose this command, but as soon as you create or drag an object, it snaps to the nearest column and row borders.

● To Shape, on the Snap submenu, turns on the To Grid command when you choose it, activating its functionality. It adds to the virtual grid the edges of any existing objects, making it easy to align objects to one other. If you turn off the To Grid command, the To Shape command is turned off as well.

● Both the To Grid and To Shape commands, on the Snap submenu, are toggles—that is, you click once to turn them on and click again to turn them off.

- If you select an object and click any of the tools on the Nudge submenu, the object moves one pixel at a time in the direction you want.

- The Align Or Distribute submenu contains commands that operate only when two or more objects are selected, arranging the selected objects relative to each other.

---

tip   **Nudge with the keyboard**

You can also use the arrow keys on your keyboard—the functional equivalent of the Nudge buttons—to nudge objects one pixel at a time. If the To Grid command is turned on, pressing an arrow key moves the selected object to the next gridline in that direction.

The Align Or Distribute submenu can be a great help when you are working with multiple objects. Suppose you have a number of objects that you want to be evenly spaced. You could start by using the Align Top command to line up one row of objects, and then choose Distribute Horizontally to space them evenly. Then use the following Align Or Distribute commands to align the rest of the objects to the newly organized row.

- **Align Left.** Lines up the left edges of all selected objects with the left edge of the leftmost object selected.

- **Align Center.** Lines up the centers of objects along a vertical axis and finds the average common centerline of all selected objects.

- **Align Middle.** Lines up the centers of objects along a horizontal axis, and finds the average common middle line of all selected objects.

- **Distribute Horizontally and Distribute Vertically.** Calculates the total amount of space between the selected objects and divides the space as equally as possible among them. The first and last objects (leftmost and rightmost, or top and bottom) do not move—all the objects in between are adjusted as necessary.

Protecting Objects

You can prevent objects from being selected, moved, formatted, or sized by choosing Format, AutoShape, clicking the Protection tab, and selecting the Locked option. You can also use the Lock Text option, which is visible only when a text box is selected, to protect the text contents of a text box. Newly drawn objects are assigned Locked protection. However, to turn on worksheet security and protection for both text boxes and new objects, you must also choose Tools, Protection, Protect Sheet. For more information about protection, see "Protecting Worksheets" on page 127.

Controlling the Display of Objects

To speed up the scrolling of your worksheet, choose Tools, Options and click the View tab. In the Objects area of the View tab, Show All is normally selected. Selecting the Show Placeholders option reduces text boxes, button objects, and embedded charts to simple patterns that indicate their locations on the worksheet. Show Placeholders increases your scrolling speed because Excel doesn't have to redraw the objects every time you scroll to a new screen. You must turn on the Show All option before you print.

Hide All suppresses the display of objects entirely, increasing screen redraw speed even more. Although you cannot directly modify objects when Hide All is turned on, some actions still change them. If anything other than Don't Move Or Size With Cells is selected on the Properties tab of the Format AutoShape dialog box, the object responds to adjustments made to the column width or row height of underlying cells.

Inserting Other Objects

The Object command on the Insert menu gives you direct access to other applications you can use to create objects. The difference between inserting a picture and inserting an object is that a picture is always static and cannot be directly edited or updated (although you can copy it to another program and edit it there), whereas an inserted object retains a connection to its source application. You can open an embedded object for editing by double-clicking it.

When you choose Insert, Object, a dialog box appears with two tabs—Create New and Create From File. The Create New tab, shown in Figure 10-24, turns on an application and then creates the object directly in the selected application. You select an application in the Object Type list. The contents of this list box vary depending on the configuration of your system and the applications you have installed.

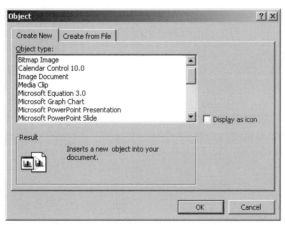

Figure 10-24. You can use the Create New tab of the Object dialog box to simultaneously insert an object and turn on the application used to create it.

Chapter 10

When you select an item in the Object Type list, a small frame is inserted in the current worksheet at the location of the active cell, and the application needed to create or edit that object type is started. For example, if you select Paintbrush Picture in the Object Type list, Microsoft Paint starts, and you can then create a new drawing or edit an existing one. Elements of the interface of the application you select appear without completely displacing the worksheet interface, as shown in Figure 10-25, in which we inserted a MIDI Sequence object. The degree to which this blending of interfaces occurs depends on the chosen application.

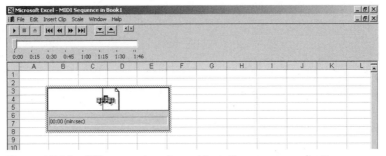

Figure 10-25. When you insert an object, the source application opens, but the Excel interface is still visible.

When you are finished editing the inserted object, click any cell in the worksheet to exit Edit mode. The object you created is inserted at the location of the active cell.

The Object dialog box's Create From File tab is shown in Figure 10-26. You can use this tab to insert an existing file as an object rather than create a new object with the Create New tab. (The object types you can embed depend on the applications installed in your computer.)

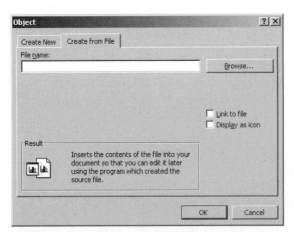

Figure 10-26. Use the Create From File tab of the Object dialog box to insert existing documents in your workbooks.

Chapter 10

Although the Link To File option on the Create From File tab isn't selected by default, you can still open the object in its source application by double-clicking it. If you select the Link To File option, the object is updated when the source file changes.

The Display As Icon option embeds the selected file in your workbook as an icon. This option is particularly convenient if an embedded object is long, large, or more easily viewed in its source application. However, if you distribute the workbook to other users, be sure the same application is available on their computers, or they will not be able to open the embedded icon for viewing.

To make changes to any embedded object, double-click the object. The source application starts and the object file opens, allowing you to make modifications.

Using Clip Art and Other Media

If you don't have the time or the inclination to create your own artwork using Excel's drawing tools, you can instantly call on the talents of numerous professional illustrators using the Insert Clip Art button on the Drawing toolbar. Clip art objects are similar to objects that you create using Excel's Drawing tools. You can resize, reposition, add borders, and sometimes even add fills and patterns to clip art objects. Besides art, you can also insert photographs, sounds, and movies into your spreadsheets for that extra wow factor. Click the Insert Clip Art button to display the Insert Clip Art task pane, shown in Figure 10-27. (Or you can choose Insert, Picture, Clip Art.)

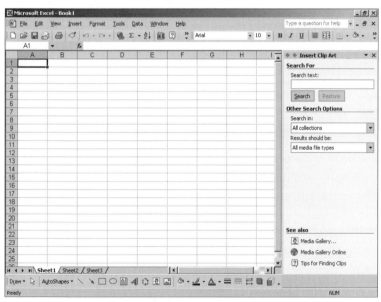

Figure 10-27. Use the Insert Clip Art task pane to add not only art, but photos, movies, or sounds to your worksheets.

newfeature!

The first time you click the Insert Clip Art button (or choose the command), Excel asks you if you want to index any existing media files that exist on your computer by displaying the Insert Clip Art dialog box . You can do this anytime later, if you prefer, or not at all. As you can see in Figure 10-28, this dialog box gives you a clue to the Insert Clip Art task pane's underlying technology, which is called the Microsoft Clip Organizer. If you click OK, the Clip Organizer catalogues everything it finds on your computer; if you click Options, the dialog box shown on the right in Figure 10-28 appears, allowing you to specify which folders you want the Clip Organizer to look in, as well as the ones you'd prefer it to ignore.

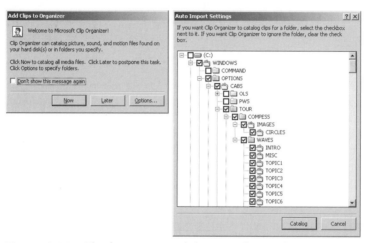

Figure 10-28. The first time you click Insert Clip Art the dialog box on the left appears. Clicking the Options button displays the dialog box on the right.

The media clips available via the Insert Clip Art task pane are catalogued not only by file name and file type, but also by keywords. Each of the media clips that come with Microsoft Office has a keyword already applied. For example, if you type **people** into the Search Text box in the Insert Clip Art task pane, a set of media clips similar to the ones in Figure 10-29 appears in the task pane. You can limit the search results by choosing items in the Search In and Results Should Be lists in the Insert Clip Art task pane, before clicking the Search button.

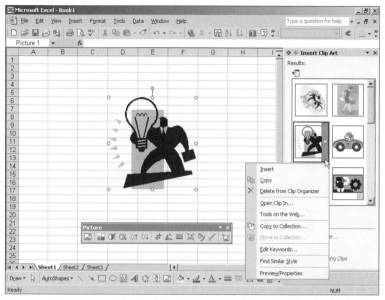

Figure 10-29. Search by keyword for a set of clips you can drag to the worksheet, or click the arrow bar on the right of a clip for a menu containing more options.

To use a clip in the Results list, drag it to the worksheet. When you hover the mouse pointer over a clip in the task pane, a gray bar with an arrow appears to the right. If you click the bar, a menu like the one in Figure 10-29 appears, giving you additional options you can apply to the selected clip. Many of the commands on this menu are self-explanatory; however, several commands could use some explanation.

- **Open Clip In** opens a different application and opens the clip for editing, if any compatible applications are registered on your computer.

- **Tools On The Web** connects you to the Microsoft Media Gallery Services Web site where, among other things, you can add additional collections of clips from the Web. Note that the Clips Online link at the bottom of the Insert Clip Art task pane also connects you to a Media Gallery Web site, although it is not necessarily the same site.

- **Copy/Move To Collection** adds or relocates the selected clip to one of your own collections, by displaying the Copy to Collection dialog box. You can create a new collection or add to an existing personal collection.

- **Edit Keywords** displays the dialog box shown in Figure 10-30 on the next page, where you can add or modify any keywords associated with the selected clip.

Chapter 10

- **Find Similar Style** searches for any clips that were created using a similar illustration style. Unfortunately, this depends on a style code embedded in each preinstalled clip, rather than a subjective artistic evaluation of the artwork (although this would probably involve a lot more computing power than most of us have on the desktop). Don't expect this command to work on clips you add from your own archives.

- **Preview/Properties** displays the Preview/Properties dialog box, which lists all the pertinent information about the clip. This is a handy way to find out the format of the clip, the keywords associated with it, and more.

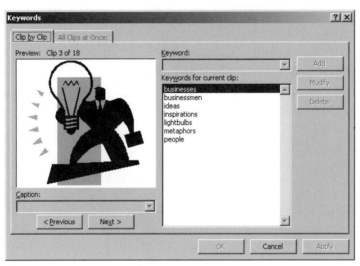

Figure 10-30. You can add or change keywords for the selected clip.

newfeature! Managing Your Clip Organizer Exhibitions

You can go straight to the source of the content displayed in the Insert Clip Art task pane by clicking the Clip Organizer link at the bottom of the task pane, which displays the dialog box similar to the one shown in Figure 10-31. (We first clicked Office Collections, and then Business, and then selected the Concepts category.) The contents of the Collection List might differ, depending on the clips catalogued on your system.

Chapter 10

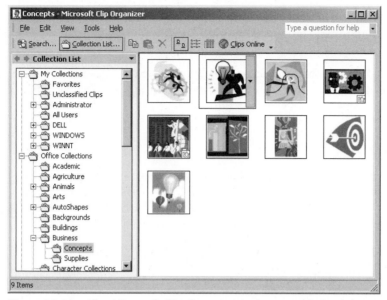

Figure 10-31. The Microsoft Clip Organizer is the wizard behind the curtain of the Import Clip Art task pane.

The Microsoft Clip Organizer isn't really a dialog box at all, but a separate application with its own interface and Help system. Although most of the functionality you need to manage your gallery is available in the menu shown in the task pane in Figure 10-29, these commands and more are also available in the menus and buttons of the Microsoft Clip Organizer. Here are a few highlights:

● Click the Search button to display a Search pane similar to the one in the Insert Clip Art task pane. Click the Collection List button to return to the list.

● Choose File, New Collection to create a new category in the Collection List. This command is only available when an icon in the My Collections group is selected.

● Choose File, Add Clips To Organizer to display the dialog box shown on the left in Figure 10-28, which enables you to catalog the clips on your computer. If you declined to do this the first time you clicked the Insert Clip Art button, you can do it this way whenever it's convenient.

● Choose File, Add Clips To Organizer, On My Own to display a dialog box similar to the Open dialog box in Excel, which you can use to locate and add specific items.

- Choose File, Add Clips To Organizer, From Scanner or Camera to open on your scanner or camera driver dialog box and import images directly from the source.

- Choose Tools, Compact to remove unused space. Clips that come with Microsoft Office XP are already compacted, but you can choose this command if you add your own clips.

Importing Graphics

You can import graphics into Excel from other programs that produce files compatible with the Windows Clipboard. There are several ways to do this, the simplest being to copy the image in the source program, and then choose Edit, Paste Special in Excel, allowing you to select from several options, as shown in Figure 10-32.

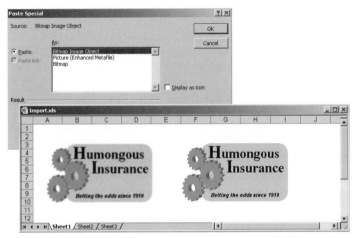

Figure 10-32. Images copied from other programs can usually be pasted in several formats using Edit, Paste Special; for example, the Bitmap Image Object format is shown on the left and the Picture format is shown on the right.

The image used in Figure 10-32 was copied from Microsoft Paint and pasted twice. First it was pasted in the default format, Bitmap Image Object, which is shown on the left. The image was pasted again using the Picture (Enhanced Metafile) format, shown on the right. As you can see, the detail is much crisper in the Picture (Enhanced Metafile) format image. This isn't to say that images are always best in Metafile format, just that you might want to try the available options to find the best results.

If the application used to create the graphic you want to import into Excel supports linking, you might be able to establish a link between the source file and the graphic. After you import the graphic into Excel, the link allows the graphic to be updated automatically if the source document changes. For more information about linking, see Chapter 21, "Linking and Embedding."

Inserting Pictures

The From File command (found by choosing Insert, Picture) allows you to embed in your workbooks graphics that have been saved in a variety of file formats in your workbooks. (The actual formats supported depend on your computer's configuration.)

The Insert Picture dialog box is functionally identical to the Open dialog box. Use the Look In box or the Navigation bar icons to the left to locate a particular graphic. The Files Of Type drop-down list allows you to zero in on a particular file type, but is set to All Pictures by default. You can choose different ways to look at files by clicking the Views button (to the left of the Tools menu button). Thumbnail view is the default. For more information about the Open dialog box, see "Opening Files" on page 44.

Inserting Organization Charts

Organization charts are used to show the chain of command in a company, or any other type of hierarchical organization. What used to require an expensive, dedicated software program can now be performed within Excel. Insert, Picture, Organization Chart inserts a rudimentary organization chart like the one shown in Figure 10-33, and displays the Organization Chart toolbar shown in Figure 10-34, which you can use to modify your freshly inserted organization chart.

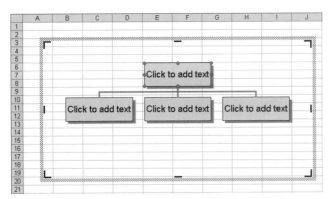

Figure 10-33. Insert, Picture, Organization Chart places a starter organization chart on your worksheet.

Insert Shape tear-off palette

AutoFormat

Figure 10-34. Use The Organization Chart toolbar to edit your organization charts.

Insert Shape is a tear-off menu you use to add more items to the organization chart. It contains three commands:

- **Subordinate** adds another box below the selected box.

- **Coworker** adds another box on the same level as the selected box.

- **Assistant** adds another box below the selected box, but offset, as shown in Figure 10-35.

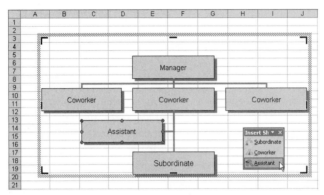

Figure 10-35. If you insert an Assistant box, it's offset from the flow of the organization chart.

The Layout menu on the Organization Chart toolbar offers a number of different standard configurations, and tools to help fit and scale the chart. The Select menu allows you to select a particular level or branch of the chart, or you can select only the assistants or the connecting lines, making formatting easier. The AutoFormat button displays the Organization Chart Style Gallery, which offers various combinations of layout and formatting.

Inserting Diagrams

When you click Insert, Diagram (or click the Insert Diagram or Organization Chart button on the Drawing toolbar), the Diagram Gallery dialog box appears, as shown in Figure 10-36. This figure also shows an example of the Target Diagram inserted on a worksheet.

> **note** The first diagram type shown in the Diagram Gallery is an organization chart, which you can also get by choosing Insert, Picture, Organization Chart, as discussed earlier.

You modify diagrams using essentially the same techniques you use to modify the layout and formatting of Organization Charts. When you select any diagram type and click OK, the corresponding diagram is inserted and the Diagram toolbar (shown in Figure 10-37) appears. This toolbar contains the same tools regardless of which type of diagram you insert, but the buttons look different, depending on the type of diagram.

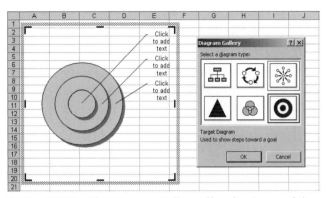

Figure 10-36. The Diagram Gallery offers five types of diagrams other than organization charts.

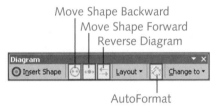

Figure 10-37. The Diagram toolbar.

The Diagram toolbar options are as follows:

- **Insert Shape** adds another copy of the standard shape to the selected diagram.

- **Move Shape Forward/Backward** changes the position of the selected item in the diagram. The name of the button is somewhat misleading, because the shape might not seem to move, but the labels shift, indicating that the labeled item has changed position.

- **Reverse Diagram** takes all items and labels and reorders them. Like the Move Shape buttons, the diagram might not change too much in appearance, but the labels indicate the reversal.

- **Layout** offers several commands to fit, scale, and change the layout.

- **AutoFormat** opens the Diagram Style Gallery dialog box. This dialog box, like the Organization Chart Style Gallery, offers a number of predesigned combinations of layouts and formats for the selected diagram type. There is a different set for each type of diagram. Figure 10-38 on the next page shows the gallery for the Target diagram.

- **Change To** converts the selected diagram to any one of the other diagram types.

321

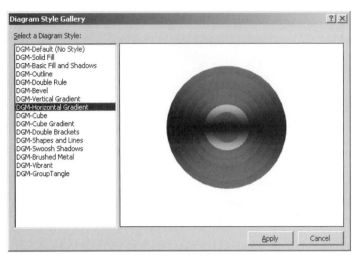

Figure 10-38. The Diagram Style Gallery offers a different set of AutoFormat options for each diagram type.

Inserting Scanned Images

Click Insert, Picture, From Scanner Or Camera to use an installed scanner or digital camera to provide a picture to insert. This button turns on the driver for your scanner or camera and opens its settings dialog box. For more information, see the instructions that came with your digital camera.

newfeature!
Formatting Pictures

In addition to AutoShapes and Text Boxes, you can add pictures to your worksheets using the Insert Picture command or the Insert Clip Art button. As with other types of graphic objects, you can size, position, and protect pictures, as well as add borders and control transparency. For more information about the Insert Picture command, see "Importing Graphics" on page 318. For more information about the Insert Clip Art button, see "Using Clip Art and Other Media" on page 313.

To format pictures, select an image and choose the first command on the Format menu—the name of this command changes depending on the type of object selected. For example, the image shown in Figure 10-39 is a pasted bitmap image. If you select it and choose Format, Picture (or double-click it), the Format Picture dialog box appears. This is similar to other object formatting dialog boxes, except that it includes a Picture tab.

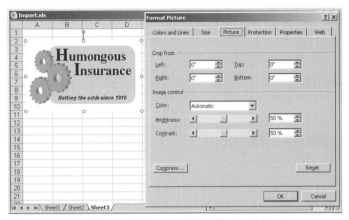

Figure 10-39. When a bitmap or Metafile is selected, you can choose Format, Picture to adjust image settings.

The Crop From settings on the Picture tab allow you to change the size of the image. This is easier to do using the Picture toolbar. The Color list in the Image Control area includes the following options:

- **Automatic** uses the original colors of the image and is the default.
- **Grayscale** changes any colors to their equivalent gray values.
- **Black & White** converts gray values less than 50 percent to white, and gray values more than 50 percent to black.
- **Washout** preserves colors but changes the brightness to 85 percent and the contrast to 15 percent, creating a watermark-like image.

The Brightness and Contrast sliders give you control over the exposure of inserted pictures. Click the Reset button to return all setting to their original values. Click the Compress button to display the Compress Pictures dialog box, which includes the following options:

- The Apply To options offer a handy way to compress all the images in your workbook at once, or only selected pictures.
- The Change Resolution options allow you to modify the resolution to Print resolution (200 dots per inch) or Web/Screen resolution (96 dots per inch).
- The Compress Pictures option applies the selected settings to the selected images.
- The Delete Cropped Areas Of Pictures option discards any non-visible portions of pictures you have cropped using the options on the Picture tab or the Crop button on the Picture toolbar. This is nonreversible.

Chapter 10

The Picture toolbar, shown in Figure 10-40, appears whenever you select a picture, unless you close it by clicking the Close button while a picture is selected. If this is the case, choose View, Toolbars, Picture to redisplay the Picture toolbar.

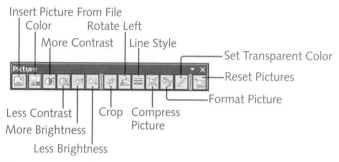

Figure 10-40. The Picture toolbar appears whenever a picture is selected.

The buttons on the Picture toolbar are as follows:

- **Insert Picture From File** displays the Insert Picture dialog box.

- **Color, Contrast, Brightness, and Reset Picture** duplicate the options of the same names on the Picture tab of the Format Picture dialog box.

- **Format Picture and Compress Picture** display the corresponding dialog boxes.

- **Rotate Left** duplicates one of the most-used commands on the Rotate or Flip submenu. (Even if you want to rotate right, you can just click this button a few more times to achieve the same effect.)

- **Line Style** displays a menu containing various point sizes and line types you can apply to the borders of the selected picture.

- **Compress Pictures** displays the Compress Pictures dialog box. For more information about the Compress Pictures dialog box, see "Formatting Pictures" on page 322.

- **Crop** duplicates options on the Picture tab, but it's much easier to use. Figure 10-41 shows that when you click the Crop button, special cropping handles appear on the selected picture. If you drag any of these handles, the size of the picture window changes, without changing the proportions of the image.

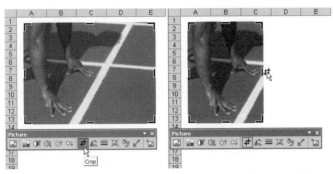

Figure 10-41. Use the Crop button to change the size of a picture window.

- **Set Transparent Color** specifies a color that becomes transparent. Often, this is used on white backgrounds in pictures like logos to allow the underlying information to show. Click the button and then click any color in the selected picture, as shown in Figure 10-42, to turn every pixel of that color transparent.

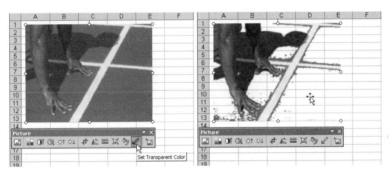

Figure 10-42. The Set Transparent Color button makes every pixel of the color you click turn invisible.

More Tricks With Objects

But wait, there's more! This section describes a few features that are hard to classify with the other drawing features. You can essentially turn any graphic object into a button by assigning a macro to it. In addition, you can take pictures of your worksheets, which can be used in other programs, or even used within Excel workbooks, where they can be either static bitmaps or dynamic windows that display what's happening in other areas of the workbook, or other workbooks.

Chapter 10

Assigning Macros to Objects

You can attach a macro to any object, allowing you to activate the macro by simply clicking the object. To attach a macro to an object, do the following:

1 Right-click the object and choose the Assign Macro command from the shortcut menu.

2 When the Assign Macro dialog box appears (shown in Figure 10-43), specify whether you want to record a new macro or assign an existing macro to the object.

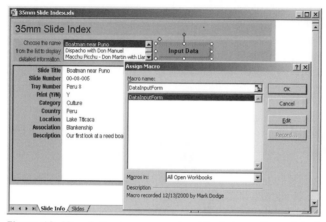

Figure 10-43. Assigning macros to objects turns them into buttons.

For more information about macros, see Part 10, "Working with Visual Basic and Macros."

Taking Pictures of your Worksheets

Excel provides techniques for taking pictures of your worksheets: the Camera button (which you can add to a toolbar), and the Copy Picture, Paste Picture, and Paste Picture Link commands that appear on the Edit menu if you press the Shift key before you choose Edit.

Using the Camera Button

Camera

With the Camera button, you can copy an image of a range of cells and paste the image anywhere in the same worksheet, another worksheet in the same workbook, or another workbook. Copying an image isn't the same as copying the cells with Edit, Copy. When you use the Camera button, you copy a linked image of the cells, not their contents. As a result, the image changes dynamically if the contents of the original cells change.

tip **Add the Camera button to a toolbar**

To add the Camera button to a toolbar, choose View, Toolbars, Customize. In the Customize dialog box, click the Commands tab, select the Tools category, and drag the Camera button onto any toolbar

Figure 10-44 shows two worksheets side by side. If you select the range G3:G16 in the Pacific Sales Summary worksheet and click the Camera button, the pointer changes from a plus sign to a cross hair. Click anywhere in Book1 to select it, and then click the cross-hair pointer where you want the upper left corner of the picture to appear. Excel embeds the picture as shown on the right in Figure 10-44.

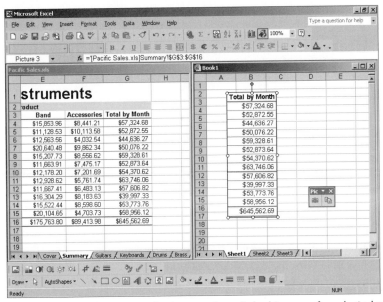

Figure 10-44. The Camera button creates a linked image of a selected range.

note Any graphic objects that might happen to be within or overlapping the selected range are also shown in the embedded picture.

After you paste the picture, you can change its size and proportions by dragging its selection handles and treat it just like any other graphic object. Changes in shape, size, or formatting do not affect the dynamic updating of the data displayed in the picture.

If you select the embedded picture, the formula bar displays a formula much like any other cell-linking formula, as shown in Figure 10-44. After you create the picture, you can edit the formula in the formula bar, and the picture changes accordingly. You can even change the reference formula to link a completely different worksheet or workbook. For example, we selected the embedded picture in Book1 and changed the

formula shown for the object from =ʻ[Pacific Sales.xls]Summary'!$G$3:$G$16 to
=ʻ[Pacific Sales.xls]Summary'!$F$3:$G$16. The picture adjusts to include the additional column, as shown in Figure 10-45. For more information about linking formulas, see "Using Cell References in Formulas" on page 356.

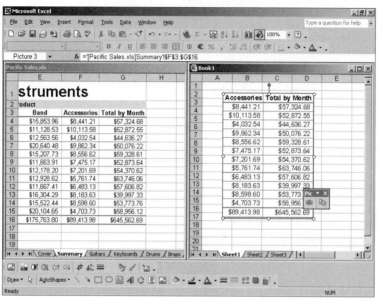

Figure 10-45. If you change the cell references in a formula for a picture
created with the Camera button, the picture changes accordingly.

The link between the source and destination documents has another distinctive and
useful characteristic. Suppose you close the Pacific Sales worksheet in Figure 10-44. If
you then double-click the embedded image in Book1, Pacific Sales opens automatically,
with the pictured range selected.

Using the Copy Picture and Paste Picture Commands

The Copy Picture command creates an image just as the Camera button does, but with
an important difference. The copied picture is static, with no links to any worksheet.
Static pictures are useful when you don't need to update data or when the speed with
which Excel recalculates the worksheet is more important. You can use the Copy Picture command to add images of worksheets and charts to reports or other documents
via the Clipboard. After you take the picture, you can paste it in another Excel document or in a document from any application that accepts Clipboard images.

To use the Copy Picture command, select the cells, object, or chart you want to copy,
hold down Shift, and choose Edit, Copy Picture. (When you hold down Shift, the Copy
command becomes Copy Picture, and the Paste command becomes Paste Picture.) The
options in the Copy Picture dialog box are as follows:

- The default option, As Shown On Screen, reproduces the selection at the moment you take the picture.

- The As Shown When Printed option reproduces the selection according to the settings in the Page Setup dialog box that control the printing of gridlines and row and column headings.

- The Picture option copies the picture in a format that can be displayed on monitors with different resolutions. This is useful if the picture will be viewed on different computers.

- The Bitmap option copies the picture in a format that is correct only when the display resolution is the same as the screen from which it was copied.

After you copy an image to the Clipboard, you can paste the image anywhere you want—in another location on the worksheet, in another worksheet, or even in a document from another application. You can paste the image into an Excel document with the Paste command, the Paste Picture command, or the Paste button on the Standard toolbar.

The Paste Picture command is similar to Copy Picture, except that you don't see the Copy Picture dialog box. Instead, the image is pasted using the As Shown When Printed option as the default format. To use this command, copy any cell or range using your favorite copying technique, and then hold down Shift and choose Edit, Paste Picture.

There is one more command that appears on the Edit menu when you hold down Shift: Paste Picture Link. This command creates a linked image just like the Camera button does, except that the resulting image also uses the As Shown When Printed format instead of the As Shown on Screen option, as the Camera button does.

Gallery of Spiffy Examples

This section includes just a few samples of what you can do in Excel. With the exception of a couple of scanned personal photos, all the effects represented here were created with the tools and clip art that come with Excel.

Figure 10-46 on the next page shows a logo for a fictitious company called Fabrikam, Inc. The logo was created using the following buttons on the Drawing toolbar:

- The Insert Diagram or Organization Chart button, Target Diagram

- The Arrow button

- The Line button

- The Rectangle button

- The Shadow Style button
- The Format AutoShape button.

Figure 10-46. A different use for a diagram.

The Pacific Musical Instruments logo shown in Figure 10-47 was created on a page with a picture applied to the background by choosing Format, Sheet, Background. Otherwise, the following tools on the Drawing toolbar were used to create the logo:

- The Text Box button.
- AutoShapes, More AutoShapes.
- Draw, Rotate or Flip, Flip Horizontal.
- The Shadow Style button.

Figure 10-47. You can do a lot with AutoShapes and Text Boxes.

Figure 10-48 shows a picture applied to the background using Format, Sheet, Background, and the following tools on the Drawing toolbar:

- AutoShapes, Callouts, Oval Callout, and Cloud Callout.
- The Fill Color button

Figure 10-48. Your friendly authors, mugging for the camera.

The Morgan Park Zoo worksheet in Figure 10-49 has an interesting argyle background created by first selecting A1:E4 and enlarging the cells by changing row heights and column widths. With the cell range still selected, we then chose Format, Cells, clicked the Border tab, and clicked both diagonal border preset buttons. Then we clicked the Patterns tab and selected a fill color. The rest of the work was done with the following tools on the Drawing toolbar:

● The Insert Clip Art button

● The Rectangle button

● The Text Box button

● The Fill Color button's Fill Effects command

Figure 10-49. You can use cell borders to create patterned backgrounds.

Figure 10-50 on the next page shows a logo for a fictitious company called Photo Cell that includes a personal photo inserted using Insert Picture, From File. Otherwise, the logo was created using the following tools on the Drawing toolbar:

- The Text Box button
- The Rectangle button
- The Line Style button
- The Shadow Style button
- The Insert WordArt button

And the following buttons on the WordArt toolbar:

- The Format WordArt, Colors and Lines, Fill Color, Fill Effects, Picture tab
- The WordArt Same Letter Heights button
- The WordArt Alignment, Stretch Justify button
- The WordArt Character Spacing, Kern Character Pairs button

Figure 10-50. You can apply a picture to WordArt as a fill color.

Figure 10-51 shows the City Power & Light logo, which makes maximum use of WordArt and its special diamond handles that allow you to change a particular dimension. In this case, we changed the angle of the italic slant in the slogan to match the swoosh in the clip art. The logo was created using the following tools on the Drawing toolbar:

- The Insert Clip Art button
- The Insert WordArt button

And the following buttons on the WordArt toolbar:

- The Format WordArt button
- The WordArt Shape button

Figure 10-51.   WordArt and clip art make a powerful combination.

Any of the graphics shown in this section can be used in workbooks, or you can use Copy Picture to copy and paste them into other documents created in other applications. For more information about the Copy Picture command, see "Using the Copy Picture and Paste Picture Commands" on page 328.

Printing and Presenting

Microsoft Excel makes it easy for you to produce polished, professional-looking reports. In this chapter, we explain how to define the layout of your printed pages, control page breaks, preview your pages for printing, and use the Report Manager. This chapter concentrates on printing worksheets, but with a few refinements, you can apply the procedures to printing charts.

> For more information about printing charts, see Chapter 24, "Basic Charting Techniques."

Controlling the Appearance of Your Pages

To set options affecting the appearance of your printed pages, choose File, Page Setup. The various tabs of the Page Setup dialog box let you set your printout's orientation, scaling, margins, headers and footers, and page numbering.

Setting Page Options

The Page tab in the Page Setup dialog box is the one you'll use most often; it contains settings that control page orientation, scaling, paper size, print quality, and page numbering. Figure 11-1 on the next page shows the Page Setup dialog box, which you display by choosing File, Page Setup.

Printing Wide or Tall

On the Page tab of the Page Setup dialog box, the Orientation setting determines whether Excel prints your worksheet vertically (using the Portrait setting) or horizontally (using the Landscape setting). When you select Portrait, pages have more room for rows but less room for columns. This setting is the default. Select Landscape if you have more columns but fewer rows on each page.

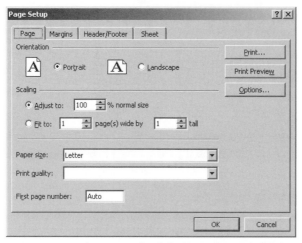

Figure 11-1. The Page tab of the Page Setup dialog box contains options, such as orientation, scaling, paper size, print quality, and page numbering.

Setting a Reduction Ratio

Using the Scaling setting on the Page tab of the Page Setup dialog box, you can override the default size of your printouts in one of two ways: by specifying a scaling factor (from 10 percent through 400 percent) or by fitting the report to a specified number of pages. Excel always scales in both the horizontal and vertical dimensions. For example, if the full size of your print area is two pages deep but only one page wide and you tell Excel to scale it to a single page, the resulting printout will be both narrower and shallower. The Fit To Page options are a great way to print a sheet that is normally just a bit too large to fit onto a single printed page. Without the Fit To Page feature, you spend a lot of time reformatting to smaller fonts or changing column widths and row heights. If you want to return to a full-size printout after selecting a scaling option, you can select the Adjust To option and type **100** in the % Normal Size box.

Specifying Paper Size and Print Quality

The Paper Size and Print Quality drop-down lists include the options available for your printer driver. Your laser printer, for example, might offer print-quality settings of 600 dpi, 300 dpi, and 150 dpi. Higher dpi settings look better but take longer to print. You might also be able to adjust these settings and more, using your printer driver's dialog box, which you can access by clicking the Options button on the Page tab of the Page Setup dialog box.

For more information about printer drivers, see "Setting Printer Driver Options" on page 351.

newfeature!

AutoLetter/A4 Paper Resizing

Excel now includes help for folks who routinely share work across international borders. In much of the world, the standard paper size is Letter (8 1/2 x 11 in.), but A4 paper (210 x 297mm) is also widely used. Now you can print sheets set for A4 paper size on printers loaded with standard Letter size paper (and vice versa), and Excel adjusts the page setup accordingly. Excel does this on-the-fly, without changing the page size setting in the Page Setup dialog box. If you want to turn this feature off, choose Tools, Options, and on the International tab, clear the Allow A4/Letter Paper Resizing check box.

Setting the First Page Number

If you want to add page numbers to your printout's header or footer—an essential element when printing multipage worksheets—use the First Page Number box on the Page tab of the Page Setup dialog box. You can enter any starting number, including 0 or negative numbers. By default, this option is set to Auto, but you can change it to any number you want.

Setting Margins

You can adjust the margins of your printouts to allow the maximum amount of data to fit on a page, and to customize the amount of space available for headers, footers, or to accommodate special requirements, such as three-hole-punched paper. The Margins tab of the Page Setup dialog box gives you control over the top, bottom, left, and right margins of your printed worksheets. As shown in Figure 11-2, the default settings are 1 inch for the top and bottom margins and 0.75 inch for the left and right margins.

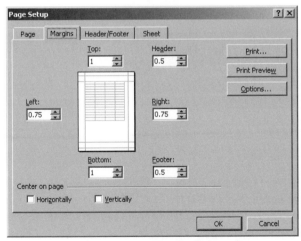

Figure 11-2. You can set the top, bottom, left, and right margins for your worksheets on the Margins tab of the Page Setup dialog box.

Chapter 11

337

When you click in any of the boxes on the Margins tab, a line appears in the sample page, displayed in the middle of the dialog box, showing you where the selected margin will appear.

If you want a header or footer to appear on each page, the top and bottom margins need to be large enough to accommodate them. For more information about setting up a header and footer, see the next section."

Centering Your Work on the Page

Excel aligns sheets to the upper left corner of the printed page by default. If you want Excel to center your printout on the page vertically, horizontally, or both, select the Center On Page options at the bottom of the dialog box (refer to Figure 11-2).

Creating a Header and Footer

On the Header/Footer tab of the Page Setup dialog box, you can provide essential information about your printout—such as file name, creation date, page number, and author's name—by including a header (printed at the top of each page) or footer (printed at the bottom of each page). By default, Excel prints footers .5 inch from the bottom edge and headers .5 inch from the top edge, but you can change this on the Margins tab of the Page Setup dialog box.

Initially, the drop-down lists that appear immediately under the words Header and Footer in the dialog box shown in Figure 11-3 offer predefined options you can use to customize your headers and footers. When you highlight an option in the drop-down list, the preview area adjacent to the list displays a sample of the selected option.

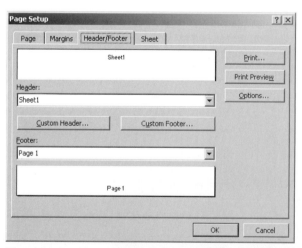

Figure 11-3. You can choose from predefined headers and footers or create your own using the Header/Footer tab of the Page Setup dialog box.

338

Creating Custom Headers and Footers

If you don't find what you need in the list of predefined headers and footers, you can create your own or modify one of Excel's. If you create custom headers or footers for the current workbook, Excel adds them to these drop-down lists. Click the Custom Header button to open the Header dialog box, shown in Figure 11-4, or the Custom Footer button to open a similar dialog box.

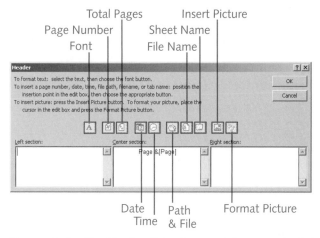

Figure 11-4. The Header dialog box contains many tools to make creating a header a snap.

---

tip   **Create a default header and footer**

If you want your header and footer to be the same on every workbook you create, you can create a default header and footer. Open a new, blank workbook, and set the header and footer the way you want them to be every time. Next, save the workbook using the name Book.xls. Store this file in the XLStart folder. Whenever you open a new workbook, it will have your header and footer already in place. For more information on the XLStart folder, see "Adding Templates to the XLStart Folder" on page 255.

Excel uses various codes to represent information that you might want to put in your headers and footers—such as the current time, current date, and current page number. Fortunately, you don't have to learn these codes to create headers and footers. Click the appropriate box (Left Section, Center Section, or Right Section) to indicate where you want the information to appear, and then click the appropriate buttons to add the information to your header or footer. Here's what each button does:

● **Font.** Displays the Font dialog box, allowing you to specify font and font style for the selected text.

339

● **Page Number.** Inserts page number in the selected section.

● **Total Pages.** Inserts the total number of pages in the selected section; typically used in conjunction with the page number in a "Page X of Y" construction.

● **Date.** Inserts the date of printing in the selected section.

● **Time.** Inserts the time of printing in the selected section.

● **Path & File.** Inserts the folder path and file name of the workbook in the selected section.

● **File Name.** Inserts only the file name of the current workbook in the selected section.

● **Sheet Name.** Inserts the name of the current worksheet in the selected section.

● **Insert Picture.** Displays the Insert Picture dialog box, allowing you to add a picture to the selected section.

● **Format Picture.** Displays the Format Picture dialog box, allowing you to adjust settings of an inserted picture.

To specify text in your header or footer, click the appropriate edit box and type your text. To divide the text between two or more lines, press Enter at the end of each line. To include an ampersand in your text, type two ampersands.

newfeature! Adding Pictures to Headers and Footers

You can now add pictures to custom headers and footers using the Insert Picture and Format Picture buttons (refer to Figure 11-4). Click the Insert Picture button to access the Insert Picture dialog box, which you use to locate the picture you want to use. When you insert the picture, Excel displays &[Picture] in the section box of the Header (or Footer) dialog box. (Unlike other header and footer codes, you can't just type in this code—you have to use the Insert Picture button.)

After you insert the picture, click the Format Picture button to specify the size, brightness, and contrast of the picture and to rotate, scale, or crop the picture. (You can't directly manipulate Header or Footer pictures—you must use the Format Picture button.) It might take some trial and error to obtain the result you want, adjusting the size of the picture as well as the top or bottom margins to accommodate it. Figure 11-5 shows a sample of a picture used in a header, displayed in Print Preview.

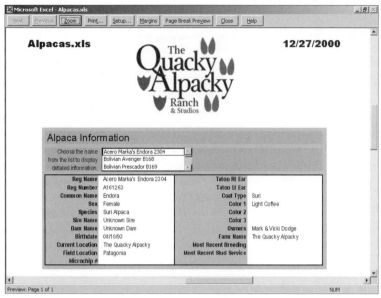

Figure 11-5. You can manipulate the fonts and even add pictures to headers and footers.

To arrive at the example shown in Figure 11-5, we did the following:

- Left section: File name added, Font changed to 16-point Arial Black

- Center section: Picture inserted, scaled to 61 percent

- Right section: Date added, Font changed to 16-point Arial Black

- On the Margins tab of the Page Setup dialog box, the Top margin set to 2.5 inches and Center On Page set to Horizontally.

Changing Fonts in Headers and Footers

Excel's default font for headers and footers is 10-point Arial. To select a different type-face, point size, or font style, select the code or text in the section you want to change and click the Font button to access the Font dialog box. Note that font options you select apply only to the highlighted code in the section box. You can assign different font options to each section, even to individual elements within each section.

Setting Sheet Options

The Sheet tab of the Page Setup dialog box, shown in Figure 11-6, controls settings specific to the active sheet. You can specify different sheet options for each sheet in a workbook.

Chapter 11

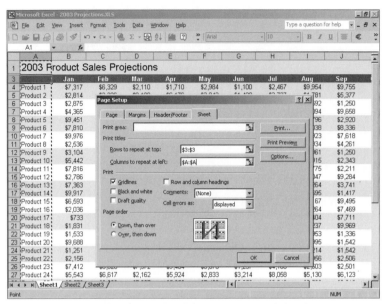

Figure 11-6. Use the Sheet tab of the Page Setup dialog box to set row and column titles to print on each page of your worksheet.

Specifying Rows and Columns to Print on Every Page

On many worksheets, the column and row labels that identify information categories are located in only the first couple of columns and top few rows. When Excel breaks up a large report into pages, those important column and row labels might appear only on the first page of the printout. You can use the Sheet tab of the Page Setup dialog box to force Excel to print the contents of one or more columns, one or more rows, or a combination of columns and rows on every page of a report. (This used to be known as the *Print Titles* feature. This was actually the name of a command that achieved the same result.)

Suppose you want to print the contents of column A and row 3 on all pages of a lengthy report. First, click the Rows To Repeat At Top box, and then click the row 3 heading, or any cell in row 3. (To select multiple contiguous row headings, drag through them.) The dialog box collapses to give you more room; to redisplay the full dialog box, click the button on the right side of the box. Click the Columns To Repeat At Left box, and then select the column A heading or any cell in column A. Figure 11-6 shows the result.

> **note** In some earlier versions of Excel, you had to be careful to exclude print title columns and rows from the print area—that is, the area of the worksheet that you were asking Excel to print. Otherwise, your titles would appear twice: once as titles and once as part of the print area. Recent versions of Excel are smart enough to recognize when print titles fall within the print area.

If you prefer to type your entries, you can enter the row numbers or column letters in the Rows To Repeat At Top box and the Columns To Repeat At Left box. To specify rows 3 and 4, for example, type **3:4**. To specify column A, type **A:A**. Note that for a single row or column, you have to type the number or letter twice, separated by a colon. You can specify separate print titles for each worksheet in your workbook. Excel remembers the titles for each worksheet.

> **note** To remove print titles, you can go back to the Page Setup dialog box and delete the title specifications. However, you might find it quicker to use the Define Name dialog box. To use the Define Name dialog box, press Ctrl-F3 and delete the name Print_Titles.

Printing Gridlines

By default, Excel does not print gridlines, regardless of whether you have them displayed on your worksheet. If you want to print gridlines, select the Gridlines check box on the Sheet tab of the Page Setup dialog box.

Printing Comments

Comments are annotations created by selecting Insert, Comment. To make sure the comments in your worksheet are included with your printout, select one of the Comments options on the Sheet tab of the Page Setup dialog box. If you select At End Of Sheet from the drop-down list, Excel adds a page to the end of the printout and prints all your notes together, starting on that new page. If you select As Displayed On Sheet, Excel prints the comments where they are located on a worksheet.

> For more on creating cell notes, see "Adding Comments to Cells" on page 266.

Printing Drafts

If your printer offers a draft-quality mode, you can obtain a quicker, though less attractive, printout by selecting the Draft Quality option on the Sheet tab of the Page Setup dialog box. This option has no effect if your printer has no draft-quality mode and is most useful for dot matrix or other slow printers.

Translating Screen Colors to Black and White

If you've assigned colors and patterns to your worksheet but you're using a black-and-white printer, you'll probably want to select the Black And White option on the Sheet tab of the Page Setup dialog box, which tells Excel to use only black and white when printing.

Chapter 11

Printing Row and Column Headings

If you select the Row And Column Headings option on the Sheet tab of the Page Setup dialog box, Excel prints row letters to the left of and column numbers on top of worksheet data. This option is handy when you're using printouts to document the structure of a worksheet.

Setting the Printing Order of Large Print Ranges

When you print a large report, Excel breaks the report into page-size sections based on the current margin and page-size settings. If the print range is both too wide and too deep to fit on a single page, Excel normally works in "down, and then over" order. For example, suppose your print range measures 120 rows by 20 columns and Excel can fit 40 rows and 10 columns on a page. Excel prints the first 40 rows and first 10 columns on page 1, the second 40 rows and first 10 columns on page 2, and the third 40 rows and first 10 columns on page 3. On page 4, Excel prints the first 40 rows and second 10 columns, and so on. If you prefer to have Excel print each horizontal chunk before moving down to the next vertical chunk, select the Over, Then Down option on the Sheet tab of the Page Setup dialog box.

Adjusting Page Breaks

Excel makes it easy to adjust the positions of page breaks. You can do this by selecting View, Page Break Preview. The resulting preview is shown in Figure 11-7. You can move page breaks by dragging them with the mouse. You can even edit your worksheet while in Page Break Preview mode.

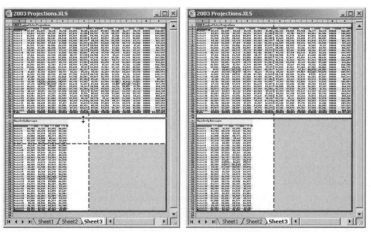

Figure 11-7. Page Break Preview shows default page breaks with dashed lines, which you can reposition by dragging with your mouse.

Using Page Break Preview allows you to see both the positions of your page breaks and the page numbers Excel will use when you print. Default page breaks—the ones that

Excel proposes to use if you don't intervene—appear as dashed lines. If you're not happy with the position of a default break, drag the line, as shown on the left in Figure 11-7. Your page break then becomes a manual page break, displayed as a solid line, as shown on the right in Figure 11-7. To return from Page Break Preview to Normal view, choose View, Normal.

---

tip   **Lose the dashed lines**

After you set your page breaks, Excel displays them in Normal view as dashed lines. If you'd rather not see these lines, choose Tools, Options, click the View tab, and then clear the Page Breaks check box.

If you attempt to extend the dimensions of a page beyond the maximum width or depth according to the current page setup, Excel scales the sheet to make it fit and displays the Adjusted values in the Scaling options shown on the Page tab of the Page Setup dialog box.

Inserting and Removing Manual Page Breaks

Spreadsheet pagination can be problematic, given the fact that rows and columns of numbers often don't fit into the 8-1/2 x 11 world of printing. This is why Excel provides yet another method you can use to manually adjust page breaks. To add a page break, select any cell of the row directly beneath or in the column directly to the right of where you want the break to occur, and then choose Insert, Page Break. If you select a cell where data appears both below and to the right, Excel applies page breaks both horizontally and vertically. To remove a break, position your mouse in the row below a horizontal break, or in the column to the right of a vertical break, and then choose Insert, Remove Page Break.

Troubleshooting

My Manual Page Breaks Don't Work

In the Page Setup dialog box, selecting the Fit To option on the Page tab can cause Excel to override manual page breaks. Fit To applies reduction sufficient to fit the entire print area into a specific number of pages. To derail this override, switch to the Adjust To option. This allows the worksheet to print according to your manual page breaks.

If you prefer the compressed Fit To "look" but still want to control page breaks, you can define the print area using multiple nonadjacent ranges—one range per page. Excel automatically prints each nonadjacent range as a separate page. There is one catch: Excel requires you to insert a blank row or column wherever you want a page break. Then you select the first range, hold down Ctrl, and select the next range. Select as many ranges (pages) as you want. Then choose File, Print Area, Set Print Area.

---

tip   **Remove all page breaks**

To reset all the page breaks on a worksheet, click the header cell at the intersection of the row and column headers to select the entire sheet, and choose Insert, Reset All Page Breaks.

Using Print Preview

The Print Preview feature gives you a glimpse of your worksheets the way they will look on paper. You can check the effect of page breaks, margins, and formatting before you needlessly waste paper with multiple test printouts. To access Print Preview, use one of the following methods:

- Choose File, Print Preview.

- Click the Print Preview button on the Standard toolbar.

- Shift-click the Print button on the Standard toolbar.

- Click the Preview button in the Print dialog box or the Print Preview button in the Page Setup dialog box.

If you're not satisfied with the appearance of your worksheet, you can access most page layout settings from within Print Preview. Click the Setup button to display the Page Setup dialog box and change any page setting.

You can also change the margins and column widths without leaving Print Preview by clicking the Margins button, as shown in Figure 11-8. To adjust a margin, drag a dotted line; to adjust a column's width, drag the column handle. As you drag, the page-number indicator in the lower left corner of the screen changes to display the name and setting for the margin or the width of the selected column. To turn off the display of margin lines and column handles, click the Margins button again.

The following buttons help you to move around within Print Preview mode:

- You can move forward or backward a page at a time by clicking the Next and Previous buttons or by pressing Page Up and Page Down. Alternatively, to move more quickly through a long document, drag the scroll box. As you drag, Excel displays the current page number in the lower left corner of the Print Preview screen.

- Click the Zoom button to display the page in roughly 100 percent Zoom— the same size that you see in Normal view. Click the Zoom button to return to the normal Print Preview whole-page view. Alternatively, you don't need to use the Zoom button at all. Click anywhere (except on a displayed margin line) and the preview zooms in; click anywhere in zoomed mode and the preview returns to whole-page view.

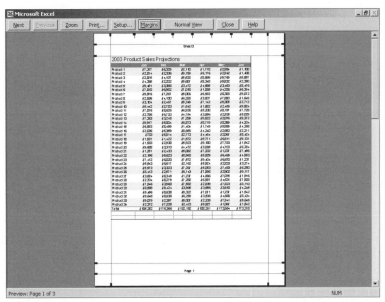

Figure 11-8. You can change the margins of a worksheet displayed in Print Preview by clicking the Margins button.

- Next to the Close button is a button entitled either Normal View or Page Break Preview, depending on the view you were using when you went into Print Preview. If you were working in Normal view when you opened Print Preview, the button is entitled Page Break Preview. If you were in Page Break Preview when you opened Print Preview, the button is called Normal View. This button opens the corresponding view when you click it.

After you're satisfied with the appearance of your document, you can click the Print button to print the document, or you can click Close to leave Print Preview and return to the previous view.

Specifying What and Where to Print

Click the Print button on the Standard toolbar, and the entire active area of the current worksheet is immediately sent to the printer. For all but the most basic of worksheets, you'll probably need to provide a bit more information, beginning with specifying exactly what you want to print. To do so, choose File, Print to display the Print dialog box.

You can print only a particular range of pages by entering the starting and ending page numbers in the From and To boxes in the Print Range area of the Print dialog box, shown in Figure 11-9 on the next page.

Chapter 11

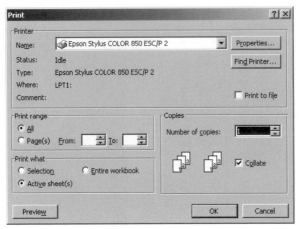

Figure 11-9. Use the Print dialog box to tell Excel what you want to print and how many copies you want.

The Print dialog box contains these additional options for specifying what, where, and how you want Excel to print:

- **Entire Workbook.** Print the entire workbook, not just the current worksheet.

- **Active Sheet(s).** Print a group of worksheets but not the entire workbook. To do so, first select the worksheets you want to print as a group before choosing File, Print. For more information about selecting a group of worksheets, see "Editing Multiple Worksheets" on page 187.

- **Selection.** Print any selected range of a worksheet.

- **Copies.** Specify the number of copies you want. You can instruct Excel to print up to 32,767 copies at a time.

- **Collate.** If your worksheet is more than one page long and you plan to print multiple copies, have Excel collate the copies for you. For example, instead of printing 5 copies of page 1, followed by 5 copies of page 2, Excel prints page 1 and page 2 together, prints the next set, and so on. Collated copies are more convenient but might take slightly longer to print.

- **Print to File.** Send the selected data to a file on disk, instead of to the printer.

tip **Find a printer on the network**

The Find Printer button shown in Figure 11-9 is useful when you are connected to a network, running Windows 2000 or later, and using Windows Active Directory Service. Click this button to search for all the printers that are available anywhere on your network.

The Name box of the Print dialog box displays the name of your default printer. To use a different printer, click the down arrow to display a list of available printers and then select the printer you want to use.

Printing to a File

The Print To File check box is in many ways an anachronism—a remnant of computing days of yore. It was often used to facilitate batch printing—that is, unattended print-ing of multiple files—back when print spooling was less widespread. You can still use Print To File if you want to print a document from a different computer on which Excel isn't installed.

When you print to a file, Excel sends the same stream of data that would normally go straight to your printer into a file on your hard disk. This isn't an Excel document file, but a printer document file. Excel saves all the necessary information from your docu-ment so that line and page breaks, spacing, and fonts (hopefully) remain the same. Unfortunately, your results can vary depending on the type of printer, the fonts you use, and the complexity of your document. For this reason, it's advisable to test printer files before relying on them for critical work.

Here's the key to making this process work: you have to use MS-DOS to send the file to your printer. In Windows 9x, you can access MS-DOS by choosing Start, Programs, MS-DOS Prompt; in Windows 2000, choose Start, Programs, Accessories, Command Prompt. At the command prompt, type

```
copy <file name> lpt1: /b
```

This assumes that the printer file is located in the same directory where you are issuing the command. You can, of course, get around this assumption by specifying a full path name instead of just a file name.

Defining a Default Print Area

When using the Active Sheet(s) option in the Print dialog box, Excel checks to see whether you have assigned the range name Print_Area on each specified sheet. If you have, Excel prints only the range to which you've assigned the name. Otherwise, Excel prints the entire active area of the selected sheet(s). If you expect to print the same area of a given sheet repeatedly, you can save yourself some steps by defining the print area. Here are the easiest ways to define the print area in Excel:

- Select the range you want to define and then choose File, Print Area, Set Print Area.

  OR

- Choose File, Page Setup, and on the Sheet tab, enter the cell range you want to print in the Print Area box.

Chapter 11

349

For more information about defining range names, see "Naming Cells and Cell Ranges" on page 371.

Suppose you have a workbook that is crowded with data, but each sheet in the work-book includes only a small area of summary information that you need to print. You can define a unique print area on each sheet in a workbook. If you select two or more sheets and print using the Active Sheet(s) option, Excel prints only the area of each sheet where you have defined a print area and prints the entire active area of any selected sheets where you haven't defined a print area.

---

tip   Take advantage of quick printing

To bypass the Print dialog box, click the Print button on the Standard toolbar or Shift-click the Print Preview button. Excel prints using the default Active Sheet(s) option.

No More Blank Page Printing

In previous versions of Excel, a sheet like the one shown here would print on four pages of paper. Only three pages include content, but the fourth page still would have printed, either as a blank page or as a page containing nothing but gridlines (if you opted to print gridlines).

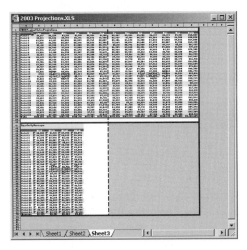

Excel 2002, however, includes something called Intelliprint, which looks at the content of the sheet and attempts to determine whether you really want the page to print. In this case, only three pages print—as you would hope.

Setting Printer Driver Options

Occasionally while working in Excel, you might need to set options that only your printer driver provides. For example, you might need to switch from automatic to manual paper feed or from one paper tray to another. You can do this by choosing Start, Settings, Printers, right-clicking the appropriate printer, and then choosing Properties. You can also set many of these options from within Excel by clicking the Properties button in the Print dialog box (refer to Figure 11-9) to open a version of the printer driver dialog box for the selected printer.

Part 5

Creating Formulas and Performing Data Analysis

Chapter 12

Building Formulas

Formulas are the heart and soul of a spreadsheet, and
Microsoft Excel offers a rich environment in which to build
complex formulas. Armed with a few mathematical operators
and rules for cell entry, you can turn a worksheet into a powerful calculator.

Formula Fundamentals

All formulas in Excel begin with an equal sign. The equal sign
tells Excel that the succeeding characters constitute a formula.
If you omit the equal sign, Excel might interpret the entry
as text.

To see how formulas work, we'll walk through some rudimentary ones. Begin by selecting blank cell A10. Then type **=10+5**
and press Enter. The value 15 appears in cell A10. Now select
cell A10, and the formula bar displays the formula you just
entered. What appears in the cell is the displayed value; what
appears in the formula bar is the underlying value, which in
this case is a formula.

Understanding the Precedence of Operators

Operators are symbols that represent specific mathematical
operations, including the plus sign (+), minus sign (-), division sign (/), and multiplication sign (*). When performing
these operations in a formula, Excel follows certain rules
of precedence:

- Expressions within parentheses are processed first.

- Multiplication and division are performed before
  addition and subtraction.

- Consecutive operators with the same level of precedence are calculated from left to right.

Enter some formulas to see how these rules apply. Select an empty cell and type
=4+12/6. Press Enter, and you see the value 6. Excel first divides 12 by 6 and then adds
the result (2) to 4. If Excel used different precedence rules, the result would be different. For example, select another empty cell and type =(4+12)/6. Press Enter, and you
see the value 2.666667. This demonstrates how you can change the order of precedence
using parentheses. The formulas in Table 12.1 contain the same values and operators,
but note the different results because of the placement of parentheses:

Table 12-1. Placement of Parentheses

Formula	Result
=3*6+12/4-2	19
=(3*6)+12/(4-2)	24
=3*(6+12)/4-2	11.5
=(3*6+12)/4-2	5.5
=3*(6+12/(4-2))	36

If you do not include a closing parenthesis for each opening parenthesis in a formula,
Excel displays the message "Microsoft Excel found an error in this formula" and provides a suggested solution. If the suggestion matches what you had in mind, simply
press Enter and Excel completes the formula for you.

When you type a closing parenthesis, Excel briefly displays the pair of parentheses in
bold. This feature is handy when you are entering a long formula and are not sure
which pairs of parentheses go together.

---

tip   **When in doubt, use parentheses**

If you are unsure of the order in which Excel will process a sequence of operators, use
parentheses—even if the parentheses aren't necessary. Parentheses also make your
formulas easier to read and interpret, which is helpful if you or someone else needs to
change them later.

Using Cell References in Formulas

A *cell reference* identifies a cell or group of cells in a workbook. When you include cell
references in a formula, the formula is linked to the referenced cells. The resulting
value of the formula is dependent on the values in the referenced cells and changes
automatically when the values in the referenced cells change.

To see cell referencing at work, select cell A1 and type the formula =**10*2**. Now select cell A2, and type the formula =**A1**. The value in both cells is 20. If at any time you change the value in cell A1, the value in cell A2 changes also. Now select cell A3, and type =**A1+A2**. Excel returns the value 40. Cell references are especially helpful when you create complex formulas.

Entering Cell References with the Mouse

You can save time and increase accuracy when you enter cell references in a formula by selecting them with the mouse. For example, to enter references to cells A9 and A10 in a formula in cell B10, do the following:

1 Select cell B10, and type an equal sign.

2 Click cell A9, and type a plus sign.

3 Click cell A10, and press Enter.

When you click each cell, a marquee surrounds the cell and a reference to the cell is inserted in cell B10. After you finish entering a formula, be sure to press Enter. If you do not press Enter and select another cell, Excel assumes that you want to include the cell reference in the formula.

The active cell does not have to be visible in the current window for you to enter a value in that cell. You can scroll through the worksheet without changing the active cell and click cells in remote areas of your worksheet as you build a formula. The formula bar displays the contents of the active cell, no matter which area of the worksheet is currently visible.

---

tip   **Redisplay the active cell**

If you scroll through your worksheet and the active cell is no longer visible, you can redisplay it by pressing Ctrl+Backspace.

Understanding Relative, Absolute, and Mixed References

Relative references—the type we've used so far in the sample formulas—refer to cells by their position in relation to the cell that contains the formula, such as "the cell two rows above this cell." *Absolute references* refer to cells by their fixed position in the worksheet, for example, the cell located at the intersection of column A and row 2. A *mixed reference* contains a relative reference and an absolute reference, for example, the cell located in column A and two rows above this cell. Absolute and mixed references are important when you begin copying formulas from one location to another in your worksheet. When you copy and paste, relative references adjust automatically, while absolute references do not. For information about copying cell references, see "How Copying and Cutting Affect Cell References" on page 360.

A relative reference to cell A1, for example, looks like this: =A1. An absolute reference to cell A1 looks like this: =$A$1. You can combine relative and absolute references to cell A1 to create these mixed references: =$A1 or =A$1.

If the dollar sign precedes only the letter (A, for example), the column coordinate is absolute and the row is relative. If the dollar sign precedes only the number (1, for example), the column coordinate is relative and the row is absolute.

When you enter or edit a formula, press F4 to change reference types quickly. The following steps show how:

1 Select cell A1, and type **=B1+B2** (but do not press Enter).

2 Press F4 to change the reference nearest to the flashing cursor to absolute. The formula becomes **=B1+$B$2**.

3 Press F4 again to change the reference to mixed (relative column coordinate and absolute row coordinate). The formula becomes **=B1+B$2**.

4 Press F4 again to reverse the mixed reference (absolute column coordinate and relative row coordinate). The formula becomes **=B1+$B2**.

5 Press F4 again to return to the original relative reference.

Creating References to Other Worksheets in the Same Workbook

You can refer to cells in other worksheets within the same workbook just as easily as you refer to cells in the same worksheet. For example, to enter a reference to cell A9 in Sheet2 into cell B10 in Sheet1, do this:

1 Select cell B10 in Sheet1, and type an equal sign.

2 Click the Sheet2 tab.

3 Click cell A9, and then press Enter.

After you press Enter, Sheet1 is made active. Select cell B10, and you will see that it contains the formula =Sheet2!A9.

The worksheet portion of the reference is separated from the cell portion by an exclamation point. Note also that the cell reference is relative, which is the default when you select cells to create references to other worksheets.

Creating References to Worksheets in Other Workbooks

You can refer to cells in worksheets in separate workbooks in the same way that you refer to cells in other worksheets within the same workbook. These references are called *external references*. For example, to enter a reference to Book2 into Book1, follow these steps:

1 Create a new workbook—Book2—by clicking the New button on the
Standard toolbar.

2 Choose Window, Arrange, Vertical.

3 Select cell A1 in Sheet1 of Book1, and type an equal sign.

4 Click anywhere in the Book2 window to make the workbook active.

5 Click the Sheet2 tab at the bottom of the Book2 window.

6 Click cell A2. Before pressing Enter to lock in the formula, your screen should
look similar to Figure 12-1.

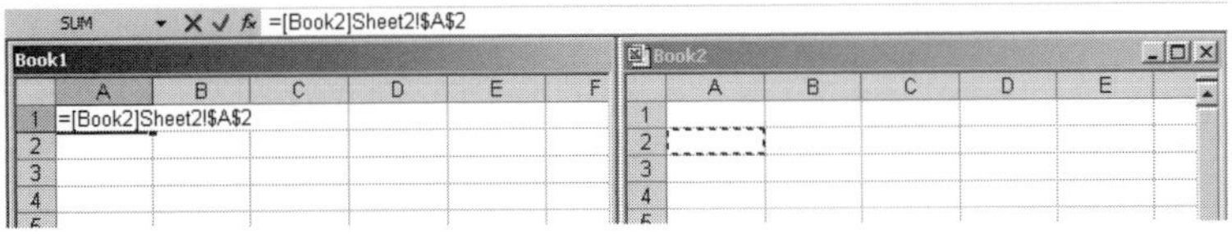

Figure 12-1. Enter external references easily by clicking the cell to which
you want to refer.

7 Press Enter to lock in the reference.

Understanding Row-Column Reference Style

In R1C1 reference style, both rows and columns are numbered. The cell reference R1C1
means row 1, column 1; therefore, R1C1 and A1 refer to the same cell. Although R1C1
reference style isn't widely used anymore, it was the standard in some spreadsheet programs, such as Multiplan. The normal reference style in Excel assigns letters to columns
and numbers to rows, such as A1 or Z100.

To turn on the R1C1 reference style, choose Tools, Options, click the General tab, and
select the R1C1 Reference Style option. The cell references in all your formulas automatically change to R1C1 format. For example, cell M10 becomes R10C13, and cell
IV65536, the last cell in your worksheet, becomes R65536C256.

In R1C1 notation, relative cell references are displayed in terms of their relationship to
the cell that contains the formula rather than by their actual coordinates. This can be
helpful when you are more interested in the relative position of a cell than in its absolute position. For example, suppose you want to enter in cell R10C2 (B10) a formula
that adds cells R1C1 (A1) and R1C2 (B1). After selecting cell R10C2, type an equal
sign, select cell R1C1, type a plus sign, select cell R1C2, and then press Enter. Excel
displays =R[-9]C[-1]+R[-9]C. Negative row and column numbers indicate that the
referenced cell is above or to the left of the formula cell; positive numbers indicate that
the referenced cell is below or to the right of the formula cell. The brackets indicate
relative references. This formula reads, "Add the cell nine rows up and one column to
the left to the cell nine rows up in the same column."

Chapter 12

A relative reference to another cell must include brackets. Otherwise, Excel assumes you're using absolute references. For example, the formula **=R8C1+R9C1** uses absolute references to the cells in rows 8 and 9 of column 1.

How Copying Affects Cell References

One of the handiest things about using references is the capability to copy and paste formulas. But you need to understand what happens to your references after you paste so that you can create formulas with references that operate the way you want them to.

Copying Relative References When you copy a cell containing a formula with relative cell references, the references change automatically, relative to the position of the cell where you paste the formula. Referring to Figure 12-2, suppose you type the formula **=AVERAGE(B4:E4)** in cell F4. This formula averages the values in the four-cell range that begins four columns to the left of cell F4.

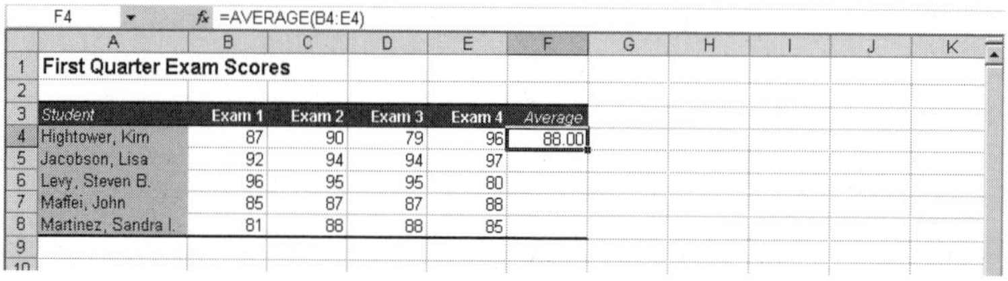

F4 =AVERAGE(B4:E4)

	A	B	C	D	E	F
1	First Quarter Exam Scores					
2						
3	Student	Exam 1	Exam 2	Exam 3	Exam 4	Average
4	Hightower, Kim	87	90	79	96	88.00
5	Jacobson, Lisa	92	94	94	97	
6	Levy, Steven B.	96	95	95	80	
7	Maffei, John	85	87	87	88	
8	Martinez, Sandra I.	81	88	88	85	

Figure 12-2. Cell F4 contains relative references to the cells to its left.

You want to repeat this calculation for the remaining rows as well. Instead of typing a new formula in each cell in column F, you select cell F4 and choose Edit, Copy. Then you select cells F5:F8, choose Edit, Paste Special, and then select the Formulas option (to preserve the formatting). The results are shown in Figure 12-3. Because the formula in cell F4 contains a relative reference, Excel adjusts the references in each copy of the formula. As a result, each copy of the formula calculates the average of the cells in the corresponding row. For example, cell F7 contains the formula **=AVERAGE(B7:E7)**.

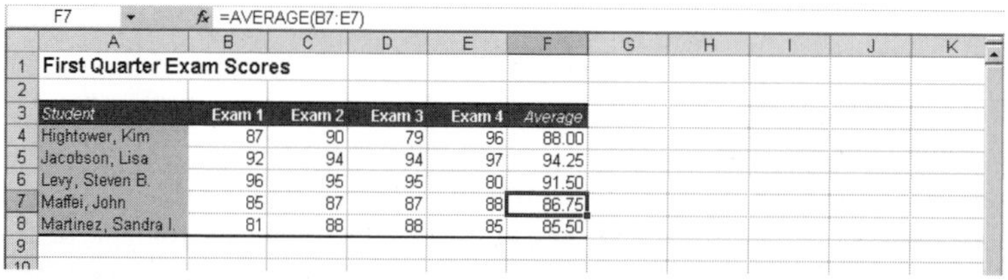

F7 =AVERAGE(B7:E7)

	A	B	C	D	E	F
1	First Quarter Exam Scores					
2						
3	Student	Exam 1	Exam 2	Exam 3	Exam 4	Average
4	Hightower, Kim	87	90	79	96	88.00
5	Jacobson, Lisa	92	94	94	97	94.25
6	Levy, Steven B.	96	95	95	80	91.50
7	Maffei, John	85	87	87	88	86.75
8	Martinez, Sandra I.	81	88	88	85	85.50

Figure 12-3. We copied the relative references from cell F4 to cells F5:F8.

Copying Absolute References If you want cell references to remain the same when you copy them, use absolute references. For example, in the worksheet on the left in Figure 12-4, cell B2 contains the hourly rate at which employees are to be paid, and cell C5 contains the relative reference formula **=B2*B5**. Suppose that you want to copy the formula in C5 to the range C6:C8. The worksheet on the right in Figure 12-4 shows what happens if you copy the existing formula to this range: You get erroneous results. Although the formulas in cells C6:C8 should refer to cell B2, they don't. For example, cell C7 contains the incorrect formula =B4*B7.

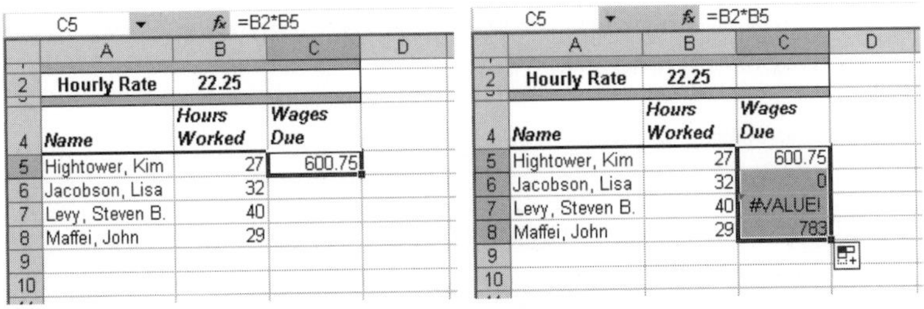

Figure 12-4. The formula in cell C5 contains relative references. We copied the relative formula in cell C5 to cells C6:C8, producing incorrect results.

Because the reference to cell B2 in the original formula is relative, it changes as you copy the formula to the other cells. To correctly apply the wage rate in cell B2 to all the calculations, you must change the reference to cell B2 to an absolute reference before you copy the formula.

To change the reference style, click the formula bar, click the reference to cell B2, and then press F4. The result is the following formula: =$B$2*B5.

When you copy this modified formula to cells C6:C8, the second cell reference, but not the first, is adjusted within each formula. In Figure 12-5, cell C7 now contains the correct formula: =$B$2*B7.

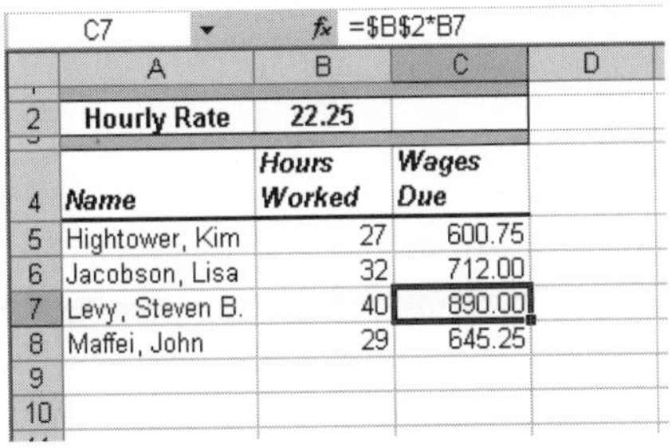

Figure 12-5. We created an absolute reference to cell B2 before copying the formula.

Copying Mixed References   You can use mixed references in your formulas to anchor a portion of a cell reference. (In a mixed reference, one portion is absolute and the other is relative.) When you copy a mixed reference, Excel anchors the absolute portion and adjusts the relative portion to reflect the location of the cell to which you copied the formula.

To create a mixed reference, you can press the F4 key to cycle through the four combinations of absolute and relative references—for example, from B2 to $B$2 to B$2 to $B2.

Chapter 12

The loan payment table in Figure 12-6 uses mixed references (and an absolute reference). You need to enter only one formula in cell C6 and then copy it down and across to fill the table. Cell C6 contains the formula = –PMT ($B6,$C$3,C$5) to calculate the annual payments on a $10,000 loan over a period of 15 years at an interest rate of 7 percent. We copied this formula to cells C6:F10 to calculate payments on three loan amounts using four interest rates.

C6	▼	fx =-PMT($B6,$C$3,C$5)				
	A	B	C	D	E	F	G

	A	B	C	D	E	F	G
1							
2		**Loan Payment Calculator**					
3		Years:	15				
4				**Loan Amount**			
5		Rate:	$ 10,000	$ 20,000	$ 30,000	$ 40,000	
6		7.00%	1,098	2,196	3,294	4,392	
7		7.50%	1,133	2,266	3,399	4,531	
8		8.00%	1,168	2,337	3,505	4,673	
9		8.50%	1,204	2,408	3,613	4,817	
10		9.00%	1,241	2,481	3,722	4,962	
11							

Figure 12-6. This loan payment table uses formulas that contain mixed references.

The first cell reference, $B6, indicates that we always want to refer to the values in column B but the row reference (Rate) can change. Similarly, the mixed reference, C$5, indicates that we always want to refer to the values in row 5 but the column reference (Loan Amount) can change. For example, cell E8 contains the formula =–PMT ($B8,$C$3,E$5). Without mixed references, we would have to edit the formulas manually in each of the cells in the range C6:F10.

Troubleshooting

Inserted Cells Are Not Included in Formulas

If you have a SUM formula at the bottom of a row of numbers, and then insert new rows between the numbers and the formula, the range reference in the SUM function doesn't include the new cells. Unfortunately, you can't do much about this. This is an age-old spreadsheet problem, but Excel attempts to correct it for you automatically. The range reference in the SUM formula will indeed not change when you insert new rows. If you type new values in the newly inserted cells, however, the range reference adjusts with each new entry. The only caveat is that you must enter the new values one at a time, starting with the cell directly below the existing list. If you begin entering values in the middle of a group of newly inserted cells, the range reference remains unaffected, although a smart tag appears, offering the option of adding the new cells to the existing formula on the smart tag actions menu. For more information about the SUM function, see "Using the SUM Function" on page 414. For more information about smart tags, see "Smart Tags" on page 4.

Editing Formulas

You edit formulas the same way you edit text entries. To delete characters in a formula, drag through the characters in the cell or the formula bar and press Backspace or Delete. To replace a character, highlight it and type its replacement. To replace a reference, highlight it and then click the new cell you want the formula to use. A relative reference is entered automatically.

You can also insert additional cell references in a formula. For example, to insert a reference to cell B1 in the formula =A1+A3, simply move the insertion point between A1 and the plus sign and either type +B1 or type a plus sign and click cell B1. The formula becomes =A1+B1+A3.

Understanding Reference Syntax

So far, we have used the default worksheet and workbook names for the examples in this book. When you save a workbook, you must give it a permanent name. If you create a formula first and then save the workbook with a new name, the formula is adjusted accordingly. For example, if you save Book2 as Sales.xls, appears in the reference, as in =[Book2]Sheet2!$A$2 changes to =[Sales.xls]Sheet2!$A$2. And if you rename Sheet2 of Sales.xls to February, the reference changes to =[Sales.xls]February!$A$2. If the referenced workbook is closed, the full path to the folder where the workbook is stored appears in the reference, as shown in the example ='C:\Work\[Sales.xls]February'!$A$2.

In the preceding example, note that apostrophes surround the workbook and worksheet portion of the reference. Excel adds the apostrophes around the path when you close the workbook. If you type a new reference to a closed workbook, however, you must add the apostrophes yourself. To avoid typing errors, open the closed workbook and click cells with the mouse to enter references so that Excel inserts them in the correct syntax for you.

Using Numeric Text in Formulas

The term "numeric text" refers to an entry that is not strictly numbers, but includes both numbers and a few specific text characters. You can perform mathematical operations on numeric text values as long as the numeric string contains only the following characters:

```
0 1 2 3 4 5 6 7 8 9 . + - E e
```

In addition, you can use the / character in fractions. You can also use the following five number-formatting characters:

```
$ , % ( )
```

You must enclose numeric text strings in quotation marks. For example, if you type the formula =$1234+$123, Excel displays an error message stating that Excel found an error in the formula you entered. (The error message also offers to correct the error for you by removing the dollar signs.) But the formula ="$1234"+'$123" produces the result 1357 (ignoring the dollar signs). When Excel performs the addition, it automatically translates numeric text entries into numeric values.

About Text Values

The term "text values" refers to any entry that is neither a number nor a numeric text value; the entry is treated as text only. You manipulate text values in the same way that you manipulate numeric values. For example, if cell A1 contains the text ABCDE and you type the formula =**A1** in cell A10, cell A10 displays ABCDE.

You can use the & (ampersand) operator to *concatenate,* or join, several text values. Extending the preceding example, if cell A2 contains the text FGHIJ and you type the formula =**A1&A2** in cell A3, cell A3 displays ABCDEFGHIJ. To include a space between the two strings, change the formula to =**A1&""&A2**. This formula uses two concatenation operators and a *literal string,* or *string constant* (a space enclosed in quotation marks).

You can use the & operator to concatenate strings of numeric values as well. For example, if cell A3 contains the numeric value 123 and cell A4 contains the numeric value 456, the formula =**A3&A4** produces the string 123456. This string is left aligned in the cell because it's considered a text value. (Remember, you can use numeric text values to perform any mathematical operation as long as the numeric string contains only the numeric characters listed on the previous page.)

Finally, you can use the & operator to concatenate a text value and a numeric value. For example, if cell A1 contains the text ABCDE and cell A3 contains the numeric value 123, the formula =**A1&A3** produces the string ABCDE123.

Practical Concatenation

Suppose you have a database of names in which the first and last names are stored in separate columns. This figure shows you how to generate a list of full names.

	A	B	C	D	E	F
	E2		▼	f_x =A2&", "&B2		
	Last Name	First Name		Full Name by First Name	Full Name by Last Name	
1						
2	Hightower	Kim		Kim Hightower	Hightower, Kim	
3	Jacobson	Lisa		Lisa Jacobson	Jacobson, Lisa	
4	Levy	Steven B.		Steven B. Levy	Levy, Steven B.	
5	Maffei	John		John Maffei	Maffei, John	
6	Martinez	Sandra I.		Sandra I. Martinez	Martinez, Sandra I.	
7						

The full names listed in columns D and E were created using formulas like the one visible in the formula bar in the preceding figure. For example, the formula in cell D2 is =**B2&" "&A2**, which concatenates the contents of the cells in columns A and B and adds a space character in between. The formula in cell E2 (shown in the figure) reverses the position of the first and last names and adds a comma before the space character.

Pretty soon, you'll be using the term *concatenate* in everyday conversation. Instead of the old ducks in a row metaphor, you'll be saying, we've got to concatenate our ducks. Caution is advised.

Using Functions: A Preview

In simplest terms, a *function* is a predefined formula. Many Excel functions are shorthand versions of frequently used formulas. For example, the SUM function adds a series of cell values by selecting a range. Compare the formula =A1+A2+A3+A4+A5+A6+A7+A8+A9+A10 with the formula =SUM(A1:A10).The SUM function makes the formula a lot shorter and easier to create.

> For more information about functions, see Chapter 13, "Using Functions." For more about the SUM function, see Chapter 14, "Everyday Functions."

Some Excel functions perform complex calculations. For example, using the PMT function, you can calculate the payment on a loan at a given interest rate and principal amount.

All functions consist of a function name followed by a set of *arguments* enclosed in parentheses. (In the preceding example, A1:A10 is the argument in the SUM function.) If you omit a closing parenthesis when you enter a function, Excel adds the parenthesis after you press Enter, as long as it's obvious where the parenthesis is supposed to go. (Relying on this feature can produce unpredictable results; for accuracy, always double-check your parentheses.)

Using the AutoSum Button

The SUM function is used more often than any other function. To make this function more accessible, Excel included on the Standard toolbar an AutoSum button, which inserts the SUM function into a cell. To check out the AutoSum feature:

1 Enter a column of numbers, like we did in Figure 12-7.

2 Select the cell below the column of numbers and click the AutoSum button. The button inserts the entire formula for you and suggests a range to sum.

3 If the suggested range is incorrect, simply drag through the correct range, and press Enter.

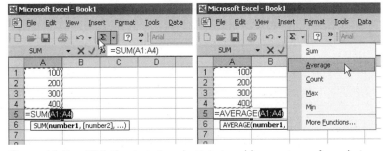

Figure 12-7. Click the AutoSum button to add a summary formula in a cell adjacent to columns or rows of numbers.

Chapter 12

365

> **tip**   **Get quick formula-free answers**
>
> Get a quick sum by selecting the cells you want to sum and then looking at the status bar, where the total of the selected range appears. Right-click the status bar total to choose whether the range is summed, averaged, or counted or whether the maximum or minimum value is displayed in the status bar. For more information, see the "Quick Totals in the Status Bar" sidebar on page 30.

newfeature!   The latest addition to the functionality of the AutoSum button is the menu that appears when you click the arrow next to the button, as shown in Figure 12-7. You can enter the Average, Count, Max, or Min function almost as easily as you can enter the Sum function—all it takes is an extra click to select the function you want from the menu. Plus, the More Functions command opens the Insert Function dialog box, where you can access any Excel function.

You can click the AutoSum button to enter several SUM functions at one time. For example, if we select cells B9:C9 in Figure 12-5 and then click the AutoSum button, Excel enters SUM formulas in both cells.

For more information, see "Using the SUM Function" on page 414.

Inserting Functions

Insert
Function

When you want to use a built-in function, click the Insert Function button—the fx button located in the formula bar. (You can also choose Insert, Function.) When you do so, the Insert Function dialog box shown in Figure 12-8 appears. For details about using the Insert Function dialog box, see "Inserting Functions" on page 408.

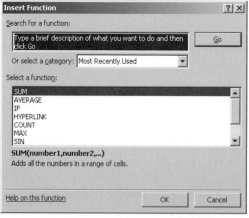

Figure 12-8.   The Insert Function dialog box gives you access to all built-in functions in Excel.

Creating Three-Dimensional Formulas

You can use references to perform calculations on cells that span a range of worksheets in a workbook. These are called *3-D, or three-dimensional, references*. Suppose you set up 12 worksheets in the same workbook—one for each month—with a year-to-date summary sheet on top. If all the monthly worksheets are laid out identically, you could use 3-D reference formulas to summarize the monthly data on the summary sheet. For example, the formula =SUM(**Sheet2:Sheet13!B5**) adds all the values in cell B5 on all the worksheets between and including Sheet2 and Sheet13. To construct this three-dimensional formula, follow these steps:

1 In cell B5 of Sheet1, type **=SUM(**.

2 Click the Sheet2 tab, and select cell B5.

3 Click the tab scrolling button (located to the left of the worksheet tabs) until the Sheet13 tab is visible.

4 Hold down the Shift key and click the Sheet13 tab. All the tabs from Sheet2 through Sheet13 change to white, indicating that they are selected for inclusion in the reference you are constructing.

5 Select cell B5.

6 Type the closing parenthesis, and then press Enter.

For more information about group editing, see "Editing Multiple Worksheets" on page 187.

You can use the following functions with 3-D references: SUM, MIN, VAR, COUNTA, PRODUCT, VARP, AVERAGE, STDEV, COUNT, MAX, and STDEVP.

Formula-Bar Formatting

You can enter spaces and line breaks in a formula to make it easier to read—without affecting the calculation of the formula. To enter a line break, press Alt+Enter. Figure 12-9 shows a formula that contains line breaks.

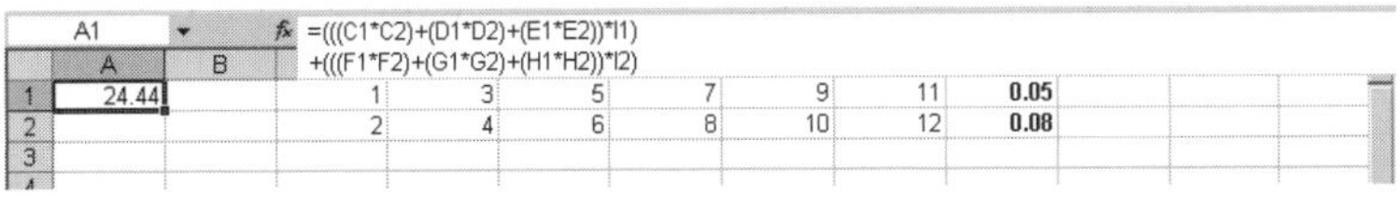

Figure 12-9. You can enter line breaks in a formula to make it more readable.

Creating Natural-Language Formulas

You can use labels instead of cell references when you create formulas in worksheet tables. Labels at the top of columns and to the left of rows identify the adjacent cells in

Chapter 12

the table when you use the labels in a formula. This is called a *natural-language formula*, which is a fairly accurate description of the way it works, providing you use language that is, well, *natural*. The spreadsheet in Figure 12-10 shows a simple sales table as an example of how this works.

> **tip** **Cross the language barrier**
>
> The capability to create natural-language formulas is an option that is normally turned on. To disable this feature, choose Tools, Options; on the Calculation tab, clear the Accept Labels In Formulas option.

B9 =SUM(Qtr 1)

	A	B	C	D	E	G	H
1	Duffy Vineyards						
2	Sales						
3	2002	Qtr 1	Qtr 2	Qtr 3	Qtr 4	Total	Average
4	Product 1	1000	1050	1100	1150	4300	1075
5	Product 2	1100	1150	1200	1250	4700	1175
6	Product 3	1200	1250	1300	1350	5100	1275
7	Product 4	1300	1350	1400	1450	5500	1375
9	Total	4600	4800	5000	5200	19600	1225
10	Average	1150	1200	1250	1300	4900	

Figure 12-10. You can use the column and row labels in a table to refer to cells and ranges in formulas.

The formulas in rows 9 and 10 might normally contain formulas with range references, such as =**SUM(B4:B7)**. But instead of a range reference, a natural-language formula uses a column label from the table, such as =**SUM(Qtr 1)**, as shown in Figure 12-10. When you use text instead of cell references in formulas, Excel looks for column and row labels that match. If Excel finds a matching label, it extrapolates what you are after, using a complex set of internal rules. For our purposes, we can say the following:

- If a formula contains a label from the same column or row where the formula resides, Excel assumes that you want to use the entire contiguous range of entries adjacent to the label (either below a column label or to the right of a row label).
- If a formula contains a label from a column or row other than the one where the formula resides, Excel assumes that you want to act on a single cell at the intersection of the labeled column or row and the column or row containing the formula.

If what you intend isn't clear, Excel displays a dialog box like the one shown in Figure 12-11, asking you to select the label.

To identify a specific cell in a natural-language formula, we use intersection. For example, the formula =**Product 2 Qtr 2** pinpoints the cell located at the intersection of the Product 2 row and the Qtr 2 column, which is—cell C5. (Note that you must enter a space between the row and column label in the formula.)

Chapter 12: Building Formulas

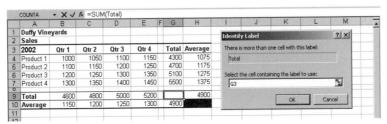

Figure 12-11. If Excel can't tell which label you want to use, the Identify
Label dialog box appears.

You can copy and paste natural-language formulas; the columns and rows to which you
refer adjust accordingly. In Figure 12-11, the formula in cell B9 was copied to cells
C9:E9. All of the formulas in the copy range adjusted so that the label for the current
column was used. For example, after copying the formula in cell B9 to the right, the
formula in cell E9 became =SUM(Qtr 4).

Note that if you copy natural-language formulas to places that do not make sense, Excel
alerts you that something is wrong. For example, if you copy the formula in cell H9 to
cell J9, Excel displays the error value NAME? because no label is available in column J.

If you change the column and row labels in tables, the labels you typed into formulas
adjust. For example, if we change the label Total in Cell G3 of Figure 12-11 to Year, the
formula in cell G9 adjusts accordingly to read =SUM(Year).

---

tip   Use names for more power

You can use plain-language formulas in the rows and columns of the worksheet that
contains the table and its labels, but you can't use labels in formulas on other
worksheets or other workbooks. If you use defined cell range names instead of labels,
you can use the names in formulas located on any sheet in any workbook

---

Getting Explicit About Intersections

In the worksheet in Figure 12-11, if you type the formula =Qtr 1*4 in cell I4, Excel
assumes that you want to use only one value in the Qtr 1 range B4:B7—the one that
lies in the same row as the formula that contains the reference. This is called *implicit
intersection*. Because the formula is in row 4, Excel uses the value in cell B4. If you enter
the same formula in cells I5, I6, and I7, each cell in that range contains the formula
=Qtr1*4, but at I5 the formula refers to cell B5, at I6 it refers to cell B6, and so on.

Explicit intersection refers to a specific cell with the help of the intersection operator.
The *intersection operator* is the space character that appears when you press the
Spacebar. If you type the formula =Qtr 1 Product 1*4 at any location on the same
worksheet, Excel knows that you want to refer to the value that lies at the intersection
of the range labeled Qtr 1 and the range labeled Product 1, which is cell B4.

Substituting Labels Automatically

Excel can substitute labels for cell references in formulas automatically, as you enter
them. To do so, you must first define the label ranges as follows:

1 Choose Insert, Name, Label. The Label Ranges dialog box shown in
Figure 12-12 appears.

2 Click the Add Label Range box, and then drag in the worksheet to select the
labels you want to define.

3 Select the Row Labels Or Column Labels option.

4 Click the Add button to add the label range to the Existing Label Ranges list.

After you define label ranges, any references to cells within those ranges are automatically replaced by natural-language labels.

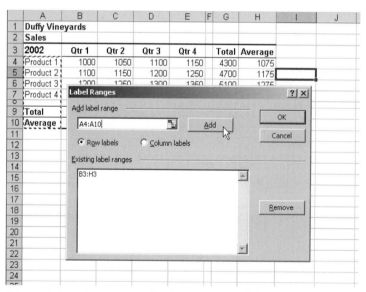

Figure 12-12. You can use the Label Ranges dialog box to substitute
labels for cell references in formulas.

When you define labels, references in existing formulas are not changed for you, but
Excel will substitute the appropriate labels when you enter new formulas. For example,
after defining the labels in Figure 12-12, you could click cell I5, type an equal sign, and
then click cell C5. Normally Excel would insert the cell reference C5 in the formula, but
instead the label intersection Qtr 2 Product 2 appears.

Naming Cells and Cell Ranges

When you find yourself repeatedly typing cryptic cell addresses, such as
Sheet3!A1:AJ51, into formulas, don't worry—Excel has a better way. Assign a short,
memorable name to the popular cell or range, and then use that name instead of the
cryptogram in formulas.

After you define names in a worksheet, those names are made available to any other
worksheets in the workbook. A name defining a cell range in Sheet6, for example, is
available for use in formulas in Sheet1, Sheet2, and so on in the workbook. As a result,
each workbook contains its own set of names. You can also define worksheet-level
names that are available only on the worksheet in which they are defined.

For more information about worksheet-level names, see "Workbook-Wide vs. Worksheet-Only
Names" on page 374.

tip   **Don't define names for simple tables**

In a simple table with row and column headings, you can use the headings themselves
in formulas located in the same rows and columns, without first having to define
names. See "Creating Natural-Language Formulas" on page 367.

Using Names in Formulas

When you use the name of a cell or a range in a formula, the result is the same as if you
entered the cell or range address. For example, suppose you entered the formula
=A1+A2 in cell A3. If you defined the name Mark as cell A1 and the name Vicki as cell
A2, the formula =**Mark+Vicki** has the same result.

Chapter 12

The easiest way to define a name follows:

1 Select a cell.

2 Click the Name box in the formula bar, as shown in Figure 12-13.

3 Type **TestName**, and then press Enter.

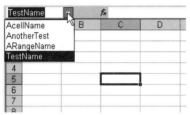

Figure 12-13. Use the Name box in the formula bar to quickly assign names to cells and ranges.

Keep the following basics in mind when using names in formulas:

● The Name box normally displays the address of the selected cell. If the selected cell or range is named, the name takes precedence over the address and is displayed in the Name box.

● When you define a name for a range of cells, the range name does not appear in the Name box unless the entire range is selected.

● When you click the Name box and select a name, the cell selection switches to the named cells.

● If you type a name that has already been defined into the Name box, Excel switches the selection instead of redefining the name.

● When you define a name, the address includes the worksheet name and the cell reference is absolute. For example, when you define the name TestName for cell C5 in Sheet1, the actual name definition is recorded as Sheet1!$C$5.

For more information about absolute references, see "Understanding Relative, Absolute, and Mixed References" on page 357.

Defining and Managing Names

Instead of coming up with new names for cells and ranges, you can simply use existing text labels to create names. Choosing Insert, Name, Define, you can use text in adjacent cells to define cell and range names, as seen in Figure 12-14 on page 22. You can choose this command also to redefine existing names.

Rules for Naming

The following rules apply when you name cells and ranges in Excel:

- All names must begin with a letter, a backslash (\), or an underscore (_).
- Numbers can be used.
- Spaces can't be used.
- Excel translates blank spaces in labels to underscores in defined names.
- Symbols other than backslash and underscore can't be used.
- Names that resemble cell references can't (for example, AB$5 or R1C7) can't be used.
- Single letters, with the exception of the letters R and C, can be used as names.

A name can contain 255 characters, but if it contains more than 253 characters, you can't select it from the Name box. Excel does not distinguish between uppercase and lowercase characters in names. For example, if you create the name Tax and then create the name TAX in the same workbook, the first name is overwritten by the second.

tip   Press Ctrl+F3 to display the Define Name dialog box instantly.

If you select the range you want to name before choosing the command, and you are happy using the adjacent label as a name, just press Enter to define the name. The next time you open the Define Name dialog box, the name appears in the Names In Workbook list, which displays all the defined names for the workbook.

You can define a name also without first selecting a cell or range in the worksheet. For example, in the Define Name dialog box, type **Test2** in the Names In Workbook box and then type =D20 in the Refers To box. Click the Add button to add the name to the list.

The Define Name dialog box remains open, and the Refers To box displays the name definition =Sheet1!D20. Excel adds the worksheet reference for you, but note that the cell reference stays relative, just as you entered it. If you do not enter the equal sign preceding the reference, Excel interprets the definition as text. For example, if you typed **D20** instead of **=D20**, the Refers To box would display the text constant ="D20" as the definition of the name Test2.

When the Define Name dialog box is open, you can insert references in the Refers To box also by selecting cells in the worksheet. If you name several cells or ranges in the Define Name dialog box, be sure to click the Add button after entering each definition. (If you click OK, Excel closes the dialog box.)

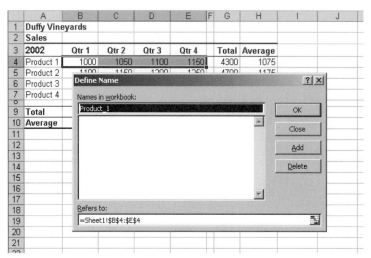

Figure 12-14. When you choose Insert, Name, Define, any label in an adjacent cell in the same row or column is suggested as a name.

Editing Names

To redefine an existing cell or range name in the Define Name dialog box, first select the name in the Names In Workbook list and then edit the cell or range reference in the Refers To box. You can either type a new reference or select a new cell or range directly in the worksheet while the Define Name dialog box is open.

To delete a name in the Define Name dialog box, select the name from the Names In Workbook list and then click Delete. Keep in mind that when you delete a name, any formula in the worksheet that refers to that name returns the error value #NAME?

Workbook-Wide vs. Worksheet-Only Names

Names in Excel are normally workbook-level. That is, a name defined in any worksheet is available for use in formulas from any other worksheet. But you can also create worksheet-level names that are available only on the worksheet in which they are defined. To define a worksheet-level name for a cell or a range of cells, precede the name with the name of the worksheet, followed by an exclamation point.

For example, to define TestSheetName as a sheet-level name in Sheet1, select the range you want, choose Insert, Name, Define, and then type **Sheet1!TestSheetName** in the Names In Workbook box. The following are some additional facts to keep in mind when working with sheet- and book-level names:

- Sheet-level names do not appear in the Name box or the Define Name dialog box in sheets other than the one in which they are defined.

Selecting Cells While a Dialog Box Is Open

The Refers To box in the Define Name dialog box contains a *collapse dialog button*, which indicates a box from which you can navigate and select cells. For example, after you click the Refers To box, you can click any other worksheet tab, drag scroll bars, and make another workbook active by choosing the workbook name in the Window menu. In addition, you can click the collapse dialog button and, sure enough, the dialog box collapses, allowing you to see more of the worksheet.

	A	B	C	D	E	F	G	H	I
1	Duffy Vineyards								
2	Sales								
3	2002	Qtr 1	Qtr 2	Qtr 3	Qtr 4		Total	Average	
4	Product 1	1000	1050	1100	1150		4300	1075	
5	Product 2	1100	1150	1200	1250		4700	1175	
6	Pr	Define Name – Refers to:						? ×	
7	Pr	=Sheet1!$B$4:$E$4							
8									
9	Total	4600	4800	5000	5200		19600	1225	
10	Average	1150	1200	1250	1300		4900		
11									

You can drag the collapsed dialog box around the screen using its title bar. When you finish, click the collapse dialog button again, and the dialog box returns to its original size.

- When you select a cell or range that you have defined with a sheet-level name, the name of the cell or range (TestSheetName, for example) appears in the Name box on the formula bar, but the name of the worksheet (Sheet1!, for example) is hidden.

- To edit a sheet-level name, make the worksheet in which the name is defined active and choose Insert, Name, Define.

- When a worksheet contains a duplicate book-level and sheet-level name, the sheet-level name takes precedence over the book-level name on the sheet where it lives.

- You can't use a duplicate book-level name in the worksheet where the sheet-level name is defined.

- You can use a sheet-level name in a formula on other worksheets by including the name, in its entirety, in the formula. For example, you could type the formula =**Sheet2!TestSheetName** in a cell on Sheet3.

Creating Names Semiautomatically

You can choose Insert, Name, Create to name several adjacent cells or ranges at once, using row labels, column labels, or both. When you choose this command, Excel displays the Create Names dialog box shown in Figure 12-15.

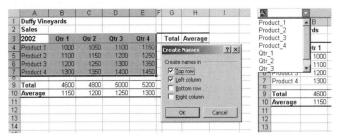

Figure 12-15. Use the Create Names dialog box to name several cells
or ranges at once using labels. The resulting names appear in the Name box.

Select the appropriate Create Names In options for the selected cells, and Excel uses the labels included in the selection to name each range. For example, Figure 12-15 shows that with A3:E7 selected, the Top Row and Left Column options in the Create Names dialog box are selected, creating a set of names for each Qtr and each Product. When you click the arrow to the right of the Name box in the formula bar, you see the names Product_1, Product_2, Product_3, and Product_4 listed. (The name Product_1, for example, is defined as the range $B$4:$E$4.)

Naming Constants and Formulas

You can create names that are defined by constants and formulas instead of by cell references. You can use absolute and relative references, numbers, text, formulas, and functions as name definitions. For example, if you often use the value 8.3 percent to calculate the sales tax, you can choose Insert, Name, Define, type the name **Tax** in the Names In Workbook box, and then type **8.3%** (or .083) in the Refers To box. Then you can use the name Tax in a formula, such as =**Price+(Price*Tax)**, to calculate the cost of items with 8.3 percent sales tax. Note that named constants and formulas do not appear in the Name box in the formula bar, but they do appear in the Define Name dialog box.

You can also enter a formula in the Refers To box. For example, you might define the name Price with a formula, such as =**Sheet1!A1*190%**. If you define this named formula while cell B1 is selected, you can then type =**Price** in cell B1, and the defined formula takes care of the calculation for you. Because the reference in the named formula is relative, you could then type =**Price** into any cell in your workbook to calculate a price using the value in the cell directly to the left. If you enter a formula in the Refers To box that refers to a cell or range in a worksheet, Excel updates the formula whenever the value in the cell changes.

Using Relative References in Named Formulas

When you are creating a named formula that contains relative references, such as
=**Sheet1!B22+1.2%**, Excel interprets the position of the cells referenced in the Refers
To box as relative to the active cell. Later, when you use such a name in a formula, the
named formula uses whatever value corresponds to the relative reference. For example,
if cell B21 was the active cell when you defined the name Tax as =**Sheet1!B22+1.2%**,
the name Tax always refers to the cell one row below the cell in which the formula is
currently located.

Creating Three-Dimensional Names

You can create three-dimensional names, which use 3-D references as their definitions.
For example, suppose you have a 13-sheet workbook containing one identical sheet for
each month plus one summary sheet. You can define a 3-D name that can be used to
summarize totals from each monthly sheet. To do so, follow these steps:

1 Select cell B5 in Sheet1 (the Summary sheet).

2 Choose Insert, Name, Define.

3 Type **Three_D** (or any name you choose) in the Names In Workbook box and
type =**Sheet2:Sheet13!B5** in the Refers To box.

4 Press Enter.

Now you can use the name Three_D in formulas that contain any of the following
functions: SUM, MIN, VAR, COUNTA, PRODUCT, VARP, AVERAGE, STDEV,
COUNT, MAX, and STDEVP. For example, the formula =**MAX(Three_D)** returns the
largest value in the three-dimensional range named Three_D. Because you used relative
references in step 3, the definition of the range Three_D changes as you select different
cells in the worksheet. For example, if you select cell C3 and display the Define Name
dialog box, =**Sheet2:Sheet13!C3** appears in the Refers To box.

> For more information on three-dimensional references, see "Creating Three-Dimensional
> Formulas" on page 367.

Pasting Names into Formulas

After you define one or more names in your worksheet, you can insert those names in
formulas using the Paste Name dialog box, which is shown in Figure 12-16 on the
next page.

Figure 12-16. Use the Paste Name dialog box to insert names in your formulas.

For example, to paste the name Product_1 into a formula:

1 Type an equal sign and then type the operators, functions, or constants of your formula.

2 Place the insertion point in the formula where you want to insert the name, and then choose Insert, Name, Paste (or press F3).

3 Select Product_1, and click OK to insert the name in the formula.

4 Type any other operands and operators to complete the formula, and then press Enter.

Creating a List of Names

In large worksheet models, it's easy to accumulate a long list of defined names. To keep a record of all the names used, you can paste a list of defined names in your worksheet by clicking the Paste List button in the Paste Name dialog box, as shown in Figure 12-17. Excel pastes the list in your worksheet beginning at the active cell.

Figure 12-17. Use the Paste List button to create a list of names and their definitions.

> **note** When Excel pastes the list, it overwrites any existing data. If you inadvertently over-write data, press Ctrl+Z to undo it.

Replacing References with Names

To replace references in formulas with their corresponding names, choose Insert, Name, Apply. Excel locates all cell and range references for which you have defined

names. If you select a single cell before you choose the Apply command, Excel
applies names throughout the active worksheet; if you select a range of cells, Excel
applies names to only the selected cells.

Figure 12-18 shows the Apply Names dialog box, which lists all the cell and range
names you have defined. If you do not want to include all the names, click a name in
the list to clear it; click it again to reselect it.

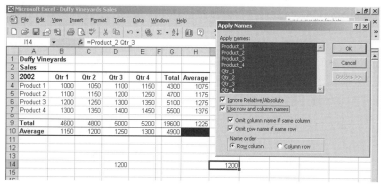

Figure 12-18. Use the Apply Names dialog box to substitute names for
cell and range references in your formulas.

Click the Options button to display all the options shown here.

Excel normally does not apply the column or row name if either is superfluous. For
example, Figure 12-18 shows a sheet after we applied names using the default options
in the Apply Names dialog box. Cell I14 is selected, and the formula bar shows that it
contains the formula =**Product_2 Qtr_3**, which before applying names contained the
formula =**D5**. Because cell I14 isn't in the same row or column as any of the defined
ranges, both the row and column names are included in the new formula. Cell D14
contained the same formula, =**D5**. But because D14 is in the same column as the referenced cell, only the row name is needed thanks to implicit intersection, resulting in the
formula =**Product_2**.

If you prefer to see both the column and row names even when they are not necessary,
clear the Omit Column Name If Same Column option and the Omit Row Name If
Same Row option.

For more information about implicit intersection, see the "Getting Explicit about Intersections"
sidebar on page 369.

The Name Order options control the order in which row and column components
appear. For example, using the Column Row option, the formula in cell I 14 in
Figure 12-18 would become =**Qtr_3 Product_2**.

Select the Ignore Relative/Absolute option to replace references with names regardless of the reference type. In general, leave this check box selected. Most name definitions use absolute references (the default when you define and create names), and most formulas use relative references (the default when you paste cell and range references in the formula bar). If you clear this option, absolute, relative, and mixed references are replaced with name definitions only if the definitions use the corresponding reference style.

The Use Row And Column Names option is necessary if you want to apply names in intersection cases, as we have shown in the examples. If you define names for individual cells, however, you can clear Use Row and Column Names to apply names to only specific cell references in formulas.

Using Go To with Named Ranges

When you choose Edit, Go To (or press F5), range names appear in the Go To dialog box, as shown in Figure 12-19. Select a name, and click OK to jump to the range referred to. Note that names defined with constants or formulas do not appear in the Go To dialog box.

Figure 12-19. Use the Go To dialog box to select a cell or range name so you can move to that cell or range quickly.

---

tip　**Jump with the Reference box**

The Go To dialog box remembers the last four places you visited. The latest location is always in the Reference box when you display the dialog box so that you can jump between two locations by pressing F5 and then pressing Enter.

Understanding Error Values

An *error value* is the result of a formula that Excel can't resolve. The seven error values are described in Table 12-2.

Table 12-2. Error Values

Error Value	Cause
#DIV/0!	You attempted to divide a number by zero. This error usually occurs when you create a formula with a divisor that refers to a blank cell.
#NAME?	You entered a name in a formula that isn't in the Define Name dialog box list. You might have mistyped the name or typed a deleted name. Excel displays this error value also if you do not enclose a text string in quotation marks.
#VALUE	You entered a mathematical formula that refers to a text entry.
#REF!	You deleted a range of cells whose references are included in a formula.
#N/A	No information is available for the calculation you want to perform. When building a model, you can type **#N/A** in a cell to show that you are awaiting data. Any formulas that reference cells containing the #N/A value return #N/A.
#NUM!	You provided an invalid argument to a worksheet function. #NUM! can indicate also that the result of a formula is too large or too small to be represented in the worksheet.
#NULL!	You included a space between two ranges in a formula to indicate an intersection, but the ranges have no common cells.

Worksheet Calculation

Excel developers used to wear t-shirts emblazoned with the battle cry "Recalc or Die." Rest assured that no developer has ever been harmed during the creation of any version of Excel. The deceptively simple process of calculation computes all formulas and then displays the results in the cells that contain them. When you change the values in the cells to which these formulas refer, Excel updates the values of the formulas as well. This updating process is called *recalculation,* and it affects only those cells containing references to cells that have changed.

By default, Excel recalculates whenever you make changes to a cell. If a large number of cells must be recalculated, the words Calculating Cells and a number appear at the left end of the status bar. The number indicates the percentage of recalculation that has

Chapter 12

been completed. You can interrupt the recalculation process by simply using commands or making cell entries; Excel pauses and then resumes recalculation when you are finished.

Recalculating Manually

To save time, particularly when you are making entries in a large workbook with many formulas, you can switch from automatic to manual recalculation; that is, Excel will recalculate only when you tell it to. To set manual recalculation, choose Tools, Options and then click the Calculation tab to display the options shown in Figure 12-20.

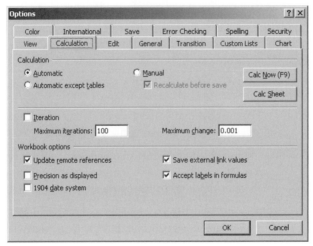

Figure 12-20. The Calculation tab of the Options dialog box controls worksheet calculation and iteration.

Here are a few things to remember about calculation options:

● To turn off automatic recalculation, select the Manual option. If you make a change that normally initiates recalculation, the status bar displays Calculate instead of recalculating automatically.

● The Recalculate Before Save option helps make sure that the most current values are stored on disk.

● To turn off automatic recalculation only for data tables, select the Automatic Except Tables option. For more information, see "Using Data Tables" on page 499.

● To recalculate all open workbooks, click the Calc Now button or press F9.

● To calculate only the active worksheet in a workbook, click the Calc Sheet button or press Shift+F9.

Copying Formulas and Pasting Only Their Resulting Values

Normally when you copy a cell that contains a formula, the formula is pasted as well, which is handy. But if you want to copy only the result, without the formula, choose Edit, Paste Special. The Paste Special dialog box appears, as shown in Figure 12-21. Among *many* other things, you can choose Paste Special to extract the results of formulas. To transfer only the resulting values of formulas, select the Values option. For more information about Paste Special options, see "Pasting Selectively Using Paste Special" on page 152.

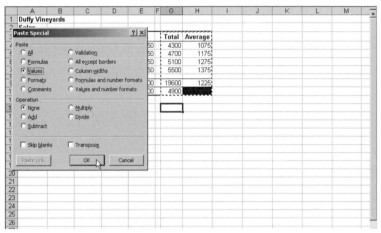

Figure 12-21.   Choose Edit, Paste Special to extract specific information from copied cells.

Evaluating Part of a Formula

You might want to see the result of just one part of a complex formula if, for example, you are tracking down a discrepancy. To change only part of a formula to a value, select the part you want to change and press F9. You can use this technique also to change highlighted cell references in formulas to their values. Figure 12-22 on the next page shows an example.

If you're just checking your figures, press the Esc key to discard the edited formula. Otherwise, if you press Enter, you replace the selected portion of the formula.

---

tip   **Use Evaluate Formula to troubleshoot**

You can also choose Tools, Formula Auditing, Evaluate Formula to troubleshoot your workbook models. For more information, see "Evaluating and Auditing Formulas" on page 258.

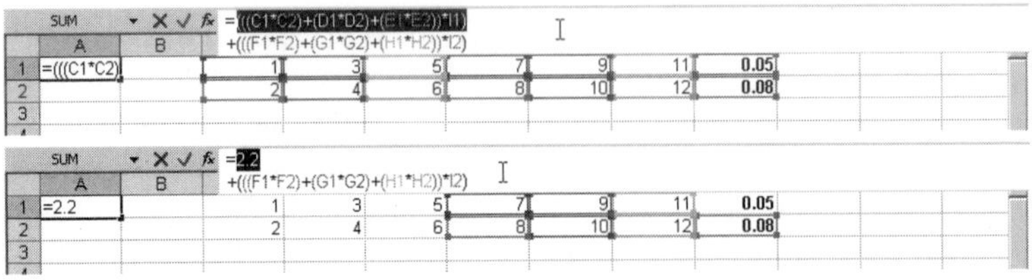

Part 5: Creating Formulas and Performing Data Analysis

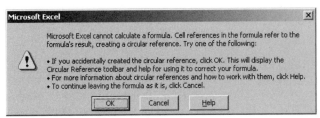

Figure 12-22. Select any part of a formula and press F9 to convert it to
its resulting value.

Using Circular References

A *circular reference* is a formula that depends on its own value. The most obvious type
is a formula that contains a reference to the same cell in which it's entered. For
example, if you type =C1-A1 in cell A1, Excel displays the error message shown in
Figure 12-23.

Figure 12-23. This error message appears when you attempt to enter a
formula that contains a circular reference.

If a circular reference warning surprises you, this usually means that you made an error
in a formula. Click OK, and look at the formula. If the error isn't obvious, check the
cells that the formula refers to.

Choose View, Toolbars, Circular Reference to help track down the problem using the
built-in auditing features of Excel. Click the Trace Precedents or Trace Dependents button to draw tracer arrows on the worksheet. These arrows show you a visual path to all
the cells involved, as shown in Figure 12-24.

Figure 12-24. Display the Circular Reference toolbar to track
down unwanted circular references.

Chapter 12: Building Formulas

If you click the Trace Precedents button, Excel draws a line from the cell that contains the formula to any cells used by the formula. Each time you click, tracer lines appear for the next level, if any of the cells used by the formula contain formulas themselves.

For additional information about auditing tools, see "Auditing and Documenting Worksheets" on page 256.

Many circular references can be resolved. Some circular formulas are useful or even essential, such as the set of circular references in Figure 12-25. These formulas are circular because the formula in cell M29 depends on the value in M30, and the formula in M30 depends on the value in M29.

	C	D	E	F	G	H	I	J	K	L	M	N	O	P
16														
17	Qty	Description								Unit Price	TOTAL			
18	1	Drum Set								$1,234.00	$ 1,234.00			
19	1	Hi-hat stand								$ 178.00	$ 178.00			
20	1	Ride Cymbal								$ 123.00	$ 123.00			
21	1	Crash Cymbal								$ 123.00	$ 123.00			
22	2	Hi-hat cymbals								$ 89.00	$ 178.00			
23	2	Cymbal Stands								$ 65.00	$ 130.00			
24	4	Pair drumsticks								$ 2.00	$ 8.00			
25														
26										SubTotal	$ 1,974.00			
27										Shipping	$ 123.00			
28	Payment	Select One...							Tax Rate(s)	8.30%	$ 163.84			
29								Over $2K Discount		-4.00%	=IF(L29<>"",ROUND(L29*M30,2),"")			
30	Comments									TOTAL	$ 2,173.88			
31	Name													

Figure 12-25. The discount formula in cell M29 is circular because it depends on the total, which in turn depends on the discount value in M29.

After you dismiss the error message shown in Figure 12-23, the formula will not resolve until you allow Excel to recalculate in controlled steps. To do so, choose Tools, Options, click the Calculation tab, shown in Figure 12-26, and then select the Iteration option. Excel recalculates all the cells in any open worksheets that contain a circular reference.

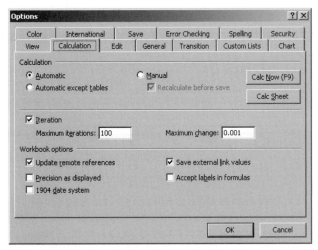

Figure 12-26. Control iterations using the Calculation tab in the Options dialog box.

Chapter 12

If necessary, the recalculation repeats the number of times specified in the Maximum Iterations box (100 is the default). Each time Excel recalculates the formulas, the results in the cells get closer to the correct values. If necessary, Excel continues until the difference between iterations is less than the number entered in the Maximum Change box (0.001 is the default). Thus, using the default settings, Excel recalculates either a maximum of 100 times or until the values change less than 0.001 between iterations, whichever comes first.

If the word Calculate appears in the status bar after the iterations are finished, more iterations are possible. You can accept the current result, increase the number of iterations, or lower the Maximum Change threshold. Excel does not repeat the Cannot resolve circular reference error message if it fails to resolve the reference. You must determine when the answer is close enough. Excel can perform iterations in seconds, but in complex circular situations, you might want to set the Calculation option to Manual; otherwise, Excel recalculates the circular references every time you make a cell entry.

The useful circular reference scenario described in this section is called *convergence*: The difference between results becomes smaller with each iterative calculation. In the opposite process, called *divergence*, the difference between results becomes larger with each calculation. Excel continues iterations until it completes the number you specify.

Understanding the Precision of Numeric Values

Excel stores numbers with as much as 15-digit accuracy and converts any digits after the fifteenth to zeros. Excel drops any digits after the fifteenth in a decimal fraction. In addition, Excel uses scientific notation to display numbers that are too long for their cells.

Table 12-3 contains examples of how Excel treats integers and decimal fractions longer than 15 digits when they are entered in cells with the default column width of 8.43 characters:

Table 12-3. Examples of Numeric Precision

Typed entry	Displayed Value	Stored Value
123456789012345678	1.23457E+17	123456789012345000
1.23456789012345678	1.234568	1.23456789012345
1234567890.12345678	1234567890	1234567890.12345
123456789012345.678	1.23457E+14	123456789012345

Excel can calculate positive values as large as 9.99E+307 and approximately as small as 1.00E-307. If a formula results in a value outside this range, Excel stores the number as text and assigns a #NUM! error value to the formula cell.

Troubleshooting

Rounded Values in My Worksheet Don't Add Up

Your worksheet can appear erroneous if you use rounded values. For example, if you use cell formatting to display numbers in currency format with two decimal places, the value 10.006 is displayed as the rounded value $10.01. If you add 10.006 and 10.006, the correct result is 20.012. If all of these numbers are formatted as currency, however, the worksheet displays the rounded values $10.01 and $10.01, and the rounded value of the result is $20.01. The result is correct, as far as rounding goes, but its appearance might be unacceptable for a particular purpose, such as a presentation.

You can correct this problem by changing the currency format, or you can choose Tools, Options and then select the Precision As Displayed option on the Calculation tab. However, you should select this option only with extreme caution because it permanently changes the underlying values in your worksheet to their displayed values. For example, if a cell containing the value 10.006 is formatted as currency, selecting the Precision As Displayed option permanently changes the value to 10.01. For more information about number formatting, see "Formatting Stuff in Cells" on page 204.

Using Arrays

Arrays are familiar concepts to computer programmers. Simply defined, an array is a collection of items. Excel is one of the few applications that facilitate array operations, in which items that comprise an array can be individually or collectively addressed in simple mathematical terms. Here is some basic array terminology you should know:

- An *array formula* acts on two or more sets of values, called *array arguments*, to return either a single result or multiple results.

- An *array range* is a block of cells that share a common array formula.

- An *array constant* is a specially organized list of constant values that you can use as arguments in your array formulas.

Arrays perform calculations in a way unlike anything else. They can be used for worksheet security, alarm monitors, linear regression tables, and much more.

One-Dimensional Arrays

The easiest way to learn about arrays is to look at a few examples. For instance, you can calculate the averages shown in Figure 12-27 on the next page by entering a single array formula.

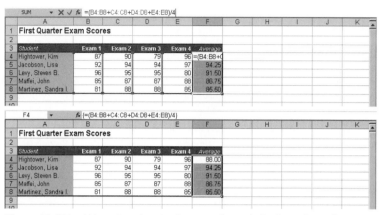

Figure 12-27. We entered a single array formula in the selected range F4:F8.

This particular example might be used to help protect the formulas from tampering because modifying individual formulas in cells that are part in an array is impossible. To enter this formula, do the following:

1 Select the range F4:F8.

2 Type the formula into the formula bar, as shown in Figure 12-27.

3 Press Ctrl+Shift+Enter.

The resulting single array formula exists in five cells at once. Although the array formula seems to be five separate formulas, you can't make changes to any one formula without selecting the entire formula—that is, the entire range F4:F8.

Array Formula Rules

To enter an array formula, first select the cell or range that will contain the results. If the formula produces multiple results, you must select a range the same size and shape as the range or ranges on which you perform your calculations.

Follow these guidelines when entering and working with array formulas:

- Press Ctrl+Shift+Enter to lock in an array formula. Excel will then place a set of curly braces around the formula in the formula bar to indicate that it's an array formula. Don't type the braces yourself; if you do, Excel interprets your entry as a label.

- You can't edit, clear, or move individual cells in an array range, nor can you insert or delete cells. You must treat the cells in the array range as a single unit and edit them all at once.

- To edit an array, select the entire array, click the formula bar, and edit the formula. Then press Ctrl+Shift+Enter to lock in the formula.

- To clear an array, select the entire array and press Delete.
- To select an entire array, click any cell in the array and press Ctrl+/.
- To move an array range, you must select the entire array and either cut and paste the selection or drag the selection to a new location.
- You can't cut, clear, or edit part of an array, but you can assign different formats to individual cells in the array. You can also copy cells from an array range and paste them in another area of your worksheet.

Two-Dimensional Arrays

In the preceding example, the array formula resulted in a vertical, one-dimensional array. You can also create arrays that include two or more columns and rows, otherwise known as two-dimensional arrays. An example is shown in Figure 12-28.

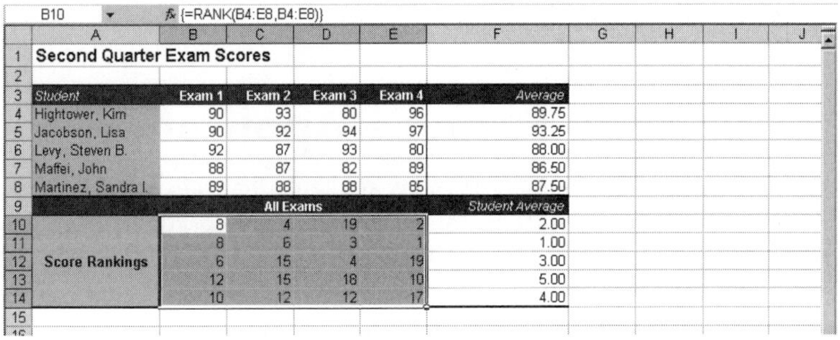
B10 {=RANK(B4:E8,B4:E8)}

	A	B	C	D	E	F
1	Second Quarter Exam Scores					
2						
3	Student	Exam 1	Exam 2	Exam 3	Exam 4	Average
4	Hightower, Kim	90	93	80	96	89.75
5	Jacobson, Lisa	90	92	94	97	93.25
6	Levy, Steven B.	92	87	93	80	88.00
7	Maffei, John	88	87	82	89	86.50
8	Martinez, Sandra I.	89	88	88	85	87.50
9		All Exams				Student Average
10	Score Rankings	8	4	19	2	2.00
11		8	6	3	1	1.00
12		6	15	4	19	3.00
13		12	15	18	10	5.00
14		10	12	12	17	4.00
15						

Figure 12-28. We used a two-dimensional array formula in B10:E14 to compute the rank of each exam score. A similar one-dimensional array is in F10:F14.

To enter a two-dimensional array, do the following:

1. Select a range to contain your array that is the same size and shape as the range you want to work with.
2. Type your formula into the formula bar, and press Ctrl+Shift+Enter.

> **tip** Unfortunately, you can't create three-dimensional arrays across multiple worksheets in workbooks.

Single-Cell Array Formulas

You can perform calculations on a vast collection of values within a single cell, using an array formula that produces a single value as a result. For example, to count the number of error values in a range of cells, you can create a single-cell array formula, as shown in Figure 12-29 on the next page.

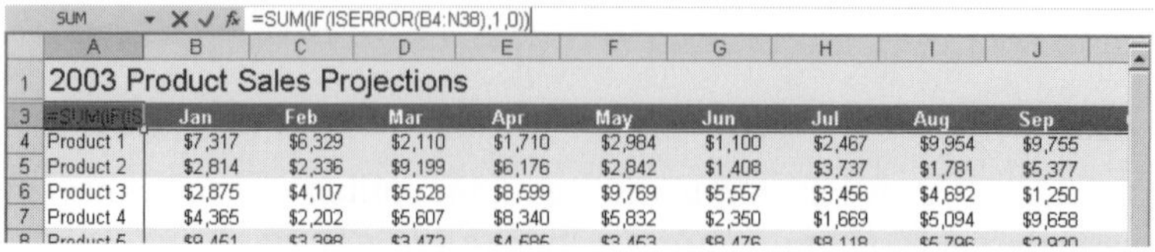

Figure 12-29. We used a single-cell array formula in A3 to count error values that appear in the range B4:N38.

In the example shown in Figure 12-29, the formula can be entered as a normal formula (press Enter) or as an array formula (press Ctrl+Shift+Enter). In this case, using an array formula makes a difference. No matter how many errors might appear in the worksheet, the nonarray version of the formula returns the value 1 because the SUM function essentially has only one argument—the result of the single ISERROR function. If you enter the same formula as an array formula, however, it returns the total number of errors because the SUM function sees an array of individual ISERROR functions instead of just one. For more on the ISERROR function, see "Using the IS Information Functions" on page 427.

A Single-Cell Array Formula Application

Suppose you want the total number of items in a table that satisfy two criteria. You want to know how many transactions of more than $1,000 occurred after a specified date. You could add a column to the table containing an IF function to find each transaction that satisfies these criteria, and then total the results of that column. A simpler way to do this is to use a single array formula like this one:
=SUM((A1:A100>37266)*(C1:C100>999)).

The 37266 in the formula is the serial date value for 1/10/2002. Enter the formula by pressing Ctrl+Shift+Enter. Each item in the first parenthetical expression evaluates to either a 1 (TRUE) or a 0 (FALSE), depending on the date; each item in the second parenthetical expression evaluates also to either a 1 or a 0, depending on whether its value is greater than 999. The formula then multiplies the 1s and 0s, and when both are TRUE, the resulting value is 1. The SUM function adds the 1s and gives you the total. You can add more criteria by adding more parenthetical elements to the formula; any expression that evaluates to false (0) eliminates that transaction because anything multiplied by 0 is 0.

You could enhance this formula in several ways. For example, replace the serial date number with the DATEVALUE function so you can use 1/10/2002 as an argument instead of having to find the date value yourself. Even better, use cell references as arguments to each element so you can type criteria into cells rather than editing the formula. For information about the DATEVALUE function, see Chapter 15, "Formatting and Calculating Date and Time."

Using Array Constants

An *array constant* is a specially organized list of values that you can use as arguments in your array formulas. Array constants can consist of numbers, text, or logical values. You must enclose an array constant in braces—{ and }—and separate its elements with commas and semicolons. Commas indicate values in separate columns, and semicolons indicate values in separate rows. The formula in Figure 12-30, for example, performs nine computations in one cell.

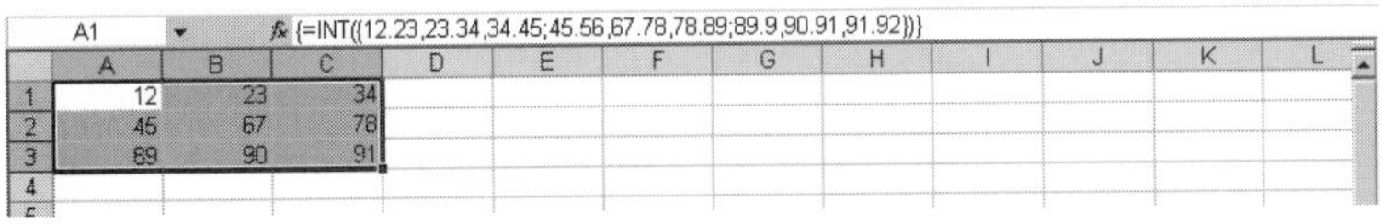

Figure 12-30. An array constant is the argument for this array formula.

To enter a formula using an array constant, follow these steps:

1 Select a range of cells the size you need to contain the result. In Figure 12-30, the argument to the INT function contains three groups (separated by semi-colons) of three values (separated by commas), which produces a three-row, three-column range.

2 Type the braces around the argument, to indicate that the enclosed values make up an array constant.

3 Press Ctrl+Shift+Enter. The resulting array formula contains two sets of curly braces—one set encloses the array constant and the other encloses the entire array formula.

When entering array constants, remember that commas between array elements place those elements in separate columns, and semicolons between array elements place those elements in separate rows. In addition, you must type curly braces to enclose the array constant.

Understanding Array Expansion

When you use arrays as arguments in a formula, all your arrays should have the same dimensions. If the dimensions of your array arguments or array ranges do not match, Excel often expands the arguments. For example, to multiply all the values in cells A1:B5 by 10, you can use either of the following array formulas:
{ =A1:B5*10} or { ={ 1,2;3,4;5,6;7,8;9,10} *10}.

Note that these two formulas are not balanced; ten values are on the left side of the multiplication operator but only one is on the right. Excel expands the second argument to match the size and shape of the first. In the preceding example, the first formula is equivalent to { =A1:B5*{ 10,10;10,10;10,10;10,10;10,10} } and the second is equivalent to { ={ 1,2;3,4;5,6;7,8;9,10} *{ 10,10;10,10;10,10;10,10;10,10} }.

When you work with two or more sets of multivalue arrays, each set must have the same number of rows as the argument with the greatest number of rows and the same number of columns as the argument with the greatest number of columns.

Linking Workbooks

Creating dynamic links between workbooks with external reference formulas provides a number of advantages. For example, you could break a large, complex company budget model into more manageable departmental models. Then you could link all the departmental workbooks (supporting workbooks) to a master budget workbook (a dependent workbook). In addition to creating more manageable and flexible models, linked workbooks can save recalculation time and memory.

This section discusses some special considerations to be aware of when working with workbooks linked by external reference formulas. For more information about external references, see "Creating References to Other Worksheets in the Same Workbook" on page 358 and "Creating References to Worksheets in Other Workbooks" on page 358.

Saving Linked Workbooks

When you create a set of linked workbooks, you should save the supporting workbooks before you save the dependent workbooks. For example, suppose you are modeling your company's 2003 budget in an unsaved workbook called Book1. When you save the workbook, you give it the name Budget 2003.

Now suppose that you have another active workbook in which you plan to enter actual (as opposed to budgeted) expenditures; you have already saved the workbook with the name Actual 2003. This workbook contains links to your Budget workbook and, therefore, is dependent on the Budget workbook for some of its information. When you first created these links, the Budget workbook was identified as Book1.

If you save Book1 as Budget 2003 while the Actual workbook is still open, all references to Book1 in the Actual workbook change automatically to Budget 2003. For example, if Actual contains the reference =[Book1]Sheet1!$A$1, the reference changes to ='[Budget 2003.xls]Sheet1'!$A$1.

If you try to close the dependent Actual 2003 workbook before you save the supporting Book1 (Budget) workbook, however, you see the warning Save Actual 2003 with references to unsaved documents? Click OK to save and close it. When you then save Book1 as Budget 2003, the references to Book1 in the Actual workbook are not updated because it's not open; the formulas continue to reference Book1. When you reopen Actual 2003, Excel displays a message box notifying you that the workbook contains links to another workbook and prompts you to update the linked information. If you click Yes, Excel is, of course, unable to find Book1. You need to find the Actual 2003 workbook so that Excel can reestablish the links.

Opening a Dependent Workbook

When you save a workbook that contains dependent formulas, Excel stores the most recent results of those formulas. If you open and edit the supporting workbook after closing the dependent workbook, the values of edited cells in the supporting workbook might be different. When you open the dependent workbook again, it contains the old values of the external references in the dependent formulas, but Excel displays an alert box with the message "This document contains links to other data sources." The alert box lets you tell Excel whether or not to read the current values from the closed workbook on the disk.

If you click Don't Update, Excel opens the dependent workbook without updating any references to the supporting workbook. All dependent formulas retain their last saved values.

If you click Update, Excel searches for the supporting workbook. If it's found, Excel reads the supporting values and updates the dependent formulas in the dependent workbook. Excel does not open the supporting workbook; it merely reads the appropriate values from it.

If Excel can't find the supporting workbook, it displays the alert "This workbook contains one or more links that cannot be updated." You can click Continue to open the workbook anyway, or you can click Edit Links to identify, in the Edit Links dialog box, a new supporting file to use.

Editing Links

You can open supporting workbooks, as well as specify different supporting workbooks, when you choose Edit, Links, which is available only when an external reference exists in the active workbook. For example, the dialog box shown in Figure 12-31 displays a link to a supporting workbook.

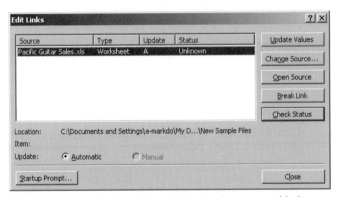

Figure 12-31. Use the Edit Links dialog box to quickly locate all your supporting workbooks.

Here is some helpful information about using the Edit Links dialog box:

● An A in the Status column indicates a link that is updated automatically.

● An M in the Status column indicates a manual link that isn't updated until you click the Update Values button.

● Click the Open Source button to open the supporting workbook.

● Click the Change Source button to select a different supporting workbook.

● Click the Break Link button to convert all existing external references in formulas to their current values. You can't undo this action, so click the Break Link button with caution.

● Click the Update Values button to fetch the latest figures from the supporting workbook without having to open it.

● You can link objects and documents created in other applications, such as Microsoft Word, to Excel worksheets and charts. When you do so, the Type box displays the application name and the object type.

InsideOut

Be careful when moving documents

Normally you should be careful about moving documents to which you have created links in workbooks. This isn't true, however, if you are using Windows 2000 (or later) or Windows NT. For example, if you create a link to text in a Word document and then change the name or location of that document, Excel still finds the source and updates the link—provided the source is stored on an NTFS (the Windows NT/2000 File System) volume. You can do this because NTFS maintains a change log, and Excel consults that log. (If you use hyperlinks, however, relocating or changing the source file breaks the link, even if the file is on an NTFS volume both before and after the change.) If you move the source document to a FAT32 (the MS-DOS/Windows File System) volume, however, Excel can't find the document.

Copying, Cutting, and Pasting in Linked Workbooks

You can use relative or absolute references to cells in other workbooks as you do in a single workbook. Relative and absolute references to cells in supporting workbooks respond to the Copy, Cut, and Paste commands and toolbar buttons in much the same way as references to cells in the same workbook do.

For example, suppose you create the formula =[**Form2**]**Sheet1**!**F1** in cell A1 in Sheet1
of Form1 and then use Copy and Paste to copy this formula to cell B1. The formula in
cell B1 becomes =[**Form2**]**Sheet1**!**G1**. The original formula changed when it was copied to cell B1 because the reference to cell F1 is relative. However, if the formula in cell
A1 of Form1 contained an absolute reference, such as =[**Form2**]**Sheet1**!**$F$1**, the reference in the copied formula would not change.

Copying and Pasting between Workbooks

When you copy a dependent formula from one workbook to another and that formula
includes a relative reference to a third workbook, the reference is adjusted to reflect the
new position of the formula. For example, suppose that cell A1 in Form1 contains the
formula =[**Form2**]**Sheet1**!**A1**. If you copy and paste that formula into cell B5 in Form3,
the result is the formula =[**Form2**]**Sheet1**!**B5**. The formula is adjusted to reflect its new
relative position.

If you copy a formula that contains an absolute reference to another workbook, the
formula remains the same. For example, suppose cell A1 in Form1 contains the formula =[**Form2**]**Sheet1**!**$A$1**. If you copy and paste that formula into cell B5 in Form3,
the resulting formula is the same.

Even if you copy a dependent formula to the workbook to which the formula refers, it's
still a dependent formula. For example, if you copy the formula =[**Form2**]**Sheet1**!**$A$1**
from cell A1 of Form1 to cell A3 on Sheet1 of Form2, the resulting formula is essentially the same, except that the book reference isn't necessary because the formula is in
the same workbook. As a result, the formula becomes =**Sheet1**!**$A$1**.

Cutting and Pasting between Workbooks

Excel does not adjust the relative references in a formula when you cut it from one
workbook and paste it in another, as it does when you copy a formula. For example,
suppose that cell A1 in Sheet1 of Form1 contains the formula =[**Form2**]**Sheet1**!**A1**. If
you cut that formula and paste it into cell B5 of Form3, the formula does not change.

Cutting and Pasting Cells Referred to by Dependent Formulas

When you cut and paste cells, Excel normally adjusts any references to those cells in the
formulas of the workbook. Dependent formulas, however, do not follow the same
rules. When you cut and paste a cell referred to by a dependent formula in a closed
workbook, that formula isn't adjusted to reflect the change.

For example, suppose you create the formula =[**Form2**]**Sheet1**!**A10** in cell A1 in
Form1. If you close Form1 and use Cut and Paste to move the entry to cell B10 of
Form2, the formula in cell A1 of Form1 remains the same. You might expect the link to

be broken because the worksheet containing the formula was closed when you modified the referenced cell. However, Excel manages to keep track of everything. When you open the workbook, the message "This document contains links to other data sources" alerts you that the data the workbook depended on has changed.

Creating Conditional Tests

A *conditional test* formula compares two numbers, functions, formulas, labels, or logical values. Conditional tests can be used to flag values that fall below or above a given threshold, for example. You can use simple mathematical and logical operators to construct logical formulas, or you can use an assortment of built-in functions. For information about using conditional test functions, see "Understanding Logical Functions" on page 424

Each of the following formulas performs a rudimentary conditional test:

```
=A1>A2
```

```
=5-3<5*2
```

```
=AVERAGE(B1:B6)=SUM(6,7,8)
```

```
=C2="Female"
```

```
=COUNT(A1:A10)=COUNT(B1:B10)
```

```
=LEN(A1)=10
```

Every conditional test must include at least one logical operator, which defines the relationship between elements of the conditional test. For example, in the conditional test A1>A2, the greater than (>) logical operator compares the values in cells A1 and A2. Table 12-4 lists the six logical operators.

Table 12-4. Logical Operators

Operator	Definition
=	Equal to
>	Greater than
<	Less than
> =	Greater than or equal to
< =	Less than or equal to
< >	Not equal to

The result of a conditional test is either the logical value TRUE (1) or the logical value
FALSE (0). For example, the conditional test =**A1=10** returns TRUE if the value in A1
equals 10 or FALSE if A1 contains any other value.

Using the Conditional Sum and Lookup Wizards

Excel includes two useful tools called wizards that help you assemble frequently used
yet confusing types of formulas. The Conditional Sum Wizard and the Lookup Wizard
are provided as *add-ins,* which are special types of macros designed to integrate
seamlessly into Excel. To see whether you have these Wizards installed, look at the
Tools menu. If you see a Conditional Sum or Lookup commands, then the respective
Wizards are installed.

If you don't see a Wizard submenu, or if one of the wizards isn't there, choose Tools,
Addins. If Conditional Sum Wizard and Lookup Wizard are on the list of available
add-ins, select both (and any others you want) and then click OK to install them. If
neither add-in is on the list, you need to run Setup to install them.

> For more information about Setup, see Appendix A, "Installing Microsoft Excel."

Creating Conditional Sum Formulas

The Conditional Sum Wizard creates formulas using the SUM and IF functions. This
wizard not only makes the construction of these formulas easier and faster, but also
shows you how these formulas are constructed so that you can build your own conditional formulas without the Wizard.

> For more information about the IF function, see "Understanding Logical Functions" on page 424.

To build a conditional formula:

1 Select the table or list containing the values you want to use, and choose Tools,
Conditional Sum to display the dialog box shown in Figure 12-32 on the next page.

 If you click anywhere in the table before you start the wizard, Excel automatically selects the current region for you. If Excel selects the correct region,
click the Next button. Otherwise, drag to select the range you want to use.
Remember to include the row and column labels. The dialog box changes to
the one shown on the left in Figure 12-33 on the next page.

2 In the Column To Sum list, select the name of the column from which you
want to extract totals.

 This is why you need to select the labels in the Step 1 dialog box. If the column
labels do not appear in the list, click the Back button and reselect the range.

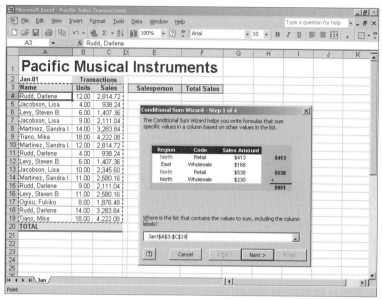

Figure 12-32. The Conditional Sum Wizard helps you construct SUM
formulas that are choosy about what they include.

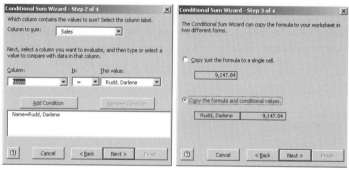

Figure 12-33. These wizard steps allow you to select the cells to
include in your calculation

3 Still in Step 2 of the Wizard, specify the condition to use in selecting the values you want to include in the total. In the Column list, select the name of
the column containing the labels you want to conditionally check, select an
operator in the Is list, and then select a value in the This Value list.

The contents of the This Value list change depending on the column selected
in the Column list. The This Value list displays only the unique values in the
selected column, ignoring duplicates.

4 Click the Add Condition button.

The criteria you specify are added to the list at the bottom of the dialog box. You can add as many as seven conditions. If you change your mind about any condition, select the condition from the list and click the Remove Condition button. When you have finished removing conditions, click the Next button.

5 In Step 3 of the Wizard, choose either Copy Just The Formula To A Single Cell, or choose Copy The Formula And Conditional Values.

---

tip **Copy the formula**

If you select the first option—Copy Just The Formula To A Single Cell—in Step 3 of the Wizard, you won't be able to copy the formula without modifying it. If you select the second option—Copy The Formula And Conditional Values—you can copy the formula without modification. When you select the second option, the resulting formula includes a relative reference to the cell containing the pasted conditional value as the logical criterion for the IF function.

---

6 Click the Next button, and then select the cell where you want to place the resulting formula.

If you chose the Copy Formula And Conditional Values option in Step 3 of the Wizard, the Wizard adds an extra step. Select the cell where you want the conditional value to go. Then click Next, and click the cell where you want the formula to go.

7 Click Finish. The resulting formula (and the optional conditional value) is pasted in the worksheet in the locations specified.

8 Click the Add Condition button.

InsideOut

Beware of the wizard

In many cases, including Step 1 of the Conditional Sum Wizard (shown in Figure 12-32), Excel attempts to select a cell range or table for you automatically. This doesn't always work the way it should. In the example worksheet shown in Figure 12-32, Excel automatically selected A1:C20, which includes a merged cell at the top; this isn't allowed. We had to select the correct range before proceeding. Excel should recognize this before automatically selecting it, but it doesn't.

You can add more conditional formulas, or if you already have a list of unique values, you can copy the formula as needed (but only if you used the Copy Formula And Conditional Values option in Step 3 of the wizard), as shown in Figure 12-34.

F4			fx {=SUM(IF($A$4:$A$19=E4,$C$4:$C$19,0))}								
	A	B	C	D	E	F	G	H	I	J	K
1	**Pacific Musical Instruments**										
2	Jan-01		Transactions								
3	Name	Units	Sales		Salesperson	Total Sales					
4	Rudd, Darlene	12.00	2,814.72		Rudd, Darlene	9,147.84					
5	Jacobson, Lisa	4.00	938.24		Jacobson, Lisa	5,394.88					
6	Levy, Steven B.	6.00	1,407.36		Martinez, Sandra I.	8,678.72					
7	Jacobson, Lisa	9.00	2,111.04		Tiano, Mike	8,444.16					
8	Martinez, Sandra I.	14.00	3,283.84		Levy, Steven B.	5,394.88					
9	Tiano, Mike	18.00	4,222.08		Ogisu, Fukiko	1,876.48					
10	Martinez, Sandra I.	12.00	2,814.72								

Figure 12-34. We added a list of unique salesperson names (conditions) in column E and copied the conditional sum formula to cells F5:F9.

InsideOut

Watch out for spaces

The Conditional Sum Wizard isn't smart about space characters. For example, if a label in the column of criteria includes an invisible space character at the end of the text string, Excel excludes it from the total, even if all the instances are the same.

Creating Lookup Formulas

The Lookup Wizard creates formulas using the INDEX and MATCH functions. Like the Conditional Sum Wizard, it makes the construction of lookup formulas easier and faster, and it also illustrates how these formulas are constructed so that you can build them yourself later. For more information about the INDEX and MATCH functions, see "Understanding Lookup and Reference Functions" on page 429. To build a lookup formula:

1 Choose Tools, Lookup to display the dialog box shown on the left in Figure 12-35.

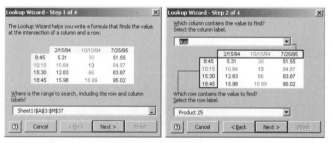

Figure 12-35. Specify the lookup range and the row and column you want to find using the first two steps of the Lookup Wizard.

> **note** The resulting formula shown in the formula bar in Figure 12-35 is enclosed in curly braces, { and }, indicating an array formula. For more information about arrays, see "Using Arrays" on page 387.

2 Select the table or list containing the values you want to use. If you click anywhere in the table before you start the Wizard, Excel automatically selects the current region for you. If Excel selects the correct region, click the Next button; otherwise drag to select the range you want to use. Remember to include the row and column labels. The dialog box changes to the one shown on the right in Figure 12-35.

3 Select the name of the column containing the value you want from the Select The Column Label list. (This is why you need to select the labels in the Step 1 dialog box.) If the labels don't appear in the list, click the Back button and reselect the range.

4 Decide whether you want the lookup parameters as well as the result to be inserted in your worksheet, as shown in Figure 12-36. Inserting the parameters (conditions) is recommended, as we will show later. Select the Copy The Formula And Lookup Parameters option, and then click Next.

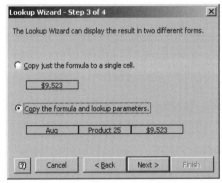

Figure 12-36. If you copy the formula to a single cell, the parameters are fixed; copying both the formula and the parameters allows you to create a lookup table.

5 Select the cell where you want to resulting formula to be placed. If you chose the Copy The Formula And Lookup Parameters option in Step 3 of the Wizard, the Wizard adds two extra steps. If you did this, select the cell where you want the first parameter to go, click Next, and click a cell from the second parameter. Then click Next and click the cell where you want the conditional formula to go.

6 Click Finish.

Figure 12-37 on the next page shows an example of how you can use the Lookup Wizard to build a lookup table.

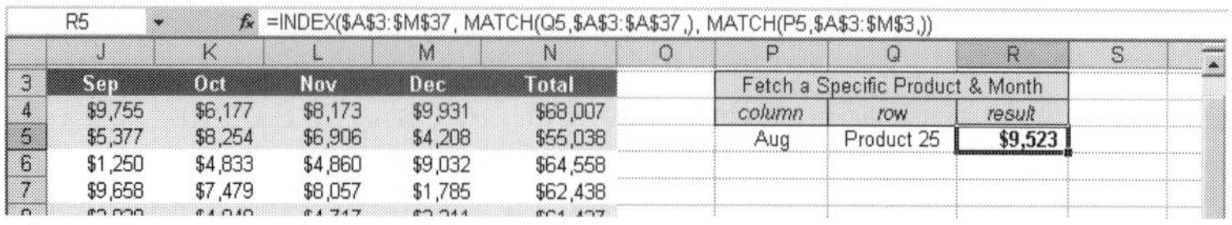

R5			*fx* =INDEX($A$3:$M$37, MATCH(Q5,$A$3:$A$37,), MATCH(P5,$A$3:$M$3,))								
	J	K	L	M	N	O	P	Q	R	S	
3	**Sep**	**Oct**	**Nov**	**Dec**	**Total**		Fetch a Specific Product & Month				
4	$9,755	$6,177	$8,173	$9,931	$68,007		*column*	*row*	*result*		
5	$5,377	$8,254	$6,906	$4,208	$55,038		Aug	Product 25	$9,523		
6	$1,250	$4,833	$4,860	$9,032	$64,558						
7	$9,658	$7,479	$8,057	$1,785	$62,438						

Figure 12-37. You can enter different months and product numbers to
change the corresponding value in cell R5.

As mentioned previously, when you select the Copy The Formula And Lookup Parameters option in Step 3 of the Lookup Wizard, the parameters are inserted in your
worksheet; in our example, we specified cells P5 and Q5. The resulting lookup formula
(in cell R5) refers to these inserted values using relative references. As you can see in
the formula bar in Figure 12-37, the first arguments for the MATCH functions are relative references to our specified cells. Used in this way, you can do two things. You can
type other valid parameters (Sept, or Product 12, or both, for example) into the
parameter cells (P5 and Q5), and the lookup formula finds the corresponding value at
the new intersection. Two, because the parameter references are relative, you can copy
the formula to additional cells and type additional parameters into cells in the same
relative locations.

Chapter 13

Using Functions

Worksheet functions are special tools that perform complex calculations quickly and easily. They work like the special keys on sophisticated calculators that compute square roots, logarithms, and statistical evaluations—except that Microsoft Excel has hundreds of these special functions. Some functions, such as SIN and FACT, are the equivalent of lengthy mathematical formulas that you would otherwise have to create by hand. Other functions, such as IF and VLOOKUP, can't be otherwise duplicated by formulas. When none of the built-in functions is quite what you need, you can create custom functions, as explained in Chapter 32, "Creating Custom Functions."

Using Excel's Built-In Function Reference

While preparing this book, we had to make some tough choices. Fully describing each of the hundreds of worksheet functions would fill an entire book—or two, perhaps. To provide the greatest benefit, we had to decide which functions to focus on and which to mention only briefly. Admittedly, we tend to devote more ink to financial, information, and lookup functions than we do to engineering or trigonometric functions. We think this makes sense for the majority of our readers. If you need more information about functions that we do not cover in great detail, Excel offers several built-in resources:

● **The online Help system** includes a detailed description of each worksheet function. Just press F1, and then type a function name to get specific help. You can also go to the Help Contents tab, Function Reference, where the functions are grouped into functional categories to help you find the one you need, as shown in Figure 13-1 on the next page.

403

Part 5: Creating Formulas and Performing Data Analysis

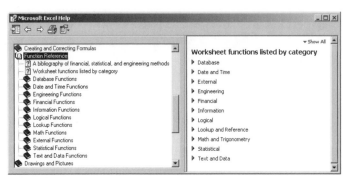

Figure 13-1. Excel's online Help system includes a comprehensive function reference.

● **The Insert Function dialog box**, shown in Figure 13-5, can be used to search through the entire list of functions if you're not sure which function you need. To display the Insert Function dialog box, click the Insert Function button.

● **The Function Arguments dialog box**, shown in Figure 13-2, provides details about the function, and the required arguments appear in the middle of the dialog box. Notice that there is also a link to the relevant Help topic at the bottom of the dialog box. To display the Function Arguments dialog box, click the Insert Function button on the formula bar *after* you type in a valid function name.

Insert Function button

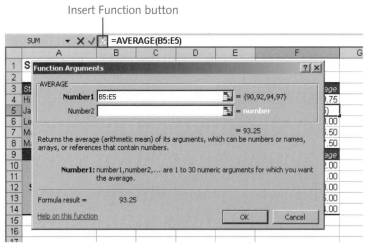

Figure 13-2. Click the Insert Function button for instant assistance with an existing function or to find a function that fills your need.

● **Function ScreenTips** (yellow tags that appear below formulas) are useful if you are unsure about the syntax of a function as you enter a formula, and you can get help without even leaving the cell. Function ScreenTips, shown in Figure 13-3, show you the correct function syntax but also include a link to the Help topic on the selected function. Just click the function name in the ScreenTip to display the relevant topic from the online Help system. If you click an argument name in the ScreenTip, the corresponding section of the formula is highlighted for you, making it easy to identify each argument. (To turn off this feature, choose Tools, Options, click the General tab, and under Settings, clear the Function ScreenTips check box.)

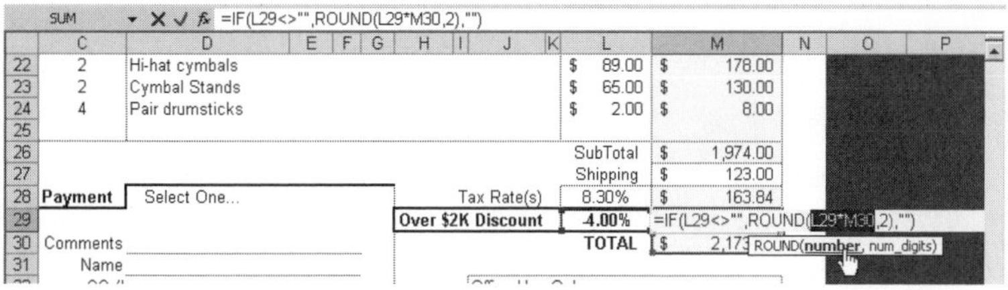

Figure 13-3. Click an argument name in the Function ScreenTip, which appears when you click an existing function, to highlight the corresponding argument in the cell.

For more on the Excel online Help system, see "Online Help Works—Really!" on page 54.

Installing the Analysis ToolPak

When you install Excel, the most commonly used functions are installed as well. However, there are additional functions available in the Analysis ToolPak, a set of add-in tools and functions designed for data analysis. This add-in includes a number of excellent worksheet functions that become available through the Insert Function dialog box, and some sophisticated, macro-based, statistical analysis tools.

To see if you have the Analysis ToolPak installed, go to the Tools menu. If the Data Analysis command is there (you might have to double-click the menu name to expand it to its full size), then you're good to go. The Data Analysis dialog box is shown on the right in Figure 13-4 on the next page. If the Data Analysis command isn't on your Tools menu, choose Tools, Add-Ins. If Analysis ToolPak is on the list of available add-ins, select it, and then click OK to install them. If the Analysis ToolPak isn't in the list of available add-ins, you'll need to run Setup to install it.

For more information on the Analysis ToolPak, see Chapter 17, "Functions for Analyzing Statistics." For more about Setup, see Appendix A, "Installing Microsoft Excel."

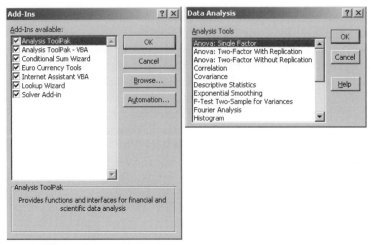

Figure 13-4. Choose Tools, Add-Ins to install the Analysis ToolPak, which includes (among other things) the Tools, Data Analysis command, whose dialog box is shown on the right.

Exploring the Syntax of Functions

Worksheet functions have two parts: the name of the function and the argument(s) that follow. Function names—such as SUM and AVERAGE—describe the operation that the function performs. Arguments specify the values or cells to be used by the function. For example, the function ROUND has the following syntax: =ROUND(*number, num_digits*) as in the formula =ROUND(M30,2). The M30 is a cell reference entered as the *number* argument—the value to be rounded. The 2 is the *num_digits* argument. The result of this function is a number (whatever M30 happens to be) rounded to two decimal places.

Parentheses surround function arguments. The opening parenthesis must appear immediately after the name of the function. If you add a space or some other character between the name and the opening parenthesis, the error value #NAME? appears in the cell.

> **note** A few functions, such as PI, TRUE, and NOW have no arguments. (These functions are usually nested in other formulas.) Even though they have no arguments, they must be followed by an empty set of parentheses, as in =NOW( ).

When you use more than one argument in a function, you separate the arguments with commas. For example, the formula =PRODUCT(C1,C2,C5) tells Excel to multiply the numbers in cells C1, C2, and C5. Some functions, like PRODUCT and SUM, take an unspecified number of arguments. You can use as many as 30 arguments in a function, as long as the total length of the formula does not exceed 1,024 characters. However, you can use a single argument, or a range that refers to any number of cells in your

worksheet, as a formula. For example, the function =SUM(A1:A5,C2:C10,D3:D17) has
only three arguments but actually totals the values in 29 cells. (The first argument,
A1:A5, refers to the range of five cells from A1 through A5, and so on.) The referenced
cells can, in turn, also contain formulas that refer to more cells or ranges.

Expressions as Arguments

You can use combinations of functions to create an expression that Excel evaluates to a
single value and then interprets as an argument. For example, in the formula
=SUM(SIN(A1*PI( )),2*COS(A2*PI( ))) the comma separates two complex expressions that are evaluated and used as the arguments of the SUM function.

Types of Arguments

In the examples presented so far, all the arguments have been cell or range references.
You can also use numbers, text, logical values, range names, arrays, and error values
as arguments.

Numeric Values

The arguments to a function can be numeric. For example, the SUM function in the
formula =SUM(327,209,176) adds the numbers 327, 209, and 176. Usually, however,
you enter the numbers you want to use in cells of a worksheet and then use references
to those cells as arguments to your functions.

Text Values

You can also use text as an argument to a function. For example, in the formula
=TEXT(NOW( ),"*mmm d, yyyy*") in the second argument to the TEXT function, *mmm
d, yyyy*, is a text argument specifically recognized by Excel. It specifies a pattern for converting the serial date value returned by NOW into a text string. Text arguments can be
text strings enclosed in quotation marks or references to cells that contain text.

For more on text functions, see "Understanding Text Functions" on page 419.

Logical Values

The arguments to a few functions specify only that an option is either set or not set;
you can use the logical values TRUE to set an option and FALSE to specify that the
option isn't set. A logical expression returns the value TRUE or FALSE to the worksheet
or the formula containing the expression. For example, the first argument of the IF
function in the formula =IF(A1=TRUE,"**Future** ", "**Past** ")&"**History**" is a logical
expression that uses the value in cell A1. If the value in A1 is TRUE, the expression
A1=TRUE evaluates to TRUE, the IF function returns Future, and the formula returns
the text Future History to the worksheet.

407

For more on logical functions, see "Understanding Logical Functions" on page 424.

Named References

You can use a range name as an argument to a function. For example, if you use the Insert, Name, Define command to assign the name QtrlyIncome to the range C3:C6, you can use the formula =**SUM(QtrlyIncome)** to total the numbers in cells C3, C4, C5, and C6.

For more on names, see "Naming Cells and Cell Ranges" on page 371.

Arrays

You can use an array as an argument in a function. Some functions, such as TREND and TRANSPOSE, require array arguments; other functions don't require array arguments but do accept them. Arrays can be composed of numbers, text, or logical values.

For more on arrays, see "Using Arrays" on page 387.

Mixed Argument Types

You can mix argument types within a function. For example, the formula =**AVERAGE(Group1,A3,5*3)** uses a range name (Group1), a cell reference (A3), and a numeric expression (5*3) to arrive at a single value. All three are acceptable.

Inserting Functions

Insert
Function

The easiest way to locate and insert built-in functions is by clicking the Insert Function button. When you do, the dialog box shown in Figure 13-5 appears.

Click the Insert Function button
to access any of Excel's built-in functions.

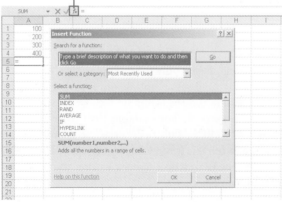

Figure 13-5. Find a function using the Insert Function dialog box.

Chapter 13: Using Functions

If you're not sure what function you need, enter a description of what you are trying to do into the Search box. For example, if you enter "I want to know how many cells contain values" and then press the Go button, the Insert Function dialog box returns a list of recommended functions, similar to the list shown in Figure 13-6. As it turns out, the first function in the list of suggestions fills the bill. If you don't find the function you're looking for, try rewording your query.

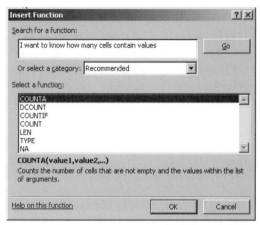

Figure 13-6. Ask a question in the Search box, and Excel suggests some possible functions you can try.

You can also select a function category from the drop-down list to display all the applicable functions available. Function categories include Financial, Date & Time, Lookup & Reference, Text, and more. The Recommended category keeps track of any functions returned as a result of using the Search box.

When you select a function, the syntax and a brief description appear at the bottom of the dialog box. You can obtain help on a function selected in the Select A Function list by clicking the Help On This Function link at the bottom of the dialog box. When you select a function and click OK, Excel enters an equal sign to start a formula in the active cell, inserts the function name and a set of parentheses, and displays the Function Arguments dialog box, shown in Figure 13-7.

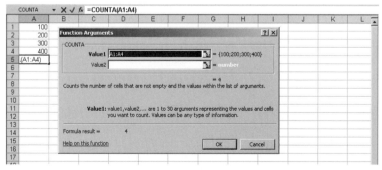

Figure 13-7. The selected function appears in the Function Arguments dialog box, where you can find more information about the function and each selected argument.

409

> **tip** **Shrink the function arguments**
>
> Drag the Function Arguments dialog box around on the screen if you need to see the cells under it. For maximum viewing, shrink the dialog box by clicking one of the collapse buttons at the right side of the boxes.

The Function Arguments dialog box contains one box for each argument of the selected function. If the function accepts a variable number of arguments (such as SUM), the dialog box grows as you enter additional arguments. A description of the argument box currently containing the insertion point appears near the bottom of the dialog box. To the right of each argument box, a display area shows the current value of the argument. This display is very handy when you are using references or defined names, as the value of each argument is calculated for you. The current value of the function (Formula Result) appears at the bottom of the dialog box.

Some functions, such as INDEX, have more than one form. When you select a function from the Insert Function dialog box that has more than one form, Excel presents the Select Arguments dialog box, shown in Figure 13-8, in which you select the form you want to use.

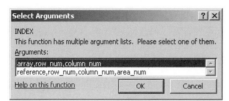

Figure 13-8. If a function has more than one form, the Select Arguments dialog box appears.

> **tip** **Get quick assistance with arguments**
>
> Type an equal sign followed by the function's name in the formula bar and then press Ctrl+A to display the Function Arguments dialog box (or the Select Arguments dialog box, if the function has more than one form).

Troubleshooting

Why Do I Get a #NAME? Error?

There are a few reasons for this error, but one of the more common is typing the function name incorrectly. Here's a good habit to acquire if you type functions yourself: Use lowercase letters. When you press Enter, Excel converts the name of the function to uppercase letters if you entered it correctly. If the letters don't change, you probably entered the name of the function incorrectly. If you're not sure of the exact name or if you continue to get an error, perhaps it's time to consult Help or use the Insert Function dialog box.

Inserting References and Names

As with any other formula, you can insert cell references and defined names into your functions easily using the mouse. For example, to enter a function in cell C11 that averages the cells in the range C2:C10, select cell C11, type =**average**(, and then select the range C2:C10. A marquee appears around the selected cells and a reference to the selected range appears in the formula. Then type the closing parenthesis. If you define named ranges, constants, or formulas in your worksheets, you can insert them into your formulas. To do this, choose Insert, Name, Paste, and then select the name you want in the Paste Name dialog box. When you click OK, the name appears at the insertion point in the formula.

Chapter 14

Everyday Functions

This chapter describes some of the more useful functions Excel has to offer. To keep this book from threatening the integrity of your bookshelf, we've had to make some hard choices about which functions to focus on. Therefore, this chapter (along with chapters 15, 16, and 17) by no means represents a comprehensive reference. But Appendix D, "Function Reference," does list every function available in Excel along with the basic information you need to put it to use as well as cross-references to any information available in this and other chapters. For details on functions not discussed here, take advantage also of the descriptive information presented in the Insert Function dialog box and the online Help system.

For more information, see Chapter 15, "Formatting and Calculating Date and Time;" Chapter 16, "Functions for Financial Analysis;" and Chapter 17, "Functions for Analyzing Statistics."

Understanding Mathematical Functions

Most of the work you do in Excel will probably involve at least a few mathematical functions. The most popular among these is the SUM function, but Excel is capable of calculating just about anything. In this section, we'll discuss some of the most used (and most useful) mathematical functions in Excel.

For more information about individual functions, see Appendix D, "Function Reference."

Using the SUM Function

The SUM function totals a series of numbers. It takes the form
=SUM(*number1, number2, …*). The *number* arguments are a series of as many as 30
entries that can be numbers, formulas, ranges, or cell references that result in numbers. SUM ignores arguments that refer to text values, logical values, or blank cells.

> **tip** **SUMmon more power**
>
> You can create powerful conditional SUM formulas using add-in tools. See "Using the
> Conditional Sum and Lookup Wizards" on page 397.

The AutoSum Button

AutoSum

Because SUM is such a commonly used function, Excel provides the AutoSum button
on the Standard toolbar. If you select a cell and click the AutoSum button, Excel creates
a SUM formula and guesses which cells you want to total. To enter SUM formulas into
a range of cells, select the cells before clicking AutoSum.

Automatic Range Expansion

Ever since the first spreadsheet program was created, one of the most common problems has been inserting cells at the bottom or to the right of a range that is already
referenced in a formula. For example, suppose you type the formula **=SUM(A1:A4)** in
cell A5, and then select row 5 and insert a new row. The new row is inserted above
the selected row, thus pushing the SUM formula down to cell A6. Any numbers in the
new inserted cell A5 are not included in the SUM formula. The previous version of
Excel changed all that. Now you can insert cells at the bottom or to the right of a
range referenced by a formula, and Excel adjusts the formulas for you *as soon as you
type values in the new inserted cells*.

This works only when you insert cells immediately to the right or below a referenced
range. Inserting cells at the top or to the left of a referenced range still involves editing the referencing formulas manually.

Using Selected Mathematical Functions

Excel has 60 built-in math and trig functions, all of which are listed in Appendix D,
"Function Reference." This section only brushes the surface, covering a few of the
more useful or misunderstood functions.

The PRODUCT and SUMPRODUCT Functions

The PRODUCT function multiplies all its arguments and can take as many as 30 arguments. Arguments that are text, logical values, or blank cells are ignored.

You can use the SUMPRODUCT function to multiply the value in each cell in one range by the corresponding cell in another range of equal size and then add the results. You can include up to 30 arrays as arguments but each array must have the same dimensions. (Non-numeric entries are treated as zero.) For example, the following formulas are essentially the same:

```
=SUMPRODUCT(A1:A4, B1:B4)
```

```
{=SUM(A1:A4*B1:B4)}
```

The only difference between them is that the SUM formula must be entered as an array by pressing Ctrl+Shift+Enter.

For more information about arrays, see "Using Arrays" on page 387.

The MOD Function

The MOD function returns the remainder of a division operation (modulus). It takes the arguments (*number, divisor*). The result of the MOD function is the remainder produced when *number* is divided by *divisor*. For example, the function =**MOD(9, 4)** returns 1, the remainder that results from dividing 9 by 4.

A MOD Example

Here's a practical use of the MOD function that you can ponder:

1   Select a cell and choose Format, Conditional Formatting.

2   Select the Formula Is option from the first condition list, and then type the formula **=MOD(ROW(), 2)=0** in the box on the right.

3   Click the Format button and select a color from the Patterns tab to create a format that applies the selected color to every other row. Note that if you select cells in an odd-numbered row, nothing seems to happen, but if you copy or apply the format to other rows, you'll see the result.

This formula checks the current row number using the ROW function, divides it by 2, and if there is a remainder (indicating an odd-numbered row), returns FALSE because the formula also contains the conditional test **=0**. If MOD returns anything but zero (a remainder), the condition tests FALSE. Therefore, formatting is applied only when the formula returns TRUE (in even-numbered rows). For more information about conditional formatting, see "Applying Conditional Formats" on page 245.

The COMBIN Function

The COMBIN function determines the number of possible combinations, or groups, that can be taken from a pool of items. It takes the arguments (*number, number_chosen*), where *number* is the total number of items in the pool and *number_chosen* is the number of items you want to group in each combination. For example, to determine how many different 12-player football teams you can create from a pool of 17 players, type the formula =COMBIN(17, 12). The result indicates that 6,188 teams could be created.

Chapter 14

---

tip   **Try your luck**

The COMBIN function can help you figure out just how slim a chance you have of getting the elusive ace-high straight flush in a game of five-card stud. The number of card combinations is expressed by the formula **=COMBIN(52, 5)**, resulting in 2,598,960. Not too bad, when you consider the odds of winning the lottery. To figure that out, you need to know the number of possible combinations when choosing 6 numbers out of a total of 49. Type the formula **=COMBIN(49, 6)**, and the result is 13,983,816 possibilities. Better keep the day job.

The RAND and RANDBETWEEN Functions

The RAND function generates a random number between 0 and 1. It's one of the few Excel functions that doesn't take an argument. Note that you must still type the parentheses after the function name. The result of a RAND function changes each time you recalculate your worksheet. If you use automatic recalculation, the value of the RAND function changes each time you make a worksheet entry.

The RANDBETWEEN function, which is available when you install the Analysis ToolPak add-in, provides more control than RAND. With RANDBETWEEN, you can specify a range of numbers within which to generate random integer values.

For information about installing the Analysis ToolPak add-in, see "Installing the Analysis ToolPak" on page 405.

The arguments (*bottom, top*) represent the smallest and largest integers that the function should use. The values for these arguments are inclusive. For example, the formula =RANDBETWEEN(123, 456) can return any integer from 123 up to and including 456.

Using the Rounding Functions

Excel includes several functions devoted to the seemingly narrow task of rounding numbers by a specified amount.

> **note** Don't confuse the rounding functions with fixed formats, such as 0 and 0.00, which are available when you choose Format, Cells and click the Number tab. When you format the contents of a cell to a specified number of decimal places, you change only the display of the number in the cell; you don't change the value. When performing calculations, Excel always uses the underlying value, not the displayed value. Conversely, the rounding functions change the values of the numbers that they operate on.

The ROUND, ROUNDDOWN, and ROUNDUP Functions

The ROUND function rounds a number to a specified number of decimal places, rounding digits less than 5 down and digits greater than or equal to 5 up. It takes the arguments (*number, num_digits*). If *num_digits* is negative, the function rounds to the left of the decimal point; if *num_digits* is 0, the function rounds to the nearest integer. For example, the formula =**ROUND(123.4567, -2)** returns 100, and the formula =**ROUND(123.4567, 3)** returns 123.457. The ROUNDDOWN and ROUNDUP functions take the same form as ROUND. As their names imply, they always round down or up, respectively.

The EVEN and ODD Functions

The EVEN function rounds a number up to the nearest even integer. The ODD function rounds a number up to the nearest odd integer. Negative numbers are correspondingly rounded down. For example, the formula =**EVEN(23.4)** returns 24, and the formula =**ODD(-4)** returns -5.

The FLOOR and CEILING Functions

The FLOOR function rounds a number down to the nearest given multiple, and the CEILING function rounds a number up to the nearest given multiple. These functions take the arguments (*number, multiple*). For example, the formula =**FLOOR(23.4, 0.5)** returns 23, and the formula =**CEILING(5, 1.5)** returns 6.

Using the Flexible MROUND Function

Suppose you want to round a number to a multiple of something other than 10—for example, rounding numbers to sixteenths so that when formatted as fractions they never appear with a denominator larger than 16. The MROUND function, included in the Analysis ToolPak, rounds any number to a multiple you specify. (See "Installing the Analysis ToolPak" on page 405

The function takes the form **=MROUND(*number,multiple*)**. For example, typing the formula **=MROUND(A1, .0625)** rounds the number displayed in cell A1 in increments of one-sixteenth. The function rounds up if the remainder after dividing *number* by *multiple* is at least half the value of *multiple*. If you want to apply this to an existing formula, just wrap the MROUND formula around it by replacing A1 (in the example) with your formula.

The INT Function

The INT function rounds numbers down to the nearest integer. For example, the formulas

```
=INT(100.01)
```

```
=INT(100.99999999)
```

both return the value 100, even though the number 100.99999999 is essentially equal to 101. When a number is negative, INT also rounds that number down to the next integer. If each of the numbers in the examples were negative, the resulting value would be –101.

The TRUNC Function

The TRUNC function truncates everything to the right of the decimal point in a number, regardless of its sign. It takes the arguments (*number, num_digits*). If *num_digits* isn't specified, it's set to zero. Otherwise, TRUNC truncates everything after the specified number of digits to the right of the decimal point. For example, the formula **=TRUNC(13.978)** returns the value 13; the formula **=TRUNC(13.978, 1)** returns the value 13.9.

newfeature!

AVERAGE vs. AVG

Other spreadsheet programs, such as Lotus 1-2-3, use the AVG statistical function to compute averages. In previous versions of Excel, typing the formula **=AVG(2,4, 5, 8)** would result in a #NAME error. Excel 2002 now accepts AVG, although when you type the function, an error dialog box appears, asking whether you want to change the function to AVERAGE. Still kind of rude, but it works. Presumably, the reason why Excel doesn't just change AVG to AVERAGE for you is so you will learn to start using the correct function name.

Cells containing text, logical values, or empty cells are ignored, but cells containing a zero value are included. Excel also includes the AVERAGEA function, which operates in the same way as AVERAGE, except it includes text and logical values in the calculation. For more information, see Appendix D, "Function Reference."

Understanding Text Functions

Text functions are some of the most useful word-processing and data-management tools you'll find anywhere—they do things that word-processing programs can't do. For example, you can use the TRIM and CLEAN functions to remove extra spaces and nonprinting characters, which is great for cleaning up imported data—a task that ranges from difficult to impossible using search and replace.

The UPPER, LOWER, and PROPER functions change the case of words, sentences, and paragraphs with no retyping. You might find yourself copying text from other documents into Excel, just so you can apply these functions. Then choose Edit, Paste Special to convert the formulas to their resulting (text) values and return the text to the original document.

In this section, we'll discuss the most useful Excel text functions.

For more information about individual functions, see Appendix D, "Function Reference."

Using Selected Text Functions

Text functions convert numeric text entries into numbers and convert number entries into text strings so that you can manipulate the text strings themselves.

The TEXT Function

The TEXT function converts a number into a text string with a specified format. Its arguments are (*value, format_text*), where *value* represents any number, formula, or cell reference; and *format_text* is the format for displaying the resulting string. For example, the formula =**TEXT(98/4,"0.00")** returns the text string 24.50. You can use any Excel formatting symbol ($, #, 0, and so on) except the asterisk (*) to specify the format you want, but you can't use the General format.

> For information about formatting symbols and codes, see Table 8-1 "Custom Format Symbols" on page 217 and Table 8-2 "Built-in Custom Format Codes" on page 219.

The DOLLAR Function

Like the TEXT function, the DOLLAR function converts a number into a string. DOLLAR, however, formats the resulting string as currency with the number of decimal places you specify. The arguments (*number, decimals*) specify a number or reference and the number of decimal places you want. For example, the formula =**DOLLAR(45.899, 2)** returns the text string $45.90 Notice that Excel rounds the number when necessary.

If you omit *decimals*, Excel uses two decimal places. If you add a comma after the first argument but omit the second argument, Excel uses zero decimal places. If you use a negative number for *decimals*, Excel rounds to the left of the decimal point.

The LEN Function

The LEN function returns the number of characters in an entry. The single argument can be a number, a string enclosed in double quotation marks, or a reference to a cell. Trailing zeros are ignored. For example, the formula =**LEN("Test")** returns 4.

The LEN function returns the length of the displayed text or value, not the length of the underlying cell contents. For example, suppose cell A10 contains the formula =**A1+A2+A3+A4+A5+A6+A7+A8** and its result is the value 25. The formula =**LEN(A10)** returns the value 2, which indicates the length of the resulting value 25. The cell referenced as the argument of the LEN function can contain another string function. For example, if cell A1 contains the function =**REPT("-*", 75)**, which enters the two-character dash and asterisk string 75 times in a cell, the formula =**LEN(A1)** returns the value 150.

The ASCII Functions: CHAR and CODE

Every computer uses numeric codes to represent characters. The most prevalent system of numeric codes is ASCII, or American Standard Code for Information Interchange. ASCII uses a number from 0 to 127 (or in some systems, to 255) to represent each number, letter, and symbol.

The CHAR and CODE functions deal with these ASCII codes. The CHAR function returns the character that corresponds to an ASCII code number; the CODE function returns the ASCII code number for the first character of its argument. For example, the formula =**CHAR(83)** returns the text S. The formula =**CODE("S")** returns the ASCII code 83. If you type a literal character as the text argument, be sure to enclose the character in quotation marks; otherwise, Excel returns the #NAME? error value.

The Clean-Up Functions: TRIM and CLEAN

Leading and trailing blank characters often prevent you from correctly sorting entries in a worksheet or a database. If you use string functions to manipulate text in your worksheet, extra spaces can prevent your formulas from working correctly. The TRIM function eliminates leading, trailing, and extra blank characters from a string, leaving only single spaces between words.

The CLEAN function is similar to TRIM, except it operates on only nonprintable characters, such as tabs and program-specific codes. CLEAN is especially useful if you import data from another program or operating system, because the translation process often introduces nonprintable characters that appear as symbols or boxes. You can use CLEAN to remove these characters from the data.

The EXACT Function

The EXACT function is a conditional function that determines whether two strings match exactly. The function ignores formatting, but it is case-sensitive, so uppercase letters are considered different than lowercase letters. If both strings are identical, the function returns TRUE. Both arguments must be literal strings enclosed in quotation marks, references to cells that contain text, numeric values, or formulas that evaluate to numeric values. For example, if cell A5 and cell A6 of your worksheet both contain the text Totals, the formula =**EXACT(A5, A6)** returns TRUE.

For information about comparing strings, see "Creating Conditional Tests" on page 396.

The Case Functions: UPPER, LOWER, and PROPER

Three functions manipulate the case of characters in text strings. The UPPER and LOWER functions convert text strings to all uppercase or all lowercase letters. The PROPER function capitalizes the first letter in each word, capitalizes any other letters in the text string that do not follow another letter, and converts all other letters to lowercase. For example, if cell A1 contains the text mike Tiano, you can type the formula =**UPPER(A1)** to return MIKE TIANO. Similarly, the formula =**LOWER(A1)** returns mike tiano, and =**PROPER(A1)** returns Mike Tiano.

Unexpected results can occur when the text contains punctuation, however. For example, if cell A1 contains it wasn't bad, the PROPER function converts it to the text It Wasn'T Bad.

Using the Substring Text Functions

The following functions locate and return portions of a text string or assemble larger strings from smaller ones: FIND, SEARCH, RIGHT, LEFT, MID, SUBSTITUTE, REPLACE, and CONCATENATE.

The FIND and SEARCH Functions

You use the FIND and SEARCH functions to locate the position of a substring within a string. Both functions return the position in the string of the character you specify. (Excel counts blank spaces and punctuation marks as characters.) These two functions work the same way, except FIND is case sensitive and SEARCH allows wildcards. Both functions take the same arguments: (*find_text, within_text, start_num*). The optional *start_num* argument is helpful when *within_text* contains more than one occurrence of *find_text*. If you omit *start_num*, Excel reports the first match it locates. For example, to locate the p in the string A Night At The Opera, you would type the formula =FIND("p", "A Night At The Opera"). The formula returns 17, because p is the seventeenth character in the string.

If you're not sure of the character sequence you're searching for, you can use the SEARCH function and include wildcards in your *find_text* string. Suppose you've used the names Smith and Smyth in your worksheet. To determine whether either name is in cell A1, type the formula =SEARCH("Sm?th", A1).If cell A1 contains the text John Smith or John Smyth, the SEARCH function returns the value 6—the starting point of the string Sm?th.

If you're not sure of the number of characters, use the * wildcard. For example, to find the position of Allan or Alan within the text (if any) stored in cell A1, type the formula =SEARCH("A*an", A1).

The RIGHT and LEFT Functions

The RIGHT function returns the rightmost series of characters from a specified string; the LEFT function returns the leftmost series of characters. These functions take the same arguments: (*text, num_chars*). The *num_chars* argument indicates the number of characters to extract from the *text* argument.

These functions count blank spaces in the text argument as characters; if text contains leading or trailing blank characters, you might want to use a TRIM function within the RIGHT or LEFT function to ensure the expected result. For example, suppose you type **This is a test** in cell A1 of your worksheet. The formula =**RIGHT(A1,4)** returns the word test.

The MID Function

You can use the MID function to extract a series of characters from a text string. This function takes the arguments (*text, start_num, num_chars*). For example, if cell A1 contains the text This Is A Long Text Entry, you can type the formula =MID(A1, 11, 9) to extract the characters Long Text from the entry in cell A1.

The REPLACE and SUBSTITUTE Functions

The REPLACE and SUBSTITUTE functions substitute new text for old text. The
REPLACE function replaces one string of characters with another string of characters
and takes the arguments (*old_text, start_num, num_chars, new_text*). Suppose cell A1
contains the text Eric Miller, CEO. To replace the first four characters with the string
Geof, type the formula =**REPLACE(A1, 1, 4, "Geof")**. The result is Geof Miller, CEO.

With the SUBSTITUTE function, you specify the text to replace. The function takes the
arguments (*text, old_text, new_text, instance_num*). Suppose cell A1 contains the text
Mandy and you want to place it in cell A2 but change it to Randy. Type this formula in
cell A2 =**SUBSTITUTE(A1,"M","R")**.

The *instance_num* argument optionally replaces only the specified occurrence of
old_text. For example, if cell A1 contains the text through the hoop, the 4 in the formula =**SUBSTITUTE(A1, "h", "l", 4)** tells Excel to substitute an l for the fourth h
found in cell A1. If you don't include *instance_num*, Excel changes all occurrences of
old_text to *new_text*.

The CONCATENATE Function

To assemble strings from up to 30 smaller strings or references, the CONCATENATE
function is the function equivalent of the & character. For example, if cell
B4 contains the text Pacific with a trailing space character, the formula
=**CONCATENATE(B4, "Musical Instruments")** returns Pacific Musical Instruments.

Troubleshooting

Concatenated Dates Become Serial Numbers

If you try to concatenate the contents of a cell formatted as a date, the result is probably not what you expect. Because a date in Excel is only a serial number, what you
normally see is a formatted representation of the date. But when you concatenate the
contents of a date-formatted cell, you get the unformatted version of the date. To
avoid this problem, use the TEXT function to convert the serial number to a recognizable form. For example, suppose cell A1 contains the text Today's Date is and cell A2
contains the function =**NOW()** and is formatted to display the date in dd/mm/yyyy
format. Nonetheless, the formula =**CONCATENATE(A1, " ", A2)** results in the value
Today's Date is 37621 (or whatever the current date serial number happens to be). To
remedy this problem, add the TEXT function as follows:
=**CONCATENATE(A1, " ", TEXT(A2, "dd/mm/yyyy"))**.

This version returns the value Today's Date is 05/01/2002 (or whatever today's date
happens to be). Note that the formula includes a space character as a separate argument (" ") between the two cell reference arguments.

Understanding Logical Functions

You use logical functions to test for specific conditions. These functions are often called *logical operators* in discussions of Boolean logic, which is named after George Boole, the British mathematician. You might have run across logical operators also in set theory, a name that was sometimes used when teaching logical concepts in high school. You use logical operators to arrive at one of two conclusions: TRUE or FALSE. We'll discuss the most useful logical functions in this section.

For more information about individual functions, see Appendix D, "Function Reference."

Using Selected Logical Functions

Excel has a rich set of logical functions, including some that are included in the Analysis ToolPak add-in. Most logical functions use conditional tests to determine whether a specified condition is TRUE or FALSE.

For information about installing the Analysis ToolPak add-in, see "Installing the Analysis ToolPak" on page 405. For more information about conditional tests, see "Creating Conditional Tests" on page 396.

Streamline Formulas Using the SUMIF Function

If you find yourself frequently using the IF function to perform conditional tests on individual rows or columns and then using the SUM function to total the results, the SUMIF function might make your work a little easier. With SUMIF, you can add specific values in a range, based on a criterion you supply. For example, you can type the formula **=SUMIF(C12:C27, "Yes", A12:A27)** to find the total of all numbers in A12:A27 in which the cell in the same row in column C contains the word Yes. This performs all the calculations you need in one cell, and eliminates having to create a column of IF formulas. For more information about SUMIF, see "The SUMIF and COUNTIF Functions" on page 473.

The IF Function

The IF function returns values based on supplied conditional tests. It takes the arguments (*logical_test*, *value_if_true*, *value_if_false*). For example, the formula =IF(A6<22, 5, 10) returns 5 if the value in cell A6 is less than 22; otherwise, it returns 10. You can nest other functions within an IF function. For example, the formula =IF(SUM(A1:A10)>0, SUM(A1:A10), 0) returns the sum of A1 through A10 if the sum is greater than 0; otherwise, it returns 0.

You can also use text arguments to return nothing instead of zero if the result is false. For example, the formula =**IF(SUM(A1:A10)>0, SUM(A1:A10), "")** returns a null string ("") if the conditional test is false. The *logical_test* argument can also consist of text. For example, the formula =**IF(A1="Test", 100, 200)** returns the value 100 if cell A1 contains the string Test or returns 200 if it contains any other entry. The match between the two text entries must be exact except for case.

The AND, OR, and NOT Functions

Three additional functions help you develop compound conditional tests: AND, OR, and NOT. These functions work with the logical operators =, >, <, >=, <=, and <>. The AND and OR functions can each have as many as 30 logical arguments. The NOT function takes only one argument. Arguments can be conditional tests, arrays, or references to cells that contain logical values.

Suppose you want Excel to return the text Pass only if a student has an average score above 75 and fewer than five unexcused absences. In Figure 14-1, we typed the formula =**IF(AND(G4<5,F4>75), "Pass", "Fail")**. This fails the student in row 5 because of the five absences. If you use OR instead of AND in the formula shown in Figure 14-1, all students would pass.

	A	B	C	D	E	F	G	H	I	J	K
	H4		*fx* =IF(AND(G4<5,F4>75),"Pass","Fail")								
1	Math Exam Scores										
2	Ms. Nagata										
3	Student	Exam 1	Exam 2	Exam 3	Exam 4	Average	Absences	Pass/Fail			
4	Hightower, Kim	87	90	79	96	88.00	2	Pass			
5	Jacobson, Lisa	92	94	94	97	94.25	5	Fail			
6	Levy, Steven B.	96	95	95	80	91.50	0	Pass			
7	Maffei, John	85	87	87	88	86.75	4	Pass			
8	Martinez, Sandra I.	81	88	88	85	85.50	1	Pass			
9											
10											

Figure 14-1.   You can create complex conditional tests using the AND function.

The OR function returns the logical value TRUE if any one of the conditional tests is true; the AND function returns the logical value TRUE only if all the conditional tests are true.

Because the NOT function negates a condition, it is usually used with other functions. NOT instructs Excel to return the logical value TRUE if the argument is false or the logical value FALSE if the argument is true. For example, the formula =**IF(NOT(A1=2), "Go"," ")** tells Excel to return the text Go if the value of cell A1 is anything but 2.

Nested IF Functions

Sometimes you can't resolve a logical problem using only logical operators and the AND, OR, and NOT functions. In these cases, you can nest IF functions to create a hierarchy of tests. For example, the formula
=IF(A1=100, "Always", IF(AND(A1>=80, A1<100), "Usually", IF(AND(A1>=60, A1<80), "Sometimes", "Who cares?")))
states, in plain language: If the value is 100, return "Always"; if the value is from 80 through 99, return "Usually"; if the value is from 60 through 79, return "Sometimes"; or finally, if none of these conditions is true, return "Who cares?".

> ## InsideOut
>
> ### Don't use too many IFs
>
> You can create formulas containing up to seven nested functions. For example, the following formula
> =IF(A1=1, 3, IF(A1=2, 6, IF(A1=3, 5, IF(A1=4, 6, IF(A1=5, 8, IF(A1=6, 7, IF(A1=7, 0, 1))))))) works just fine in Excel, but if you add one more IF function, you'll get an error.
>
> Nested IF formulas are a common conditional test, but the seven-function limit might cause some problems, especially if you're converting data from a program that allows a greater number of nested functions, such as Lotus 1-2-3. You'll have to either break long formulas into two cells or approach the task differently, perhaps by using lookup functions. For more information, see "The Lookup Function" on page 432 and "The Address Functions" on page 433.

Other Uses for Conditional Functions

You can use all the conditional functions described in this section as stand-alone formulas. Although you usually use functions, such as AND, OR, NOT, ISERROR, ISNA, and ISREF, within an IF function, you can use formulas, such as
=AND(A1>A2, A2<A3), also to perform simple conditional tests. This formula returns the logical value TRUE if the value in A1 is greater than the value in A2 and the value in A2 is less than the value in A3. You might use this type of formula to assign TRUE and FALSE values to a range of numeric database cells and then use the TRUE and FALSE conditions as selection criteria for printing a specialized report.

Understanding Information Functions

The information functions could be called the internal monitoring system in Excel. Although they perform no specific calculations, you can use them to find out about elements of the Excel interface and then use that information elsewhere. We'll discuss the most useful of these functions in this section.

For more information about individual functions, see Appendix D, "Function Reference."

Using Selected Information Functions

Information functions allow you to gather information about the contents of cells, their formatting, and the computing environment as well as perform conditional tests for the presence of specific types of values.

The TYPE and ERROR.TYPE Functions

The TYPE function determines whether a cell contains text, a number, a logical value, an array, or an error value. The result is a code for the type of entry in the referenced cell: 1 for a number (or a blank cell), 2 for text, 4 for a logical value (TRUE or FALSE), 16 for an error value, and 64 for an array. For example, if cell A1 contains the number 100, the formula =**TYPE(A1)** returns 1. If A1 contains the text Microsoft Excel, the formula returns 2.

Like the TYPE function, the ERROR.TYPE function detects the contents of a cell, except it detects different types of error values. The result is a code for the type of error value in the referenced cell: 1 for #NULL!, 2 for #DIV/0!, 3 for #VALUE!, 4 for #REF!, 5 for #NAME!, 6 for #NUM!, and 7 for #N/A. Any other value in the referenced cell returns the error value #N/A. For example, if cell A1 contains a formula that displays the error value #NAME!, the formula =**ERROR.TYPE(A1)** returns 5. If A1 contains the text **Microsoft Excel**, the formula returns #N/A.

The COUNTBLANK Function

The COUNTBLANK function counts the number of empty cells in the specified range, which is its only argument. This function is tricky because formulas that evaluate to null text strings, such as =" ", or to zero might seem empty, but they aren't and therefore won't be counted.

Using the IS Information Functions

You can use the ISBLANK, ISERR, ISERROR, ISLOGICAL, ISNA, ISNONTEXT, ISNUMBER, ISREF, and ISTEXT functions to determine whether a referenced cell or range contains the corresponding type of value. In addition, the ISEVEN and ISODD functions are available if you've installed the Analysis ToolPak.

For information about installing the Analysis ToolPak add-in, see "Installing the Analysis ToolPak" on page 405.

All IS Information functions take a single argument. For example, the ISBLANK function takes the form =**ISBLANK**(*value*). The *value* argument is a reference to a cell. If
value refers to a blank cell, the function returns the logical value TRUE; otherwise, it
returns FALSE.

InsideOut

Be aware of IS anomalies

Although you can use a cell range (rather than a single cell) as the argument to any IS
function, the result might not be what you expect. For example, you would think the
ISBLANK function would return TRUE if the referenced range is empty or FALSE if the
range contains any values. Instead, its behavior depends on where the range is in
relation to the cell containing the formula. If the argument refers to a range that inter-
sects the row or column containing the formula, ISBLANK uses implicit intersection to
arrive at the result. In other words, the function looks at only one cell in the referenced range, and only if it happens to be in the same row or column as the cell
containing the function. The function ignores the rest of the range. If the range shares
neither a row nor a column with the formula, however, the result is always FALSE.
For more about intersection, see the "Getting Explicit about Intersections" on
page 369.

An ISERR Example

You can use ISERR to avoid getting error values as formula results. For example, suppose you want to call attention to cells containing a particular character string, such as
12A, resulting in the word Yes appearing in the cell containing the formula. If the
string isn't found, you want the cell to remain empty. You can use the IF and FIND
functions to perform this task, but if the value isn't found, you get a #VALUE! error
rather than a blank cell.

To solve this problem, add an ISERR function to the formula. The FIND function
returns the position at which a substring is found within a larger string. If the substring
isn't there, FIND returns #VALUE!. The solution is to add an ISERR function, such as
=**IF(ISERR(FIND("12A", A1)), " ", "Yes")**. Because you're not interested in the error,
which is simply a by-product of the calculation, this traps the error, leaving only the
results that you are interested in.

> **note** When you enter numeric values as text, such as **="21"**, the IS function, unlike other functions, does not recognize them as numbers. Therefore, the formula **=ISNUMBER("21")** returns FALSE.

Understanding Lookup and Reference Functions

Lookup and reference functions help you utilize your own worksheet tables as sources of information to be used elsewhere in formulas. You can use three primary functions to look up information stored in a list or a table or to manipulate references: LOOKUP, VLOOKUP, and HLOOKUP. Some powerful lookup and reference functions in addition to these three are available; we describe many of them in this section.

> For more information about individual functions, see Appendix D, "Function Reference."

Using Selected Lookup and Reference Functions

VLOOKUP and HLOOKUP are nearly identical functions that look up information stored in tables you have constructed. VLOOKUP and HLOOKUP operate in either vertical or horizontal orientation (respectively), but LOOKUP works either way.

When you look up information in a table, you normally use a row index and a column index to locate a particular cell. Excel derives the first index by finding the largest value in the first column or row that is less than or equal to a lookup value you supply and then uses a row number or column number argument as the other index. Make sure the table is sorted by the row or column containing the lookup values.

> **tip Create automated lookup formulas**
>
> You can create powerful lookup formulas using add-in tools. (The tools don't actually use any of the Lookup functions.) For more information, see "Using the Conditional Sum and Lookup Wizards" on page 397.

These functions take the following forms:

```
=VLOOKUP(lookup_value, table_array, col_index_num, range_lookup)
```

```
=HLOOKUP(lookup_value, table_array, row_index_num, range_lookup)
```

Table 14-1 lists LOOKUP function arguments and their descriptions. The LOOKUP function takes two forms, the first is called the *vector form*, and the second is called the *array form*:

```
=LOOKUP(lookup_value, lookup_vector, result_vector)
```

```
=LOOKUP(lookup_value, array)
```

Table 14-1. Lookup Function Arguments

Argument	Description
lookup_value	The value, cell reference, or text (enclosed in quotation marks) that you want to find in a table or a range.
table_array	A cell range or name that defines the table to look in.
row_index_num *col_index_num*	The row or column number of the table from which to select the result, counted relative to the table (not according to the actual row and column numbers).
range_lookup	A logical value that determines whether the function matches the lookup_value exactly or approximately. Type FALSE to match the lookup_value exactly. The default is TRUE, which finds the closest match.
lookup_vector	A one-row or one-column range that contains numbers, text, or logical values.
result_vector	A one-row or one-column range that must be the same size as lookup_vector.
array	A range containing numbers, text, or logical values to compare with lookup_value.

The difference between the lookup functions is the type of table each function uses: VLOOKUP works only with vertical tables (tables arranged in columns); HLOOKUP works only with horizontal tables (tables arranged in rows). The *array form* of LOOKUP can be used with either horizontal or vertical tables, and the *vector form* can be used with single rows or columns of data.

The array form of LOOKUP determines whether to search horizontally or vertically based on the shape of the table defined in the *array* argument. If there are more columns than rows, LOOKUP searches the first row for *lookup_value*; if there are more rows than columns, LOOKUP searches the first column for *lookup_value*. LOOKUP always returns the last value in the row or column containing the *lookup_value*; you can specify a row or column number using VLOOKUP or HLOOKUP.

The VLOOKUP and HLOOKUP Functions

For the VLOOKUP and HLOOKUP functions, whether a lookup table should be considered vertical or horizontal depends on where the comparison values (the first index) are located. If the values are in the leftmost column of the table, the table is vertical; if they are in the first row of the table, the table is horizontal. (In contrast, LOOKUP uses the shape of the table to determine whether to use the first row or column as the comparison values.) The comparison values can be numbers or text, but they must be arranged in ascending order. No comparison value should be used more than once in a table.

The *index_num* argument (sometimes called the *offset*) provides the second index and tells the lookup function which column or row of the table to look in for the function's result. The first column or row in the table has an index number of 1; therefore, the *index_num* argument must be greater than or equal to 1 and must never be greater than the number of rows or columns in the table. For example, if a vertical table is three columns wide, the index number can't be greater than 3. If any value does not meet these rules, the function returns an error value.

You can use the VLOOKUP function to retrieve information from the table in Figure 14-2.

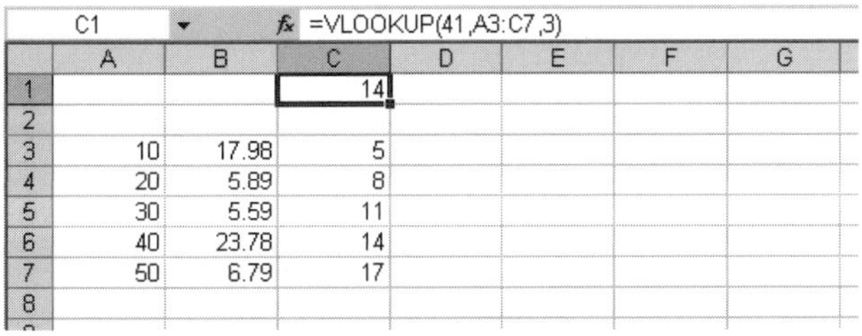

C1 =VLOOKUP(41,A3:C7,3)

	A	B	C	D	E	F	G
1			14				
2							
3	10	17.98	5				
4	20	5.89	8				
5	30	5.59	11				
6	40	23.78	14				
7	50	6.79	17				
8							

Figure 14-2. You can use the VLOOKUP function to retrieve information from a vertical table like this one.

Remember that these lookup functions normally search for the greatest comparison value that is less than or equal to the lookup value, not for an exact match between the comparison values and the lookup value. If all the comparison values in the first row or column of the table range are greater than the lookup value, the function returns the #N/A error value. If all the comparison values are less than the lookup value, however, the function returns the value that corresponds to the last (largest) comparison value in the table, which might not be what you want. If you require an exact match, type **FALSE** as the *range_lookup* argument.

The worksheet in Figure 14-3 shows an example of a horizontal lookup table using the HLOOKUP function.

	A1	▾		*fx* =HLOOKUP(6,B2:E7,3)			
	A	B	C	D	E	F	G
1	101						
2		3	6	10	16		
3		5	100	99	1		
4		10	101	98	2		
5		25	105	95	3		
6		30	110	94	2		
7		35	125	90	1		
8							

Figure 14-3. You can use the HLOOKUP function to retrieve
information from a horizontal table like this one.

The LOOKUP Function

The LOOKUP function has two forms, *vector* and *array*, as described previously. In
both forms, it's similar to VLOOKUP and HLOOKUP and follows the same rules, but
is available in two forms, *vector* and *array*, described in Table 14-1.

Like HLOOKUP and VLOOKUP, the *vector form* of LOOKUP searches for the largest
comparison value that isn't greater than the lookup value. It then selects the result
from the corresponding position in the specified result range. The *lookup_vector* and
result_vector arguments are often adjacent ranges, but they don't have to be when you
use LOOKUP. They can be located in separate areas of the worksheet, and one range
can be horizontal and the other vertical. The only requirement is that they must have
the same number of elements.

For example, consider the worksheet in Figure 14-4, where the ranges are not parallel.
Both the *lookup_vector*, A1:A5, and the *result_vector*, D6:H6, have five elements.
The *lookup_value*, 3, matches the entry in the third cell of the *lookup_vector*, making
the result of the formula the entry in the third cell of the result range: 300.

	A7	▾		*fx* =LOOKUP(3,A1:A5,B6:F6)			
	A	B	C	D	E	F	G
1	1						
2	2						
3	3						
4	4						
5	5						
6		100	200	300	400	500	
7	300						
8							

Figure 14-4. The vector form of the LOOKUP function can
retrieve information from a nonparallel cell range.

The *array form* of LOOKUP is similar to VLOOKUP and HLOOKUP but works with
either a horizontal or a vertical table, using the dimensions of the table to figure out
the location of the comparison values. If the table is taller than it is wide or the table is

square, the function treats it as a vertical table and assumes that the comparison values are in the leftmost column. If the table is wider than it is tall, the function views the table as horizontal and assumes that the comparison values are in the first row of the table. The result is always in the last row or column of the specified table; you can't specify column or row numbers.

Because HLOOKUP and VLOOKUP are more predictable and controllable, you'll generally find using them preferable to using LOOKUP.

The ADDRESS Function

The Address function provides a handy way to build a reference from numbers. It takes the arguments (*row_num, column_num, abs_num, a1, sheet_text*). For example, the formula =ADDRESS(1, 1, 1, TRUE, "Data Sheet") results in the reference 'Data Sheet'!$A$1. (For a complete explanation of the ADDRESS function, see Appendix D, "Function Reference."

The CHOOSE Function

You use the CHOOSE function to retrieve an item from a list of values. The function takes the arguments (*index_num, value 1, value 2, ...*) and can include up to 29 values. The *index_num* argument is the position in the list you want to return; it must be positive and can't exceed the number of elements in the list. The function returns the value of the element in the list that occupies the position indicated by *index_num*. For example, the function =CHOOSE(2, 6, 1, 8, 9, 3) returns the value 1, because 1 is the second item in the list. (The *index_num* value itself isn't counted as part of the list.) You can use individual cell references for the list, but you can't specify ranges. You might be tempted to create a function, such as =CHOOSE(A10, C1:C5), to take the place of the longer function in the preceding example. If you do, however, the result is a #VALUE! error value.

The MATCH Function

The MATCH function is closely related to the CHOOSE function. However, whereas CHOOSE returns the item that occupies the position in a list specified by the *index_num* argument, MATCH returns the position of the item in the list that most closely matches a lookup value.

tip You can create powerful lookup formulas using add-in tools that use the MATCH
function. See "Using the Conditional Sum and Lookup Wizards" on page 397.

This function takes the arguments (*lookup_value*, *lookup_array*, *match_type*), where
lookup_value and the items in the *lookup_array* can be numeric values or text
strings, and *match_type* defines the rules for the search, as shown in Table 14-2 on the
next page.

Table 14-2. MATCH Function Arguments

match_type	Description
1 (or omitted)	Finds the largest value in the specified range (which must be sorted in ascending order) that is less than or equal to *lookup_value*. If no items in the range meet these criteria, the function returns #N/A.
0	Finds the first value in the specified range (no sorting necessary) that is equal to *lookup_value*. If no items in the range match, the function returns #N/A.
-1	Finds the smallest value in the specified range (which must be sorted in descending order) that is greater than or equal to *lookup_value*. If no items in the range meet these criteria, the function returns #N/A.

When you use MATCH to locate text strings, you should specify a *match_type* argument of 0 (an exact match). You can then use the wildcards * and ? in the *lookup_value* argument.

The INDEX Function

The INDEX function has two forms: an array form, which returns a value, and a reference form, which returns a cell reference. The forms of these functions are

```
=INDEX(array, row_num, column_num)
```

```
=INDEX(reference, row_num, column_num, area_num)
```

tip You can create powerful lookup formulas with add-in tools that use the INDEX function. See "Using the Conditional Sum and Lookup Wizards" on page 397.

The *array form* works only with an array argument; it returns the value of the result, not the cell reference. The result is the value at the position in *array* indicated by *row_num* and *column_num*. For example, the formula =INDEX({10,20,30;40,50,60} , 1, 2) returns the value 20, because 20 is the value in the cell in the second column and first row of the array.

note Each form of the INDEX function offers an advantageous feature. Using the reference form of the function, you can use multiple, nonadjacent areas of the worksheet as the *reference* lookup range. Using the array form of the function, you can get a range of cells, rather than a single cell, as a result.

The *reference form* returns a cell address instead of a value and is useful when you want to perform operations on a cell (such as changing the cell width), rather than on its value. This function can be confusing, however, because if an INDEX function is nested in another function, that function can use the value in the cell whose address is returned by INDEX. Furthermore, the reference form of INDEX doesn't display its result as an address; it displays the value(s) in that address. Remember that the result is an address, even if it doesn't look like one.

Here are a few guidelines to keep in mind when using the INDEX function:

- If you type 0 as the *row_num* or *column_num* argument, INDEX returns a reference for the entire row or column, respectively.

- The *reference* argument can be one or more ranges, which are called areas. Each area must be rectangular and can contain numbers, text, or formulas. If the areas are not adjacent, you must enclose the *reference* argument in parentheses.

- The *area_num* argument is needed only if more than one area is included in *reference*. It identifies the area to which the *row_num* and *column_num* arguments will be applied. The first area specified in *reference* is designated area 1, the second area 2, and so on.

Let's consider some examples to see how all this works. Figure 14-5 shows an example of an INDEX function. The formula in cell A1 uses the row coordinate in cell A2 and the column coordinate in cell A3 to return the contents of the cell in the third row and second column of the specified range.

435

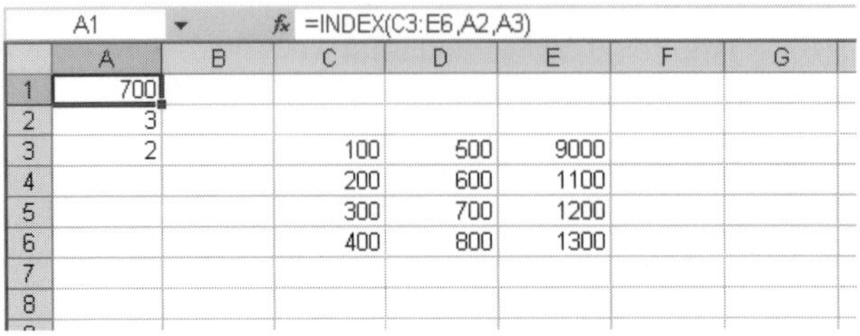

Figure 14-5. Use the INDEX function to retrieve the address
or value in a cell where information is located.

The following example is a bit more tricky. Using the same worksheet in Figure 14-5,
the formula =**INDEX(C3:E6, 0, 2)** displays the #VALUE! error value because the
row_num argument of 0 returns a reference to the entire column specified by the
column_num argument of 2, or the range D3:D6. Excel can't display a range as the
result. However, try nesting this formula in another function, as follows:
=**SUM(INDEX(C3:E6, 0, 2))**. The result is 2600, the sum of the values in D3:D6. This
illustrates the utility of obtaining a reference as a result.

Now let's see how the INDEX function works with multiple ranges in the *reference*
argument. (When more than one range is used, you must enclose the argument in
parentheses.) For example, in the formula =**INDEX((A1:C5,D6:F10), 1, 1, 2)**, the *reference* range comprises two areas: A1:C5 and D6:F10. The *area_num* argument (2) tells
INDEX to work on the second of these areas. This formula returns the address D6,
which is the cell in the first column and first row of the range D6:F10. The displayed
result is the value in that cell.

The INDIRECT Function

The INDIRECT function returns the contents of a cell using its reference. It takes the
arguments (*ref_text, a1*), where *ref_text* is an A1-style or R1C1-style reference, or a cell
name. The *a1* argument is a logical value indicating which type of reference you're using. If *a1* is FALSE, Excel interprets *ref_text* as R1C1 format; if *a1* is TRUE or omitted, Excel interprets *ref_text* as A1 format. For example, if cell C6 of your worksheet
contains the text value **B3** and cell B3 contains the value 2.888, the formula
=**INDIRECT(C6)** returns the value 2.888. If your worksheet is set to display R1C1-
style references, and cell R6C3 contains the text reference "R3C2" and cell R3C2 contains the value 2.888, the formula =**INDIRECT(R6C3, FALSE)** also returns the value
2.888.

The ROW and COLUMN Functions

The result of the ROW and COLUMN functions is the row or column number, respectively, of the cell or range referred to by the function's single argument. For example,
the formula =**ROW(H5)** returns the result 5. The formula =**COLUMN(C5)** returns the
result 3 because column C is the third column on the worksheet.

If the argument is omitted, the result is the row or column number of the cell that contains the function. If the argument is a range or a range name and the function is entered as an array by pressing Ctrl+Shift+Enter, the result of the function is an array that consists of the row or column numbers of each row or column in the range. For example, suppose you select cells B1:B10, type the formula =ROW(A1:A10), and then press Ctrl+Shift+Enter to enter the formula in all cells in the range B1:B10. That range will contain the array result { 1;2;3;4;5;6;7;8;9;10}, the row numbers of each cell in the argument.

The ROWS and COLUMNS Functions

The ROWS and COLUMNS functions return the number of rows or columns, respectively, referenced by the function's single argument in a reference or an array. The argument is an array constant, a range reference, or a range name. For example, the result of the formula =ROWS({100,200,300;1000,2000,3000}) is 2, because the array consists of two rows (separated by a semicolon). The formula =ROWS(A1:A10) returns 10, because the range A1:A10 contains ten rows. And the formula =COLUMNS(A1:C10) returns 3, because the range A1:C10 contains three columns.

The AREAS Function

You can use the AREAS function to determine the number of areas in a reference. *Areas* refer to individual cell or range references, not regions. The single argument to this function can be a cell reference, a range reference, or several range references. If you use several range references, you must enclose them in a set of parentheses so that Excel doesn't misinterpret the commas that separate the ranges. (Although this function takes only one argument, Excel still interprets unenclosed commas as argument separators.) For example, suppose you assign the name Test to the group of ranges A1:C5,D6,E7:G10. The function =AREAS(Test) returns the number 3, the number of areas in the group.

The TRANSPOSE Function

The TRANSPOSE function changes the horizontal or vertical orientation of an array. It takes a single argument, *array*. If the argument refers to a vertically oriented range, the resulting array is horizontal. If the range is horizontal, the resulting array is vertical. The first row of a horizontal array becomes the first column of the vertical array result, and vice versa. You must type the TRANSPOSE function as an array formula in a range that has the same number of rows and columns as the *array* argument has columns and rows, respectively.

> **tip** For quick and easy transposition, select the range you want to transpose, press Ctrl+C to copy the range, choose Edit, Paste Special, and then click the Transpose option.

Chapter 15

Formatting and Calculating Date and Time

You can use date and time values to date-stamp documents and to perform date and time arithmetic. Creating a production schedule or a monthly billing system is relatively easy with Microsoft Excel. Although Excel uses numeric values to count each nanosecond, starting from the beginning of the 20th century, you can use formatting to display those numbers in whatever form you want.

Understanding How Excel Records Dates and Times

Excel assigns serial values to days, hours, minutes, and seconds, which makes it possible for you to perform sophisticated date and time arithmetic. The basic unit of time in Excel is the day. Each day is represented by a serial date value from 1 through 65,380. The base date, represented by the serial value 1, is Sunday, January 1, 1900. When you enter a date in your worksheet, Excel records the date as a serial value that represents the number of days between the base date and the specified date. For example, the date January 1, 2002 is represented by the serial value 37,257, representing the number of days between the base date—January 1, 1900—and January 1, 2002.

The time of day is a decimal value that represents the portion of a day that has passed from its beginning—12:00 midnight—to the specified time. Therefore, the time 12:00 noon is represented by the value 0.5, because the difference between midnight and noon is exactly half a day. The time/date combination 2:09:03 PM, October 23, 2002, is represented by the serial value 37552.5896180556, because October 23, 2002, is day number

37,552 (counting January 1, 1900 as day number 1), and the interval between midnight and 2:09:03 PM amounts to .5896180556 of a whole day.

> **tip** **Display the serial date value**
>
> You can see the serial value of a formatted date by selecting the cell containing the date and pressing Ctrl+Shift+tilde (~). To return the cell to its date format, choose Edit, Undo.

Using the 1904 Date System

If you transfer documents between Excel for the Macintosh and Excel for Windows, the proper date system for the worksheet is set for you. When the date system changes, existing serial date values display different dates, but the underlying values do not change. If you change date systems after you have begun entering dates in a worksheet, all your dates will be off by four years.

You can change the base date (the date that corresponds to the serial value 1) from January 1, 1900—used by Excel for Windows—to January 2, 1904—used by Excel for the Macintosh. Choose Tools, Options, click the Calculation tab, and select the 1904 Date System option.

When you select this option, the serial date values in your worksheet remain the same, but the display of all dates changes so that the serial values of any dates you enter in your Excel for Windows worksheets match corresponding serial values from Excel for the Macintosh worksheets. If you transfer information into Excel for Windows from a worksheet created in Excel for the Macintosh, selecting this option ensures that Excel evaluates the serial date values correctly. In this book, we use the 1900 date system.

Entering Dates and Times

Although Excel records dates and times as serial date values, you don't have to enter them that way. You can manipulate dates and times in your worksheet formulas just as you manipulate other types of values. You enter date values in formats that Excel automatically applies. To enter date values in this way, type the date in one of the following formats: **d/m/yy, m/d/yy, d-mmm-yy, d-mmm,** or **mmm-yy.** (You can also enter 4-digit years for any of these formats.)

> **tip** **Adjust regional number settings**
>
> You can change the default date, time, currency, and numbering settings through the Regional Options control (or Regional Settings, depending on your system) in the Windows Control Panel.

If your entry doesn't match any of the built-in date or time formats, Excel picks the format that's most similar to your entry. For example, if you enter **1 Dec**, you see the formatted entry 1-Dec in the cell. In the formula bar, the entry appears as 12/1/2002 (if the current year is 2002) so you can edit the date more easily.

You can also enter times in a time format. Select a cell and type the time in one of the following forms: **h:mm AM/PM, h:mm:ss AM/PM, h:mm, h:mm:ss,** or the combined date and time format, **m/d/yy h:mm.** Notice you must separate the hours, minutes, and seconds of the time entries by colons.

> For more information about custom formats, see "Creating Your Own Date and Time Format on page 445.

If you don't include AM, PM, A, or P with the time, Excel uses the 24-hour (military) time convention. In other words, Excel always assumes that the entry **3:00** means 3:00 AM, unless you specifically enter **PM.**

tip   Insert an instant date or time stamp

Enter the current date in a cell or formula by holding down Ctrl and pressing the semi-colon (;) key. The date stamp is entered in the current short-date format, as set in Control Panel. Enter the current time in a cell or formula by holding down Ctrl and Shift together and pressing the colon (:) key. The time stamp is entered in h:mm AM/PM format. (Of course, the colon and semicolon occupy the same key—the Shift key changes the formula to a time stamp.)

InsideOut

Change the magic crossover date

December 31, 2029 is the default magic crossover date—that is, the last day that Windows assumes is in the future if you enter the year using only two digits. For example, if you type **12/31/29** into a cell, Microsoft Windows assumes that you mean the year 2029. If, however, you type **1/1/30** into a cell, Windows interprets it to mean January 1, 1930.

You can change this magic crossover date by changing the setting on the Date tab of the Regional Options control (or Regional Settings, depending on your system), which is accessed from the Windows Control Panel. Of course, you're still limited to a 100-year span; if you change the last date Windows recognizes as being in the future, the corresponding beginning date—January 1, 1900—changes accordingly. Therefore, if you need to enter century-spanning dates, you should get into the habit of typing the full four-digit year to avoid surprises.

Entering a Series of Dates

You can create an evenly spaced series of dates in a row or column in several ways, but the job is especially easy when you use the Fill handle. Suppose you want to create a series of dates in row 1. The series begins with March 1, 2002, and the dates must be exactly one month apart.

If you enter **3/1/2002** in cell A1 and drag the Fill handle to the right, Excel extends the series of dates incrementally by days, as shown in Figure 15-1. After you drag, Excel displays a smart tag adjacent to the selection. Click the smart tag to display the smart tag action menu shown in Figure 15-1, which displays a number of AutoFill options; select Fill Months to convert the already-extended day series into a month series.

For more about smart tags, see "Smart Tags" on page 4.

For more about smart tags, see "Smart Tags" on page 4.

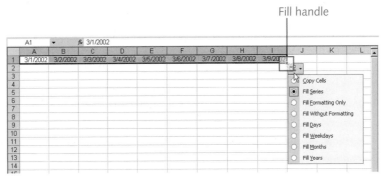

Figure 15-1. After you drag the Fill handle to extend a date series, use the smart tag action menu to adjust the series.

If you drag the Fill handle by right-clicking it, a shortcut menu that is similar to the smart tag action menu appears. You can use this shortcut menu to select a fill command before performing any fill action. If what you want to do isn't represented on the menu, click the Series command at the bottom of the shortcut menu to display the Fill Series dialog box.

You can use the Series command to tend a series of dates with a bit more flexibility than using the Fill handle. To use this approach, type the starting date, select the range of cells you want to fill (including the starting date), and choose Edit, Fill, Series to display the Fill Series dialog box shown in Figure 15-2.

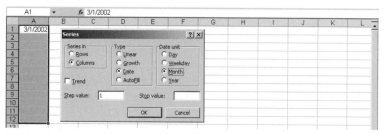

Figure 15-2. Use the Series dialog box to create date series.

When extending a series of dates, remember the following:

- You can use the Series In options to choose whether to extend the selected date across the current row or down the current column.

- You can use the Step Value option to specify the interval between cells. For example, by typing **2** in the Step Value box and selecting Month in the Date Unit section, you can create a series of dates occurring every other month. By typing a negative number in the Step Value box, you can create a series that decreases (goes backward in time).

- You can use the Stop Value box to set an ending date for the series. Using this method, you can use the Series command without having to figure out how many cells to select in advance. For example, to enter a series of dates that extends from 1/1/02 through 12/31/04, type **1/1/02** into a cell. Then select that cell, display the Series dialog box, select the Columns option, and type **12/31/04** in the Stop Value box. Excel extends a series of dates following the original cell from 4/1/00 to 12/1/01.

For more information on the AutoFill and the Series command, see "Filling and Creating Data Series" on page 174.

Extending an Existing Date Series

The AutoFill feature uses the selected cells to determine the type of series you intend to create when you drag the Fill handle. AutoFill copies text and nonsequential values and increments sequential numeric values. Because dates are stored as serial values, AutoFill extends them sequentially, as illustrated in Figure 15-3 on the next page.

Chapter 15

	A	B	C	D	E	F	G	H
1	Selected Values		Resulting Series					
2								
3	9:00	10:00	11:00	12:00	13:00	14:00	15:00	
4	2001	2002	2003	2004	2005	2006	2007	
5	1/1/2002	2/1/2002	3/1/2002	4/1/2002	5/1/2002	6/1/2002	7/1/2002	
6	1/1/2002	3/1/2002	5/1/2002	7/1/2002	9/1/2002	11/1/2002	1/1/2003	
7	1-Jan	2-Jan	3-Jan	4-Jan	5-Jan	6-Jan	7-Jan	
8	Dec-02	Dec-03	Dec-04	Dec-05	Dec-06	Dec-07	Dec-08	
9	Dec-02	Dec-04	Dec-06	Dec-08	Dec-10	Dec-12	Dec-14	
10	Product 1	Product 2	Product 3	Product 4	Product 5	Product 6	Product 7	
11	Sat	Mon	Wed	Fri	Sun	Tue	Thu	
12	1 1/2	2 3/4	4	5 1/4	6 1/2	7 3/4	9	
13								

Figure 15-3. Starting with the values in the Selected Values area, we created the values to the right by dragging the Fill handle.

When you use the Fill handle to extend the value in a single selected cell, Excel assumes you want to increment the numeric value in each cell. (If you want to copy the cell instead, hold down Ctrl while dragging the Fill handle.) Notice that in Figure 15-3 the entries in rows 7 through 11 contain text values. AutoFill recognizes text entries for days and months and extends them as if they were numeric values. In addition, when a cell contains a mixed text and numeric entry (as in row 10), AutoFill copies the text portion, if it's not the name of a month or day, and extends the numeric portion, if it occurs at either end of the entry.

Formatting Dates and Times

After you enter a date or time in a cell, you can choose Format, Cells and click the Number tab to change its format using any of Excel's built-in formats. Choose Date or Time in the Category box to display the list of available formats in the Type box on the right. A preview of the format appears in the Sample box in the upper right corner, as shown in Figure 15-4.

> **note** At the top of the list of Date and Time formats are several that begin with an asterisk (*). These formats respond to changes in the settings available on the Date and Time tabs in the Windows Control Panel's Regional Options control (or Regional Settings, depending on your system). All other formats remain unaffected by these Control Panel settings.

Most of the Date and Time formats are easy to understand, but there are a few special formats:

● The 13:30 and 13:30:55 time formats use the 24-hour (military) time convention.

● The 30:55.2 time format displays only minutes and seconds; fractions of seconds are displayed as a decimal value.

● The 37:30:55 time format displays elapsed time.

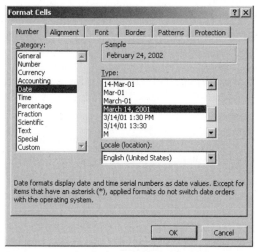

Figure 15-4. Use the Number tab of the Format Cells dialog box to apply date and time formats to cells.

Creating Your Own Date and Time Formats

To supplement the standard Date and Time formats, you can create custom formats using the same technique you use for creating custom numeric formats.

> For more information about custom numeric formats, see "Creating Custom Formats" on page 215.

For example, you can create a format that displays all the available date and time information. The entry **2/24/02** would appear as Sunday, February 24, 2002 0:00:00.0. To create this format, follow these steps:

1 Select the cell that contains the date.

2 Choose Format, Cells (or press Ctrl+1) and click the Number tab.

3 Select the Custom category.

4 Highlight the entry in the Type list and type the following custom format code: **dddd mmmm dd, yyyy h:mm:ss.0**.

5 Click OK. Excel stores the new format in the Type list for the Custom category and displays the date using the new format in the selected cell.

You can use the same procedure to display only a portion of the date or the time information available. For example, if you create the format mmmm, Excel displays the date 2/24/2002 as the word February.

Table 15-1 shows the formatting codes you can use to create custom date and time formats. Be sure to keep two things in mind. First, Excel assumes that m means months. If, on the other hand, you enter the code m immediately after an h, or the code mm immediately after an hh, Excel displays minutes instead of months. Second, if you include one of the codes AM/PM, am/pm, A/P, or a/p in a time format, Excel uses the 12-hour time convention; if you omit these codes, Excel uses the 24-hour (military) time convention.

After you add a custom date or time format to the Type list, you can apply it to any date or time entry. Select the Custom category and select the format you entered from the Type list (new custom formats appear at the bottom of the list), and click OK to apply the format.

Measuring Elapsed Time

You can enclose time codes in brackets, as listed at the bottom of the Table 15-1, to display more than 24 hours, more than 60 minutes, or more than 60 seconds in a time value. The brackets must always appear around the first code in the format. Excel provides one built-in elapsed time code, [h]:mm:ss, available only in the Custom category Type list. Other valid codes for measuring elapsed time include [mm]:ss and [ss].

Bracketed codes have no effect if you use them in any position of the format other than first. For example, if you use the code h:[mm]:ss, Excel ignores the brackets and displays the time using the normal h:mm:ss format.

> **note** One format in the Time category on the Number tab of the Format Cells dialog box
> represents elapsed time: 37:30:55. This is the same as the [h]:mm:ss format in the
> Custom category.

Suppose you want to determine the elapsed time between two dates. Type the following formulas in cells A1, A2, and A3, respectively: **11/23/02 13:32**, **11/25/02 23:59**, and **=A2-A1**.

If you apply the built-in format [h]:mm:ss to cell A3, the result of the formula is 58:27:00—the elapsed time between the two dates. If you apply the standard h:mm:ss format to cell A3 instead, the result is 10:27:00—the difference between the two times. Without the elapsed time format code, Excel ignores the difference in dates.

Chapter 15: Formatting and Calculating Date and Time

Table 15-1.   Codes for Creating Custom Date and Time Formats

Code	Display
General	Number in General (serial value) format
d	Day number without leading zero (1–31)
dd	Day number with leading zero (01–31)
ddd	Day-of-week abbreviation (Sun–Sat)
dddd	Complete day-of-week name (Sunday–Saturday)
m	Month number without leading zero (1–12)
mm	Month number with leading zero (01–12)
mmm	Month name abbreviation (Jan–Dec)
mmmm	Complete month name (January–December)
yy	Last two digits of year number (00–99)
yyyy	Complete four-digit year number (1900–2078)
h	Hour without leading zero (0–23)
hh	Hour with leading zero (00–23)
m	Minute without leading zero (0–59)
mm	Minute with leading zero (00–59)
s	Second without leading zero (0–59)
ss	Second with leading zero (00–59)
s.0	Second and tenths of a second without leading zero
s.00	Second (without a leading zero) and hundredths of a second without leading zero
ss.0	Second (without a leading zero) and tenths of a second with leading zero
ss.00	Second and hundredths of a second with leading zero
AM/PM	Time in AM/PM notation
am/pm	Time in am/pm notation
A/P	Time in A/P notation
a/p	Time in a/p notation
[ ]	Brackets display the absolute elapsed time when used to enclose a time code, as in [h].

Troubleshooting

I Can't Enter a Number of Hours Over 9999!

Suppose you have a worksheet in which you keep a running total of flying time for pilots, using Excel's time formats. Whenever you try to enter a number of hours over 9999 (which isn't uncommon), Excel treats the entry as text. What's wrong?

Nothing is wrong—that's just a built-in limitation of Excel. Here are a couple of ways to work with this limitation:

- First, use an elapsed time format. Choose Format, Cells, click the Number tab, select the Custom category, and then choose [h]:mm:ss in the Type list to apply the one built-in elapsed time format. If you don't need to record seconds, you can delete :ss. Elapsed time formats can store and display an unlimited number of hours.

- Second, if you need to enter more than 9999 hours at a time, you'll have to break it into two smaller chunks and enter it in two cells.

You should also know that when you enter a time greater than 24 hours (even 24:01), Excel adds a date in the formula bar. Unless the number of hours entered exceeds a year's worth, the added date will be sometime in 1900; you'll just have to live with that. Fortunately, this date doesn't show in the cell unless you format it to.

Calculating with Date and Time

Because Excel records dates as serial date values, you can use dates in formulas and functions as you would any other value. Suppose you want to find the date that falls exactly 200 days after July 4, 2002. If cell A1 contains the entry 7/4/02, you can use the following formula to compute the date 200 days later, which is 1/20/03 (or 37,641): **=A1+200**.

As another example, suppose you want to find the number of weeks between October 31, 2001, and May 13, 2002. Use the formula =(("**5/13/02**")-("**10/31/01**"))/7, which returns approximately 27.7 weeks.

You can also use times in formulas and functions; however, the results of time arithmetic are not as easy to understand as the results of date arithmetic. For example, you can determine how much time has elapsed between 8:22 AM and 10:45 PM with the formula =""**22:45**"-"**8:22**". The result is .599306, which can be formatted using a 24-hour time format (one that doesn't include AM/PM) to display 14:23. Excel displays the result relative to midnight.

Suppose you want to determine the time that is 2 hours, 23 minutes, and 17 seconds after 12:35:23 PM. The formula =("**12:35:23 PM**")+("**2:23:17**") returns the correct answer, .624074, which can be formatted as 14:58:40. In this formula, 2:23:17 represents not an absolute time (2:23:17 AM) but an interval of time (2 hours, 23 minutes, and 17 seconds). This format is perfectly acceptable to Excel.

Troubleshooting

Excel Displays My Time as #####!

Excel can't display negative numbers as dates or times. If the result of a date or time calculation is negative, and you attempt to display this result in a date or time format, you will see a cell full of number signs, no matter how you widen the cell. This typically happens when you subtract a later time of day from an earlier time of day. You can work around the problem by converting the result to elapsed hours. To do that, multiply the result by 24 and display it in a numeric format, not a date or time format.

Working with Date and Time Functions

Using Excel's date and time functions, you can perform worksheet calculations quickly and accurately. For example, if you use your worksheet to calculate your company's monthly payroll, you might use the HOUR function to determine the number of hours worked each day and the WEEKDAY function to determine whether employees should be paid at the standard rate (for Monday through Friday) or at the overtime rate (for Saturdays and Sundays). In this section, you explore a few (but not all) of Excel's date and time functions in detail. For a complete list of functions available in Excel, see Appendix D, "Function Reference."

Using the TODAY and NOW Functions

You can enter =**TODAY**( ) into a cell or a formula to insert the serial value of the current date. If you enter the function into a cell with the General format (which is the default), the resulting value is displayed in mm/dd/yyyy format. Although this function takes no arguments, you must remember to include the empty parentheses. (You'll remember that *arguments* are variables that supply the values a function needs to perform its calculations. Arguments are placed between the parentheses of functions that require them.)

Similarly, you can enter =**NOW**() into a cell or formula to insert the current date and time. This function also takes no arguments. The result of the function is a serial date and time value that includes an integer (the date) and a decimal value (the time). Excel doesn't update the value of NOW continuously. If the value of a cell that contains the NOW function isn't current, you can update the value by recalculating the worksheet. (You recalculate the worksheet by making a new entry or by pressing F9.) Excel also updates the NOW function whenever you open or print the worksheet.

The NOW function is an example of a *volatile* function—that is, a function whose calculated value is subject to change. Anytime you open a worksheet that contains one or more NOW functions and close the worksheet, Excel prompts you to save your changes regardless of whether you've made any, because the current value of NOW has changed since the last time you used the worksheet. (Another example of a volatile function is RAND.)

For more on the RAND function, see "The RAND and RANDBETWEEN Functions" on page 416.

Using the WEEKDAY Function

The WEEKDAY function returns the day of the week for a specific date and takes the arguments (*serial_number, return_type*). The *serial_number* argument can be a serial date value; a reference to a cell that contains either a date function or a serial date value; or text, such as 1/27/00 or January 27, 2000. If you use text, be sure to enclose the text in quotation marks. The function returns a number that represents the day of the week that the specified date falls on. The optional *return_type* argument determines the way the result is displayed. Table 15-2 lists the available return types.

Table 15-2. Return Type Codes

If return_type is	WEEKDAY returns
1 or omitted	A number from 1 through 7 where 1 is Sunday and 7 is Saturday
2	A number from 1 through 7 where 1 is Monday and 7 is Sunday
3	A number from 0 through 6 where 0 is Monday and 6 is Sunday

tip **Use a custom day-of-week format**

You might want to format a cell containing the WEEKDAY function with a custom day-of-week format, such as **dddd**. By applying this custom format, you can use the result of the WEEKDAY function in other functions and still have a meaningful display on the screen.

Using the YEAR, MONTH, and DAY Functions

The YEAR, MONTH, and DAY functions return the value of the year, month, and day portions of a serial date value. All three take a single argument, which can be a serial date value; a reference to a cell that contains either a date function or a serial date value; or a text date enclosed in quotation marks. For example, if cell A1 contains the date 3/25/2002, the formula =**YEAR(A1)** returns the value 2002, the formula =**MONTH(A1)** returns the value 3, and the formula =**DAY(A1)** returns the value 25.

Using the HOUR, MINUTE, and SECOND Functions

Just as the YEAR, MONTH, and DAY functions extract the value of the year, month, and day portions of a serial date value, the HOUR, MINUTE, and SECOND functions extract the value of the hour, minute, and second portions of a serial time value. For example, if cell B1 contains the time 12:15:35 PM, the formula =**HOUR(B1)** returns the value 12, the formula =**MINUTE(B1)** returns the value 15, and the formula =**SECOND(B1)** returns the value 25.

Using the DATEVALUE and TIMEVALUE Functions

Excel's DATEVALUE function translates a date into a serial value. You must enter the single argument as text, using any date from 1/1/1900 to 12/31/9999, and you must add quotation marks around the text. You can enter the argument using any of Excel's built-in Date formats; however, if you enter the date without a year, Excel uses the current year from your computer's internal clock. For example, the formula =**DATEVALUE("December 31, 2010")** returns the serial value 40,543.

Similarly, the TIMEVALUE function translates a time into a decimal value. You must enter its single argument as text. You can use any of Excel's built-in Time formats, but you must add quotation marks around the text. For example, the formula =**DATEVALUE("December 31, 2010")** returns the decimal value 0.6875.

Working with Specialized Date Functions

Excel includes a set of specialized date functions that perform operations such as calculations for the maturity dates of securities, for payroll, and for work schedules. The functions described in this section are available only if you install the Analysis ToolPak add-in.

For information about installing the Analysis ToolPak add-in, see "Installing the Analysis ToolPak" on page 405.

Chapter 15

Using the EDATE and EOMONTH Functions

You can use the EDATE function to calculate the exact date that occurs an indicated number of months before or after a given date. It takes the arguments (*start_date, months*), where *start_date* is the date you want to use as a starting point, and *months* is an integer value that indicates the number of months before or after the start date. If the *months* value is positive, the function returns a date after the start date; if the *months* value is negative, the function returns a date before the start date. For example, to find the date that falls exactly 23 months after June 12, 2001, enter the formula =EDATE("6/12/01", 23), which returns the value 37,753, or May 12, 2003.

The EOMONTH function returns a date that is an indicated number of months before or after a given date. Although EOMONTH is similar to EDATE and takes the same arguments, the value returned is always rounded up to the last day of the month. For example, to calculate the serial date value that is the last day of the month 23 months after June 12, 2001, enter the formula =**EOMONTH("6/12/2001", 23)**, which returns 37,772, or May 31, 2003.

Using the YEARFRAC Function

The YEARFRAC function calculates a decimal number that represents the portion of a year that falls between two given dates. This function takes the arguments (*start_date, end_date, basis*), where *start_date* and *end_date* specify the period of time you want to convert to a fractional year. The *basis* argument is the type of day count you want to use, as described in Table 15-3.

Table 15-3.   Basis Codes

If *basis* is	YEARFRAC returns
0 (or omitted)	30/360, or 30 days per month and 360 days per year, as established in the United States by the National Association of Security Dealers (NASD)
1	Actual/actual, or the actual number of days in the month(s)/actual days in the year
2	Actual/360
3	Actual/365
4	European 30/360

For example, to determine the fraction of a year that falls between 4/12/02 and 12/15/02, you can enter the formula =YEARFRAC("4/12/02", "12/15/02"). This formula returns 0.675, based on the default 30-day month and 360-day year.

Using the WORKDAY and NETWORKDAYS Functions

The WORKDAY and NETWORKDAYS functions are invaluable for anyone who calculates payroll and benefits or determines work schedules. Both functions return values based on working days, excluding weekend days. In addition, you can choose whether to include holidays and specify the exact dates.

The WORKDAY function returns the date that is an indicated number of working days before or after a given date. This function takes the arguments (*start_date*, *days*, *holidays*), where *start_date* is the date you want the function to count from, and *days* is the number of workdays before or after the start date, excluding weekends and holidays. Use a positive value for days to count forward from the start date; use a negative value to count backward. The optional *holidays* argument can be an array or a reference to a cell range that contains any dates that you want to exclude from the calculation. If you leave *holidays* blank, the function counts all weekdays from the start date. For example, to determine the date that is 100 working days, not counting holidays, from the current date, use the formula =**WORKDAY(NOW( ),100)**.

Similarly, the NETWORKDAYS function calculates the number of working days between two given dates. It takes the arguments (*start_date*, *end_date*, *holidays*). For example, to determine the number of working days between January 15, 2002 and June 30, 2002, use the formula =**NETWORKDAYS(1/15/02", "6/30/02")**, which results in a value of 119.

Chapter 16

Functions for Financial Analysis

The financial functions that are provided with Microsoft Excel allow you to perform common business calculations, such as net present value and future value, without building long and complex formulas. These functions are the heart of spreadsheets—the word "spreadsheet" itself refers to the seemingly antiquated system of using special grid paper to track financial information. Functions have taken the place of the old ten-key calculator sequences ("algorithms") used by accounting professionals before computers revolutionized the discipline.

> **note** Many of the financial functions discussed in this chapter are included in the Analysis ToolPak add-in. For information about accessing the Analysis ToolPak add-in, see "Installing the Analysis ToolPak" on page 405.

Calculating Investments

Most financial functions accept similar arguments. To streamline this section, we'll define the common arguments in Table 16-1 on the next page and explain any differences in how you can use them in the individual function descriptions. Another list of common arguments accompanies the section on depreciation.

For quick details on specific functions, see Appendix D, "Function Reference."

Table 16-1. Investment Function Arguments

Argument	Description
Future value	The value of an investment at the end of the term (0 if omitted)
Inflow 1, inflow 2, inflow n	Periodic payments when individual amounts differ
Number of periods	Term of investment
Payment	Periodic payments when individual amounts are the same
Type	When payment is to be made (0 if omitted); 0 = at end of period; 1 = at beginning of period
Period	Number of an individual periodic payment
Present value	Value of investment today
Rate	Discount rate or interest rate
Guess	A starting interest rate for iterative calculations (10 percent if omitted)
Finance rate	The rate at which you borrow money to purchase an investment
Reinvestment rate	The rate at which you reinvest cash received from an investment

The PV Function

Present value is one of the most common methods for measuring the attractiveness of a long-term investment. Present value is today's value of the investment. It's determined by discounting the inflows (payments received) from the investment back to the present time. If the present value of the inflows is greater than the cost of the investment, the investment is a good one.

The PV function computes the present value of a series of equal periodic payments or of a lump-sum payment. (A series of equal payments is often called an ordinary annuity.) This function takes the arguments *(rate, number of periods, payment, future value, type)*; for definitions of these arguments, see Table 16-1. To compute the present value of a series of payments, enter a value for the *payment* argument, or to compute the present value of a lump-sum payment, enter a value for the *future value* argument. For an investment with both a series of payments and a lump-sum payment, use both arguments.

Here's a real-world example of how this function works: Suppose you are presented with an investment opportunity that returns $1,000 each year over the next five years. To receive this annuity, you must invest $4,000. Are you willing to pay $4,000 today to earn $5,000 over the next five years? To decide whether this investment is acceptable, you need to determine the present value of the stream of $1,000 payments you will receive.

Because you could invest your money in a money-market account at 4.5 percent, we'll use 4.5 percent as the discount rate of the investment. (Because this discount rate is a sort of hurdle over which an investment must leap before it becomes attractive to you, it's often called the hurdle rate.) To determine the present value of this investment, use the formula =**PV(4.5%, 5, 1000)**, which returns the value -4389.98, meaning that you should be willing to spend $4,389.98 now to receive $5,000 over the next five years. Because your investment is only $4,000, you can surmise that this is an acceptable investment.

Suppose you're offered $5,000 at the end of five years instead of $1,000 for each of the next five years. Is the investment still as attractive? To find out, use the formula =**PV(4.5%, 5, , 5000)**. (Include a comma as a placeholder for the unused *payment* argument.) This formula returns the present value -4012.26, which means that, at a hurdle rate of 4.5 percent, you should be willing to spend $4,012.26 to receive $5,000 in five years. Although the proposal isn't as attractive under these terms, it's still acceptable because your investment is only $4,000.

The NPV Function

The NPV function calculates the net present value, which is another common method for determining the profitability of an investment. In general, any investment that yields a net present value greater than zero is considered profitable. This function takes the arguments *(rate, inflow 1, inflow 2,...)*; for definitions of these arguments, see Table 16-1. You can use as many as 29 inflow values as arguments, but you can include any number of values by using an array as an argument.

NPV differs from PV in two important respects. Whereas PV assumes constant inflow values, NPV allows variable payments. The other major difference is that PV allows payments and receipts to occur at either the beginning or end of the period, whereas NPV assumes that all payments and receipts are evenly distributed and that they occur at the end of the period. If the cost of the investment must be paid up front, you should not include the cost as one of the function's inflow arguments but should subtract it from the result of the function. On the other hand, if the cost must be paid at the end of the first period, you should include it as a negative first inflow argument. Let's consider an example to help clarify this distinction.

Chapter 16

Suppose you are contemplating an investment on which you expect to incur a loss of
$55,000 at the end of the first year, followed by gains of $95,000, $140,000, and
$185,000 at the ends of the second, third, and fourth years. You will invest $250,000 up
front, and the hurdle rate is 12 percent. To evaluate this investment, use the formula
=NPV(12%, -55000, 95000, 140000, 185000) -250000.

> **note** The result, -6153.65, tells you not to expect a net profit from this investment. Note
> that the negative values in this formula indicate the money you spend on your invest-
> ment. (You can use the Goal Seek command to determine what initial cost or interest
> rate would justify the investment.) For more information about this command, see
> "using the Goal Seek Command" on page 515.

This formula does not include the up-front cost of the investment as an argument for
the NPV function. However, if you make the initial $250,000 investment at the end of
the first year, the formula is **=NPV(12%,(-250000-55000), 95000, 140000, 185000)**.
The result, $20,632.07, would suggest that this might be a profitable investment.

The FV Function

The FV function determines the future value of an assessment and is essentially the
opposite of present value, computing the value at some future date of an investment
that makes payments as a lump sum or as a series of equal periodic payments. This
function takes the arguments *(rate, number of periods, payment, present value, type)*; for
definitions of these arguments, see Table 16-1. Use the *payment* argument to compute
the future value of a series of payments and the *present value* argument to compute the
future value of a lump-sum payment.

Suppose you're thinking about starting an IRA. You plan to deposit $2,000 in the IRA
at the beginning of each year, and you expect the average rate of return to be 9 percent
per year for the entire term. Assuming you're now 30 years old, how much money will
your account accumulate by the time you're 65? Use the formula
=FV(9%, 35, -2000, , 1) to learn that your IRA balance will be $470,249.45 at the end
of 35 years.

Now assume that you started an IRA account three years ago and have already accumu-
lated $7,500 in your account. Use the formula **=FV(9%, 35, -2000, -7500, 1)** to learn
that your IRA will grow to $623,354.20 at the end of 35 years.

In both of these examples, the *type* argument is 1, because payments occur at the
beginning of the period. Including this argument is particularly important in financial
calculations that span many years. If you omit the *type* argument in the preceding formula, Excel assumes that you add money to your account at the end of each year and
returns the value $584,526.27—a difference of $38,828!

The PMT Function

The PMT function computes the periodic payment required to amortize a loan over a specified number of periods. This function takes the arguments *(rate, number of periods, present value, future value, type)*; for definitions of these arguments, see Table 16-1.

Suppose you want to take out a 25-year mortgage for $100,000. Assuming an interest rate of 8 percent, what will your monthly payments be? First divide the 8-percent interest rate by 12 to arrive at a monthly rate (0.66667 percent). Next convert the number of periods into months by multiplying 25 by 12 (300). You can include these computations as arguments using the formula =**PMT((8%/12), (25*12), 100000)** to compute the monthly mortgage payment, which turns out to be -$771.82. (The result is negative because it's a cost to you.)

Troubleshooting

PMT Function Produces Unrealistic Results

Sometimes you might find that the PMT function seems to produce unrealistic results—such as payments that are excessively large. As is the case with all functions used for calculating investments, make sure you are using the same units for both the *rate* and *nper (number of periods)* arguments. If, for example, you type **8%** for the rate, you must enter the *nper* argument in years, because 8 percent is an annual rate. If you type **8%** for the rate and **360** as the term, Excel returns the payment required to amortize a loan at either 8 percent per month for 30 years or 8 percent per year for 360 years! You can resolve your problem by either dividing 8 percent by 12 (which is the standard way of expressing a loan) or typing **30** for *nper*, indicating the term in years. Note, however, that these two options are not equivalent—they yield very different results because of the way interest is calculated. You should use the same units that your lender uses, which is probably annual interest rate divided by 12 and *nper* expressed in months.

The IPMT Function

The IPMT function computes the interest part of an individual payment made to repay an amount over a specified time period, with constant periodic payments and a constant interest rate. This function takes the arguments *(rate, period, number of periods, present value, future value, type)*; for definitions of these arguments, see Table 16-1.

Suppose you borrow $100,000 for 25 years at 8 percent interest. The formula =**IPMT((8/12)%, 1, 300, 100000)** tells you that the interest component of the payment due for the first month is -$666.67. The formula =**IPMT((8/12)%, 300, 300, 100000)** tells you that the interest component of the final payment of the same loan is -$5.11.

The PPMT Function

The PPMT function is similar to the IPMT function, except that it computes the principal component of an individual payment when a loan is repaid over a specified time with constant periodic payments and a constant interest rate. If you compute both IPMT and PPMT for the same period, you can add the results to obtain the total payment. The PPMT function takes the arguments *(rate, period, number of periods, present value, future value, type)*; for definitions of these arguments, see Table 16-1.

If you borrow $100,000 for 25 years at 8 percent interest, the formula =**PPMT((8/12)%, 1, 300, 100000)** tells you that the principal component of the payment for the first month of the loan is –$105.15. The formula =**PPMT((8/12)%, 300, 300, 100000)** tells you that the principal component of the final payment of the same loan is –$766.70.

The NPER Function

The NPER function computes the number of periods required to amortize a loan, given a specified periodic payment. This function takes the arguments *(rate, payment, present value, future value, type)*; for definitions of these arguments, see Table 16-1.

Suppose you can afford mortgage payments of $1,000 per month and you want to know how long it will take to pay off a $100,000 loan at 8 percent interest. The formula =**NPER((8%/12), –1000, 100000)** tells you that your mortgage payments will extend over 165.34 months.

If the payment is too small to amortize the loan at the indicated rate of interest, the function returns an error value. The monthly payment must be at least equal to the period interest rate times the principal amount; otherwise, the loan will never be amortized. For example, the formula =**NPER((8/12)%, -600, 100000)** returns the #NUM! error value. In this case, the monthly payment must be at least $666.67 to amortize the loan (although it would take a couple of lifetimes worth of payments at that amount).

The RATE Function

The RATE function determines the rate of return of an investment that generates a series of equal periodic payments or a single lump-sum payment. This function takes the arguments *(number of periods, payment, present value, future value, type, guess)*; for definitions of these arguments, see Table 16-1. You use either the *payment* argument to compute the rate for a series of equal periodic payments or the *future value* argument to compute the rate of a lump-sum payment.

Suppose you're considering an investment that will pay you five annual $1,000 payments. The investment costs $3,000. To determine the actual annual rate of return on your investment, use the formula =**RATE(5, 1000, -3000)**. This formula returns 20 percent, an excellent rate of return on this investment.

> **note** The RATE function uses an iterative process to compute the rate of return. The function begins by computing the net present value of the investment at the *guess* rate. If that first net present value is greater than zero, the function selects a higher rate and repeats the net present value calculation; if the first net present value is less than zero, the function selects a lower rate for the second iteration. RATE continues this process until it arrives at the correct rate of return or until it has gone through 20 iterations. For more information about iteration, see "Using Circular References" on page 384.

If you receive the #NUM! error value when you enter the RATE function, Excel probably cannot calculate the rate within 20 iterations. Try entering a different *guess* rate to give the function a running start. A rate from 10 percent through 100 percent usually works.

The IRR Function

The IRR function determines the internal rate of return of an investment, which is the rate that causes the net present value of the investment to equal zero. In other words, the internal rate of return is the rate that causes the present value of the inflows from an investment to equal the cost of the investment.

Internal rate of return, like net present value, is used to compare one investment opportunity with another. An attractive investment is one whose net present value, discounted at the appropriate hurdle rate, is greater than zero. Turn that equation around and you can see that the discount rate required to generate a net present value of zero must be greater than the hurdle rate. Thus, an attractive investment is one for which the discount rate required to yield a net present value of zero—that is, the internal rate of return—is greater than the hurdle rate.

The IRR function takes the arguments *(values, guess)*. (For definitions of these arguments, see Table 16-1.) The *values* argument is an array or a reference to a range of cells that contain numbers. Only one *values* argument is allowed, and it must include at least one positive and one negative value. IRR ignores text, logical values, and blank cells. IRR assumes that transactions occur at the end of a period and returns the equivalent interest rate for that period's length. The *guess* argument is optional, but if you receive the #NUM! error value, try including a *guess* to help Excel reach the answer.

Suppose you agree to buy a condominium for $120,000 and rent it to someone else. Over the next five years, you expect to receive $25,000, $27,000, $35,000, $38,000, and $40,000 in net rental income. You can set up a simple worksheet that contains your investment and income information. Enter the six values into cells A1:A6 of the worksheet. (Be sure to enter the initial $120,000 investment as a negative value.) Then the formula =IRR(A1:A6) returns the internal rate of return of 11 percent. If the hurdle rate is 10 percent, you can consider this condominium purchase a good investment.

The MIRR Function

The MIRR function calculates the modified internal rate of return of an investment. The difference from the IRR function is that MIRR takes into account the cost of the money you borrow to finance the investment. MIRR assumes that you'll reinvest the cash it generates and that transactions occur at the end of a period. It then returns the equivalent interest rate for that period's length.

The MIRR function takes the arguments *(values, finance rate, reinvestment rate)*. (For definitions of these arguments, see Table 16-1.) The *values* argument must be an array or a reference to a range of cells that contain numbers. This argument represents a series of payments and income occurring at regular periods. You must include at least one positive and one negative value in the *values* argument. For example, if cells A1 through A6 contain the values -120000, 25000, 27000, 35000, 38000, and 40000, the formula =**MIRR(A1:A6, 10%, 8%)** returns a modified internal rate of return of 10 percent.

Calculating Depreciation

Depreciation has an enormous effect on the bottom line of any business, and accurate calculation of depreciation is crucial if you want to avoid triggering a detailed scrutiny of your records by the IRS. These functions help you precisely determine the depreciation of an asset for a specific period. Table 16-2 lists the common arguments used in these functions:

Table 16-2. **Depreciation Function Arguments**

Argument	Description
Cost	Initial cost of the asset
Life	Length of time the asset will be depreciated
Period	Individual time period to be computed
Salvage	Asset's remaining value after it has been fully depreciated

The SLN Function

The SLN function determines the straight-line depreciation for an asset for a single period. This depreciation method assumes that depreciation is uniform throughout the useful life of the asset. The cost or basis of the asset, less its estimated salvage value, is deductible in equal amounts over the life of the asset. This function takes the arguments *(cost, salvage, life)*. (For definitions of these arguments, see Table 16-2.)

Suppose you want to determine the depreciation for each year of a machine that costs $8,000 new, has a life of 10 years, and has a salvage value of $500. The formula =SLN(8000, 500, 10) tells you that each year's straight-line depreciation is $750.

The DDB and DB Functions

The DDB (double declining balance) function computes an asset's depreciation at an accelerated rate—more in the early periods and less later. Using this method, depreciation is computed as a percentage of the net book value of the asset (the cost of the asset less any prior years' depreciation).

The function takes the arguments *(cost, salvage, life, period, factor)*; for argument definitions, see Table 16-2. All DDB arguments must be positive numbers, and you must use the same time units for life and period; that is, if you express life in months, period must also be in months. The *factor* argument is optional and has a default value of 2, which indicates the normal double-declining balance method. Using 3 for the *factor* argument specifies the triple-declining balance method.

Suppose you want to calculate the depreciation of a machine that costs $5,000 new and that has a life of five years (60 months) and a salvage value of $100. The formula =DDB(5000, 100, 60, 1) tells you that the double-declining balance depreciation for the first month is $166.67. (Note that *life* is expressed in months.) The formula =DDB(5000, 100, 5, 1) tells you that the double-declining balance depreciation for the first year is $2,000.00. (Note that *life* is expressed in years.)

Chapter 16

The DB (declining balance) function is similar to the DDB function except that it uses the fixed declining balance method of depreciation and can calculate depreciation for a particular period in the asset's life. It takes the arguments *(cost, salvage, life, period, month)*. The *life* and *period* arguments must use the same units. The optional *month* argument is the number of months depreciated in the first year, which, if omitted, is 12—a full year. For example, to calculate the real depreciation for the first period on a $1,000,000 item with a salvage value of $100,000, a life of six years, and seven months in the first year, use the formula =**DB(1000000, 100000, 6, 1, 7)**, which returns $186,083.33.

The VDB Function

The VDB (variable declining balance) function calculates the depreciation of an asset for any complete or partial period, using either the double-declining balance or another accelerated-depreciation factor that you specify.

This function takes the arguments *(cost, salvage, life, start, end, factor, no switch)*; for argument definitions, see Table 16-2. The *start* argument is the period after which depreciation will be calculated, and *end* is the last period for which depreciation will be calculated. These arguments determine the depreciation for any length of time during the life of the asset. The *life*, *start*, and *end* arguments must all use the same units (days, months, or years). The optional *factor* argument is the rate at which the balance declines. If you omit *factor*, Excel assumes that the argument is 2 and uses the double-declining balance method. The optional *no switch* argument is a value that specifies whether to switch to straight-line depreciation when the straight-line depreciation is greater than the declining balance. If you omit *no switch* or type **0** (**FALSE**), Excel switches to straight-line; to prevent the switch, type **1** (**TRUE**).

Suppose that you purchased a $15,000 asset at the end of the first quarter of the current year and that this asset will have a salvage value of $2,000 after five years. To determine the depreciation of this asset next year (the fourth to seventh quarters of its use), use the formula =**VDB(15000, 2000, 20, 3, 7)**. The depreciation for this period is $3,760.55. The units used here are quarters. Notice that the *start* argument is 3, not 4, because we are jumping over the first three periods to start in the fourth.

The SYD Function

The SYD function computes an asset's depreciation for a specific time with the sum-of-the-years'-digits method. The SYD function takes the arguments *(cost, salvage, life, period)*. (For definitions of these arguments, see Table 16-2.) You must use the same units for life and period. Using the sum-of-the-years'-digits method, depreciation is calculated on the cost of the item less its salvage value. Like the double-declining balance method, the sum-of-the-years'-digits method is an accelerated depreciation method.

Suppose you want to determine the depreciation of a machine that costs $15,000, has a life of three years, and a salvage value of $1,250. The formula =**SYD(15000, 1250, 3, 3)** tells you that the sum-of-the-years'-digits depreciation for the third year is $2,291.67.

Analyzing Securities

Excel offers a group of functions designed for specific tasks relating to the computation and analysis of various types of securities. All these functions are part of the Analysis ToolPak. For more information about the Analysis ToolPak, see "Installing the Analysis ToolPak" on page 405.

Many of these functions share similar arguments. We'll describe the most common ones in Table 16-3 to avoid revisiting the same information in the function discussions that follow.

Table 16-3. Security-Analysis Function Arguments

Argument	Description
Basis	Day count basis of the security. If omitted, defaults to 0, indicating US (NASD) 30/360 basis. Other basis values include: 1 = actual/actual 2 = actual/360 3 = actual/365 4 = European 30/360
Coupon	The security's annual coupon rate
Frequency	Number of coupon payments made per year: 1 = annual, 2 = semiannual, 4 = quarterly
Investment	Amount of investment in the security
Issue	Issue date of the security
Maturity	Maturity date of the security, which must be greater than the settlement date
Par	Par value (face value) of the security; $1000 if omitted
Price	Price of the security
Rate	Interest rate of the security at the issue date, which must be greater than or equal to zero
Redemption	Value of the security at redemption
Settlement	Settlement date of the security (the day you have to pay for it), which must be greater than the issue date
Yield	Annual yield of the security, which must be greater than or equal to zero

You can enter dates by using any of the following : the date's serial number, the date enclosed in quotation marks, or a reference to a cell that contains a date. For example, you can enter June 30, 2000, as the serial date value 36707, as "6/30/00", or as a reference to a cell containing this date. If the security-analysis function results in a #NUM! error value, be sure that the dates are in the correct form and that they meet the criterion described in Table 16-3.

For more information about serial date values, see "Understanding How Excel Records Dates and Times" on page 439.

The DOLLARDE and DOLLARFR Functions

One of this pair of functions converts the familiar fractional pricing of securities to decimals, and the other converts decimals to fractions. The DOLLARDE function takes the arguments *(fractional dollar, fraction)*, and the DOLLARFR function takes the arguments *(decimal dollar, fraction)*. The *fractional dollar* argument is the value you want to convert expressed as an integer, followed by a decimal point and the numerator of the fraction you want to convert. The *decimal dollar* argument is the value you want to convert expressed as a decimal. The *fraction* argument is an integer indicating the denominator you want to use in the conversion. For the DOLLARFR function, fraction is the unit that the function should use when converting the decimal value, effectively rounding the decimal number to the nearest half, quarter, eighth, sixteenth, thirty-second, and so on.

For example, the formula =**DOLLARDE(1.03, 32)** translates as 1+3/32, which is equivalent to 1.09375. On the other hand, the formula =**DOLLARFR(1.09375, 32)** returns the result 1.03.

The ACCRINT and ACCRINTM Functions

The ACCRINT function returns the interest accrued by a security that pays interest on a periodic basis. This function takes the arguments *(issue, first interest, settlement, rate, par, frequency, basis)*; where first interest indicates the date on which interest is first accrued; for other argument definitions, see Table 16-3. For example, suppose a Treasury bond has an issue date of March 1, 2002, a settlement date of April 1, 2002, a first interest date of September 1, 2002, a 7-percent coupon rate with semiannual frequency, a par value of $1,000, and a basis of 30/360. The accrued interest formula is =**ACCRINT("3/1/02", "9/1/02", "4/1/02", 0.07, 1000, 2, 0)** which returns 5.833333, indicating that $5.83 accrues between March 1, 2002, and April 1, 2002.

Similarly, the ACCRINTM function returns the interest accrued by a maturity security (a type of security with not only a rhyming name, but which also pays interest at maturity). This function takes the arguments *(issue, settlement, rate, par, basis)*. Using the preceding example with a maturity date of July 31, 2006, the accrued interest formula is =ACCRINTM("3/1/02", "7/31/06", 0.07, 1000, 0), which returns 309.1667, indicating that the $1,000 bond will pay $309.17 interest on July 31, 2006.

The INTRATE and RECEIVED Functions

The INTRATE function calculates the rate of interest, or discount rate, for a fully invested security. This function takes the arguments *(settlement, maturity, investment, redemption, basis)*; for argument definitions, see Table 16-3. For example, suppose a bond has a settlement date of March 31, 2002, and a maturity date of September 30, 2002. A $1,000,000 investment in this bond will have a redemption value of $1,032,324, using the default 30/360 basis. The bond's discount rate formula is =INTRATE("3/31/02", "9/30/02", 1000000, 1032324, 0), which returns 0.064648, or 6.46 percent.

Similarly, the RECEIVED function calculates the amount received at maturity for a fully invested security, and takes the arguments *(settlement, maturity, investment, discount, basis)*. Using the preceding example with a 5.5 percent discount rate, the formula =RECEIVED("3/31/02", "9/30/02", 1000000, 0.055, 0) returns the mature value $1,028,277.63.

The PRICE, PRICEDISC, and PRICEMAT Functions

The PRICE function calculates the price per $100 of face value of a security that pays interest on a periodic basis. This function takes the arguments *(settlement, maturity, rate, yield, redemption, frequency, basis)*; for argument definitions, see Table 16-3. For example, suppose a bond's settlement date is March 31, 2002, its maturity date is July 31, 2002, and the interest rate is 5.75 percent, with semiannual frequency. The security's annual yield is 6.50 percent, its redemption value is $100, and it's calculated using the standard 30/360 basis. The bond price formula is =PRICE("3/31/02", "7/31/02", 0.0575, 0.065, 100, 2, 0), which returns $99.73498.

Similarly, the PRICEDISC function returns the price per $100 of face value of a security that is discounted, instead of paying periodic interest. This function takes the arguments *(settlement, maturity, discount, redemption, basis)*. Using the preceding example with the addition of a discount amount of 7.5 percent, the formula =PRICEDISC("3/31/02", "7/31/02", 0.075, 100, 0) returns a price of $97.50.

Finally, the PRICEMAT function returns the price per $100 of face value of a security that pays its interest at the maturity date. This function takes the arguments *(settlement, maturity, issue, rate, yield, basis)*. Using the preceding example with a settlement date of July 31, 2002, an issue date of March 1, 2002, and the maturity date changed to July 31, 2003, the formula =PRICEMAT("7/31/02", "7/31/03", "3/31/02", 0.0575, 0.065, 0) returns $99.18.

Chapter 16

The DISC Function

The DISC function calculates the discount rate for a security and takes the arguments *(settlement, maturity, price, redemption, basis)*. (For argument definitions, see Table 16-3.) For example, suppose a bond has a settlement date of June 15, 2002, a maturity date of December 31, 2002, a price of $96.875, and a $100 redemption value, and uses the standard 30/360 basis. The bond discount rate formula =DISC("6/15/02", "12/31/02", 96.875, 100, 0) returns 0.057398, or 5.74 percent.

The YIELD, YIELDDISC, and YIELDMAT Functions

The YIELD function determines the annual yield for a security that pays interest on a periodic basis and takes the arguments *(settlement, maturity, rate, price, redemption, frequency, basis)*; for definitions of these arguments, see Table 16-3. For example, suppose a bond has a settlement date of February 15, 2002, a maturity date of December 1, 2002, a coupon rate of 5.75 percent with semiannual frequency, a price of $99.2345, and a $100 redemption value, and uses the standard 30/360 basis. The annual bond yield formula =YIELD("2/15/02", "12/1/02", 0.0575, 99.2345, 100, 2, 0) returns 0.067406, or 6.74 percent.

The YIELDDISC function, on the other hand, calculates the annual yield for a discounted security. It takes the arguments *(settlement, maturity, price, redemption, basis)*. Using the preceding example but changing the price to $96.00, the bond yield formula =YIELDDISC("2/15/02", "12/1/02", 96, 100, 0) returns 0.052448, or 5.25 percent.

The YIELDMAT function calculates the annual yield for a security that pays its interest at maturity. This function takes the arguments *(settlement, maturity, issue, rate, price, basis)*. Using the arguments from the YIELD example but adding an issue date of January 1, 2002, and changing the price to $99.2345, the yield-at-maturity formula =YIELDMAT("2/15/02", "12/1/02", "1/1/02", 0.0575, 99.2345, 0) returns 0.067178, or 6.72 percent.

The TBILLEQ, TBILLPRICE, and TBILLYIELD Functions

The TBILLEQ function calculates the bond-equivalent yield for a Treasury bill. It takes the arguments *(settlement, maturity, discount)*. (For argument definitions, see Table 16-3.) For example, suppose a Treasury bill has a settlement date of February 1, 2002, a maturity date of July 1, 2002, and a discount rate of 8.65 percent. The formula for calculating the bond yield that is equivalent to the yield of a Treasury bill =TBILLEQ("2/1/02", "7/1/02", 0.0865) returns 0.091, or 9.1 percent.

You use the TBILLPRICE function to calculate the price per $100 of face value for a Treasury bill. This function takes the arguments *(settlement, maturity, discount)*. Using the preceding example, the formula to calculate the price per $100 of face value, =TBILLPRICE("2/1/02", "7/1/02", 0.0865), returns 96.3958, or $96.40.

Finally, the TBILLYIELD function calculates a Treasury bill's yield. It takes the arguments *(settlement, maturity, price)*. Using the preceding example with its result, a price of $96.40, the yield formula =**TBILLYIELD("2/1/02", "7/1/02", 96.40)** returns the yield 0.0896, or 8.9 percent.

The COUPDAYBS, COUPDAYS, COUPDAYSNC, COUPNCD, COUPNUM, and COUPPCD Functions

The following group of functions performs calculations relating to bond coupons. For all the sample formulas in this section, we'll use as our example a bond with a settlement date of March 1, 2002, and a maturity date of December 1, 2002. Its coupons are payable semiannually, using the actual/actual basis (that is, a *basis* argument of 1). All these functions take the same arguments: *(settlement, maturity, frequency, basis)*. (For definitions of these arguments, see Table 16-3.)

The COUPDAYBS function calculates the number of days from the beginning of the coupon period to the settlement date. Using our sample data, the formula =**COUPDAYBS("3/1/02", "12/1/02", 2, 1)** returns 90.

The COUPDAYS function calculates the number of days in the coupon period that contains the settlement date. Using our sample data, the formula =**COUPDAYS("3/1/02", "12/1/02", 2, 1)** returns 182.

The COUPDAYSNC function calculates the number of days from the settlement date to the next coupon date. Using our sample data, the formula =**COUPDAYSNC("3/1/02", "12/1/02", 2, 1)** returns 92.

The COUPNCD function calculates the next coupon date after the settlement date. Using our sample data, the formula =**COUPNCD("3/1/02", "12/1/02", 2, 1)** returns 37408, or June 1, 2002.

The COUPNUM function calculates the number of coupons payable between the settlement date and the maturity date and rounds the result to the nearest whole coupon. Using our sample data, the formula =**COUPNUM("3/1/02", "12/1/02", 2, 1)** returns 2.

The COUPPCD function calculates the coupon date before the settlement date. Using our sample data, the formula =**COUPPCD("3/1/02", "12/1/02", 2, 1)** returns 37226, or December 1, 2001.

The DURATION and MDURATION Functions

The DURATION function calculates the annual duration for a security whose interest payments are made on a periodic basis. Duration is defined as the weighted average of the present value of the bond's cash flow and is used as a measure of how a bond's price responds to changes in the yield. This function takes the arguments *(settlement, maturity, coupon, yield, frequency, basis)*. (For argument definitions, see Table 16-3.)

Chapter 16

For example, suppose a bond has a settlement date of January 1, 1998, a maturity date of December 31, 2003, a semiannual coupon rate of 8.5 percent, a yield of 9.5 percent, and uses the default 30/360 basis. The resulting formula
=**DURATION("1/1/98", "12/31/03", 0.085, 0.095, 2, 0)** returns a duration of 4.78708.

The MDURATION function calculates the annual modified duration for a security with interest payments made on a periodic basis, adjusted for market yield per number of coupon payments per year. This function takes the arguments *(settlement, maturity, coupon, yield, frequency, basis).* Using the values from the DURATION formula, the modified duration formula looks like this:
=**MDURATION("1/1/94", "12/31/99", 0.085, 0.095, 2, 0)**, and returns a value of 4.57.

Chapter 17

Functions for Analyzing Statistics

Microsoft Excel provides a wide range of features that can help you analyze statistical data. A number of functions that assist in simple analysis tasks, such as AVERAGE, MEDIAN, and MODE, are built into the program. If the built-in statistical functions aren't enough, you can turn to the Analysis ToolPak, an add-in module that provides a collection of functions and tools to augment the built-in analytic capabilities of Excel. You can use these tools to create histograms, rank-and-percentile tables, extract samples from a data set, perform regression analysis, generate special random-number sets, apply Fourier and other transformations to your data, and more. In this chapter, we'll explore statistical analysis functions built into Excel, as well as those included with the Analysis ToolPak.

For more information, see "Installing the Analysis ToolPak" on page 405.

Analyzing Distributions of Data

In statistics, a collection of measurements is called a distribution. Excel has several methods that you can use to analyze distributions: built-in statistical functions, the sample and population statistical functions, or the rank and percentile functions together with the Rank and Percentile tool.

note You can also analyze distributions using the Descriptive Statistics and Histogram tools, both of which are included in the Analysis Toolpak add-in. For more information about using the Analysis Toolpak tools, see "Using the Analysis Toolpak Data Analysis Tools" on page 483.

Using Built-In Statistical Functions

You use the built-in statistical functions to analyze a group (or population) of measurements. In this section, the discussion is limited to the most commonly used statistical functions.

> **note** Excel also offers the advanced statistical functions LINEST, LOGEST, TREND, and GROWTH, which operate on arrays. For more information, see "Understanding Linear and Exponential Regression" on page 477.

The AVERAGE Function

The AVERAGE function computes the arithmetic mean, or average, of the numbers in a range by summing a series of numeric values and then dividing the result by the number of values. This function takes the arguments *(number1, number2, ...)*, can include up to 30 arguments, and ignores blank cells and cells containing logical and text values. For example, to calculate the average of the values in cells B4 through B15, you could use the formula
=(B4+B5+B6+B7+B8+B9+B10+B11+B12+B13+B14+B15)/12, but it's obviously more efficient to enter =AVERAGE(B4:B15).

> For more information about this function, see the sidebar "AVERAGE vs. AVG" on page 419.

The MEDIAN, MODE, MAX, MIN, and COUNT Functions

These functions all take the same arguments: essentially just a cell range or a list of numbers separated by commas, such as *(number1, number2, ...)*, and they can accept up to 30 arguments, ignoring text, error values, and logical values. Here's a brief description of each:

- **MEDIAN** computes the median of a set of numbers. The median is the number in the middle of the set; that is, an equal number of values are higher and lower than the median. If the numbers specified include an even number of values, the value returned is the average of the two that lie in the middle of the set.

- **MODE** determines which value occurs most frequently in a set of numbers. If no number occurs more than once, MODE returns the #N/A error value.

- **MAX** returns the largest value in a range.

- **MIN** returns the smallest value in a range.

- **COUNT** tells you how many cells in a given range contain numbers, including dates and formulas that evaluate to numbers.

> **note** To count all nonblank cells, regardless of what they contain, you can use the COUNTA function. For more information about this function, see the sidebar entitled "The A Functions" on page 474.

The SUMIF and COUNTIF Functions

The SUMIF function is similar to SUM but first tests each cell using a specified conditional test before adding it to the total. This function takes the arguments (*range, criteria, sum_range*). The *range* argument specifies the range you want to test, the *criteria* argument specifies the conditional test to be performed on each cell in the range, and the *sum_range* argument specifies the cells to be totaled. For example, if you have a sheet with a column of month names defined using the range name Months and an adjacent column of numbers named Sales, use the formula =SUMIF(**Months,** "**June**", **Sales**) to return the value in the Sales cell that is adjacent to the label June. Alternatively, you can use a conditional test formula, such as =SUMIF(**Sales,** "**>=999**", **Sales**), to return the total of all sales figures that are more than $999.

> **tip**   **SUMmon more conditional power**
>
> You can use the Conditional Sum Wizard add-in to help you construct formulas. For more information, see "Using the Conditional Sum and Lookup Wizards" on page 397.

Similarly, COUNTIF counts the cells that match specified criteria and takes the arguments *(range, criteria)*. Using the same example, you can find the number of months in which sales fell below $600 using a conditional test, as in the formula =COUNTIF(**Sales,** "**<600**").

> For more information about conditional tests, see "Creating Conditional Tests" on page 396. For more about using range names, see "Naming Cells and Cell Ranges" on page 371.

Using Functions that Analyze Rank and Percentile

Excel includes several functions that extract rank and percentile information from a set of input values: PERCENTRANK, PERCENTILE, QUARTILE, SMALL, LARGE, and RANK.

The PERCENTRANK Function

The PERCENTRANK function returns a percentile ranking for any member of a data set. You can use this function to create a percentile table that's linked to the input range so that the percentile figures are updated if the input values change. We used this function to create the percentile ranking in column E of Figure 17-1 on the next page.

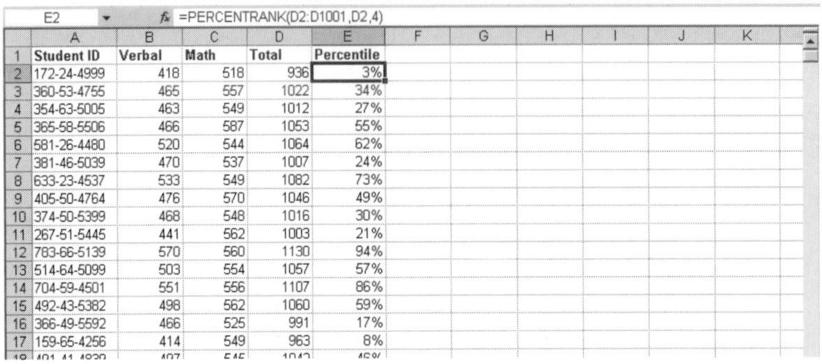

E2 =PERCENTRANK(D2:D1001,D2,4)

	Student ID	Verbal	Math	Total	Percentile
2	172-24-4999	418	518	936	3%
3	360-53-4755	465	557	1022	34%
4	354-63-5005	463	549	1012	27%
5	365-58-5506	466	587	1053	55%
6	581-26-4480	520	544	1064	62%
7	381-46-5039	470	537	1007	24%
8	633-23-4537	533	549	1082	73%
9	405-50-4764	476	570	1046	49%
10	374-50-5399	468	548	1016	30%
11	267-51-5445	441	562	1003	21%
12	783-66-5139	570	560	1130	94%
13	514-64-5099	503	554	1057	57%
14	704-59-4501	551	556	1107	86%
15	492-43-5382	498	562	1060	59%
16	366-49-5592	466	525	991	17%
17	159-65-4256	414	549	963	8%

Figure 17-1. PERCENTRANK links percentile figures to input values.

The PERCENTRANK function takes the arguments *(array, x, significance)*. The *array* argument specifies the input range (which is D2:D1001, in our example), and *x* specifies the value whose rank you want to obtain. The *significance* argument, which is optional, indicates the number of digits of precision you want; if omitted, results are rounded to three digits (*0.xxx* or *xx.x%*).

The A Functions

Excel includes a set of functions that give you more flexibility when calculating data sets that include text or logical values. These functions are AVERAGEA, COUNTA, MAXA, MINA, STDEVA, STDEVPA, VARA, and VARPA, all of which accept a series of up to 30 arguments *(value1, value2, ...)*.

Normally, the non-A versions of these functions ignore cells containing text values. For example, if a range of 10 cells contains one text value, AVERAGE ignores that cell and divides by 9 to arrive at the average, whereas AVERAGEA considers the text value part of the range and divides by 10. This is helpful if you always want to include all referenced cells in your calculations, especially if you use formulas that return text flags, such as none, if a certain condition is met. For more information about STDEVA, STDEVPA, VARA, and VARPA, see "Using Sample and Population Statistical Functions" on page 476.

The PERCENTILE and QUARTILE Functions

You use the PERCENTILE function to determine which member of an input range stands at a specified percentile ranking, and takes the arguments *(array, k)*. You must express the percentile *k* as a decimal fraction between 0 and 1. For example, to find out which score in Figure 17-1 represents the 87th percentile, you can use the formula **=PERCENTILE(D2:D1001, 0.87)**.

The QUARTILE function, which takes the arguments *(array, quart)*, works much like the PERCENTILE function, except that it returns the value that represents the lowest percentile, or any quarter-percentile in the input set. The *array* argument specifies the input range. The *quart* argument specifies the value to be returned, as shown in Table 17-1.

Table 17-1. The Quart Argument

Quart	Returns
0	Lowest value
1	25th-percentile value
2	Median (50th-percentile) value
3	75th-percentile value
4	Highest value

InsideOut

Use MIN, MEDIAN, and MAX

QUARTILE is a powerful function, but if you don't need to return 25th or 75th percentile values, you will get faster results using other functions, particularly when working with large data sets. Use the MIN function instead of QUARTILE(*array*, 0), the MEDIAN function instead of QUARTILE(*array*, 2), and the MAX function instead of QUARTILE(*array*, 4).

The SMALL and LARGE Functions

The SMALL and LARGE functions return the *k*th smallest and *k*th largest values in an input range; both take the arguments *(array, k)*, where *k* is the position from the largest or smallest value to the value in the array you want to find. For example, to find the 15th highest score in Figure 17-1, you can use the formula =**LARGE(D2:D1001, 15)**.

The RANK Function

The RANK function returns the ranked position of a particular number within a set of numbers, and takes the arguments *(number, ref, order)*. The *number* argument is the number for which you want to find the rank, *ref* is the range containing the data set, and *order* optionally ranks the number as is if it were in a ranking list in an ascending or descending (the default) order. For example, to find out which ranking the score 1200 has in the data set in Figure 17-1, you can use the formula =**RANK(1200, D2:D1001)**.

By default, the highest value is ranked 1, the second highest is ranked 2, and so on. If RANK can't find an exact match between its first argument and an input value, it returns the #N/A error value.

Using Sample and Population Statistical Functions

Variance and standard deviation are statistical measurements of the dispersion of a group, or population, of numbers. The standard deviation is the square root of the variance. As a rule, about 68 percent of a normally distributed population falls within one standard deviation of the mean, and about 95 percent falls within two standard deviations. A large standard deviation indicates that the population is widely dispersed from the mean; a small standard deviation indicates that the population is tightly packed around the mean.

Four statistical functions—VAR, VARP, STDEV, and STDEVP—compute the variance and standard deviation of the numbers in a range of cells. Before you calculate the variance and standard deviation of a group of values, you must determine whether those values represent the total population or only a representative sample of that population. The VAR and STDEV functions assume that the values represent only a sample of the total population; the VARP and STDEVP functions assume that the values represent the total population.

Calculating Sample Statistics: VAR and STDEV

The VAR and STDEV functions compute variance and standard deviation, assuming that their arguments represent only a sample of the total population. These functions both take the arguments *(number1, number2, ...)*, and accept up to 30 arguments. The worksheet in Figure 17-2 shows exam scores for five students and assumes that the scores in cells B4:E8 represent only a part of the total population.

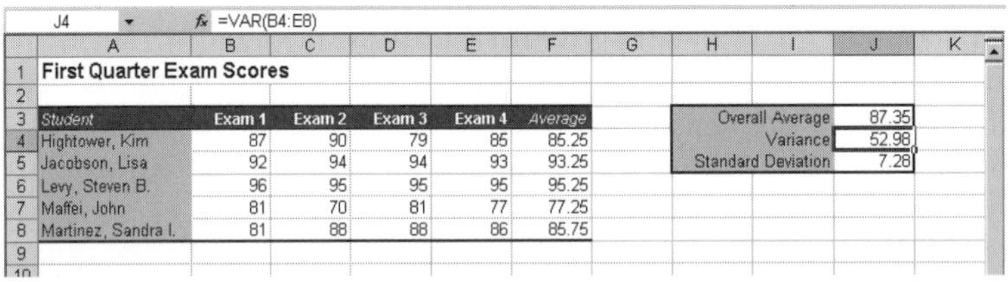
J4 =VAR(B4:E8)

Student	Exam 1	Exam 2	Exam 3	Exam 4	Average
Hightower, Kim	87	90	79	85	85.25
Jacobson, Lisa	92	94	94	93	93.25
Levy, Steven B.	96	95	95	95	95.25
Maffei, John	81	70	81	77	77.25
Martinez, Sandra I.	81	88	88	86	85.75

Overall Average	87.35
Variance	52.98
Standard Deviation	7.28

Figure 17-2. The VAR and STDEV functions measure the dispersion of sample exam scores.

Cell J4 uses the VAR function =VAR(B4:E8) to calculate the variance for this sample group of test scores. Cell J5 uses the STDEV function =STDEV(B4:E8) to calculate the standard deviation.

Assuming that the test scores in the example are normally distributed, we can deduce that about 68 percent of the students (the general-rule percentage) achieved scores between 80.07 (the average 87.35 minus the standard deviation 7.28) and 94.63 (87.35 plus 7.28).

Calculating Total Population Statistics: VARP and STDEVP

If the numbers you're analyzing represent an entire population rather than a sample, use the VARP and STDEVP functions to calculate variance and standard deviation. These functions both take the arguments *(number1, number2, ...)*, and accept up to 30 arguments.

Assuming that cells B4:E8 in the worksheet, shown in Figure 17-2, represent the total population, you can calculate the variance and standard deviation with the formulas =**VARP(B4:E8)** and =**STDEVP(B4:E8)**. The VARP function returns 50.33, and the STDEVP function returns 7.09.

---

tip   **Include text and blanks**

The STDEV, STDEVP, VAR, and VARP functions do not include text values or blank cells in their calculations. If you want to include blanks and/or text, use the A versions: STDEVA, STDEVPA, VARA, and VARPA. For more information, see the sidebar "The A Functions" on page 474.

Understanding Linear and Exponential Regression

Excel includes several array functions for performing linear regression—LINEST, TREND, FORECAST, SLOPE, and STEYX—and exponential regression—LOGEST and GROWTH. These functions are entered as array formulas and they produce array results. You can use each of these functions with one or several independent variables. The following list provides a definition of the different types of regression:

- **Linear regression** produces the slope of a line that best fits a single set of data. Based on a year's worth of sales figures, for example, linear regression can tell you the projected sales for March of the following year by giving you the slope and y-intercept (that is, the point where the line crosses the y-axis) of the line that best fits the sales data. By following the line forward in time, you can estimate future sales, if you can safely assume that growth will remain linear.

- **Exponential regression** produces an exponential curve that best fits a set of data that you suspect does not change linearly with time. For example, a series of measurements of population growth will nearly always be better represented by an exponential curve than by a line.

● **Multiple regression** is the analysis of more than one set of data, which
often produces a more realistic projection. You can perform both linear
and exponential multiple regression analyses. For example, suppose you
want to project the appropriate price for a house in your area based on
square footage, number of bathrooms, lot size, and age. Using a multiple
regression formula, you can estimate a price, based on a database of information gathered from existing houses.

Regressing into the Future?

The concept of regression might sound strange because the term is normally associated with movement backward, whereas in the world of statistics, regression is often
used to predict the future. Simply put, regression is a statistical technique that finds a
mathematical expression that best describes a set of data.

Often businesses try to predict the future using sales and percent-of-sales projections
based on history. A simple percent-of-sales technique identifies assets and liabilities
that vary along with sales, determines the proportion of each, and assigns them percentages. Although using percent-of-sales forecasting is often sufficient for slow or
steady short-term growth, the technique loses accuracy as growth accelerates.

Regression analysis uses more sophisticated equations to analyze larger sets of data
and translates them into coordinates on a line or curve. In the not-so-distant past,
regression analysis was not widely used because of the large volume of calculations
involved. Since spreadsheet applications, such as Excel, began offering built-in regression functions, the use of regression analysis has become more widespread.

Calculating Linear Regression

The equation $y = mx + b$ algebraically describes a straight line for a set of data with
one independent variable where x is the independent variable, y is the dependent
variable, m represents the slope of the line, and b represents the y-intercept. If a line
represents a number of independent variables in a multiple regression analysis to an
expected result, the equation of the regression line takes the form
$y = m_1 x_1 + m_2 x_2 + ... + m_n x_n + b$ where y is the dependent variable, x_1 through x_n are n independent variables, m_1 through m_n are the coefficients of each independent variable, and
b is a constant.

The LINEST Function

The LINEST function uses this more general equation to return the values of m_1
through m_n and the value of b, given a known set of values for y and a known set of
values for each independent variable. This function takes the form **LINEST**
(*known_y's, known_x's, const, stats*).

The *known_y's* argument is the set of y-values you already know. This argument can be a single column, a single row, or a rectangular range of cells. If *known_y's* is a single column, each column in the *known_x's* argument is considered an independent variable. Similarly, if *known_y's* is a single row, each row in the *known_x's* argument is considered an independent variable. If *known_y's* is a rectangular range, you can use only one independent variable; *known_x's* in this case should be a range of the same size and shape as *known_y's*. If you omit the *known_x's* argument, Excel uses the sequence 1, 2, 3, 4, and so on.

The *const* and *stats* arguments are optional. If either is included, it must be a logical constant—either TRUE or FALSE. (You can substitute 1 for TRUE and 0 for FALSE.) The default settings for *const* and *stats* are TRUE and FALSE, respectively. If you set *const* to FALSE, Excel forces b (the last term in the straight-line equation) to be 0. If you set *stats* to TRUE, the array returned by LINEST includes the following validation statistics.

se_1 through se_n	Standard error values for each coefficient
Se_b	Standard error value for the constant b
r^2	Coefficient of determination
se_y	Standard error value for y
F	F statistic
Df	Degrees of freedom
ss_{reg}	Regression sum of squares
ss_{resid}	Residual sum of squares

Before creating a formula using LINEST, you must select a range large enough to hold the result array returned by the function. If you omit the *stats* argument (or set it explicitly to FALSE), the result array encompasses one cell for each of your independent variables and one cell for b. If you include the validation statistics, the result array looks like the following example. After selecting a range to contain the results array, type the function and then press Ctrl+Enter to enter the function in each cell of the result array.

m_n	m_{n-1}	...	m_2	m_1	b
se_n	se_{n-1}	...	se_2	se_1	se_b
r^2	se_y				
F	df				
ss_{reg}	ss_{resid}				

Note that, with or without validation statistics, the coefficients and standard error values for your independent variables are returned in the opposite order from your input data. For example, if you have four independent variables organized in four columns, LINEST evaluates the leftmost column as x_1, but it returns m_1 in the fourth column of the result array.

Figure 17-3 shows a simple example of the use of LINEST with one independent variable. The entries in column B of this worksheet represent monthly product demand for a small business. The numbers in column A represent the months in the period. Suppose you want to compute the slope and y-intercept of the regression line that best describes the relationship between the demand and the months. In other words, you want to describe the trend of the data. To do this, select the range F6:G6, type the formula =**LINEST(B2:B19, A2:A19)**, and press Ctrl+Shift+Enter. The resulting number in cell F6 is 20.613, the slope of the regression line; the number in cell G6 is 4002.065, the y-intercept of the line.

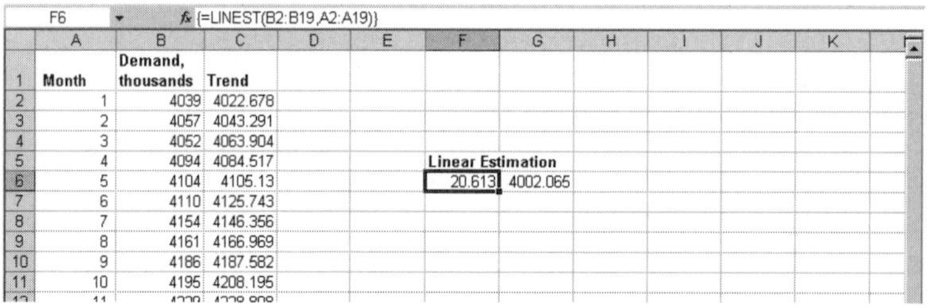

Figure 17-3. The LINEST function computes the slope and y-intercept of a regression line.

> **note** The LINEST and LOGEST functions return only the y-axis coordinates used for calculating lines and curves. The difference between them is that LINEST projects a straight line and LOGEST projects an exponential curve. You must be careful to match the appropriate function to the analysis at hand. The LINEST function might be more appropriate for sales projections, and the LOGEST function might be more suited to applications, such as statistical analyses or population trends. For more information, see "The LOGEST Function" on page 483.

The TREND Function

LINEST returns a mathematical description of the straight line that best fits known data. TREND finds points that lie along that line and that fall into the unknown category. You can use the numbers returned by TREND to plot a trend line—a straight line that helps make sense of actual data. You can also use TREND to extrapolate, or make intelligent guesses about, future data based on the tendencies exhibited by known data. (Be careful. Although you can use TREND to plot the straight line that best fits the known data, TREND can't tell you if that line is a good predictor of the future.

Validation statistics returned by LINEST can help you make that assessment.) The
TREND function takes the form =TREND(*known_y's, known_x's, new_x's, const*).

The first two arguments represent the known values of your dependent and independent variables. As in LINEST, the *known_y's* argument is a single column, a single row,
or a rectangular range. The *known_x's*, argument also follows the pattern described for
LINEST. The third and fourth arguments are optional. If you omit *new_x's*, the
TREND function considers *new_x's*, to be identical to *known_x's*. If you include const,
the value of that argument must be TRUE or FALSE (or 1 or 0). If const is TRUE,
TREND forces *b* to be 0.

To calculate the trend-line data points that best fit your known data, simply omit the
third and fourth arguments from this function. The results array will be the same size
as the *known_x's*, range. In Figure 17-4, we used TREND to find the value of each point
on the regression line that describes the data set from the example in Figure 17-3. To
create these values, we selected the range C2:C19 and entered
=TREND(B2:B19, A2:A19) as an array formula using Ctrl+Shift+Enter.

	C2		▼	*fx* {=TREND(B2:B19,A2:A19)}									
	A	B	C	D	E	F	G	H	I	J	K	
1	Month	Demand, thousands	Trend									
2	1	4039	4022.678									
3	2	4057	4043.291									
4	3	4052	4063.904									
5	4	4094	4084.517			Linear Estimation						
6	5	4104	4105.13			20.613	4002.065					
7	6	4110	4125.743									
8	7	4154	4146.356									
9	8	4161	4166.969									
10	9	4186	4187.582									
11	10	4195	4208.195									
12	11	4229	4228.808									

Figure 17-4. The TREND function creates a data series that can be plotted
as a line on a chart.

To extrapolate from existing data, you must supply a range for *new_x's*. You can supply
as many or as few cells for *new_x's*, as you want. The result array will be the same size
as the *new_x's*, range. In Figure 17-5 we used TREND to calculate demand for the 19th,
20th, and 21st months. To arrive at these values, we entered the numbers 19 through 21
in A21:A23, selected C21:C23, and entered =TREND(B2:B19, A2:A19, A21:A23) as an
array formula.

	C21		▼	*fx* {=TREND(B2:B19,A2:A19,A21:A23)}									
	A	B	C	D	E	F	G	H	I	J	K	
1	Month	Demand, thousands	Trend									
2	1	4039	4022.678									
3	2	4057	4043.291									
4	3	4052	4063.904									
5	4	4094	4084.517			Linear Estimation						
6	5	4104	4105.13			20.613	4002.065					
7	6	4110	4125.743									
18	17	4368	4352.486									
19	18	4389	4373.099									
20												
21	19		4393.712									
22	20		4414.325									
23	21		4434.938									
24												

Figure 17-5. TREND can predict the sales figures for months 19, 20, and 21.

The FORECAST Function

The FORECAST function is similar to TREND, except that it returns a single point along a line rather than returning an array that defines the line. This function takes the form =FORECAST(*x, known_y's, known_x's*).

The *x* argument is the data point for which you want to extrapolate a value. For example, instead of using TREND, we can use the FORECAST function to extrapolate the value in cell C23 in Figure 17-4 by entering the formula =FORECAST(21, B2:B19, A2:A19) where the *x* argument refers to the 21st data point on the regression line. You can use this function if you want to calculate any point in the future.

The SLOPE Function

The SLOPE function returns the slope of the linear regression line. The slope is defined as the vertical distance divided by the horizontal distance between any two points on the regression line. Its value is the same as the first number in the array returned by the LINEST function. In other words, SLOPE calculates the trajectory of the line used by the FORECAST and TREND functions to calculate the values of data points. The SLOPE function takes the form =SLOPE(*known_y's, known_x's*).

To find the slope of the regression line that describes the data set from the example shown in Figure 17-5, we can enter =SLOPE(B2:B19, A2:A19) as an array. This returns a value of 20.613.

The STEYX Function

The STEYX function calculates the standard error of a regression, a measure of the amount of error accrued in predicting a y for each given x. This function takes the form =STEYX(**known_y's, known_x's**). If we apply this function to the worksheet shown in Figure 17-5, the formula =STEYX(B2:B19, A2:A19) returns a standard error value of 12.96562.

Calculating Exponential Regression

Unlike linear regression, which plots values along a straight line, exponential regression describes a curve by calculating the array of values needed to plot it. The equation that describes an exponential regression curve is

$$y = b * m_1^{x1} * m_2^{x2} * \ldots * m_n^{xn}$$

If you have only one independent variable, the equation is

$$y = b * m^x$$

The LOGEST Function

The LOGEST function works like LINEST, except that you use it to
analyze data that is nonlinear, and it returns the coordinates of an exponential curve
instead of a straight line. LOGEST returns coefficient values for each independent variable plus a value for the constant b. This function takes the form
=LOGEST(known_y's, known_x's, const, stats).

LOGEST accepts the same arguments as the LINEST function and returns a result array
in the same fashion. If you set the optional stats argument to TRUE, the function also
returns validation statistics. For more information about the LOGEST function's underlying equations and its arguments, see "The LINEST Function" on page 478.

---

note The LINEST and LOGEST functions return only the y-axis coordinates used for calculating lines and curves. The difference between them is that LINEST projects a straight
line and LOGEST projects an exponential curve. You must be careful to match the
appropriate function to the analysis at hand. The LINEST function might be more
appropriate for sales projections, and the LOGEST function might be more suited to
applications, such as statistical analyses or population trends.

The GROWTH Function

Where the LOGEST function returns a mathematical description of the exponential
regression curve that best fits a set of known data, the GROWTH function finds points
that lie along that curve. The GROWTH function works like its linear counterpart, TREND,
and takes the form **=GROWTH(*known_y's, known_x's, new_x's, const*)**. For more information about the GROWTH function's arguments, see "The TREND Function" on page 480.

Using the Analysis
Toolpak Data Analysis Tools

If you performed a complete installation of Excel, the Analysis ToolPak is available each
time you start Excel. You can access the tools installed with the Analysis ToolPak by
choosing Tools, Data Analysis to display the dialog box shown in Figure 17-6.

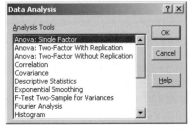

Figure 17-6. The Data Analysis dialog box presents a list of tools.

Using the Descriptive Statistics Tool

The Descriptive Statistics tool provides a table of statistics for one or more sets of input values. For each variable in the input range, this tool's output range includes a detailed list of statistics, as shown in Figure 17-7.

	A	B	C	D	E	F	G	H	I
1	99.39954			Column1					
2	97.44463								
3	100.4885		Mean	100.0501282					
4	102.5529		Standard Error	0.064578902					
5	102.3967		Median	100.034272					
6	103.4663		Mode	103.4662662					
7	95.63282		Standard Deviation	2.042164194					
8	99.53164		Sample Variance	4.170434595					
9	102.19		Kurtosis	-0.388877776					
10	97.8266		Skewness	0.048003657					
11	98.61959		Range	11.57037332					
12	96.61914		Minimum	94.46110451					
13	96.30618		Maximum	106.0314778					
14	98.04474		Sum	100050.1282					
15	98.45299		Count	1000					
16	95.76414		Largest(75)	103.0917454					
17	98.86415		Smallest(75)	97.10988959					
18	99.1919								
19	100.2697								
20	99.26901								
21	99.34602								

Figure 17-7. We generated 1000 normally distributed random numbers, using 100 as the mean and 2 as the standard deviation, and then verified their normalness with the Descriptive Statistics tool.

To use the Descriptive Statistics tool, choose Tools, Data Analysis, select Descriptive Statistics, and click OK. The dialog box shown in Figure 17-8 appears.

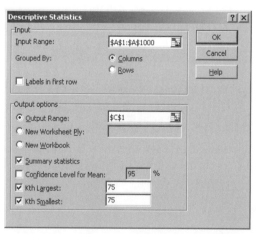

Figure 17-8. Use the Descriptive Statistics tool to create a table of statistics.

The Descriptive Statistics tool requires an input range that consists of one or more variables, and an output range. You must also indicate whether the variables are to be arranged by column or by row. If you include a row of labels, be sure to select the

Chapter 17: Functions for Analyzing Statistics

Labels In First Row option. Excel then uses the labels to identify the variables in its output table. Only select the Summary Statistics option if you want a detailed output table as shown in Figure 17-7; otherwise, leave this check box empty.

For more information about random numbers, see "Generating Random Number" on page 490.

Like the other tools in the Analysis ToolPak, Descriptive Statistics creates a table of constants. If a table of constants doesn't suit your needs, you can obtain most of the same statistical data from other Analysis ToolPak tools or from formulas that use Excel's worksheet functions. The statistics and formulas are listed in Table 17-3.

Table 17-3. Descriptive Statistics Formulas

Statistic	Formula
Mean	=AVERAGE(*number1*, *number2*, ...)
Standard error	Similar to =STEYX (*known_y's*, *known_x's*) but uses the ±-distribution rather than the standard normal distribution.
Median	=MEDIAN(*number1*, *number2*, ...)
Mode	=MODE(*number1*, *number2*, ...)
Standard deviation	=STDEV(*number1*, *number2*, ...)
Variance	=VAR(*number1*, *number2*, ...)
Kurtosis	=KURT(*number1*, *number2*, ...)
Skewness	=SKEW(*number1*, *number2*, ...)
Range	=MAX(*number1*, *number2*)- MIN (*number1*, *number2*, ...)
Minimum	=MIN(*number1*, *number2*, ...)
Maximum	=MAX(*number1*, *number2*, ...)
Sum	=SUM(*number1*, *number2*, ...)
Count	=COUNT(*value1*, *value2*, ...)
*k*th largest	=LARGE(*array, k*)
*k*th smallest	=SMALL(*array, k*)
Confidence	Similar to =CONFIDENCE (*alpha, standard_dev, size*) but uses a different algorithm.

Chapter 17

Creating Histograms

A histogram is a chart (usually a simple column chart) that takes a collection of measurements and plots the number of measurements (called the frequency) that fall
within each of several intervals (called bins).

To see how the Histogram tool works, we'll use a table of 1000 SAT test scores. (The input
range must contain numeric data only.) To see a breakdown of the total scores at 50-point
intervals, begin by setting up the distribution bins shown in column F of Figure 17-9.

	A	B	C	D	E	F	G	H	I	J	K
1	Student ID	Verbal	Math	Total							
2	172-24-4999	418	518	936		600					
3	360-53-4755	465	557	1022		650					
4	354-63-5005	463	549	1012		700					
5	365-58-5506	466	587	1053		750					
6	581-26-4480	520	544	1064		800					
7	381-46-5039	470	537	1007		850					
8	633-23-4537	533	549	1082		900					
9	405-50-4764	476	570	1046		950					
10	374-50-5399	468	548	1016		1000					
11	267-51-5445	441	562	1003		1050					
12	783-66-5139	570	560	1130		1100					
13	514-64-5099	503	554	1057		1150					
14	704-59-4501	551	556	1107		1200					
15	492-43-5382	498	562	1060		1250					
16	366-49-5592	466	525	991		1300					
17	159-65-4256	414	549	963		1350					
18	491-41-4839	497	545	1042		1400					
19	826-63-4690	581	519	1100		1450					

Figure 17-9. Column F contains the distribution bins.

The distribution bins don't have to be equally spaced as are the ones in Figure 17-9, but
they must be in ascending order. Choose Tools, Data Analysis, and select the Histogram
tool. The Histogram dialog box is shown in Figure 17-10.

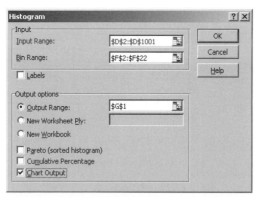

Figure 17-10. This dialog box appears after you select
the Histogram tool from the Data Analysis dialog box.

The Histogram tool can take three items of information: the location of the data (in
this case, D2:D1001), the location of the bins (F2:F22), and the upper left cell of the
range where you want the analysis to appear (G1). After you click OK, Excel writes its
analysis in columns G and H, as shown in Figure 17-11.

Chapter 17: Functions for Analyzing Statistics

	A	B	C	D	E	F	G	H	I	J	K
1	Student ID	Verbal	Math	Total			Bin	Frequency			
2	172-24-4999	418	518	936		600	600	0			
3	360-53-4755	465	557	1022		650	650	0			
4	354-63-5005	463	549	1012		700	700	0			
5	365-58-5506	466	587	1053		750	750	0			
6	581-26-4480	520	544	1064		800	800	0			
7	381-46-5039	470	537	1007		850	850	0			
8	633-23-4537	533	549	1082		900	900	3			
9	405-50-4764	476	570	1046		950	950	48			
10	374-50-5399	468	548	1016		1000	1000	155			
11	267-51-5445	441	562	1003		1050	1050	329			
12	783-66-5139	570	560	1130		1100	1100	291			
13	514-64-5099	503	554	1057		1150	1150	150			
14	704-59-4501	551	556	1107		1200	1200	23			
15	492-43-5382	498	562	1060		1250	1250	1			
16	366-49-5592	466	525	991		1300	1300	0			
17	159-65-4256	414	549	963		1350	1350	0			
18	491-41-4839	497	545	1042		1400	1400	0			
19	826-63-4690	581	519	1100		1450	1450	0			

Figure 17-11. This analysis tells us that 3 scores were at least 900 but less than 950, 48 are at least 950 but less than 1000, and so on.

note If you want, leave the Bin Range box blank. Excel then creates evenly distributed bin intervals using the minimum and maximum values in the input range as beginning and endpoints. The number of intervals is equal to the square root of the number of input values.

Here are a few things to keep in mind when using the Histogram tool:

- In the Frequency column, the histogram reports the number of input values that are equal to or greater than the bin value but less than the next bin value.

- The last value in the table reports the number of input values equal to or greater than the last bin value.

- Select the Pareto option in the Histogram dialog box to sort the output in descending order.

- Select the Cumulative Percentage option to create a table that lists the cumulative percentages of each bin level.

InsideOut

Beware of bin formulas

Notice that the Histogram tool duplicates your column of bin values in the Bin column, which is convenient if you place the output somewhere else in your workbook. But because the Histogram tool copies the bin values, it's best if the bin range contains numeric constants rather than formulas. If you do use formulas, be sure they don't include relative references; otherwise, when Histogram copies the range, the formulas might produce unwanted results.

Chapter 17

Part 5: Creating Formulas and Performing Data Analysis

If you select the Chart Output option in the Histogram dialog box, the Histogram tool simultaneously generates a chart like the one shown in Figure 17-12 along with the frequency distribution table. (We enlarged the chart to make it easier to see.)

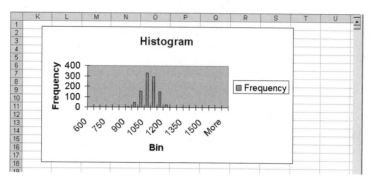

Figure 17-12. The Histogram tool can automatically create a column chart like this one.

> For everything you need to know about charts, see Part 8, "Creating Charts."

Analyzing Distribution with the FREQUENCY Function

The Histogram tool generates a set of numeric constants. If you'd rather create formulas linked to the input values, you can use the built-in FREQUENCY array function, which calculates the number of times specified values occur in a population, and takes the arguments *(data_array, bins_array)*. Figure 17-13 shows the FREQUENCY function applied to the data shown in Figure 17-8.

	A	B	C	D	E	F	G	H	I	J	K
						f_x (=FREQUENCY(D2:D1001,F2:F20))					
1	Student ID	Verbal	Math	Total							
2	172-24-4999	418	518	936		600	0				
3	360-53-4755	465	557	1022		650	0				
4	354-63-5005	463	549	1012		700	0				
5	365-58-5506	466	587	1053		750	0				
6	581-26-4480	520	544	1064		800	0				
7	381-46-5039	470	537	1007		850	0				
8	633-23-4537	533	549	1082		900	3				
9	405-50-4764	476	570	1046		950	48				
10	374-50-5399	468	548	1016		1000	155				
11	267-51-5445	441	562	1003		1050	329				
12	783-66-5139	570	560	1130		1100	291				
13	514-64-5099	503	554	1057		1150	150				
14	704-59-4501	551	556	1107		1200	23				
15	492-43-5382	498	562	1060		1250	1				
16	366-49-5592	466	525	991		1300	0				
17	159-65-4256	414	549	963		1350	0				
18	401-41-4830	407	545	1042		1400	0				

Figure 17-13. Use the FREQUENCY function to link the distribution analysis to the input data.

To use the FREQUENCY function, set up a column of bin values, just as you would with the Histogram tool, and then select the entire range where you want the output to appear, which in our example would be G2:G21—the cells in column G that are directly adjacent to the bin values in column F. (This range must be a column, because FREQUENCY can't use a row or multicolumn range as its output range.) Then enter the formula, specifying the input range as the first argument and the bin range as the second. Press Ctrl+Shift+Enter to lock in the array formula. For more information about arrays, see "Using Arrays" on page 387.

Using the Rank and Percentile Tool

Suppose you want to rank the scores shown in Figure 17-9. You could rank the scores by sorting the data in descending order, with the best score at the top and the worst score at the bottom of the column. To find the rank of any score, you might want to create an ascending series of numbers beside the sorted scores, with 1 beside the best score and 1000 beside the worst.

The Analysis ToolPak includes a Rank And Percentile tool that not only performs these tasks for you but also creates percentile figures for each value in your input range. To use this tool, choose Tools, Data Analysis, and select Rank And Percentile. The Rank And Percentile dialog box is shown in Figure 17-14.

> **note** If the Data Analysis command does not appear on the full Tools menu (double-click the menu name), see "Installing the Analysis ToolPak" on page 405.

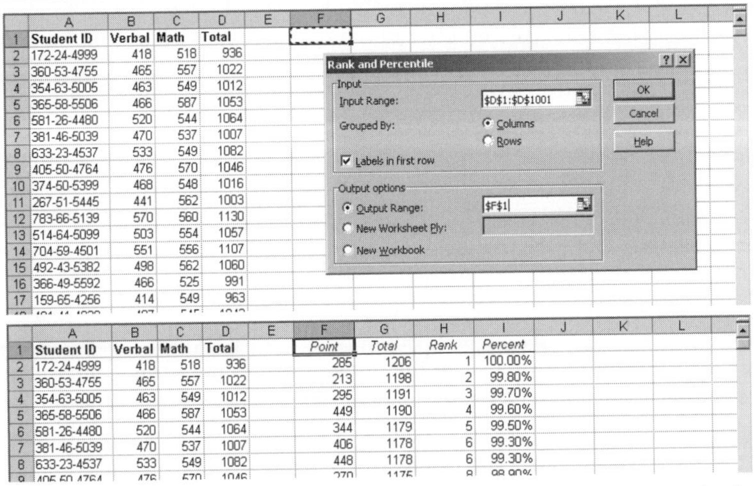

Figure 17-14. Use the Rank And Percentile tool to generate an output table like the one shown in the lower figure.

Here are some hints to remember when using the Rank And Percentile tool:

- It's best to use the Labels In First Row option in the Rank And Percentile dialog box, and then include the column heading in the input range. This way, the second column in the output table uses the same label. If you do not include the label in the input range, the output column is labeled Column1.

● In Figure 17-14, we analyzed a single column of data, but we could analyze the Verbal, Math, and Total columns together. In that case, we would specify the input range B1:D1001, and the tool would generate 12 columns of output, 4 for each input column.

● You can also have the output table placed on a new sheet or workbook, which is a good idea if you select multiple columns of input data resulting in a large output table.

● Here's how to read the output of the Rank And Percentile tool, shown at the bottom of Figure 17-14. The first row of the output table (F2:I2) tell us that the 285th item in the input range is a total score of 1206, which ranks first and is better than 100 percent of the other scores.

Correlating Tables

The input and output tables, shown in the bottom graphic of Figure 17-14, share a common column of data—the Total column—and the exact same number of rows. But because the two tables are sorted differently, the rows don't match up. The easiest solution is to sort the output table by the Point column; in this context, point indicates the position of the corresponding data point in the input range. Therefore, sorting the output table by the Point column puts it in the same order as the input table, as shown at the top of the following figure.

	A	B	C	D	E	F	G	H	I	J
1	Student ID	Verbal	Math	Total		Point	Total	Rank	Percent	
2	172-24-4999	418	518	936		1	936	972	2.70%	
3	360-53-4755	465	557	1022		2	1022	657	33.90%	
4	354-63-5005	463	549	1012		3	1012	726	26.60%	
5	365-58-5506	466	587	1053		4	1053	447	54.60%	
6	581 26 4490	520	544	1064		5	1064	370	61.70%	

	A	B	C	D	E	F	G	H	I
1	Student ID	Verbal	Math	Total	Rank	Percent			
2	172-24-4999	418	518	936	972	2.70%			
3	360-53-4755	465	557	1022	657	33.90%			
4	354-63-5005	463	549	1012	726	26.60%			
5	365-58-5506	466	587	1053	447	54.60%			
6	581 26 4490	520	544	1064	370	61.70%			

If you want to add information from the output table to the existing input table, you can delete the Point column (because the Point column simply indicates the row number) and the Total column (because the input table already has a Total column) in the output table, and then delete the blank column, creating a single table, as shown at in the bottom graphic in the preceding figure.

Generating Random Numbers

The built-in random-number function, RAND, generates a uniform distribution of random real numbers between 0 and 1. In other words, all values between 0 and 1 share the same probability of being returned by a set of formulas based on the RAND function. Because the sample is relatively small, the distribution is by no means perfectly uniform. Nevertheless, repeated tests demonstrate that the RAND function doesn't favor any position within its spectrum of distribution. For more information, see "The RAND and RANDBETWEEN Functions" on page 416.

Troubleshooting

Random Numbers Keep Changing

The RAND function is one of Excel's *volatile* functions—that is, it recalculates every time the sheet recalculates, which happens every time you make an entry in a cell. If you want to generate a set of random numbers and then "freeze" them, select all the RAND formulas in your sheet then choose Edit, Paste Special, and choose the Values option to replace the volatile formulas with stable values. Better yet, instead of using the RAND function, you can use the Tools, Data Analysis, Random Number Generation tool, which produces constants instead of formulas.

You can use the random-number component of the Analysis ToolPak to create sets of random numbers that are not uniformly distributed, and then use the Histogram tool to sort and plot the results. These random-number sets are useful for Monte Carlo decision analysis and other kinds of simulations. Six distribution types are available: Uniform, Normal, Bernoulli, Binomial, Poisson, and Discrete (user-defined). In addition, you can use the Patterned Distribution option to create non-random numbers at specified intervals. To use the Random Number Generation tool, choose Tools, Data Analysis, and select Random Number Generation. Excel presents a dialog box like the one shown in Figure 17-15.

Figure 17-15. The Parameters area of the Random Number Generation dialog box changes to reflect the distribution type you select.

Here are a couple of important points regarding the use of the Random Number Generation tool:

- In the Number Of Variables and Number Of Random Numbers boxes, you indicate how many columns of numbers you want and how many numbers you want in each column. For example, if you want 10 columns of 100 numbers each, specify 10 in the Number Of Variables box and 100 in the Number Of Random Numbers box.

- You can also specify a seed value. However, each time you generate a random-number set with a particular distribution type using the same seed value, you get the same sequence of numbers; therefore, you should specify a seed value only if you need to be able to reproduce a random-number sequence.

Random Number Distribution Methods

In the Random Number Generation dialog box, the parameters shown directly below the Distribution list change, depending on the type of distribution you select. As Figure 17-15 shows, when you select Uniform Distribution, you can specify the beginning and end points of the distribution in the Between/And boxes.

Distributing Random Numbers Uniformly

This option asks you to specify two numbers between (and including) which to generate a set of random numbers, and works much the same way as the RANDBETWEEN function, generating an evenly distributed set of real numbers. You can use this option as a more convenient alternative to RAND if you want endpoints other than 0 and 1 or if you want sets of numbers to be based on the same seed value.

Distributing Random Numbers Normally

Normal Distribution has the following characteristics:

- One particular value, the mean, is more likely to occur than any other value.

- Values greater than the mean are as likely to occur as values less than it.

- Values close to the mean are more likely to occur than values distant from the mean.

To generate normally distributed random numbers, you specify two parameters: the mean and the standard deviation. The standard deviation is the average absolute difference between the random numbers and the mean. (Approximately 68 percent of the values in a normal distribution will fall within one standard deviation of the mean.)

Generating Random Numbers Using Bernoulli Distribution

The Bernoulli Distribution option simulates the probability of success of a number of trials, given that all trials have an equal probability of succeeding and that the success of one trial has no impact on the success of subsequent trials. (Note that success in this context has no value implication. In other words, you can use this distribution to simulate failure as readily as success.) All values in the Bernoulli distribution's output are either 0 or 1.

The probability that each cell will return a 1 is given by the distribution's sole parameter—P Value—for which you supply a number from 0 to 1. For example, if you want a sequence of 100 random Bernoulli values whose most likely sum is 27, you define a 100-cell output range and specify a P Value of 0.27.

Generating Random Numbers Using Binomial Distribution

The Binomial Distribution option simulates the number of successes in a fixed number of trials, given a specified probability rate. As with the Bernoulli Distribution option, the trials are assumed to be independent; that is, the outcome of one has no affect on any other. To generate binomially distributed numbers, you specify Number of Trials and the P Value (probability) that any trial will succeed. (Again, success in this context has no value implication. In other words, you can use this distribution to simulate failure as readily as success.)

For example, suppose you make 10 sales presentations a week; you close the sale 20 percent of the time; and you would like to know what your success rate might be over the next year. Type **50** (for 50 working weeks in the year) in the Number Of Random Numbers box, 0.2 in the P Value box, and 10 in the Number Of Trials box to learn that you can expect to make no sales four weeks in the coming year.

Generating Random Numbers Using Poisson Distribution

The Poisson Distribution option simulates the number of times an event occurs within a particular time span, given a certain probability of occurrence. The occurrences are assumed to be independent; that is, each occurrence has no effect on the likelihood of others.

The Poisson Distribution option takes a single parameter, Lambda, which represents the expected outcome of an individual occurrence. For example, suppose you receive an average of 10 service calls a day. You want to know how often you can expect to get 18 or more service calls in a day over a year. To get this information, type **260** (52 weeks times 5 days) in the Number Of Random Numbers box and 10 in the Lambda box (the expected average). You can then use the COUNTIF function to count the number of times 18 shows up in the output range. For more information, see "The SUMIF and COUNTIF Functions" on page 473.

Generating Random Numbers Using Discrete Distribution

Use the Discrete Distribution option to create a custom distribution pattern by specifying a table of possible outcomes along with the probability associated with each outcome. The probability values must be between 0 and 1, and the sum of the probabilities in the table must equal 1. To use the Discrete Distribution option, specify the possible outcomes and their probabilities as a two-column range whose reference is the only parameter used by this option.

For example, you could create a custom distribution pattern to generate random snow-shovel sales patterns based on a two-column input range: Month Number and Probability of Snow.

Generating Semi-Random Numbers Using Patterned Distribution

The Patterned Distribution option in the Random Number Generation dialog box generates numbers that are both random and part nonrandom. Selecting the Patterned Distribution option displays the dialog box shown in Figure 17-16.

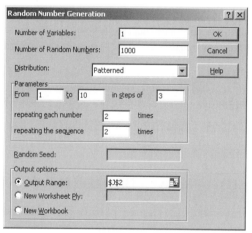

Figure 17-16. The Patterned Distribution option creates an arithmetic series with operational repetitions.

You can think of the Patterned Distribution option as a fancy Series command. It creates one or more arithmetic series with optional internal repetitions. For example, to create the series 1, 1, 4, 4, 7, 7, 10, 10, 1, 1, 4, 4, 7, 7, 10, complete the dialog box as shown in Figure 17-16, requesting two sequences of the numbers 1 through 10, using a step interval of 3, and repeating each number twice within each cycle.

If the step interval takes the series beyond the specified upper value, the output range includes the upper value because the last interval is truncated. For example, if you specify a step interval of 4 and the numbers 1 through 10, Excel creates the series 1, 5, 9, and 10.

Sampling a Population of Numbers

The Sampling tool extracts a subset of numbers from a larger group (or population) of numbers. From an input range, you can sample a specified number of values at random or at every *n*th value. The Sampling tool copies the extracted numbers to an output range you specify. To use the Sampling tool, choose Tools, Data Analysis, and select Sampling. Figure 17-17 shows the dialog box that appears.

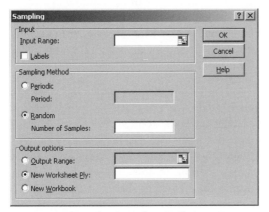

Figure 17-17.   The Sampling tool extracts a
random or periodic subset of a numeric population.

The values in the input range must be numeric. They can include blank values and dates, provided the dates are entered as numbers, not text. For example, to simplify a chart of daily commodity prices, you can use the Sampling tool to extract every *n*th data point and then create a new plot from the extracted data.

---

tip   **Sample text values**

To perform the equivalent of sampling from a range containing text values, set up a series of ascending integers beginning at 1 in a column alongside the text values, and then use the Sampling tool to extract numbers from this series. Then you can assemble a list of sampled text values by using the resulting numbers as arguments to the INDEX function. For more information, see "The INDEX Function" on page 434.

Calculating Moving Averages

A moving average is a forecasting technique that simplifies trend analysis by smoothing fluctuations that occur in measurements taken over time. These fluctuations can be caused by random noise that is often a by-product of the measurement technique. For example, measurements of the height of a growing child will vary with the accuracy of the ruler and whether the child is standing straight or slouching. You can take a series of measurements, however, and smooth them over time, resulting in a curve that reflects the child's actual growth rate. Fluctuations in measurements can result from other temporary conditions that introduce bias. Monthly sales, for example, might vary with the number of working days in the month or the absence of a star salesperson who takes a vacation.

Suppose you have created the 18-month demand curve shown in Figure 17-18. To generate a less noisy trend line from this data, you can plot a six-month moving average. The first point in the moving average line is the average of the first six monthly figures (January through June 2000). The next point averages the second-through-seventh monthly figures (February through July 2000), and so on. You can use the Moving Average tool to perform this analysis for you. To do so, choose Tools, Data Analysis, and select Moving Average to display the dialog box shown in Figure 17-19.

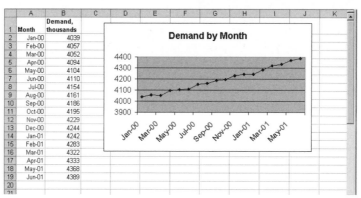

Figure 17-18. We'll use this 18-month demand curve to demonstrate Excel's Moving Average tool.

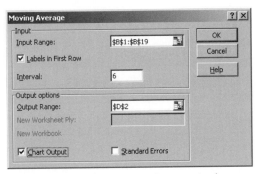

Figure 17-19. The Moving Average tool
helps smooth out bumpy curves to reveal the trend.

The Moving Average tool requires three pieces of information: the input range that
contains the data you want to analyze, the output range where the averaged data will
appear, and the interval over which the data is averaged. To determine a three-month
moving average, for example, specify an interval of 3.

Figure 17-20 shows a six-month moving average superimposed over the original
demand curve in Figure 17-18. The Moving Average tool produced the data in column
C, which was used to create the straighter plot line in the chart. Notice that the first five
cells in the tool's output range contain #N/A error values. Where the interval is n, you
will always have $n-1$ #N/A error values at the beginning of the output. Including those
values in a chart presents no problem, because Excel leaves the first area of the plot
line blank.

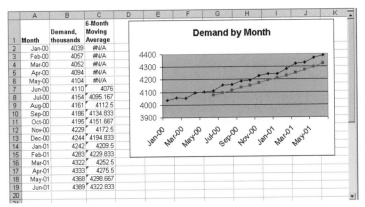

Figure 17-20. The Moving Average tool provides a better perspective
of the overall trend.

> **tip**   **Stow the flags**
>
> Notice that each cell containing a moving average value in Figure 17-20 displays a flag in the upper left corner of the cell. This is an error flag; after you select the cell, a *smart tag action menu* appears alerting you that the formula omits adjacent cells. In this case, it's OK. To remove the flags, select all the flagged cells, click the smart tag to display its menu, and then choose the Ignore Error command.

Chapter 18

Performing What-If Analysis

One of the most important benefits of spreadsheet software is that it performs a what-if analysis quickly and easily. Change key variables, and instantly see the effect. For example, if you're using Microsoft Excel to decide whether to lease or purchase a car, you can test your financial model with different assumptions about interest rates and down payments, and you can see the effects of varying rates on bottom-line costs you will pay, such as the total interest. Excel offers a number of advanced what-if features, which are discussed in this chapter.

Using Data Tables

A data table, or sensitivity table, summarizes the impact of one or two variables on formulas that use those variables. You can choose Data, Table to create two kinds of data tables: a table based on a single input variable that tests the variable's impact on more than one formula, or a table based on two input variables that tests their impact on a single formula.

Data Tables Based on One Input Variable

Suppose you're considering buying a house that requires you to take on a 30-year, $200,000 mortgage, and you need to calculate monthly payments on the loan for several interest rates. A one-variable data table, such as the one shown in Figure 18-1 on the next page, can give you the information you need.

C2	▼		*fx* =PMT(A2/12,360,C1)									
	A	B	C	D	E	F	G	H	I	J	K	
1		Loan Amount:	200,000									
2			($555.56)									
3		6.0%										
4		6.5%										
5		7.0%										
6		7.5%										
7		8.0%										
8		8.5%										
9												
10												

Figure 18-1. Begin building the data table by entering the interest rates and the PMT function in the worksheet.

To create this table, enter the interest rates you want to test, as shown in cells B3:B8 in Figure 18-1. This is the *input range*, because it contains the input values you want to test. Enter the loan amount in a cell outside the data table area. We entered $200,000 in cell C1. This allows us to easily change the loan amount to test various scenarios. Enter the formula that uses the input variable. In this case, enter the formula =PMT(A2/12, 360, C1) in cell C2. In this formula, A2/12 is the monthly interest rate, 360 is the term of the loan in months, and C1 refers to the cell containing the loan principal.

> **note** Notice that the formula in cell C2 refers to cell A2, which is blank. Because A2 is blank, the function returns a spurious result: the payment required to amortize the loan at an interest rate of 0 percent. Cell A2 is a placeholder through which Excel will feed the values in the input range to create the data table. Because Excel never changes the underlying value of this cell, this placeholder can be any cell outside the table range.

After you have entered the inputs and the formula, select the data table—the smallest rectangular block that includes the formula and all the values in the input range. In this case, select the range B2:C8, and then choose Data, Table.

In the Table dialog box, shown in Figure 18-2, specify the location of the input cell in the Row Input Cell or Column Input Cell box. The *input cell* is the placeholder cell referred to by the table formula—in this example, A2. If the input values are arranged in a row, enter the input cell reference in the Row Input Cell box. If the values in the input range are arranged in a column, as in our example, use the Column Input Cell box.

Figure 18-2. Use the Table dialog box to specify the input cell.

After you click OK, Excel enters the results of the table formula (one result for each
input value) in the available cells of the data table range. In this example, Excel enters
six results in the range C3:C8, as shown in Figure 18-3.

C8		fx (=TABLE(,A2))								
	A	B	C	D	E	F	G	H	I	J	K
1		Loan Amount:	200,000								
2			($555.56)								
3		6.0%	-1199.10								
4		6.5%	-1264.14								
5		7.0%	-1330.60								
6		7.5%	-1398.43								
7		8.0%	-1467.53								
8		8.5%	-1537.83								
9											
10											

Figure 18-3. The monthly loan payments for each interest rate now
appear in the data table.

When you create this data table, Excel enters the array formula { =**TABLE(,A2)**} in each
cell in the *results range* C3:C8. In the sample table, the formula computes the results of
the PMT function using each of the interest rates in column B. After you have built the
table, you can change the loan amount or any of the interest rate values to see the
results immediately.

> **note** The TABLE function is an internal function, meaning that you can't select it in the
> Insert Function dialog box, or enter it manually.

Single-Variable Tables with More than One Formula

When you create a single-variable data table, you can include as many output formulas
as you want. If your input range is in a column, enter the second output formula
directly to the right of the first one, the third to the right of the second, and so on. You
can use different formulas for different columns, but they must all use the same
input cell.

Suppose you're thinking about buying a house that would require you to take out an
$180,000 mortgage. You want to know what your monthly payments would be on that
mortgage at each of the interest rates in the input range, and you want to be able to
compare these payments with those for the $200,000 mortgage calculated in Figure 18-3.
You can expand the table in Figure 18-3 to include both formulas.

To add a new formula to the existing data table, enter the new formula in cell D2. For
this example, we entered =**PMT(A2/12, 360, D1)**. This formula must also refer to cell
A2, the same input cell as in the first formula. Then type **$180,000** in cell D1, select the
table range B2:D8; choose Data, Table; and enter the same input cell reference ($A$2)
in the Column Input Cell box. Figure 18-4 on the next page shows the result.

	D2	▾		*fx* =PMT(A2/12,360,D1)									
	A	B	C	D	E	F	G	H	I	J	K	
1		Loan Amount:	200,000	180,000								
2			($555.56)	($500.00)								
3		6.0%	-1199.10	-1079.19								
4		6.5%	-1264.14	-1137.72								
5		10.0%	-1755.14	-1579.63								
6		7.5%	-1398.43	-1258.59								
7		8.0%	-1467.53	-1320.78								
8		8.5%	-1537.83	-1384.04								
9												
10												

Figure 18-4. This data table computes the monthly payments on two
different loan amounts at various interest rates.

Data Tables Based on Two Input Variables

Suppose you want to build a data table that computes the monthly payment on a
$200,000 mortgage, but this time you want to vary not only the interest rate but also
the term of the loan. You want to know what affect changing the interest rate to 6, 6.5,
7, 7.5, 8, or 8.5 percent and changing the term to 15, 20, 25, or 30 years (180, 240, 300,
or 360 months) will have on your monthly payment.

To create this table, you can again enter six interest rates in cells B3:B8, and then enter
the second set of input values—the loan terms, in months—in a row above and to the
right of the first set, as shown in Figure 18-5.

After you enter the loan amount in a cell outside the table area (cell I2 in this example)
you can create the table formula. Because this is a two-variable table, the formula must
be entered in the cell at the intersection of the row and column that contain the two
sets of input values—cell B2, in this example. Although you can include as many formulas as you want in a single-variable data table, you can include only one output formula in a two-variable table. The formula for the table in this example is
=PMT(A2/12, B1, I2).

You'll notice immediately that the formula in cell B2 returns the #DIV/0! error value.
This is because the two blank cells, A2 and B1, when used as arguments, produce a
number that is either too large or too small for Excel to represent. As you'll see, this
spurious result does not affect the performance of the table.

	B2	▾		*fx* =PMT(A2/12,B1,I2)								
	A	B	C	D	E	F	G	H	I	J	K	L
1				Months					Loan Amount:			
2		#DIV/0!	180	240	300	360			200,000			
3		6.0%										
4		6.5%										
5		7.0%										
6	Rates	7.5%										
7		8.0%										
8		8.5%										
9												
10												

Figure 18-5. Cell B2 contains the formula for this two-variable table.

Finally, select the data table—the smallest rectangular block that includes all the input
values and the table formula. In this example, the table range is B2:F8. Choose Data,
Table, and specify the (empty) input cells. Because this is a two-variable table, you

must define two input cells. For this example, enter the reference for the first input cell, $B$1, in the Row Input Cell box, and then enter the reference for the second input cell, $A$2, in the Column Input Cell box. Figure 18-6 shows the result, with a little formatting added for easier reading.

	C3	▾	f_x {=TABLE(B1,A2)}									
	A	B	C	D	E	F	G	H	I	J	K	L
1					Months				Loan Amount:			
2			#DIV/0!	180	240	300	360			200,000		
3			6.0%	-1687.71	-1432.86	-1288.60	-1199.10					
4			6.5%	-1742.21	-1491.15	-1350.41	-1264.14					
5		Rates	7.0%	-1797.66	-1550.60	-1413.56	-1330.60					
6			7.5%	-1854.02	-1611.19	-1477.98	-1398.43					
7			8.0%	-1911.30	-1672.88	-1543.63	-1467.53					
8			8.5%	-1969.48	-1735.65	-1610.45	-1537.83					
9												
10												

Figure 18-6. This data table calculates the monthly payments using various interest rates and terms.

Troubleshooting

The Results in My Two-Input Data Table Are Wrong

Be careful not to reverse the input cells in a two-variable table. If you do, Excel uses the input values in the wrong place in the table formula, which creates a set of meaningless results. For example, if you reverse the input cells in the example shown in Figure 18-6, Excel uses the values in the input range C2:F2 as interest rates and the values in the input range B3:B8 as terms, resulting in monthly payments in the 20 million dollar range!

To make sure you're using the correct input cells, you need to look at the formula. In our example formula **=PMT(A2/12, B1, I2)**, you can tell that cell A2 is the column input cell because A2 appears in the first argument which is *rate*. Because the rates are arranged in a column, A2 is the column input cell.

Editing Tables

Although you can edit the input values or formulas in the left column or top row of a table, you can't edit the contents of any individual cell in the results range because the data table is an array. If you make a mistake when you set up a data table, you must select all the results; choose Edit, Clear, and then recompute the table.

You can copy the table results to a different part of the worksheet. You might want to do this to save the table's current results before you change the table formula or variables. In Figure 18-7 on the next page, we copied the values from C3:F8 to C10:F15. The copied values are constants, not array formulas. Excel automatically changes the results of the table from a set of array formulas to their numeric values if you copy the results out of the table range.

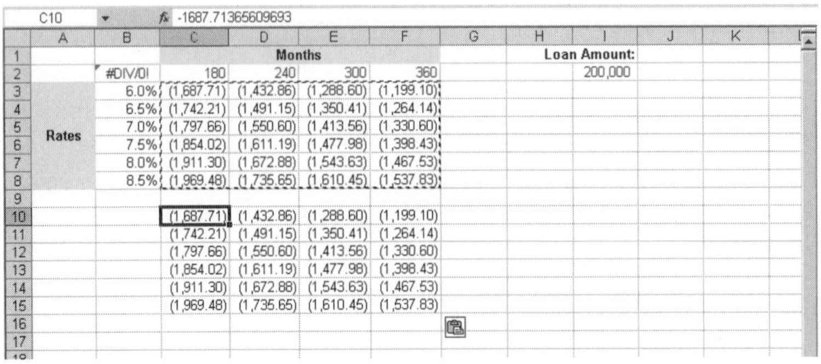

Figure 18-7. Copying the results range to another part of the worksheet transfers the numeric values, not the formulas used to compute them.

Using the Scenario Manager

To model more complicated problems than data tables can handle, involving as many as 32 variables, you can call on the services of the Scenario Manager by choosing Tools, Scenarios. A *scenario* is a named combination of values assigned to one or more variable cells in a what-if model. The worksheet in Figure 18-8 is a what-if model, set up so that you can enter variable figures and watch the effect on dependent computed values. The Scenario Manager records, tracks, and applies combinations of variable values.

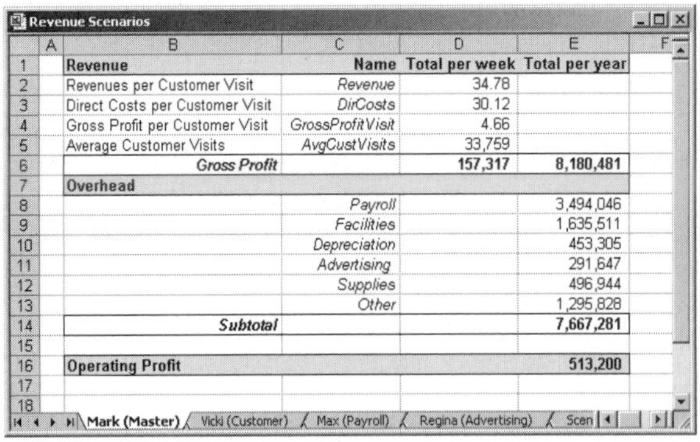

Figure 18-8. We'll use the Scenario Manager to model the effects of changing values in D2:D3, D5, and E8:E13 of this worksheet.

Here are some of the things you can do with the Scenario Manager:

- Create multiple scenarios for a single what-if model, each with its own sets of variables. You can create as many scenarios as your model requires.

- Distribute a what-if model to other members of your group so that they can add their own scenarios. Then you can collect the multiple versions and merge all the scenarios into a single worksheet.

- Track changes made to scenarios easily with Scenario Manager's version-control features by recording the date and the user name each time a scenario is added or modified.

- Print reports detailing all the changing cells and result cells.

- Password-protect scenarios from modification, and even hide them from view.

- Examine relationships between scenarios created by multiple users, using Scenario Summary and PivotTable Reports. For more on PivotTables, see Chapter 30, "Analyzing Data with PivotTable Reports."

Imagine that you manage a grocery store whose profit picture is modeled by the worksheet in Figure 18-8. The numbers in D2:D5, and E8:E13 are historic averages; column C contains the range names applied to the relevant cells in columns D and E. You're interested in testing the impact of changes in these cells on the bottom line in cell E16.

---

tip   **Name the cells**

Cell references are OK, but before you begin using the Scenario Manager, it's a good idea to name the cells you plan to use for your variables, as well as any cells containing formulas whose values depend on your variable cells. This step isn't required, but it makes the scenario reports, as well as some of the dialog boxes, more intelligible. For more information, see "Naming Cells and Cell Ranges" on page 371.

Defining Scenarios

To define a scenario, follow these steps:

1   Choose Tools, Scenarios.

2   In the Scenario Manager dialog box, shown in Figure 18-9 on the next page, click the Add button.

Figure 18-9. When you choose Tools, Scenarios,
the Scenario Manager dialog box is displayed.

3 In the Add Scenario dialog box, shown in Figure 18-10, type a name for your
scenario. (Note that as soon as you enter cell references in the Add Scenario
dialog box, the title of the dialog box changes to Edit Scenario.)

---

tip **Name the Normal scenario**

It's a good idea to define the values you begin with as a scenario before changing any
of them. You can name this scenario something like Starting Values or Last Year. If you
don't name the starting scenario, you'll lose your original what-if assumptions when
you display the new changing cell values in your worksheet.

Figure 18-10. Here we entered the references of the changing cells
individually by selecting each one with the mouse and separating one
reference from the next with a comma.

4 In the Changing Cells box, type or select the cells you plan to vary. Select nonadjacent cells and ranges by pressing the Ctrl key before selecting the cells or by separating their references or names with commas, as shown in Figure 18-10.

5 Click OK to create the first scenario. The Scenario Values dialog box appears, displaying a box for each changing cell. If you have named the changing cells, the names are displayed adjacent to the boxes, as shown in Figure 18-11; otherwise, the references of the changing cells are displayed.

6 To complete a scenario, edit these values, but for this example, leave the values as they are and just click OK.

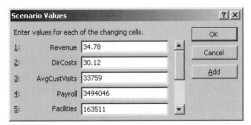

Figure 18-11. Because we previously named each changing cell, the names appear in the Scenario Values dialog box.

---

tip **Use temporary formulas**

In each box, you can enter either a constant or a formula. For example, to increase the value of the first variable in Figure 18-12, click in front of the value in the first variable's box and type =1.1* to create a formula that multiplies the current value by 1.1. (Note that although you can enter formulas in the Scenario Values dialog box, Excel alerts you that the formulas are converted to their resulting values after you click OK.)

---

7 To create another scenario, click Add to return to the Add Scenario dialog box.

Browsing Your Scenarios

Select a scenario name in the Scenario Manager dialog box, and click the Show button (or use the Scenario box, if you added it to a toolbar). The Scenario Manager replaces the variable values currently in the worksheet with the values you specified when you created the scenario. Figure 18-12 on the next page shows the example worksheet with a scenario showing average customer visits increased by 5 percent and revenues per customer visit decreased by 5 percent.

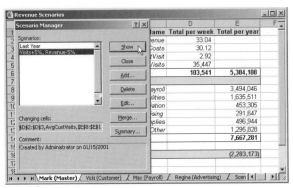

Figure 18-12. Clicking the Show button replaces your current
worksheet values with the values of a specified scenario.

The Scenario Manager dialog box remains on screen while you use the Show button so
that you can look at the results of other scenarios without returning to the worksheet.
If you click Close or press Esc to close the Scenario Manager dialog box, the values
from the last scenario you browsed remains in the worksheet. (A good reason to create
a starting values scenario, as mentioned earlier.)

Adding, Editing, and Deleting Scenarios

Scenarios are saved with all other worksheet data when you save. Each worksheet in a
workbook can contain its own set of scenarios. In the Scenario Manager dialog box,
you add new scenarios by clicking Add, and you edit existing scenarios by clicking
Edit, which displays the Edit Scenario dialog box (which is the same as the Add Scenario dialog box shown in Figure 18-10). You can change the name of the selected
scenario, and add or remove changing cells. The Delete button in the Scenario Manager
dialog box works as expected, removing the selected scenario from the list.

Tracking Changes

If someone edits a scenario, Excel adds a Modified By entry to the Comment box in the
Scenario Manager dialog box, beneath the Created By entry that appears when a scenario is first added. Each time a scenario is modified, Excel adds the name of the user
and the date of modification. This information is particularly helpful if you route your
what-if models to others and then merge their scenarios into a single what-if model, as
discussed in the following section.

Track comment modifying

When you edit scenarios, you can modify the contents of the Comment box; those modifications persist in all dialog boxes, including the creation and modification dates. You might not want this to happen, if you really want to track changes or prevent tampering. But if you create a summary report, the original modification information appears when you expand the outline to show the comments adjacent to each scenario name. If you don't want these comments modified, make sure you take advantage of the preventative measures discussed in "Protecting Worksheets" on page 127.

Routing and Merging Scenarios

If part of your job is to develop what-if models or projections for your company, you probably spend a lot of time gathering information about trends and market forces that might affect the company in the future. Often you need input from several people, each of whom knows about a particular aspect of the business, such as payroll costs or sales trends. Excel includes two features to make this sort of information-gathering task easier: document routing and scenario merging.

If you are connected to a network that uses a compatible electronic mail system, you can choose File, Send To, Routing Recipient to attach the current workbook to an electronic mail message. Compatible electronic mail systems include Microsoft Outlook, Microsoft Mail, Lotus cc:Mail, and any other electronic mail application that comply with the Messaging Application Programming Interface (MAPI) or Vendor Independent Messaging (VIM) standards. Alternatively, you can route workbooks using the Internet via Web documents and FTP sites.

For more on using routing slips, see "Routing Workbooks to a Workgroup Using Electronic Mail" on page 544. For more on using the Internet with Excel, see Chapter 20, "Transferring Files to and from Internet Sites."

If you are not connected to a network with a compatible electronic mail system, you can make copies of the worksheet containing your what-if model and distribute the copies to your coworkers the old-fashioned way—on floppy disks.

For example, suppose you want to distribute a what-if model to your coworkers: Vicki has expertise on customer trends, Max knows the payroll story, and Regina keeps track of advertising. You can consolidate their contributions using the routing slip approach, if available, or distribute individually named copies of the workbook to each person. After your coworkers add their what-if scenarios and return the workbook or workbooks, you can merge the scenarios into a master worksheet. Simply open all the workbooks containing the scenarios you want, open the worksheet where you want the result to go, and click the Merge button in the Scenario Manager dialog box. When you do so, a dialog box like the one in Figure 18-13 appears.

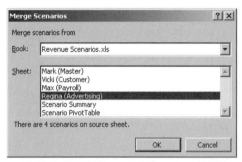

Figure 18-13. Clicking Merge in the Scenario Manager dialog box displays the Merge Scenarios dialog box, with which you can import scenarios from any sheet in any open workbook.

InsideOut

Request only the data you need

Merging scenarios works best if the basic structure of all the worksheets is identical. Although this uniformity isn't a strict requirement, merging scenarios from worksheets that are laid out differently can cause changing cell values to appear in unexpected locations. For this reason, and because it's generally difficult to ascertain the skill level of everyone contributing data, you might try a different approach. Distribute a questionnaire requesting only the data you need, use external cell references to link the requested data with the appropriate locations in your master worksheet, and create the scenarios yourself.

In the Merge Scenarios dialog box, you select the workbook and worksheet from which you want to merge scenarios. As shown in Figure 18-13, if you select a worksheet in the Sheet list, a message at the bottom of the dialog box tells you how many scenarios exist on that worksheet. When you click OK, the scenarios on that worksheet are copied to the active worksheet. After merging all the scenarios from your coworkers, the Scenario Manager dialog box for this example looks like the one shown in Figure 18-14.

Chapter 18: Performing What-If Analysis

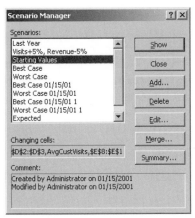

Figure 18-14. The merged scenarios now appear in the same
worksheet; if an identically named scenario is merged, Excel
appends a creator name, date, or number to the name.

Notice in Figure 18-14 that the Comment box displays the name of the creator and
modifier of the selected scenario. Notice also that the Scenarios list includes similarly
named scenarios. In this example, all the coworkers used the same three scenario
names—Expected, Best Case, and Worst Case—and Excel avoided conflicts by appending the creation date when it encountered duplicate names. Excel also used numbers to
distinguish merged scenarios that were created on the same date, as shown by the last
two Best Case scenarios shown in Figure 18-14. You can use the Edit button to rename
the scenarios if you want.

Each group of scenarios provided by the coworkers uses different changing cells. Vicki's
scenarios change the values in cells D2, D3, and D5, whereas Max's scenarios change
only the value in E8 and Regina's scenarios change only the value in E11. You can
display these different scenarios together and watch how the combinations affect the
bottom line.

The Scenario Express

The quickest and easiest way to define and display scenarios is to use the Scenario
box—a control that you can add to a toolbar. Choose View, Toolbars, choose Customize, click the Commands tab, and then choose the Tools category. Scroll down to find
the Scenario box and drag it to any toolbar. The Scenario box lists all the scenarios
defined on the active worksheet. If you want to display a scenario, click the down arrow next to the Scenario box and choose the name of the scenario you want to show
in the drop-down list.

Creating Scenario Reports

The Revenue Scenarios workbook with its merged scenarios has become a somewhat complex what-if model. However, you can create models that are far more complex, which can include as many scenarios as you want (or as many as your computer can handle) with up to 32 variables per scenario. The Scenario Manager's summary reports help you keep track of all the possibilities, and the PivotTable Report option gives you additional what-if functionality by allowing you to manipulate the elements of the report.

Clicking the Summary button in the Scenario Manager dialog box displays the dialog box shown in Figure 18-15. Use it to create reports that show the values each scenario assigns to each changing cell.

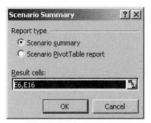

Figure 18-15. Use the Scenario Summary dialog box to specify the type of report and the result cells you want to see.

At the bottom of the dialog box, you identify result cells that you want to appear in the report, separated by commas. You want cells that are dependent on the most changing cells—in this case, the Operating Profit value in cell E16, as well as cell E6, the yearly Gross Profit value.

The Scenario Summary Report

The Scenario Summary is a fully formatted report placed on a new worksheet, as shown in Figure 18-16. (We adjusted column widths and wrapped text in the row 3 headings for better readability.)

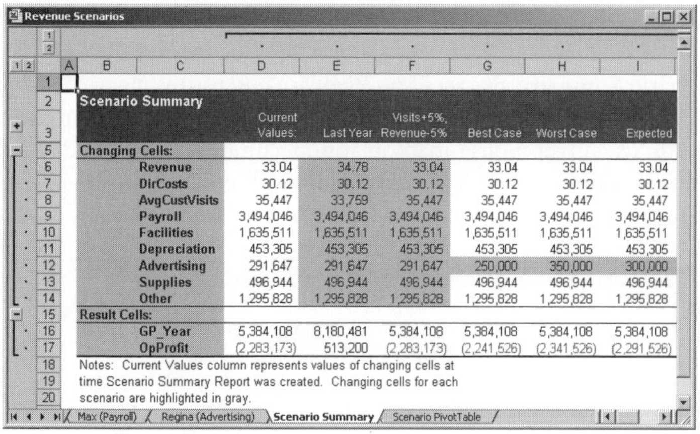

Chapter 18: Performing What-If Analysis

Figure 18-16. The Scenario Summary option creates a report in a
new worksheet named Scenario Summary.

In Figure 18-16, notice that all the changing cell values in columns E and F are shaded
in gray. The shading indicates cells that change in the scenario whose name appears at
the top of the column.

Notice also that outlining symbols appear above and to the left of the summary report,
allowing you to show and hide details. As you can see in Figure 18-17, clicking the outline
plus sign symbol displays hidden data—the contents of the Comment box in the Scenario
Manager dialog box, including the creation and modification date of each scenario.

For information about working with worksheet outlines, see "Outlining Worksheets" on
page 272.

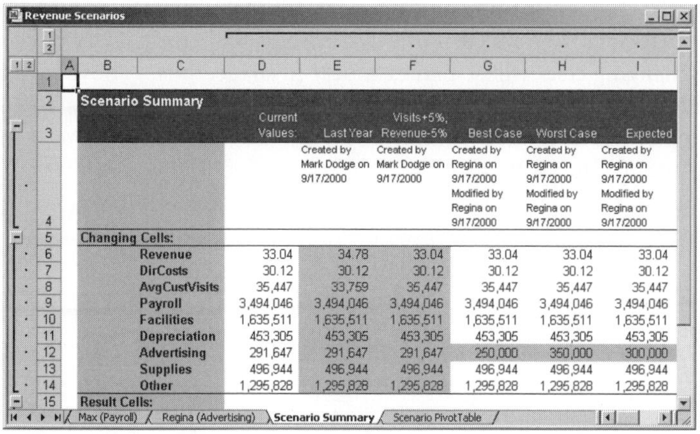

Figure 18-17. The comments entered into the Scenario Manager
dialog box are hidden in row 4 of the Scenario Summary Report.

Chapter 18

The Scenario PivotTable Report

Like the Scenario Summary, the Scenario PivotTable Report is created as a new worksheet in your workbook. However, PivotTables are what-if tools in their own right, allowing you to use direct mouse-manipulation techniques to mix and match different scenarios in the report and watch the effects on result cells. Figure 18-18 shows a Scenario PivotTable Report created from a version of the Revenue Scenarios workbook.

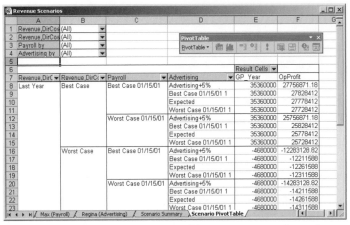

Figure 18-18. The Scenario PivotTable Report manipulates the actual data in the report.

> For more about PivotTables and the PivotTable toolbar, see Chapter 30, "Analyzing Data with PivotTable Reports."

The report cells containing numeric data represent the result cells as they would appear given the scenarios as they are currently displayed in the report. The row boxes initially display the changing cells, whose names appear in shaded boxes above the names of each scenario in which the changing cells are included. The result cells initially appear across the top of the table. To try a different arrangement, you drag any of the shaded boxes from one area to another.

InsideOut

Use Scenario Summary reports

PivotTables are powerful analysis tools best suited to complex what-if models that include scenarios with different sets of changing cells created by different people. The more one-dimensional your what-if model the less useful a PivotTable becomes. PivotTables take longer to create and consume more memory than Summary reports. If you create all the scenarios yourself and use the same set of changing cells in each, you might find it easier to use Scenario Summary reports because you won't be able to make use of the advantages offered by the PivotTable.

Using the Goal Seek Command

By choosing Tools, Goal Seek, you can compute an unknown value that produces the result you want. For example, suppose you want to know the maximum 30-year mortgage you can afford if the interest rate is 6.5 percent and if you must limit your monthly payments to $2,000. To use the Goal Seek command to answer this question, first set up the problem using trial values. For example, in the mortgage problem shown in Figure 18-19, a $500,000 mortgage would require monthly payments in excess of the $2,000 target.

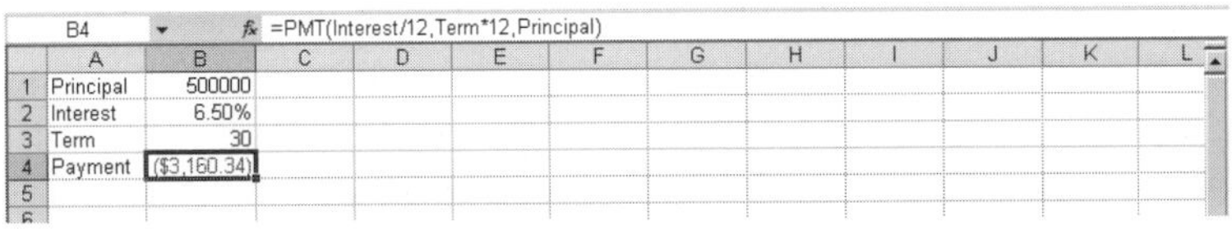

	B4	▾	fx	=PMT(Interest/12,Term*12,Principal)									
	A	B	C	D	E	F	G	H	I	J	K	L
1	Principal	500000										
2	Interest	6.50%										
3	Term	30										
4	Payment	($3,160.34)										
5												
6												

Figure 18-19. Use the Goal Seek command to find the maximum mortgage you can borrow if you want to keep your payments under a certain limit.

Here's how to perform goal seeking on this problem:

1 Define names for the cells B1:B4 by selecting cells A1:B4, choosing Insert, Name, Create, clicking the Left Column option, and then clicking OK.

2 Select the formula cell—in this case, B4—to make it the active cell.

3 Choose Tools, Goal Seek to display the Goal Seek dialog box shown in Figure 18-20 on the next page.

Part 5: Creating Formulas and Performing Data Analysis

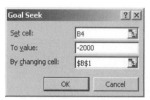

Figure 18-20. To use goal seeking, complete the Goal Seek dialog box.

4 Accept the value in the Set Cell box (make sure it specifies the cell containing the formula). In the To Value box, type the maximum value you want as the result of the formula—in this case, **-2000**. (You enter a negative number because the payment represents cash spent rather than received.)

5 In the By Changing Cell box, type the reference or click the cell in the worksheet whose value is unknown—in this case, cell B1 (the Principal value). Alternatively, if you have assigned a name, such as Principal, to cell B1, you can type that name in the By Changing Cell box.

6 Click OK, or press Enter. Excel displays the Goal Seek Status dialog box shown in Figure 18-21. The answer you are looking for appears in the cell specified in the By Changing Cell box.

7 To enter this value in the worksheet, click OK in the Goal Seek Status dialog box. To restore the value that was in B1 before you used the Goal Seek command, click Cancel.

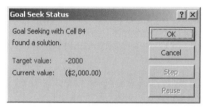

Figure 18-21. The Goal Seek Status dialog box informs you when a solution is found.

Excel uses an iterative technique to perform goal seeking. It tries one value after another for the variable cell specified in the By Changing Cell box until it arrives at the solution you requested. The mortgage problem we just looked at can be solved quickly. Other problems might take longer, and some might not be solvable at all.

While Excel is working on a complex goal-seeking problem, you can click Pause in the Goal Seek Status dialog box to interrupt the calculation, and then click Step to display the result of each successive iteration. A Continue button appears in the dialog box if you are solving a problem in this stepwise fashion. To resume full-speed goal seeking, click Continue.

Precision and Multiple Solutions

Suppose you enter the formula =A2^2 in cell A1 of a blank worksheet and then use the Goal Seek command to find the value of A2 that will make A1 equal to 4. (In other words, in the Goal Seek dialog box, type $A$1 in the Set Cell box, 4 in the To Value box, and $A$2 in the By Changing Cell box.) The result, shown in Figure 18-22, might be surprising. Excel seems to be telling you that the closest value it can find to the square root of 4 is 2.000023.

By default, the Goal Seek command stops when it has either performed 100 iterations (trial solutions) or found an answer that comes to within 0.001 of your specified target value. If you need greater precision than this, you can change the default limits by choosing Tools, Options, clicking the Calculation tab, and then changing the Maximum Iterations value to a number higher than 100, the Maximum Change value to a number less than 0.001, or both.

For more information about worksheet calculation options, see Chapter 12, "Building Formulas."

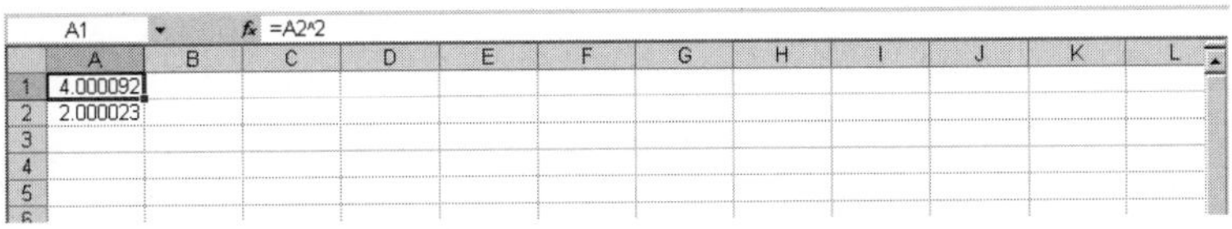

A1		f_x =A2^2										
	A	B	C	D	E	F	G	H	I	J	K	L
1	4.000092											
2	2.000023											
3												
4												
5												
6												

Figure 18-22. The Goal Seek command returns this result when asked to find the square root of 4.

This example illustrates another factor you should be aware of when you use the Goal Seek command. The Goal Seek command finds only one solution, even though your problem might have several. In this case, the value 4 has two square roots: +2 and -2. In situations like this, the Goal Seek command gives you the solution with the same sign as the starting value. For instance, if you start with a value of -1 in cell A2, the Goal Seek command reports the solution as -1.999917, instead of +2.000023.

Using the Solver

The Goal Seek command is handy for problems that involve an exact target value that depends on a single unknown value. For problems that are more complex, you should use the Solver add-in. The Solver can handle problems that involve many variable cells and can help you find combinations of variables that maximize or minimize a target cell. It also specifies one or more constraints—conditions that must be met for the solution to be valid.

Chapter 18

note The Solver is an add-in. If you performed a full installation of Excel, the Tools menu includes the Solver command. If you don't find that command on the Tools menu, choose Tools, Add-Ins, and then select Solver Add-In in the Add-Ins list. If Solver isn't in the list, you'll need to rerun Setup. For more information running Setup, see Appendix A, "Setting Up Microsoft Excel."

As an example of the kind of problem that the Solver can tackle, imagine you are planning an advertising campaign for a new product. Your total budget for print advertising is $12,000,000; you want to expose your ads at least 800 million times to potential readers; and you've decided to place ads in six publications—we'll call them Pub1 through Pub6. Each publication reaches a different number of readers and charges a different rate per page. Your job is to reach the readership target at the lowest possible cost with the following additional constraints:

- At least six advertisements should run in each publication.
- No more than a third of your advertising dollars should be spent on any one publication.
- Your total cost for placing advertisements in Pub3 and Pub4 must not exceed $7,500,000.

Figure 18-23 shows one way to lay out the problem.

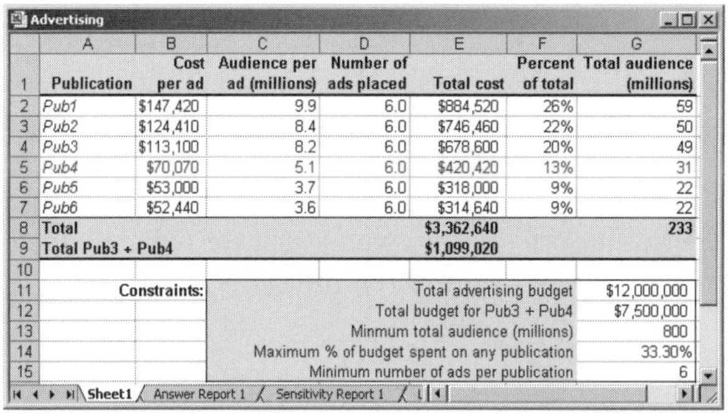

	A	B	C	D	E	F	G
1	Publication	Cost per ad	Audience per ad (millions)	Number of ads placed	Total cost	Percent of total	Total audience (millions)
2	Pub1	$147,420	9.9	6.0	$884,520	26%	59
3	Pub2	$124,410	8.4	6.0	$746,460	22%	50
4	Pub3	$113,100	8.2	6.0	$678,600	20%	49
5	Pub4	$70,070	5.1	6.0	$420,420	13%	31
6	Pub5	$53,000	3.7	6.0	$318,000	9%	22
7	Pub6	$52,440	3.6	6.0	$314,640	9%	22
8	**Total**				**$3,362,640**		**233**
9	**Total Pub3 + Pub4**				**$1,099,020**		
10							
11		**Constraints:**				Total advertising budget	$12,000,000
12						Total budget for Pub3 + Pub4	$7,500,000
13						Minmum total audience (millions)	800
14						Maximum % of budget spent on any publication	33.30%
15						Minimum number of ads per publication	6

Figure 18-23. You can use the Solver to determine how many advertisements to place in each publication to meet your objectives at the lowest possible cost.

note This section provides only an introduction to the Solver. A complete treatment of this powerful tool is beyond the scope of this book. For more details, including an explanation of the Solver's error messages, see Excel's online Help system. For background material on optimization, we recommend two textbooks: *Management Science* by Andrew W. Shogan (Englewood Cliffs, New Jersey: Prentice-Hall, 1988) and *Operations Research, Applications and Algorithms* by Wayne L. Winston (Boston: PWS-Kent Publishing Co., 1991).

You might be able to work out this problem yourself by substituting many alternatives for the values currently in D2:D7, keeping your eye on the constraints, and noting the impact of your changes on the total expenditure figure in E8. In fact, that's what the Solver does for you—but it does it more rapidly, and it uses some analytic techniques to home in on the optimal solution without having to try every conceivable alternative.

Choose Tools, Solver to display the dialog box shown in Figure 18-24. To complete this dialog box, you must give the Solver three pieces of information: your objective, or target (minimizing total expenditure), your variables or changing cells (the number of advertisements you will place in each publication), and your constraints (the conditions summarized at the bottom of the worksheet in Figure 18-23).

Figure 18-24. Use the Solver Parameters dialog box to set up your problem.

Stating the Objective

In the Set Target Cell box, you indicate the goal, or target, that you want Solver to achieve. In this example, you want to minimize your total cost—the value in cell E8—so you specify your objective by typing **E8** in the Set Target Cell box. In this example, because you want the Solver to set your target cell to its lowest possible value, you select Min as the Equal To option.

---

tip **Name everything**

It's a good idea to name all the important cells of your model before you put the Solver to work. If you don't name the cells, the Solver's reports construct names based on the nearest column-heading and row-heading text, but these constructed names don't appear in the Solver dialog boxes. For more information, see "Naming Cells and Cell Ranges" on page 371.

You don't have to specify an objective. If you leave the Set Target Cell box blank, click the Options button, and select the Show Iteration Results option, you can use the Solver to step through some or all the combinations of variable cells that meet your constraints. You will then receive an answer that solves the constraints but isn't necessarily the optimal solution.

> For more information about the Show Iteration Results option, see "Viewing Iteration Results" on page 525.

Specifying Variable Cells

The next step is to tell the Solver which cells to change. In our example, the cells whose values can be adjusted are those that specify the number of advertisements to be placed in each publication, or cells D2:D7. Alternatively, you can click Guess, and the Solver proposes the appropriate changing cells based on the target cell you specified.

Specifying Constraints

The last step, specifying constraints, is optional. To specify a constraint, click the Add button in the Solver Parameters dialog box and complete the Add Constraint dialog box. Figure 18-25 shows how you express the constraint that total advertising expenditures (the value in cell E8 in the model) must be less than or equal to the total budget (the value in cell G11).

Figure 18-25. Click the Add button in the Solver Parameters dialog box to add constraints.

Figure 18-26 shows how the Solver Parameters dialog box looks after all your constraints have been specified. Notice that the constraints are listed in alphabetical order, not necessarily in the order in which you defined them.

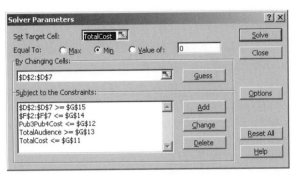

Figure 18-26. The Solver lists the constraints in alphabetical
order and uses defined cell and range names whenever possible.

Notice also that two of the constraints have range references on the left side of the
comparison operator. The expression $D$2:$D$7>=$G$15 stipulates that the value of
each cell in D2:D7 must be 6 or greater, and the expression $F$2:$F$7<=$G$14 stipulates that the value of each cell in F2:F9 must be no greater than 33.30 percent. Each
of these expressions is a shortcut way of stating six separate constraints. If you use this
kind of shortcut, the constraint value on the right side of the comparison operator
must be a single cell reference, a range of the same dimensions as the range on the left
side, or a constant value.

After completing the Solver Parameters dialog box, click Solve. In the advertisement
campaign example, the Solver succeeds in finding an optimal value for the objective
cell while meeting all the constraints and displays the dialog box shown in Figure 18-27.
The values displayed in your worksheet at that time result in the optimal solution. You
can leave these values in the worksheet by selecting the Keep Solver Solution option
and clicking OK, or you can restore the original values by clicking the Restore Original
Values option and clicking OK (or by clicking Cancel). You also have the option of
assigning the solution values to a named scenario. The solution values shown in
Figure 18-27 indicate that you will expose your target audience to your advertisements
800 million times.

	A	B	C	D	E	F	G
1	Publication	Cost per ad	Audience per ad (millions)	Number of ads placed	Total cost	Percent of total	Total audience (millions)
2	Pub1	$147,420	9.9	6.0	$884,520	8%	59
3	Pub2	$124,410	8.4	6.0	$746,460	7%	50
4	Pub3	$113,100	8.2	33.0	$3,736,174	33%	271
5	Pub4	$70,070	5.1	53.3	$3,736,174	33%	272
6	Pub5	$53,000	3.7	34.0	$1,801,773	16%	126
7	Pub6	$52,440	3.6	6.0	$314,640	3%	22
							800

Solver Results

Solver found a solution. All constraints and optimality
conditions are satisfied.

Reports
Answer
Sensitivity
Limits

○ Keep Solver Solution
○ Restore Original Values

OK   Cancel   Save Scenario...   Help

sing budget	$12,000,000
ub3 + Pub4	$7,500,000
ce (millions)	800
publication	33.30%
publication	6

Figure 18-27. When the Solver succeeds, it presents the
Solver Results dialog box.

Chapter 18

Specifying Integer Constraints

Notice that in Figure 18-27, Solver arrived at 53.3 for the Number of Ads Placed in Pub4. Unfortunately, because it's not possible to run three-tenths of an advertisement, the solution isn't practical.

To stipulate that your ad-placement variables be restricted to whole numbers, invoke the Solver and click the Add button in the Solver Parameters dialog box. In the Add Constraint dialog box, you select the range that holds your ad placement numbers—D2:D7. Display the drop-down list in the middle of the dialog box and select *int*. The Solver inserts the word integer in the Constraint box, as shown in Figure 18-28. Click OK to return to the Solver Parameters dialog box.

Figure 18-28. To specify an integer constraint, select the item labeled *int* in the drop-down list.

Note that when converting numbers to integers, Excel effectively rounds down; the decimal portion of the number is truncated. The integer solution shows that by placing 53 ads in Pub4, you can buy an additional ad in Pub5. For a very small increase in budget, you can reach an additional 2 million readers.

InsideOut

Determine whether you need integer constraints

Adding integer constraints to a Solver problem can geometrically increase the problem's complexity, resulting in possibly unacceptable delays. The example discussed in this chapter is relatively simple and does not take an inordinate amount of time to solve, but a more complex problem with integer constraints might pose more of a challenge for the Solver. Certain problems can only be solved using integer constraints. In particular, integer solutions are useful for problems in which variables can assume only two values, such as 1 or 0 (yes or no), but you can also use the bin (binary) option in the drop-down list in the middle of the Change Constraint dialog box.

Chapter 18

Saving and Reusing the Solver Parameters

If you save a workbook after using the Solver, all the values you entered in the Solver's dialog boxes are saved along with your worksheet data. You do not need to reenter the parameters of the problem if you want to continue working with it during a later Excel session.

Each worksheet in a workbook can store one set of Solver parameter values. To store more than one set of Solver parameters with a given worksheet, you must use the Solver's Save Model option. To use this option, follow these steps:

1 Choose Tools, Solver.

2 Click the Options button, and then in the Solver Options dialog box, shown in Figure 18-29, click Save Model. Excel prompts you for a cell or range in which to store the Solver parameters on the worksheet.

3 Specify a blank cell by clicking it or typing its reference, and then click OK. The Solver pastes the model beginning at the indicated cell and inserting formulas in as many of the cells below it as necessary. (Be sure that the cells below the indicated cell do not contain data.)

4 To reuse the saved parameters, click Load Model in the Solver Parameters dialog box, and then specify the range in which you stored the Solver parameters.

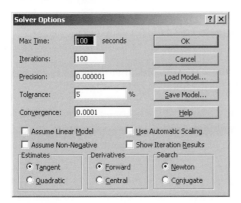

Figure 18-29. The Load Model and Save Model buttons in the Solver Options dialog box provide a way to store and retrieve your Solver parameters.

You'll find it easiest to save and reuse Solver parameters if you assign a name to each save model range immediately after you use the Save Model option. You can then specify that name when you use the Load Model option.

For more information about naming, see "Naming Cells and Cell Ranges" on page 371.

Chapter 18

Assigning the Solver Results to Named Scenarios

An even better way to save your Solver parameters is to save them as named scenarios using the Scenario Manager. As you might have noticed, the Solver Results dialog box includes a Save Scenario button. Click this button to assign a scenario name to the current values of your variable cells. This option provides an excellent way to explore and perform further what-if analysis on a variety of possible outcomes.

For more information about scenarios, see "Using the Scenario Manager" on page 504.

Other Solver Options

The Solver Options dialog box contains several options that might need some explanation:

- The Max Time and Iterations boxes tell the Solver, in effect, how hard to work on the solution. If the Solver reaches either the time limit or the number of iterations limit before finding a solution, calculation stops and Excel asks you whether you want to continue. The default settings are usually sufficient for solving most problems, but if you don't reach a solution with these settings, you can try adjusting them.

- The Precision setting is used by the Solver to determine how closely you want values in the constraint cells to match your constraints. The closer this setting is to the value 1, the lower the precision is. If you specify a setting that is less than the default 0.000001, it results in a longer solution time.

- The Tolerance setting applies only to problems that use integer constraints and represents a percentage of error allowed in the solution.

- The Estimates, Derivatives, and Search options are best left at their default settings, unless you understand linear optimization techniques. If you want more information about these options, click the Help button in the Solver Options dialog box.

Linear Models

A linear optimization problem is one in which the value of the target cell is a linear function of each variable cell; that is, if you plot XY charts of the target cell's value against all meaningful values of each variable cell, your charts are straight lines. If some of your plots produce curves instead of straight lines, the problem is nonlinear.

The Assume Linear Model option can be turned on only for what-if models in which all the relationships are linear. Models that use simple addition and subtraction and worksheet functions, such as SUM, are linear in nature. However, most models are nonlinear. They are generated by multiplying changing cells by other changing cells, by using exponentiation or growth factors, or by using nonlinear worksheet functions, such as PMT.

The Solver can solve linear problems more quickly if you click the Options button in the Solver Parameters dialog box and then select the Assume Linear Model option. If you select this option for a nonlinear problem and then try to solve the problem, however, the Solver Results dialog box displays the message "The conditions for Assume Linear Model are not satisfied." If you are not sure about the nature of your model, it's best not to use this option.

The Importance of Using Appropriate Starting Values

If your problem is nonlinear, you must be aware of one important detail: your choice of starting values can affect the solution generated by the Solver. With nonlinear problems, you should always do the following:

- Set your variable cells to reasonable approximations of their optimal values before running the problem.

- Test alternative starting values to see what impact, if any, they have on the Solver's solution.

Viewing Iteration Results

If you're interested in exploring many combinations of your variable cells, rather than only the combination that produces the optimal result, you can take advantage of the Solver's Show Iteration Results option. Click the Options button in the Solver Parameters dialog box, and select the Show Iteration Results option in the Solver Options dialog box. After each iteration, the Show Trial Solution dialog box appears, which allows you to save the scenario and then either stop the trial or continue with the next iteration.

You should be aware that if you use the Show Iteration Results option, the Solver pauses for solutions that do not meet all your constraints as well as for sub-optimal solutions that do.

Generating Reports

In addition to inserting optimal values in your problem's variable cells, the Solver can summarize its results in three reports: Answer, Sensitivity, and Limits. To generate one or more reports, select the names of the reports in the Solver Results dialog box. Select the reports you want, and then click OK. (Hold down Ctrl to select more than one.) Each report is saved on a separate worksheet in the current workbook.

The Sensitivity Report

The Sensitivity report provides information about how sensitive your target cell is to changes in your constraints. This report has two sections: one for your variable cells and one for your constraints. The right column in each section provides the sensitivity information.

Each changing cell and constraint cell is listed in a separate row. The Changing Cell area includes a Reduced Gradient value that indicates how the target cell would be affected by a one-unit increase in the corresponding changing cell. Similarly, the Lagrange Multiplier column in the Constraints area indicates how the target cell would be affected by a one-unit increase in the corresponding constraint value.

The Answer Report

The Answer report lists the target cell, the variable cells, and the constraints. This report also includes information about the status of and slack value for each constraint. The status can be Binding, Not Binding, or Not Satisfied. The *slack value* is the difference between the solution value of the constraint cells and the number that appears on the right side of the constraint formula. A binding constraint is one for which the slack value is 0. A nonbinding constraint is a constraint that was satisfied with a nonzero slack value.

> **note** If you select the Assume Linear Model option in the Solver Options dialog box, the Answer Report is the only report that the Solver produces for you (the Limits and Sensitivity reports are not meaningful when using integer constraints).

The Limits Report

The Limits report tells you how much the values of your variable cells can be increased or decreased without breaking the constraints of your problem. For each variable cell, this report lists the optimal value as well as the lowest and highest values that can be used without violating constraints.

Troubleshooting

The Solver Can't Solve My Problem

The Solver is powerful but not miraculous. It might not be able to solve every problem you give it. If the Solver can't find the optimal solution to your problem, it presents an unsuccessful completion message in the Solver Solution dialog box. The most common unsuccessful completion messages are the following:

Solver could not find a feasible solution. The Solver is unable to find a solution that satisfies all your constraints. This can happen if the constraints are logically conflicting or if not all the constraints can be satisfied (for example, if you insist that your advertising campaign reach 800 million readers on a $1 million budget). In some cases, the Solver also returns this message if the starting values of your variable cells are too far from their optimal values. If you think your constraints are logically consistent and your problem is solvable, try changing your starting values and rerunning the Solver.

The maximum iteration limit was reached; continue anyway? To avoid tying up your computer indefinitely with an unsolvable problem, the Solver is designed to pause and present this message after it has performed its default number of iterations without arriving at a solution. If you see this message, you can resume the search for a solution by clicking Continue, or you can quit by clicking Stop. If you click Continue, the Solver begins solving again and does not stop until it finds a solution, gives up, or reaches its maximum time limit. If your problems frequently exceed the Solver's iteration limit, you can increase the default iteration setting by choosing Tools, Solver, clicking the Options button, and entering a new value in the Iterations box.

The maximum time limit was reached; continue anyway? This message is similar to the iteration-limit message. The Solver is designed to pause after a default time period has elapsed. You can increase this default by choosing the Solver command, clicking Options, and modifying the Max Time value.

Part 6

Collaboration and the Internet

Collaborating with Excel

In the past, if you wanted to share your worksheets with other people, you copied everything onto floppy disks, carried them down the hall (or flipped them over the partition), and handed them to the person you wanted to share them with. This system (still effective!) was known affectionately as "sneakernet." The lucky few who worked in large companies might have been connected to a network. These days, small companies and those who work at home have networks, and everyone can take advantage of the global network known as the Internet. Microsoft Excel 2002 makes it easier than ever to get connected and provides easy-to-use tools that can help foster the synergy that is the hallmark of effective collaboration.

Sharing Files Using a Network

If you're connected to a network or to the Internet or if you're running Microsoft Outlook or Microsoft Exchange, using the features described in this section can make sharing information a lot easier.

Saving and Retrieving Files on Remote Computers

Using the Save In drop-down list on the Save As dialog box, you can save a workbook on any available network drive or at an FTP (File Transfer Protocol) site or Web folder on the Internet. The dialog box that is displayed when you choose File, Open contains a Look In drop-down list similar to the Save In list. You can use this list to retrieve workbooks saved on the network or on the Internet.

Retrieving Busy Files Automatically

When you try to open a file that resides on a network drive while another user has the file open, Excel displays the File In Use dialog box, which allows you to open the file in read-only mode. If the file was saved with password protection, you must also enter the appropriate password. Figure 19-1 shows the File In Use dialog box that appears when you attempt to open a file that's in use.

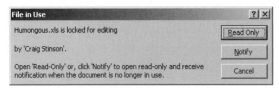

Figure 19-1. The File In Use dialog box appears when you try to open a busy file.

If you click the Notify button in the File In Use dialog box, Excel opens your file in read-only mode but alerts you when the file becomes available for read-write access. At that point, you see the dialog box shown in Figure 19-2.

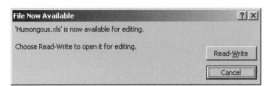

Figure 19-2. The File Now Available dialog box alerts you when the file is no longer in use.

Sharing Workbooks on a Network

It has always been possible to share Excel files on a network. You just had to make sure that you coordinated your efforts to avoid having more than one person open a file at the same time. Now Excel allows two or more people to work on the same workbook simultaneously, using the Share Workbook command.

When you select the Allow Changes By More Than One User At The Same Time check box shown in Figure 19-3 and click OK, Excel displays a confirmation prompt and then saves the workbook. This is necessary because the workbook must be saved as "sharable" before another user can open it. After the workbook has been saved, the bracketed word [Shared] appears in the title bar whenever anyone opens the workbook, and it remains until sharing is turned off.

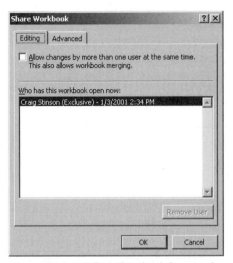

Figure 19-3. Select the check box to share the workbook.

> **tip** To change the name that appears in another user's Shared Workbook dialog box when you work with a shared file, choose Tools, Options, click the General tab, and edit the User Name box.

Of course, there are inherent risks when people work at the same time in the same place. Conflicts can arise when several people are making changes that affect the same cells. When someone saves changes, Excel not only saves the workbook but also updates it if other users saved any changes. A dialog box informs you that your changes have been incorporated. After you save, changes that have been made by other people are outlined with a colored border, and a special cell comment explains who did what when. When you point to the cell, a comment box displays this information, as shown in Figure 19-4. Note that the triangular comment indicator appears in the upper left corner of the cell instead of in the upper right corner, as it does for standard cell comments.

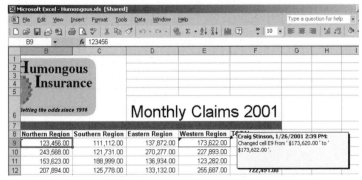

Figure 19-4. Cells changed by others in a shared workbook are outlined, and a comment is attached.

533

> **note** Change tracking, which determines whether outlines and comment boxes appear in your worksheet, is turned on by default. You can control it by choosing Tools, Track Changes, Highlight Changes, and selecting the Track Changes While Editing check box. Make sure this box is selected before the worksheet is first saved for sharing if you want to be able to track and review changes later.

What You Can and Can't Do with a Shared Workbook

There are limitations to what you can do when a workbook is shared. Shared workbooks can be edited using Excel 97 and later versions only. Earlier versions, such as Microsoft Excel 7 for Windows 95, don't support shared editing.

When a workbook is opened for sharing, you can enter text and numbers, change cell formatting, edit formulas, and copy, paste, and move data by dragging with the mouse. You can insert columns and rows, but you can't insert blocks of cells. You can't merge cells, insert charts or other objects, create hyperlinks, assign passwords, insert automatic subtotals, create outlines, create data tables or PivotTables, or insert worksheets. You can't do anything with macros except run them, although you can record macros if they are stored in a different, nonshared workbook. The Conditional Formatting, Scenarios, and Data Validation commands are disabled for a workbook in shared mode (although you can still see their effects), as are most of the buttons on the Drawing toolbar.

When you save a shared file, Excel checks for conflicts and determines whether any mediation is called for. Usually, a dialog box appears after you save the file that informs you that changes made by other users have been incorporated. However, if others' changes involve any of the same cells you changed, the mediator arrives in the form of the Resolve Conflicts dialog box shown in Figure 19-5.

> **note** When setting up a multiuser workbook, establish some working guidelines and design the workbook for maximum safety. For example, each person could have a separate named worksheet in the workbook, each worksheet reflecting a specific area of responsibility. Then you could create a separate consolidation worksheet that pulls together all the relevant data from the personal sheets to present it in the necessary format. For more information, see "Consolidating Worksheets" on page 278.

Figure 19-5. If more than one person changes the same cells, the last person to save changes might get to decide which ones to keep.

For each conflict identified, the Resolve Conflicts dialog box specifies the cells involved and allows you to decide whose changes to keep. You can resolve conflicts individually or use the buttons at the bottom of the dialog box to select all the changes entered by you or others.

Note that conflicts can exist only between the last saved version and the version you are trying to save. If more than two users have made changes to the same cells, each person who saves the workbook gets to decide who wins the conflict of the moment. You can, however, revisit all the conflicts and accept or reject them individually later.

For more information, see "Reviewing Changes" on page 539.

Using Advanced Sharing Options

You can change some aspects of the default behavior of shared workbooks. To do so, choose Tools, Share Workbook and click the Advanced tab of the Share Workbook dialog box (see Figure 19-6 on the next page). Each shared workbook user can set these options individually. Use the first section on the Advanced tab to specify the length of time you want to keep track of changes, or whether you want to track them at all.

note Turning off change tracking detracts from your ability to merge workbooks. For more information, see "Merging Workbooks" on page 541.

535

Figure 19-6. Use the Advanced tab to determine the way changes are handled.

In the Update Changes section, select when you want updates to occur. Normally when users save a file, their changes are saved, and their copy of the workbook is also updated with any changes made by others. The Automatically Every option is handy, allowing you to specify how often updates occur automatically. When you choose automatic updating, the normal procedure is as described previously: Your changes are saved, and changes made by others are incorporated into your copy. You also can select the Just See Other Users' Changes option, which gives you the ability to hold your changes back until you decide to save them, while at the same time updating your file at regular intervals with any changes recorded by others.

As mentioned previously, when conflicts arise, the Resolve Conflicts dialog box shown in Figure 19-5 appears. If you select The Changes Being Saved Win in the Conflicting Changes Between Users section on the Advanced tab of the Share Workbook dialog box, however, all conflicts are essentially resolved in favor of the last user to issue the Save command.

The Include In Personal View check boxes allow you to change the print settings and any views set using the AutoFilter or Advanced Filter command on the Data menu. With these check boxes selected, each person who has a shared workbook open can have different print and filter settings, which are recalled the next time that person opens the shared workbook.

> **tip** **Password-protect before you share**
>
> You can use the standard Excel password-protection options with shared workbooks, but you must apply the password before sharing. Choose File, Save As, click the Tools button, and then choose the General Options command. In the File Sharing area, you can enter a password for opening the workbook and another password for making modifications to the workbook. Then you can disseminate the necessary passwords to members of your workgroup. For more information about file protection, see "Protecting Files" on page 41.

Tracking Changes

Change tracking in Excel is closely linked with shared workbooks. If you choose Tools, Track Changes, Highlight Changes, and then select the Track Changes While Editing check box, you put your workbook into shared mode. The workbook is saved, just as if you had chosen the Share Workbook command. Even if you select the Don't Keep Change History option on the Advanced tab of the Share Workbook dialog box, as shown in Figure 19-6, you can still turn change tracking back on by using the Track Changes commands. When you choose Tools, Track Changes, Highlight Changes, the dialog box shown in Figure 19-7 appears.

> **tip** **Track changes without sharing**
>
> You don't have to share a workbook to be able to track the changes you make yourself. Just turn on change tracking and save the resulting shared workbook in an unshared folder on your own hard disk instead of on a shared network location.

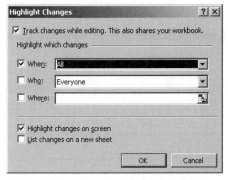

Figure 19-7. Use the Highlight Changes command to show what's been done in a shared workbook.

You control which changes you want highlighted. Use the When drop-down list to select whether you want to see all the changes made since the workbook was first shared, only those changes that you haven't yet reviewed, those that have been made since the last time you saved, or those that have been made since a date you specify. The Who options include Everyone, Everyone But Me, and the name of every individual who has made changes to the shared workbook. If you want, you can enter a specific cell or range in the Where box. If you select a range before opening the Highlight Changes dialog box, its address is displayed in the Where box when you click the adjacent check box. If you select the check box next to the Where option, you can drag to select the cells directly on the worksheet while the dialog box is still open.

Normally the changes are highlighted on the screen with cell borders and attached cell comments. Clear the check box to turn off the Highlight Changes On Screen option. You can also create a History worksheet detailing all the changes made. To do so, select the List Changes On A New Sheet option. The resulting worksheet is inserted after the last worksheet in the workbook, as shown in Figure 19-8.

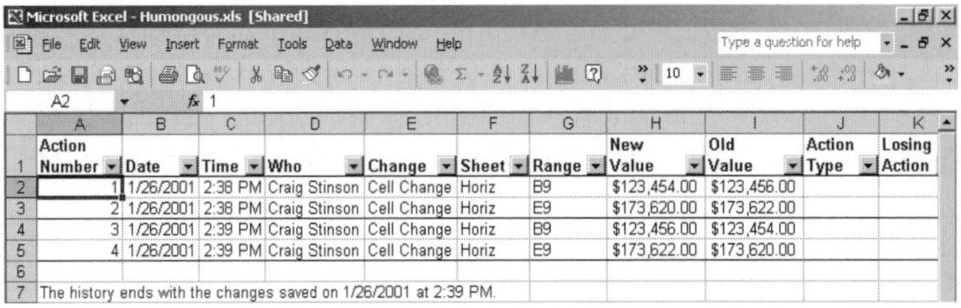

Figure 19-8. You can choose to create a History worksheet detailing the changes made to a shared workbook.

> **note** Formatting changes aren't recorded in the change history.

The History worksheet is a special locked worksheet that can be displayed only when a worksheet is in shared mode. The worksheet disappears when you turn off sharing. If you subsequently restart a shared workbook session, the history starts fresh, and any changes recorded in previous sharing sessions are lost.

> **tip** To keep track of the change history after discontinuing the sharing session, copy the contents of the locked History worksheet and paste them into another worksheet.

538

Protecting the Change History

If you want to ensure that every change made during a sharing session is documented, choose Tools, Protection, Protect Shared Workbook. When you do, the dialog box shown in Figure 19-9 appears.

Figure 19-9. You can ensure that change tracking is protected in a shared workbook.

If you click Sharing With Track Changes and then click OK, change tracking for the shared workbook is protected so no one in your workgroup can turn it off directly. However, anyone can turn off the protection by choosing Tools, Protection, Unprotect Shared Workbook. To eliminate this possibility, you can enter a password in the Protect Shared Workbook dialog box. But you must do this when the workbook is not in shared mode. Then anyone who tries to turn off protection must enter the identical, case-sensitive password.

> **tip** If you successfully enter a password to turn off Protect For Sharing mode, not only is protection turned off, but the workbook is also removed from sharing. Note that this isn't the case unless there is a password. When you remove a workbook from sharing, you cut off anyone else who has the workbook open, and the change history is erased.

Reviewing Changes

You can decide at any time to go through each change that has been made to the shared workbook, provided the Track Changes While Editing check box was selected in the Highlight Changes dialog box when the worksheet was first saved for sharing. Choosing Tools, Track Changes, Accept Or Reject Changes displays the dialog box shown in Figure 19-10 on the next page. The drop-down lists are similar to those on the Highlight Changes dialog box, except that in the When list, the only options available are Not Yet Reviewed and Since Date.

Figure 19-10. Use this dialog box to specify which changes you want to review.

When you click OK, the dialog box shown in Figure 19-11 appears, and the first change that meets the criteria you specified in the Select Changes To Accept Or Reject dialog box is highlighted on the worksheet. The dialog box describes the change, who made it, and the time it was made. At this point, you can accept or reject the change or you can accept or reject all the changes. After you have accepted or rejected all the changes, you cannot review them again. You can, however, still display the History worksheet.

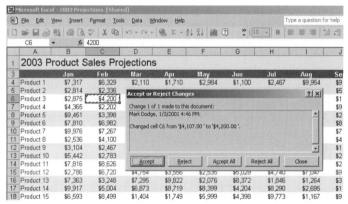

Figure 19-11. Each change is highlighted and described, allowing you to accept or reject it.

Canceling the Shared Workbook Session

You can discontinue the sharing session at any time by clearing the Allow Changes By More Than One User option on the Editing tab of the Share Workbook dialog box. (Anyone else using the shared workbook can also do this; no one "owns" the right to enable or disable sharing.) Several things happen when you do this. First, the change history is lost. If you subsequently start a new sharing session, the history starts fresh. Any other users who still have the shared workbook open won't be able to save their changes to the same file. They'll be in read-only mode, but Excel won't inform them of that until they attempt to save, at which time the Save As dialog box will appear. Even if you turn sharing off and then turn it back on again while another person still has the file open, the person won't be able to share the file until he or she closes and reopens it.

540

You can click The Remove User button on the Editing tab of the Share Workbook dialog box if you want to disconnect someone from the sharing session manually. Doing this maintains the change history for the master workbook. You'll probably want to warn the person you're disconnecting, of course.

Combining Changes Made to Multiple Workbooks

Another way to share a workbook is to make a separate copy of the workbook for each person in your workgroup. This might be a good option if not everyone in your group has access to the same network server or there aren't any network or Internet file-sharing options available to you. In this scenario, after all the distributed copies have been updated with each person's changes, someone collects the copies and merges everyone's work into a master workbook.

Merging Workbooks

You can merge workbooks that were created equal—that is, a set of workbooks created from the same master. When you merge workbooks, all changes made to the merged workbooks are merged into the master workbook. Merging workbooks, like change tracking, is closely linked with the shared workbooks feature; you can merge only workbooks that have been saved with sharing turned on.

The following procedure explains how to set up your workbooks for distribution and eventual merging:

1 Open the workbook you want to distribute.

2 Choose Tools, Share Workbook.

3 On the Editing tab of the Share Workbook dialog box, select the Allow Changes By More Than One User At the Same Time check box.

4 Click the Advanced tab, and make sure that there is a sufficient number of days specified in the Keep Change History For box for all the members of your workgroup to finish their edits and for you to collect and merge the workbooks. If you are unsure about how long to specify, enter a large number, such as **500**. If this time limit is exceeded, you will not be able to merge workbooks.

5 Click OK to save the workbook in shared mode.

6 Choose File, Save As and save additional copies of the workbook under different names—one for each person on your distribution list. Because sharing is turned on, each copy you save is also in shared mode.

7 Distribute the copies to the members of your group.

541

After you have prepared, distributed, and collected the edited workbooks, you are ready to merge by following these steps:

1 Open the workbook you want to use as the master workbook. All the changes made to the other workbooks you merge will be replicated in the master workbook. This workbook must have been saved from the same original shared workbook, just as the workbooks you distributed were.

2 Make sure none of the other workbooks you want to merge are open, and then choose Tools, Compare And Merge Workbooks to display the dialog box shown in Figure 19-12.

3 Select the files you want to merge.

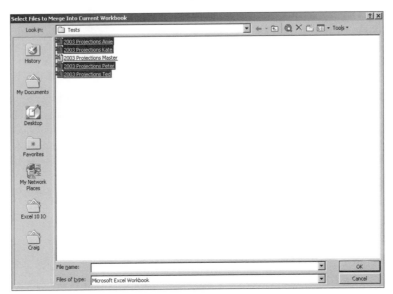

Figure 19-12. When the master workbook is already open, select the other workbooks to merge.

The workbooks you select in the Select Files To Merge Into Current Workbook dialog box are merged one by one, in the order in which they appear in the dialog box. All changes made to the merged workbooks are, in turn, made to the master workbook. You can accept and reject changes and display the History worksheet, just as you can with shared workbooks, as described in "Tracking Changes" on page 537.

> **note** Although merging workbooks combines all changes from a set of workbooks, consolidation combines only values from a set of worksheets. (These worksheets can be in different workbooks.) The Consolidate command can assemble information from as many as 255 supporting worksheets into a single master worksheet. For more information about the Consolidate command, see "Consolidating Worksheets" on page 278.

Mailing Workbooks Using Electronic Mail

Excel provides built-in features to take advantage of electronic mail. If Microsoft Outlook, Microsoft Exchange, or another compatible mail program is present, the commands on the File, Send To submenu become available. When you choose the Mail Recipient command, Excel asks whether you want to send a message with the current workbook as an attachment or whether you want to send the active sheet of the current workbook as the body of the message. A simple mail message is shown in Figure 19-13 with an Excel workbook attached.

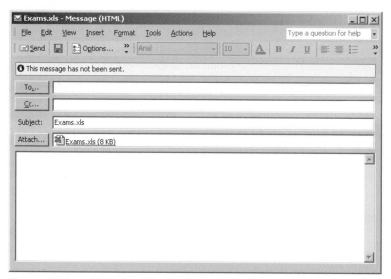

Figure 19-13. Choosing File, Send To, Mail Recipient starts your mail program and either attaches the current workbook or displays the current worksheet.

> **tip** You can also send mail using the Send To Mail Recipient button on the Reviewing toolbar.

When you click the Send button, the message and attached copy of the workbook or worksheet are sent to the recipients listed in the To box. When the message is received, the recipients double-click the Excel icon to open the workbook. Note that any subsequent changes you make to the workbook aren't reflected in the sent copy.

Sending a Workbook for Review

Choosing File, Send To, Mail Recipient (For Review) provides you with an easy way to circulate a workbook for comments and changes by members of your workgroup. Ideally this command should be used with workbooks that you have set up for sharing. The message you send includes a hyperlink to the current workbook in its current storage location. Recipients can then add their own changes and return the workbook to you.

Before presenting a mail form, the Mail Recipient (For Review) command asks whether you would like to attach a copy of the current file, in addition to displaying the hyperlink. Answer yes if you are sending to offline recipients who won't have access to the file at its current storage location.

Routing Workbooks to a Workgroup Using Electronic Mail

If you are working on a project that involves a group of people whose input is crucial, you can route a workbook to the group using electronic mail. When you choose File, Send To, Routing Recipient, the Routing Slip dialog box shown in Figure 19-14 is displayed.

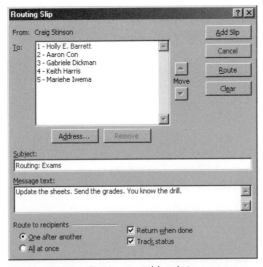

Figure 19-14. Route a workbook to a group using the Routing Recipient command.

544

The Routing Recipient command offers several advantages over the Mail Recipient command. For example, the Routing Recipient command allows you to specify sequential routing. That is, if you construct a list of recipients using the Address button and select the One After Another option at the bottom of the dialog box, the workbook will be sent to the first person on the list. When that person has finished, the workbook will automatically be forwarded to the next person on the list. The To list shows you the sequence, which you can modify by selecting a name in the list and clicking the Move buttons. Alternatively, you can choose to route the workbook to all recipients at the same time by selecting All At Once.

To send the message off on its appointed rounds, click the Route button on the Routing Slip dialog box. To attach the routing slip to the workbook, click the Add Slip button. Using the latter method allows you to continue working. When you're ready to send the message, choose the Next Routing Recipient command (which replaces the Mail Recipient command when you have a routed workbook open) on the Send To submenu. The dialog box shown in Figure 19-15 appears. If you click OK, the workbook is sent to the next person on your routing slip. You can also choose the second option, Send Copy Of Document Without Using The Routing Slip. If you do, a mail window appears as if you had chosen the Mail Recipient command, allowing you to send the workbook to anyone you choose. The original routing slip remains, and you can still send it to the next recipient on the list.

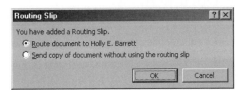

Figure 19-15. This dialog box appears when you begin routing your workbook.

You can also reopen and edit the routing slip itself to include more or fewer people in the distribution by choosing the Other Routing Recipient command (which replaces the Add Routing Slip command when you have a routed workbook open). If the Track Status option in the Routing Slip dialog box is selected, you will receive notification each time the workbook is forwarded so you can keep track of its progress. If the Return When Done option is selected, the workbook is automatically returned to you in the mail after it has made its rounds.

newfeature!
Using a SharePoint Team Services Site

SharePoint Team Services is an Internet-based system for facilitating team communication and collaboration, introduced with Microsoft Office XP. SharePoint requires a Web server equipped with Microsoft FrontPage Server Extensions 2002 and Microsoft Office Server extensions. If you have access to a SharePoint site, you can use the site as a workgroup document repository. You can also participate in threaded discussions with other members in your team. Figure 19-16 on the next page shows the home page for a sample SharePoint site.

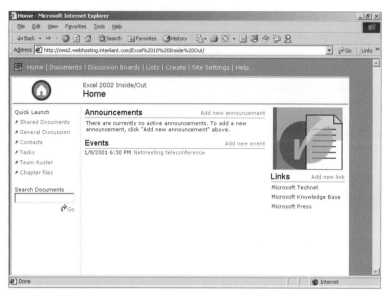

Figure 19-16. The home page for a SharePoint site makes team communication and collaboration easier.

Downloading and Uploading Documents

Your SharePoint site presumably includes at least one, and potentially many more than one, document library. These are folders to which you can save files or from which you can retrieve them. The sample SharePoint site shown in Figure 19-16 includes two document libraries, Shared Documents and Chapter Files. Links to these folders appear in the Quick Launch section of the home page.

To retrieve a file from your SharePoint site, you can navigate to the appropriate document library and click the link for the file that you want. A dialog box will appear, giving you the option of opening the selected file from its current location or saving it to disk. If you open it from its current location, the file appears in your Web browser (replacing the SharePoint site). If it's an Excel file, the Web browser's menus and toolbars are merged with those of Excel, making all of Excel's functionality available to you as you work.

To upload a file to a document library, navigate to the library and click the Upload Document link. (This link might be renamed, depending on how your site is designed, but presumably the site will have some link designed for file uploading.) On the ensuing page you can click Browse, navigate to your file, and then click Save and Close (or a similarly named link) to send the file on its way.

Using Web Folders or Network Places for File Transfer

As an alternative to uploading and downloading in the manner described in the last section, you can set up a Web folder (in Windows 98, Windows NT 4, or Windows NT 4 Server) or a Network Place (in Windows 2000 or later or Windows Me). After you have set up a Web folder or Network Place, you can interact with your SharePoint site via Windows Explorer or directly from Excel.

Setting Up a Web Folder for a SharePoint Document Library

To set up a Web Folder in Windows 98 or any edition of Windows NT 4, follow these steps:

1 Open My Computer.

2 Double-click Web Folders.

3 Double-click Add Web Folder.

4 In the Add Web Folder dialog box, type the URL for the document library on your SharePoint site.

5 Supply your user name and password if prompted.

6 Click Finish.

Setting Up a Network Place for a SharePoint Document Library

To set up a Network Place in Windows 2000 (or later) or Windows Millennium Edition, follow these steps:

1 Open My Network Places.

2 Double-click Add Network Place.

3 In the first dialog box of the Add Network Place Wizard, type the URL of your SharePoint document library.

4 Supply your user name and password if prompted.

5 Type a name for your new Network Place, and then click Finish.

After you have created a Web Folder or Network Place, you can use it as you would any other local or remote folder. That is, you can open it in Windows Explorer or in Excel's Open or Save As dialog box. Figure 19-17 on the next page shows Excel's Save As dialog box with the Shared Documents library on our sample SharePoint site.

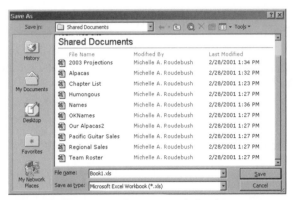

Figure 19-17. In Excel's Save As dialog box, we've navigated to a Network Place for our SharePoint document library.

Using NetMeeting with Excel

Microsoft NetMeeting is a program that lets you establish an online conference with one or more other users. In a NetMeeting session, you can chat (communicate in real time via the keyboard), talk (provided you have a microphone), share images via camera in something approximating real time, transfer files, manipulate a shared white board, and operate a remote computer.

NetMeeting is integrated with Excel via commands on the Tools, Online Collaboration menu. The Meet Now command allows you to launch a session directly. The Schedule Meeting command allows you to schedule a NetMeeting session, using Microsoft Outlook's Calendar facility.

When you choose Tools, Online Collaboration, Meet Now, NetMeeting initially displays its Find Someone dialog box, which consists of a Select A Directory drop-down list and a window displaying the contents of the currently selected directory. Microsoft Internet Directory, the default, displays the names of your MSN Messenger Service contacts (if any), along with their current status (online or offline). You can initiate a session with an online MSN Messenger Service contact by clicking that person's name.

Alternatives to Microsoft Internet Directory include Windows Address Book and History. Selecting Windows Address Book displays the names of any contacts in your address book for whom you have stored NetMeeting contact information. Selecting History displays the names of persons with whom you have had recent NetMeeting sessions.

In addition, you can enter the name of any Internet Locator Service (ILS) directory. An ILS directory is a list of NetMeeting users (and users of similar programs) who are currently logged onto that directory. Logging onto an ILS directory supplies the directory with your current IP address (which NetMeeting requires to initiate a session), plus your name and other information that you choose to supply. You can find a list of ILS servers at *www.netmeet.net/bestservers.asp*.

Using Web Discussions

If you have access to a Web server running Microsoft Office Extensions, you can take advantage of a collaboration feature called Web Discussions. This allows you to associate threaded discussions with particular Excel documents stored on the Office-extended server. The discussion threads are stored in separate files and can be merged with the documents when you view those documents on the server.

To use Web Discussions, begin by choosing Tools, Online Collaboration, Web Discussions. A special toolbar appears at the bottom of your Excel window. (You can't move this toolbar, and you won't find it listed on the View, Toolbars menu. Unlike other toolbars in Microsoft Office applications, it doesn't have a Close box. To close it, click the Close tool.) If this is your first session with the Office-extended server, you need to specify the server's location by choosing Discussions, Discussion Options.

After you connect to the server, you can add comments to the current document by choosing Discussions, Insert About The Workbook. The dialog box shown in Figure 19-18 appears. Type a title and a comment, and then click OK. Figure 19-19 on the next page shows a document with an associated Web discussion. (The document is stored on our sample SharePoint site.)

To reply to an existing comment in a Web discussion thread, click the document icon to the right of the comment. From the menu that appears, click Reply.

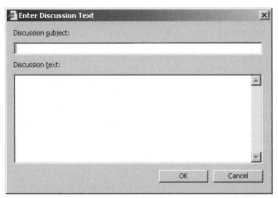

Figure 19-18.   In Excel's Save As dialog box, we've navigated to a Network Place for our SharePoint document library.

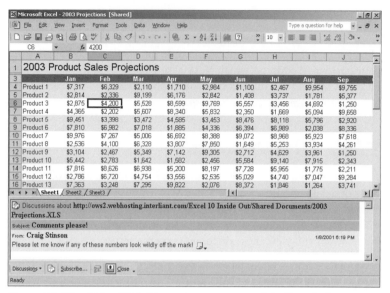

Figure 19-19. Using Web Discussions, you associate threaded commentary with a document stored on an Office-extended Web server.

Subscribing to Documents on an Office-Extended Server

To subscribe to a document means to request automatic notification via e-mail of changes to that document. You can subscribe to a document stored on a Web server running Microsoft Office Extensions by opening that document, choosing Tools, Online Collaboration, Web Discussions, and then clicking the Subscribe tool on the Web Discussions toolbar. The dialog box shown in Figure 19-20 appears.

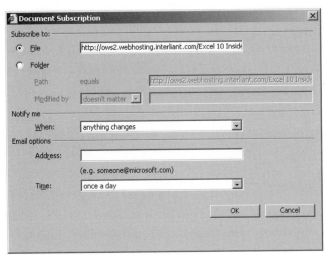

Figure 19-20. In the Document Subscription dialog box, you can indicate what kind of events merit notification and how often you want to be notified.

Use options in the When box to specify the kinds of events of which you want to be notified. In the Time box, you can indicate how often you want to be notified. The default is Once A Day, but you can change that to either once a week or whenever a change occurs.

Transferring Files to and from Internet Sites

Chapter 19, "Collaborating with Excel," dealt with (among many other topics) the SharePoint Team Services facility from Microsoft—an effective way to use the Internet for team collaboration. You can use SharePoint Team Services facility from Microsoft bulletin board, a place to schedule meetings (virtual and otherwise), and a central location for links to team resources, in addition to a convenient repository for shared Office documents.

This chapter looks at the subject of Internet storage from a more general perspective. You explore uploading Excel files to FTP and Web sites (as well as downloading them from such places, of course). We also review the various ways that Excel saves documents in HTML and spreadsheet XML (Extensible Markup Language).

For information about setting up queries to retrieve tabular data from Web sites, see Chapter 29, "Working with External Data."

Working with FTP Sites

Before you can connect to an FTP site, you have to specify the location of the site and (if the site doesn't accept anonymous access) provide logon information. To do this, follow these steps:

1 Choose File, Save As or File, Open.

2 In the Save As or Open dialog box, open the Look In list (at the top of the dialog box).

553

3 Near the bottom of the list, you'll find the entry FTP Locations. Below that is an entry labeled Add/Modify FTP Locations. Select this entry.

4 Fill out the Add/Modify FTP Locations dialog box, shown in Figure 20-1.

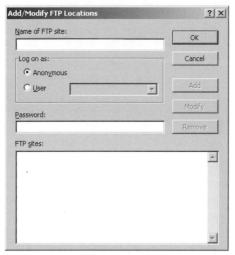

Figure 20-1. Before you can interact with an FTP site, you have to supply its particulars in this dialog box.

In the Name Of FTP Site box, enter either the URL for the FTP site you want to use or its IP address (if you know it). If you enter a URL that Excel recognizes as an FTP site, Excel adds the prefix ftp:// for you. For example, if you type **ftp.microsoft.com** as your URL, Excel correctly fills out the box as *ftp://ftp.microsoft.com*.

If your FTP site does not require that you supply a name and password to connect, the site allows *anonymous* access. You can leave the Log On As Anonymous option selected in that case. If your site requires that you log on, select the User option, type your user name, and type your password in the Password box. When you have finished filling out the specs for your FTP site, click Add, and then click OK.

Be aware that regardless of how you log on to an FTP site, you might or might not have both read and write privileges at the site. You might, for example, be able to download documents from the site but not upload to it.

After you have established an FTP site via the Add/Modify FTP Locations dialog box, you can use that site as you would any other local or network folder (assuming, of course, that you are connected to the Internet and have the requisite access permissions). The new FTP site is now a folder within your FTP Locations folder and will appear in the Look In list of Excel's Save As and Open dialog boxes, under the heading FTP Locations. You can navigate to subfolders within the new FTP folder, just as you would navigate to subfolders on your own hard disk.

Adding a Site to Your My Places Bar

For easier access to an FTP site (or any other folder), you can add it to your My Places bar, the navigation panel at the left edge of the Save As and Open dialog boxes. Follow these steps:

1 In the Save As or Open dialog box, open the Look In list and choose FTP Locations.

2 In the main window of the dialog box (which now displays the FTP Locations folder), select your FTP site.

3 Choose Tools, Add To "My Places."

The new FTP site now has an icon on the My Places bar, where its URL or IP address is undoubtedly wider than the bar itself. You can make the icon name intelligible by right-clicking it, choosing Rename, and entering something short and sweet—such as **MS FTP Site**. Figure 20-2 shows an FTP site on the My Places bar.

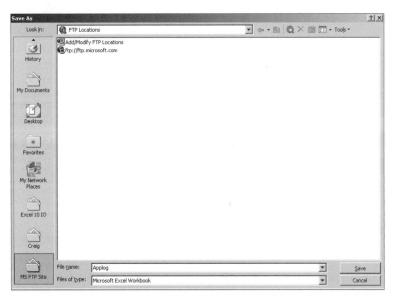

Figure 20-2. You can add an FTP site to your My Places bar and replace its lengthy URL with a "friendly" name.

To remove an FTP site (or any other custom item) from the My Places bar, right-click it and choose Remove. To remove an FTP site from the FTP Locations folder, right-click it in the FTP Locations folder and choose Remove from the shortcut menu. You also can return to the Add/Modify FTP Locations dialog box, select the site and click Delete.

Adding an FTP Site to My Network Places

Provided you're running Windows 2000 (or later) or Windows ME, you have another way to make an FTP site more accessible. You can add it to your My Network Places folder.

To add an FTP site to My Network Places, follow these steps:

1 Open the My Network Places folder on your desktop.

2 Double-click Add Network Place to launch the Add Network Place Wizard.

3 In the first wizard dialog box, type the URL or IP address for your site. If you're entering a URL, be sure to include the ftp:// prefix; the wizard will assume an http:// prefix if you don't.

4 In the second wizard dialog box, indicate whether you log on anonymously or not. If you don't log on anonymously, clear the check box. You won't be able to enter a password, but you will be able to supply your user name, and your site will prompt for the password when you connect.

5 In the third wizard dialog box, supply the name that you want to appear in My Network Places.

When your site has taken up residence in My Network Places, you can get to it from Excel's Save As or Open dialog box by clicking My Network Places on the My Places bar. You also can add it to the My Places bar directly, following the instructions given in the last section.

Troubleshooting

I Can't Add an FTP Site to My Network Places

Excel and other Office applications include an Add Network Place Wizard, accessible from within the Save As or Open dialog box. To get to it, choose File, Save As or File, Open; click My Network Places on the My Places bar, and double-click Add Network Place. Unfortunately, the wizard accepts http:// sites (ordinary Web sites) only and rejects any URLs that don't begin with http://. To add your FTP site to My Network Places, start with the My Network Places folder on your desktop.

Working with HTTP (Web) Sites

If you have access to a private or public Web site that supports the Distributed Authoring and Versioning (DAV) Internet protocol, Microsoft Office Server Extensions, or Microsoft FrontPage Server Extensions 2002, you can save Excel files to and retrieve them from that site. You can use the site as a repository for shared documents, as an offline storage location (for backup purposes, perhaps), or as a place to park documents that you plan to use while traveling. With your files stored on a Web site, you can retrieve them from anywhere, provided you have access to a computer running Excel 2002 (and to the Internet, of course).

You can access Excel documents on Web sites by typing a URL into the Open or Save As dialog box. For example, you could type *http://communities.msn.com/MyStuff/Files/Alpacas.xls* into Excel's Open dialog box to retrieve a file named Alpacas.xls from an MSN Communities site called MyStuff. It's not likely you'll want to do that much typing, though. The simpler method is to add the Web site to your My Network Places folder (in Windows 2000 or later, or in Windows Me) or to your Web Folders (in Windows 98).

To add a Web site to your My Network Places folder, you can begin by clicking My Network Places on the My Places bar of Excel's Save As or Open dialog box. After the My Network Places folder opens, click Add Network Place to summon the Add Network Place Wizard, which will guide you through the remaining steps. Alternatively, you can double-click My Network Places on your desktop, choose Add Network Place, and interact with the wizard that appears in that context. The two wizards are not identical, but both are self-explanatory. (The biggest difference is that the wizard supplied via the Excel dialog boxes accepts HTTP URLs only, and the one accessible via Windows Explorer allows you to create shortcuts to FTP sites as well.)

To create a Web folder from Excel, while running in Windows 98, use these steps:

1 Choose File, Save As or File, Open.

2 Click Web Folders in the My Places bar.

3 Click Create New Folder. The Add Web Folder Wizard dialog box appears, as shown in Figure 20-3.

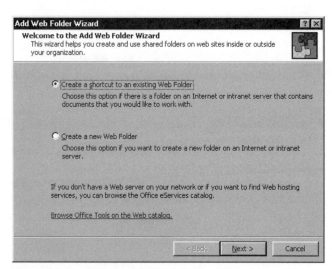

Figure 20-3. Use the Add Web Folder Wizard to create a conveniently accessible shortcut to a Web site in Windows 98.

557

4 Select Create A New Web Folder, and click Next.

5 In the ensuing dialog box, supply the URL and a friendly name for your Web site.

Using MSN Communities for File Storage

MSN Communities offers free Web storage (suitable for Excel and other Microsoft Office documents) to anyone. Storage can be either private (available to you and selected invitees only) or public. You can create your own storage site by navigating to *http://communities.msn.com/filecabinets* (see Figure 20-4) and following the instructions you find there.

Figure 20-4. MSN Communities provides free Web storage for your documents.

Saving and Publishing Excel Files in HTML

When you save an XLS file to a Web or FTP site, other users can read that file only if they have Excel. To save Excel data to the Internet or to an intranet site in such a way that users can read the data in their Web browsers, you need to save it in HTML, the markup language of the Internet.

Considering the Options

When it comes to posting Excel documents to the Internet, Excel gives you lots of choices. You can save a file or publish it; you can save or publish it with or without interactivity. However you save or publish it, you can send the whole workbook to HTML, or just a part of it. You also can choose to use or ignore a Web Archive format introduced with this version of Excel. The following sections present some questions to consider as you work your way through the maze of options.

Do You Want Interactivity?

If you save your spreadsheet document without interactivity, users will be able to look at the numbers and charts but will not be able to change or reformat them. If you save with interactivity, users will be able to change numbers, formulas, and formatting, much as if you had given them a native Excel file. They won't be able to make permanent changes to the underlying HTML file, of course, but while they're reading your work in their browsers, they'll be able to play what-if with your worksheets.

Excel offers three interactive components:

- Spreadsheet
- Chart
- PivotTable Report

You choose which of these components you want to use when you create an HTML file with interactivity. Figures 20-5, 20-6, and 20-7 illustrate the three interactive components.

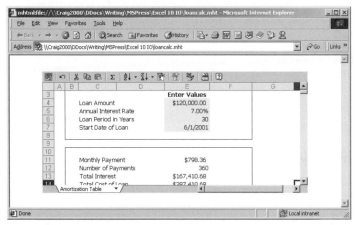

Figure 20-5.   The spreadsheet component, one of three interactive components, lets viewers change cell values and formatting.

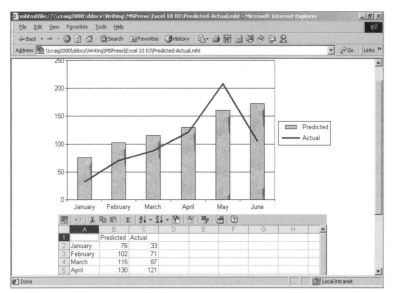

Figure 20-6. The chart component lets viewers change numbers and see their effects on the graph.

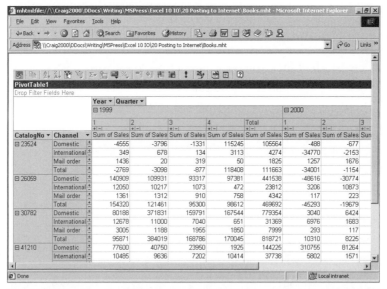

Figure 20-7. The PivotTable component lets viewers rearrange table fields to view different slices of your data.

To work with any of these interactive components, your viewers must have Microsoft Internet Explorer 4.01 or later, as well as the Microsoft Office Web Components. Microsoft Office XP ships with both, but users without Office XP might be out of luck. Users without the required components don't see a noninteractive version of your data—they see an error message. Therefore, if you're publishing Excel work to HTML for consumption by the public at large, you definitely shouldn't use interactivity. (When you save without interactivity, users can open the resulting HTML files in any Web browser.)

On the other hand, if you're publishing to a company intranet or some other environment where you know your viewers have Office XP, interactivity can be extremely handy. With the spreadsheet component, for example, you can set up a model that lets users enter their own assumptions (interest, inflation, or sales growth, for example) and use your spreadsheet logic to test their effects. With the chart component, users can change numbers and see what happens graphically. With the PivotTable component, users can rearrange tabular data to see different "slices" of the information you provide.

note If your worksheet relies on external data and you want users to be able to refresh the data within their Web browsers, you must save the application with PivotTable interactivity. Queries to external data cannot be refreshed on the spreadsheet component.

Your decision to use interactivity or not might be affected by factors other than whether your users have the required Office components. Not everything you do on an Excel spreadsheet can be translated effectively to the relevant interactive component. For example, the interactive spreadsheet component does not support wrapped text, so your neatly formatted worksheet that relies on wrapped text will look considerably less neat on conversion to the interactive component. Similarly, certain kinds of charts look great in the interactive chart component, and others are downright unusable. The spreadsheet component produces an oddly constrained window on the Web page, regardless of what resolution you're using when you perform the conversion (refer to Figure 20-5).

Microsoft has improved all three interactive components in this version of Excel. This time around, for example, the spreadsheet component retains references to named cells, ranges, and formulas. In the previous version, named references were converted to ordinary cell-address references. In Excel 2002, unlike with Excel 2000, it's possible to save entire workbooks using spreadsheet interactivity. Unless the application that you're posting to the Web or your intranet absolutely requires interactivity, however, you should certainly test the static approach as well as the interactive, to see which meets your needs better.

Note that some spreadsheet features can't be converted to either a static Web page or an interactive one. If Excel sees features in your workbook that it can't carry over to the HTML file, it warns you with a message similar to the one shown here.

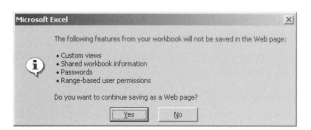

Usually the items you see in a message like this are features that wouldn't make sense in a Web-browser context. You'll be alerted anyway and given the opportunity to back out.

> **note** Choose File, Web Page Preview to see what your current worksheet will look like as a static (noninteractive) Web page. The Web Page Preview command doesn't create a permanent disk file; it pours the active worksheet into your Web browser as a temporary HTML file, deleting the file when you close the browser. If you're comparing interactive and static approaches to a given application, you can save yourself a few steps by using Web Page Preview to check out the static version.

To Save or To Publish?

When you publish a document to HTML, Excel creates a new HTML file (or updates an existing one) but leaves you in the original XLS version. If you select an AutoRepublish option, the program will update the HTML copy every time you save new changes to the XLS file. When you merely save the document in HTML, as opposed to publishing it, Excel closes the XLS file and leaves you to work (in Excel, not in the Web browser!) in the HTML file. In other words, it does a simple Save As operation, switching the format of your file in the process—exactly as it would if you chose File, Save As and saved your current document as a text file.

If you're converting a document to HTML to make it available to Internet or intranet users, you'll want to publish, not save. That way, you can ensure that your viewers always have the latest version. Each time you save changes to the original document, Excel will immediately transfer the changes to your Web or intranet site.

On the other hand, if you want to post an entire workbook to HTML without interactivity, you must save, not publish. To publish an entire workbook, you have to use the interactive spreadsheet component. Don't ask why!

Web Page or Web Archive?

In Excel 2000, if you saved an entire workbook to HTML, the resulting .htm file was saved in the folder you specified, and a large number of supporting documents were also saved in a new subfolder of that folder. (The supporting documents would include one HTML file for each worksheet in the workbook, another HTML file for displaying worksheet tabs, a cascading style sheet file, an XML file describing the structure of the workbook, various graphics files, and in some cases quite a bit more.) The file prolif-eration resulting from this approach was not only inconvenient—it could be hazardous as well. If one or more of the supporting files were damaged or lost, browsers would probably be unable to display the Web page correctly.

You now have the option of saving an entire workbook as a single Web archive file. The resulting file (which has the extension .mht) might be large, but at least it's only one file. This is an option you should exercise—unless you have some compelling reason to stick with the old format.

Excel 2002 doesn't create Web archive files by default, but you can make it do so. In the Save As dialog box, choose Tools, Web Options. On the Browsers tab, select Save New Web Pages As Web Archives. When you save changes to an existing Web page that uses the older multiple-file format, Excel will continue saving in that format. New docu-ments will be saved as Web archives, however.

Saving an Entire Workbook Without Interactivity

As mentioned, if you want to post an entire workbook to HTML and you don't want to use the interactive spreadsheet component, you need to save, not publish. To do this, follow these steps:

1 Choose File, Save As Web Page.

2 In the Save As dialog box, select Entire Workbook and clear Add Interactivity.

3 Supply a file name and location.

4 Choose Web Page or Web Archive in the Save As Type list, and click Save. Figure 20-8 shows, in Internet Explorer, a workbook saved in this manner.

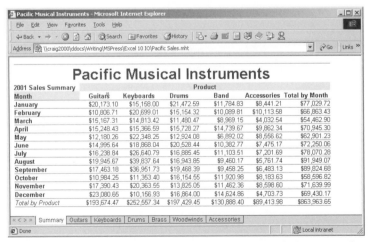

Figure 20-8. A workbook saved to HTML looks much the way it does in Excel.

As you can see in the figure, the resulting HTML file includes worksheet tabs. They look a little different from the ones you know and love, but they function the same way. The worksheet in the figure has horizontal gridlines—but only because the original spreadsheet was formatted to include these lines as cell borders. When Excel converts an XLS file to HTML, it drops the spreadsheet grid (along with the row-and-column frame), so if you think gridlines will help your viewer read a table, add them by choosing Format, Cells before you convert to HTML.

Cell B3, the heading Guitars in the original document, has a cell note. The note is carried over to the HTML file, marked by a tiny red flag. When a cursor hovers over the flag in Internet Explorer, the note shows in a pop-up window.

Changing the Title

When you use a Web browser to view an Excel file saved to HTML, the browser normally displays the file's name in the title bar. If you want something different to appear in the browser's title bar, click Change Title in the Save As dialog box before you click Save. In the ensuing dialog box, you can supply an alternative title.

Publishing Without Interactivity

To publish Excel data without interactivity, start by deciding what part of your workbook you want to publish. If you're publishing an entire worksheet or chart sheet, open that sheet. If you're publishing a worksheet range, select that range.

Choose File, Save As Web Page. Excel responds with a Save As dialog box, modified to include some HTML-relevant options. Click the Publish button in this dialog box. The Publish As Web Page dialog box, shown in Figure 20-9, appears.

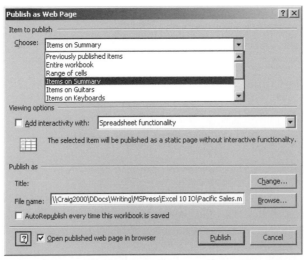

Figure 20-9. Use the Publish As Web Page dialog box to specify which part of your workbook you want to save and whether you want interactivity.

The drop-down Choose list includes all the worksheet elements that you can publish. If you've published this worksheet before, an item called Previously Published Items is available, along with the individual worksheets and chart sheets. If you selected a range before choosing Save As Web Page, the Choose list will display Range Of Cells, and another box below it will identify the selected range. You can modify this range, of course, by spelling out or pointing out a different range.

The AutoRepublish Every Time This Workbook Is Saved check box is clear by default. If you want your Web site to stay current with changes you make in the XLS file, be sure to select this check box before you click Publish.

The Open Published Web Page In Browser check box is selected by default. It's handy; if you don't clear it, you'll get an immediate look at your new Web page in your own browser when you click Publish.

Publishing with Interactivity

To publish Excel data with interactivity, follow the same steps as for publishing without interactivity, but select the Add Interactivity With check box. In the list adjacent to this check box, tell Excel which interactive component you want to use. (Depending on what part of your workbook you're publishing, you might not have a choice.)

If you're publishing an ordinary worksheet table, as opposed to a PivotTable, Excel 2002 gives you the option of saving it with either spreadsheet interactivity or PivotTable interactivity. The latter option doesn't make much sense (your viewer won't have anything to pivot), unless the worksheet table happens to be an external query range. In that case, if you want the viewer to be able to refresh the data in his or her browser, you need to save with PivotTable interactivity.

Note that when you publish with spreadsheet interactivity, external-reference formulas are converted to their current values. Other formulas, including those that reference cells or ranges by name, should remain intact.

newfeature!
Opening and Saving Files in XML

Excel 2002 supports XML, an important data interchange format. You can load any generic XML document into Excel by choosing File, Open and selecting XML Files in the Files Of Type list. You can save a spreadsheet in Spreadsheet XML, an XML format developed by Microsoft, by choosing File, Save As, and choosing XML Spreadsheet from the Files Of Type list.

Using the Interactive Web Components

Figure 20-10 on the next page shows a workbook saved with spreadsheet interactivity. This is the same workbook that is depicted without interactivity in Figure 20-8. Now, as you can see, the workbook appears within a traditional spreadsheet frame, looking a bit as it did in Excel. But only a bit! The Excel-like worksheet tabs have been replaced by a single tab with a menu. The spreadsheet component calls this the *sheet selector*. Click the sheet selector, and choose from the shortcut menu to switch to a different worksheet.

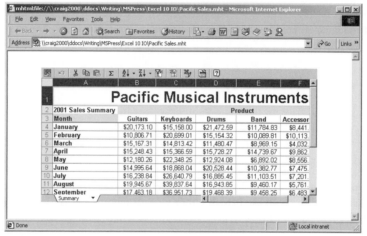

Figure 20-10. The workbook shown without interactivity in Figure 20-8 appears here with spreadsheet interactivity.

Rather than merge Excel menus with Web-browser menus, the interactive spreadsheet component relies on shortcut menus and a single, fixed toolbar. Many of the tools on this toolbar are familiar, although some probably are not.

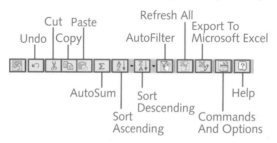

The two Sort tools have drop-down arrows beside them; click an arrow to specify a sorting field. (You can sort on only one column at a time, and only by row.) Click the AutoFilter tool if you want to see only those rows that meet some criterion. The Refresh All tool is meaningful only with the interactive PivotTable component.

For more information about using AutoFilters, see "Using the AutoFilter Command" on page 722.

Figure 20-11 shows the four-tabbed dialog box that appears when you either click the Commands And Options tool or right-click any part of the worksheet and choose Commands And Options from the shortcut menu. Most of the functionality that's available in the spreadsheet component is found somewhere in this dialog box. (Not all, however! To sort or filter, for example, you need to use the toolbar or the shortcut menu.)

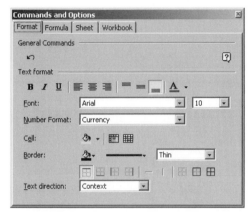

Figure 20-11. Almost all the spreadsheet component's functionality is accessible via this dialog box.

On the Formula tab, you can inspect either the formula behind the selected cell (if there is a formula) or the cell's full value. (You can see the same information by merely double-clicking the cell.) Also on the Formula tab, you can see a list of the worksheet's defined names—and add new ones if you are so inclined.

The Sheet tab includes a Find command and a set of Show/Hide options. You can suppress the display of row headers, column headers, and gridlines here. You can even flip the worksheet so that column A appears at the right, column B to its left, and so on.

The Workbook tab includes more Show/Hide options (horizontal and vertical scroll bars, sheet selector, and toolbar), options for switching between automatic and manual recalculation, and a list of the workbook's sheets. You can change sheet names here, hide selected sheets, and alter the order in which sheets appear.

Figure 20-12 on the next page shows a chart published with chart interactivity. Unlike the one shown in Figure 20-6, this one includes a toolbar above the chart. Excel does not display this toolbar by default. We added it to the published file by right-clicking the chart and choosing Toolbar from the shortcut menu.

The reason Excel doesn't ordinarily display this toolbar is that most of the tools (all except, Undo, Legend, and Help) are dimmed. The same toolbar is available for use with Interactive PivotChart Reports—and it's useful in that context.

When you display an ordinary chart (not a PivotChart) with chart interactivity, you can modify the underlying data, but you can't reformat the chart (other than to suppress the legend display). Note that Excel displays the supporting data even if the chart originated on a chart sheet, not as an embedded chart.

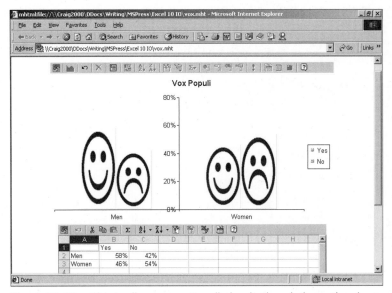

Figure 20-12. This toolbar can optionally be displayed above the chart component.

The user interface for the interactive PivotTable component is considerably more complex than the spreadsheet and chart interfaces—and requires an understanding of PivotTables. We'll take up that topic in Chapter 30, "Analyzing Data with PivotTables Reports."

Linking and Embedding

Microsoft no longer uses the term object linking and embedding (OLE) to describe its technology for creating "compound" documents—that is, documents that integrate data from multiple applications. But the technology is still there, and if you work with the full suite of Microsoft Office applications, you will undoubtedly have occasions to take advantage of it.

Part of the reason that OLE has disappeared from Microsoft's formal vocabulary is that linking and embedding capability is nearly universal in major Microsoft Windows applications now, and it ostensibly works so well that you seldom have to think about what you're doing. Nevertheless, it is important to have a general understanding of the differences between embedding and linking, to know when it's appropriate to use one form of integration as opposed to the other, and to know how to fix matters in the event that a link becomes broken.

Embedding vs. Linking

When you *embed* another application's data in Excel, your Excel document stores a complete copy of the source data. Because you have a complete copy of the source data (the paragraph from Microsoft Word, for example, or the voice annotation you created in Sound Recorder), that information remains intact even if the source is destroyed or becomes otherwise unavailable. But the embedded copy becomes completely independent from the source. The source might change, but the embedded copy does not (unless you edit it, of course).

When you *link* your Excel document to some external data, your document records pointers to the source of that data. If the source changes, your workbook can change accordingly.

569

Whether it changes automatically to match the source, or only when you request an update, depends on options that you set. In any event, your Excel document retains a connection with the source.

If the information you link or embed is text or a graphic, Excel "renders" it (makes it visible on your worksheet) if it can (that is, if it's in a format that Excel recognizes) and if you have not explicitly asked for an iconic display. Otherwise, Excel displays an icon that represents the linked or embedded information. When you double-click the icon, Excel renders the information (plays the sound clip or video, for example), provided an application capable of rendering it is available.

In some cases, Excel might display only some of a text document that you link or embed. If you link or embed a multipage Word document, for example, your work-book displays the first page only. To see the rest, double-click that first page.

Because embedding typically records more information in your Excel document than linking does, embedding tends to generate larger files. If minimizing file size matters, you should favor linking over embedding. You should also link if you need to have Excel update your workbook when the source data changes.

On the other hand, if you need to fetch some information from a document on a net-work server so that you can take it on the road, obviously you'll want to embed it, not link to it. Otherwise, Excel won't be able to find it when you're disconnected from the server.

Embedding vs. Static Pasting

What's the difference between embedding something and doing an ordinary paste from the Clipboard?

If you paste text into Excel from Notepad (an application that doesn't support embed-ding), that text arrives as though you typed it directly into the active worksheet cell. (If the text spans multiple lines, Excel delivers each new line to a new cell in the current column.) If you embed text from Word, the embedded text becomes an object, similar in some ways to a shape created via the Drawing toolbar. As Figure 21-1 shows, when the embedded text is selected, the word Object, followed by a number, appears in the name box, and an EMBED formula appears on the formula line. A rectangle with white handles surrounds the object itself, allowing you to reposition or resize it. (By choosing Format, Object, you can modify or eliminate the rectangle line and format the object in various other ways.)

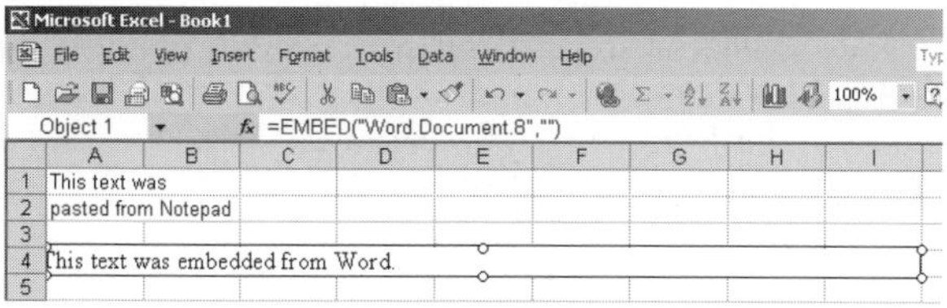

Figure 21-1. Pasting text statically enters it into worksheet cells; embedding creates an object.

More important, perhaps, if you double-click the embedded object, you can edit it using the application that created it. If you double-click the Word object in Figure 21-1, for example, Excel displays a thick border around the embedded text. The normal Excel menus and toolbars are replaced by Word's menus and toolbars, and if you've chosen to display the ruler in Word, the ruler appears inside the embedded object. At this point, you are essentially in Word, although the Excel context remains visible. When you have finished using Word to edit the object, you can click outside it (back on the worksheet), and the Word paraphernalia disappears.

This kind of object editing is called *editing in place*. Not all applications that support embedding offer it. If you double-click an object embedded from an application that doesn't support editing in place, Excel launches a more-or-less normal copy of that application. (It might include a command on its File menu for updating your Excel document with the changes you make.)

In cases where embedding and static pasting are both options, you should favor embedding if you want to retain the ability to edit the material in its native application—or if you want to be able to apply object formatting commands to the incoming material.

Embedding and Linking from the Clipboard

When you copy data to the Clipboard, the source application typically posts the data to the Clipboard in a variety of formats. When you choose Paste Special in Excel (or in another application, if you're not pasting into Excel), the Paste Special dialog box allows you to choose among all the formats currently on the Clipboard that Excel (or the receiving application) can accept. Here is an example to illustrate the process.

The source data in this example is a Microsoft PowerPoint slide. By opening the View menu in the Windows 2000 ClipBook Viewer (clipbrd.exe), you can see the names of the formats in which PowerPoint has posted this data, as shown in Figure 21-2 on the next page. The formats that aren't grayed out (Picture and Enhanced Metafile) are formats that the ClipBook Viewer application knows how to render. All the formats listed in gray below Enhanced Metafile are available for receiving applications, even though ClipBook Viewer itself can't render them.

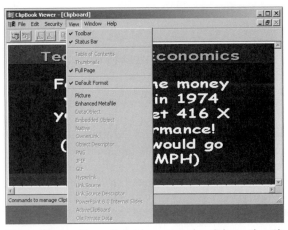

Figure 21-2. PowerPoint has posted a slide to the Clipboard in many different formats, only two of which the Windows 2000 ClipBook Viewer can render.

Choosing Paste Special in Excel while this PowerPoint slide is on the Clipboard shows you what formats Excel can accept. In this case, as Figure 21-3 shows, Excel gives a choice of six formats.

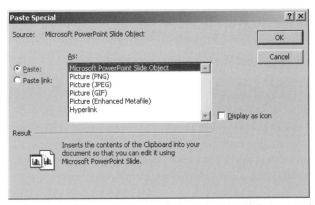

Figure 21-3. Excel can paste the PowerPoint slide in six of the many formats that PowerPoint posted to the Clipboard.

In many cases, the format that appears first in the Paste Special dialog box is the default format—the one that you would get by choosing Paste or pressing Ctrl+V. If the Clipboard data can be embedded, Excel is likely to make the embedding format the default. If you need to be certain, however, you shouldn't depend on these generalizations; use Paste Special instead of Paste.

If a format listed in the Paste Special dialog box includes the word Object, choosing that format embeds the Clipboard data. All the other formats produce a static paste. If you're not sure what a format is or does, select it in the Paste Special dialog box and read the descriptive text below the format list.

InsideOut

Don't Bother Pasting a Bitmap Object

If you copy a bitmap to the Clipboard, choose Paste Special in Excel, and then select the Bitmap Image Object format, Excel pastes a picture instead of embedding a bitmap object. Microsoft has acknowledged this bug but says it will not be fixed in Excel 2002. To embed a bitmap, choose Insert, Object (described later in this chapter) instead of Paste Special.

As Figure 21-3 shows, the Paste Special dialog box includes two option buttons, Paste and Paste Link. To link your source data, select Paste Link. Excel will render your source data in whatever format you have selected and also create a link to the source.

Figure 21-4 shows a block of text paste-linked from Word into Excel. Notice that Excel identifies this as an object (as it does for embedded text). But instead of the EMBED formula that you saw with the embedded text (refer to Figure 21-1), Excel creates an external-reference formula, similar to the kind of formula it creates if you reference a cell in an external Excel workbook. For reasons that aren't at all clear, the linked object also gets a green rotation handle in addition to the usual white handles. You can use the green handle to slant or invert the text block.

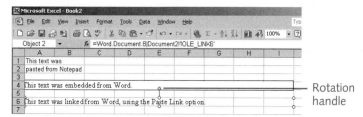

Rotation handle

Figure 21-4. When you link data, Excel creates an external-reference formula similar to the formula it would use to reference a cell in another worksheet.

The Paste Link option button in Excel's Paste Special dialog box is not available for all the formats that Excel can paste. If it's not available for the data and format you want, try linking by choosing Insert, Object instead of Paste Special. For more information, see "Embedding and Linking with the Object Command" on page 574.

573

InsideOut

Don't Link to a Hyperlink

Curiously, if you copy Word data to the Clipboard and choose Paste Special in Excel, you'll find that you can select the Hyperlink format and also the Paste Link option button. Linking to a hyperlink sounds like a meaningless operation, and it is. It also generates a long-lasting hourglass followed by an error message. This bug has been around at least since Excel 2000.

As mentioned, if you embed or link a format that Excel cannot render, the incoming data is represented by an icon. In some cases, you can also ask for iconic representation of data that Excel can render. Displaying an icon instead of the rendered data is an excellent choice if you want the user of your Excel document to have access to external information but not be distracted by it. The icon takes up little space on your worksheet, and you can add text beside it to explain its purpose.

To link or embed information from the Clipboard and display it as an icon, use the Paste Special command, select the format you want, and select the Display As Icon check box. Note that this check box is not available for all formats.

Embedding and Linking with the Object Command

Choosing Insert, Object allows you to embed an object that doesn't exist as Clipboard data. As Figure 21-5 shows, the Object dialog box has two tabs, Create New and Create From File. Using the Create New tab, you can create an object from scratch and then embed it. Using the Create From File tab, you can either embed or link an entire file.

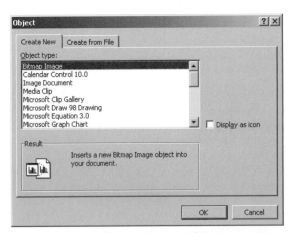

Figure 21-5. By choosing Insert, Object, you can create embeddable objects or link or embed entire files.

Chapter 21

The list on the Create New tab includes document types that are probably familiar, such as Bitmap Image and Microsoft Word Document, as well as the names of OLE server applications installed on your system. If you choose a document type and click OK, Excel launches the application associated with that document type. If the application in question supports editing in place, Excel's menus (except for the File menu) and toolbars will be replaced by those of the application, and you will be able to create your object in a window that appears on your Excel worksheet. If the application does not support editing in place, the full application appears in a separate window. After you create your object, you can send the new object to your Excel worksheet by choosing a command on the application's File menu.

For example, suppose you want to embed a new sound annotation in your Excel document. You could do it as follows:

1 Choose Insert, Object.

2 On the Create New tab, select Wave Sound and click OK. Excel launches Sound Recorder (or whatever other application you have associated with the Wave Sound document type).

3 In Sound Recorder, you record your annotation.

4 From Sound Recorder's File menu, choose Exit & Return To Book1 (assuming your workbook is Book1).

The OLE Server names on the Create New tab represent applications whose sole purpose is to create embeddable objects. If you choose Calendar Control 10.0, for example, Excel displays a calendar on your worksheet. If you choose Microsoft Equation 3.0, the Microsoft Equation Editor program appears, allowing you to create and embed a mathematical, chemical, or other technical expression as an object on your Excel worksheet. As Figure 21-6 shows, the Microsoft Equation Editor is an application that supports editing in place. It replaces Excel's menus and displays its elaborate palette of symbol toolbars.

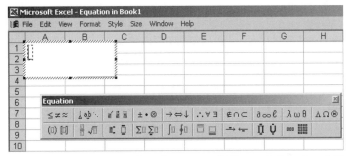

Figure 21-6. You can take advantage of Microsoft Equation Editor and other OLE server applications by choosing Insert, Object.

On the Create From File tab of the Object dialog box, you can type the name of a file or use the Browse button to locate it. To embed the file, click OK. To create a link to it, select the Link To File check box. To display an embedded or linked object as an icon, select the Display As Icon check box.

Using the Create From File tab of the Object dialog box, you can embed or link any file into your Excel document. If you embed a file type that's not listed on the Create New tab, the resulting EMBED formula references the Windows Packager application. This application (packager.exe) is a "wrapper" that encapsulates the embedded file. When you double-click the object on your worksheet, Packager executes the file, an action equivalent to double-clicking it in a Windows Explorer window. If the file is associated with an application, your file appears in the context of that application. If it's not associated with an application, a Run With dialog box appears. In the Run With dialog box, you can choose an application with which to open the file.

If you link a file type that doesn't appear on the Create New tab, the linking formula references the file directly. In this case, double-clicking the link object is exactly like double-clicking the file in a Windows Explorer window.

Launching Programs from within an Excel Document

You can choose Insert, Object to place an icon on your worksheet that launches another program. Simply reference the program's executable file on the Create From File tab. Be aware that if you embed the executable, you get the whole executable, which is likely to be a very large file. Embed a program such as PowerPoint, and you've suddenly got a megabyte-plus Excel document. Linking gets the job done without significantly magnifying your file size.

Managing Links

If an Excel workbook includes links to other documents, you can choose Edit, Links to summon the dialog box shown in Figure 21-7. The Edit Links dialog box lists all links in the current file, including links created by formula references to cells in other worksheets.

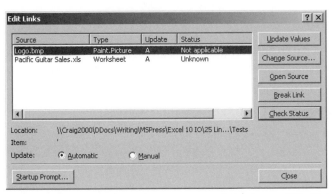

Figure 21-7. To update, alter, or sever a link, choose Edit, Links.

Choosing Automatic or Manual Update

The Automatic and Manual option buttons, near the bottom of the dialog box, control the manner in which your links are updated. If you choose Automatic (the only choice available for links with other Excel documents), your link is updated whenever the source changes. This automatic updating occurs instantaneously with some source applications and takes a while longer with others. Theoretically, you don't need to concern yourself with refreshing the link; Windows will perform that duty for you. If you find that the updating occurs more frequently than you want it to (or if the process intrudes on your concentration in any way), you might want to switch from Automatic to Manual. With updating set to Manual, you can force an update by choosing Edit, Links, selecting the link, and clicking Update Values.

Updating on File Open

Regardless of your Update setting, Excel normally gives you the option of performing an update when you open the file. It does this by presenting the dialog box shown here.

If you'd rather not be bothered with this question every time you open a file containing links, choose Edit, Links, and click Startup Prompt. You can then decide whether Excel will update your links on startup—without being prompted each time. Note that the startup prompt setting is document-specific.

Fixing Broken Links

If Excel tries to update a link and can't find the source file, it presents an error message. If this difficulty occurs when you open your Excel document, the message looks like the one shown here.

Clicking the Edit Links button takes you to a file-browser dialog box, which you can use to help Excel locate your file (assuming you know where it is). If the problem occurs while you're working in your Excel document, you'll see a different message, in a dialog box that lacks the Edit Links button. After closing the dialog box, choose Edit, Links, select the troubled link, and click Change Source.

> **note**   You can disconnect a linked object from its source in either of two ways. You can delete the object's link formula, or you can choose Edit, Links, select the link, and click Break Link. Either way, your linked object remains on the worksheet, but Excel converts it from an object to a picture.

Linking vs. Hyperlinking

Hyperlinking, discussed in Chapter 20, "Posting Excel Documents to the Internet," is an alternative way to connect an Excel document with an external file. (You can also use hyperlinking to connect an Excel document with a Web site or document, of course.) If you want your Excel document to reference supplementary information without making that information obtrusive, you can do it with a hyperlink as easily as with an OLE link displayed as an icon.

Which method you prefer is likely to be a matter of taste. Most people looking at your Excel document will find a hyperlink self-explanatory, but some might not know immediately how to use an OLE link. On the other hand, an iconic OLE link might more easily grab a viewer's attention. OLE links also are self-repairing—in some cases, at least. (If you rename or move a target of an OLE link, Windows can sometimes update the link information so that Excel still finds the linked file.) Hyperlinks are not self-repairing. If you think the target of a link might get renamed or moved, it's safer to use an OLE link.

Using Hyperlinks

Chapter 21, "Linking and Embedding," discussed one method of creating links between Excel documents and other documents. The method described there, sometimes called *paste-linking,* relies on Microsoft's object linking and embedding technology. When you paste-link a document onto an Excel worksheet, you see either that document (sometimes only a portion of it) or an icon representing the document. When changes are made to the linked document, its representation in Excel changes. When you double-click the paste-linked document (or its iconic stand-in), Excel starts the application that created the document.

In this chapter, you look at a newer way to forge links in Excel documents, one that relies on the familiar conventions of the Internet world. The newer method is, of course, hyperlinking. A hyperlink in an Excel workbook behaves like a hyperlink in your Web browser; a single click of the link opens the target of the link. Typically, that's another document somewhere—on the World Wide Web, on your own hard disk, or on a local area network server.

Hyperlinks in Excel can look like text hyperlinks in Web pages. That is, a hyperlink can be a simple word or phrase, underlined and colored to distinguish it from other text in your workbook. After you click such a link, the color ordinarily changes, marking the fact that you've already visited that link's target.

Just as links on Web pages can be attached to graphics instead of text, so can they in Excel. Not only can you assign an Excel hyperlink to a drawing object or imported image, you can even assign it to a toolbar icon or menu command. If you've got a favorite Web site that you often leave Excel to visit, and if there's also an Excel menu command or tool that you never use, you can change the text of the menu command to the name of your favorite Web site and assign a hyperlink to the command. That way the hyperlink will be available, regardless of what Excel file you're working with.

Here's a short inventory of nifty things you can do with hyperlinks in Excel:

- **Link to Web sites.** You'll find the ability to link to Web pages particularly useful if you use Excel to generate material on the Web. When you post your Excel document to your Web server, you can already have the appropriate links to related pages in place.

- **Link to other existing documents.** Let's say you're a realtor with a worksheet that summarizes your current listings portfolio. You have pictures of each house, but the pictures don't fit neatly into worksheet cells. Create hyperlinks to the pictures instead. You can assign the hyperlinks to cells containing the multiple listing service numbers or street addresses. Or suppose you're looking for a way to catalog your digital photo collection. Although you can use file and folder names to describe photo contents, dates, or locations, there are limits to how much information you can supply in a file name. Consider setting up an Excel table instead, with hyperlinks from descriptive information to individual photo files.

- **Link to a document that doesn't yet exist.** Well, maybe this one isn't *so* nifty. But you can do it. Excel will create the document when you click the link.

- **Link to another place in the current document.** Perhaps you've built a complex worksheet for someone else to use. You can help that person navigate your masterpiece by supplying a table of hyperlinks.

- **Link to an e-mail message.** You can create a contact list in Excel and hyperlink each name to the person's e-mail address. When you click the link, Excel launches your default e-mail program, with the envelope already addressed.

---

newfeature!

tip   Edit hyperlinks easily

If you've used hyperlinks in earlier versions of Excel, you probably know that it was a little awkward to select the link for editing (without opening it, that is). It's easier in Excel 2002. Simply click and hold. After about a second, the mouse cursor will change from a hand to a normal cell selector (the fat, white plus sign). Release the mouse button, and the link is yours to edit.

Creating a Hyperlink in a Cell

If you're creating a hyperlink to a Web site and you already know the site's URL, you don't even have to choose Insert, Hyperlink. Type the URL into a cell, and Excel will turn it into the appropriate hyperlink. If the URL begins with www, Excel assumes it's an HTTP (Web site) URL. If the URL doesn't start with www, you need to include the prefix http://. (If the URL uses some other prefix, such as ftp://, you must, of course, type that.)

Troubleshooting

Excel Doesn't Turn My URLs into Hyperlinks!

Excel turns obvious URLs into hyperlinks by default. If it doesn't perform this service for you, you need to adjust an AutoCorrect setting. Choose Tools, AutoCorrect Options, click the AutoFormat As You Type tab, and select the Internet And Network Paths With Hyperlinks check box.

Turning Ordinary Text into a Hyperlink

To turn text other than a URL into a hyperlink, select it and choose Insert, Hyperlink (or select it and press Ctrl+K). The dialog box shown in Figure 22-1 appears. (If you've used the Hyperlink command in previous versions of Excel, you'll note some small design changes in this dialog box.)

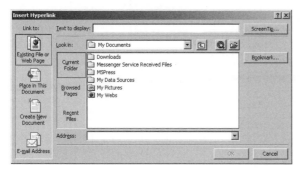

Figure 22-1. You can use the Insert Hyperlink dialog box to link to a file or Web page.

Use the following steps to create a hyperlink in a worksheet cell:

1 In the Address box, type the target of the link (the place to which you'll be taken when you click the link).

2 In the Text To Display box, enter the text of the hyperlink. Excel will display this text underlined in your worksheet cell. (This box is probably already filled out when you get to the Insert Hyperlink dialog box.)

3 Click ScreenTip to supply the ScreenTip that should appear when your mouse hovers over the cell. This might be a "friendly" name for a Web site, or a description of a file's contents. If you omit this step, Excel uses a default ScreenTip that identifies the target of the link.

> **note** Because PivotTable cells move when a PivotTable Report is rearranged, you cannot assign a hyperlink to a cell within a PivotTable.

Linking to a Web Site

To create a link to a Web site, supply the URL in the Address box of the Insert Hyperlink dialog box. The dialog box makes this easy. The drop-down arrow next to the Address box reveals the URLs of places you've recently visited (along with file names that you've recently used for hyperlinks). If you don't find what you're looking for there, click the Browsed Pages button. That shows the names (rather than the URLs) of recently visited sites (see Figure 22-2). From one list or the other, you'll probably find the site you want to link to.

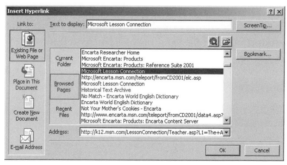

Figure 22-2. The Browsed Pages button reveals the names of sites you've recently visited.

If you don't find your site via the Address list or Browsed Pages—or if you're not sure you've found the right site—click the Browse The Web button (next to the folder icon above the Browsed Pages list). This action launches your Web browser. Use the browser to navigate to the page you want. When you return to Excel, the Insert Hyperlink dialog box will contain the address of that site.

Note that if you're linking to a Web site from your desktop, the Address box must include the appropriate protocol prefix (http:// or ftp://, for example). If you're creating a link that will be used on a Web site, a target address that isn't fully qualified will be assumed to be relative to the current page.

Troubleshooting

But I Don't Want That Hyperlink

Sometimes a URL is just a URL, and you don't want to launch your browser every time you touch it with your mouse. Right-click the cell in question, and choose Remove Hyperlink from the shortcut menu.

Linking to a Location in the Current Document

To link to a location in the current document, click Place In This Document in the Insert Hyperlink dialog box. As Figure 22-3 shows, you can link to any sheet or to a named cell or range. If you select a sheet name, use the Type The Cell Reference box to identify the cell on that sheet to which you want to link. Excel links to A1 by default.

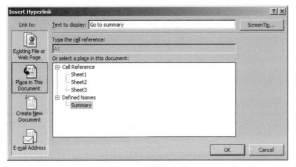

Figure 22-3. You can create a link to any sheet, named range, or cell on the current worksheet.

Linking to an Existing File

To create a link to another file, click the Existing File Or Web Page button in the navigation bar at the left side of the Insert Hyperlink dialog box. Then either type the path of the file in the Address box, or use the Browse For File button (the open folder) to find the file.

If you're linking to an Excel file, you can also click the Bookmark button to specify a location within that file. You can specify a sheet name or a named cell or range. The Bookmark button won't help you if you're linking to other kinds of documents.

Linking to a New File

To create a link to a new file, click Create New Document in the navigation bar at the left side of the Insert Hyperlink dialog box. As Figure 22-4 shows, the dialog box then changes to reveal a pair of option buttons. With one, you create the file immediately; with the other, you create the file the first time you click the hyperlink.

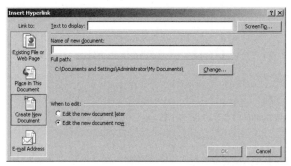

Figure 22-4. You can link to a file that doesn't yet exist—and create it either immediately or the first time you click the hyperlink.

Linking to an E-Mail Message

By clicking the E-Mail Address button in the navigation bar at the left side of the Insert Hyperlink dialog box, you can create a hyperlink that opens your e-mail program and fills out the envelope for a new message. Figure 22-5 shows how the Insert Hyperlink dialog box appears after you click E-Mail Address. If you use this feature occasionally, the Recently Used E-Mail Addresses portion of the dialog box will list previous addressees, and you can resend to a former recipient by selecting from the list. If the address you want isn't there, though, you have to type it on the E-Mail Address line; Excel won't open your address book for you.

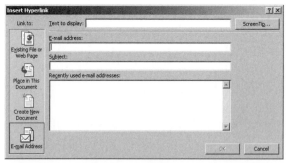

Figure 22-5. You can use this form of the Insert Hyperlink dialog box to create a mailto: link.

You can specify multiple addresses on the E-Mail Address line. Use semicolons to separate the addresses. You can also include a subject by filling out the Subject line.

Assigning a Hyperlink to a Graphic, Toolbar Button, or Menu Command

You can assign a hyperlink to a drawing object or imported picture. Simply select the object and choose Insert, Hyperlink (or press Ctrl+K). You cannot assign a hyperlink to an embedded chart or chart element, however.

Use the following steps to assign a hyperlink to a toolbar icon:

1 Choose View, Toolbars, Customize. (Or right-click any toolbar, and choose Customize.)

2 If the tool you want to use is visible, right-click it with the Customize dialog box open. If it's not visible, add it to an open toolbar (or display a toolbar on which it is visible), and then right-click it.

3 Choose Assign Hyperlink, Open from the shortcut menu to open the Insert Hyperlink dialog box.

When you assign a hyperlink to a toolbar icon, you don't get the opportunity to specify a ScreenTip. Excel uses the target of the link as the ScreenTip.

For information about customizing toolbars, see "Customizing Toolbars and Menus" on page 65.

InsideOut

The Insert Hyperlink Command Is Dimmed

For reasons that aren't entirely clear, most tools can accept hyperlinks, but some cannot. If the Hyperlink command isn't available, you'll have to choose other tools.

Use the following steps to assign a hyperlink to a menu command:

1 Choose View, Toolbars, Customize.

2 In the Customize dialog box, navigate to the menu command you want to use and right-click it.

3 Choose Assign Hyperlink, Open from the shortcut menu.

For more information about customizing menus, see "Customizing Toolbars and Menus" on page 65.

Editing, Removing, and Deleting a Hyperlink

To change anything having to do with a hyperlink, right-click the link and choose Edit Hyperlink from the shortcut menu. (If the link is assigned to a toolbar icon or menu command, you need to choose View, Toolbars, Customize first.) Doing this transports you to the Edit Hyperlink dialog box, which is the same as the Insert Hyperlink dialog box.

To remove a hyperlink (that is, disconnect it from its erstwhile target), right-click it and choose Remove Hyperlink from the shortcut menu. To delete a hyperlink, you can select it and press the Delete key. That removes the link, but, unfortunately, it leaves the link formatting in place. If your link was blue and underlined, the next text you enter in that cell will also be blue and underlined. To remove the link *and* its formatting, select it and choose Edit, Clear, All.

Formatting a Hyperlink

You can use the Format, Cells command or a toolbar icon to change the appearance of a cell containing a hyperlink. If you change the text color of the link, the cell will retain the color you choose, regardless of whether you've clicked the link. If you remove the underline from the link, the link will remain without the underline even after you follow the link. To change the default hyperlink formatting, choose Format, Style. In the Style dialog box, choose Hyperlink or Followed Hyperlink and make your changes.

Using the HYPERLINK Function

The HYPERLINK function creates a hyperlink in a worksheet cell, based on arguments you supply. The syntax is

`=HYPERLINK(link_location,friendly_name)`

In this syntax, *link_location*, a required argument, is a text value that specifies the target of the link, and *friendly_name*, an optional argument, is the text that will appear in the cell. If *friendly_name* is omitted, it is assumed to be the same as *link_location*. Either argument can be a cell reference. Here are a couple of examples:

`=HYPERLINK("http://www.microsoft.com","Microsoft Web Site")`

`=HYPERLINK("[\\myserver\myfile.xls]Sheet2!B29")`

The first example displays the text "Microsoft Web Site" as a hyperlink that connects to *www.microsoft.com*. Note that you must include the http:// prefix in the *link_location* argument. The second example creates a hyperlink that takes you to cell B29 on Sheet2 of Myfile.xls, stored on \\myserver.

The most likely use for the HYPERLINK function is to construct a link target from text in another cell. For example, if you want a set of links to jump to different servers at different times, you could enter the current server name in a cell and then build HYPERLINK formulas with absolute references to that cell. By changing the cell contents, you could then update all the HYPERLINK formulas at once.

Part 7

Integrating Excel with Other Applications

Chapter 23

Integrating Excel with Word and PowerPoint

Its many presentation features notwithstanding, Microsoft Excel is at heart an analytical tool. When it comes time to organize information and present it to others, you're likely to turn to two other programs in the Microsoft Office XP suite, Microsoft Word and Microsoft PowerPoint. Naturally, these programs are designed to work hand-in-glove with Excel, so you can easily do your number crunching in Excel and transfer the results to Word or PowerPoint when you need to make a verbal or visual presentation.

In this chapter, we'll survey the few points you need to know when incorporating your Excel tables and charts into Word and PowerPoint documents. We'll also show how you can use contact lists stored in Excel to generate form letters, mailing labels, and envelopes in Word.

Using Excel Tables in Word Documents

You can create tables directly in Word, of course, but you have to fuss with Table menu commands to do it. If your tables consist of more than a few rows or columns, you'll find it simpler to build them in Excel and then transfer them to your Word documents. You can use the following methods to move a worksheet range from Excel into Word:

- Copy the Excel data to the Clipboard, and then use Paste or Paste Special in Word to paste the table in the format of your choice, with or without a link to the source data.

- Choose Insert, Object in Word.

- Choose Insert, File in Word.

Pasting an Excel Table from the Clipboard

If you copy an Excel worksheet range to the Clipboard, and then (before closing your Excel document) paste it into a Word document using Ctrl+V, your data arrives in HTML format. Assuming your source material does not include graphical elements, it should look as it did in Excel. Word preserves your font, numeric, column-width, and row-height formatting; recognizes merged cells that extend across multiple columns; and so on. Graphical images on your worksheet are not conveyed to Word in this format, however; if you need to preserve these elements, use Paste Special in Word, not Paste. For more information, see "Using Paste Special to Control the Format of Your Table" on the next page.

Data pasted in the HTML format becomes a table in Word, and you can alter its appearance by means of commands on Word's Table menu. The presence or absence of gridlines in this table is determined by your current settings in Word, not by whether you've made worksheet gridlines visible in Excel. You can add or remove gridlines in Word by using Table, Show Gridlines, or Table, Hide Gridlines. Note, however, that if you choose Format, Cells to add gridlines to your range in Excel before transferring the information to the Clipboard, Excel formatting is maintained, even if you choose Table, Hide Gridlines in Word.

> **note** If you copy an Excel range and then close your Excel document before pasting it into Word, the default paste format changes from HTML to Formatted Text (RTF), another format that preserves the original appearance of your table in Word but abandons any graphical elements associated with it. For a description of the differences between HTML and RTF, see the section "Using Formatted Text (RTF) and HTML Format" on page 595.

When you paste your data into Word, a smart tag appears with the menu shown here.

Using this smart tag's menu, you can abandon the formatting your table had in Excel, opting instead for Word's current default table formatting style or plain text. If you go for plain text, Word treats your data as ordinary text lines, using tab characters to separate columns. Typically this means that numbers and words that lined up neatly on your Excel worksheet no longer do in your Word document.

The smart tag menu also allows you to create a link between your pasted table and its original Excel source, so that if the source changes, the table in Word can change accordingly. If you choose to link, you can either maintain Excel's formatting (Keep Source Formatting And Link To Excel) or apply Word's current defaults (Match Destination Table Style And Link To Excel). There are other ways to forge links with Excel tables, so we'll defer that discussion until later, in the section "Paste-Linking an Excel Table into Word" on page 596.

Using Paste Special to Control the Format of Your Table

For maximum control over the way in which Word pastes tabular data from Excel, copy your Excel range to the Clipboard. Then leave the workbook open in Excel while you choose Edit, Paste Special in Word. You see the Paste Special dialog box shown in Figure 23-1. (If you close the Excel workbook before choosing Edit, Paste Special in Word, all but the text formats become unavailable.)

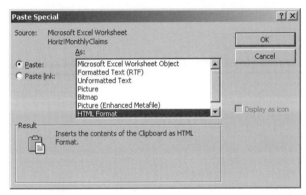

Figure 23-1. Word can paste an Excel range in any of these formats and in unformatted Unicode text.

With any of the formats displayed in the Paste Special dialog box, you can either paste or paste-link. We'll look at the latter operation in a moment, in the section "Paste-Linking an Excel Table into Word" on page 596. The next sections describe the available paste formats:

- Microsoft Excel Worksheet Object.

- Formatted Text (RTF) and HTML Format.

- Unformatted Text and Unformatted Unicode Text.

- Picture, Bitmap, and Picture (Enhanced Metafile).

593

Using the Microsoft Excel Worksheet Object   Pasting the Worksheet Object format embeds your Excel table in your Word document, with any graphical elements that happened to be included in your Excel selection. Your table should look the same in Word as it did in Excel, because the object format preserves Excel's gridlines setting.

The principal value of the Worksheet Object format, apart from the fact that it keeps graphical elements associated with worksheet cells, is that it allows you to edit the pasted table using Excel's commands and features, not Word's. For example, if you want to apply a custom numeric format to your data after pasting it as an object into Word, you can do that by double-clicking the object.

Word allows editing in place of embedded Excel objects. If you double-click an embedded Excel object in Word, the menus in Word change temporarily to those of Excel, as shown in Figure 23-2. After you edit the object and click in any other part of the Word document, Excel's menus are replaced by Word's.

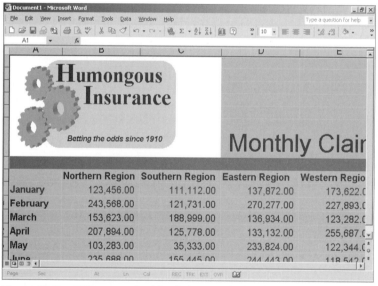

Figure 23-2.   When you double-click an embedded Excel object, Word's menus are replaced by Excel's, allowing you to use Excel formatting and editing features to modify the object.

An important peculiarity to note about Excel objects embedded into Word documents is that Excel embeds the entire workbook, not only the selection that you copied to the Clipboard. The sheet tabs at the bottom of Figure 23-3 illustrate this point. Although the editing window that appears in Word when you double-click the Excel object has the same dimensions as the original selection in Excel, you can scroll to any part of the current worksheet and even switch to another worksheet in the same workbook. When you return to Word (by clicking off the embedded object), Word treats any scrolling you do as an edit of the embedded object. If you switch from Sheet1 to Sheet2 while you're editing, you'll see Sheet2 when you return to your Word document.

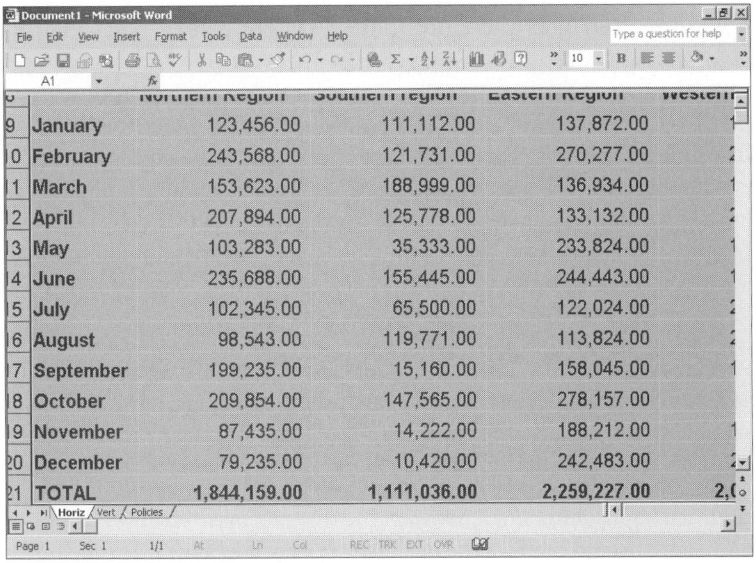

Chapter 23: Integrating Excel with Word and PowerPoint

Figure 23-3. Word embeds the entire Excel workbook, not only the selection
that you copied to the Clipboard.

---

tip **Pare before you paste**

Because Word embeds the entire workbook when you paste an Excel selection as an
object, and because embedding adds to the size of the receiving document, it's a good
idea to eliminate everything you don't need before you embed. If the table you want
to embed in your Word document is part of a large Excel workbook, copy it first to an
empty workbook. Then copy it to the Clipboard and embed it in Word.

Using Formatted Text (RTF) and HTML Format   Formatted Text (RTF) and HTML
Format preserve the font and numeric formatting of your Excel selection. They differ
in the way they preserve that formatting. Formatted Text (RTF) uses *rich-text format*, a
method of encoding formatting information that has been available for a long time in
Microsoft Office and other kinds of documents. HTML (Hypertext Markup Language)
is Word's default format (the one you get when you press Ctrl+V) and also the programming language of the World Wide Web. Both formats generate tables in Word,
maintaining the cell alignment that you had in Excel and allowing for manipulation via
Word's Table menu. Neither format includes graphical elements that were part of your
Excel selection.

HTML is more likely to render the formatting of your Excel selection accurately than
RTF. But you might want to experiment to see which format suits your purposes more
effectively. If you don't like the results you get, choose Edit, Undo and try again with a
different format.

Using Unformatted Text and Unformatted Unicode Text   Use Unformatted Text and Unformatted Unicode Text when you do not want your Clipboard data to become a table in Word. Both formats transfer data from the Clipboard as though you had typed it directly into your Word document, using tab characters between the columns of your original Excel selection and return characters at the ends of lines. Ordinarily, the result is that data that was aligned neatly in Excel is no longer aligned in Word. Use the Unicode format if your data includes characters outside the normal ANSI range— for example, characters from non-Latin alphabets. Otherwise, it doesn't matter which of these two formats you use.

Using Picture, Bitmap, and Picture (Enhanced Metafile)   Picture, Bitmap, and Picture (Enhanced Metafile) formats produce more-or-less faithful graphical representations of your original Excel selection (including, of course, any graphical elements associated with it). Because the results are pictures, not tables, you can modify them with tools on Word's Picture toolbar.

You can learn about differences between the formats by selecting each one in the Paste Special dialog box and reading the explanatory text that appears at the bottom of the dialog box. These pearls from Microsoft tell you, among other things, that the Picture format uses the least amount of memory and loads the quickest, but that the Bitmap format gives you the nearest visual equivalent of your original Excel selection. You should take such generalizations with a grain of salt and experiment to see which works best for you.

Paste-Linking an Excel Table into Word

You can paste-link any of the formats shown in Figure 23-1 and described in the preceding sections by selecting the Paste Link option in the Paste Special dialog box. When you do this, Word creates a field that references the source of your Excel data. The field is a code (comparable to an external-reference formula in Excel) that tells the application how to update the data if you request a manual update. The code also tells the application how to locate the data for editing if you double-click the linked information on your Word document. You can see the code by choosing Tools, Options in Word, clicking the View tab, and selecting the Field Codes check box.

Links from Excel into Word are automatic by default, which means that any time the Excel source is changed, the Word document is automatically adjusted. You can switch to manual linking by choosing Edit, Links, selecting the linked item, and selecting the Manual Update option in Word. In the Links dialog box, as shown in Figure 23-4, you can also click Break Link to disassociate the Word data from its Excel source, or Change Source to point the link to different data.

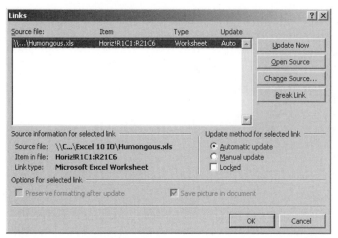

Figure 23-4. In Word's Links dialog box, you can switch between manual and automatic updating, modify the link specification, or break the link.

If you're using manual updating, you can also force an update by clicking Update Now in the Links dialog box. A simpler way to update your table is to select it and press F9.

Linking to Named Ranges

It is extremely important that you make sure Word identifies the source of an Excel link by means of a range name, not by an ordinary range reference. Otherwise, if the source table changes location for any reason (for example, if someone inserts or deletes a few rows), the link will no longer reference the original table. For information about naming ranges, see "Defining and Managing Names" on page 372.

If the worksheet range has a name at the time you copy it to the Clipboard, Word will reference it by name when you perform your paste-link. If it is not named, Word will reference it by cell address, using R1C1 notation. If you subsequently assign a name to the range in Excel and perform a manual update, Word will continue to reference it by address, not by name.

To fix the reference by hand, do the following.

1 Choose Edit, Links in Word.

You'll see a dialog box similar to the one shown in Figure 23-4, and in the Item column for your link, you'll find the R1C1 address of the source table.

2 Click Change Source.

A file-browser dialog box will appear.

3 Click the Item button in this dialog box to get to the Set Item dialog box, shown here.

4 Delete the R1C1 range reference, type your new range name, and click OK. You'll be returned to the file-browser.

5 Select the name of the file in which your table resides, and click Open.

6 Back in the Links dialog box, click OK, and your link will henceforth know its name.

Linking with Hyperlinks

An alternative way to create a link between a Word document and an Excel document is to use hyperlinks. With an Excel range on the Clipboard, you can choose Edit, Paste As Hyperlink in Word. As Figure 23-5 shows, each cell in the copied range becomes a separate, individual hyperlink. Each hyperlink points to the upper left corner cell (not necessarily the active cell) in the copied range. Formats are preserved (but each cell gets a hyperlink underline unless you change the way Word normally displays hyperlinks); graphical elements are omitted from the copy.

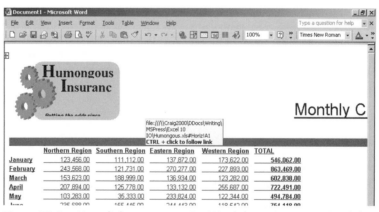

Figure 23-5. Hyperlinks can connect a Word document to an Excel document, but they are not updated when the source changes.

The principal disadvantage of using hyperlinks instead of OLE links (that is, paste-linking) is that hyperlinks don't get updated when the source changes. A hyperlink can make it easy for you or another user to find your way back to the data source, but it provides no assurance that your Word document is faithful to the source.

Using the Object Command

The Clipboard methods just described are fine for importing existing Excel tables into Word documents. If you're creating a table from scratch, you have the option of using an alternative method—by choosing Insert, Object in Word. When you choose Insert, Object, the Object dialog box opens. Click the Create New tab, and then select Microsoft Excel Worksheet, Word displays a window into a blank Excel worksheet, as Figure 23-6 shows.

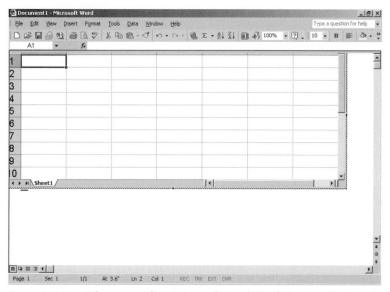

Figure 23-6. When you select Microsoft Excel Worksheet on the Create New tab of Word's Object dialog box, a window into Excel appears in your Word document.

Here you can create your table, taking advantage of all of Excel's formatting and calculation tools. When your table is ready for inclusion in your Word document, click outside the Excel window. The result is an Excel object embedded in your Word file—exactly what you get if you create the table initially in Excel, copy it to the Clipboard, and then choose Microsoft Excel Worksheet Object from Word's Paste Special dialog box.

The table that Word embeds will have the same row-and-column dimensions as the Excel window in which you created the table. That is, empty cells will be embedded along with populated ones. If you have to scroll to populate certain cells, some of your Excel table will not be embedded. In short, you need to adjust the size of the Excel window so that it includes all the rows and columns that you want in Word—and no more.

While you're working in the Excel window, it is possible to choose File, Open in Excel to open an existing workbook. When you do this, the workbook you open is transferred as formatted text (not as an object) into a new Word document, exactly as if you opened a new document in Word and chose Insert, File. We'll look at this approach to importing Excel tables in the next section.

599

The Object dialog box displayed when you choose Insert, Object also has a Create From File tab. Here you can specify an existing Excel file and embed (or link) the entire file into your Word document.

Using the File Command

By choosing Insert, File in Word, you can copy an entire Excel workbook—or a specified portion of a workbook—to a Word file. You can't copy embedded charts, chart sheets, or any other graphical elements with this technique, but you can copy the contents of any cell or range of cells. The result in Word is a table that maintains all the formatting of the original.

To use this feature, follow these steps:

1 Choose Insert, File.

2 In the file browser that appears, set the Files Of Type field to All Files, and then select your Excel file.

The Open Worksheet dialog box shown in Figure 23-7 appears.

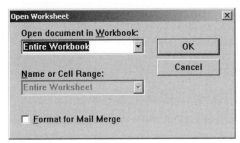

Figure 23-7. With Word, you can import an entire Excel file or only a particular worksheet or range.

3 To import the entire Excel workbook, click OK.

Each populated worksheet in the imported file will appear, one after the other, with a single line space separating the worksheets. Unpopulated regions of your worksheets and blank worksheets are omitted. Blank rows and columns above and to the left of populated regions are not imported.

To restrict the import to a particular worksheet, select it in the Open Document In Workbook field. When you specify anything but Entire Workbook in this field, the Name or Cell Range field becomes available. To restrict the import to a particular range, type that range in this field.

> ## Troubleshooting
>
> ### My Range is Invalid
>
> Unfortunately, although the Name Or Cell Range field clearly implies that you can specify the name of a range on the worksheet you want to import, the fact is that you can't. You'll get an "invalid range" error if you try. This bug has no workaround; you have to specify a range address, not a range name.

Using Excel Charts in Word Documents

You can insert an Excel chart into a Word document by copying it from the Clipboard or by choosing Insert, Object in Word. If you paste an Excel chart from the Clipboard into your Word document, the chart arrives in picture format. The smart tag menu that appears gives you the option of switching to an embedded chart object or to a chart object linked to the source file.

As with an Excel table, you can choose Edit, Paste Special in Word to control the format in which your chart is pasted into Excel. If you copied your chart from a chart sheet in your Excel document, your format choices are Microsoft Excel Chart Object, Picture, Bitmap, and Picture (Enhanced Metafile). Pasting the Object format embeds the entire Excel document, not just the chart sheet, so this option has the potential to enlarge your Word document dramatically (particularly if your workbook includes a lot of information in addition to the chart you copied). The other three options generate pictures. As mentioned, Microsoft says the Picture format consumes the least amount of memory, but you should experiment to see which generates the most satisfactory image in your Word document. If you copy from an embedded chart (you must first select the chart's Chart Area to do this), the Picture and Bitmap options become unavailable.

> ## Troubleshooting
>
> ### My Chart is Truncated!
>
> If you copy a chart-sheet chart sized to fit the window frame and you're working in a high-resolution mode, you might be trying to move more pixels onto the Clipboard than your system can accommodate. When you paste a chart into Word under these circumstances, your chart might be truncated. To correct the problem, go back to Excel, move the chart onto a worksheet (right-click the chart, choose Location from the shortcut menu, and specify a worksheet), and then copy the resulting embedded chart. If you still get a truncated chart in Word, try reducing the size of the embedded chart in Excel.

To edit a chart object embedded in your Word document, double-click it. Because Word embeds the entire Excel document from which the chart originated, you'll have access to both the chart and its supporting data when you enter Edit mode. Thus you can change both the appearance of the chart (that is, its formatting characteristics) and the data the chart depicts.

If the chart object you're editing started out as an embedded chart in Excel (that is, a chart not displayed on a separate chart sheet), you'll find that when you enter Edit mode, Excel displays the chart on a separate chart sheet. Don't be dismayed by this; Excel isn't doing anything to the layout of the Excel workbook from which you imported the chart. In fact, it's not touching that workbook; when you edit an embedded chart object, you're working only with that embedded copy, not with the original document.

To paste-link an Excel chart into a Word document, choose Edit, Copy in Excel to post the chart to the Clipboard. Then choose Edit, Paste Special in Word. Select the format in which you want the chart rendered, select the Paste Link option, and then click OK. You can paste-link any format except Picture (Enhanced Metafile).

You can also embed an Excel chart by choosing Insert, Object in Word and then selecting Microsoft Excel Chart on the Create New tab of the Object dialog box. Word initially displays a dummy Excel chart that plots food, gas, and motel expenses for the months January through June (see Figure 23-8). Knowing that this is not likely to be exactly the chart you had in mind, it also takes you directly into Edit mode. There you'll find a single worksheet (Sheet1) and a chart sheet containing the dummy chart. You can overwrite the expense-report information on Sheet1 with the data you want to plot.

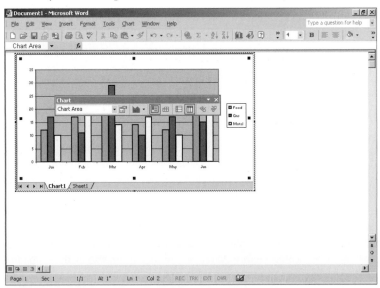

Figure 23-8. Not knowing what you want to plot, Word generates a dummy expense-report chart when you choose Insert, Object.

Using Excel to Supply
Mail-Merge Data to Word

Microsoft Word includes a Mail Merge Wizard that facilitates the batch creation of letters, e-mail messages, envelopes, mailing labels, and directories. You can use Excel tables (as well as many other types of data source) to supply names, addresses, phone numbers, and so on, for use by the Wizard.

> **note** If you have used mail-merge tools in earlier versions of Word, you'll find that they've changed significantly in Word 2002.

Before you feed data from Excel into Word's Mail Merge Wizard, be sure your Excel worksheet is well structured for this purpose. Your table should meet the following criteria:

- Each column in the first row should be a field name, such as Title, Salutation, First Name, Middle Name, Last Name, Address1, Address2, and so on.

- Each field name should be unique.

- Every piece of information that you want to be able to manipulate separately in your merge document should be recorded in a separate field. In a form letter, for example, you probably want to work with first and last names separately, so that you can use them both in an address block, but use the last name only (with a salutation or title) at the beginning of the letter. Therefore, your Excel table should have separate fields for first name and last name.

- Each row should provide information about a particular item. In a mailing list, for example, each row would include information about a particular recipient.

- Your table should have no blank rows.

To use Word's Mail Merge Wizard, follow these steps:

1 Choose Tools, Letters And Mailings, Mail Merge Wizard.

2 The Wizard has six steps. To use an Excel table, choose Use An Existing List and click the Browse button in step 2.

3 Navigate to the file you want to use, and click Open.

4 The Select Table dialog box that appears (see Figure 23-9 on the next page) includes an entry for each worksheet in your Excel workbook, with a dollar sign appended to each sheet name. Specify the worksheet that contains the records you want to merge, and click OK.

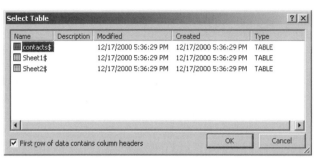

Figure 23-9. In the Select Table dialog box, you specify the worksheet that contains the records you want to merge.

5 The Mail Merge Recipients dialog box appears (see Figure 23-10), allowing you to sort and filter the data source. Initially the check box to the left of each record is selected, which means that all records will be included in your merge. To remove particular items, clear their check boxes. (If you want only a few records, you can start by clicking the Clear All button. Then you can select just those records you want to include.)

Figure 23-10. In the Mail Merge Recipients dialog box, you can filter and sort the data source.

For more efficient filtering, you can use the arrows to the left of each field name. These function like the auto-filter feature in Excel, although, for reasons we can only guess, they employ a markedly different user interface. To restrict the list to a particular set of records (all those with zip codes greater than or equal to 90000, for example), click the arrow next to any field (no, it doesn't have to be the field you care about), choose Advanced, and then fill out the Filter And Sort dialog box shown in Figure 23-11.

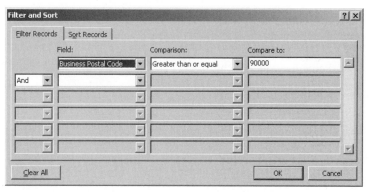

Figure 23-11. We've used the Filter And Sort dialog box to limit our list to ZIP codes that start with 9.

In the Field field, choose the field that will be your filtering criterion. In the Comparison field, choose a comparison operation, and in the Compare To field, specify a comparison value. If you need more than one filtering criterion, select And or Or at the start of the second line, and then continue with more field names, operators, and comparison criteria.

You can use the Sort Records tab to change the order in which your data will be fed to the mail-merge mechanism. If you're sorting by one field only, however, you'll find it simpler to click the field heading in the Mail Merge Recipients dialog box (refer to Figure 23-10). Click a heading to generate an ascending sort by that heading; a second click turns it into a descending sort.

When you have your data as you want it, click OK to return to the Wizard. In the remaining three steps, you can create your merge document (the document that uses your data records), preview the results, and then carry out the merge. For more information about using Word's Letters And Mailings tools, including the Mail Merge Wizard, consult *Microsoft Word Version 2002 Inside Out*, also published by Microsoft Press.

Using Excel Tables in PowerPoint

You can insert an Excel range into a PowerPoint slide by pasting it from the Clipboard or by choosing Insert, Object in PowerPoint. With an Excel table on the Clipboard, PowerPoint's default paste format (the one you get by pressing Ctrl+V) is Microsoft Excel Worksheet Object—which means you get an entire Excel workbook embedded in your PowerPoint slide. If you get this result unintentionally, click the smart tag, and choose one of the alternatives offered on the smart tag menu—Table or Picture Of Table. Table uses the HTML format, and Picture Of Table uses the Picture format. This last conserves memory and is probably ideal when you need to add Excel data to a slide but don't care about the ability to edit that data.

If editing is important, you'll probably want to stick with the default object format and not worry about the impact this makes on the size of your PowerPoint file. When you want to edit the table, double-click it. PowerPoint supports editing in place, so you'll remain in PowerPoint, but you'll be able to use Excel's formatting and calculation features.

To paste formats other than the object format, picture, or HTML, choose Edit, Paste Special in PowerPoint, instead of Edit, Paste. Your format options are similar to those available in Word. For more information, see the section "Using Paste Special to Control the Format of Your Table" on page 593. Note, however, that the Formatted Text (RTF) option does not preserve the appearance that your table has in Excel. This option appears, in fact, to be exactly the same as Unformatted Text.

You'll also want to use Paste Special if you need to link your PowerPoint slide to the Excel file that provided the pasted table.

To create a new Excel table from scratch within a PowerPoint slide, choose Insert, Object, choose the Create New option, and select Microsoft Excel Worksheet. PowerPoint adds a single-worksheet workbook to the current slide and takes you directly into Edit mode, where you have access to all of Excel's formatting and other features, as shown in Figure 23-12. When you've finished creating your Excel table, click any other part of the slide to return to PowerPoint.

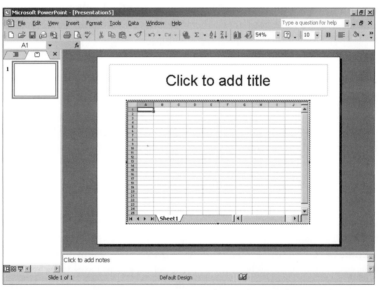

Figure 23-12. When you select Microsoft Excel Worksheet in the Object dialog box, a window into Excel appears in your PowerPoint document.

Using Excel to create charts for your PowerPoint slides is essentially like using Excel to create tables. You can copy an Excel chart to the Clipboard and then paste it into PowerPoint, or you can choose Insert, Object and select Microsoft Excel Chart. If you use the latter route, PowerPoint presents you with the same gas, oil, and motel expense chart that we saw earlier in this chapter (refer to Figure 23-8), with a different set of colors than Word uses. You can modify the associated worksheet to generate the chart you need.

If you paste a chart from the Clipboard onto a PowerPoint slide, PowerPoint embeds your entire Excel workbook by default. Using the smart tag menu, you can switch to a picture of the chart—which should suit your needs fine if you won't subsequently need to edit the chart.

Part 8

Creating Charts

Basic Charting Techniques

Microsoft Excel includes a powerful and versatile charting engine. Over the years, Microsoft has continued to add both more analytic features and more presentation capabilities to this component of the program. You can now choose from an extensive variety of common business and technical chart types, and you can enhance the appearance of your charts with pictures, clip art, WordArt text, lines, arrows, and many other devices that help make a stronger visual impact.

This chapter covers the basics of chart creation. Chapter 25, "Enhancing the Appearance of Your Charts," shows you how to tailor the appearance of a chart as well as how to add your own customized chart types to the program's list of chart types. We also look at some ways to simplify the appearance of your charts in order to create more immediate impact on others.

In Chapter 26, "Working with Chart Data," we look at the procedures for modifying the content of your charts—adding and removing data, adding trendlines and error bars, and so on. In Chapter 27, "Advanced Charting Techniques," we discuss some of the less obvious things that you can do with Excel charts—such as creating charts that update automatically as you extend their source data.

Creating a New Chart

The snappiest way to create a chart is to select some data and press F11. Excel blasts your data—no questions asked—into whatever chart style is the current default, placing the result on a new chart sheet.

The F11 shortcut is a holdover from the earliest days of Excel, when all charts lived on separate chart sheets and before the invention of wizards. Nowadays the way Excel "expects" you to

611

create a chart is by selecting some data and clicking the Chart Wizard tool on the Standard toolbar. (Alternatively, choose Insert, Chart.) These actions awaken the wizard, which presents a sequence of four helpful dialog boxes.

If you're the kind of person who likes to get things done in a hurry, you might want to remember the F11 technique. You can always modify the resulting default chart—and even relocate it back to your worksheet if you don't want it on a separate chart sheet. (To move a chart from a separate chart sheet to a worksheet location, choose Chart, Location and select the second option. Excel deletes the chart sheet after moving the chart.)

Before we look at what the wizard has to offer, here are some points to note about data selection: As usual in Excel, you can select only a single cell in a block of data, and the program will figure out the extent of your data block correctly and automatically. But if you choose to select the entire block yourself, instead of a single cell, be sure you've really got the whole thing—that, for example, you haven't omitted any of the row or column headings. That way the wizard will often—maybe even usually—get the category-axis and legend labels right.

---

tip   **Add a blank row**

If you expect to be adding more data to your graph as time goes by, consider including a blank row at the bottom of the original selection. If you add data later by inserting a new row above this blank row and putting the new data in the incoming row, your chart will automatically incorporate the new data. There are other ways to create "dynamic" charts that automatically update themselves when your data expands, but this approach is the simplest.

Step 1: Choosing a Chart Type

The wizard's Step 1 dialog box, shown in Figure 24-1, presents a gallery of chart types and sub-types. Notice the Press And Hold To View Sample button and that the dialog box includes two tabs, Standard Types and Custom Types.

Below the gallery on the right side of the dialog box, Excel presents a short description of each standard chart sub-type. If the description isn't clear, or if you simply want to see what your data will look like in the current sub-type, click Press And Hold To View Sample. Excel responds by showing you what you'd see if you went straight to the Finish button. (The preview might not be exact because of differences in aspect ratio.)

On the Custom Types tab, you'll find a gallery of fancy customized charts. If you're new to charting in Excel, you can get an idea of some of the program's formatting power by strolling through this custom gallery. Note that the big window on the right side of the dialog box shows each custom chart type with your own data.

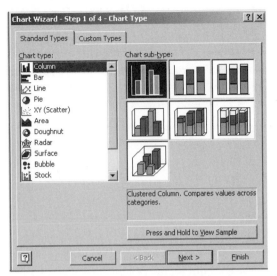

Figure 24-1. Use the wizard's first dialog box to select a chart type and sub-type.

After you've created your own customized charts, you can add them to the Custom Types tab of this dialog box. To add a customized chart, right-click the chart, choose Chart Type, go to the Custom Types tab, click User-Defined, and then click Add.

Step 2: Specifying the Data to Plot

In the wizard's Step 2 dialog box, shown in Figure 24-2, you can confirm that Excel has properly understood your data selection. In most cases, you'll find that it has—but not in all cases. If the program has misunderstood your intentions, you should be able to tell at a glance by looking at the sample window at the top of the Data Range tab.

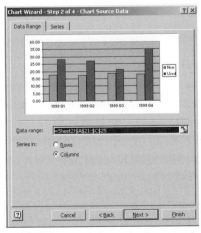

Figure 24-2. In the wizard's second dialog box, you can confirm that the program has properly parsed your data selection.

If you intended to plot a larger or smaller range than you see in the sample window, you can set matters right on the Data Range line. If the program plotted columns as data series when you wanted rows instead, you can fix that with the Rows and Columns options. In Figure 24-2, for example, the program has given us two data series, each consisting of four points. If instead we wanted four data series, each consisting of two points, we would select the Rows option.

---

tip **Plot multiple areas**

The data you plot does not have to lie in contiguous ranges. You could, for example, plot every other column in a data block. To select noncontiguous ranges, hold down Ctrl while you select each range. Then activate the Chart Wizard.

Excel parses your data selection on the assumption that you want more points than series. For example, if you plot a selection that consists of three columns and 20 rows, the program will assume that the columns represent series and that the rows represent points. If the number of rows and columns in your selection is the same, Excel plots by row—making each row a data series.

The Series tab of the Step 2 dialog box allows you to make additional corrections. For example, suppose you've given Excel a two-column range to plot, in which the first column consists of years. Excel has erroneously construed the years to be a data series. Figure 24-3 illustrates the problem.

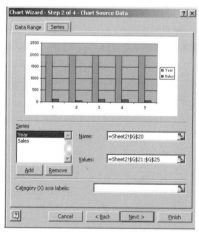

Figure 24-3. Excel has mistakenly plotted year labels as a data series. We can use the Series tab of the Step 2 dialog box to fix the problem.

The Series list on the Series tab shows the name of each data series. The names here are the labels that will appear in your chart's legend if you decide to include a legend. When you select a name in the Series list, the Name field shows the worksheet cell from which Excel derived the name of the selected series, and the Values field shows the cells that contribute data to this series. The Category Axis Labels field, meanwhile, shows which cells Excel is using for the labels that appear along the category axis. In Figure 24-3, this field is blank; Excel will use default category-axis labels (1, 2, 3, and so on) instead of worksheet text.

To correct the problem shown in Figure 24-3, we need to select the Year series and click the Remove button. Then we need to select the Category Axis Labels field and enter the range that contains our year labels.

InsideOut

Be aware of dates

If you select a column of years and select one or more unlabeled columns of numbers, Excel will not recognize that you want the years to be category-axis labels. Instead it will treat the years as a data series. Amazingly enough, it will do this even if you have applied the Text format to your years. You could prefix each year with an apostrophe as you enter it on the worksheet, but, unfortunately, Excel will think you have made a mistake when you do this. The best way to handle this is to use the Series tab of the Step 2 dialog box. If Excel has made a mistake and treated category-axis labels as a data series, you can correct it there. (See "Step 2: Specifying the Data to Plot," page 613.)

Step 3: Choosing Chart Options

The wizard's third dialog box is where you make your first aesthetic decisions—such as whether to include gridlines, a legend, or data labels. You can also add titles to your chart and its axes here. Each tab in the dialog box shows you the effect of your decisions immediately. Bear in mind as you work through this dialog box that you can always change your mind later.

Specifying Chart and Axis Titles

The Titles tab lets you assign a title for the chart and descriptive text for each axis. Excel displays the text using default fonts, alignments, and positions. Any titles you create become ordinary text-box objects, and you can reposition, realign, reformat, and edit them after the chart has been created.

Note that the Excel charting user interface does not give you a way to derive title text from worksheet cells. That is, you can't type a cell reference in a title field. Presumably that's because Excel's designers assumed that you would have no need for a dynamic title (one that would change as a worksheet cell changed). If that assumption was wrong in your case, you can rectify the matter by writing a short VBA (Visual Basic for Applications) procedure that copies a cell's contents into the active chart's title. Something like the following does the trick:

```
Sub GetTitleFromA1()
    Dim strTitleText As String
    StrTitleText = Range("a1").Value
    With ActiveChart
        .HasTitle = True
        .ChartTitle.Text = strTitleText
    End With
End Sub
```

InsideOut

Add the title manually

Excel is pretty smart about recognizing category-axis labels and series names (legend labels) in your chart-data selection. But it's not clever at all about getting chart titles from your data selection. You'll have to add the title manually, using the Chart Wizard's Step 3 dialog box. Moreover, if your data includes only one chart series and a text item appears above that series, Excel will treat that text as both a series name and a chart title—almost certainly not what you want. You'll have to fix that in the Step 3 dialog box as well.

Displaying or Hiding Axes

In all chart types except for pie and doughnut charts, Excel includes value and category axes by default. (Typically, the value axis is what your algebra teacher would have called the *y*-axis, and the category axis is the *x*-axis.) Certain chart types include a secondary value axis by default; see the Line—Column on 2 Axes type on the Custom Types tab of the Step 1 dialog box for an example. Whatever Excel proposes to give you, however, you may choose to omit if your needs suggest a leaner, axis-free appearance. Note, however, that if you choose to omit an axis—by clearing its check box on the Axes tab of the Step 3 dialog box—all labels associated with that axis are suppressed as well.

For more information about changing the appearance of axes, see "Working with Axes" on page 639.

Category vs. Time Scaling

In most cases, if your category-axis data consists of dates, Excel recognizes that and automatically applies "time scaling," as opposed to "category scaling," to the axis. Time scaling differs from category scaling in the following ways:

● Excel positions all data points in accordance with their chronological locations. For example, if a time-scaled axis includes points for January 1,

Chapter 24

January 2, and January 6, the January 2 point appears closer to the January 1 point than to the January 6 point.

- Excel automatically plots time-series points in chronological order, whether or not the data range is sorted chronologically.

- Excel uses the smallest time difference between your data points as its base unit, but you can switch to a larger base unit to get a different perspective on your data. For example, if you plot daily stock prices, Excel uses 1 day as its base unit. But you can switch to a weekly or monthly view by changing the base unit. For information about changing the base unit, see "Changing the Base Unit" on page 646.

In most cases, time scaling is a great convenience to you, and you should accept Excel's decision to apply it. If you prefer category scaling, however, select the Category option on the Axes tab of the Step 3 dialog box. (The default selection here is Automatic, which means "let Excel decide.")

InsideOut

Use fully qualified dates

You might suppose that if you plotted including a column with the text labels Jan, Feb, Mar, and so on, Excel would recognize the month names and give you time scaling by default. It will not. Although Excel knows that Jan, Feb, and Mar are members of a series (you can drag the fill handle to extend those labels through the rest of the year), the charting engine doesn't realize that those labels have anything to do with the calendar. To get time scaling with month labels, abbreviated or otherwise, enter the values on the worksheet as fully qualified dates—for example, 1,1,2001; 2,1,2001; and so on. Format them to taste (the custom numeric format *mmm* will give you three-letter month abbreviations), and then plot.

Manual Scaling and Other Axis Formatting Options

Excel insists on scaling the value axis to begin at 0 (or below 0 if you're plotting negative numbers), even if all your values are in the stratosphere. This often results in a chart where all the values are scrunched together in a narrow visual range and where differences between one value and the next are hard to discern. Unfortunately, you can't override the default scaling while you're creating your chart. But you can do it later; see "Working with Axes" on page 639.

You can also use procedures described in Chapter 25 "Enhancing the Appearance of Your Charts" to change the font and alignment of axis labels, to change the numeric formatting used for values and dates, and to change the tick-mark interval, line style, or color of your axes.

Displaying Gridlines

Most of Excel's chart types use some gridlines by default. You can add gridlines or remove them by clicking the Gridlines tab of the Step 3 dialog box.

Major gridlines emanate from axis subdivisions called major tick marks. Minor gridlines are drawn from further subdivisions known as minor tick marks. Excel determines the positions of these tick marks automatically, but you can use formatting commands to change their positions. You can also alter the colors of the gridlines themselves.

Note that the Gridlines tab doesn't appear if you're building a pie or doughnut chart, because these chart types do not use axes.

Be aware that major value-axis gridlines in certain kinds of three-dimensional charts make data points appear to have less than their true value. In Figure 24-4, for example, the data points have the exact integer values 5, 6, 7, 8, 9, and 10. But the gridlines make each point appear to be about 0.25 less. The data markers are drawn to the height they would have in a simple two-dimensional view, whereas the gridlines are drawn in three-dimensional perspective. To avoid confusing the viewer of this kind of chart, you might want to add data labels that show each point's actual value.

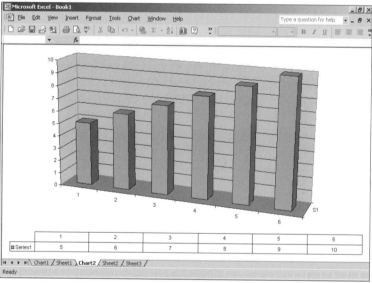

Figure 24-4. Each point on this chart is an integer, but the gridlines make the points appear to be somewhat less than their true value.

Displaying or Hiding a Legend

Excel normally displays a legend on the right side of the chart. You can choose a different location for the legend or dispense with it altogether by clicking the Legend tab in the Step 3 dialog box. The Legend tab offers five standard locations: Bottom, Corner Top, Right, and Left. You're not limited to those locations, however; once you've created the chart, you can move its legend around at will with your mouse.

Displaying Data Labels

The Chart Wizard can attach various kinds of labels to data markers. Pie and doughnut slices, for example, can be identified with percentages, absolute values, or both. Columns in a column graph and markers in a line graph can have labels indicating the value of each point or the category-axis text associated with each point, and so on. Excel does not display data labels by default. To add them, click the Data Labels tab in the Step 3 dialog box, shown in Figure 24-5.

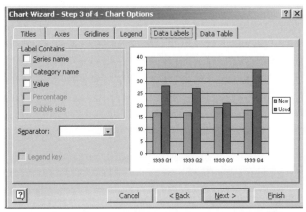

Figure 24-5. The Chart Wizard lets you assign certain kinds of labels to data points.

As the figure shows, the Chart Wizard does not provide a way to label data points with text other than category-axis labels. You can use other descriptive text, but the process is laborious. First create a chart using one of the built-in data-label options. Then select each label in turn and replace it with the text you actually want to use.

For a VBA procedure to automate this process, using the contents of a worksheet range for the label text, see "Generating Useful Data Labels on XY (Scatter) Charts" on page 637.

Adding a Data Table

Depending on the type of chart you're creating, Excel might give you the option of including a data table along with the chart. A data table is simply a table of the values from which the chart is derived. To include a data table, click the Data Table tab in the Step 3 dialog box, shown in Figure 24-6 on the following page.

Chapter 24

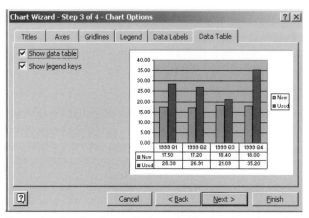

Figure 24-6. Excel can display a table showing the values from which a chart is built.

Note that if you decide to include a data table, you can also include legend keys beside each data series. Legend keys show the color or marker style used for each series. If you include the legend keys, you can probably dispense with the legend itself, leaving yourself more room for the plot.

InsideOut

Paste-link a picture for greater table flexibility

Unlike other optional chart elements, such as legends and titles, a data table can appear only in one position—directly below the chart. You can't drag a data table into some other location.

Step 4: Telling Excel Where to Put Your Chart

Excel can create your new chart either as an object embedded on a worksheet or as a separate chart sheet. The fourth and final dialog box presented by the Chart Wizard lets you express your preference. However you decide, you can always change your mind later by right-clicking the chart and choosing Location from the shortcut menu.

Creating Combination (Overlay) Charts

Sometimes you'll find that a chart with multiple data series becomes more intelligible if you plot one or more series in a style that contrasts with the other series. For example, you might want to plot one series as columns and another as a line. To create this kind of overlay chart, first see if the combination you're looking for is already represented on the Custom Types tab of the Chart Wizard's Step 1 dialog box. If it's not, follow these steps

1 Create the chart using one of the standard chart types.

2 On the finished chart, right-click the data series that you want to appear in a contrasting style.

3 From the shortcut menu, choose Chart Type.

4 Select the style you want, and select the Apply To Selection check box.

5 Click OK.

Note that while you can make some truly awful combination charts this way (try a mixture of bars and columns, for example), Excel draws the line at particular combos. No matter how much you may desire it, for example, you cannot combine a pie chart with a line chart.

Changing a Chart's Size and Position

If you place the chart as an object on an existing worksheet, Excel creates the chart in a default size and position. The chart becomes a worksheet object, and you can change its size as you would that of any other object, by selecting it and dragging handles. You can move it by dragging any part of the chart outside its plot area.

To change a chart's size while keeping its center stationary, hold down Ctrl while you drag. To change a chart's size while maintaining its current aspect ratio, hold down Shift while you drag a corner handle.

When you resize a chart, Excel adjusts the size of all chart text. If you're not happy with the adjustment, you can use formatting commands to increase or decrease the text size.

If you place the new chart on a separate chart sheet, Excel creates it at a standard size. By default, the chart is resized as you resize the window. If you prefer to have the chart stay at the same size when you resize the window, activate the chart sheet, choose Tools Options, go to the Chart tab, and clear the Chart Sizes With Window Frame check box.

> **note** If you use chart sheets and you sometimes change screen resolution, be sure to keep the Chart Sizes With Window Frame check box (on the Chart tab of the Options dialog box) selected. Otherwise, when you switch to a lower resolution, a chart that neatly filled the frame at the higher resolution will become partly invisible at the lower resolution

Plotting Hidden Cells

Excel normally ignores any hidden rows or columns in a chart's data range. If you want hidden cells to be plotted, create the chart in the normal way. Select any element of the chart, choose Tools, Options, go to the Chart tab, and then clear the Plot Visible Cells Only check box.

InsideOut

Don't hold down Ctrl

If you select the chart object rather than an element of the chart, the Plot Visible Cells Only check box is unavailable. If you see clear (white) handles around the perimeter of the chart, you've selected the chart object. Be sure you're not holding down Ctrl, and then select again.

Handling Missing Values

Excel normally skips over any missing points (blank cells) in your data range. You have two other options:

- Plot the missing points as zeros.
- Interpolate the missing points.

If you interpolate, Excel draws a straight line to bridge the gap created by a missing value; it does not actually interpolate a new point. Hence, this option is meaningful only in line, xy (scatter), and radar charts, and only in data series that connect points with lines (that is, it's not meaningful in a series that uses unconnected markers).

To change the way Excel handles missing points in a chart, select the chart, choose Tools, Options, go to the Chart tab (see Figure 24-7), and choose an option button under Plot Empty Cells As.

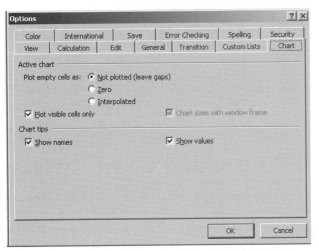

Figure 24-7. On the Chart tab of the Options dialog box, you can change the way Excel handles missing points in a data range.

Changing the Default Chart Type

Excel's "factory" default chart type is a two-dimensional clustered column chart—that is, a vertical bar chart in which series are plotted side by side along a single category axis. To make a different type of chart the default

1 Create a chart.

2 Select the chart, and choose Chart, Chart Type.

3 In the Chart Type dialog box, click Set As Default Chart.

Charts that use two or more chart types (for example, a chart that plots one series as columns and another series as a line) cannot be the default chart type. Other kinds of customized chart types can be the default, however. If you find yourself using a particular combination of chart formatting settings again and again, add that chart to the Custom Types tab of the Chart Type dialog box, and then make your new custom type the default.

Printing Charts

To print a chart that appears on a separate chart sheet, simply activate the sheet and follow the printing procedures described in Chapter 10. To print an embedded chart object, you can do either of the following:

- To print the chart by itself, select it and then choose File, Print.

- To print the chart with surrounding worksheet data, select any part of the worksheet, but not the chart. Then choose File, Print.

Saving, Opening, and Protecting Charts

Charts are saved with the workbook in which they reside. To save a chart, simply save the workbook file. After you create a chart, you can choose Tools, Protection to lock the worksheet or chart sheet containing the chart. Then other people can't change the sheet and, therefore, the chart. The Protection command works the same way for both worksheets and chart sheets.

Working with Embedded Chart Objects

As mentioned, a chart embedded on a worksheet is an "object," just like an embedded picture, calendar control, or anything else that you might add to your worksheet via the Insert, Object command. You can assign a macro to it, and move it forward or back relative to other objects, by using the same kinds of actions that you would apply to other kinds of objects. For details about working with objects, see Chapter 9, "Advanced Formatting and Editing Techniques."

The one important point you have to remember about working with a chart object is that to select it *as an object*, you need to hold down Ctrl while you click. Otherwise, you'll be selecting an element of the chart, not the entire object. When you've selected the object, white (clear) handles appear around its perimeter, and a name, such as "Chart 1," appears in the name box. If you see black handles around the chart, you've selected the chart area (an element of the chart), not the chart object.

From the VBA perspective, an embedded chart is a member of the ChartObjects class, whose parent is the worksheet on which the chart resides. You could select a chart, for example, with something like the following:

```
Worksheets("Sheet1").ChartObjects("Chart1").Select
```

You can give an embedded chart a descriptive name by Ctrl-selecting it and typing over the default name that appears in the name box. In the foregoing example, if you named your chart "My cool radar chart," you could access it using ChartObjects("My cool radar chart"), instead of ChartObjects("Chart1").

Enhancing the Appearance of Your Charts

After you've created a chart, you can do many things to modify its appearance. Microsoft Excel offers a wide assortment of commands for tailoring your charts to suit your tastes, presentation needs, and company's visual standards. Those commands are the subject of this chapter.

Working with the Chart Menu and Chart Toolbar

The first step in customizing any chart is to select it. If you saved the chart on a separate chart sheet, open that sheet. If you embedded it on a worksheet, select it there. When you open a chart sheet or select a chart object, Excel replaces the Data menu with the Chart menu and displays a handy Chart toolbar, shown in Figure 25-1 on the next page.

The first four commands on the Chart menu open dialog boxes that are almost identical to the four dialog boxes presented by the Chart Wizard. Thus you can use the Chart menu to revise any decision you make while creating your chart. (You can also return to the full Chart Wizard by selecting your chart and clicking the Chart Wizard tool on the Standard toolbar.) If you create a column chart, for example, and decide you'd rather have a bar chart, select the Chart Type command from the Chart menu. This takes you to a dialog box almost identical to the one pictured in the first step of the Chart Wizard. If you want to add titles to your axes, choose Chart, Chart Options, and then click the Titles tab. Any chart-building choice you can make using the Chart Wizard, you can also make after the fact using the Chart menu.

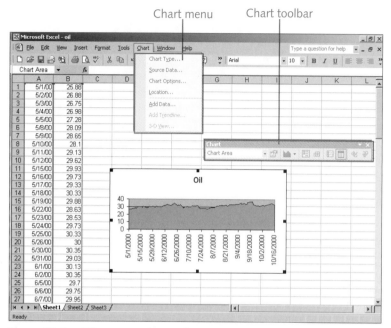

Chart menu   Chart toolbar

Figure 25-1. When you select a chart, Excel displays a Chart menu and a Chart toolbar.

Figure 25-2 lists each of the Chart toolbar's features. This toolbar normally appears whenever you select a chart and disappears when you select anything else. Most users find it helpful and unobtrusive. Unfortunately, unlike the Office Assistant, it's not smart enough to jump out of the way if you drag a chart on top of it. If the toolbar's presence becomes an irritant, you can click its Close box to send it packing. To make the toolbar visible again, right-click any toolbar and select Chart. (Alternatively, choose View, Toolbars, Chart.) Note that if you dismiss the Chart toolbar while you have a chart selected, Excel assumes that you really don't like the thing and doesn't bother you with it the next time you create or select a chart.

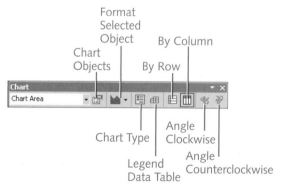

Format
Selected
Object   By Column

Chart
Objects   By Row

Chart Type | Angle
           | Clockwise

Legend | Angle
Data Table | Counterclockwise

Figure 25-2. The Chart toolbar's most useful feature is the Chart Objects list, which you can use to select an element of your chart for formatting purposes.

As with any other toolbar, you can move, dock, or reshape the Chart toolbar. Tug on its bottom border, for example, and the toolbar transforms itself from a long, narrow rectangle into a square-like shape. Moreover, like other floating toolbars in Excel 2002, the toolbar fades gracefully into semitransparency if you ignore it for a while.

If you use certain tools on the Chart toolbar often but others never, consider removing the tools you never use. Right-click the toolbar (or any other toolbar), choose Customize, and then drag away the tools you don't want. To restore the deleted tools, right-click a toolbar, choose Customize, click the Toolbars tab, select Chart, and click Reset.

Selecting Chart Elements

To change the appearance of any chart element, such as the legend or the category axis, first select the element (or right-click it to access its shortcut menu directly). Sometimes, in a complex chart, the easiest way to do this is to select the item in the Chart Objects list, on the Chart toolbar. If you select the object by clicking directly on the chart, you can confirm that you've selected the item you want by glancing at the Chart Objects list or the Name box (to the left of the formula bar near the upper left corner of your screen). The ScreenTip that appears when you hover over a chart element can also assist you in making the right selection. If you don't see a ScreenTip when you hover, this feature is probably turned off. You can turn it back on by choosing Tools, Options, clicking the Chart tab, and selecting Show Names.

Copying Formats from One Chart to Another

Most of this chapter is devoted to procedures for changing the appearance of particular chart elements. However, if you've already got one chart set up just the way you want it, you can use that chart as a model for others.

To transfer the formats of one chart to another:

1 Select the chart area of the chart whose formats you want to copy.

2 Choose Edit, Copy. If the Copy command is unavailable, you haven't selected the chart area of the source chart.

3 Select the other chart.

4 Choose Edit, Paste Special, and select the Formats option.

Note that when you copy formats from one chart to another, you copy all formatting decisions, including any scaling choices you made. If your second chart plots values in a different range from your first chart, chances are you're not going to be satisfied with the outcome of the format copy. Not to worry; adjust the scaling on the second chart after you've completed the copy operation.

Adding a Customized Chart to the Chart Wizard Gallery

If you want to use a particular combination of chart formats repeatedly, it's best to create a new entry in Excel's chart type gallery. First create the chart that you want to serve as a model for other charts. Select the chart, and then choose Chart, Chart Type. Click the Custom Types tab, click the User-Defined option in the Select From group, and click Add. In the Add Custom Chart Type dialog box, supply a name for the custom chart and (if you like) a description of it.

To delete a customized chart from the gallery, return to the gallery, click the User-Defined option, select the name of the customized chart type you want to delete, click the Delete button, and then answer the confirmation prompt.

Repositioning Chart Elements with the Mouse

You can move the chart title, axis titles, data labels, and legend by dragging them with the mouse. You can also use your mouse to explode a pie slice or doughnut bite. Note, in particular, that you can adjust the positions of individual data labels without moving an entire series of labels and that, although the Chart Wizard can create a legend in certain fixed positions, you're free to drag the legend anywhere, even into the middle of the chart itself.

To restore the default position of an object, drag it back to its original position. To re-create the default position more precisely, first delete the object, and then re-create it. For example, if you drag the legend onto the middle of a chart and then decide it really looked better in its original location, click the Legend tool on the Chart toolbar twice. The first click deletes the customized legend, and the second click re-creates a standard legend.

Unfortunately, although you can move data labels at will, you have no such freedom with the tick-mark labels that appear along your axes. You can rotate these (the Angle Clockwise and Angle Counterclockwise tools on the Chart toolbar provide one easy way), but you cannot pick them up and drop them elsewhere. In addition, you cannot do anything with individual axis labels; you can modify them only as a group. Therefore, if you want to change the color of a particular label or move it inside the plot area, you're out of luck. You need to create individual text annotations to serve as axis labels.

> **tip** **Don't forget the obvious**
>
> With all Excel's chart formatting dialog boxes and toolbar tools, it's easy to overlook the obvious: you can often delete an object by selecting it and pressing Delete. In particular, you can remove the default dull gray background on your plot area by selecting the plot area and pressing Delete.

Moving and Resizing the Plot Area

The *plot area* is the part of your chart that displays data, whereas the *chart area* is the area surrounding the plot area. You can use the mouse to change the size, position, and aspect ratio of the plot area. For example, if Excel puts a bigger frame around your chart than you want, select the plot area and drag it outward. If you don't like the default distribution of the plot area and surrounding white space, use your mouse to adjust it.

Figure 25-3 shows a chart in which the default aspect ratio of the plot area has been altered. The chart presents a forecast; it seems appropriate to put the plot area on the right side of the chart area, with a right-aligned caption on the left.

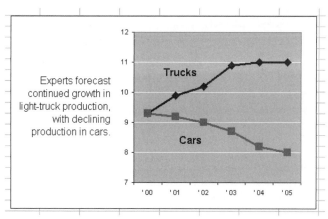

Figure 25-3. Although Excel centers the plot area within the chart area by default, you don't have to stick to that arrangement if it doesn't suit you.

Working with Titles

As you saw in Chapter 24, "Basic Charting Techniques," the Chart Wizard's third dialog box creates titles for your chart and each of your chart's axes. You can return to this dialog box after you've created your chart by selecting any part of the chart and choosing Chart, Chart Options. There you can add, delete, or edit titles.

Creating a Two-Line Title

One thing you cannot do in the Chart Wizard and the Chart Options dialog box is create a multiline title. You can break a one-line title into two or more lines after you have created it, however. Click the title once, pause, and then click again. The first click selects the title, and the second puts an insertion point into the text of the title. Position the insertion point where you want a line break to appear, and then press Enter.

Formatting a Title

To change the font, color, border, background, or alignment of a title—double-click it. Alternatively, you can right-click it and choose Format Chart Title or select it and choose Format, Selected Chart Title. All these routes access the Format Chart Title dialog box, shown in Figure 25-4.

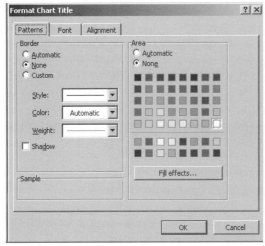

Figure 25-4. Use the Format Chart Title dialog box to alter the font, border, background, and alignment of a selected chart title.

On the Patterns tab, you can specify a border or a background for your title. Excel gives you neither by default. You can also tell Excel to put a shadow around your title. Note that if you select the Shadow check box, Excel switches the Border selection from None to Automatic—which means that it gives you a border in the default color and line weight. You're not obligated to have a border just because you choose to have a shadow, however. You can return the Border setting to None to achieve a three-dimensional look for the title.

The Area section of the Patterns tab determines what goes behind your title text. If you select Automatic, Excel gives you the default setting, which typically means white and opaque. If you select None, the background color for your title is the same as the color behind the title. If you drag the title onto a gray plot area, for example, the background

Chapter 25

for your title becomes gray. This is not the same as making the title background transparent. If there are gridlines on that plot area, the gridlines don't show through the title background—unless you've also selected the Transparent option on the Font tab. If you choose a colored background, your title's background will be opaque, even if you do select Transparent on the Font tab.

By clicking the Fill Effects button on the Patterns tab, you can also specify a background pattern or picture for your title. That's right; you can put wallpaper behind your title. The Fill Effects feature functions the same way in this context as it does in the plot area and chart area. For more information about the Fill Effects feature, see "Formatting Background Areas" on page 661.

On the Font tab, you can change the typeface, size, and color of your title. You can also add other effects, such as boldface, italics, superscripts, and subscripts. The Auto Scale check box on the Font tab, selected by default, determines whether Excel adjusts the point size of your title whenever you adjust the size of the chart. If you do not want this adjustment to occur, clear the Auto Scale check box.

Using the Alignment tab, shown in Figure 25-5, you can change not only the alignment of your title but also its orientation. By default, Excel displays your chart title and the title assigned to your horizontal axis (usually the category axis) with 0-degree orientation—in other words, the title lies horizontally. The vertical axis receives an upward-reading vertical title. You can change the tilt of any of these titles by dragging the red diamond in the Orientation control. For more precise tilting, you can adjust the Degrees spin box. Alternatively, you can create a vertical title made up of ordinary horizontal letters by selecting the vertical Text option in the Orientation control.

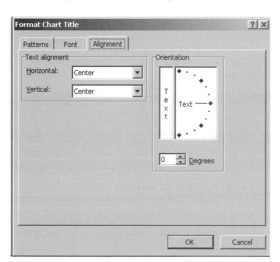

Figure 25-5. To change the orientation and alignment of your titles, click the Alignment tab.

The idea of a diagonal chart title might seem silly at first. Remember, however, you can drag the title onto the plot area if you want. A slanted title on the plot area can make a stylish chart annotation, as Figure 25-6 shows. Normally you use text boxes or WordArt for chart commentary, but the alignment options aren't available for text boxes, and using WordArt is a bit more complicated than rotating a title.

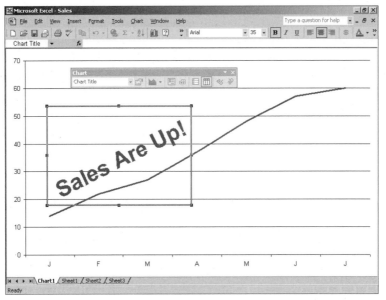

Figure 25-6. An angled title can make a stylish chart annotation.

InsideOut

Size the chart first

If you decide to play with tilted titles in large sizes—like the one shown in Figure 25-6—it's a good idea to size your chart to taste before you add the title. Excel isn't always as sharp as you might like about resizing an altered title when you resize its containing chart.

Formatting Individual Characters in a Title

By formatting title characters individually, you can make your titles look like ransom notes. Figure 25-7 shows one possible use for individual-character formatting; the characters in the word *up* have been elevated via the superscript option. (We've also increased their point size.)

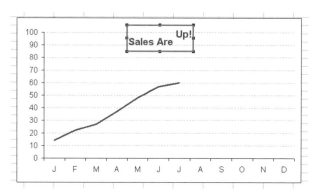

Figure 25-7. Applying the Superscript attribute to the word "Up" helps make the point.

To change the appearance of one or more characters in a title, select the title, pause, and then select the characters you want to change. With the characters selected, choose Format, Selected Chart Title. The dialog box that appears has only a Font tab. (In other words, you can't change the background characteristics of selected characters.)

InsideOut

Ignore the Properties Tab

This dialog box also includes a Properties tab. Changes here affect the whole chart, not just the selected characters. The Properties tab doesn't belong in this dialog box (yes, it's a bug), so it's best to ignore it.

Adding Text Annotations

To add a text annotation to your chart, select any part of the chart and type. Your words appear on Excel's formula bar as you type; when you press Enter, they appear within a text box. Using the handles at the perimeter of the box, you can move the annotation to whatever location suits your purposes. If you change the size or location of your chart, Excel does its best to maintain the position of your annotation relative to other components of the chart, but it cannot do this perfectly. If you're planning to annotate your charts with text, the best practice is to finalize the size and position of the chart before adding your text.

You can also add text annotations by clicking the Text Box tool on the Drawing toolbar, drawing out a rectangle on the chart, and typing within the resulting rectangle. This approach is functionally equivalent to the approach just described.

Note that text boxes produce plain text. You can format text box words and letters individually (using the same methods that you use to format individual characters of a title), but you can't drag the text into decorative shapes or generate multicolored letters. For those kinds of adornments, you need the WordArt tool. For more information about using WordArt, see "Creating WordArt" on page 298.

To delete a text annotation, select its bounding rectangle and press Delete. If the text box doesn't go away, you probably selected the text itself, not the box. Try again.

Working with Data Labels

If you neglected to add data labels to your chart while you were working your way through the Chart Wizard, you can do so after the fact by selecting any part of the chart, choosing Chart, Chart Options, and clicking the Data Labels tab. You can also use the Data Labels tab of the Chart Options dialog box to modify the contents of your labels. The labeling options for most chart types are Series Name, Category Name, and Value (see Figure 24-5 on page 619.). In pie and doughnut charts, you can also display each point's percentage of the total points—a useful option.

If your chart has more than one series, asking for data labels in the Chart Wizard or the Chart Options dialog box creates labels for all your series. If you want to label some series but not all, first create your chart without labels. Then select the series you want to label, choose Format, Selected Data Series, and click the Data Labels tab. You'll find the same options there as in the Chart Wizard or the Chart Options dialog box. The only drawback to adding labels this way is that you can't see your labels until you leave the dialog box. (In the Chart Wizard or Chart Options dialog box, your selections take effect immediately—and that can be particularly useful if you're not sure what the various labeling options do.)

Label Positioning and Alignment Options

To change the position or alignment of a set of data labels, select them on the chart, choose Format, Selected Data Labels, and click the Alignment tab. The dialog box that appears, shown in Figure 25-8, is similar to the one shown in Figure 25-5 with one crucial difference: the Label Position list. Use this list to tell Excel where you want your labels to sit in relation to your data markers. Available options vary by chart type. Figure 25-8 shows the options for column and bar charts.

When displaying outside-positioned data labels on pie or doughnut charts, Excel draws leader lines if the pie slice (or doughnut bite) happens to be narrower than the label, as shown in Figure 25-9. Here the Brand C and Brand B slices were too narrow to accommodate their labels; consequently, Excel moved the labels away from the slices and drew leader lines. Alternatively, you can select your chart, choose Chart, Chart Options, click the Data Labels tab, and clear the Show Leader Lines check box.

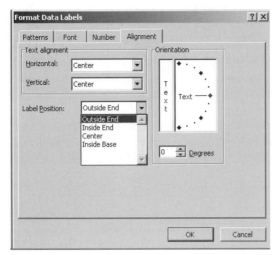

Figure 25-8. Excel allows you to position data labels in various ways, depending on the chart type.

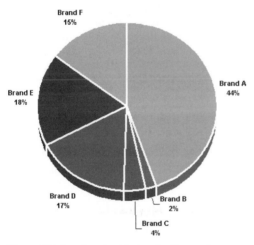

Figure 25-9. Excel adds leader lines where appropriate to pie-chart data labels.

If your labels display more than one item—Series Name and Value, for example—you might want Excel to display the items on separate lines. To do this, select your chart, choose Chart, Chart Options, click the Data Labels tab, and select New Line in the Separator box.

InsideOut

Prepare for the unexpected effect

If you've chosen to display label items on separate lines, you might be surprised to see what Excel does with your labels if you decide to angle them. The program starts by ignoring your New Line request and displaying the entire label on a single angled line. If the labels display two items, Excel puts the second item in parentheses. (It does not do this if the label displays three items.) Having the second item enclosed in parentheses is attractive—so much so that you might wonder why this choice isn't available for ordinary horizontal labels!

Numeric Formatting Options for Data Labels

If your data labels include numbers, you can apply any numeric format to those numbers. If you don't like the format that Excel gives you by default, select the labels, choose Format, Selected Data Labels, and click the Number tab. Along with the usual built-in and custom formatting options, you'll find a check box labeled Linked To Source. Select this check box if you want your data labels to always have the same numeric format as the worksheet cells from which Excel derives them.

Font and Patterns Options for Data Labels

The Patterns and Font tabs of the Format Data Labels dialog box (the dialog box shown in Figure 25-8) work like their counterparts in other formatting dialog boxes. Use the Font tab to change the labels' typeface, style, or color. Use the Patterns tab to add borders or shadows, or to format background areas for your data labels. Note that Excel ordinarily changes your labels' point size if you adjust the size of the chart. Clear the Auto Scale check box on the Font tab if you'd rather Excel didn't do this.

Editing Data Labels

You can change the content of data labels to whatever you please. You can even link labels to worksheet cells so that the labels change as those cells change. This process is awkward, however, because you have to change each label individually.

To change the content of a label, click it once, pause, and then click it again. The first click selects the entire series of labels; the second refines the selection to a particular label. After you have a particular label selected, begin typing. Excel replaces the current label with whatever you type.

To link a label to a worksheet cell, enter a sheet-qualified cell reference on the formula bar, such as =**Sheet1!A1**. The sheet name is required, even if the chart is embedded on the same worksheet as the cell reference.

Positioning and Formatting Data Labels Individually

To adjust any aspect of an individual data label's formatting, click the label once, pause, and then click it again. Now choose Format, Selected Data Labels.

Figure 25-10 shows the same pie chart as Figure 25-9, but with individually formatted data labels. We started by choosing an inside position for the entire series. Then we dragged the Brand C and Brand B labels out of the chart because their slices didn't accommodate inside labels. (Excel kindly gave us leader lines for these labels, even though we weren't using default positioning.) To improve the contrast with colored slices, we formatted each inside label in boldface and white. (We also changed a few of the slice colors. Excel's default colors include light tones as well as dark ones, and the light ones don't work well with white text.)

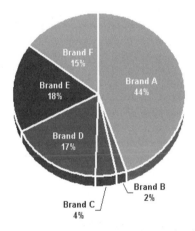

Figure 25-10. This chart has individually formatted data labels.

Generating Useful Data Labels on XY (Scatter) Charts

The data labels that Excel makes available for xy (scatter) charts are not terribly useful, as Figure 25-11 on the next page makes clear. This figure uses the Series Name data-label option, which applies the name of the series to each label on the chart. The other two options, X Value and Y Value, aren't much better.

In a case like this, use a set of text labels lying elsewhere on the worksheet—typically adjacent to the numeric data. In the example shown in Figure 25-11, the labels that would be meaningful are in the range A2:A6.

You can adjust each label on the chart individually—and that's not difficult in this case, because the chart has only five points. If you had to do this on a larger chart, or do it on a daily basis on charts of any size, you might begin to feel a little annoyed.

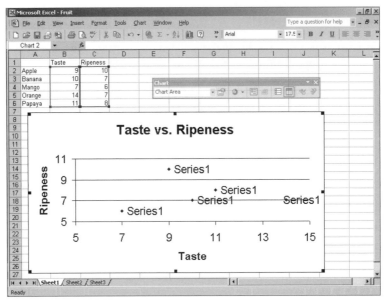

Figure 25-11. Excel's built-in labeling options for xy (scatter) charts are disappointing.

The following bit of Visual Basic code can help:

```
Sub XYLabeler()
    Dim LabelRange As Range
    Dim i as Integer, Pts As Integer

    Set LabelRange = Application.InputBox _
        (prompt:="Data Label Range?", Type:=8)
    ActiveChart.ApplyDataLabels
    Pts = ActiveChart.SeriesCollection(1).Points.Count
    For i = 1 to Pts
        ActiveChart.SeriesCollection(1).Points(i).Datalabel.Characters.Text _
        = LabelRange(i)
    Next I
End Sub
```

To use this code, press Alt+F11 to open the Visual Basic Editor (VBE). In the window titled Project–VBAProject, select the name of your workbook. (Press Ctrl+R if you don't see this window.) From the VBE menu bar, choose Insert, Module. In the new module window that appears, type the code. Return to Excel, select the chart you want to label, and choose Tools, Macro, Macros. Select XYLabeler in the list that appears and click Run. When prompted, select the range that you want to supply the labels and then click OK. (If your chart is on a chart sheet, you need to click the worksheet tab on which your labels reside and then select the range.)

> **caution** This is quick-and-dirty code, and it presents an ugly VBA error message if you fail to select a chart before running the macro. It's also designed to label a single data series.

> For more information about using macros and Visual Basic, see Part 10, "Working with Visual Basic and Macros."

Figure 25-12 shows the result of using this macro to apply the labels in A2:A6. As you can see, the label text is now OK, but the placement of some of the labels is less than ideal. In particular, Excel insists on planting the Orange label on top of its data point, no matter how wide we make the chart. It's almost inevitable that you'll want to make some adjustments by hand. For more information about manually adjusting data labels, see "Positioning and Formatting Data Labels Individually" on page 637.

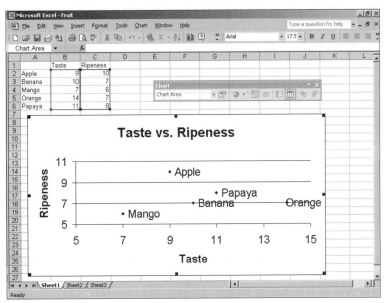

Figure 25-12. Our macro applied the contents of A2:A6 as data labels, but we still need to move a few of them by hand.

Working with Axes

Excel gives you a great deal of control over the format, position, and scale of your charts' axes. You can specify the line style, color, and weight of the axes, as well as the presence or absence of tick marks and tick labels. You can also override Excel's default scaling and establish the positions at which vertical and horizontal axes intersect.

Specifying the Line Style, Color, and Weight

To change the line style, color, or weight of an axis, select it, choose Format, Format Selected Axis, and then click the Patterns tab, shown in Figure 25-13. The default axis is a thin, solid black line, but you can choose from eight line styles and four weights. Note that Excel draws your tick marks in the same style as your axis. Therefore, if you choose a heavy red line for the axis, you'll have heavy red tick marks as well—unless, of course, you opt for no tick marks.

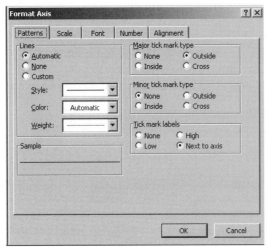

Figure 25-13. Change the properties of an axis by clicking the Patterns tab in the Format Axis dialog box.

Specifying the Position of Tick Marks and Tick-Mark Labels

Tick marks are short lines that either cross or abut an axis at regular intervals. Like the lines that mark inches and fractions of inches along a ruler, tick marks help define the axis scale. Tick marks come in two degrees, major and minor. Minor tick marks delineate subdivisions between major tick marks.

Tick-mark labels are the labels that identify positions along the axis. In Figure 25-14, for example, the value-axis tick-mark labels are the currency figures at the left edge of the chart. The category-axis tick-mark labels are Quarter 1, Quarter 2, and so on.

By default, Excel displays major tick marks on the outside of axes and does not display minor tick marks. Excel displays a tick-mark label for each major tick mark, adjacent to an axis. To reposition tick marks or tick-mark labels, select the appropriate axis, choose Format, Format Selected Axis, and click the Patterns tab, shown in Figure 25-13.

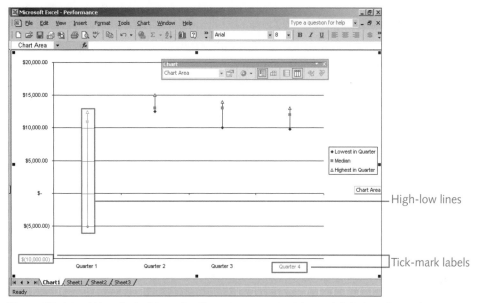

Figure 25-14. We selected Low for the category-axis tick-mark labels to keep them out of the plot area.

You will probably want to reposition your tick-mark labels in charts where the category and value axes intersect somewhere other than the lower left corner of the chart. In Figure 25-14, for example, the inclusion of negative values causes the category axis to cross the value axis above the bottom of the chart. If the category-axis tick-mark labels remained in their default stations—adjacent to the axis—they'd be in the middle of the plot area. Therefore, we selected Low in the Tick-Mark Labels section of the Patterns tab of the Format Axis dialog box.

Changing the Numeric Format Used by Tick-Mark Labels

When you first create a chart, Excel links the numeric format of your value-axis tick-mark labels to that of the source data. Create a chart from data with the Currency format, for example, and Excel applies the Currency format to the labels on your value axis. Change the format of the source data, and the labels stay in step.

You can override that linkage by applying a specific numeric format to your tick-mark labels. Clicking a Formatting toolbar tool does the trick, as does selecting one of the options on the Number tab of the Format Axis dialog box. After you explicitly format your axis labels, Excel no longer copies formatting changes from the source data to the chart. To relink the format of your tick-mark labels with that of the source data, revisit the Number tab of the Format Axis dialog box and select the Linked To Source check box.

Scaling Axes Manually

You're not obligated to use the default axis scaling that Excel uses. You can specify your own maximum and minimum values, change the positions of major and minor tick marks (as well as the gridlines that can extend from those tick marks), and switch between normal and logarithmic scaling.

Scaling a Value Axis Manually

To scale a value axis manually, select it, choose Format, Format Selected Axis, and click the Scale tab of the Format Axis dialog box, shown in Figure 25-15. When you enter new values in any of the first four boxes of this dialog box, Excel clears the associated Auto check box. To restore a default scaling parameter, reselect its Auto check box.

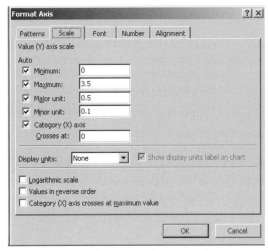

Figure 25-15. Click the Scale tab on the Format Axis dialog box to scale a selected value axis manually or to restore a default scaling parameter.

Setting Minimum and Maximum Values　When all the values in your chart are positive, Excel's default value axis begins at 0 and ends somewhere above the highest value in the chart. If all the values are negative, the scale normally begins somewhere below the lowest value and ends at 0. If the chart includes both positive and negative values, the default scale starts below the lowest value and ends above the highest.

In a chart containing only positive values, you can zoom in on the plot area by changing the value in the Minimum box from 0 to a number that approximates the lowest value in the chart. In a chart containing only negative values, you can zoom in by making a similar change to the value in the Maximum box.

Changing the Position of Tick Marks and Gridlines　The Major Unit and Minor Unit values on the Scale tab of the Format Axis dialog box determine the position of major and minor tick marks, if you choose to display them. For example, to increase

642

Chapter 25

the space between gridlines, increase the value in the Major Unit box, the Minor Unit box, or both.

Changing the Intersection of the Category Axis   By default, the category axis crosses the value axis at 0. To position it elsewhere, type a value other than 0 in the Category (X) Axis Crosses At box. Excel then clears the associated Auto check box. To restore the normal axis position, reselect the Auto check box.

You can also modify the position of the category axis by selecting the Category (X) Axis Crosses At Maximum Value box at the bottom of the dialog box. Excel then displays the axis at the top of the chart (unless you also select the Values In Reverse Order box).

Using Logarithmic Scaling   In a logarithmic scale, each power of 10 is separated by the same distance along the axis. For example, in a logarithmic scale that runs from 1 through 10,000, the numbers 1, 10, 100, 1,000, and 10,000 are equally spaced. Scientific and other types of technical charts can often benefit from logarithmic scaling. To use logarithmic scaling, select the Logarithmic Scale check box on the Scale tab of the Format Axis dialog box. To restore linear (nonlogarithmic) scaling, clear this check box.

In a logarithmic scale, the lowest value is 1. You cannot plot negative and 0 values. If you apply logarithmic scaling to a chart that contains negative or 0 values, Excel displays an error message and removes those values from the chart. To restore them, restore linear scaling.

Reversing the Value-Axis Scale   You can turn the value-axis scale upside down so that the highest values appear near the bottom of the chart and the lowest values appear near the top. This option is convenient if all your chart values are negative and you're interested primarily in the absolute value of each point. You might also find it handy in cases where lower values are considered better—for example, in a chart that plots your golf score over time. To reverse the scale, select the Values In Reverse Order check box on the Scale tab.

Scaling a Non–Time-Scaled Category Axis Manually   To scale a non–time-scaled category axis manually, select it, choose Format, Format Selected Axis. Then click the Scale tab of the Format Axis dialog box, shown in Figure 25-16 on the next page.

Changing the Intersection of the Value Axis   By default, the value axis crosses the category axis to the left of the first category's data markers. However, you can position its crossing point elsewhere. Type a value other than 1 in the Value (Y) Axis Crosses At Category Number box. To restore the normal position of the axis, change this value back to 1.

You might want to consider moving the value axis to the middle of a chart if that chart's purpose is to compare two sets of values (see Figure 25-17 on the next page for an example). Here we've put a 2 in the Value (Y) Axis Crosses At Category Number box, telling Excel to draw the value axis to the left of category 2 (Bob).

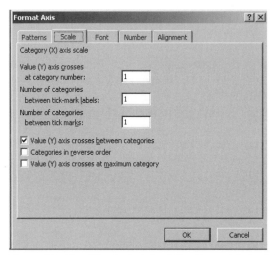

Figure 25-16. The Scale tab of the Format Axis dialog box also changes the scaling of a selected non–time-scaled category axis.

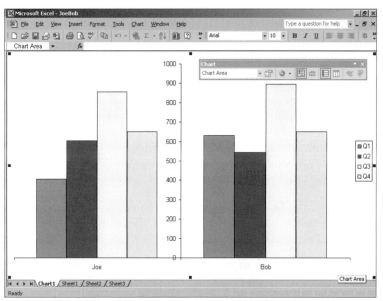

Figure 25-17. When a chart compares two sets of values, it can be helpful to position the value axis between the two sets.

Changing the Intervals Between Category Labels Excel displays one category label for each data cluster (or for each data point in a single-series chart). If the chart has many data points, the program draws the labels at an angle so they don't overlap. If you specify horizontal alignment (on the Alignment tab of the Format Axis dialog box), Excel skips a certain number of labels to avoid overlap. If, despite these measures, you still find your horizontally aligned labels overlapping or if you just want to see fewer labels, enter a number other than 1 in the Number Of Categories Between Tick-Mark Labels box. If you enter 2, for example, Excel displays a label for every other category. If you enter 3, Excel displays labels for every third category, and so on.

Changing the Intervals Between Tick Marks and Gridlines   The value in the Number Of Categories Between Tick Marks box determines the position of major tick marks along the category axis. By default, Excel creates a major tick mark for every category name. You can make them appear less frequently if you enter a value greater than 1 in this box.

The presence or absence of tick marks along the category axis doesn't have much of an impact on the appearance of your chart. However, major gridlines emanate from major tick marks; therefore, if you display major category-axis gridlines (on the Chart Options dialog box), you can control the frequency at which they appear by altering the interval between tick marks.

Excel draws minor category-axis gridlines halfway between each pair of major gridlines. You cannot independently customize this interval.

Changing Where the First Point Appears   The Value (Y) Axis Crosses Between Categories option determines where the first point in each series appears relative to the value axis. Excel selects this option by default for bar and column charts and clears it for area and line charts. As a result, Excel draws bar and column charts with a space between the axis and the first marker, and area and line charts with their first markers flush against the value axis.

Reversing the Category-Axis Scale   You can invert the category-axis scale so that Excel places the first category on the right side of the chart and the last category on the left. This option is convenient if you want to emphasize the last category. To reverse the scale, select the Categories In Reverse Order check box.

Scaling a Time-Scaled Category Axis Manually

The scaling options for time-scaled category axes are different from those used for ordinary category axes. To see these options, select a time-scaled category axis, choose Format, Format Selected Axis, and click the Scale tab, shown in Figure 25-18 on the next page.

Changing the Minimum and Maximum   By default, Excel makes your earliest time value the minimum point on the scale and the latest time value the maximum. By specifying different values for these parameters, you can zoom in on a subset of your data. For example, if your chart plots monthly information from January through December, you can focus on the third quarter by changing the Minimum value to 7/1 of the year in question and the Maximum value to 9/1. Furthermore, if you want to show that the current year's results are still unknown, you can extend the maximum to a date beyond the date of your last data point. Excel then compresses the plot into the left side of the chart, leaving white space on the right.

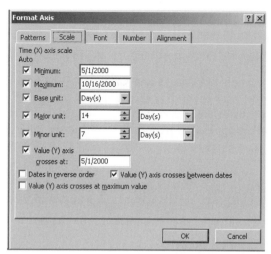

Figure 25-18. You can change the appearance of a time-scaled chart dramatically using the parameters in this dialog box.

Changing the Major and Minor Units   The Major Unit setting determines the spacing of major tick marks, tick-mark labels, and major gridlines. To move labels and gridlines farther apart, increase the value of the Major Unit by choosing a number in the left spin box and a time unit in the right. Note, however, that the Major Unit value must not be smaller than the Base Unit value.

The Minor Unit setting determines the spacing of minor tick marks and minor gridlines. You can increase or decrease the interval between these items by specifying different values in the two Minor Unit spin boxes.

Changing the Base Unit   The Base Unit setting determines the granularity of your time-scaled chart. If your chart plots monthly figures, for example, and you change the Base Unit to Day(s), Excel displays nearly a month's worth of blank space between each pair of data points, as shown in Figure 25-19. Going in the other direction, by increasing the Base Unit value, you can achieve a form of consolidation, as Figure 25-20 shows.

The first of these two charts plots daily oil prices. The Base Unit remains where Excel set it when the chart was created—at Day(s). Switching the Base Unit to Month(s) in the second chart allows you to see the high and low price and the start point and end-point of oil prices during each month. (To make the chart more meaningful, you can also change the Number format of the category-axis tick marks from m/d to mmm or mmmm so that you can see abbreviated or spelled-out month names instead of the first date in each month.)

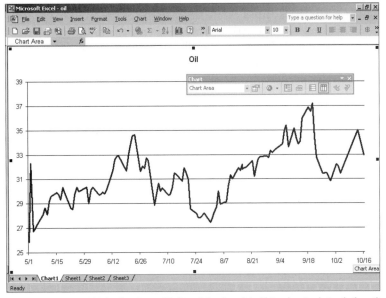

Figure 25-19. With the Base Unit set to Day(s), this chart plots daily oil prices.

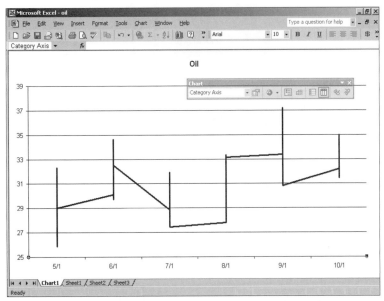

Figure 25-20. Changing the Base Unit to Month(s) shows the range over which prices varied during each month.

Setting the Value-Axis Cross Point and Reversing the Scale   The remaining scaling options for time-scaled category axes are comparable to those for value axes, as discussed in "Scaling a Value Axis Manually" on page 642. You can use these options to reverse the plotting order of your data and to specify the point at which the category and value axes cross.

Scaling the Series Axis Manually   The series axis appears only in certain three-dimensional charts, such as the one shown in Figure 25-21. When each series appears on a separate plane, Excel displays two axes along the floor of the chart and a third axis straight up from the floor. One of the axes along the floor of the chart becomes the category (x) axis and the other becomes the series (y) axis. The axis with the Q1, Q2, Q3, and Q4 labels in Figure 25-21 is the series axis.

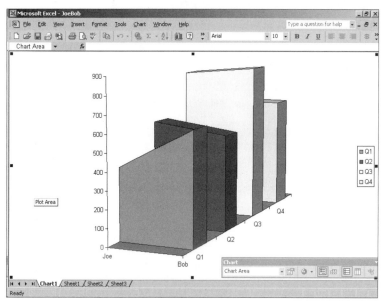

Figure 25-21.   This three-dimensional area chart has a series axis, as well as a value and a category axis.

You can change the scale of a series axis by selecting it, choosing Format, Format Selected Axis, and then clicking the Scale tab. As Figure 25-22 shows, your options are few. To increase the space between series labels, type a number greater than 1 in the Number Of Series Between Tick-Mark Labels box. To increase the space between tick marks (and gridlines), type a value greater than 1 in the Number Of Series Between Tick Marks box. To reverse the order in which Excel plots the series, select the Series In Reverse Order check box. This last option might be useful if the points in your first series obscure those in subsequent series. You can also deal with this problem by rotating the chart.

For information about rotating a chart, see "Changing the Rotation" on page 668.

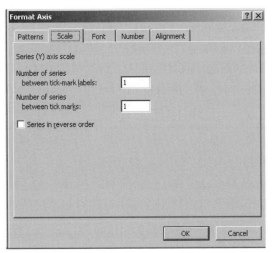

Figure 25-22. Use the Scale tab to change the scale of a select series axis.

Adding, Removing, and Formatting Gridlines

Gridlines help define your plot area, making it easier to see the magnitude of your chart markers. To add gridlines to a chart, choose Chart, Chart Options, and then click the Gridlines tab of the Chart Options dialog box. Major gridlines connect to major tick marks, and minor gridlines connect to minor tick marks. You can change the position of both kinds of tick marks (and thus the number of gridlines that appear) in both of the following ways:

● Select the axis whose gridlines you want to change, and then choose Format, Format Selected Gridlines.

● Select a gridline from the set you want to change, and then choose Format, Format Selected Gridlines.

Either way, you come to the Scale tab of the Format Gridlines dialog box. On the Scale tab, change the values in the Major Unit and Minor Unit boxes to change the spacing of the gridlines.

To change the line style, weight, or color of a set of gridlines, change the corresponding settings on the Patterns tab of the Format Gridlines dialog box (access by selecting one of the gridlines and choosing Format, Format Selected Gridlines). To restore the default appearance of the gridline, select Automatic on the Patterns tab.

Formatting Data Series and Markers

Excel provides plenty of options for formatting the appearance and arrangement of both entire data series and individual markers within a series. Many of these options apply to all charts, whereas others are for specific chart types. You'll look at the generally applicable options first, followed by options for specific chart types.

> **tip**   **Format markers individually**
>
> You can apply many formatting options to data markers both singularly and as a whole series. To select a single marker, first select its series. Then click the marker you want to format. If Excel cannot apply your formatting command to the individual marker, it applies it to the entire series.

Assigning a Series to a Secondary Value Axis

A secondary value axis makes it possible to plot series that fall within widely divergent value ranges. The secondary axis, usually positioned on the right side of the chart, can have a completely different scale from the primary axis. You can assign as many series as you like to the secondary axis.

To switch a series from the primary axis to a secondary axis (creating the secondary axis in the process if you don't already have one) or to move a secondary-axis series back to the primary axis, select the series, choose Format, Selected Data Series, and click the Axis tab of the Format Data Series dialog box. Make your selection in the Plot Series On section of this dialog box.

Using Two or More Chart Types in the Same Chart

You can create many different kinds of overlay charts in which you have plotted one or more data series in a chart type that contrasts with the remaining data series. Figure 25-23 shows an example of such a chart. Because this chart isn't comparing apples with apples (or Joe with Bob, as in Figure 25-17), plotting the two series in contrasting chart types makes sense.

To change the chart type that you have assigned to a series, select the series, choose Chart, Chart Type, and select from Excel's chart-type gallery. Be aware that Excel cannot overlay certain subtypes over other subtypes. For example, you can't combine a three-dimensional area chart with a two-dimensional column chart. You should also realize that certain permitted overlays don't work aesthetically.

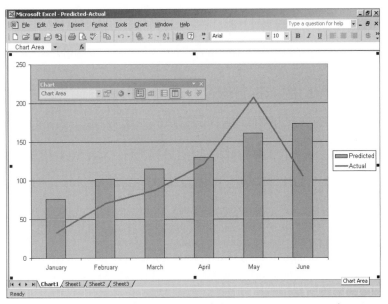

Figure 25-23. Excel makes it easy to plot series in contrasting chart types.

Changing the Series Order

Excel normally plots series following the column or row order of the data on your worksheet, but you're not obliged to stick with the default order. To change the series order for your chart, select any of its data series, choose Format, Selected Data Series, and then click the Series Order tab, shown in Figure 25-24.

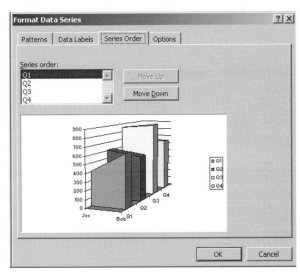

Figure 25-24. Using the Series Order tab, you can determine the order in which Excel presents the series on your chart.

If you want to change this chart so that the most recent quarter appeared in front, with the remaining series in the order Q3, Q2, Q1, you select Q1 in the Series Order list and click the Move Down button three times. Then you select Q2 and move it down two positions, and so on.

Changing the series order is one way to make a partially obscured series visible in a three-dimensional chart. You can also improve the readability of this kind of chart by changing its viewing angle. For information on how to do this, see "Changing Three-Dimensional Viewing Angles" on page 667.

Toggling the Column/Row Orientation

Excel usually makes the appropriate decision about whether to plot your series by row or by column. However, you can overrule it easily by clicking the By Row or By Column button on the Chart toolbar. You can use these buttons to switch instantly between the two orientations. If you'd rather not use the toolbar, choose Chart, Source Data, click the Range tab, and then select either the Series In Rows or Series In Columns option.

Changing Colors, Patterns, Fills, and Borders for Markers

To change the color, pattern, fill, or border for a marker or set of markers, select the series or marker, choose Format, Selected Data Series (or Format Selected Data Point, if you selected a single marker), and then click the Patterns tab of the resulting dialog box. Your choices here are essentially the same as your choices for formatting the background areas of your chart. For example, you can add pictures to your data markers, using the same procedures you use to make a picture serve as a background for your entire chart. For more information about formatting with pictures, see "Formatting Background Areas" on page 661.

Using the Invert If Negative Option

In the Patterns dialog box for many types of data series, you'll find a check box labeled Invert If Negative. If you select this option for a series, Excel displays any negative markers within that series in a contrasting color.

The Invert If Negative option changes negative values to white. That usually contrasts well with the colors that charting engine in Excel uses by default. (However, negative values in all the data series on the same chart all look the same—white.) If you happen to build a chart with white data markers, the Invert If Negative option gives you no inversion at all, as Figure 25-25 shows.

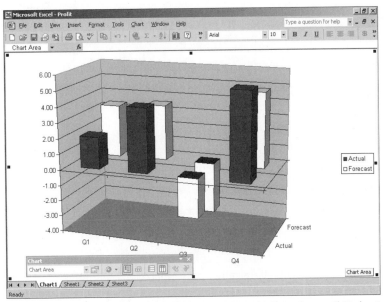

Figure 25-25. We applied Invert If Negative to both series on this chart, but the white series remains white, even when values are negative.

Using the Vary Colors By Point (Slice) Option

Charts that plot a single series might or might not use distinct colors for each point in the series. By default, Excel varies colors by point in pie and doughnut charts, but not in column or bar charts. You can override the default by means of the Vary Colors By Point check box, which you'll find on the Options tab of the Format Data Series dialog box.

Adjusting Marker Spacing in
Two-Dimensional Column and Bar Charts

To adjust the spacing of markers in a two-dimensional column or bar chart, select a series (any series will do), choose Format, Selected Data Series, and then click the Options tab, shown in Figure 25-26 on the next page. The Overlap option controls the distribution of markers within a cluster, and the Gap Width option determines the space between clusters. The default settings for the kind of chart shown in Figure 25-26 are 0 percent overlap and 150 percent gap width. As a result, Excel displays markers within a cluster side by side, with no overlap and no space between them, and places a space between clusters equal to 1.5 times the width of an individual marker.

To create overlap, specify a value greater than 0 and not greater than 100 in the Overlap box. To change the amount of space between clusters, enter a value from 0 through 100 in the Gap Width box. The smaller the gap width, the wider your bars or columns become. By specifying a 0 percent gap width, you can create a step chart—a bar or column chart in which you have all the markers lined up next to each other, with no intervening spaces.

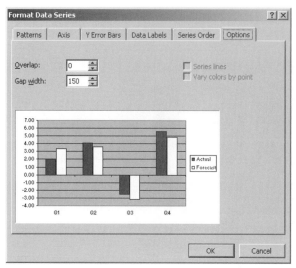

Figure 25-26. Use the Options tab to adjust marker spacing.

In certain kinds of charts, particularly the kind that depicts reality versus expectations, creating partial overlap between series can produce some interesting effects. Figure 25-27 shows a chart with 60 percent overlap between the Actual and Forecast series. We've also reduced the gap width from 150 to 50.

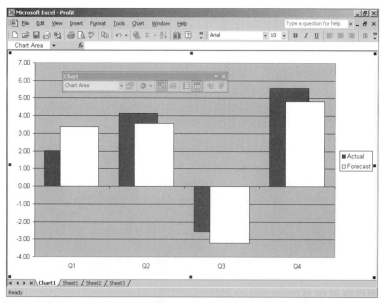

Figure 25-27. Overlapping data series can sometimes create a pleasing effect.

Adjusting Marker Spacing in Three-Dimensional Charts

In three-dimensional charts that use a series axis, three parameters control the spacing of markers. Gap depth and gap width specify the relative intermarker space along the series axis and category axis, respectively, whereas chart depth determines the relative length of the series axis. Reducing gap depth or gap width brings markers closer together; increasing these values moves the markers farther apart. Increasing chart depth generates a chart that appears to recede further into the page, whereas decreasing chart depth flattens the chart.

To change any of these parameters, select any series from a three-dimensional chart, and choose Format, Selected Data Series. Then click the Options tab, shown in Figure 25-28.

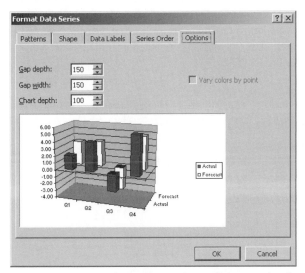

Figure 25-28. Excel provides an immediate sample of any parameter changes you make.

You'll find that achieving the right look in a three-dimensional chart is a matter of balance. Increasing the chart depth, for example, can produce a more dramatic three-dimensional look, but tends to scrunch the chart along its value axis. If experimentation leads you astray, you can restore the original look by setting the gap width and gap depth to 150 and the chart depth to 100.

---

tip **Delete the legend**

By default, Excel creates legends even for charts with series axes. The legend is superfluous unless you have done away with your series-axis tick-mark labels. Furthermore, it significantly reduces the amount of space available to the chart. If you don't need it, you can produce a better-looking chart by deleting it.

Adding Series Lines in Stacked Column and Bar Charts

Series lines connect markers in stacked column or bar charts. They can help you follow the changes in magnitude of markers that don't originate on the category axis. To add series lines, click any series in a stacked column or bar chart, choose Format, Selected Data Series, click the Options tab, and then select the Series Lines check box. Note that Excel draws series lines for each series in the chart, not just the one you selected.

Changing Marker Shapes in Three-Dimensional Column and Bar Charts

In certain three-dimensional column and bar charts, you can switch the marker shape of individual series to cubes, cylinders, cones, or pyramids. To do this, select the series or individual marker you want to change, choose Format, Format Selected Data Series (or Format Selected Data Point, if you selected a single marker), and then click the Shape tab, shown in Figure 25-29.

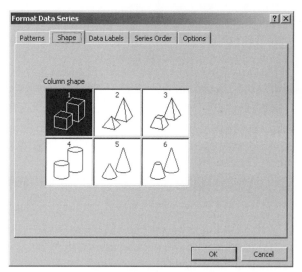

Figure 25-29. Select one of the shapes on the Shape tab to change an individual marker or series of markers.

Options 2 and 3 are similar to one another, as are options 5 and 6. The difference is that with options 3 and 6, only the data marker with the largest absolute value in the series has the pointed top. The others are truncated (see Figure 25-30).

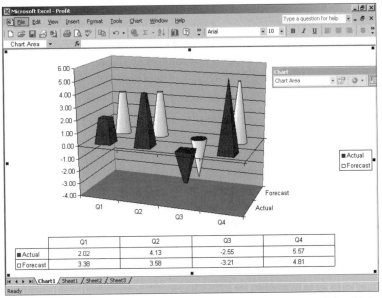

Figure 25-30. With the marker styles used in this chart, Excel should draw the markers with the largest absolute values full size and truncate the others; unfortunately, Excel doesn't always perform this correctly.

caution Unfortunately, Excel doesn't always seem to know which marker deserves the pointed top. In Figure 25-30, the Forecast marker with the largest absolute value is at Q4 (4.81), but Excel gave Q3 (–3.21) the pointed cone. Interestingly, the Q3 Forecast value in this chart is the point with the *lowest* absolute value!

Smoothing the Lines in Line and XY (Scatter) Charts

Excel can apply smoothing to line and xy (scatter) chart series. To use this feature, select the series you want to smooth. Choose Format, Selected Data Series, click the Patterns tab, and then select the Smoothed Line check box. Note that this smoothing option isn't the same as the exponential smoothing feature available via the Analysis ToolPak.

Changing Line and Marker Styles in Line, XY (Scatter), and Radar Charts

To change the style, weight, or color of the lines in a line, xy (scatter), or radar chart, select the series you want to change, choose Format, Selected Data Series, and then click the Patterns tab. In the dialog box that appears, you can also change the style, color, and size of your markers—or eliminate the markers from your series.

Adding High-Low Lines and Up and Down Bars to Line Charts

High-low lines are straight lines that extend between the highest and lowest points in a cluster. You can use them to indicate the range over which a value varies. Figure 25-14 illustrates the use of high-low lines. High-low lines are available only in two-dimensional line charts.

Up and down bars are rectangles drawn between corresponding points of two or more line series. Excel fills the bars with one color or pattern if the first series is higher than the last and with a contrasting color or pattern when the opposite is true. Use up and down bars in charts that track opening and closing prices (so-called candlestick charts), but you can add them to any two-dimensional line chart that includes at least two data series.

To add high-low lines or up and down bars to a chart, select any series, choose Format, Selected Data Series, click the Options tab, and then select either the High-Low Lines check box, the Drop Lines check box, or both.

When you use the Up/Down Bars option, you also can modify your chart's gap width. This option is normally available only with bar and column charts, but Excel treats a line chart with up and down bars as a kind of column chart. Increasing the Gap Width parameter makes the up and down bar rectangles narrower, and decreasing this parameter makes the bars wider.

To change the appearance of your high-low lines and up and down bars, select one of them and choose Format, Selected Data Series. You can change the color, weight, and style of your high-low lines and the color, pattern, and border of your up and down bars. You can even format the up and down bars with a texture or picture.

For more information about adding a texture or picture to up and down bars, see "Formatting Background Areas" on page 661.

Adding Drop Lines to Area and Line Charts

Drop lines are straight lines that extend from a data point to the category axis. Drop lines are particularly useful in multiple-series area charts, but you can add them to any two-dimensional or three-dimensional line or area chart. Select a series, choose Format, Selected Data Series, click the Options tab, and then select the Drop Lines check box.

Exploding Pie Slices and Doughnut Bites

You can use your mouse to detonate pies and doughnuts. Click a marker and drag it away from the chart's center. (You can explode only the outermost ring of a doughnut chart, however. The inner rings are impervious.) To implode, drag a marker back toward the center.

Note that when you drag a pie slice or doughnut bite, the whole pie or doughnut comes apart. If you just want to drag a particular marker away from the rest of the chart, click that marker twice (with a pause between clicks). After you have a single marker selected, drag it.

Using Formatting and Split Options in Pie-Column and Pie-Pie Charts

Pie-column and pie-pie charts are pie charts in which Excel splits out one or more series into a second chart—a column chart or a second pie chart. The second chart provides a more detailed look at a portion of the first chart.

To convert an ordinary pie chart into a pie-pie or pie-column chart, select any part of the chart and choose Chart, Chart Type. You'll find the pie-pie and pie-column sub-types on the right side of the Pie gallery.

By default, Excel derives the detail portion of your pie-pie or pie-column chart from the last two series of the main chart. However, Excel has many other options for split-ting the chart. To see these options, select a series point from an existing pie-pie or pie-column chart, choose Format, Selected Data Series, and then click the Options tab. Figure 25-31 shows some of your choices.

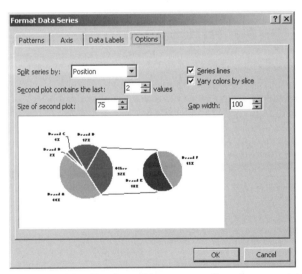

Figure 25-31. Excel provides many options for organizing and formatting a pie-pie or pie-column chart.

You can split your chart by position (the last n points in a series go to the detail chart), by absolute value (all points less than n go to the detail chart), or by percent value (all slices less than n percent of the total go to the detail chart). Alternatively, you can select Custom in the Split Series By list, and then drag slices from the main chart to the detail chart. However you choose to split, your options are the same for both pie-pie and pie-column charts. The only difference between the two kinds of chart lies in the shape of the detail component. However you choose to split, Excel redraws the main chart to show a single slice representing all the slices shown in the detail chart. By default, Excel draws series lines from the edges of this single slice of primary chart to the entire detail chart. You can remove the series lines by clearing the Series Lines check box.

Excel makes the diameter of the detail pie or the detail column 75 percent of the height of the main chart. To change these relative sizes, enter a different percentage value in the Size Of Second Plot spin box. You can also move the detail plot closer or farther away from the main plot by entering larger or smaller values in the Gap Width spin box.

Changing the Angle of the First Pie Slice or Doughnut Bite

By default, Excel draws the beginning radius for the first marker in a doughnut or pie series at a 45-degree angle from the vertical. In other words, if the pie or doughnut were a clock face, the first radius would point toward a spot midway between one o'clock and two o'clock. You can change the angle by selecting a series point, choosing Format, Selected Data Series, clicking the Options tab, and modifying Angle Of First Slice.

Working with Data Tables

You can add a data table to a chart by selecting the chart, choosing Chart, Chart Options, clicking the Data Table tab, and selecting Show Data Table. The resulting data table shows the numbers from which the chart was derived and is particularly useful when the chart is located on a separate chart sheet.

Unfortunately, you can't move or format the data table. You can create a more flexible equivalent to the Data Table option as follows:

1 Copy the source data for the chart.

2 Select the chart.

3 Hold down the Shift key and choose Edit, Paste Picture. (The Paste Picture command does not appear on the Edit menu unless you hold down the Shift key.)

4 Size and position the picture of the source data.

5 In the formula bar, type a reference to the source data. For example, if the source data occupies Sheet1!A1:D5, type **=Sheet1!A1:D5**. Press Enter.

Now you have a picture of your source data, linked to that source data. If the data changes, so does the picture. If you change the formatting of the source data, the picture changes to match. You can move the table picture anywhere you want, including onto the chart.

Formatting Background Areas

Excel provides a rich set of options for formatting the background areas of your charts—including the plot area, the chart area, and the walls and floors of three-dimensional charts. You can also apply these formatting options to legends, to the background areas of text objects (titles and data labels), and to certain kinds of chart markers—including columns, bars, pyramids, cones, cylinders, areas, bubbles, pie slices, and doughnut bites.

You can access all the formatting options described in this section from the Fill Effects dialog box. (To get there, select the chart element in question, and then choose the first command on the Format menu.) On the Patterns tab, click the Fill Effects button.

Filling an Area with a Color Gradient

A color gradient is a smooth progression of color tones from one part of an area to another—such as from the top of a column marker to the bottom. Color gradients can give your chart areas a classy, professional appearance.

Excel offers two basic kinds of color gradients—one-color gradients and two-color gradients. In a one-color gradient, adding or subtracting luminosity varies the chosen color so that you typically obtain a progression from white to black, with varying shades of the chosen color between. In a two-color gradient, Excel varies the balance of the chosen colors so that the first color predominates at one point and the second at another.

If you opt for a two-color gradient, you can either specify the two colors yourself or choose from a palette provided by Excel. The preset palette includes atmospheric choices, such as Early Sunset and Fog; choices that mimic familiar materials, such as Mahogany and Parchment; and a variety of other interesting color combinations.

In any case, to specify a color gradient, click the Gradient tab in the Fill Effects dialog box. You'll see the dialog box shown in Figure 25-32 on the next page.

Select the gradient you want by clicking one of the options in the Colors section of this dialog box. When you make your selection, Excel displays the appropriate number of color pickers. (If you select Preset, Excel displays a list of its designer offerings.)

In the bottom portion of the dialog box, choose a basic shading style—such as horizontal or vertical—and a variant of that style. The Variants boxes show samples, in your chosen colors, of the basic shading style you selected.

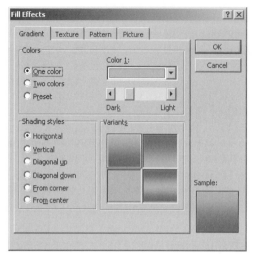

Figure 25-32. You can choose from many preset color gradients or create your own.

Filling an Area with a Pattern

Like a two-color gradient, a pattern provides a mix of two colors—called, in this case, the foreground color and the background color. However, in a pattern, Excel varies the two colors in accordance with a repeating geometrical design selected from the Pattern tab. Figure 25-33 shows the Pattern tab of the Fill Effects dialog box.

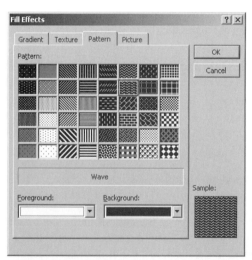

Figure 25-33. Use the Pattern tab to apply a repeating geometrical design to your background area.

Use the dialog box to select foreground and background colors; you will see samples of the available patterns in your chosen colors. The name of the selected pattern appears above the foreground and background colors, and a larger sample of the selection appears in the lower right corner of the dialog box.

Filling an Area with a Texture or Picture

If you don't care for solids, gradients, and patterns, why not fill your background areas or data markers with textures or pictures? You can use images in a wide variety of supported formats, or you can use one of the 24 texture images supplied by Excel. The latter evokes familiar materials, such as oak, marble, and cloth. For example, Figure 25-34 shows a fish fossil texture applied to a chart's plot area.

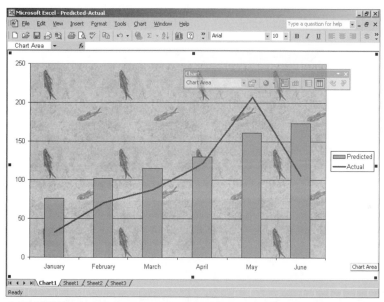

Figure 25-34. We've applied a fish fossil texture to the plot area of this chart.

To apply a texture to an area, click the Fill Effects button, click the Texture tab, and then select a texture from the gallery. If you don't find a satisfactory texture there, click Other Textures. In the ensuing dialog box, you can select any supported graphic file (Enhanced Metafile, Windows Metafile, JPEG, PNG, BMP, GIF, Compressed Windows Enhanced Metafile, Compressed Windows Metafile, Compressed Macintosh PICT, Kodak Photo CD, PC Paintbrush, CorelDraw, CGM, EPS, FPX, WordPerfect Graphics, Tag Image, Macintosh PICT, and Photodraw) available on your system. Excel treats the specified image as repeating wallpaper—as if you used it as wallpaper on your desktop. If you want a single image, instead of a repeating image, use the Picture tab instead of the Texture tab.

Troubleshooting

I Can't Get Rid of the Background Texture?

Okay, you've figured out that fish fossils don't really enhance the presentation-worthiness of your chart. Now what? You might suppose that somewhere on that Texture (or Picture) dialog box there would be an "off" button. There isn't. If Excel's Undo command isn't available, you can remove the texture, or picture, by selecting the formatted area and then choosing Edit, Clear. Alternatively, return to the Patterns dialog box. Instead of clicking Fill Effects button, select None in the Area section.

If you prefer to use a single image, click the Picture tab, click Select Picture, and then find the image you want. Excel supports the same formats here as on the Texture tab. After you select an image, it appears on the Picture tab (see Figure 25-35).

Figure 25-35.   Use the Picture tab instead of the Texture tab if you want a single image, not a set of tiled images, to appear on your chart area or plot area.

> **note**   If you try to drag an image file from Windows Explorer onto a chart element, Windows changes your mouse pointer to a plus sign, which generally signifies that you're about to perform a drag-and-drop operation. Unfortunately, dragging and dropping has no effect in this context

When you apply a picture, as opposed to a texture, to an area other than a data marker, Excel uses a single copy of that image and adjusts the image's size and aspect ratio as necessary to fill the background area. In many cases, that adjustment of size or aspect ratio produces unsatisfactory results. If you need an untiled image and don't want

Excel to expand or compress it, put the image on the worksheet itself (not the chart), and then embed the chart on top of the image. We'll cover that approach in more detail in a moment.

When you apply a picture to a data marker, Excel gives you a choice of three formatting options. Stretch (the default) displays one copy of your picture for each marker and stretches the picture to fit. Stack displays as many copies of the picture as needed to fill the marker, leaving each copy at its original size. Use Stack And Scale To to make as many copies of the picture as needed to represent some number of units along the value axis.

Figure 25-36 shows a chart with stretched pictures applied to column markers. We could have effectively used either of the other two options here—Stack or Stack And Scale To—but the vertical distortion of the happy and sad faces, exaggerating the smiles and frowns, adds a mildly comedic touch that does no harm and might help the chart make its point.

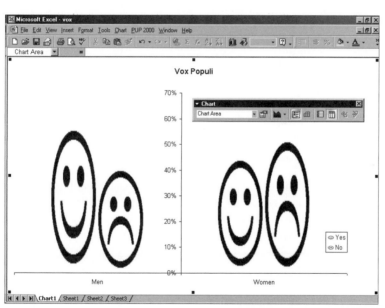

Figure 25-36. Pictures applied to column or area markers can reinforce the message you're trying to convey.

As Figure 25-35 shows, the Picture dialog box includes an Apply To section, with check boxes for Sides, Front, and End. These check boxes become available if you're formatting three-dimensional column or bar markers. Figure 25-37 on the next page shows an example of a chart with a picture applied to the ends of three-dimensional columns.

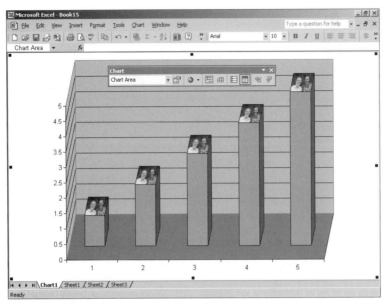

Figure 25-37. With three-dimensional columns and bars, you can assign a picture to the ends or sides, as well as to the fronts, of your markers.

Troubleshooting

I Can't Center a Picture at its Original Size

Images on plot areas or chart areas are either tiled (if you use the Texture tab) or resized to fit (if you use the Picture tab). The charting component of Excel doesn't give you the option to insert a picture at its original size, centered on the plot area or the chart area. To circumvent this limitation, you can insert your image directly onto the worksheet (by choosing Insert, Picture), and then plot a transparent chart on top of the image. You can also work in the other direction: create a chart, and then drag an image on top of it. Figure 25-38 shows an example of a chart superimposed over a clip-art image.

tip Use the Picture toolbar

One additional advantage of combining chart and image on the worksheet is that you can use the Picture toolbar to fine-tune the image. If the picture threatens to over-power the chart, for example, you can reduce its brightness or contrast—or convert it to a watermark.

Chapter 25

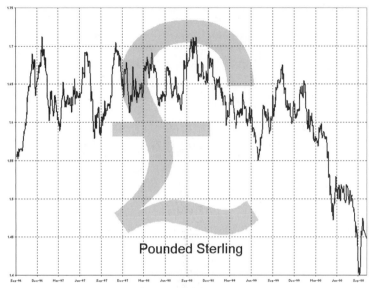

Figure 25-38. Superimposing a chart over an image—clip art or other format— on the worksheet keeps the image centered at its original size.

Changing Three-Dimensional Viewing Angles

The simplest way to change the viewing angle of a three-dimensional chart is to select one of the chart's corners and drag it with the mouse. While you're dragging, Excel displays an outline of the chart. (If you want to see an outline that includes the data markers, hold down Ctrl while you drag.) This direct-manipulation approach is simple, but you also can easily turn an intelligible chart into something quite the opposite. If you change your mind, click the Undo button.

For more precise viewing-angle adjustment, choose Chart, 3-D View. The 3-D View dialog box, shown in Figure 25-39 on the next page, provides separate controls for modifying your chart's elevation, rotation, perspective, and height.

Adjusting the Elevation

The Elevation setting changes your viewing angle relative to the floor of the chart. The default setting is 15, and you can specify any value from –90 through 90. (With three-dimensional pie charts, you're limited to values from 10 through 80.) A setting of 90 places you directly above the chart, as if you were looking down on the tops of markers. With a –90 setting, you look up through the chart's floor (which, incidentally, is always transparent regardless of how you format it). To change the elevation, type a number in the Elevation box or click the large up or down arrow button in the upper left corner of the dialog box.

667

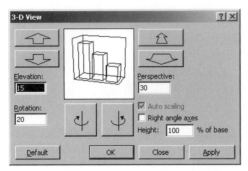

Figure 25-39. Use the 3-D View dialog box for precise control of each three-dimensional viewing parameter.

Changing the Rotation

Imagine that Excel has anchored your chart to a turntable. The Rotation setting spins the turntable. Technically, the rotation setting specifies the angle formed by the category axis and a line drawn horizontally across your screen. The default angle is 20 degrees (except for pie charts, where it's 0). You can specify any angle from 0 through 360 by entering it in the Rotation box or by clicking the clockwise and counterclockwise buttons to the right of the Rotation box.

Changing the Height

The Height setting changes a chart's value-axis-to-category-axis ratio. The default is 100 percent; you can select any value from 5 through 500. The higher the value, the taller your chart. This option is unavailable for three-dimensional bar and column charts.

Changing the Perspective

The Perspective setting determines the apparent depth of three-dimensional area, column, line, and surface charts (as long as the Right Angle Axes option isn't selected). The default setting is 30, but you can specify any value from 0 through 100. Low values make the chart look flatter, as if you were looking at the chart through a telescope or telephoto lens. High values have the opposite effect, making it appear as if you were looking through the wrong end of a pair of binoculars or through a wide-angle lens.

The default setting specifies that the far side of the chart is 30 percent smaller than the near side. This means that with a rotation of 0, the back of the floor is 30 percent narrower than the front of the floor. Similarly, if the elevation is 90, the bottom of the tallest column in a three-dimensional column chart is about 30 percent smaller than the top of the column.

To change the Perspective setting, type a new number in the Perspective box or click the up or down arrow buttons above the Perspective box. You can also eliminate all perspective from a chart by selecting the Right Angle Axes option.

Changing the Axis Angle and Scale

The Right Angle Axes option sets the axes at right angles independent of chart rotation or elevation. To see axes in perspective, turn off this option. For three-dimensional column charts, Excel always turns off this option.

Auto Scaling is available only if you have the Right Angle Axes option selected. When you change a two-dimensional chart into a three-dimensional chart, Excel sometimes draws it smaller. For charts with right-angle axes and a rotation of less than 45 degrees, the Auto Scaling option scales the three-dimensional chart so it's closer in size to the two-dimensional version.

Working with Chart Data

Charts have a way of changing over time. New data arrives, old data becomes obsolete or irrelevant, and new visual comparisons become meaningful. In this chapter, you look at Microsoft Excel's procedures for working with the data that drives your charts. You'll see how to add new points and series to a chart, how to change the order in which Excel plots your series, and how to plot multilevel categories of information. You also look at Excel's features for adding trend lines and error bars.

Excel can also create charts from PivotTable data. These charts reorganize themselves as you pivot the source data. For more information about using PivotCharts, see Chapter 30, "Analyzing Data with PivotTable Reports."

Adding Data

Excel provides several ways to add data to a chart. We'll look at the simplest methods first.

Figure 26-1 on the next page plots data through May 2. This figure also shows a week's worth of data that we haven't yet added to the chart. Notice that, because the plot area is selected, Excel drew two rectangles around the chart's source data. The first rectangle, in column A, outlines the worksheet range that the chart is using for its category-axis labels. The second rectangle, encompassing columns B through E, outlines the four data series. Excel uses purple for the first rectangle and blue for the second, to help you distinguish the two.

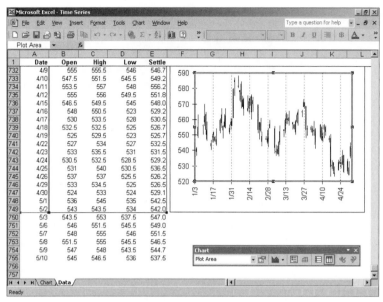

Figure 26-1. When you select the chart area or the plot area, Excel outlines the source data on your worksheet.

To extend the chart so that it includes the new data in rows 750 through 755, drag the Fill handle in the lower right corner of either rectangle. Alternatively, you can use drag-and-drop. Select the new data, including its category-axis labels (column A in Figure 26-1). Position your mouse on the border of the selection so that the mouse pointer changes to an arrow. Then drag the selection to anywhere on the chart. Excel confirms the addition by extending the rectangles to include the new data.

These methods work fine if your chart and its data are close together on the same worksheet. If they're not, you can use standard copy-and-paste procedures. Select the new data, and then choose Edit, Copy. Next, select the chart, and choose Edit, Paste. Alternatively, you can use Chart, Add Data. The Add Data dialog box appears, as shown in Figure 26-2. Fill in the dialog box by typing or selecting the range of new data.

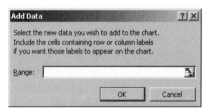

Figure 26-2. Type the new data range here or select it on your worksheet.

Adding a new series is like adding new points to existing series: select the data series you want to add, copy it, and then paste it onto the chart (or drag the selection to the chart). If the new data series is adjacent to the existing data, Excel has no difficulty figuring out that you want to add a new series rather than some new points. Even when the new data is somewhere else, Excel might still be able to add the data correctly. For example, in Figure 26-3, Excel correctly pasted the selected data as a new series because the selection has the same layout as the original data—a column and the same row positions as the existing three series.

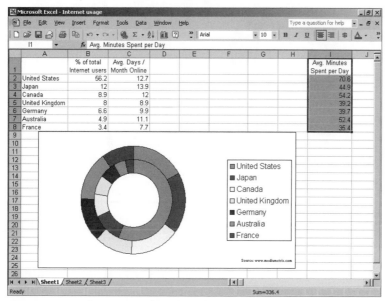

Figure 26-3. If you paste the selected range onto the chart, Excel knows you want to add a series.

However, if you were trying to add the new data seen in I10:I17 in Figure 26-4 on the next page, Excel would no longer be sure what you wanted to do. In that case, it would display the Paste Special dialog box that you see in the figure. The options in the Paste Special dialog box would be set to represent Excel's best guess about your intentions, but you would need to confirm them.

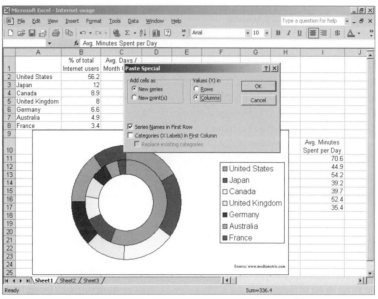

Figure 26-4. When Excel isn't sure how to parse new data dragged onto an existing chart, it displays the Paste Special dialog box.

---

tip **Include a blank row in your chart**

If you frequently extend the data series in a chart, consider incorporating a blank row at the end of the data columns. When you need to add new points, insert a new row above this blank row and add the data to the new row. Excel then incorporates the new data in your chart. If your chart uses a time-series axis, you don't need to bother with the blank row (provided you don't mind having at least one point out of sort order in your source range). Insert a new row above the last row in the data range and add your new information in that new row. Excel incorporates the new data and sorts it properly on the chart. For more information about automating the addition of data to existing charts, see "Using Named Ranges to Create Dynamic Charts" on page 687.

Removing Data

The simplest way to remove a data series from a chart is to select the series on the chart itself and press Delete. This method works even if you've refined the selection to a single point in the series; delete that point and the whole series is gone. If you want to work harder, you can choose Chart, Source Data, click the Series tab, select the series in question, and click Remove. What you *don't* want to do is try to delete the series by clearing or deleting the source data on the worksheet. Your chart will still reference the empty or nonexistent cells.

To delete points from either end of all the series in a chart, select the chart area or the plot area, and then drag the Fill handle at one of the corners of either the purple or blue bounding rectangle that surrounds your data. To remove points from a particular series, select that series, and then drag the blue Fill handle. If the Fill handle isn't visible, you can always choose Chart, Source Data and make your changes there.

By dragging the Fill handles inward at both ends of a chart's data-bounding rectangles, you can make the chart zoom in on a selected portion of your data set. In the chart shown in Figure 26-1, for example, you could create a more detailed view of the downward wave between February 2 and March 7 by dragging the top Fill handle down and the bottom Fill handle up so that only that range is selected. Alternatively, because this is a time-scaled category axis, you could select the category axis, choose Format, Selected Axis, and change the Minimum and Maximum boxes on the Scale tab.

Changing or Replacing Data

If you drag the lower or upper *perimeter* of a data-bounding rectangle, rather than its Fill handle, Excel moves both the start and endpoint of your series. This can be an effective way to obtain detailed views of a chart's data across the whole range of available data.

To switch to an entirely different set of data, select any part of your chart, and then choose Chart, Source Data. You can adjust the entire chart at once (all series) by using the Data Range box on the Data Range tab, or you can work with individual series on the Series tab.

---

tip **Switch the data source to a PivotTable**

In earlier versions of Excel, you were not permitted to switch the data set from an ordinary worksheet table to a PivotTable. Not any more: now, if you choose Chart, Source Data to change the data source to a PivotTable, Excel gives you a PivotChart. However, after you've created your PivotChart, you still can't switch the data source back to an ordinary worksheet table—unless the reversal of your first action is still available using Undo. For more about PivotTables and PivotCharts, see Chapter 30, "Analyzing Data with PivotTable Reports."

Plotting or Marking Every nth Point

Figure 26-5 on the next page shows a two-series line chart that has become difficult to read because the data points are too close together. (Each series now has 100 points; it's easy to imagine how much less effective this chart would become if its series grew to multiple hundreds of points.) Redrawing the series lines without markers wouldn't solve the problem in this hypothetical case; some points are required, but perhaps not all. One way around the difficulty is to plot only the points at some regular interval— every fifth point, for example. Another way is to plot all the points but suppress most of the markers.

Chapter 26

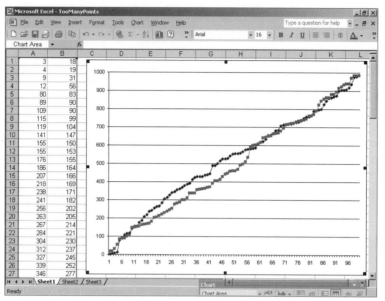

Figure 26-5. The hundreds of markers in this line chart run together and make the chart difficult to read.

To plot only every fifth point, you can take advantage of the fact that Excel normally refrains from plotting hidden points. The Plot Visible Cells Only check box determines whether Excel plots hidden points. Access this setting by choosing Tools, Options and then clicking the Chart tab. Excel selects this check box by default.

Hiding groups of rows by hand is tedious in a large set, but we can use Excel's AutoFilter feature to do the hiding for us. Fill a range adjacent to the last chart column (cells C1:C100 in Figure 26-5) with the formula =**MOD(ROW(),5)**.

Because this formula returns the remainder of the current row number divided by 5, every fifth cell in the range will hold the value 0. By using the AutoFilter feature to display only those rows in which the value in column C is 0, you can make Excel plot only every fifth data point. Figure 26-6 shows the result (the MOD formulas in column C are conveniently covered by the chart).

The principal disadvantage of the solution shown in Figure 26-6 is that the displayed points are now joined by straight lines, regardless of what the hidden values might be. A second disadvantage is that the category axis now asserts that we have only 21 points in our data sets—which is not the case.

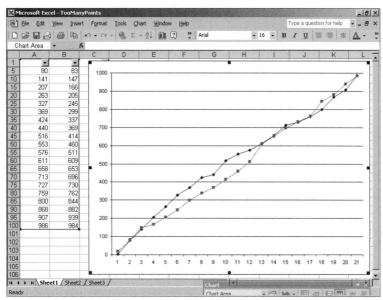

Figure 26-6. We've simplified the chart shown in Figure 26-5 by using AutoFilter to hide rows.

To plot all the data but display markers only for every fifth point, we could manually select points 1, 2, 3, 4, 6, 7, 8, 9, and so on, and format those points to be displayed without markers. Unfortunately, we'd have to do that one point at a time—clearly an odious assignment, given a large set of data.

A better solution is to use a macro, such as the following, to automate the marking of intermittent data points:

```
Sub MarkEveryNthPoint()
    Dim n as Integer, s as Integer, t as Integer
    n = InputBox("Value of n?", "Mark every nth point")
    Application.ScreenUpdating = False
    For s = 1 to ActiveChart.SeriesCollection.Count
        For t = 1 to ActiveChart.SeriesCollection(s).Points.Count
            If t Mod n <> 0 then
            ActiveChart.SeriesCollection(s).Points(t).MarkerStyle = xlNone
            End If
        Next t
    Next s
End Sub
```

To use this macro, press Alt+F11 to invoke the Visual Basic Editor (VBE). In the Project window (press Ctrl+R if the Project window isn't visible), select the name of your workbook. Then choose Insert, Module. In the new module, type the code shown previously. Return to your workbook and select the chart; choose Tools, Macro, Macros, MarkEveryNthPoint, and then click Run. In the dialog box that appears, enter the value of *n* that you want to use, and then click OK. The macro deletes the markers from all points other than those that are even multiples of *n*. As Figure 26-7 shows, the macro simplifies the chart while leaving all the source data visible.

> For more information about creating and using macros, see Chapter 31, "Recording Macros."

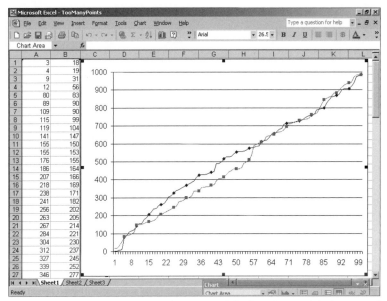

Figure 26-7. We've used a macro to simplify this chart, while leaving all the source data visible.

Changing the Plot Order

To change the order in which series are plotted, select any series and choose Format, Selected Data Series; then click the Series Order tab, shown in Figure 26-8. Use the Move Up and Move Down buttons to manipulate the series order.

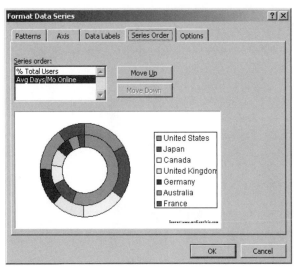

Figure 26-8. Use the Series Order tab of the Format Data Series dialog box to change the order in which Excel plots series.

Using Multilevel Categories

Excel allows you to categorize your categories. This sounds redundant, but a quick example illustrates the technique. Suppose you want to plot the data shown in Figure 26-9 (The resulting chart is shown in Figure 26-10 on the next page). The series are months and the categories are the sales offices located in different cities. The city sales are further classified by state, however.

The ability to create multilevel charts appeared first in Excel 97, the version immediately before the one with which Excel introduced PivotCharts. PivotCharts—charts derived from PivotTables—are an alternative way to create multilevel charts, and they have certain advantages over the simpler multilevel charts discussed here.

		January	February	March
Salespeople by office				
Washington	Seattle	13	13	14
Washington	Spokane	6	8	10
Oregon	Portland	12	12	12
Oregon	Eugene	2	2	2
California	San Francisco	11	13	15
California	Los Angeles	14	18	2
California	San Diego	16	16	11

Figure 26-9. This worksheet uses multilevel categories; city sales offices are grouped by the states in which the cities are located.

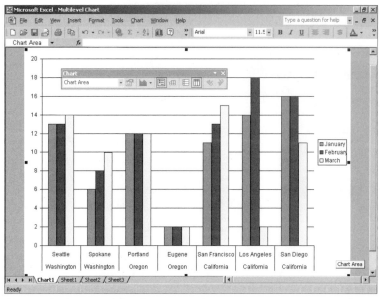

Figure 26-10. A multilevel category chart uses two or more sets of category names to label the category axis.

Before you can create a PivotChart, you have to have a PivotTable, and creating a PivotTable requires that your data be laid out on the worksheet in a particular manner. To create a PivotTable from the data shown in Figure 26-9, for example, you need to organize your worksheet like the one shown here.

	A	B	C	D
1	**State**	**City**	**Month**	**Employees**
2	Washington	Seattle	January	13
3	Washington	Seattle	February	13
4	Washington	Seattle	March	14
5	Washington	Spokane	January	6
6	Washington	Spokane	February	8
7	Washington	Spokane	March	10
8	Oregon	Portland	January	12

After creating the PivotTable, you could generate the PivotChart shown in Figure 26-11. If the information you need to plot is relatively simple and you already have it organized in a manner not conducive to PivotTable creation, you're probably better off using the multilevel charting capability discussed earlier.

For more information about creating PivotTables and PivotCharts, see Chapter 30, "Analyzing Data with PivotTable Reports."

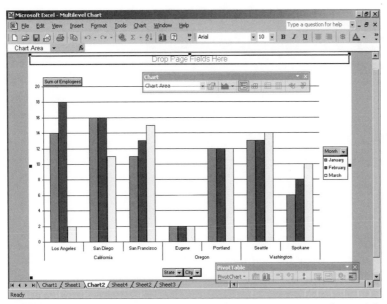

Figure 26-11. PivotCharts like this are an alternative way to plot multilevel data.

Adding Trend Lines

A *trend line* is a line that describes the general tendency of a data series. It can be a moving average, a linear-regression line, or a line generated by one of various kinds of nonlinear curve-fitting methods.

To add a trend line to a series in an area, bar, column, line, or xy (scatter) chart, first select the series, and then choose Chart, Add Trendline. (This command appears only when a series is selected.) Excel displays the Add Trendline dialog box shown in Figure 26-12 on the next page.

To specify how Excel should draw the trend line, select one of the Trend/Regression Type options. If you select Polynomial, indicate the highest power (from 2 through 6) for the independent variable in the adjacent Order box. If you select Moving Average, indicate the number of periods Excel should use in its calculations in the adjacent Period box.

After you've indicated the type of trend or regression line Excel should draw, select the Options tab if you want a name for the trend line to appear in the chart legend. Provided you're not working with a moving average, you can also use the Forward and Backward spin boxes on the Options tab to extrapolate the trend line. For linear, polynomial, and exponential trend lines, you can also set the y-intercept in the Set Intercept box. You can also display the regression equation and the R-squared value beside the trend line plot.

Chapter 26

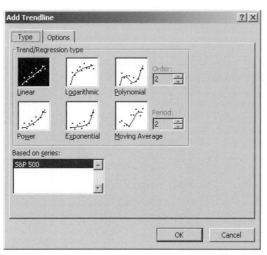

Figure 26-12.   Using the Add Trendline dialog box, you can add six different types of trend lines to your data series.

You can add as many trend lines to a series as you please. To format a trend line, select it and choose Format, Format Selected Trendline. Note that Excel does not create a new data set on your worksheet when you add a trend line to the chart. You can do that yourself, of course, using statistical functions or averaging formulas. For information about using statistical functions and averaging formulas, see Chapter 17, "Functions for Analyzing Statistics."

Adding Error Bars

When you chart statistical or experimental data, it's often helpful to indicate the confidence level of your data. Excel's error bar feature makes this easy. To add error bars to a data series in an area, bar, column, line, or xy (scatter) chart, select the series, choose Format, Selected Data Series, and then click the Y Error Bars tab, shown in Figure 26-13.

You can set error bars to show the actual data point value plus some number, minus some number, or both plus and minus some number. Use the options in the Display section to indicate which of these error bar styles you want. Use the Error Amount options—Fixed Value, Percentage (of the data point value), Standard Deviation(s), Standard Error, and Custom (a number specified manually)—to calculate the amount depicted by the error bar.

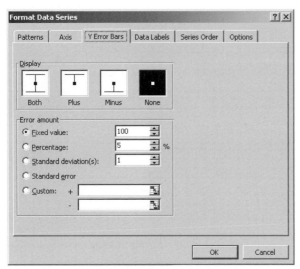

Figure 26-13. Using the Format Data Series dialog box, you can customize error bars to illustrate the potential error for each data point in a series.

What-If Charting: Dragging Markers to Change Data

Because charts are linked to worksheet cells, you can use them to construct visual what-if scenarios with your data. For example, if you set up a break-even analysis in a worksheet and then plot fixed costs, variable costs, total costs, and gross margin in a chart, you can change fixed-cost assumptions in the worksheet and immediately see the effect on the gross-margin line in the chart.

You can also reverse this process in two-dimensional bar, column, line, and xy (scatter) charts. You can drag chart data markers—including picture markers—up or down and have Excel adjust the underlying worksheet. In the break-even analysis, for example, you can drag the chart's gross-margin line up so that it crosses 0 at a different point, and then find out on the worksheet how much you would need to reduce your fixed costs to achieve the increase in profit. This process is called *graphical goal seeking.*

Let's look at a simple example. Suppose that you created the break-even analysis chart shown in Figure 26-14 on the next page. The Profit (Loss) line of this chart (the line with asterisk markers) shows that, given the current assumptions, you can expect to break even some time around the beginning of period 6.

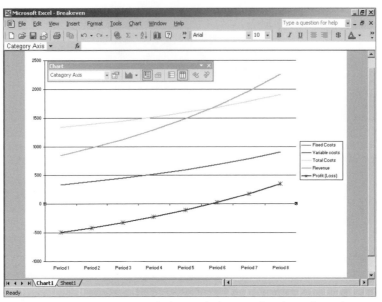

Figure 26-14. Tampering with the profit line on this chart shows how it affects the assumptions on your worksheet.

Suppose you want to know what it would take to reach the break-even point by the beginning of period 4. To find out, you can select the period 4 data point (select the profit line once, pause, and then select the fourth marker on that line), and drag it up so that its value changes to 0. As Figure 26-15 shows, Excel provides feedback about the value of the point you're dragging, as well as dotted lines from the current position of the point to the points immediately preceding and following it.

When you release the mouse button to drop the marker in its new location, Excel either changes the source item on the worksheet (if that item is a constant value) or displays the Goal Seek dialog box (if the item is a calculated value). In this example, profit is a calculated value, so the Goal Seek dialog box shown in Figure 26-16 is displayed.

By filling out the Goal Seek dialog box, you can see how much you have to change some of the underlying assumptions to reach your target. The example shown in Figure 26-16 instructs Excel to change the initial (period 1) revenue expectation (the value in E2) so that the profit (loss) for period 4 (cell F5) becomes 0.

Naturally, you can also do this directly from the worksheet. However, some people prefer working visually. Excel's what-if charting feature accommodates that preference.

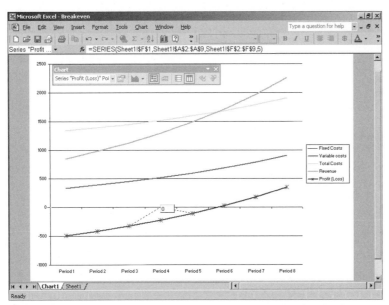

Figure 26-15.   As you drag a data point, Excel provides feedback about how far you moved.

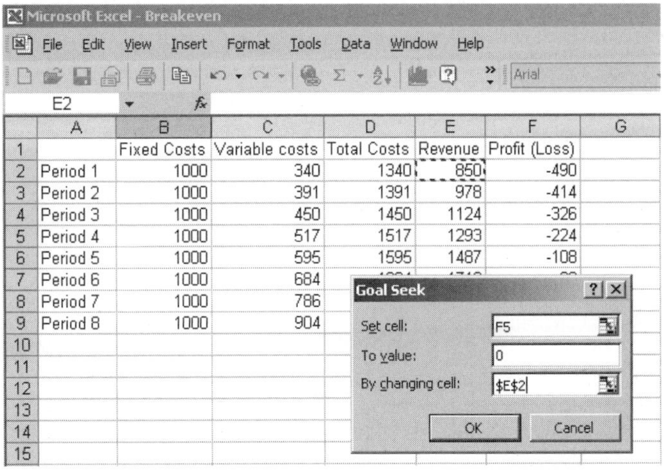

Figure 26-16.   Because the dragged point was a calculated value, Excel responds to the action by displaying the Goal Seek dialog box.

Advanced Charting Techniques

In this chapter, you explore assorted topics that don't fall neatly into the preceding three chapters. You look at a couple of Excel's more exotic chart types, consider the use of Excel for creating Gannt charts, and learn ways to make Excel perform some formatting feats that it would rather not. Let's begin with a technique for making your charts stay current as you add to their source data.

Using Named Ranges to Create Dynamic Charts

If you select a chart's series and look at Excel's formula line, you see that a series is generated by a formula that uses the SERIES function. SERIES is a special kind of function that's used only in this context, to define a chart series. You can't use it on the worksheet, and you can't incorporate worksheet functions or formulas into its arguments.

For all chart types except bubble, the SERIES function has the arguments listed in Table 27-1 on the next page.

In bubble charts, the SERIES function takes an additional argument, which specifies the bubble sizes.

Each of these SERIES function arguments corresponds to a field on the SERIES tab of the Source Data dialog box. Figure 27-1 on the next page illustrates these relationships. The name argument for this SERIES formula is Sheet1!$B$1 and appears in the Name field of the dialog box. (Because Sheet1!$B$1 contains the label Price, the series is identified as Price in the Series field of the dialog box.) The category_labels argument is Sheet1!$A$2:$A$1056 and appears in the Category(X) Axis

Labels field. The values argument is Sheet1!$B$2:$B$1056 and can be found in the Values field. Because the chart has only one series, the *order* argument is 1. This default plot order is reflected by the position of the Price series in the Series field of the dialog box.

Table 27-1. SERIES Function Arguments

Argument	Required/Optional	Specifies
name	Optional	The name that appears in the legend
category_labels	Optional	The labels that appear on the category axis (if omitted, Excel uses consecutive integers as labels)
values	Required	The values that Excel will plot
order	Required	The plot order for the series

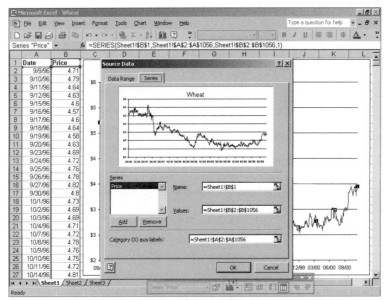

Figure 27-1. Each argument in a chart's SERIES formula appears as a field on the Series tab of the Source Data dialog box.

Why Does Any of This Matter?

Because it's possible—and sometimes desirable—to apply range names to some of these SERIES arguments. By using range names you can more easily switch a chart from plotting one set of data to an entirely different set. More important, by creating a dynamic range name and using that as a SERIES argument, you can create a dynamic chart. All charts are dynamic in the sense that they change to reflect changes in their source data. But by using dynamic range names, you can also make a chart automatically plot new data as it's added to your worksheet or automatically plot a subset of the worksheet data—for example, the most recent 30 points.

As you might know, all names in Excel are formula names, not range names. Typically, the formulas resolve to range references. For example, if you select A1:A10 on Sheet1, and use the Define command to create a name for your range selection, Excel defines the name as

```
=Sheet1!$A$1:$A$10
```

By incorporating certain functions into the formula that defines a name, you can make that name reference different worksheet ranges, depending on worksheet conditions.

Plotting New Data Automatically

The chart shown in Figure 27-1 plots Sheet1!$A$2:$A$1056 as category-axis labels and Sheet1!$B$2:$B$1056 as values for the Price series. To make this chart automatically incorporate new data points added in columns A and B, you create the following names on Sheet1:

Name	Definition
Date	=OFFSET(Sheet1!$A$1,1,0,COUNTA($A:$A)-1)
Price	=OFFSET(Sheet1!$B$1,1,0,COUNTA($B:$B)-1)

For information about defining names, see "Defining and Managing Names" on page 372.

These formulas say, in effect, give me a range that starts one row below A1 (or B1) and whose number of rows is one less than the number of populated cells in column A (or column B). As more cells in columns A and B become populated, the formula automatically resolves to an expanding range. (Obviously, the range incorporates the new data only if that data appears in cells immediately below the existing data. Of course, for this technique to give the desired result, the remainder of columns A and B must be empty.)

After you've defined these dynamic names, you can apply them to your chart's SERIES formula in either of two ways:

- By selecting the chart series that you want to modify, and then editing the SERIES formula on the formula bar.

- By selecting the chart, choosing Chart, Source Data, going to the Series tab, and making changes to the appropriate dialog-box fields.

InsideOut

You cannot apply the names by choosing Insert, Name, Apply; it just doesn't work in this context.

Working in the dialog box is simpler, but whichever way you decide to work, changes in one venue are copied to the other. Whichever way you go, leave the sheet references in place. For example, if the Values field says =Sheet1!$B$2:$B:1056, leave the Sheet1! part alone and replace the absolute range address with your new range name. If the name is unique in your workbook, Excel will eventually display it as a workbook-level name, as Figure 27-2 shows.

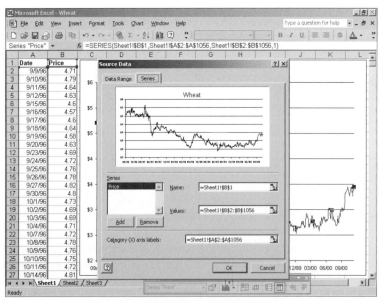

Figure 27-2. When you replace the absolute range references in the Values and Category (X) Axis Labels fields with dynamic names, this chart incorporates new data.

Plotting Only the Most Recent Points

If you want to plot only the most recent 30 points in the example price chart, you modify your names to look like this:

Name	Definition
Date	=OFFSET(Sheet1!$A$1,COUNTA($A:$A)-30,0,30
Price	=OFFSET(Sheet1!$B$1,COUNTA($B:$B)-30,0,30)

These formulas tell Excel to start at the 30th row from the end of the populated area and create a range encompassing 30 rows and 1 column.

> **caution** If you delete a name that has been applied to a chart series, the series is no longer valid. Excel does not restore the range reference that used to be equivalent to the deleted name.

Using Arrays to Create a Static Chart

Under some circumstances you might want to "freeze" a chart so that it no longer updates itself. The most likely reason to do this is to create a snapshot of your data at some point in time—either as a baseline or as a scenario case.

One way to produce such a chart is to copy the source data somewhere and either hide or protect the worksheet on which it resides. A safer way is to convert all range references in all the chart's SERIES formulas to arrays. To do so, select a series on the chart you want to freeze. A SERIES formula should appear on Excel's formula bar. Press F2 to edit the formula, and then press F9. Excel replaces all range references (including names) to arrays of constants. These constants are impervious to anything that occurs subsequently on the worksheet. The only way you can "unfreeze" a chart that's been made static in this manner is to edit the SERIES formula again (or make the equivalent edits in the Source Data dialog box).

Using Bubble Charts

A *bubble chart* is a scatter chart in which each data point provides three pieces of information instead of two. In the more common form of scatter chart, the *xy chart,* the position of each point is determined by two attributes, its *x* value and its *y* value. The same is true in a bubble chart, except that in a bubble chart each point is a bubble, the size of which is determined by the point's third attribute. An example will clarify.

In Figure 27-3, the table at A1:D6 includes three columns of data—number of competitors, sales in millions, and market share. The position of each bubble on the chart below the table is determined by its value in column B and column C. The size of each bubble is determined by its value in column D.

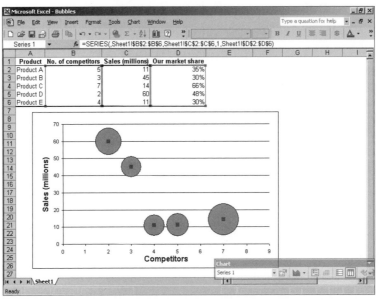

Figure 27-3. In this bubble chart, bubble sizes are determined by values in column D, and the positions of the bubbles are determined by values in columns B and C.

When you select a bubble chart series, Excel displays three bounding rectangles instead of the usual two. The third, green, rectangle indicates the bubble-size range. The SERIES formula that appears on the formula line includes a fifth argument to specify the bubble-size range, and the Series tab of the Source Data dialog box includes an additional field called Sizes.

If you select a bubble series, choose Format, Selected Data Series, and click the Options tab, you find some additional formatting options (see Figure 27-4). In the Size Represents area, you can choose whether to have your bubble-size range specify bubble area or bubble width (in practice, there's not much difference between the two options). Using the Show Negative Bubbles check box, you can opt to include bubbles for negative values. Such values are normally not plotted (not even as simple points). If you select the check box, Excel plots the negative values as unfilled bubbles to ensure contrast with your positive values. On the Options tab, you can also change the scale used to size your bubbles.

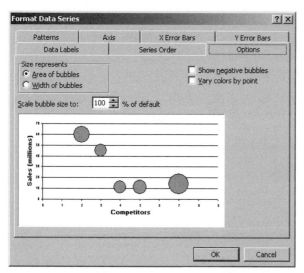

Figure 27-4. Bubble series come with additional formatting options.

The big shortcoming of Excel's bubble charts is the same one that plagues its xy (scatter) charts: the program doesn't know how to create meaningful data labels. If you choose Chart, Chart Options, and click the Data Labels tab, you find an option to display each point's bubble size as a data label. This is potentially useful information, but the default position for these labels, to the right of the bubbles, can easily plant a bubble's label in the center of a neighboring bubble (see Figure 27-5 on the next page). To get around this problem, you must first create the labels. Then select the labels, choose Format, Selected Data Labels, click the Alignment tab, and choose something different (Center, perhaps) in the Label Position field.

What's worse, the labels you're most likely to want—in the example, the product names in column A—aren't available at all as standard options. You can enter your own labels manually, following the procedure described in "Editing Data Labels" on page 636. You also can use the VBA procedure in "Generating Useful Data Labels on XY (Scatter) Charts" on page 637 to apply the text in a range (A2:A6, for example) as data labels.

In the example chart, you might want both the product name (column A) and the market share (column D) to appear in your data labels. The best approach is to concatenate the values in columns A and D into a new range of cells. For example, by entering the formula =A2&","&TEXT(D2,"0%") into cell E2 and then replicating this formula down to E6, you create a column containing the product name, followed by a comma and a space, followed by an appropriately formatted market-share value. You then can use this column with the Data Labeler macro listed in Chapter 25, "Enhancing the Appearance of Your Charts," to generate your labels.

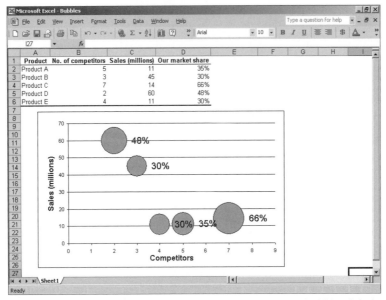

Figure 27-5. With data labels in their default position, a bubble's label can easily land inside a neighboring bubble.

As you'll see in the next section, Excel's radar chart type can also position data points according to their values on three scales. Radar charts can plot points with many more than three attributes, but they work well only when all attributes fall roughly within the same numeric range. In a bubble chart, the x, y, and bubble-size values can occupy totally distinct orders of magnitude—as they do, in fact, in Figure 27-3.

Using Radar Charts

A *radar chart* is a chart in which each data point gets a separate copy of a single value axis, with the axis copies distributed radially around a center point. Because each series gets its own value-axis copy, the chart has no need for a category axis. Figure 27-6 shows one of these remarkable creatures.

The three series, Strength, Agility, and Endurance, have 15 data points each. Hence, the chart has 15 copies of the value axis. Only one of these copies, the one that points straight up toward the label Alexander, bears tick-mark labels. In all other respects, each axis copy has the same formatting and scaling—and this is a requirement of the chart type. The series are identified by their marker types (round for Strength, square for Agility, triangular for Endurance) and by their line colors. The lines and markers can be formatted or removed, as they can on line charts.

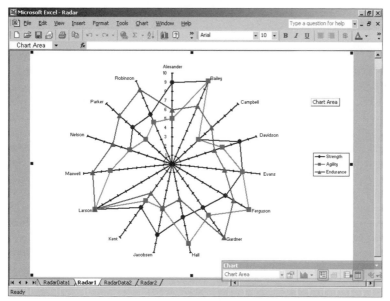

Figure 27-6. Because this radar chart plots 15 points for each of three data series, the plot uses 15 separate copies of the value axis.

The chart in Figure 27-6 plots the data shown here.

	A	B	C	D
1		Strength	Agility	Endurance
2	Alexander	9	5	6
3	Bailey	10	10	7
4	Campbell	4	4	6
5	Davidson	8	6	5
6	Evans	8	8	6
7	Ferguson	7	10	8
8	Gardner	6	7	10
9	Hall	6	9	4
10	Jacobsen	8	5	5
11	Kent	6	5	4
12	Larson	10	10	10
13	Maxwell	7	7	9
14	Nelson	5	5	7
15	Parker	6	4	8
16	Robinson	6	5	9

If you leave the lines in place, each series becomes a closed polygon, and by studying the shapes of the polygons you can divine the message of the chart. In Figure 27-6, for example, all three polygons pooch out at the Larson point, telling us that Larson has a high degree of all three attributes. The three lines fold inward, about halfway to the center, on the Kent point, suggesting that Kent has a moderate amount of each attribute—and so on.

Chapter 27

When you create a radar chart, Excel draws major value-axis gridlines by default. The gridlines make it easier to determine the magnitude of each data point but more difficult to discern the shapes of the series (see Figure 27-7). If the lines diminish the effectiveness of your chart, choose Chart, Chart Options, click the Gridlines tab, and clear the appropriate check box.

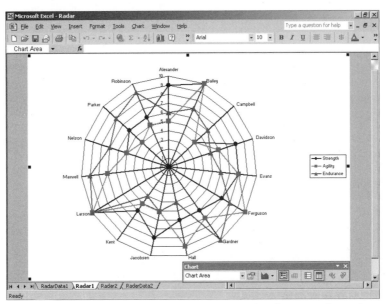

Figure 27-7. Gridlines, drawn by default, give the chart a spider-web appearance and can sometimes make the chart hard to read.

Charts of any type are easier to understand, the fewer points and series they plot. With a radar chart, in particular, it's a good idea to limit the number of series. With a three-series chart, for example, the three value-axis copies appear at right angles to one another and resemble the familiar x-y-z coordinate system. The series polygons, meanwhile, are triangles and can be visualized as intersecting planes. Such a chart (see Figure 27-8) is probably easier to understand than the one shown in Figure 27-6.

In all events, the radar chart is suitable only for data series that fall within a common numeric range. Because you can't plot outlying series on a second value axis, as you can in other chart types, the radar chart is essentially useless for plotting values in widely separated orders of magnitude.

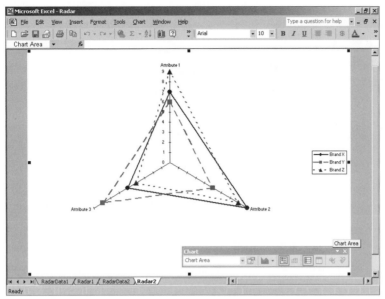

Figure 27-8. With radar charts, even more than other chart types, it's best to keep things simple.

Creating Gannt Charts

The recommended way to create a Gannt chart is with a project-management program, such as Microsoft Project. But if you *must* do it in Excel, you can—sort of. Figure 27-9 shows a primitive Gannt chart created in Excel.

This chart uses Floating Bars, an option on the Custom Types tab of the Chart Type dialog box. It plots two series—a start date and a duration. The start date is plotted as an offset from some date. Task 1, for example, begins 0 days from this reference point, Task 2 starts 4 days from the reference point, and so on. This first series is formatted to be invisible (that is, it's formatted with no border and no fill). The duration series is plotted as horizontal bars stacked on top of the start-date series. Hence, each point in the duration series is offset horizontally by the value of the corresponding point in the start-date series.

You can't tell by the grayscale image in Figure 27-9, but the Floating Bars chart type uses a forest-green gradient fill for the chart area. The tick-mark labels for both axes, meanwhile, are reversed out against this dark background. If you're not keen on green, you might want to play with the formatting.

You might also want to reverse the plot order on the category axis so that the first task appears at the top and the last at the bottom (the conventional order for Gannt charts). To do this, select the category axis, choose Format, Selected Axis, click the Scale tab, and select Categories In Reverse Order.

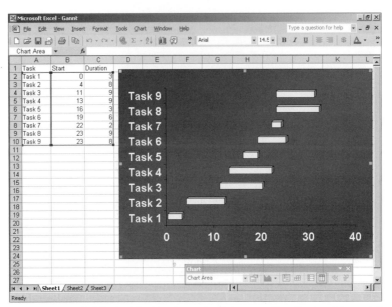

Figure 27-9. With the Floating Bars chart type on the Custom Types tab, you can create a simple Gannt chart.

The value-axis labels—0, 10, 20, 30—represent the number of days elapsed since the chart's reference date. You'd probably rather see actual dates there, but Excel won't accommodate you. (Because this is a value axis, you can't use the SERIES formula or the Source Data dialog box to tell Excel to get its labels from a different range.) The best you can do if you really want to see dates is suppress the normal tick-mark–label display (select the value axis, choose Format, Selected Axis, click the Patterns tab, and select None in the Tick Mark Labels group), and create text boxes to display your dates. That's a great deal of hand labor, unfortunately.

You need to do some similar tinkering, using the Drawing toolbar, if you want dependency arrows and other Gannt-chart paraphernalia. But if you really wanted that sort of thing, you'd have used a project-management program in the first place, right?

Assorted Formatting Issues

Although Excel's charting engine has a lot more presentation power now than it did in earlier versions, at heart it remains an analytical tool. It's more likely to turn out graphs that would have pleased your high-school algebra teacher than the kinds of attention-grabbing charts you find in business magazines or boardroom presentations.

Tuning an Excel chart for maximum impact often entails simplification—getting rid of chart elements that Excel wants to give you by default. For example, if the message of your chart is rising sales, perhaps that message is best conveyed by a bright and heavy chart line accompanied by a couple of snappy text boxes. Maybe you don't need axes, gridlines, or borders around the plot and chart areas. If you decide to keep the gridlines, you might want to tone them down a bit—for example, by replacing the solid black lines with gray dots. Maybe you can manage without that gloomy gray backdrop that comes free of charge with standard Excel chart offerings.

In the following paragraphs, you look at a few things that Excel's charts don't do gracefully—and at ways to work around the program's limitations.

Tick-Mark Labels Without Axes

If you've ever deleted a chart axis, you've undoubtedly noticed that the tick-mark labels disappeared along with the axis. What if you want labels but not axes? Instead of deleting the axis, select it, choose Format, Selected Axis, and click the Patterns tab. In the Lines section of the dialog box, choose None.

Tick-Mark Labels on the Plot Area

A stylish way to simplify a chart is to remove the value axis and tuck the tick-mark labels under gridlines on the plot area. Unfortunately, Excel makes this difficult to do. You can almost achieve the desired effect by moving the value axis onto the chart (select the category axis; choose Format, Selected Axis; click the Scale tab; and enter 2 in the Value (Y) Axis Crosses At Category Number field), hiding the axis (select the value axis; choose Format, Selected Axis; click the Patterns tab; and in the Lines section choose None), and then increasing the tick-mark labels' point size but making them subscripts. (You have to make them subscripts or they sit on top of the gridlines.) Figure 27-10 shows the result.

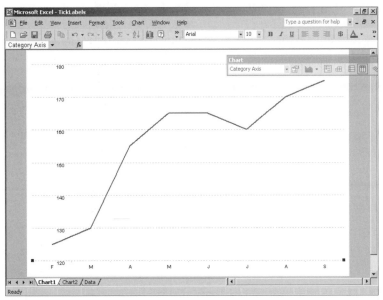

Figure 27-10. You can tuck tick-mark labels under gridlines by moving the value axis to the right, hiding the axis, and then displaying the labels as subscripts.

The problem is that on a typical chart, this technique moves the labels too far inward. More satisfactory results can be achieved by dispensing with the tick-mark labels and re-creating them as hand-positioned text boxes. This is the method used in Figure 27-11.

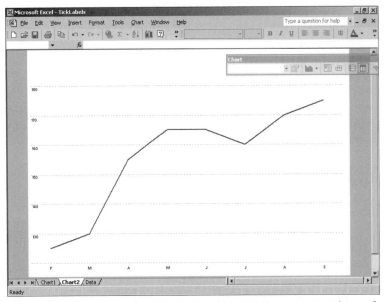

Figure 27-11. A better, but not easier, solution is to create text boxes for your tick-mark labels and then position them by hand.

Formatting Selected Gridlines or Tick-Mark Labels

You can individually select and format data markers and data labels; but when it comes to formatting gridlines or tick-mark labels, Excel offers no such convenience. If you want to see particular gridlines and not others, or particular tick-mark labels, there's no remedy but to use text boxes for the labels or the Drawing toolbar for the gridlines. You also need the Drawing toolbar if you want exceptionally thick axes or gridlines.

Staggered Tick-Mark Labels

The winner-loser chart shown in Figure 27-12 displays tick-mark labels to the left of positive bars and to the right of negative bars. Too bad Excel doesn't let you do this!

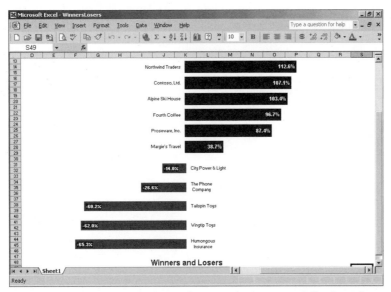

Figure 27-12. This winner-loser chart is two charts carefully aligned.

The chart, of course, is really two charts, carefully positioned so that their category axes line up. The lower chart has its tick-mark labels in the High position (select its axis, choose Format, Selected Axis, click the Patterns tab, and select High in the Tick Mark Labels section of the dialog box). This sort of arrangement works out well if both charts have the same number of points. Then you can give each chart's series the same overlap and gap width, and all the bars will look as if they came from the same chart. If you have many more positive bars than negative, or vice versa, you probably need to plot some dummy values in the set with fewer points and then format the dummy values and their data labels to be invisible.

Plotting Your Own Projection (Extrapolation) Line

Excel's TrendLine feature extrapolates a data set to forecast future values, but it does so by applying regression analysis to your existing data—and, of course, it draws a regression line for the past as well as the projection into the future. Suppose you want only the projection—and want to use your own guesstimates, never mind the math.

In that case, you plot two data series—one for history, the other for fortune-telling. If you make sure that both sets share a common data point (the September value, in Figure 27-13), the twain will meet. Format the second line in a contrasting line style, and you've got your projection.

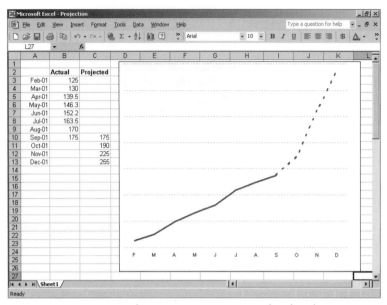

Figure 27-13. You can draw your own projection line by plotting two series with a common data point.

Part 9

Managing Databases and Lists

Managing Information in Lists

Spreadsheets are great for making lists—phone lists, client lists, task lists, transaction lists, lists of assets and liabilities, you name it. In fact, years ago, Microsoft began asking people how they used Excel (as distinguished, perhaps, from what the product's designers had expected them to do). The researchers discovered not only that list management was the number one spreadsheet activity, but that a lot of users did nothing but create and maintain lists of various sorts. Accordingly, Excel's designers over the years have added more and more features to simplify the building, maintenance, and use of lists. You explore Excel's many list-related features in this chapter.

Building and Maintaining a List

To function effectively, a list should have the following characteristics:

- The top row should consist of labels, with each label describing the contents of the column beneath it. Each label should be unique.

- Each column should contain the same kind of information.

- Each type of information that you want to be able to sort by, search on, or otherwise manipulate individually, should be in a separate column.

- The list should not contain blank rows or columns.

- Ideally, the list should occupy a worksheet by itself. If that's not possible, separate the list from any other information on the worksheet by at least one blank row and column.

Figure 28-1 shows an example of a seven-column list. Each column in this list records a particular kind of information—a *field*, in database terminology. The top row holds unique field labels. We've separated first and last names, in case we want to extract last names only or use the first and last names separately in a mail-merge process. The list has no blank rows or columns and occupies a worksheet by itself.

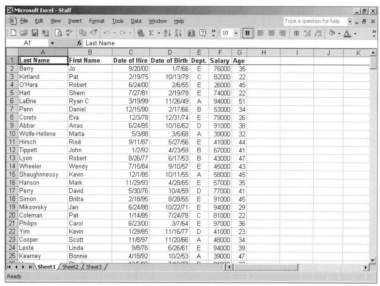

Figure 28-1. Each column in a list should contain a particular kind of information, and the first row should consist of labels describing the columns' contents.

We've used Excel's Freeze Panes column to lock the top row so it remains visible as we scroll downward through the list. Excel marks the pane boundary with a rule.

For information about freezing panes, see "Freezing Panes" on page 124.

You can make the top row bold to set it off visually from the rest of the list. This is helpful to whoever uses your list (including yourself), but Excel doesn't require it. Because the first and second rows in the list in Figure 28-1 contain different kinds of information—columns C and D , for example, have text in the top row and dates below—Excel recognizes the top row as a *header* row. If you sort your list, Excel is smart enough to keep the header row in place while it rearranges the rest of the list. If you create a PivotTable Report from your list, Excel will use the labels in the top row as field names.

Using Range Names in Your List

You might find it handy to have names assigned to the columns of your list. That way, if your list includes one or more columns of calculated data, you can make the formulas involved easier to read. For example, the list shown in Figure 28-1 has one calculated column—Age. We calculated values in this column by subtracting date of birth from today's date (giving us the number of days the person has been alive), dividing by 365.25 (to get the number of years), and then applying the INT function to the result of this division. You could write =INT((TODAY()-D2)/365.25) at G2, and then replicate downward, but writing =INT((TODAY()-Date_of_Birth)/365.25) makes the formula easier to understand.

Even though the name Date_of_Birth is assigned to the entire D column, each formula in column G that references Date_of_Birth references only the D-column value in its own row. Excel is smart that way; if a formula or function that expects a single value references a range name encompassing multiple values, Excel plucks only the value from the current row or column if it can.

Assigning names to the columns of your list is easiest if the header row (the row containing your field labels) is at the top of the worksheet, in row 1. If your list is set up that way, begin by selecting the entire columns. In Figure 28-1, for example, you drag the mouse across the column headings for columns A through G (not the labels in row 1, but the letters A through G in the worksheet frame). This creates a selection extending from A1 to G65536. Next, while this range is selected, choose Insert, Name, Create. In the Create Names dialog box, be sure that Top Row is selected and that the other three check boxes are clear. Click OK.

Excel responds by creating the following names:

Last_Name	Sheet1!$A$2:$A$65536
First_Name	Sheet1!$B$2:$B$65536
Date_of_Hire	Sheet1!$C$2:$C$65536
Date_of_Birth	Sheet1!$D$2:$D$65536
Dept.	Sheet1!$E$2:$E$65536
Salary	Sheet1!$F$2:$F$65536
Age	Sheet1!$G$2:$G$65536

In this example we assigned the column names to the entire columns, not just from row 2 to the current bottom of our list. Doing so costs nothing and accommodates the addition of new rows to the list. If our names extended only to the current last row and we copied our Age formula (which references the name Date_of_Birth) into new rows, that formula would return a #VALUE! Error.

Chapter 28

In Figure 28-1, had we also used the values in each row of column A to name that row, we could have taken advantage of Excel's nifty intersection operator (the space character) to extract bits of information from the list on an ad hoc basis. If row 21 were named Philips, for example, we could determine Philips's salary with the formula =**Philips Salary**.

The intersection operator creates a reference consisting of all the cells common to both its operand ranges. Because only one cell is common to both the range named Philips and the range named Salary, the simple formula just cited returns the item we want.

Unfortunately, naming rows based on their first-column contents is usually not as simple and reliable as naming columns based on field headings. For one thing, this technique runs aground if you don't have unique entries in the first column of each row. A much more serious problem occurs if you sort the list. Excel doesn't update name definitions just because you happen to shuffle your data. So if you sort the list in Figure 28-1 into alphabetical order by last name, writing =**Philips Salary** would almost certainly fetch someone else's salary, not that of Philips.

Using (or Disabling) Excel's List-Building Aids

Excel offers the following features to simplify the task of list creation:

- Automatic format and formula extension.
- AutoComplete for cell values.
- The Pick From List command.
- Move on Enter.
- Custom Lists.

Most users find these features to be a great convenience, but if you happen to be one who does not, you can disable or ignore them, as described later in this section.

Automatic Format and Formula Extension

Excel looks for patterns as you build or extend a list. If you enter a text value in a column, for example, and the text in the same column in the three preceding rows happens to be italic, Excel will make the current text italic to match. If you're adding a new row to a list and a particular column in at least four of the immediately preceding rows has a calculated value, Excel will perform the calculation for you in the current row as well.

One of the cooler things about the formula-extension feature is that Excel doesn't try to generate the formula until all the required operands are present. In earlier versions of Excel and other spreadsheets, users often copied formulas into the rows below an existing list so that they wouldn't have to recopy the formulas each time they added a new row. Typically, those formulas referenced other values in the current row, and if those referenced values weren't present, the formulas would return error constants (such as #VALUE!) or other kinds of erroneous results. (The age formula in column G of Figure 28-1, for example, would evaluate Date_of_Birth as 0 if that column were blank, returning an age in excess of 100.) With formula completion, you don't have to worry about missing operands.

The format-extension feature breaks down under certain circumstances—usually when it collides with some other convenience feature. If you apply an AutoFormat to the existing rows of a list, for example, Excel doesn't extend the AutoFormat appropriately. Thus, if your current row has a nice thick rule at the bottom, courtesy of an Auto-Format, that thick rule will not get up and move as you append rows. (You need to re-apply the AutoFormat after adding rows or add your new rows within the list, rather then appending them to the bottom.) If you enter dates by typing a recognized date formulation (such as 11/16/88), those dates won't assume the format of dates in previous rows. If you copy data from the Clipboard, Excel doesn't deploy the extension feature at all.

If for some reason you don't fancy having formats and formulas extended automatically, choose Tools, Options. On the Edit tab, clear the Extend List Formats And Formulas check box.

AutoComplete for Cell Values

Certain columns of lists typically repeat the same information. For example, if your Region column has four possible entries—North, South, East, and West—and encompasses hundreds of rows, you could be typing those same four words an average of 100 times apiece. AutoComplete to the rescue! If Excel notices that you're starting to enter something you've entered before (in the current column), it offers to complete the job for you. With your four regions, you have to type only **N**, **S**, **E**, or **W** and then press Enter, Tab, or a cursor key to accept Excel's completion.

If AutoComplete gets in your way for any reason, you can turn it off. Choose Tools, Options, click the Edit tab, and clear Enable AutoComplete For Cell Values.

For more about AutoComplete, see "Letting Excel Help with Typing Chores" on page 195.

Move on Enter

By default, Excel moves the selection down one row when you terminate a cell entry by pressing Enter. If you create a new row in a list by pressing the Right Arrow or Tab key after each cell entry, and then press Enter when you get to the end of the row, your Enter key becomes like the carriage-return key on a typewriter; it takes you to the leftmost cell in the next row. Most users like this. If you don't, choose Tools, Options, click the Edit tab, and clear Move Selection After Enter.

Chapter 28

> **tip** **Press Ctrl+Enter to avoid moving**
>
> To use the Enter key without moving, hold down Ctrl while you press Enter. Excel terminates the current entry but does not move the selection.

Custom Lists

Use custom lists to repeat particular sequences of entries by dragging the fill handle. If you need to create lists repeatedly that include the entries Pitcher, Catcher, First Base, and so on, in consecutive rows, you can simplify the task by creating a custom list.

> For information about creating and using custom lists, see "Creating Custom Lists" on page 178.

Validating Data Entry

You can choose Data, Validation to ensure that new or edited entries to a list (or any other worksheet range) meet the criteria you want. You can specify the type of data you'll allow (whole numbers, dates, or times, for example), as well as the range of acceptable values. You can even set up a list of allowed values (the names of your operating divisions, for example) and have Excel create a drop-down list of those values. Whoever uses your list then can select a valid entry from the drop-down list.

Your validation rules can be mandatory or merely cautionary. If the rule is mandatory, Excel will refuse to accept an entry that doesn't meet the standards you set. If the rule is cautionary, Excel will display a dialog box (with a default message or one that you supply) and give the user a chance to redo the cell entry.

When you set up the validation rule for a cell or range, you can also specify a prompt that appears whenever the validated cell is active. For example, you can have a prompt say "This cell requires an integer between 1 and 10." By choosing Data, Validation you can create such a prompt even without creating a validation rule. If you just want to generate advisory prompts that guide someone who's using your list, without forcing that person to enter particular kinds of values, the Validation command is the simplest method available.

To set up validation criteria, select the range of cells where you want the criteria to apply, and then choose Data, Validation. (Excel's automatic format and formula extension features do not replicate validation settings, so you must begin by selecting all the rows you expect your list to populate.) Excel presents the Data Validation dialog box, shown in Figure 28-2.

Troubleshooting

Excel Ignores My Validation Rules

Even with validation rules in place, Excel turns a blind eye to the following kinds of entries: data pasted from the Clipboard, data that you copy by dragging a cell's fill handle, and data that you copy or move by dragging. (If you copy a cell in the previous row by means of the Ctrl+Shift+' or Ctrl+' keyboard shortcut, however, Excel does validate the entry.) If you overwrite a validated cell by one of these methods, Excel not only accepts the entry, it also overwrites the target cell's validation rule without whatever rules (typically none) had been applied to the source cell. In short, foolproof it's not.

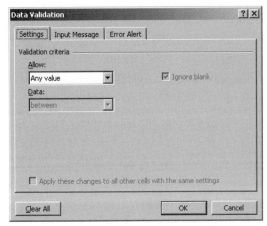

Figure 28-2. You can use validation rules to ensure that users put the right kinds of data into your list.

Specifying Data Type and Acceptable Values

To specify the kind of data you'll allow, open the Allow list on the Settings tab. You can choose from the following types: Any Value, Whole Number, Decimal, List, Date, Time, Text Length, and Custom. After you choose a data type, Excel modifies the dialog box so you can enter additional information about the chosen type. If you choose Whole Number, for example, you'll be asked to specify both a minimum and maximum acceptable value.

---

tip   **Force a text entry**

You'll notice that the list of data types that appears on the Settings tab doesn't include a Text type. Text Length is on the list, but Text Length doesn't create a requirement for text. It merely creates a length requirement (for example, more than 5 characters but fewer than 50) that will be applied in the event that text is entered. To require text, choose Custom. Then enter **=ISTEXT(address)** as your custom formula (where **address** is the address of the cell you're validating).

Supplying a List of Acceptable Values To set up a list of acceptable values, choose List from the Allow list, and then specify the worksheet range where your list appears. For example, if you want the user to enter only North, South, East, or West in cell A1, you can type those four values in some other part of your workbook—for example, the range Z1:Z4. Then you select A1, choose Data, Validation, choose List from the Allow list, and specify **Z1:Z4** as your list range.

Using a Formula to Validate Input To use a formula for validation, choose Custom from the Allow list and specify a formula in the Formula box that appears. The formula should reference the cell that you're validating (and other cells if appropriate) and should evaluate to TRUE or FALSE. For example, to ensure that cell A1's value is greater than that of cell B1, select A1, choose Data, Validation, choose Custom from the Allow list, and then specify =A1>B1 in the Formula box.

To specify more than one validating criterion, use the AND function, the OR function, or both. For example, to ensure that C1 is greater than A1 but less than B1, enter =AND(C1>A1,C1<B1).

If you select a range of cells before choosing Data, Validation, Excel updates all relative references appropriately. For example, if you select A1:A10 and enter =A1>B1 as your validation formula, Excel ensures that A1 is greater than B1, A2 is greater than B2, and so on. To make a reference absolute, add the appropriate dollar signs. For example, to make all values in A1:A10 greater than B1, change the formula to =A1>$B$1. As usual, you can press the F4 key after typing a cell reference to make that reference absolute.

Specifying an Input Message (Prompt)

To supply an input prompt to guide your user, click the Input Message tab in the Data Validation dialog box. You have the opportunity to specify both the content of the message and the title of the window in which it's delivered. The message will be displayed as a comment beside the validated cell whenever the user selects that cell.

Specifying Error Alert Style and Message

If you do no more than supply validation criteria for a cell or range, Excel displays a standard error message when the user enters invalid data and forces the user to retry or cancel (canceling leaves the cell's previous value in place). To supply your own error message, click the Error Alert tab in the Data Validation dialog box. In the dialog box that appears, you can enter title and text for your message.

You can also use the Error Alert tab to specify the style of message that appears. Your choices are Stop, Warning, and Information. These three message styles display different icons beside your message text, and they have differing consequences for the user as well. If your message style is Stop (the default), the user is forced to retry or cancel. If you choose Warning, the user will be told that his or her entry is invalid but will be given the chance to leave it in the cell anyway. If you choose Information, the user will be told about the error but will not be given a retry option.

Using Excel's Form Command to Work with Lists

You can add new information to a list by moving to the first blank row below the list and typing, but you might find it easier to choose Data, Form. The Form command generates a dialog box that can help you—or someone else who uses the list you design—add data to and otherwise manipulate your list. Figure 28-3 shows this data-entry form in the context of the staff list shown in Figure 28-1.

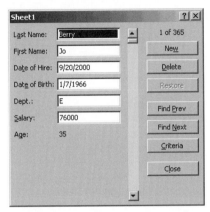

Figure 28-3.   The Form command generates a no-frills dialog box for manipulating information in a list.

At the top of the form, Excel displays the name of the worksheet (not the workbook) that contains the list on which the form is based. Immediately below this title bar are all the list's column headings. If you already entered some rows in your list, you see the entries for the first row of data alongside the column headings. (The form always shows the first row's data initially, regardless of which cell in the list is currently active.)

In Figure 28-3, the data for the first six fields appears in edit boxes. The value for the last field, Age, does not appear in an edit box, because this value is the result of a calculation. You can use the form to change any noncalculated value in the list.

Adding Rows

To add a new row to your list, click the New button. Excel displays a blank form, in which you can enter the values for your new row. To add another row, click New again; to return to the worksheet, click Close.

When you add rows to your list with the Form command, Excel expands the list downward without affecting any cells outside the list. If expanding the list will overwrite existing data, Excel alerts you and refuses to accept new data.

Chapter 28

Finding Records

You can use the Criteria button to locate particular records (rows) in the list. In response, Excel displays a new form that includes edit boxes for all fields, including those that result from a calculation (see Figure 28-4). If you enter criteria in more than one edit box, clicking Find Next or Find Prev locates records that satisfy all criteria. (As you'll see, Excel offers other ways to search for records, including methods for finding records that satisfy any, rather than all, of your criteria.) With the criteria shown in Figure 28-4, you can find all Department C employees of age 50 or younger whose salaries are at least $90,000.

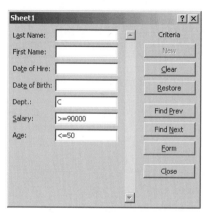

Figure 28-4. When you click Find Next or Find Prev, Excel takes you to the next (or previous) record that satisfies all three criteria.

When entering a text criterion, be aware that Excel appends an implicit asterisk wildcard to your criterion. Entering **B** in the Last Name box, for example, makes Excel look for all last names that begin with B.

When you enter date criteria, you can use any format that Excel recognizes as a date. To locate birthdays of January 1, 1980 or later, for example, you could enter >1/1/80, >**January 1, 1980,** or any of a variety of other recognizable formulations.

Sorting Lists and Other Ranges

Excel provides numerous ways to sort worksheet ranges. You can sort by columns or rows, in ascending or descending order, and with capitalization considered or ignored. (When you sort by rows, the rows of your list are rearranged, and the columns remain in the same order. When you sort by columns, the opposite kind of rearrangement occurs.) You can even define custom sorting sequences so that, for example, your company's division names always appear in a particular order, regardless of their alphabetic sequence.

Chapter 28: Managing Information in Lists

Sorting on a Single Column

To sort on a single column—the Last Name column in Figure 28-1, for example—
select one cell anywhere within that column. Then click either the Sort Ascending
button on the Standard toolbar (to arrange the column in ascending numeric or
alphabetic order) or the Sort Descending button (to do the opposite). Excel sorts in
the order you want on the column in which the selection resides.

If this is the first time you've sorted the current list, the Sort dialog box, shown in Figure 28-5,
appears with default options. If you've sorted the list before, the dialog box will display the
sort parameters you last used.

Figure 28-5. Excel recognizes the extent of your
list and the presence or absence of a header row.

If your list includes a header row that should remain in place while the other rows are
sorted, Excel usually recognizes that fact and selects the Header Row option at the bottom of the dialog box. If the program, for some reason, fails to notice a header row and
selects No Header Row instead, you can correct it before clicking OK.

Excel also assumes that the column containing the active cell is the one on which you
want to sort, and it fills out the Sort By box with either the label at the top of that column (if you have a header row) or the letter designation of that column. Because users
tend to prefer ascending sorts, it also selects the Ascending option button by default. To
carry out the sort, make any necessary adjustments to these settings and then click OK.

---

tip   **Save toolbar space**

The Standard toolbar includes two sorting buttons, one for ascending sorts, the
other for descending sorts. You can make either tool do double duty. For a
descending sort, hold down Shift while you click the Ascending Sort button. For an
ascending sort, hold down Shift while you click the Descending Sort button. If
you're short of space on the toolbar, you can eliminate the Descending Sort
button and use the Shift key to reverse the default sort direction.

Chapter 28

Part 9: Managing Databases and Lists

Sorting on More than One Column

You can sort on as many as three columns at once. To sort on more than one column, fill out one or both of the Then By boxes in the Sort dialog box. For example, to sort the staff list shown in Figure 28-1 first in descending order by Salary and then in ascending order by Last Name, you fill out the dialog box as shown in Figure 28-6. Excel then rearranges the list as shown in Figure 28-7.

Figure 28-6. To sort on two columns, you supply the names of the column headings in the Sort By and Then By boxes.

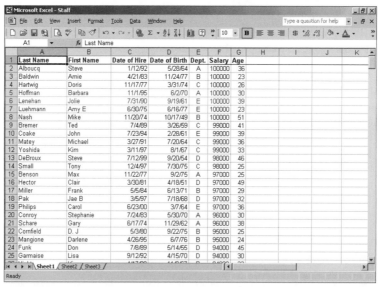

Figure 28-7. The rows are now arranged in descending order by Salary, with rows of common salary in ascending order by Last Name.

Sorting on More than Three Columns

Should you ever need to sort on more than three columns, you can do so by performing successive single-column or multiple-column sorts. Sort the least important column first. Then repeat the sort on the next-least important column, and so on.

Sorting Only Part of a List

If you select a single cell before choosing Data, Sort, Excel scans the area surrounding the selected cell, highlights the entire contiguous range of cells, and assumes you want to sort that entire range. If you want to sort only part of a list, start by selecting only those rows and columns you want to sort. Then choose Data, Sort. To sort rows 10 through 20 in Figure 28-1, for example, you start by selecting A10:G20.

You can't specify a sort range in the Sort dialog box. You must select the range before you open the dialog box. The dialog box itself doesn't indicate the range that Excel is about to sort. Check your worksheet immediately after a sort and use the Undo command if you don't like what you get.

Sorting by Columns

Thus far, our examples have involved sorting by row—leaving the columns alone. You also can sort by columns, leaving the order of the rows alone.

To sort by columns, follow these steps:

1. Choose Data, Sort.
2. Click the Options button in the Sort dialog box, and select the Sort Left to Right option.
3. Click OK to return to the main part of the Sort dialog box.
4. Fill out the boxes and option buttons in the Sort dialog box, and click OK.

Figures 28-8 and 28-9 (on the next page) show a worksheet before and after a left-to-right sort.

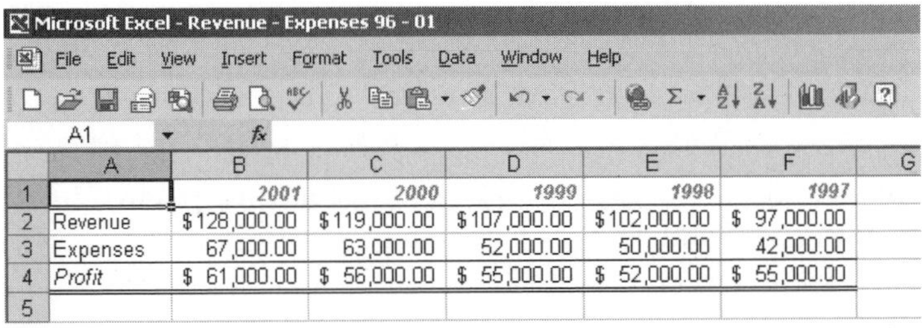
Microsoft Excel - Revenue - Expenses 96 - 01
File Edit View Insert Format Tools Data Window Help
A1
A B C D E F G
1 2001 2000 1999 1998 1997
2 Revenue $128,000.00 $119,000.00 $107,000.00 $102,000.00 $ 97,000.00
3 Expenses 67,000.00 63,000.00 52,000.00 50,000.00 42,000.00
4 Profit $ 61,000.00 $ 56,000.00 $ 55,000.00 $ 52,000.00 $ 55,000.00
5

Figure 28-8. The years are in descending order in this simple financial worksheet.

Chapter 28

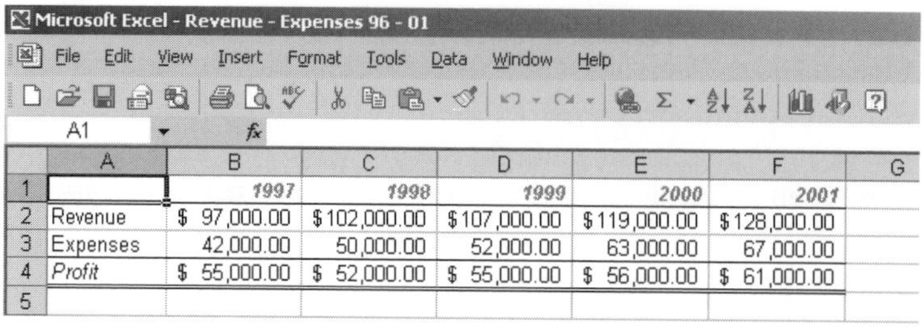

	A	B	C	D	E	F	G
		1997	*1998*	*1999*	*2000*	*2001*	
1							
2	Revenue	$ 97,000.00	$ 102,000.00	$ 107,000.00	$ 119,000.00	$ 128,000.00	
3	Expenses	42,000.00	50,000.00	52,000.00	63,000.00	67,000.00	
4	*Profit*	$ 55,000.00	$ 52,000.00	$ 55,000.00	$ 56,000.00	$ 61,000.00	
5							

Figure 28-9. Use the Sort Left To Right option to reorder the years into an ascending sequence.

To perform this sort, follow these steps:

1 Select B1:F4.

2 Choose Data, Sort.

3 Click the Options button in the Sort dialog box.

4 Make sure that Sort Left To Right is selected, and then click OK twice.

It's best to select all the data you want to sort, rather than just a single cell, when you're sorting laterally. If you select only one cell, Excel will propose to sort everything in the worksheet, including the labels in your first column. In other words, Excel doesn't recognize row headings in column-oriented sorts.

Sorting Cells That Contain Formulas

You need to exercise caution when sorting cells that contain formulas with cell references. If you sort by row, references to other cells in the same row will be correct after the sort, but references to cells in other rows of the list will no longer be correct.

Similarly, if you sort by column, references to other cells in the same columns will be correct after the sort, but references to cells in other columns will be broken. With either kind of sort, relative references to cells outside the list will be broken by the sort.

The before-and-after illustration in Figure 28-10 demonstrates the hazards of sorting ranges that contain formulas. Row 5 of the worksheet calculates the year-to-year change in profit, using relative-reference formulas. Cell C5, for example, uses the formula =C4-B4 to calculate the difference between the profits for 1998 and 1997. Each of the other formulas also references the cell directly to its left.

After sorting by column, each formula in row 5 of this figure still references the cell to the left, but now we have a #VALUE! error in B5, because B4 tries to subtract the text *Profit* from the number 61,000.

Figure 28-10. Sorting this worksheet laterally has broken the formulas in row 5.

Interestingly, if you carry out this sort manually—by picking up each column and moving it to its new location—Excel updates the formulas appropriately after each move. If you do it by choosing Data, Sort, Excel is unable to make the necessary adjustments.

To avoid the problems associated with sorting ranges containing formulas, observe the following rules:

- In formulas that reference cells outside the sort range, use only absolute references.

- When sorting by row, avoid formulas that reference cells in other rows. If you must use such formulas, reference cells by name, not by address.

- When sorting by column, avoid formulas that reference cells in other columns. If you must use such formulas, reference cells by name, not by address.

Understanding Excel's Default Sorting Sequence

To avoid surprises, you should understand the following points about the way Excel sorts:

- Excel sorts cells according to their contents, not their formats. This means, for example, that a date cell displaying November 16, 2000 will be sorted ahead of a date cell displaying 12/27/2000 (because the first date has a lower numeric value), even though numbers occur before letters in the ANSI and Unicode character-encoding sequences.

- Numeric values are sorted ahead of text values. The value 98052 would therefore be sorted ahead of the value 1 Microsoft Way, because the former is a number and the latter is text.

(continued)

> **Understanding Excel's Default Sorting Sequence** *(continued)*
>
> ● Text (and text that includes numbers) is sorted in the following order:
>
> 0 1 2 3 4 5 6 7 8 9 (space) ! " $ % & ( ) * , . / : ; ? @ [\ ] ^ _ ` { | } ~ + < = >
> a b c d e f g h i j k l m n o p q r s t u v w x y z
>
> ● Apostrophes and hyphens are usually ignored. If two values are identical except for the presence of a hyphen in one, however, the value without the hyphen is sorted ahead of the value with the hyphen.
>
> ● Logical values are sorted after text, and FALSE is sorted before TRUE.
>
> ● Error values (#DIV/0!, #NAME?, #VALUE, #REF!, #N/A, #NUM!, and #NULL!) are sorted after logical values. Excel regards all error values as equivalent; that is, it leaves them in the order it finds them.
>
> ● Blanks are placed last, in both ascending and descending sorts.

Sorting Months, Weekdays, or Custom Lists

Excel normally sorts text in alphabetical order, but it can sort on the basis of any of its custom lists if you want it to. The program includes four custom lists by default (Sun, Mon, Tues, …; Sunday, Monday, Tuesday, …; Jan, Feb, Mar, …; and January, February, March, …). If you have a column consisting of these day or month labels, you can sort them in their proper chronological order. If you've created other custom lists, you can sort text fields in the order of those lists as well.

> For information about creating and using custom lists, see "Creating Custom Lists" on page 178.

To sort on the basis of a custom list, click Options in the Sort dialog box, and then open the First Key Sort Order list. The four default custom lists will appear there, along with any others that you have created.

Custom lists can serve as the basis for first-key sorting. If you want to sort first by some other field (one that doesn't contain a custom list) and then by your custom list, you need to carry out two separate sorts. First sort by the custom-list field, and then sort by your other field.

Performing a Case-Sensitive Sort

Normally, when Excel sorts text, it disregards case variants entirely. In other words, the program regards the letter A as exactly equivalent to the letter a. You can change this behavior by choosing Options in the Sort dialog box and then selecting the Case Sensitive check box.

If you're familiar with the standard character-encoding systems used by Windows (ANSI or Unicode), you might suppose that turning on the case-sensitive option would cause Excel to sort all capital letters before all lowercase letters. That, after all, is how those character-encoding systems are constructed. (The capital alphabet occupies the range 65 through 90 (decimal notation), and the lowercase alphabet resides at 97 through 122.) The case-sensitive option does not cause Excel to perform a "straight" ANSI or Unicode sort. Instead it makes the program put lowercase variants ahead of capital variants *of the same letter.*

For example, suppose the range A1:A4 holds the following four text values:

Pine

pine

Tree

tree

If you perform a default (not case-sensitive) ascending sort on these four cells, their order will remain unchanged, because *p* comes before *t* and Excel disregards the variation in case. If you sort again with the case-sensitive option on, the order becomes

pine

Pine

tree

Tree

because *p* now comes before *P* and *t* comes before *T*. In a conventional ANSI sort, you'd get

Pine

Tree

pine

tree

because all capitals come before all lowercase letters.

Making Case-Sensitive Sorting the Default

Because Excel has to work a little harder to perform case-sensitive sorts, the feature is off by default. If you don't customarily sort gigantic lists, you might find that case-sensitive sorting is worth an extra few milliseconds. Sorting options are worksheet-specific, however, so you can't change Excel's default behavior by setting the option on a single worksheet (or by selecting a check box somewhere in the Options dialog box). To make case-sensitive sorting the default, do the following:

1 On each sheet of a blank workbook, enter some data—any data—into two contiguous cells. (You have to do this, because Excel won't let you visit the Sort dialog box until you've selected some data that it can sort.)

2 On each sheet, choose Data, Sort, click Options, and select Case Sensitive. Click OK twice to carry out the sort.

3 Delete the data on each sheet.

4 Save the workbook as a template, using the name BOOK, in your XLStart folder.

Filtering a List

To *filter* a list means to hide all the rows except those that meet specified criteria. Excel provides two filtering commands—AutoFilter, for simple criteria, and Advanced Filter, for more complex criteria. You can also use the Advanced Filter command to extract a subset of your list to another part of your workbook.

Using the AutoFilter Command

To use the AutoFilter command, first select any cell in your list. Then choose Data, Filter, AutoFilter. Excel displays drop-down arrows next to each of the column headings in your list. Clicking the arrow next to any heading reveals a list of the column's unique values, which you can use to specify filtering criteria.

---

tip   **Display arrows for selected columns**

In the typical situation, you want to apply filtering criteria to one or perhaps two of your columns, not to all. If you select a single cell in a list and choose Data, Filter, AutoFilter, Excel displays drop-down arrows atop each column, shrinking the visible part of the column headers in the process. To limit the arrows to particular columns, select only those column headings (the columns must be adjacent to one another). Then choose Data, Filter, AutoFilter.

Let's look at an example. Suppose that from the list shown in Figure 28-1, you'd like to see only those rows in which Dept. is B. To generate this subset, you choose Data, Filter, AutoFilter, and then select B from the drop-down list next to the Dept. heading. The result looks like Figure 28-11.

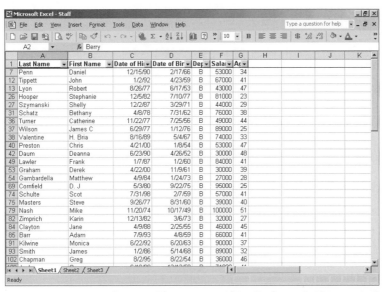

Figure 28-11. Use the AutoFilter command to display only those rows in which Dept. is B.

From the gaps in the row numbers shown in Figure 28-11, you can tell that Excel has hidden the rows that didn't meet the filtering criterion. To remind you that you have filtered your list, Excel also displays the filtered row numbers in a contrasting color.

---

tip **Use the name _FilterDatabase**

After you use the AutoFilter or Advanced Filter command, the range to which you applied the command is named _FilterDatabase. You can reselect the entire list by pressing F5 and typing **_filterdatabase** in the Go To dialog box.

Determining How Many Rows Pass the Filter

Immediately after you perform an AutoFilter operation, Excel sometimes displays, on the status bar, the number of rows that have met your criteria. This information is ephemeral, however. Fortunately, you can use the SUBTOTAL function to arrive at this number. The formula =**SUBTOTAL(3,A:A)-1** returns the number of visible, occupied cells in column A (minus 1, because you don't need to count the header row). (The SUBTOTAL function ignores rows that are hidden by a filtering process. It does *not* ignore rows that are hidden via formatting commands.)

The first argument, 3, causes SUBTOTAL to apply the COUNTA function, which counts all occupied cells. The second argument, A:A in our example, references a column in the list. Assuming the list has no blank cells, you get the same result if you substitute any other column in the list for A:A.

> For more information about the SUBTOTAL function, see "Using the SUBTOTAL function" on page 739.

Using AutoFilter Criteria in More than One Column

You can specify AutoFilter criteria for your list in as many columns as you want. Filter your list on one column, filter the resulting list on another column, and so on. Each successive application of the AutoFilter command refines the list further, so that the result includes only those rows that meet all your criteria. To see rows that meet any of your criteria, you need to use the Advanced Filter command.

Using AutoFilter to Find the Top or Bottom n Items

You can use the AutoFilter feature to find the top or bottom *n* items in a numeric column, or those items that make up the top or bottom *n* percent of a column's total. Click the drop-down arrow for the column and then select Top 10 from the list. Excel displays the dialog box shown in Figure 28-12.

Figure 28-12. Use the Top 10 dialog box to zero in on the top or bottom *n* list elements.

The Top 10 AutoFilter dialog box has three boxes. In the first, you can select either Top or Bottom. In the second, you can specify any number between 1 and 500. In the third, you can select either Items or Percent.

Using AutoFilter to Display Blank or Nonblank Entries

If a column contains blank cells, you find the entries Blanks and NonBlanks at the bottom of its AutoFilter drop-down list. If you want to locate those rows in which a particular column has no entry, specify Blanks as your criterion. If you want to exclude rows with blank entries, specify NonBlanks.

Using the Custom Option to Specify More Complex Criteria

The example in Figure 28-11 used a single equality comparison for its criterion. That is, we asked Excel to display only those rows in which the Dept. field was equal to a particular value, B. With the help of the Custom option, you can filter on the basis of an inequality or find rows that fall within a range of values. To use the Custom option, open the drop-down list for the column you're interested in and select Custom. You see the Custom AutoFilter dialog box shown in Figure 28-13.

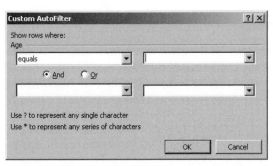

Figure 28-13. Use the Custom AutoFilter dialog box to apply more complex AutoFilter criteria to a single column.

You can enter one or two criteria in the Custom AutoFilter dialog box, and you can select from a full range of Excel's relational operators. The list boxes on the left side of the dialog box provide a selection of relationships (Equals, Does Not Equal, Is Greater Than, and so on), and the list boxes on the right allow you to select the values that appear in your list. You can, of course, type directly into the boxes on the right, if you prefer that to fishing through the list for a value.

Suppose, for example, that you want to see all the members of your Staff list with salaries greater than or equal to 90,000 as well as all those with salaries less than or equal to 30,000. After displaying the Custom AutoFilter dialog box for the Salary column, choose Greater Than Or Equal To in the upper left box and specify **90000** in the upper right box. Select the Or option button, and then choose Less Than Or Equal To in the lower left box and specify **30000** in the lower right box. If you neglect to choose the Or option button, you ask Excel for the names of employees who made both 90,000 or more and 30,000 or less, and you get an empty list.

Finding an Alphabetical Range of Text Values

To find all the text values in a column that fall within a particular range of letters, use the AutoFilter feature's Custom option and specify two criteria joined by And. For example, to find all last names beginning with B, C, or D, filter the Last Name column and specify Is Greater Than B and Is Less Than E in the Custom AutoFilter dialog box.

Using Wildcards in Custom Criteria

The Custom AutoFilter dialog box accepts two kinds of wildcard characters. You can use the asterisk (*) to represent any sequence of characters or the question mark (?) to represent any single character. For example, to find all last names starting with B, you can specify Is Equal To B* in the Custom AutoFilter dialog box. To include a literal question mark or asterisk in a filter, precede the ? or * with a tilde (~).

Removing AutoFilter Criteria

To remove an AutoFilter criterion for a particular column, Select (All) in the drop-down list. To remove all AutoFilters currently in effect, choose Data, Filter, Show All. To remove the AutoFilter drop-down arrows, choose Data, Filter, AutoFilter—thereby removing the check mark next to the AutoFilter command.

Using the Advanced Filter Command

In contrast to the AutoFilter command, the Advanced Filter command allows you to do the following:

- Specify criteria involving two or more columns and the conjunction OR.

- Specify three or more criteria for a particular column, where at least one OR conjunction is involved.

- Specify computed criteria (for example, all employees whose salaries are more than 25 percent greater than the median salary).

In addition, the Advanced Filter command can be used to extract rows from the list, placing copies of those rows in another part of the current worksheet.

InsideOut

Extract only to the current worksheet

For some reason, you cannot extract rows from a list and place them on a separate worksheet. Your criteria range can be on a different worksheet, but your extract range cannot. After you extract a set of rows, you can, of course, copy or move it to another location.

Specifying a Criteria Range

The Advanced Filter command, unlike AutoFilter, requires that you specify filtering criteria in a worksheet range separate from your list. Because entire rows are hidden when the filter is executed, it's inadvisable to put the criteria range *alongside* the list. Instead, put it above the list or on a separate worksheet. A criteria range must consist of at least two rows. Enter one or more column headings in the top row and your filtering criteria in the second and subsequent rows. With the exception of computed criteria, the headings in your criteria range must be spelled exactly like those in your list. (Capitalization and formatting don't have to match, but spelling does.) To ensure accuracy, the best way to create these headings is by selecting the column headings in your list and then using the Copy and Paste commands.

Keep in mind that a criteria range does not have to include headings for every column in the list. Columns that are not involved in the selection process don't have to be part of the criteria range.

An Example Using Two Columns Joined by OR

Figure 28-14 shows a list of homes for sale. (The underscored items in column A are hyperlinks to pictures of the houses.) Suppose that you're interested in homes with lot size (column H) of at least two acres. You'll also consider homes on smaller lots if they're in the elementary-school district U (column O). To filter the list so that homes meeting either criterion are shown, begin by creating the criteria range shown in Figure 28-15 on the next page. We've created this criteria range above the list, on three newly inserted rows.

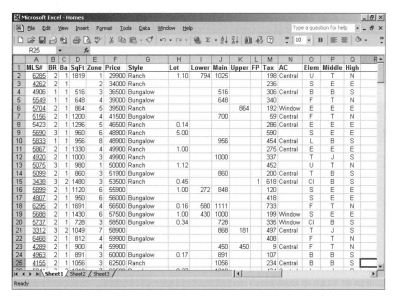

Figure 28-14. Use the Advanced Filter command to locate homes within this list that meet specific criteria.

Part 9: Managing Databases and Lists

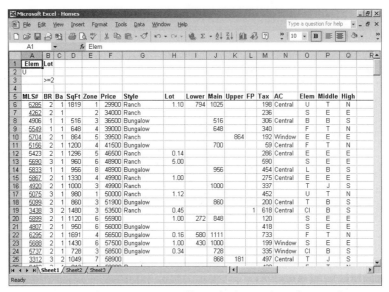

	A	B	C	D	E	F	G	H	I	J	K	L	M	N	O	P	Q	R
1	Elem	Lot																
2	U																	
3		>=2																
4																		
5	MLS#	BR	Ba	SqFt	Zone	Price	Style	Lot	Lower	Main	Upper	FP	Tax	AC	Elem	Middle	High	
6	6285	2	1	1819	1	29900	Ranch	1.10	794	1025			198	Central	U	T	N	
7	4262	2	1		2	34000	Ranch						236		S	E	E	
8	4906	1	1	516	3	36500	Bungalow			516			306	Central	B	B	S	
9	5549	1	1	648	4	39000	Bungalow			648			340		F	T	N	
10	5704	2	1	864	5	39500	Ranch				864		192	Window	E	E	E	
11	5156	2	1	1200	4	41500	Bungalow			700			59	Central	F	T	N	
12	5423	2	1	1296	5	46500	Ranch	0.14					286	Central	E	E	E	
13	5690	3	1	960	6	48900	Ranch	5.00					590		S	E	E	
14	5833	1	1	956	8	48900	Bungalow			956			454	Central	L	B	S	
15	5867	2	1	1330	4	49900	Ranch	1.00					275	Central	E	E	E	
16	4920	2	1	1000	3	49900	Ranch			1000			337		T	J	S	
17	5075	3	1	980	1	50000	Ranch	1.12					452		U	T	N	
18	5099	2	1	860	3	51900	Bungalow			860			200	Central	T	B	S	
19	3438	3	2	1480	3	53500	Ranch	0.45				1	618	Central	Cl	B	S	
20	5899	2	1	1120	6	55900		1.00	272	848			120		S	E	E	
21	4807	2	1	950	6	56000	Bungalow						418		S	E	E	
22	6295	2	1	1691	4	56500	Bungalow	0.16	580	1111			733		F	T	N	
23	5688	2	1	1430	6	57500	Bungalow	1.00	430	1000			199	Window	S	E	E	
24	5737	2	1	728	3	58500	Bungalow	0.34		728			335	Window	Cl	B	S	
25	3312	3	2	1049	7	58900				868	181		497	Central	T	J	S	

Figure 28-15. This criteria range filters the list to show homes that are either on lots of at least 2 acres or that are within elementary-school district U.

You then choose Data, Filter, Advanced Filter and fill out the Advanced Filter dialog box, as shown in Figure 28-16. Excel responds by displaying the filtered list shown in Figure 28-17. Some of the Lot fields in that filtered list are blank because the original list didn't include lot-size information about all the homes. Excel treats the blanks as zeros (and therefore less than 2) and includes them only if their Elem fields contain U.

Figure 28-16. In the Advanced Filter dialog box, select Filter The List, In-Place, and specify the addresses of your list and your criteria range.

Chapter 28: Managing Information in Lists

	A	B	C	D	E	F	G	H	I	J	K	L	M	N	O	P	Q
1	Elem	Lot															
2	U																
3		>=2															
4																	
5	MLS#	BR	Ba	SqFt	Zone	Price	Style	Lot	Lower	Main	Upper	FP	Tax	AC	Elem	Middle	High
13	5690	3	1	960	6	48900	Ranch	5.00					590		S	E	E
17	5075	3	1	980	1	50000	Ranch	1.12					452		U	T	N
33	5892	2	1	753	7	64900	Ranch						720	Window	U	T	N
46	5734	2	1	750	10	69900		0.14		750			717	Window	U	T	N
60	6446	2	1	1627	3	73900	Bungalow	4.27	469	1158			465	Central	L	B	S
68	4446	3	1	960	10	75000	Ranch	0.32		960			334		U	T	N
82	5077	3	2	1200	10	79200	Ranch			1200				Central	U	T	N
92	5372	3	2	2214	10	79900	Ranch	5.00	756	1458			2247	Central	M	T	N
101	4960	3	1	1050	10	79900	Ranch			1050		1	610	Central	U	T	N
102	4022	3	1	1028	10	79900	Ranch	0.68		1068			490	Window	U	T	N
124	4111	3	1	1123	7	86500	Ranch			1123		1	351	Central	U	T	N
141	3933	3	1	1450	7	89900	Ranch	0.40		1450		1	973	Central	U	J	N
147	5332	2	2	1824	10	89900	Ranch		910	914			751	Central	U	T	N
160	6508	4	2	1412	10	92500	Ranch	0.24		1412			1498	Central	U	T	N
163	3990	3	3	2001	3	93000	Ranch	3.34		2001			621	Central	G	B	S
182	6172	3	2	1120	3	99000	Ranch	5.00		1120			720	Central	CI	B	S
187	160	3	2	1450	10	99500	Ranch		500	950			1494	Central	U	T	N
190	6207	3	2	1352	6	99900		4.13		1352		1	464	Central	A	T	N
195	5164	3	1	3007	4	99900	Ranch	5.00	1314	1693			1141	Central	A	T	N
205	6327	4	2	1700	10	101900	Ranch		620	1080			1695	Central	U	T	N

Figure 28-17. Excel responds with a list filtered to show just the homes you're interested in.

Like AutoFilter, the Advanced Filter command hides all rows that don't pass the filter. It also displays the qualifying row numbers in a contrasting color. You can use the formula =SUBTOTAL(3,A:A) to find out how many rows have met your criteria (assuming that column A is included in your filtered list).

In Figure 28-15, notice that the two criteria are specified on separate lines. This tells Excel to find rows that meet either criterion. If you put the two criteria on the same line, you ask for just those rows that meet both criteria. In other words, criteria on the same line are joined by AND, and criteria on separate lines are joined by OR. You can put as many separate criteria as you like in a criteria range.

Both criteria are specified as simple text values. The value U under the Elem heading tells Excel to get any rows with Elem values that begin with the letter U. (In other words, there's an implied asterisk wildcard after that U.) If you want the filter to allow only values that match the letter U exactly, you enter ="=U". This clumsy-looking formulation causes the cell to display =U and has the effect of removing the implied asterisk wildcard.

The value >=2 under the Lot heading tells Excel to get rows with Lot values equal to or greater than 2. You can use any of the relational operators >, <, >=, or <= in a numeric criterion. If you want an exact match (all lot sizes of exactly two acres, for example), enter the number, without an operator.

Be aware that a blank cell in a criteria range means "accept any value for this column." If you accidentally include a blank row in the criteria range, you get an unfiltered list.

> **tip** **Navigate with Criteria**
>
> Provided your criteria range is on the same worksheet as your list, Excel assigns the name Criteria to it immediately after you use it. You can use this behavior as a navigational tool. If you need to return to a criteria range to edit it, you can get there by pressing F5 and choosing Criteria in the Go To dialog box.

An Example Using Three ORs on a Column

Now let's suppose that you want to filter the list to show all houses in three elementary-school districts—U, F, or T. You include only the Elem field in the criteria range and enter the letters U, F, and T on three separate rows immediately below the heading. The Advanced Filter command then generates the list shown in Figure 28-18.

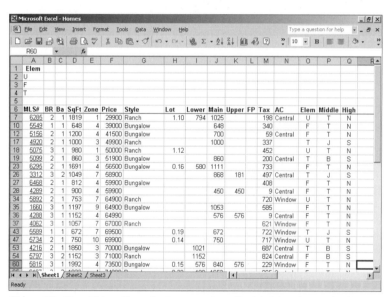

Figure 28-18. Using the criteria range in cells A1:A4 reduces the list to those houses in elementary-school districts U, F, or T.

An Example Using Both OR and AND

If you want to see all houses in middle-school district T or J that are at least 2000 square feet, you set up the criteria range as in Figure 28-19. The criterion >=2000 appears in cells B2 and B3, because for each of the middle-school districts (T and J), you want to see only houses of 2000 square feet or more.

Chapter 28

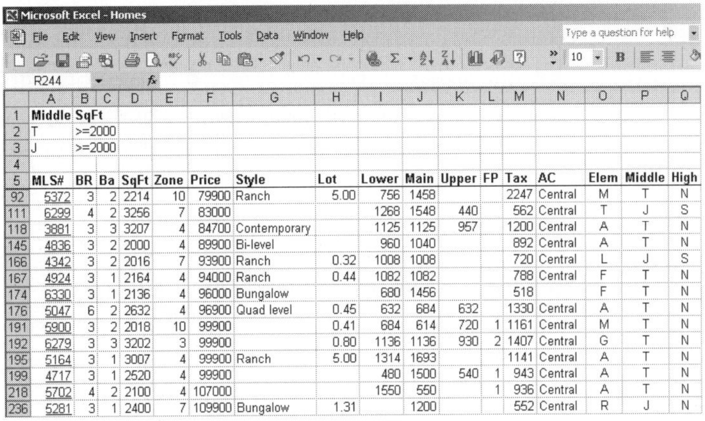

Microsoft Excel - Homes

	A	B	C	D	E	F	G	H	I	J	K	L	M	N	O	P	Q
1	Middle	SqFt															
2	T	>=2000															
3	J	>=2000															
4																	
5	MLS#	BR	Ba	SqFt	Zone	Price	Style	Lot	Lower	Main	Upper	FP	Tax	AC	Elem	Middle	High
92	5372	3	2	2214	10	79900	Ranch	5.00	756	1458			2247	Central	M	T	N
111	6299	4	2	3256	7	83000			1268	1548	440		562	Central	T	J	S
118	3881	3	3	3207	4	84700	Contemporary		1125	1125	957		1200	Central	A	T	N
145	4836	3	2	2000	4	89900	Bi-level		960	1040			892	Central	A	T	N
166	4342	3	2	2016	7	93900	Ranch	0.32	1008	1008			720	Central	L	J	S
167	4924	3	1	2164	4	94000	Ranch	0.44	1082	1082			788	Central	F	T	N
174	6330	3	1	2136	4	96000	Bungalow		680	1456			518		F	T	N
176	5047	6	2	2632	4	96900	Quad level	0.45	632	684	632		1330	Central	A	T	N
191	5900	3	2	2018	10	99900		0.41	684	614	720	1	1161	Central	M	T	N
192	6279	3	3	3202	3	99900		0.80	1136	1136	930	2	1407	Central	G	T	N
195	5164	3	1	3007	4	99900	Ranch	5.00	1314	1693			1141	Central	A	T	N
199	4717	3	1	2520	4	99900			480	1500	540	1	943	Central	A	T	N
218	5702	4	2	2100	4	107000			1550	550		1	936	Central	A	T	N
236	5281	3	1	2400	7	109900	Bungalow	1.31		1200			552	Central	R	J	N

Figure 28-19. To display 2000-square-foot houses in middle-school district T or J, repeat the >=2000 criterion in each line of the criteria range.

tip **Change filters without Show All**

Each time you use the Advanced Filter command, Excel re-examines the entire list rather than only the rows that passed the most recent filter. Therefore, you don't have to use the Show All command before changing the filter. If you want to refine a filter set—that is, filter the filtrate—add your new criteria to the previous criteria range and filter again.

Applying Multiple Criteria to the Same Column

To apply two or more criteria to the same column, repeat the column in your criteria range. For example, to retrieve rows with Price values between 50,000 and 90,000, your criteria range would look like this:

Price	Price
>=50000	<=50000

To exclude rows with prices in this range but admit everything else, you'd set up this criteria range:

Price	Price
<=90000	>=90000

Using Computed Criteria

Computed criteria involve any test other than a simple comparison of a column's value to a constant. Asking Excel to find houses with prices under $200,000 does not require a computed criterion. Asking for houses with prices below the median price of all houses in the list does.

When setting up a computed criterion, observe these rules:

- The column heading above a computed criterion must *not* be a copy of a column heading in the list. This heading can be blank, or it can be anything you want—other than a heading that already appears in the list.
- References to cells outside the list should be absolute.
- References to cells inside the list should be relative—unless you're referencing all the cells in a column.

Let's look at some examples. The next three sections explore referencing cells within the list, referencing a cell outside the list, and referencing all rows in a column.

Referencing Cells Within the List In cell A2 of Figure 28-20, we used the formula =F6/D6<50 to find all houses with prices per square foot below $50. Notice that the heading above the criterion (at cell A1) is not a copy of any heading in the list, and that the formula uses relative references to fetch values from within the list. F6 and D6 are the relevant values from the first row of the unfiltered list. Excel therefore begins by dividing F6 by D6 and comparing the result with 50. Because the references are relative, it continues by dividing F7 by D7, F8 by D8, and so on.

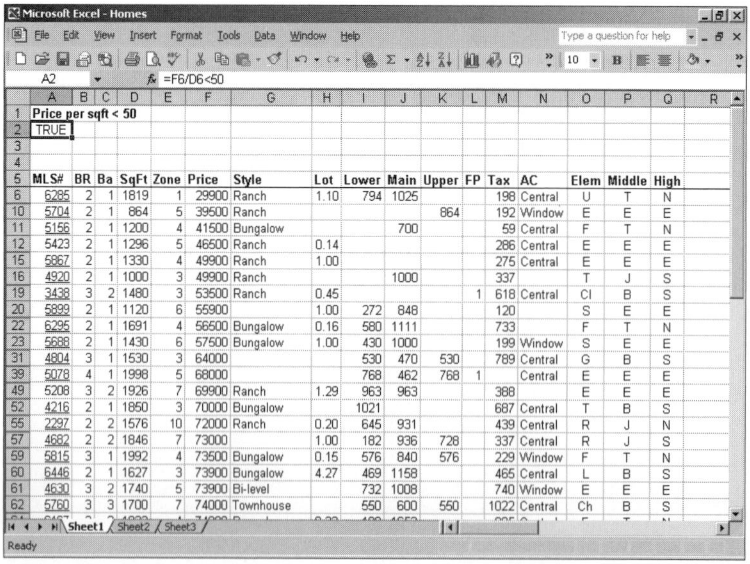

Microsoft Excel - Homes

A2 =F6/D6<50

	A	B	C	D	E	F	G	H	I	J	K	L	M	N	O	P	Q
1	**Price per sqft < 50**																
2	TRUE																
3																	
4																	
5	**MLS#**	**BR**	**Ba**	**SqFt**	**Zone**	**Price**	**Style**	**Lot**	**Lower**	**Main**	**Upper**	**FP**	**Tax**	**AC**	**Elem**	**Middle**	**High**
6	6285	2	1	1819	1	29900	Ranch	1.10	794	1025			198	Central	U	T	N
10	5704	2	1	864	5	39500	Ranch				864		192	Window	E	E	E
11	5156	2	1	1200	4	41500	Bungalow			700			59	Central	F	T	N
12	5423	2	1	1296	5	46500	Ranch	0.14					286	Central	E	E	E
15	5867	2	1	1330	4	49900	Ranch	1.00					275	Central	E	E	E
16	4920	2	1	1000	3	49900	Ranch			1000			337		T	J	S
19	3438	3	2	1480	3	53500	Ranch	0.45				1	618	Central	CI	B	S
20	5899	2	1	1120	6	55900		1.00	272	848			120		S	E	E
22	6295	2	1	1691	4	56500	Bungalow	0.16	580	1111			733		F	T	N
23	5688	2	1	1430	6	57500	Bungalow	1.00	430	1000			199	Window	S	E	E
31	4804	3	1	1530	3	64000			530	470	530		789	Central	G	B	S
39	5078	4	1	1998	5	68000			768	462	768	1		Central	E	E	E
49	5208	3	2	1926	7	69900	Ranch	1.29	963	963			388		E	E	E
52	4216	2	1	1850	3	70000	Bungalow		1021				687	Central	T	B	S
55	2297	2	2	1576	10	72000	Ranch	0.20	645	931			439	Central	R	J	N
57	4682	2	2	1846	7	73000		1.00	182	936	728		337	Central	R	J	S
59	5815	3	1	1992	4	73500	Bungalow	0.15	576	840	576		229	Window	F	T	N
60	6446	2	1	1627	3	73900	Bungalow	4.27	469	1158			465	Central	L	B	S
61	4630	3	2	1740	5	73900	Bi-level		732	1008			740	Window	E	E	E
62	5760	3	3	1700	7	74000	Townhouse		550	600	550		1022	Central	Ch	B	S

Sheet1 Sheet2 Sheet3

Ready

Figure 28-20. The criterion in A2 returns all houses with prices per square foot less than $50.

Chapter 28

The formula in A2 happens to return TRUE, because the result of that initial calculation (involving F6 and D6) is TRUE. It doesn't make any difference what that criterion formula returns, however; in fact, as you'll see, it can even return an error value.

In some rows of the unfiltered list, the SqFt column is blank. Dividing by a blank cell always returns the #DIV/0! error constant. This is not a problem. When Excel looks at a row with a blank SqFt value, it compares #DIV/0! with 50, and the result of that comparison is itself #DIV/0! Because the comparison doesn't yield a TRUE result, the row containing the blank SqFt value is excluded from the filter set—which is, presumably, the outcome you want.

If you've assigned names to the columns of your list, you can use those names instead of first-row cell references in your computed criterion. In other words, with the names SqFt and Price assigned to the appropriate columns, the formula at A2 reads =Price/SqFt<50.

This formula returns #VALUE! in A2 (because the formula appears above the list instead of alongside it), but the filter works fine anyway. (You could suppress the error value by pressing Ctrl+Shift+Enter to put an array formula in A2, but then the filter would *not* work!)

Referencing a Cell Outside the List   The criterion formula in A2 of Figure 28-21 compares prices against the median price, which is stored outside the list, in H1. (The median is calculated with the formula =MEDIAN(*price*), where *price* is a name assigned to all cells in the Price column.) The reference to H1 is absolute. If it were not, Excel would compare the price in the first row of the list to H1, the price in the second row to H2, and so on—not what you want.

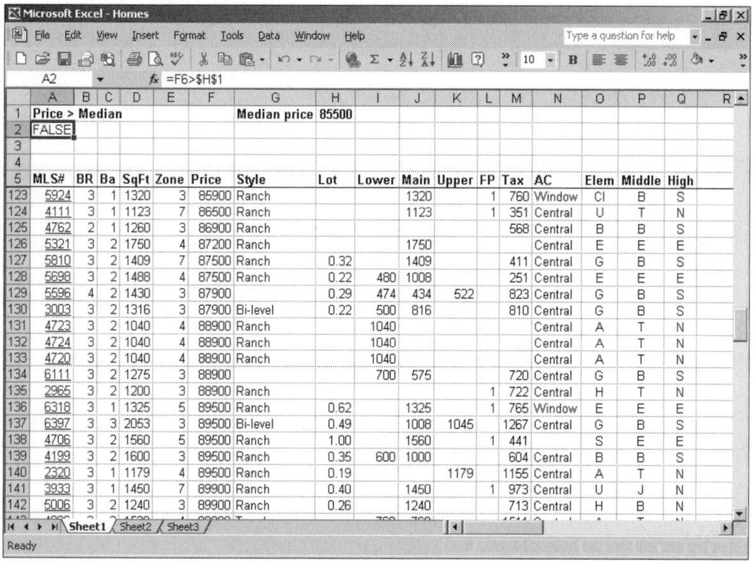

Figure 28-21.   This criterion in A2 uses an absolute reference, because the referenced cell, H1, lies outside the list.

Referencing All Rows in a Column If you change the formula in A2 of Figure 28-21 to =F6>MEDIAN($F$6:$F$238), you get the same set of rows as shown in Figure 28-21. In this case the MEDIAN function references cells within the list, but the reference has to be absolute. Otherwise, Excel looks at F6:F238, and then F7: F239, and so on. (You could drop the absolute reference to column F and make the row references absolute. If you use the F4 shortcut to create the absolute references, however, it's just as easy to make the whole thing absolute.)

Extracting Filtered Rows

The Advanced Filter dialog box includes an option for copying the selected rows to another worksheet location, instead of displaying a filtered list. To copy rows rather than display them, select the Copy To Another Location option in the Advanced Filter dialog box and supply the name or address of the range where you want the information to appear in the Copy To edit box.

The easiest way to specify the Copy To range is to click a blank cell in your worksheet where you want the range to start. Be sure the cell has plenty of blank space below and to the right of it. Excel then copies your list's column headings and all the rows that meet the Advanced Filter criteria to the range that begins with the cell you specified. Be careful, though; any data already stored in the selected range will be overwritten. Alternatively, if you specify a range of cells, Excel copies the rows that pass the filter but stops when the range is full.

> **tip** **Use Extract as a navigational aid**
>
> When you specify a Copy To range in the Advanced Filter dialog box, Excel assigns the name Extract to that range. You can use this name as a navigational aid. For example, when you need to return to the range to change column headings, press F5 and then select Extract in the Go To dialog box.

To copy only certain columns of your list to a new location, create copies of the headings for those columns. Then specify the headings (not only the first cell but the entire set of copied headings) as your Copy To range.

The Unique Records Only Option The Unique Records Only option in the Advanced Filter dialog box adds an additional filter to whatever you specify in your criteria range. It eliminates rows that are duplicates in every respect (not just duplicates in the columns that you happen to be extracting, but duplicates in all columns). The Unique Records Only option works only in conjunction with the Copy To Another Location option.

Using Subtotals to Analyze a List

Choose Data, Subtotals to apply aggregate formulas to groups of entries in a list. A typical application of the Subtotal command might be to add up sales by salesperson or customer, or expenses by payee or budget category. This command can do as its name suggests—add subtotal lines for each group of entries in a list. It also can supply other aggregate calculations at a group level. For example, you can use the Subtotals command to calculate the average of the values in a particular column for each group of rows, the number of rows in each group, the maximum or minimum value per group, the standard deviation for each group, and so on.

The Subtotals command provides one method for accomplishing these tasks. Another method is the PivotTable And PivotChart Report command, which is covered in Chapter 30, "Analyzing Data with PivotTables Reports." Excel's PivotTable feature is far more versatile than its subtotaling feature.

Figure 28-22 shows a list of transactions that includes fields for date, payee, budget category, and amount. The list is currently sorted by date. To determine how much was spent in each category, start by sorting the list by category. Then choose Data, Subtotals, and fill out the Subtotal dialog box, as shown in Figure 28-23.

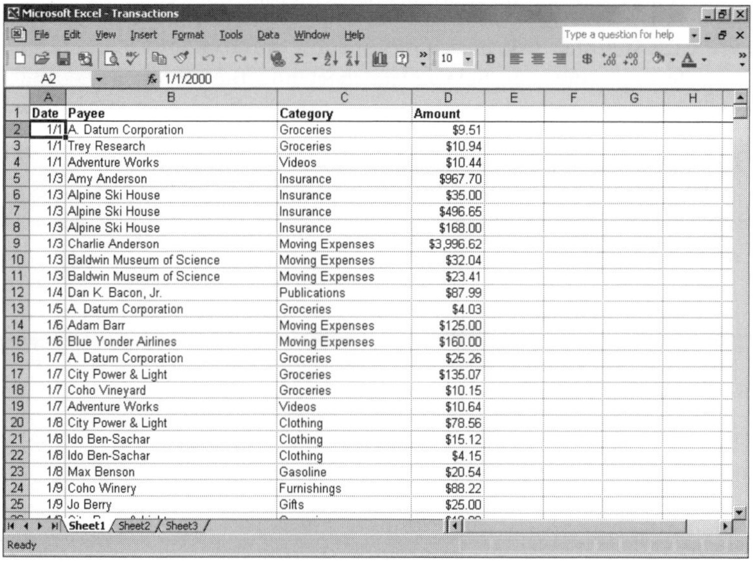

	Date	Payee	Category	Amount
2	1/1	A. Datum Corporation	Groceries	$9.51
3	1/1	Trey Research	Groceries	$10.94
4	1/1	Adventure Works	Videos	$10.44
5	1/3	Amy Anderson	Insurance	$967.70
6	1/3	Alpine Ski House	Insurance	$35.00
7	1/3	Alpine Ski House	Insurance	$496.65
8	1/3	Alpine Ski House	Insurance	$168.00
9	1/3	Charlie Anderson	Moving Expenses	$3,996.62
10	1/3	Baldwin Museum of Science	Moving Expenses	$32.04
11	1/3	Baldwin Museum of Science	Moving Expenses	$23.41
12	1/4	Dan K. Bacon, Jr.	Publications	$87.99
13	1/5	A. Datum Corporation	Groceries	$4.03
14	1/6	Adam Barr	Moving Expenses	$125.00
15	1/6	Blue Yonder Airlines	Moving Expenses	$160.00
16	1/7	A. Datum Corporation	Groceries	$25.26
17	1/7	City Power & Light	Groceries	$135.07
18	1/7	Coho Vineyard	Groceries	$10.15
19	1/7	Adventure Works	Videos	$10.64
20	1/8	City Power & Light	Clothing	$78.56
21	1/8	Ido Ben-Sachar	Clothing	$15.12
22	1/8	Ido Ben-Sachar	Clothing	$4.15
23	1/8	Max Benson	Gasoline	$20.54
24	1/9	Coho Winery	Furnishings	$88.22
25	1/9	Jo Berry	Gifts	$25.00

Figure 28-22. Use the Subtotals command to analyze this list of transactions.

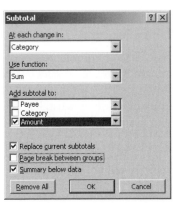

Figure 28-23. Filling out the Subtotal dialog box produces subtotals for each budget category.

By completing the dialog box as shown in Figure 28-23, you ask Excel to do the following:

- Create a new aggregation formula for each change in the Category column.

- Build the formula with the SUM function and apply it to the Amount column (that is, add up the amounts in each group).

- Place the subtotals below each group and a grand total at the bottom. (If you clear the Summary Below Data check box, the subtotals appear above each group, and a grand total appears at the top of the list.)

The result of this work is shown in Figure 28-24.

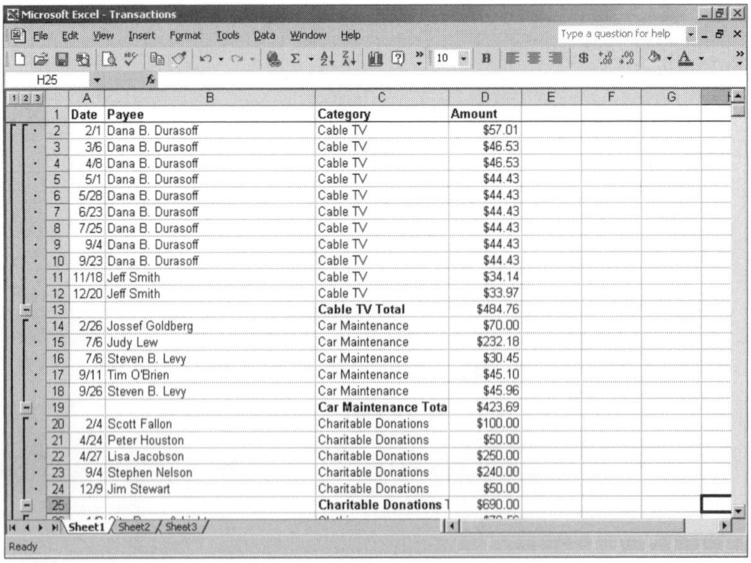

Figure 28-24. The list now includes subtotals for each budget category.

Notice that Excel outlines the subtotaled list. You can use the outline symbols to control the level of detail that's visible. Clicking the row 1 level symbol changes the display to show only the grand total. Clicking the row 2 level symbol shows only the subtotals (see Figure 28-25).

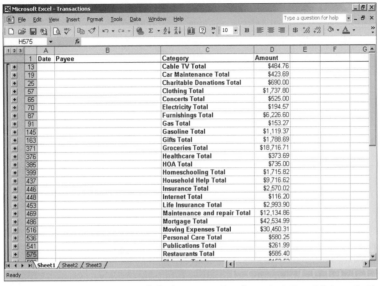

Figure 28-25. When you click the row 2 level symbol, Excel lists only the subtotals.

You can also use the outline to sort the list by the values of the subtotals. For example, with only the subtotals visible, as in Figure 28-25, you can sort by the Amount column to see which budget categories put the largest dent in your wallet.

For more information about working with outlines, see "Outlining Worksheets" on page 272.

Subtotaling on More than One Column

Suppose you want to subtotal by payee within each budget-category grouping. To do that, you choose Data, Subtotals again. Choose the appropriate column and aggregation formula (Payee and Sum, in this case), and be sure to clear the Replace Current Subtotals check box. Figure 28-26 on the next page shows the subtotals by payee and category.

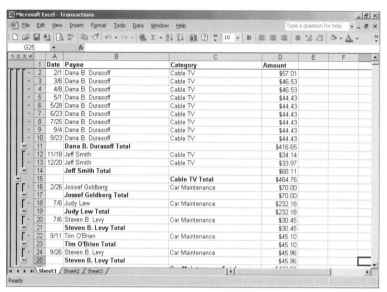

Figure 28-26. You now have subtotals by Payee within each Category.

Subtotaling with More than One Aggregation Formula

You can apply more than one subtotaling function to a given category. For example, after displaying totals by payee, you might also want to see average or maximum expenditures per payee. To add a second aggregation formula, choose Data, Subtotals, choose the appropriate function, and clear the Replace Current Subtotals check box.

Using Automatic Page Breaks

The Page Break Between Groups in the Subtotal dialog box (refer to Figure 28-23) is handy if you plan to print your subtotaled list. When you select this check box, Excel prints each group on a separate page.

Removing or Replacing Subtotals

To remove the subtotals and outline, open the Subtotal dialog box and select Remove All. To replace the current subtotals, open the Subtotal dialog box and be sure the Replace Current Subtotals check box is selected.

Grouping by Date

The Subtotals command is not adept at grouping items by date. If you want to create subtotals by month for the list shown in Figure 28-22, you need to create an additional Month column in the list. You might be tempted to apply the format *mmm* to the data in column A (or to a copy of it) and then to try creating subtotal breaks when the resulting month name changed. It won't work. Excel looks only at the actual value of cells, not at their formatted appearance, when deciding where to make the breaks.

You can insert a new column B and then write formulas of the form =MONTH(A2) in the cells of the new column. Then you can group by the resulting month numbers. If you want to see month names instead of numbers, you can write formulas in this form =CHOOSE(MONTH(A2,"Jan","Feb","Mar","Apr" …), but this entails a lot of typing. A better solution is to use a PivotTable. With a PivotTable, you can group dated items by year, quarter, month, week, and many other intervals.

For details, see "Grouping Items in Date or Time Ranges" on page 811.

Using the SUBTOTAL Function

The Subtotals command uses the SUBTOTAL function to perform its calculations. The SUBTOTAL function has the following syntax:

SUBTOTAL(function_num, ref1, ref2, …)

The function_num argument can be any number from 1 to 11; it tells the function which kind of calculation to apply, according to the scheme in the following table.

Function_Num	Function
1	AVERAGE
2	COUNT
3	COUNTA
4	MAX
5	MIN
6	PRODUCT
7	STDEV
8	STDEVP
9	SUM
10	VAR
11	VARP

Unlike ordinary applications of these eleven operations, the SUBTOTAL function skips over nested subtotals as well as rows hidden via Data, Filter, AutoFilter or Data, Filter, Advanced Filter.

Probably the most important thing to know about the SUBTOTAL function is that the Subtotals command applies it correctly and you don't need to worry about it. If you want to switch a calculation, for example, from a sum to an average, you can do so by modifying the SUBTOTAL formula that choosing Data, Subtotals gives you—in this case changing the function_num argument from 9 to 1.

Using Functions to Extract Details from a List

Excel provides a number of functions that can help you retrieve particular bits of information from your lists. You'll survey those functions in the remainder of this chapter.

The Database Statistical Functions

The database statistical functions include DAVERAGE, DCOUNT, DCOUNTA, DGET, DMAX, DMIN, DPRODUCT, DSTDEV, DSTDEVP, DSUM, DVAR, and DVARP. Each of these functions, with the exception of DGET, is the counterpart of a normal statistical function. DSUM is the counterpart of SUM, DVAR, of VAR, and so on.

The difference between the database statistical functions and their counterparts is that the database statistical functions operate only on those members of a range that meet stated criteria. You formulate the criteria by means of a criteria range, just as you would if you were performing an advanced filter operation.

For more information, see "Using the Advanced Filter Command" on page 726.

The database statistical functions all have the following syntax:
FUNC TION(database,field,criteria).

The first argument specifies the list to be examined. The second argument specifies the field (column) from which you want to retrieve a value. You can specify this either as the address of the field's column heading or as the text of that column heading. The third argument references your criteria range, and this must be a range of cells on the worksheet. Unlike some other spreadsheet programs, Excel does not permit you to specify the criterion as a text string within the function.

Figure 28-27 illustrates the DAVERAGE function. The formula at H3 is =**DAVERAGE(A6:G371,"Salary"A1:A2)**. The range A6:G371 contains the staff list. Salary is the heading for one of the list columns (we could have referenced this by address, F6, but Salary makes the formula more readable). A1:A2 is the criteria range.

The criterion is that Age is greater than or equal to 40, so the DAVERAGE formula returns the average salary for all employees over 40.

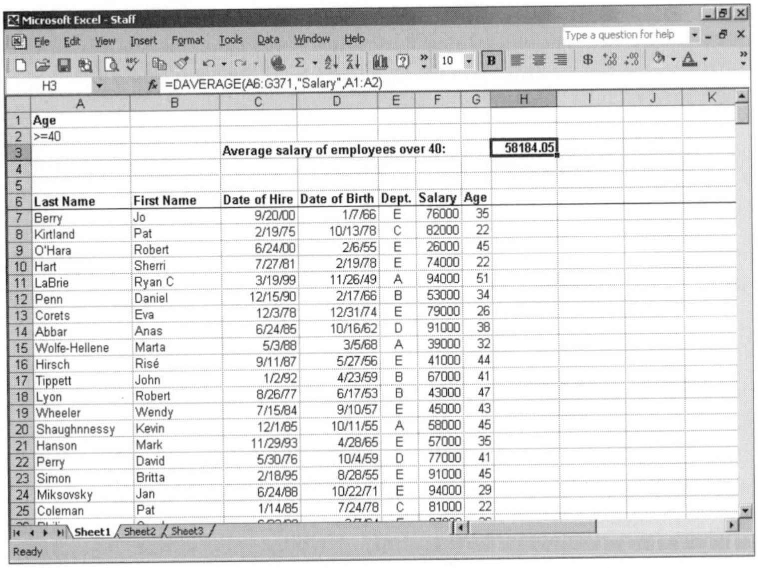

	A	B	C	D	E	F	G	H
1	Age							
2	>=40							
3			Average salary of employees over 40:					58184.05
4								
5								
6	Last Name	First Name	Date of Hire	Date of Birth	Dept.	Salary	Age	
7	Berry	Jo	9/20/00	1/7/66	E	76000	35	
8	Kirtland	Pat	2/19/75	10/13/78	C	82000	22	
9	O'Hara	Robert	6/24/00	2/6/55	E	26000	45	
10	Hart	Sherri	7/27/81	2/19/78	E	74000	22	
11	LaBrie	Ryan C	3/19/99	11/26/49	A	94000	51	
12	Penn	Daniel	12/15/90	2/17/66	B	53000	34	
13	Corets	Eva	12/3/78	12/31/74	E	79000	26	
14	Abbar	Anas	6/24/85	10/16/62	D	91000	38	
15	Wolfe-Hellene	Marta	5/3/88	3/5/68	A	39000	32	
16	Hirsch	Risé	9/11/87	5/27/56	E	41000	44	
17	Tippett	John	1/2/92	4/23/59	B	67000	41	
18	Lyon	Robert	8/26/77	6/17/53	B	43000	47	
19	Wheeler	Wendy	7/15/84	9/10/57	E	45000	43	
20	Shaughnnessy	Kevin	12/1/85	10/11/55	A	58000	45	
21	Hanson	Mark	11/29/93	4/28/65	E	57000	35	
22	Perry	David	5/30/76	10/4/59	D	77000	41	
23	Simon	Britta	2/18/95	8/28/55	E	91000	45	
24	Miksovsky	Jan	6/24/88	10/22/71	E	94000	29	
25	Coleman	Pat	1/14/85	7/24/78	C	81000	22	

Figure 28-27. The database statistical functions are useful for analyzing list information that meets particular criteria; this example uses DAVERAGE to find the average salary of workers 40 and over.

With the exception of DGET, all the database statistical functions work the same way. DGET is only slightly different. The DGET function returns the value of any cell in a column that meets the criteria expressed in a criteria range. If no cell meets the criteria, the function returns #VALUE!. If more than one cell meets the criteria, the function returns #NUM!.

You can use the ISERROR function to trap an error-generating DGET formula. For example, this formula returns the text "Data not available" if no items or more than one item met the criteria: **=IF(ISERROR(DGET(A6:G371,"Salary",A1:A2),"Data not available", DGET(A6:G371,"Salary",A1:A2))**. If you want to distinguish between the two possible types of errors, you can add the ERROR.TYPE function into the mix. ERROR.TYPE returns 3 if its reference is #VALUE! and 6 if its reference is #NUM!.

COUNTIF and SUMIF

Unlike the database statistical functions, the COUNTIF and SUMIF functions let you specify your criteria directly within the formula. Both functions are limited to simple comparison criteria, however.

COUNTIF takes the form =*COUNTIF(range,criteria)* where *range* is the range whose values you want to count and *criteria* is a text value expressing the required criterion. To count the number of Dept. E employees in the list shown in Figure 28-27, for example, you could use the formula =**COUNTIF(E6:E371,"E")**.

To count the number of employees who are 40 or older, you could use =**COUNTIF(G6:G371,">=40")**.

Note that the *range* argument references only the column you're testing, not the entire list. If you substituted A6:G371 for G6:G371 in the formula just cited, the resulting count would include everything in the Date Of Hire and Date Of Birthday fields and the over-40 Age items, because those hire dates and birth dates are all numbers greater than 40.

The SUMIF function takes the form =*SUMIF(range, criteria, sum_range)*.

Here the *criteria* argument is applied to *range*, and *sum_range* is the range whose values you want to add. For example, to calculate the total spent on salaries for workers below the age of 30 (using the list shown in Figure 28-27), you could use the formula =**SUMIF(G6:G371,"<30",F6:F371)**.

This formula says, "For every cell in G6:G371 whose value is less than 30, tally the corresponding value in column F."

Because an average is a sum divided by a count, you can use SUMIF and COUNTIF together to calculate averages. For example, the formula =**SUMIF(G6:G371,"<30",F6:F371)/COUNTIF(G6:G371,"<30")**.

returns the average salary paid to employees under 30.

Using the Conditional Sum Wizard

The Conditional Sum Wizard is an add-in that walks you through the process of summing items that meet one or more criteria. If you've installed it, you can run it by choosing Tools, Conditional Sum. If you don't find this command, you need to install the wizard. You can do that by choosing Tools, Add-ins, and selecting Conditional Sum Wizard.

The one advantage of using the Conditional Sum Wizard over using the SUMIF function is that the wizard permits multiple criteria. In Step 2 of the wizard's sequence of dialog boxes (see Figure 28-28), you select a criterion by choosing from drop-down lists and then clicking Add Condition, and you can repeat this process as often as you like.

Chapter 28

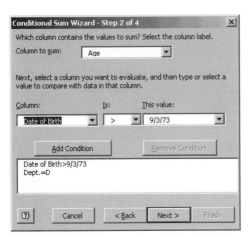

Figure 28-28. You specify criteria in the Conditional Sum Wizard by choosing from lists.

Interestingly, the Conditional Sum Wizard does not generate SUMIF formulas. Instead it uses array formulas. If you're interested in learning more about how array formulas work, you might want to generate some conditional sums this way and study the resulting formulas.

For more about array formulas, see "Using Arrays" on page 387.

COUNTBLANK

The formula =COUNTBLANK(*range*) returns the number of cells in *range* that are either empty or contain formulas that return null strings. If your application would be invalidated by the presence of blank elements in particular columns of a list, you might want to use one or more COUNTBLANK formulas as flags.

VLOOKUP and HLOOKUP

The VLOOKUP function searches for a specified value in the leftmost column of a table, and then returns a value from the same row in a specified other column of that table. The function has the following syntax:
VLOOKUP(lookup_value,table,column_number,[range_lookup]).

where *lookup_value* is the value the function searches for, *table* is the range in which the function searches, and *column_number* is the column from which the function returns a value. The optional *range_lookup* argument controls the manner in which function searches.

Chapter 28

Figure 28-29 shows the use of VLOOKUP to determine the amount of tax due, based on taxable income and filing status. The formula in this case is *=VLOOKUP(I4,taxtable,3)*.

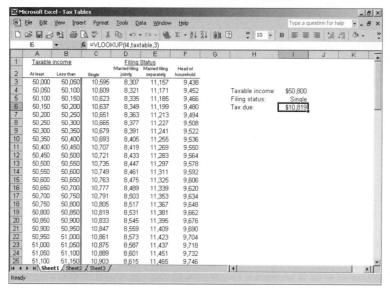

Figure 28-29. Use VLOOKUP to fetch the value in the third column of the row containing 50800, the value of cell I4.

The first argument, I4, is a reference to a cell containing the taxable income—in this case, 50,800. The second argument, taxtable, is a name assigned to the range A3:F102. The VLOOKUP will search the leftmost column of this range, column A, until it finds the value 50800. The third argument, 3, tells the function to return a value from column 3. VLOOKUP finds the value 50800 in row 19 of column A, moves across to the third column in that row (that is, moves two columns to the right), and returns the value it finds there, 10819.

If the fourth argument is either TRUE or omitted, VLOOKUP searches the leftmost column until it locates the largest value that is either less than or equal to *lookup_value*. If the fourth argument is FALSE, VLOOKUP returns #N/A unless it finds an exact match in the leftmost column. With the fourth argument TRUE or omitted, the leftmost column must be sorted in ascending order. With the fourth argument FALSE, no sort is required. Because the example omits the fourth argument, it would return 10819 if the value in I4 were anything between 50800 and 50849 (rounding to the nearest dollar).

The example uses a numeric *lookup_value*, but the function also accommodates text lookups. If you're using text as a *lookup_value*, you'll probably want to set the fourth argument to FALSE so that the function will return values based on exact matches only.

HLOOKUP works exactly like VLOOKUP, except that it's used with horizontally arranged lookup tables instead of vertical ones. The function searches the top row of such a table and returns a value from a specified row below the top row.

Using the Lookup Wizard

The Lookup Wizard is an add-in that walks you through the process of finding a value in a vertical table that's in a column to the right of some specified value in the table. In other words, it provides an alternative to building a formula with the VLOOKUP function. If you've installed the Lookup Wizard add-in, you can run it by choosing Tools, Wizard, Lookup. If you don't find this command, you need to install the wizard. You can do that by choosing Tools, Add-ins, and selecting Lookup Wizard.

Unlike the VLOOKUP function, however, the Lookup Wizard requires an exact match in the leftmost column of the lookup table. That's because it constructs its formula using the MATCH and INDEX functions, instead of the VLOOKUP or HLOOKUP function. We'll look at MATCH and INDEX next.

MATCH and INDEX

Like VLOOKUP and HLOOKUP, the MATCH function searches a range that you specify for a particular value that you specify. Unlike these other functions, however, MATCH returns the position within the range at which it finds the *lookup_value* argument. For example, if the item you're looking for is the fifth item in the range, MATCH returns the number 5—not the item itself.

The syntax for MATCH is **MATCH(lookup_value,lookup_array,[match-type])**.

The *lookup_value* argument can be any value (text or numeric) or a reference to a cell containing any value. The *lookup_array* argument can be a column, a row, or an array specified within the formula. The optional *match-type* argument is 1 by default and can be any of the following:

Match-type	**Effect**
1	MATCH looks for the largest value smaller than lookup_value. Lookup_array must be sorted in ascending order.
0	MATCH looks for exact matches only and returns #N/A if there is no exact match. Lookup_array need not be sorted.
-1	MATCH looks for the smallest value greater than lookup_value. Lookup_array must be sorted in descending order.

The MATCH function is often used to provide an argument to the INDEX function. The INDEX function returns the item at a specified row and column position within a range. The syntax is **INDEX(array,row_number,column_number)** or **INDEX(reference,row_number,column_number,area_number)**.

In the first syntax, array can be a range or an array specified within the formula. In the second syntax, *reference* can be a single range or multiple noncontiguous ranges; if multiple ranges are specified, *area_number* indicates which of the specified ranges INDEX should search.

If *array* or *reference* is a single column, the *column_number* argument can be omitted. If *array* or *reference* is a single row, the *row_number* argument can be omitted. If the combination of *column_number* and *row_number* points to a cell or value lying outside *array* or *range*, the function returns #REF!

In Figure 28-30, the formula at D2 uses MATCH and INDEX to look up the value for Eva Corets's salary. The formula reads
=INDEX(A6:G371,MATCH(C2,A6:A371),MATCH(D1,A6:G6)).

The *array* argument for INDEX is A6:G371, the address of our staff list. The *row_number* argument is supplied by MATCH(C2,A6:A371), which returns 8, because Corets (the value of C2) is at the eighth position within A6:A371. The *column_number* argument is supplied by MATCH(D1,A6:G6), which returns 6, because Salary (the value of D1) is at the sixth position within A6:G6. The INDEX function therefore returns 79000, the value lying at the intersection of the eighth row and sixth column of A6:A371.

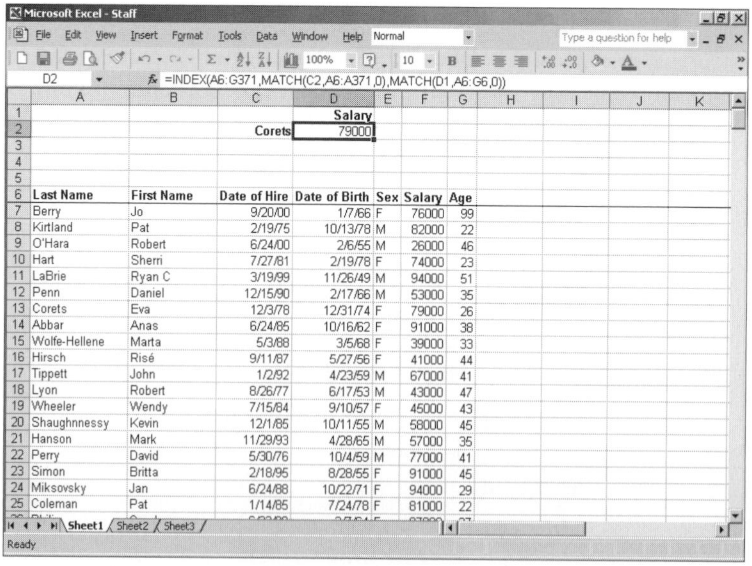

Figure 28-30. We've used INDEX in conjunction with MATCH to return the value at a particular intersection within the staff list.

If the *row_number* argument for INDEX is 0, INDEX returns an array consisting of all the values in the column specified by *column_number*. Similarly, if *column_number* is 0, INDEX returns an array of the values in the row specified by *row_number*. You could therefore fetch Ms. Corets's entire row from the staff list by selecting a range of seven horizontally contiguous cells and array-entering the formula
=INDEX(A6:G371,MATCH("Corets",A6:A371,0),0).

Note that the MATCH component of this formula needs to include a *match_type* argument of 0, because we need an exact match with the text "Corets".

Using INDEX with a List Control to Create a Data Browser

Armed with an understanding of the INDEX function, you can use a list box control on a worksheet to create an attractive data browser. Figure 28-31 illustrates this idea. The fields in the form at B6:G15 use the value of B5 as a *row_number* argument for an INDEX formula, which retrieves a value from the list on the pacadata worksheet.

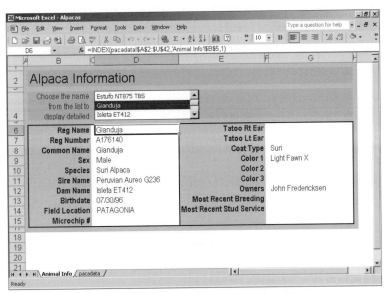

Figure 28-31. The list box control at D4 is linked to B5.

We've added a list box control to this worksheet and placed it atop cell D4. This list box control is linked to cell B5, which is scrunched into a narrow row and made invisible by a gray band. In the form at B6:G15, the cells in columns D and G use the value of B5 as a *row_number* argument for an INDEX formula, which in turn retrieves data from the list stored on the pacadata worksheet. At D6, for example, we have the formula
=INDEX(pacadata!$A$2:$U$42,'Animal Info'!$B$5,1).

Because the item currently selected in the list box control, Gianduja, is the fifteenth item in the list, cell B5 contains (invisibly) the value 15. The INDEX formula therefore retrieves the item at the intersection of row 15 and column 1 in pacadata!A2:U42. The

747

formula in cell D7 looks just like the one in D6, except that it uses a *column_number* argument of 2, and so on.

Figure 28-31 shows the browser on a normal-looking worksheet, complete with row and column headings. To make the browser look a little classier (and less spreadsheet-like), you can choose Tools, Options, click the View tab, and clear the Row & Column Headers check box.

To create a list box control, follow these steps:

1 Choose View, Toolbars, Forms.

2 On the Forms toolbar, select the list box item, and drag out a rectangle to position the control on the worksheet.

3 Right-click the new control and choose Properties.

4 On the Control tab of the Format Control dialog box (see Figure 28-32), fill out the Input Range and Cell Link boxes. The Input Range box specifies a worksheet range containing the items you want to appear in your list box. The Cell Link box specifies a cell that will record the position within Input Range of the item that is currently selected in the list control box.

5 Select the Single option button. This ensures that the user of your browser will be able to select only one item at a time.

6 Click OK.

Figure 28-32. With the properties shown here, the list control box will display the items listed in pacadata!A2:U42. The number of the item selected (its position within the list) will be returned in cell B5.

Chapter 29

Working with External Data

Microsoft Excel is a superb tool for analyzing data, but before you can do any analysis, you have to get the data into Excel. In many cases, the information you need to work with resides somewhere "outside"—in a mainframe text file, on a Web site, or in a database program such as Oracle or Microsoft Access. Excel provides excellent tools for importing that information onto your worksheets; those tools are the subject of this chapter.

Opening Text and dBase Files

The simplest way to bring external data onto an Excel worksheet is to choose File, Open. Data stored in comma-delimited or space-delimited text files, or in files in the DBF (dBase) format can be opened directly in this manner. To work with data in one of these formats, you can choose File, Open, and then select the appropriate file type—Text Files or dBase Files—in the Files Of Type box of the Open dialog box.

Excel assumes that dBase files will have the extension .dbf, and that text files will have one of the following extensions: .prn, .txt, or .csv. If your file doesn't have one of these extensions—for example, if you want to work with a text file that has the extension .log or .asc—select All Files in the Files Of Type box. Excel determines a file's type by its data, not by its name, so it doesn't make any difference what the file name extension is; Excel will read it if it can and let you know if it can't.

The Open command, of course, brings the entire text or dBase file into Excel, and it does so as a one-time transaction. If you want to look only at particular records in a text or dBase file, or if you want to create a range in Excel that can be refreshed (periodically or on demand) to keep in step with changes to the source data, you don't want to use the Open command. Use a query instead.

For more information about queries, see "Using a Query to Import Data" on page 754.

Importing a dBase document is straightforward. Each field in the dBase document becomes a column in Excel; each record becomes a row. Import of text files stored as comma-separated values (files that typically have the extension .csv) is similarly straightforward. Each time Excel encounters a comma in the original document (unless the comma appears between a pair of quotation marks), the import routine skips to a new column. Where a Return-Linefeed combination occurs in the text file, Excel begins a new row. A file of this kind is also said to be *comma-delimited*.

When you choose File, Open to bring text or dBase information into Excel, the data arrives as a new file (as opposed to a range of data imported into an existing workbook). When you save such a file, Excel will give you the option of converting it to a native Excel file. You'll want to exercise this option if you've made any change to the file that cannot be preserved in the file's original (text or dBase) format.

PRN files created by one of the MS-DOS versions of Lotus 1-2-3 are not comma-delimited but *fixed-width*. That is, alignment of columns is achieved in the text file by the insertion of a variable number of space characters, rather than by commas or some other delimiting character. When you open a text file that is not comma-delimited (or that's ambiguous for any other reason), you are greeted by the Text Import Wizard, shown in Figure 29-1.

Figure 29-1. The Text Import Wizard lets you tell Excel how to parse your text file.

Using the Text Import Wizard

The Text Import Wizard allows you to show Excel how to parse your text file. You get to tell the program what character or character combination (if any) is used to delimit columns, what kind of data appears in each column, and what character set was used to create the original file. You can also use the Text Import Wizard to exclude one or more rows at the top of your file—an option that's often useful.

The wizard's first screen, shown in Figure 29-1, presents a preview of the data that Excel is about to import. It also indicates Excel's best estimation of whether your file is delimited or fixed-width. You'll find that the wizard is usually on the money with this first guess—but if it's mistaken, you can set it straight. (If you're not sure, just go on to the second screen. When you get there, you'll know whether the program was wrong, and you can go back to the first screen to fix the problem.)

Before you click Next to leave the first screen, check to make sure the program has recognized what character set your file uses. If the file was created in a Windows program, the File Origin box should be set to Windows (ANSI). If the file was created in an MS-DOS-based program, choose MS-DOS, PC-8 or 437: OEM United States, if it was created using the United States character set. If it was created on a Macintosh, choose Macintosh. If it was created in some other computing environment, it's probably safe to choose Windows (ANSI). If the file was created in a character set other than the one your own Windows user account is using, try to find that character set in the File Origin drop-down list.

While you're still in the wizard's first screen, use the Start Import At Row spin box to eliminate any header rows that you can live without in Excel. Header rows make it hard for Excel to parse your file correctly, so you can do the program (and yourself) a good turn by lopping them off here.

The Text Import Wizard's second screen looks something like either Figure 29-2 or Figure 29-3, shown on the next page, depending on whether your file is delimited or fixed-width. In both cases, the vertical lines in the Data Preview window show how Excel proposes to split your file into columns. The Data Preview window regrettably shows a paltry 5 rows at a time and 65 characters per row. It cannot be made to show more, but you can look at other parts of the file by using the scroll bars.

Chapter 29

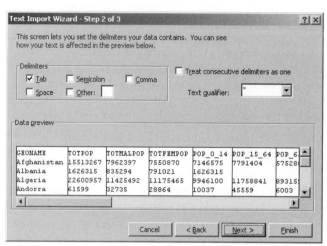

Figure 29-2. If your file is delimited, the wizard's second screen indicates what character Excel has recognized as the delimiter, and the Data Preview window shows how Excel will parse your file.

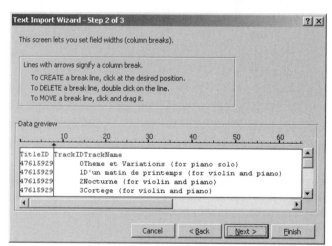

Figure 29-3. If your file is fixed-width, be sure to check the Data Preview window; you can fix Excel's mistakes by manipulating the vertical bars.

If your file is delimited, the wizard's second screen indicates what character Excel regards as the delimiter. In Figure 29-2, for example, the program has correctly divined that the file in question is tab-delimited. Most of the time, Excel gets this right. If it does not in your case, you can select a different check box and see the effect immediately in the Data Preview window. You can also select more than one check box to indicate that your file is delimited by multiple characters. If you select two or more check boxes, Excel breaks to a new column whenever it sees any of your choices.

Chapter 29: Working with External Data

A separate check box lets you stipulate that consecutive delimiting characters should be regarded as a single delimiter. You'll find that this option sometimes saves the day with tab-delimited files. The original creator of the file might occasionally have used two or more tabs to skip to the next column when the current column's contents were short. That strategy might disrupt your alignment in Excel unless you tell the program to treat consecutive delimiters as a single delimiter.

Excel is much more likely to be at sea when trying to parse a fixed-width file. In the file shown in Figure 29-3, for example, the program initially sees only one column break in the first 65 characters because of the right-alignment of the numbers 0, 1, 2, and 3 in rows 2 through 5. Fortunately, it's easy to fix a problem like this. Drag vertical lines to the left or right to reposition them. To create a column break where one doesn't yet exist (between the 0 and the word Theme in row 2 of Figure 29-3, for example), click in the appropriate place. To remove a column break that shouldn't be there at all, double-click it.

The wizard's third screen, shown in Figure 29-4, lets you specify the data type of each column. Your choices are limited to General (which treats text as text and numbers as numbers), Text (which treats all contents in a row as text, even in rows that appear to be numeric), Date, and Do Not Import column (Skip.) Excel initially assigns the General designation to all columns, and you'll probably want to override that presumption in some cases. For example, if your file happens to have a text field that begins with a hyphen, Excel will regard the hyphen as a minus sign and attempt to turn your text into a formula. You can avoid errors by indicating that the field is Text.

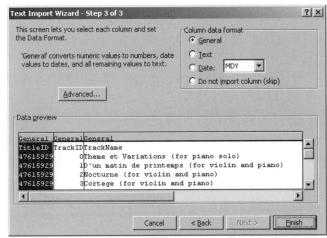

Figure 29-4. You can use the wizard's third screen to control the data type of each column.

Chapter 29

> **tip** **Watch out for credit card numbers**
>
> Sixteen-digit credit card numbers present a problem unless they're parsed as text. If Excel thinks they're really numbers, it turns the last digit into a 0 because it can handle only 15 digits of precision.

The third screen also includes an Advanced button. By clicking here, you can change the way the wizard handles commas and periods in numeric data. By default, Excel uses the settings specified in the Regional Settings section of Control Panel. If your text file was created under other assumptions, you'll need to make some adjustments in the Advanced Text Import Settings dialog box.

> **tip** **Parse Clipboard text**
>
> Occasionally when working with text data, you might find long text strings that need to be broken into separate columns. This can happen, for example, if you paste text into Excel from the Clipboard. To parse such data, select it and choose Data, Text To Columns. You'll be back in the Text Import Wizard again. The wizard wears a different title bar in this case but works the same way as before.

Using a Query to Import Data

Choosing File, Open is fine for bringing into Excel an entire text or DBF file. When the data you require resides in a server database, such as SQL Server or Oracle, or when you need to fetch information from tables in a relational database such as Microsoft Access, you need a query.

When you import data by means of a query, you can limit the import to records that meet particular criteria. Moreover, the incoming data becomes a "data range" on the current worksheet, allowing you to refresh the query periodically or when the need arises.

Database queries in Excel are accomplished through the intermediation of Microsoft Query, a querying tool supplied with Microsoft Office. Query generates statements in the SQL language and passes those statements to the data source, while shielding you from the need to master SQL yourself. If your query is relatively simple, you might not need to interact directly with Query; instead you can formulate your request by means of a four-step wizard that acts as a front end to Query.

Using Excel's query mechanism, you can retrieve data from any database program for which a current Open Database Connectivity (ODBC) or OLE DB driver is installed. ODBC is a standard interface for connecting with database programs. OLE DB, which has nothing to do with object linking and embedding, is a newer interface for the same purpose. (OLE DB has some capabilities that ODBC does not, and Excel connects to ODBC data sources by means of OLE DB.) Excel ships with support for SQL Server, SQL Server OLAP Services, Access, Visual FoxPro, Oracle, dBase, text, and a few other sources. There's even a driver for querying data stored in external Excel tables.

Reusing an Existing Query

If you have already set up a database query for yourself, the specifications for that query might be stored in a file, available for reuse. To open such a query, choose Data, Import External Data, Import Data. Excel responds by displaying the Select Data Source dialog box, a file browser that resembles an ordinary Open dialog box (see Figure 29-5).

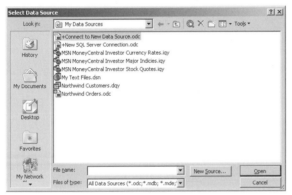

Figure 29-5. To reuse an existing query, choose Data, Import Data, and select from this dialog box.

In reality, this isn't quite an ordinary browser because, although the Look In line says My Data Sources (which is a subfolder of your My Documents folder), the files listed in the dialog box can come from the Queries subfolder of your Office10 folder and the folder Program Files\Common Files\ODBC\Data Sources, as well as from My Documents\My Data Sources.

The Select Data Source dialog box on your system probably includes the first five items shown in Figure 29-5: +Connect To New Data Source, +New SQL Server Connection (the plus signs are there to ensure that these items appear at the top of the list), and the three MSN MoneyCentral items. If additional queries or connection files have been set up on your system, they will also appear here. In Figure 29-5, we've added three items: My Text Files, Northwind Customers, and Northwind Orders. My Text Files and Northwind Orders are connection files; they tell Excel how to connect with an external data source. Northwind Customers is a query file; it contains more specific information about which tables and fields to retrieve from an external source, as well as how the incoming data should be filtered and sorted.

File name extensions are visible in Figure 29-5 because we've used a setting in Windows Explorer to make them so. You might not see extensions on your own system, but you will see different icons for different file types. (Use the Views drop-down list, next to Tools on the dialog box's toolbar, to switch to Large Icons view if you want to get a better look at the different icons.) Icons that look like one of the two shown here represent connection files, and for all intents and purposes, there is no difference between the two. (They've been created in different ways, but they're functionally equivalent.) Both allow you to establish a connection with an external database source.

Icons that look like this one represent Internet (Web) queries. Launching one of these fetches data from a particular Web site.

> For more information about Web queries, see "Using Web Queries to Retrieve Internet Data" on page 781.

Icons that look like this one represent database queries. Launching one of these executes a query against one or more remote database tables.

When you launch an existing database query, depending on how that query was set up, you might be presented with a Select Table dialog box. Make your selection from the tables listed there, and click OK. You also can go directly to the Import Data dialog box, shown in Figure 29-9. Tell Excel where you want the imported data to land, and then click OK.

> **note** In the Import Data dialog box, you can also click Properties to adjust settings that affect the behavior of the import, or Edit Query, to modify the query specifications. Certain kinds of queries, those that prompt for parameters when run, also make available the Parameters button. If you don't want to check out these options now, you can return to them any time after executing the query. See "Modifying a Query's Refresh Behavior and Other Properties" on page 761 and "Editing a Query" on page 763.

Creating a New Database Query

The first step in creating a database query is to create a connection to the data source. Start by choosing Data, Import External Data, Import Data. In the Select Data Source dialog box, you can either select +Connect To New Data Source or click the New Source Button, near the bottom of the dialog box. Both of these actions take you to the same place, the Data Connection Wizard shown in Figure 29-6.

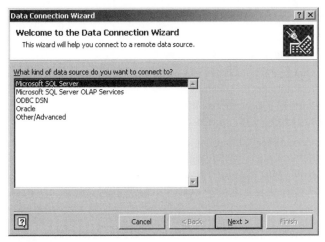

Figure 29-6. The Data Connection Wizard solicits the information it needs to connect to an external data source.

If the data source you need is not listed here, you probably need to get to it by selecting ODBC DSN and clicking Next, or by selecting Other/Advanced and clicking Next. The ODBC DSN item leads to a list of ODBC sources accessible via OLE DB. The Other/Advanced item leads to a long list of sources accessible directly via OLE DB.

> **note** If you can't find the data source you need under either ODBC DSN or Other/Advanced, see "Creating a New DSN File" on page 758.

After you identify the source of your data, you need to provide the Data Connection Wizard with whatever additional information it requires. This will probably include the location of the server, your logon credentials, and the name of a data table. If you're not sure how to work your way through the rest of the wizard's screens, you might need to get help from your database administrator.

Creating a New DSN File

If the data source you need isn't available via Data, Import External Data, Import Data, you might be able to find it by choosing Data, Import External Data, New Database Query. After choosing this command, take the following steps:

1 Double-click <New Data Source>. The Create New Data Source dialog box that appears has four boxes that must be filled out in order.

2 Supply your own name for the data source in the first box. (This name will be used to save a new DSN file when you finish.)

3 Select a driver in the second box.

4 Click the Connect button that appears in step 3. This generates a new dialog box, in which you might be asked to specify a version of the driver you're using. (For example, if you choose the dBase driver, you'll be asked to choose between dBase 5.0 and dBase IV.)

5 If the files you want to access are in the current folder, leave Use Current Directory selected. Otherwise, clear this check box and click Select Directory to tell Excel where your files live.

6 In step 4 of the previous dialog box, select a default table in the specified folder (directory).

Note that if you choose the Text driver, Excel will regard each text file in the specified folder as a "table." If you choose the Excel driver, each named range in the specified Excel file will be regarded as a "table." Be sure that the Excel data you want to query lies in a named range on the external Excel worksheet. Otherwise, you'll get an error message saying that the specified file has no tables.

After you have finished all these steps, you'll have a new DSN file in your My Data Sources folder. Open this file to execute your query.

Creating a Simple Example

Let's look at a simple query against the Northwind database that's included as a sample file with Microsoft Access. If you have Access and the sample Northwind database, installed, you'll probably find Northwind.mdb in the Samples subfolder of your Office10 folder. Northwind includes many tables; we'll query only one, the Customers table.

Start with the following steps:

1 Choose Data, Import External Data, Import Data, and then click the New Source button in the Select Data Source dialog box.

2 In the initial screen of the Data Connection Wizard, select ODBC DSN and click Next.

3 In the wizard's second screen, select MS Access Database, and click Next. This brings you to the Select Database dialog box shown in Figure 29-7.

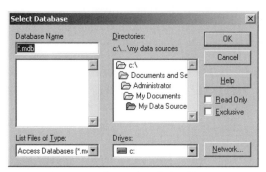

Figure 29-7. We'll use this dialog box to navigate to our MDB file.

After navigating to Northwind.mdb and clicking OK, you come to a list of tables contained in the MDB file (see Figure 29-8). The Connect To A Specific Table check box is selected by default, which means that Excel assumes you'll want your query description to point to a particular table within Northwind.mdb. You're not obliged to do this, however. By clearing this check box, you could create a general-purpose Northwind query that would prompt you for a particular table at the time the query was executed.

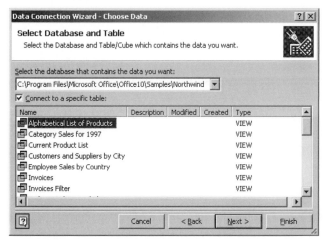

Figure 29-8. We can leave this check box selected and pick a specific table, or clear the check box and be prompted for a table when we execute the query.

Leaving the check box selected, scroll down to the Customers table and click Next. After two more wizard screens, you wind up back in the Select Data Source dialog box, which, this time, shows your new connection file. After selecting the new connection file and clicking Open, you arrive, finally, at the Import Data dialog box shown in Figure 29-9 on the next page.

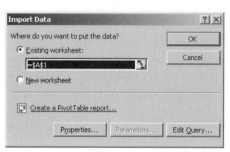

Figure 29-9. As a final step, tell Excel where you want the queried data to appear.

You're almost there. The main business of the Import Data dialog box is to get the location where you want the imported data to appear. That might be all you need to do here. If you want, though, you can deliver your imported data into a PivotTable Report by clicking the Create A Pivot Table Report link. (PivotTables are discussed in Chapter 30, "Analyzing Data with PivotTables.") You can also use the Properties button to modify the behavior of the query in certain ways or the Edit Query button to invoke the Query Wizard. We'll discuss the Query Wizard and query properties later in this chapter (see "Editing a Query" on page 763, and "Modifying a Query's Refresh Behavior and Other Properties" on page 761.) The Parameters button, dimmed in our example, is used with queries that prompt for additional information at the time the query is executed. Internet queries that fetch current stock prices and prompt for a ticker symbol on execution are an example. Figure 29-10 shows the result of your query against the Customers table of Northwind.mdb.

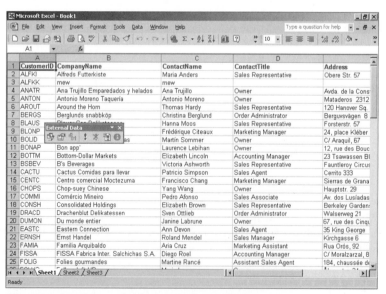

Figure 29-10. The query has arrived at cell A1.

The query looks like an ordinary Excel list, and, for the most part, it is. You can apply Excel's native filtering commands (discussed in Chapter 28, "Managing Information in Lists") to this list, change the formatting, perform calculations with the data, and so on. The difference between this and an ordinary Excel list is that Excel remembers where the data came from and can refresh it (update it with the latest values from the external source) periodically or on demand.

In short, you can consider the imported data to be occupying a range with a special property—the ability to be refreshed. Excel doesn't do much to bring this to your attention, however. The only way that you can tell that this range is special is by examining the Data menu or the External Data toolbar that appears by default when you execute a new query (see Figure 29-11.) When the active cell lies within a data range, the Import External Data, Edit Query And Data, Import External Data, and Data Range Properties commands become available, as do their counterparts on the External Data toolbar.

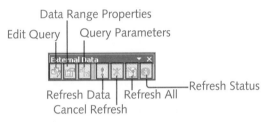

Data Range Properties
Edit Query | Query Parameters

Refresh Data | Refresh All
Cancel Refresh
Refresh Status

Figure 29-11. The External Data toolbar.

Modifying a Query's Refresh Behavior and Other Properties

Choosing Data, Import External Data, Data Range Properties (or clicking its toolbar equivalent) summons the query's properties dialog box, shown in Figure 29-12 on the next page. Here you can specify how and when you want your query to be refreshed. By default, Excel refreshes only on demand—when you click the red exclamation point on the External Data toolbar or choose Data, Refresh Data. The check boxes in the Refresh Control section of the properties dialog box give you additional options. To refresh periodically, select Refresh Every and specify a time interval. To get the latest data when you open your file, select Refresh Data On File Open. When you select this check box, you also get the option to remove the external data when you close the file. You might as well accept this, because Excel's going to refresh the data when you reopen the file anyway. (Incidentally, the check box that becomes available, Remove External Data From Worksheet Before Saving, is mislabeled. The data is removed only on file closure, not whenever you save.)

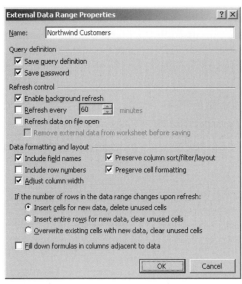

Figure 29-12. The External Data Range Properties dialog box lets you control refresh behavior and other matters.

By default, Excel performs data refresh in the background, allowing you to do other work while your data range is being updated. This is probably a useful option when your data is housed in a server database and the refresh process takes a while. If you're not taking advantage of background refresh, however, you might want to clear the Enable Background Refresh check box to see whether there's a noticeable speed improvement in the refresh.

The following sections discuss other tasks you can do by modifying settings in the External Data Range Properties dialog box.

Turning the Data Range Back into an Ordinary Range   If you no longer need query refresh, you can save some overhead by clearing the Save Query Definition check box. Excel dissociates your data from its external source and turns the range back into an ordinary Excel list.

Saving Your Password   If the Save Password check box is selected, Excel remembers your logon information and refrains from prompting you every time you refresh. This is convenient but potentially hazardous. If the external data is for your own eyes only, be aware that selecting this check box allows anyone with access to your computer to refresh the data.

Using Your Own Field Names   By default, Excel uses the field names in the external data source, displaying those field names in the first row of the data range. If you prefer to use different field names, clear the Include Field Names check box. Then create your own field-name row atop the data range.

Including Row Numbers   If you select the Include Row Numbers check box, Excel creates a new column at the left side of the data range and displays row numbers there (beginning with 0 for the first row). The rows are numbered according to the sort order you choose when you execute the query and can help you return to this order if you change the sorting in Excel.

Using Other Formatting and Layout Options   Excel adjusts column widths by default so that all records are fully visible. Clear Adjust Column Width if you don't want this behavior. Changes that you make in Excel to the appearance of your data—such as filtering, sorting, formatting, or rearrangement of columns—are preserved when you refresh. Clear the remaining two check boxes in the Data Formatting And Layout area if you want Excel to discard such changes on refresh.

Controlling Overwrite Behavior   By default, Excel makes sure that a query refresh never overwrites data lying outside the data range. If you have anything below the data range (a practice you should avoid, in any case), Excel inserts new rows as necessary to avoid overwrite. If a subsequent refresh results in a smaller data range, Excel deletes the unused cells, thereby maintaining a constant amount of white space between the bottom of the data range and whatever lies below.

The alternative possibilities, available via the set of option buttons near the bottom of the dialog box, are to clear cells when the data range shrinks (leaving empty cells and not moving the data below) or to ignore the whole question and just let overwriting occur.

Using Automatic Formula Extension   The last check box in the properties dialog box provides a very useful feature. If, after performing a query, you add a calculated field of your own, either within or adjacent to the data range, Excel subsequently treats that column as part of the data range, extending the formulas as necessary when a refresh generates additional rows, removing calculated cells when a refresh produces a smaller data range, and so on.

For example, suppose that in Figure 29-10, you wanted to add a column that would display only the last name of your contacts. You could insert a new column to the right of the ContactName column, and enter the following formula in the new cell D2: =RIGHT(C2,LEN(C2)-FIND(" ",C2)). On refresh, Excel would extend that formula through all the rows of the data range.

Automatic formula extension is not on by default. To use it, select the Fill Down Formulas In Columns Adjacent To Data check box.

Editing a Query

In our simple example, we've imported an entire Access table, including all fields and without sorting or filtering the external data. We can use Excel to filter and sort the data, of course, but in a real-world situation, with a query against a large external data table, it's better to do the filtering and sorting outside Excel. The server on which the database resides is likely to do this work more efficiently, and sending a filtered data set over the network reduces network traffic.

To import a filtered subset of an external data table, or to sort the table before it arrives, you need to edit the query. Editing the query also allows you to switch to a different table or to exclude particular fields from the imported data.

To edit a query after you already have the data in Excel, choose Data, Import External Data, Edit Query (or click its toolbar equivalent). To edit a query before importing the data, click Edit Query in the Import Data dialog box, shown in Figure 29-9. Either way, your action opens the Query Wizard, the friendly front end to Microsoft Query. The Query Wizard's first screen is shown in Figure 29-13.

> **note** If your query cannot be edited in the Query Wizard, you will be taken straight into Microsoft Query. For information about using Query, see "Working Directly with Microsoft Query" on page 768.

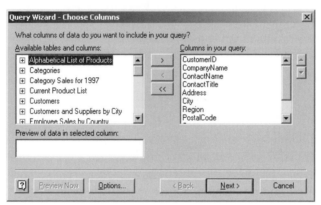

Figure 29-13. Choosing Edit Query takes you to the Query Wizard, a friendly interface for Microsoft Query.

Choosing Tables and Fields   In the wizard's first dialog box, you see a list of tables on the left and selected fields on the right. Outline controls appear to the left of table names. Click a plus sign to expand a table and reveal its fields; click a minus sign to collapse an expanded table.

To add a field to your query, select it on the left and click the right-pointing arrow. To add an entire table, select the table's name on the left and click the right-pointing arrow. To remove a field, select it on the right and click the left-pointing arrow. To remove all fields at once, click the double-arrow.

If you add a second or subsequent table to your query, Microsoft Query performs a *join* operation on the selected tables, if it can. Query joins related tables when it recognizes a primary key field in one table and a field with the same data type (and typically, but not necessarily, the same field name) in the other table. For an example of a query that involves two joined tables, see "Working Directly with Microsoft Query" on page 768.

Filtering Records After specifying tables and fields and clicking Next, you arrive at the wizard's Filter Data screen, shown in Figure 29-14. Here you can specify one or more filter criteria. This is an optional step; if you skip it, Query returns all records from the selected tables.

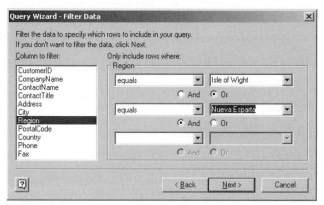

Figure 29-14. Filters, specified in the wizard's second dialog box, select the records that meet your criteria.

A filter criterion has three components: a field name, a relationship, and a value. You can specify as many as three criteria for each field, connected by And or Or. The list at the left side of the dialog box includes all the names of your selected fields. The drop-down lists in the center include a long list of available relationships, and the drop-down lists at the right include all the available values for the selected field. Figure 29-14 shows how the wizard's second screen would look if you wanted to see only those records in which the Region field equaled either Isle of Wight or Nueva Esparta.

---

tip   **For more relationships, use query directly**

The Query Wizard offers a long list of relational operators for building filtering criteria. If you use Microsoft Query directly, four additional relationships are available: Is One Of, Is Not One Of, Is Between, and Is Not Between. These additional operators are designed to work with two or more values—something that the wizard doesn't accommodate. For example, Is Between and Is Not Between both require two values. Is One Of and Is Not One Of can use a list of values. For more information, see "Working Directly with Microsoft Query" on page 768.

Troubleshooting

The Query Wizard Won't Let Me Get Rid of a Filter

The Query Wizard is a little clumsy when it comes to letting you remove filters. There's no Delete button. Clicking Back to return to the previous screen, and then clicking Next to come back to the Filtering screen doesn't get it done (the previous filter is still there). Clicking Cancel either bails out of the entire edit process or takes you to Microsoft Query, neither of which is what you probably want. To get rid of a criterion, open its relationship list and select the blank entry at the top of the list.

If you filter on two or more different fields, you'll find that when you select the second field, the wizard removes the first criterion from view. You can tell that you've applied a criterion to a field, however, by looking at the left window of the dialog box. Filtered fields appear there in boldface.

tip Because the wizard accepts up to three criteria per field, you can use it to generate some pretty marvelous filters. But it's a whole lot easier to see what you're doing if you use the full Query interface for multifield filtering. For details, see "Working Directly with Microsoft Query" on page 768.

Sorting Records After you finish filtering and click Next, the wizard presents its Sort Order screen, shown in Figure 29-15. Sorting is optional, of course. If you decline, Query returns records in the order in which they're stored in the external database file.

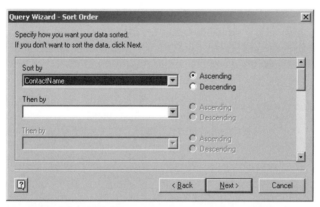

Figure 29-15. Use the Sort Order screen to arrange the records that are returned to Excel.

To sort, begin by clicking the Sort By list. There you'll find the name of each field in the table you're querying. Select a field, and then click the Ascending or Descending option to the right of the list. You can sort on as many fields as you want. To remove a sort item, select the blank entry at the top of the drop-down list. In Figure 29-15, we've asked for records sorted in ascending order by ContactName.

Saving the Query or Moving to Microsoft Query   The wizard's final screen, shown in Figure 29-16, provides two important options. The Save Query button allows you to name and save your query as a DQY file. The resulting DQY file encapsulates all the selections you've made in the construction of your query—your choice of tables and fields, your filters, and your sorting specifications. Note that this is different from the ODC file you might have made earlier. An ODC file records information required to achieve a connection with an external data source; a DQY file records query specifications.

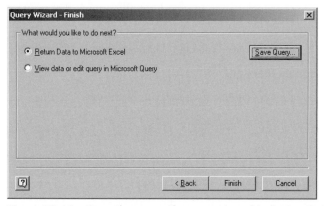

Figure 29-16.   Save the query if you want, and indicate whether you want to return directly to Excel or go on to the full Microsoft Query for further processing.

If you want to be able to reuse this query in another workbook, be sure to save it. If you save it in the default location, the resulting DQY file will appear in the My Data Sources folder when you choose Data, Import External Data, Import Data. Your query will also now be available via Data, Import External Data, New Database Query (even though at this point it's not a new database query). You'll find it on the Queries tab of the Choose Data Source dialog box.

The other option in the wizard's last screen lets you move to the full Microsoft Query for further processing. For information about why you might want to do this and how to use Query, see the following section. If you don't want to move on to Query, select Return Data To Microsoft Excel and click Finish.

> **tip**   After you've created a DQY file, you can execute it from any Windows Explorer window, just as you can an XLS file.

Chapter 29

Working Directly with Microsoft Query

The Query Wizard is an ideal tool for creating relatively simple queries, but it doesn't provide access to all of Microsoft Query's power. You'll need to work directly with Query if your query uses criteria involving calculations (other than simple comparisons) or if you want to create a query that prompts the user for one or more parameters when run. Query, but not the Query Wizard, also lets you do the following:

- Filter on the basis of fields that you don't intend to import into Excel—that is, fields that are not included in the *result set,* the records that meet your current criteria.

- Filter using Is One Of, Is Not One Of, Is Between, or Is Not Between.

- Limit the result set to unique entries.

- Perform aggregate calculations, such as totals or averages.

- Create your own joins between tables.

- Edit a query's SQL code.

Getting to Query

If the query you want to edit is already stored in a DQY file, you can open it in Microsoft Query using either of the following methods:

- Choose Data, Import External Data, Import Data. Open a DQY file. In the Import Data dialog box (see Figure 29-9), click Edit Query. When the Query Wizard arrives, click Cancel. When asked whether you want to continue editing in Microsoft Query, click Yes.

- Choose Data, Import External Data, New Database Query. Clear the check box at the bottom of the Choose Data Source dialog box. Click the Queries tab and open a query.

If you've just finished creating your query in the Query Wizard and want to open it in Microsoft Query for further editing, select View Data Or Edit Query In Microsoft Query in the Query Wizard's Finish screen.

If you are already working with imported data and you want to edit the query in Query, choose Data, Import External Data, Edit Query (or its toolbar equivalent). If you land in the Query Wizard instead of Query, click Cancel. When asked whether you want to continue editing in Microsoft Query, click Yes.

Figure 29-17 shows Query with a query against three tables from Northwind.mdb. The tables are Products, Categories, and Suppliers. The Products table is joined to the Categories table in the CategoryID field and to the Suppliers table in the SupplierID field. The query shows selected fields from these tables, revealing products by category and supplier (CompanyName), along with some price and inventory information.

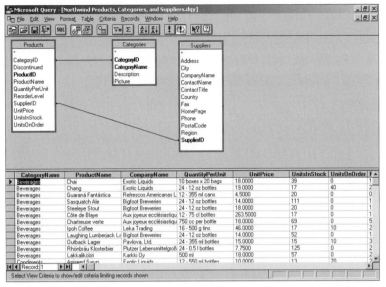

Figure 29-17. We're using Query to edit a query against three tables in Northwind.mdb.

Note that Query's window is divided into two panes—one for tables and one for data. The tables pane shows a window for each table that's currently involved in the query. The data pane shows the result set.

Shortly you'll see that Query can also accommodate a third pane, in which filtering criteria are specified. All these panes, as well as the individual table windows, are independently sizable and movable. We've bumped the data pane down a bit from its default position to make more room for the Suppliers and Products tables, and we've stretched them so that we wouldn't have to scroll to see all their fields. You'll find that Query seldom gives you an ideal window layout when it starts up, so you'll want to manipulate it to get the view you need.

Adding and Removing Tables

To add a table to Query's data pane, choose Table, Add Tables. The Add Tables dialog box lists all the tables available in the data source you're working with. To add a table, select it and click Add. You can add as many as you like before closing the Add Tables dialog box. To remove a table, select it in the table pane, and then choose Table, Remove Table.

Working with Joins

If Query doesn't already have your tables joined appropriately, you can create your own joins by dragging. If you click a field in one table, and then drag to a field in another, Query creates a join based on those fields and draws a line to indicate that it has done so. You can inspect and modify joins, and create new ones, by double-clicking any join line or by choosing Table, Joins. Figure 29-18 shows the Joins dialog box for the query shown in Figure 29-17.

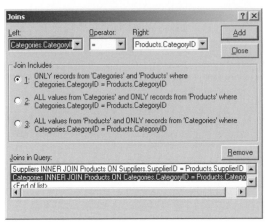

Figure 29-18. The Joins dialog box tells you exactly how your tables are joined and lets you modify the joins or create new ones.

If you're not sure what's joined to what or what the effect of a join is, it's a good idea to visit the Joins dialog box. The Join Includes section of the dialog box provides a pretty clear description of what's going on. By working with the Left, Operator, and Right fields, you can also modify the ways in which your tables are joined.

Adding, Removing, and Moving Fields

To add a field to your data pane, double-click it in a table window. To add all fields from a table, double-click the asterisk at the top of the table window.

To remove a field, select its heading (this action selects the entire field) and press Delete. To move a field from its current location, first select its heading. Then drag it to the position you want.

---

tip **Hide selected fields without removing them from the query**

If you find yourself scrolling horizontally a lot but don't want to rearrange your fields, you can hide fields that you temporarily don't need to see. Select a field, and then choose Format, Hide Columns. To redisplay a hidden field, choose Format, Show Columns, select the field in the Show Columns dialog box, and then click Show.

Renaming Fields

By default, Query uses the names of your fields as field headings. If these field names are short and cryptic, you might want to supply different headings.

Select the column you want to change, and then choose Records, Edit Column. In the Edit Column dialog box, enter a new heading in the Column Heading field.

Sorting the Result Set

Query initially displays records in the order in which they are stored in the external data source. You can change their order by choosing Records, Sort. Figure 29-19 shows the Sort dialog box with the ProductName field selected. (The dialog box, like others in Query, qualifies field names with the tables to which they belong; it says Products.ProductName, because the ProductName field is part of the Products table.)

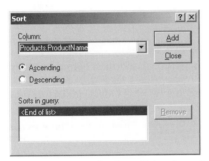

Figure 29-19. The Sort dialog box displays the current sort order and lets you add fields from a drop-down list.

The Sorts In Query section of the dialog box indicates what sort specification, if any, is currently in effect. In Figure 29-19, the list is empty, indicating that the result set is currently unsorted. The Column drop-down list at the top of the dialog box lists all the table fields available for sorting. When you add a field to the Sorts In Query list, Query performs the sort immediately but leaves the dialog box open in case you want to sort on additional fields. You can sort on as many as you please.

For multiple-field sorts, sort first on the most important sort field. Then sort on your secondary field, and so on. Figure 29-20 on the next page shows the result set sorted first by Suppliers.CompanyName and then by Products.ProductName. (The Asc abbreviation in the Sorts In Query list indicates ascending sorts.) The records now are alphabetized by supplier, with records of a common supplier alphabetized by product name.

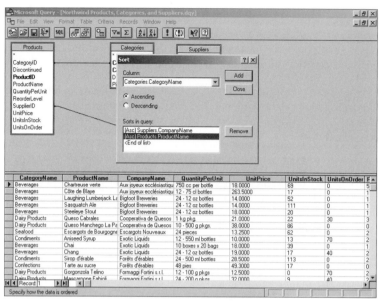

Figure 29-20. We've sorted first by supplier name, and then by product name.

When you click the Add button in the Sort dialog box, Query adds your new sort field above the currently selected field in the Sorts In Query list. If you accidentally add a field in the wrong order, select it and click Remove. Then add the field in the correct position.

Sorting with the Toolbar   The Sort icons on Query's toolbar look like their counterparts in Excel but work differently. You can add a sort to the current sort list by holding down the Ctrl key when you click a Sort icon. If you do not hold down Ctrl, clicking a Sort icon replaces the current sort with the new one.

Filtering the Result Set

Query provides a variety of methods by which you can filter the result set so that it includes only the records you're interested in. As with the Query Wizard, you create a filter by specifying one or more criteria—conditions that particular fields must meet.

Creating Exact-Match Criteria   The simplest kind of criterion is one in which you stipulate that a field exactly equal some value. Query makes it extremely easy to create such criteria:

1   Select a field value that meets your exact-match criterion.

2   Click the Criteria Equals button on the toolbar (see Figure 29-21).

Chapter 29: Working with External Data

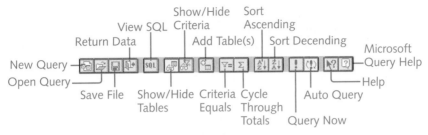

Figure 29-21. The Microsoft Query toolbar.

For example, suppose you want to filter the result set shown in Figure 29-17 to include only those records in which the CompanyName field is Karkki Oy. To do this, select any record in the CompanyName field that already equals Karkki Oy and click the Criteria Equals button. Query responds by displaying the criteria pane (if it's not already displayed) and applying the new filter to the table, as shown in Figure 29-22.

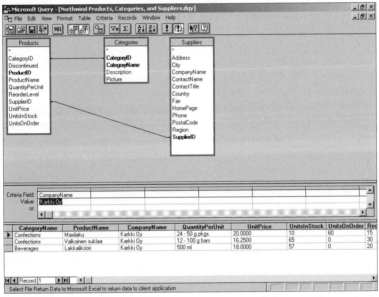

Figure 29-22. When we clicked the Criteria Equals button, Query displayed the criteria pane and applied the filter to the result set.

---

tip **Switch to a different match**

After you use the Criteria Equals button to specify an exact-match criterion, you can quickly switch to a different match. Type a new value in the criteria pane to replace the current one.

Part 9: Managing Databases and Lists

If you used Excel's Advanced Filter command (discussed in Chapter 28, "Managing Information in Lists"), you'll notice that Query's criteria pane looks a lot like a criteria range in an Excel worksheet. Field headings appear in the top row, and criteria are stated in subsequent rows. Although you can enter new criteria or edit existing ones directly in the criteria pane, it's not necessary, because Query's menu commands take care of entering information in the criteria pane for you. In fact, you don't need to have the criteria pane on your screen at all.

> **tip**   **Hide panes**
>
> To remove the criteria pane, click the Show/Hide Criteria button on the Query toolbar or choose View, Criteria. To remove the Tables pane, click Show/Hide Tables or choose View, Tables.

Automatic Query vs. Manual Query

By default, Query updates the result set every time you add a new field to the data pane, rearrange the order of the existing fields in the data pane, change a sort specification, or change a filter criterion. (If you're working in the criteria pane, the query is executed as soon as you click away from the current criteria-pane cell.) In response to these actions, Query creates a new SQL statement and executes that statement against your data source. (You can see the SQL code—and edit it, if you have a mind to do that—by clicking the View SQL button on the toolbar.) If your data source is particularly large or network traffic is high, Automatic Query can cause annoying delays. You can turn off the Automatic Query feature so that Query executes the current SQL statement only when you ask it to.

You can determine whether Automatic Query is on by checking whether the Auto Query button on the toolbar is selected (has a "pushed in" appearance) or not. To turn the feature off, click the Auto Query button or choose Records, Automatic Query.

To execute the current query in manual query mode, click the Query Now button or choose Records, Query Now.

Using Multiple Exact-Match Criteria   To generate a query that uses exact-match criteria in two or more fields, repeat the process just described for the second and each subsequent criterion. For example, to filter the result set in Figure 29-17 to show only those records with CompanyName equal to Exotic Liquids and Category Name equal to Beverages, you could select Exotic Liquids in the CompanyName field, click Criteria Equals, and then select Beverages in the CategoryName field and click Criteria Equals again. As Figure 29-23 shows, the criteria pane would then show the two criteria on the same line. Just as with an Excel criteria range, criteria on the same line are treated by Query as if they are connected by the AND operator.

Chapter 29: Working with External Data

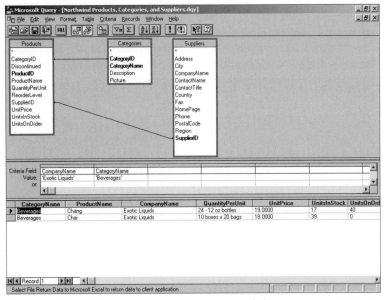

Figure 29-23. When you use the Criteria Equals button in two separate fields, Query's filter admits only those records that meet both criteria.

Using Menu Commands to Specify Exact-Match Criteria If you'd rather use menu commands than toolbar buttons, you can specify an exact-match criterion as follows:

1 Select a field value that meets your specification.

2 Choose Criteria, Add Criteria. In the Add Criteria dialog box, click Add.

Removing Criteria The simplest way to remove a filter criterion is to select the criterion's heading in the criteria pane and press Delete. To remove all criteria and restore the unfiltered result set, choose Criteria, Remove All Criteria.

Specifying Comparison Criteria To specify a comparison criterion, follow these steps:

1 Choose Criteria, Add Criteria. You'll see a dialog box similar to the one shown in Figure 29-24.

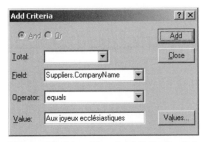

Figure 29-24. The Add Criteria dialog box lets you select fields, comparison operators, and values.

In the Add Criteria dialog box, you can construct your criteria by selecting options from various drop-down lists. For example, you can select a field from the Field list and then select an operator, such as *Is Greater Than*, from the Operator list. You can also enter a value in the Value text box by typing it or clicking the Values button and selecting from the list.

> **note** For comparison criteria that don't involve computed fields, be sure the Total field in the Add Criteria dialog box is blank, as it is in Figure 29-24. For more information on the Total field, see "Filtering on Calculated Fields" on page 780.

2 When you have filled out the Field, Operator, and Value fields, click Add.

Query responds by creating the appropriate entry in the criteria pane and, if Automatic Query is on, executing the new query. The Add Criteria dialog box remains open so that you can specify more criteria.

3 To add another criterion, select the And option or the Or option at the top of the dialog box, and then enter the information as before.

4 When you've finished entering criteria, click Close.

Filtering on Fields That Are Not in the Result Set   Your filter criteria can be based on fields that are not currently displayed in the result set. The Field list in the Add Criteria dialog box includes all fields in all active tables, not only the fields that you plan to return to Excel.

Limiting the Result Set to Unique Entries   To limit the result set to unique entries, choose View, Query Properties. In the Query Properties dialog box, select Unique Values Only. You can make this selection before or after you create your filter.

Comparing Fields   Your comparison criteria can compare the value in one field to that in another. For example, to display records where UnitsInStock is less than ReorderLevel, you would fill out the Add Criteria dialog box as shown in Figure 29-25. (We've changed the result set fields to show only the product name, company name, contact, and phone.) Note that you have to type a field name in the Value box.

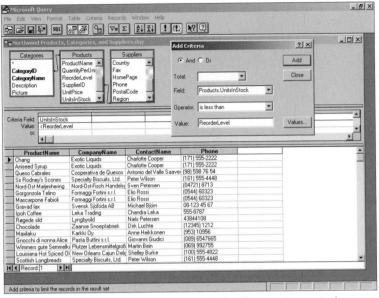

Figure 29-25. This criterion returns records where units on stock are below reorder level.

Performing Aggregate Calculations

You can analyze your result thoroughly after you get the data back onto the Excel worksheet. If you prefer, however, you can have Query do some of the calculating for you. With Query, you can make aggregate calculations (sums, averages, counts, and so on) the basis of filtering criteria.

Query refers to all calculations as *totals*, although summing values is only one of the functions available. The aggregate functions that are common to all database drivers are AVG (average), COUNT, MIN (minimum), and MAX (maximum). Your driver might support additional functions.

Cycling Through the Totals   One way to perform aggregate calculations is by clicking the Cycle Through Totals button on Query's toolbar. For example, to find the total of the UnitsOnOrder field, you would do this:

1 Display only the UnitsOnOrder field in the data pane and remove all filtering criteria from the criteria pane.

2 Select the UnitsOnOrder field and click the Cycle Through Totals button.

Chapter 29

As Figure 29-26 shows, Query responds by displaying the total in the data pane.

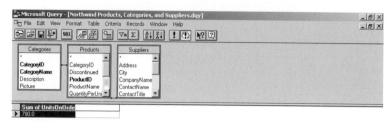

Figure 29-26. We used the Cycle Through Totals button to calculate the total units on order.

Cycling Through the Functions   In the previous example, clicking Cycle Through Totals a second time changes the aggregate function from SUM to AVG, and the number shown in the data pane changes accordingly. Successive clicks on the Cycle Through Totals button result in the count, the minimum, and the maximum. One more click returns the result set to its unaggregated state.

> **note**   Not all the aggregate functions are available for every field type.

Using Menu Commands   If you prefer menus to tools, you can use the Edit Column command:

1 Choose Records, Edit Column. (Alternatively, double-click the field heading.)

2 In the Edit Column dialog box (see Figure 29-27), select the function you want from the Total list.

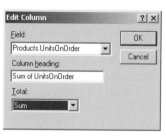

Figure 29-27. Instead of clicking Cycle Through Totals, you can use Records, Edit Column.

Chapter 29: Working with External Data

Aggregating Groups of Records In addition to grand totals, you can also calculate totals for groups of records. For example, to find out how many units are on order for each supplier company, you would do the following:

1 In the data pane, display the CompanyName field followed by the UnitsOnOrder field.

2 Select the UnitsOnOrder field and click Cycle Through Totals.

As Figure 29-28 shows, Query displays one record for each company and shows the total units on order for each.

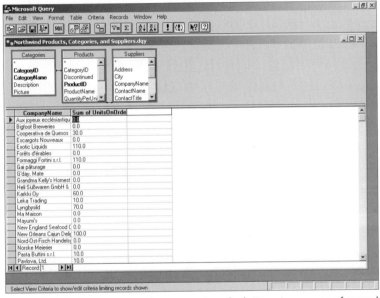

Figure 29-28. You can apply aggregate calculations to groups of records; here we calculated the total units on order per company.

Using More than One Aggregate Field You can add as many aggregate fields to your result as you need. To display both sums and averages for a numeric field, for example, you can drag that field to the data pane twice. Use the Cycle Through Totals button to apply the function you want to each copy of the field.

Filtering on Calculated Fields A field that performs an aggregate calculation is called a *calculated* field. You can use calculated fields as the basis for filtering criteria. To base a criterion on a calculated field in the Add Criteria dialog box, use the Total drop-down list to select the function you want. (If you're entering the criterion directly in the criteria pane, type the function name and enclose the field name in parentheses.) Figure 29-29 shows a criterion that returns the names of companies for whom the total products on order is greater than or equal to 20.

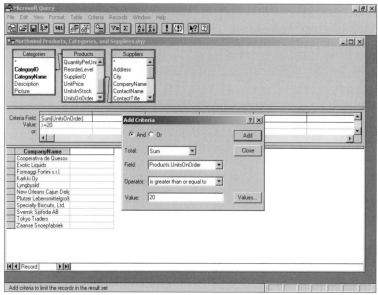

Figure 29-29. We've filtered the supplier list to show only those companies with twenty or more products on order.

Creating a Parameter-Based Query

A parameter-based query is one in which a filter criterion is based upon a value sup-plied by the user when the query is executed. To do this, first turn the Auto Query feature off by clicking the Auto Query button on the toolbar. Then specify a criterion in the normal way—either with the Add Criteria dialog box or by entering values directly in the criteria pane. Instead of entering a value, though, type a left bracket character, a prompt of your choosing, and a right bracket character. (The prompt must not be identical to the field name, although it can include the field name.) When you execute the query, either from within Query or from Excel, a dialog box containing your prompt appears. Figure 29-30 shows a parameter-based query.

Chapter 29: Working with External Data

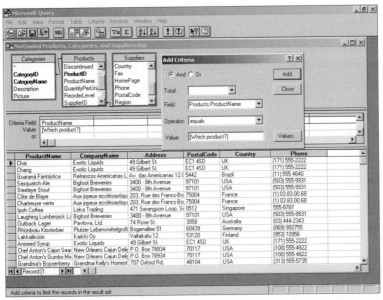

Figure 29-30. When executed, this query will prompt the user for a product name.

Saving a Query

To store your query specification in a reusable DQY file, choose File, Save. This step is optional. If you do not save the query, you will still be able to refresh it from the data range that it creates on your Excel worksheet. You will have to re-create it if you want to use it on another worksheet, however.

Returning the Result Set to Excel

To return your data to Excel, choose File, Return Data To Microsoft Excel. The Import Data dialog box (refer to Figure 29-9) will appear, asking you where you want the data returned.

newfeature!
Using a Web Query to Return Internet Data

Web queries let you grab specific information, such as stock prices, sports scores, or your company's current sales data, from the Internet or an intranet. Queries can be set up either to prompt you for the data you want (for stock ticker symbols, for example) or to get the same information every time they're executed. You can try out Web queries using a set of sample queries that come with Excel 2002.

If you're familiar with the Web query feature in Excel 2000, you'll find it was completely overhauled for the current version of Excel. Excel's new graphical interface for creating Web queries lets you build a query by pointing to the data you want. As before, you can refresh the query at any time or at regular intervals, and you can save the query in an IQY file for reuse in other worksheets. You no longer need to understand how the target Web page is built to construct a query to it.

Using an Existing Web Query

To run an existing Web query—one of the samples supplied with Excel or one that you or someone else has already set up—choose Data, Import External Data, Import Data, and open one of the IQY files listed there. (They all start with MSN MoneyCentral.) When the Import Data dialog box appears, specify a location for the incoming Web data. If the Parameters button is available, you can click it to arrive at a dialog box similar to the one shown in Figure 29-31.

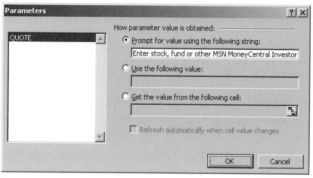

Figure 29-31. You can supply parameters to a Web query by filling out this dialog box, or you can let the query prompt you when it runs.

To supply parameters via the Parameters dialog box, either select the second option button and type one or more parameters, or select the third option and specify a worksheet range containing your parameters. If you specify a multi-cell range, Excel parses the range moving across and then down.

If you use a worksheet range to feed parameters to your Web query, you can also stipulate that the query be refreshed automatically any time the worksheet range changes. To do this, check the Refresh Automatically When Cell Value Changes check box.

Some queries might include more than one item in the list on the left side of the dialog box. A query designed to get financial planning information, for example, might ask you to supply parameter values for several different variables. In such a case, you would select a variable in the list on the left, read the prompt that appears beside the first option, supply a value or a worksheet range, and then move on to the next item in the list—and so on.

Figure 29-32 shows an example of data returned by one of the Web queries supplied with Excel 2002. Note that this query is set up to return the names of market indexes as hyperlinks. Clicking a hyperlink takes you to a relevant page in the MSN MoneyCentral Investor Web site.

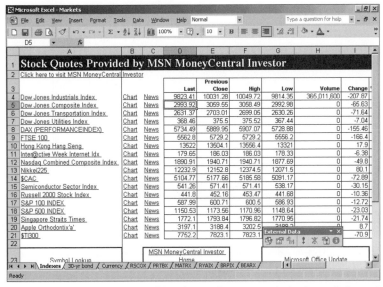

Figure 29-32.   Data returned by this Web query includes hyperlinks and AutoFilters.

Creating Your Own Web Query

Excel now provides four easy ways to construct a Web query:

- Choosing Data, Import External Data, New Web Query command

- Copying and pasting information from your Web browser

- Right-clicking in Microsoft Internet Explorer and selecting Export to Microsoft Excel

- Choosing Edit with Microsoft Excel in Internet Explorer

Using the New Web Query Command

To create a Web query with the New Web Query command, use the following steps:

1   Choose Data, Import External Data, New Web Query. The New Web Query form, shown in Figure 29-33 on the next page, appears. The New Web Query form is a specialized Web browser, and your home page appears in its window.

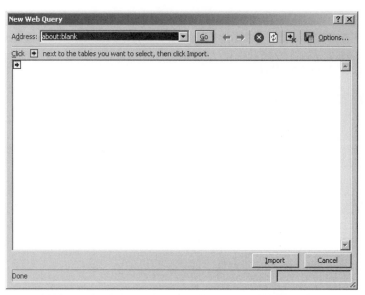

Figure 29-33. The New Web Query form is a specialized Web browser.

2 If you know the URL of the Web site you want to query, you can type or paste it into the Address field. (Unfortunately, the New Web Query form doesn't include a Favorites menu.)

3 Click Go; your Web site appears in the main window, as Figure 29-34 shows.

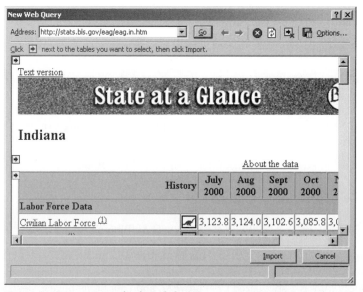

Figure 29-34. We've displayed the site we want to query in the New Web Query form.

Yellow boxes with arrows appear along the left edge of the window. Each of these boxes represents a section of the Web site that you can import into Excel. As you hover your cursor over any of these yellow boxes, a thick bounding rectangle indicates the section of the site that you will be importing if you select the yellow box. You can select any or all yellow boxes.

Saving the IQY File and Setting Formatting Options   After making your selections, you can click Import to transform your selections into a query. But before you do so, you might want to save the query (making it a reusable IQY file) or check out the menu of options. To save the query in its current form, click the Save Query tool, directly to the left of the word Options on the New Web Query form's toolbar. To set options, click Options. Figure 29-35 shows the Web Query Options dialog box.

Figure 29-35.   Among other things, the Web Query Options dialog box lets you control how much of the Web site's formatting Excel should preserve.

In the Formatting section of the dialog box, choose None to import the data as plain text. Choose Rich Text Formatting Only to preserve hyperlinks and merged cells in the Web data. Choose Full HTML Formatting to retrieve as much as possible of the original Web site's formatting. Figure 29-36 on the next page shows a Web site queried with full HTML formatting. Note the inclusion of hyperlinks in the downloaded data.

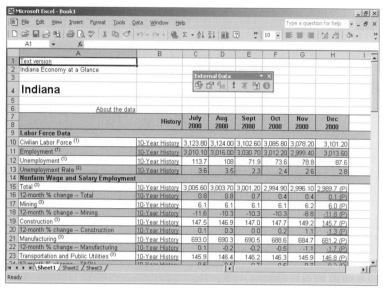

Figure 29-36. Because we queried this site using full HTML formatting, the downloaded data includes active hyperlinks and other welcome formatting characteristics.

If you make a formatting choice, import your data, and don't like the results, you can always return to the Web Query Options dialog box. In Excel, choose Data, Import External Data, Edit Query. This returns you to the New Web Query form (now titled Edit Web Query). Click Options on the toolbar to get back to the Web Query Options dialog box.

Copying and Pasting from the Web Browser

The method for creating a Web query just described is fine if you're starting in Excel and if you know the URL of the target site. But you can also start from the Web browser. Select the data you want, press Ctrl+C to copy it, click a fresh Excel worksheet, and press Ctrl+V to paste. You'll see a smart tag icon near the lower right corner of the pasted data. Open its menu, shown here, and choose Create Refreshable Web Query. Your data selection will appear in the New Web Query form.

Chapter 29

Using Internet Explorer's Export To Microsoft Excel Command

If your Web browser is Internet Explorer, you can also create a Web query by right-clicking a Web page and choosing Export To Microsoft Explorer from the shortcut menu. (If you don't see this command on the shortcut menu, you probably already have something selected in Internet Explorer. Clear your selection and try again.) The Export to Microsoft Explorer command begins by creating a new instance of Excel (it does this to avoid overwriting Excel data you might already be working with). If you right-clicked something that Internet Explorer recognizes as an HTML table, it transfers that table directly onto Sheet1!A1 as a new Web query. If you clicked anywhere other than an HTML table, the command opens Excel's New Web Query form.

Using Internet Explorer's Edit With Microsoft Excel Command

Finally, you can use the Edit With Microsoft Excel command on Internet Explorer's Standard Buttons toolbar to transfer the entire current Web page into Excel's New Web Query form. To get to this command, open the drop-down arrow next to this toolbar icon.

Like the Export to Microsoft Excel command just described, this command launches a new instance of Excel.

Analyzing Data with PivotTable Reports

A PivotTable Report is a special kind of table that summarizes information from selected fields of a data source. The source can be an Excel list, a relational database file, an OLAP cube, or multiple "consolidation ranges" (multiple ranges containing similar data, which the PivotTable can assemble and summarize). When you create a PivotTable, you specify which fields you're interested in, how you want the table organized, and what kinds of calculations you want the table to perform. After you have built the table, you can rearrange it to view your data from alternative perspectives. This ability to "pivot" the dimensions of your table—for example, to transpose column headings to row positions—gives the PivotTable its name and its unusual analytical power.

PivotTables are linked to the data from which they're derived. If the PivotTable is based on external data (data stored outside of Excel), you can choose to have it refreshed at regular time intervals, or you can refresh it whenever you need to by clicking a button on the PivotTable toolbar.

A Simple Example

Figure 30-1 on the next page shows a list of sales figures for a small publishing firm. The list is organized by year, quarter, catalog number, distribution channel, units sold, and sales receipts. The data spans a period of eight quarters (1999 and 2000), and the firm uses three distribution channels—domestic, international, and mail order. With just a few keystrokes you can turn this "flat" list into a table that provides useful information at a glance. One of the many possible arrangements for this PivotTable is shown in Figure 30-2 on the next page.

789

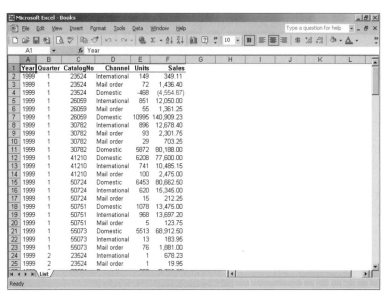

Figure 30-1. It's difficult to see the bottom line in a flat list like this; turning the list into a PivotTable will help.

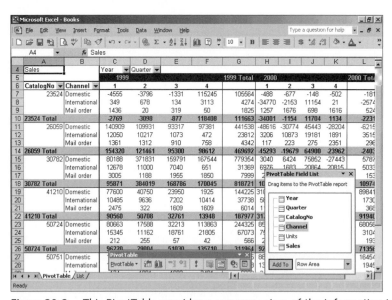

Figure 30-2. This PivotTable provides a summary view of the information in Figure 30-1.

In Figure 30-2, the Year and Quarter fields have been positioned along the table's *column axis*, and the CatalogNo and Channel fields have taken up positions along the *row axis*. The body of the table displays the total sales numbers for each column-and-row intersection. Cell H7, for example, shows that the total domestic sales in the first quarter for the book whose catalog number is 23524 were negative $488—meaning that returns outnumbered sales for that title, in that time period, in that distribution channel.

Excel displays a field-list window along with the PivotTable. The six fields of the list in Figure 30-1 appear in this window. Rearranging the PivotTable is as simple as dragging field headings from this window into new positions.

---

tip **Hide the PivotTable field list**

The PivotTable Field List window is new with Excel 2002. If you find it distracting, you don't have to look at it. To hide it, click its Close button. To redisplay it, click Show Field List on the PivotTable toolbar. With the field list hidden, you can rearrange your PivotTable by dragging field headings from their row, column, and page positions.

Rows 10, 14, 18, 22, and 26 in Figure 30-2 display subtotals for the various items in the CatalogNo field. Column G displays subtotals for the four quarters of 1999. Beyond the boundaries of the figure lie additional subtotals, and at the outer edges, the PivotTable includes a grand total column and a grand total row. If you scrolled the table in Figure 30-2 to the bottom cell in column C, for example, you would find the total first quarter 1999 sales for all titles across all distribution channels. The PivotTable And PivotChart Report command creates these subtotals and grand totals automatically, unless you tell it not to.

The PivotTable shown in Figure 30-2 makes it easy to find almost all the information recorded in the list in Figure 30-1. The only details that do not appear are the unit sales. If you had wanted to make the table a bit more complex, you could have shown those also. Suppose, however, that instead of more detail, you want less. The PivotTable can accommodate that need as well. Figure 30-3 shows one of the many ways in which the table in Figure 30-2 can be modified to focus on a particular section of the data. Here we have transposed the Channel field from the row axis to the column axis and moved both the Year and Quarter fields to the *page axis*. Moving these fields to the page axis allows you to "zoom in" on the numbers for a particular year and quarter. When you want to see a different time period, you can select a different year or quarter from the drop-down lists next to the Year and Quarter field headings.

Chapter 30

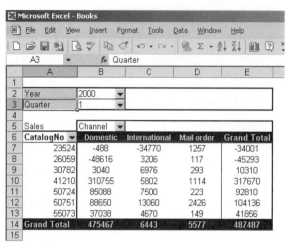

Figure 30-3. Using a PivotTable, you can focus on a particular section, or "slice," of your data.

Creating a PivotTable

You can create PivotTables from four kinds of data:

- An Excel list
- An external data source
- Multiple "consolidation" ranges (separate Excel lists that the PivotTable And PivotChart Report command will consolidate as it builds your PivotTable)
- Another PivotTable

In the example that follows, we'll create a PivotTable from the Excel list shown in Figure 30-1. For information about creating a PivotTable from an external data source, see "Creating a PivotTable from External Data" on page 821. For information about creating a PivotTable from multiple consolidation ranges, see "Using a PivotTable to Consolidate Ranges" on page 823. For information about basing one PivotTable on another, see "Building a PivotTable from an Existing PivotTable" on page 828.

Starting the PivotTable And PivotChart Wizard

To create a PivotTable from an Excel list, begin by selecting any cell within the list from which you want to create your table. Then choose Data, PivotTable And PivotChart Report. This action displays the PivotTable And PivotChart Wizard, which prompts you to follow these steps:

1 Specify the type of data source on which the table will be based and whether you want to create a PivotTable or a PivotChart Report.

2 Indicate the location of your source data.

3 Indicate where you want the table to appear.

After your complete these steps, you work with the PivotTable Field List to specify which fields you want in your table, how you want the table organized, and what calculations you want the table to perform.

Step 1: Specifying the Type of Data Source

The wizard's initial dialog box is shown in Figure 30-4.

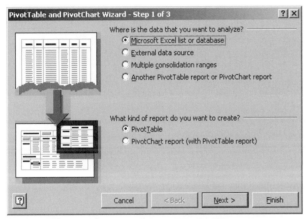

Figure 30-4. The PivotTable And PivotChart Wizard lets you work with four kinds of data sources.

Notice that Excel uses graphics on the left side of this dialog box to confirm your selection. If you select External Data Source, for example, the picture on the left changes to show a mainframe computer transferring data to a desktop terminal. If you choose PivotChart, the image in the lower left corner of the dialog box changes from a table to a chart.

Step 2: Indicating the Location of Your Source Data

After you indicate your data source type and click Next, the wizard asks for the location of your data. If you're basing your PivotTable on an Excel list and you selected a cell in that list before invoking the wizard, the wizard already knows the location of your data and merely asks you to confirm. The wizard's second dialog box, in that case, looks something like the one shown in Figure 30-5 on the next page.

Part 9: Managing Databases and Lists

Figure 30-5. Indicate or confirm the location of your data in step 2.

If your data source is an Excel list, you must include a unique field name at the top of each column. If your data source is an Excel list that isn't currently open, you can click the Browse button to find it.

Step 3: Telling the Wizard Where to Put Your PivotTable

In the wizard's last dialog box, shown in Figure 30-6, you indicate where you want your PivotTable.

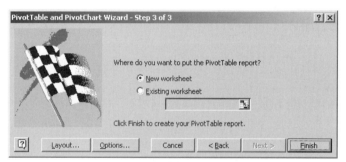

Figure 30-6. To create your table on an existing worksheet, enter a range name or reference in the text box.

To put the table on a new worksheet (always a safe choice), select the New Worksheet option. Otherwise, select Existing Worksheet and supply a range reference or name in the text box.

Before clicking Finish, you can click Options and specify such things as a time interval for automatic refresh of your table. But you can always return to the Options dialog box later.

---

tip **Use the wizard to move a PivotTable**

After you create a PivotTable, you can easily move it. Select any cell in the table, and then choose Data, PivotTable And PivotChart Report. Then select New Worksheet or specify a new address.

Troubleshooting

An Insufficient Memory Message Appears after Step 3 of the PivotTable And PivotChart Wizard

If you get an Insufficient Memory message when you click Finish in the wizard's Step 3 dialog box, and if your PivotTable is based on a query of external data, try recreating the PivotTable. Before you click Finish again, click Options in the Step 3 dialog box. In the PivotTable Options dialog box, select Optimize Memory.

If Optimize Memory doesn't solve the problem, re-create the table and click Layout in the Step 3 dialog box. Drag one or more fields to the page axis. Then double-click a page-field heading. In the PivotTable Field dialog box, click Advanced. In the PivotTable Field Advanced Options, select Query External Data Source As You Select Each Page Field Item.

If these measures still don't allow you to create the table, you need to simplify the table. Try importing fewer fields or filtering the external data to import fewer records.

Laying Out the PivotTable

After you've finished with the Step 3 dialog box, Excel displays a blank table layout similar to the one shown in Figure 30-7. Now all that's left for you to do is to drag field headings from the PivotTable Field List to the appropriate places on the PivotTable layout. To create the PivotTable shown in Figure 30-2, for example, you would drag the Channel and CatalogNo field headings to the row axis, the Quarter and Year headings to the column axis, and the Sales heading to the data area. The table in Figure 30-2 does not use the page axis.

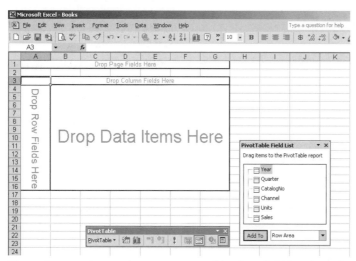

Figure 30-7.   To populate your PivotTable, drag field headings from the PivotTable Field List to the table's axes and data area.

You can put as many fields as you like in any of the areas of the layout. To remove a field, drag its heading off the layout.

---

tip **Keep the PivotTable menu handy**

The first button on the PivotTable toolbar, the button labeled PivotTable, opens a menu that includes commands not found on Excel's default Data menu. It's handy to have that menu in sight as you work with your PivotTable. However, if you object to having toolbars reduce your working area on screen, you can find the PivotTable menu's commands on the shortcut menu that appears when you right-click a cell in your PivotTable.

Pivoting a PivotTable

To pivot, or rearrange, a PivotTable, drag one or more field headings. To move a field from the column axis to the row axis, for example, all you have to do is drag its heading from the column area to the row area.

In addition to transposing columns and rows, you can change the order in which fields are displayed on the column or row axis. For example, using Figure 30-2 as an example, you can drag the Channel heading to the left of the CatalogNo heading to produce the table shown in Figure 30-8.

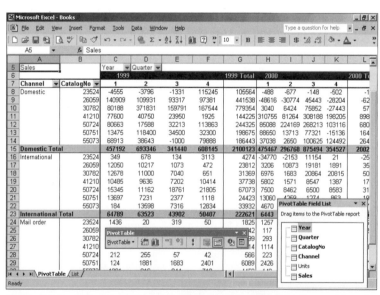

Figure 30-8. We reorganized the table by dragging the Channel heading to the left of the CatalogNo heading.

> **tip** **Use menu commands to move fields**
>
> When you're dragging a field heading from one place to another within a particular table axis, Excel might not understand what you want if you don't drop the field heading in precisely the right place. If you prefer, you can use a menu command to do the job. To move Channel to the left of CatalogNo in Figure 30-2, you can select the Channel heading, click PivotTable on the PivotTable toolbar, and then choose Order, Move Left.

Using the Page Axis

When you display a field on either the row axis or column axis, you can see all of that field's items just by scrolling through the table. On the page axis, however, each field can show only one item at a time. In Figure 30-3, you see only the 2000 item for the Year field and the 1 item for the Quarter field. To see other items in a field, select from that field's drop-down list. By selecting each entry in the list in turn, you can see a two-dimensional slice corresponding to each value in the field in the Page area.

Displaying Totals for a Field in the Page Area

At the top of each field's drop-down list, you'll find the (All) option. You can select this option to display total values for each field on the page axis. Figure 30-9 shows the result of selecting the (All) option for the Year and Quarter fields shown in Figure 30-3.

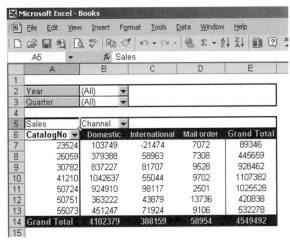

Figure 30-9. Select (All) in a field's drop-down list to see total values for that field.

Moving Page Fields to Separate Workbook Pages

Even though a PivotTable might include a page axis, the table is stored on only one workbook page. By choosing the Show Pages command, however, you can create a series of linked PivotTables, each of which can show one item in a page field. You'll find the Show Pages command on the PivotTable menu (the first button on the PivotTable toolbar).

Selecting Items to Display on the Row and Column Axes

Initially, when you drag a field heading to either the row axis or the column axis, your PivotTable displays all items for that field. In Figure 30-9, for example, all three distribution channels appear along the column axis and all seven catalog numbers appear along the row axis. To limit the display to particular items, click the drop-down arrow at the right side of the field heading, make your selections from the set of check boxes that appear, and then click OK.

> **note** You can also use an AutoShow feature to limit the display to particular items, based on their values. See "Showing the Top or Bottom Items in a Field" on page 807.

Creating a PivotChart

You can create a PivotChart by using the PivotTable And PivotChart Wizard (see Figure 30-4). Or you can first create a PivotTable and then, while any cell in the table is selected, click the Chart Wizard button on the PivotTable toolbar. If you take the first approach, Excel creates both a new PivotTable and a new PivotChart. If you take the second approach, Excel creates a PivotChart based on the current PivotTable.

Either way, the chart and table are linked. Changes to one are reflected in the other. Figure 30-10 shows a PivotChart that's linked to the PivotTable shown in Figure 30-9. Notice that the page fields of the PivotTable shown in Figure 30-9 appear at the upper left corner of the PivotChart, and the table's row and column fields appear as the category and value axes of the chart, respectively.

You can rearrange a PivotChart exactly as you would a PivotTable—by dragging field headings from one axis to another. (Because chart and table are always in lockstep with one another, you can also rearrange a chart by rearranging the table to which it's linked.) To add fields, drag them from the PivotTable Field List. To remove fields, drag them off the chart. To limit the display to particular items in a field, select those items in the field's drop-down list.

Chapter 30: Analyzing Data with PivotTable Reports

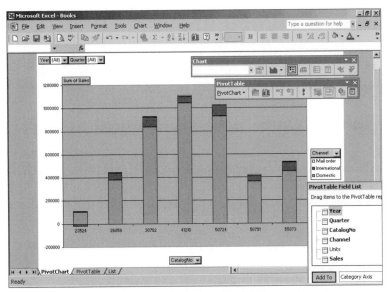

Figure 30-10. PivotCharts are linked to PivotTables and can be rearranged as easily as PivotTables can.

Note that although the PivotChart shown in Figure 30-10 includes only one field on the category axis and one on the value axis, you can display more than one. Figure 30-11 shows the same chart rearranged to include both the Channel and CatalogNo fields on the category axis and both the Year and the Quarter fields on the value axis.

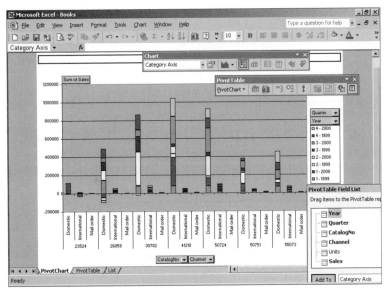

Figure 30-11. This PivotChart includes two fields on the category axis and two on the value axis.

Chapter 30

Refreshing a PivotTable

PivotTables are not updated each time a change occurs in their source data. To update a table, select any cell in the table and choose Data, Refresh Data, or click the red exclamation point on the PivotTable toolbar.

Refreshing on File Open

If you want Excel to refresh your PivotTable every time you open the workbook in which it resides, choose PivotTable, Table Options. (The PivotTable menu is on the PivotTable toolbar.) Then select the Refresh On Open check box in the PivotTable Options dialog box. If you want to prevent Excel from updating the table each time you open the workbook (for example, if the table is based on a time-consuming query of external data), be sure this check box is cleared.

Selecting Elements of a PivotTable

To select a single cell in a PivotTable, click it in the normal way—that is, while the mouse pointer is a fat white cross. To select a field item in such a way that all identical items and all associated data are also selected, position your mouse on the edge of the item so that the mouse pointer turns into a small black arrow, and then click.

For example, if you position your mouse at the left edge of cell B7 in Figure 30-2 and click while the pointer is a small black arrow, Excel selects all Domestic items (B7, B11, B15, and so on) and all the Domestic data. A second click in the same place now refines the selection so that only the first Domestic item (B7) and *its* data (C7:M7) are selected.

This sounds more complicated than it really is. Three principles are all you need to remember:

- For a single-cell selection anywhere in the table, click in the normal way.

- For a "structured" selection—that is, a selection of an item and all like items, click while the mouse pointer is a small black arrow. For row items, position the mouse at the left edge of the cell. For column items, position the mouse at the top edge of the cell.

- To refine a selection so that only some like items are selected, click a second time.

Formatting a PivotTable

You can use standard formatting commands to modify the appearance of cells in a PivotTable. Excel retains your formatting preferences when you pivot your table, provided you have not cleared the Preserve Formatting check box in the PivotTable Options dialog box. If you find your formats disappearing when you pivot, choose PivotTable, Table Options, and select the Preserve Formatting check box.

Note that, although you can apply conditional formatting to PivotTable cells, Excel does not maintain this kind of formatting when you pivot—regardless of how the Preserve Formatting check box is set.

Using AutoFormat with PivotTables

Excel provides 21 autoformatting options for PivotTables. You can apply these by selecting any cell in a table and choosing PivotTable, Format Report (or clicking the Format Report tool on the PivotTable toolbar). To remove autoformatting from a PivotTable, open the AutoFormat dialog box and select None; it's the last option in the gallery.

Changing the Numeric Format for the Data Area

To change the format of numbers in the data area, select any cell in the data area. Then click the Field Settings tool on the PivotTable toolbar (or choose PivotTable, Field Settings). In the PivotTable Field dialog box (shown in Figure 30-12), click Number, and then select the format you want. If your data area includes more than one field, you need to format each field separately.

Figure 30-12. Click Number in the PivotTable Field dialog box to apply a numeric format to all cells in a data field.

Chapter 30

Changing the Way a PivotTable Displays Empty Cells

Empty cells in a PivotTable are normally displayed as empty cells. For example, if cell F2 in Figure 30-1 were empty, cell C8 in Figure 30-2 would also be empty, because it would have no data to report. If you prefer, you can have your PivotTable display 0 or some text value (for example, NA) in cells that would otherwise be empty. To do this, take the following steps:

1 Select any cell in the PivotTable.

2 Choose PivotTable, Table Options.

3 In the PivotTable Options dialog box, select the For Empty Cells, Show check box. Then type a **0** or whatever other value you want to see in the edit box to the right of this check box.

Changing the Way a PivotTable Displays Error Values

If a worksheet formula references a cell containing an error value, that formula returns the same error value. The same is normally true in PivotTables. Error values in your source data propagate themselves into the PivotTable. If you prefer, you can have error values generate blank cells or text values.

To change the way a PivotTable responds to source-data errors, take these steps:

1 Select any cell in the PivotTable.

2 Choose PivotTable, Table Options.

3 In the PivotTable Options dialog box, select For Error Values, Show. If you want error values to generate blanks, leave the edit box empty. If you want them to generate a text value, type the text in the edit box.

Merging Labels

Figure 30-13 shows the same PivotTable as Figure 30-2, but with its outer field labels centered over or beside the corresponding inner field labels. The catalog number headings in column A of Figure 30-13 are centered vertically beside the channel headings in column B, and the year headings in row 6 are centered horizontally above the quarter headings in row 7. To achieve this effect, choose PivotTable, Table Options. In the PivotTable Options dialog box, select the Merge Labels check box.

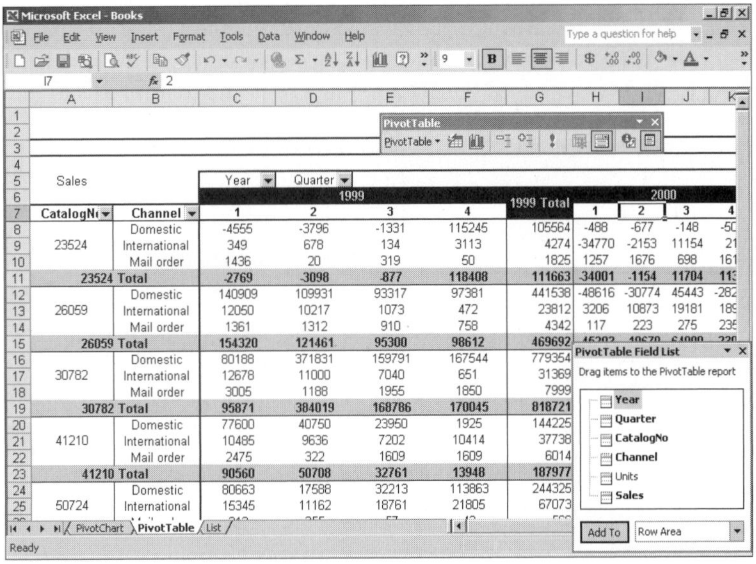

Figure 30-13. You can use the Merge Labels option to center outer field headings beside and above inner field headings.

Using Multiple Data Fields

If you add a second field to the data area of your table, Excel displays subtotals for each field. Figure 30-14 shows an example.

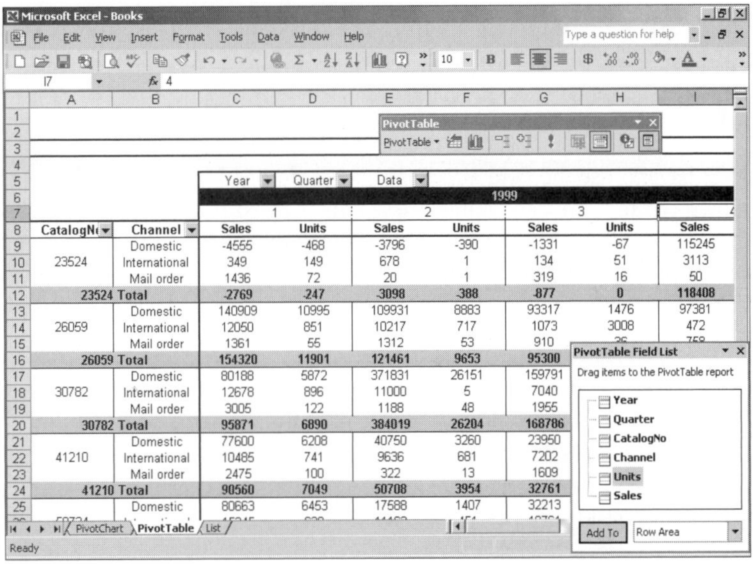

Figure 30-14. We've added a second field, Units, to the data area.

Notice that the table now includes a new field heading called Data. As with other field headings, you can further rearrange the table layout by dragging the new field heading, as Figure 30-15 shows. We moved the Data heading from the column axis to the row axis.

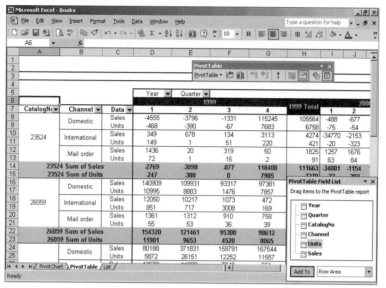

Figure 30-15. The Data field heading that appears whenever the data area has more than one field can be repositioned just as any other field heading can.

To remove a data field when you have more than one, drag the Data field button off the row column or page axis of the table. This clears all data items from the table. Then drag those fields that you want to restore from the PivotTable Field List to the data area.

Renaming Fields and Items

You don't have to use the field and item names supplied by the PivotTable And PivotChart Wizard. You can change these names by editing the field heading or any occurrence of the item in the PivotTable. When you change the name of an item in this manner, all other occurrences of the item are changed as well. For example, you can change the CatalogNo heading to Title in Figure 30-15 by selecting the heading in cell A7, typing **Title**, and then pressing Enter.

> **caution** Don't change a field heading in your PivotTable to the name of another field in your data source. Doing so will have unintended consequences.

Sorting Items

If you sort field items using the standard Sort command, Excel will sort all instances of your field items and preserve the sort order when you pivot the table. For example, to generate a descending sort of the Channel items as shown in Figure 30-15, you could select cell B7, choose Data, Sort, and specify a descending sort. Excel would then present the Channel items in the order Mail Order, International, Domestic in every place where those items occur.

You can also sort field items using an AutoSort feature. Like the standard Sort command, AutoSort rearranges table material across all instances and preserves the order you want even when you move fields from axis to axis. However, the AutoSort feature gives you the additional option of sorting field items on the basis of their data values. For example, using AutoSort, you can sort the Channel items in Figure 30-15 on the basis of the Sum Of Sales data or the Sum Of Units value. You could arrange the table so that, for each CatalogNo item, the channel with the highest sales totals appears first and the channel with the lowest sales totals appears last.

AutoSort takes precedence over the standard Sort command. That is, if you turn AutoSort on for a field, you will not be able to sort that field by choosing Data, Sort unless you subsequently turn AutoSort off.

Using AutoSort

To use AutoSort for a field, follow these steps:

1 Select an item in the field or the field's heading.

2 Click the Field Settings button on the PivotTable toolbar (or choose PivotTable, Field Settings).

3 Click the Advanced button.

4 In the PivotTable Field Advanced Options dialog box, shown in Figure 30-16 on the next page, choose the Ascending or Descending option, and then select the field you want to sort from the Using Field drop-down list. For example, to sort Channel items from those with highest sales to those with lowest, you would select the Descending option and Sum Of Sales.

To turn AutoSort off, return to the PivotTable Field Advanced Options dialog box. Under AutoSort Options, choose Manual.

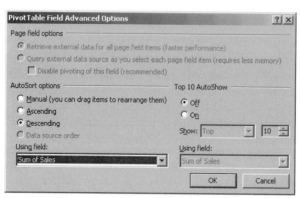

Figure 30-16.   Use the PivotTable Field Advanced Options dialog box to choose AutoSort and AutoShow options.

Rearranging Items by Hand

As long as AutoSort is off, you're free to rearrange items by dragging them. For example, in Figure 30-15, if you want to see the Channel items for CatalogNo 23524 in the order International, Mail Order, Domestic, you would do the following:

1 Select the International heading under CatalogNo 23524.

2 Position the mouse pointer on the upper boundary of the cell so that the pointer changes to a four-headed arrow.

3 Drag upward, releasing the mouse above the Mail Order item.

Note that the rearrangement just described affects only the 23524 CatalogNo item. The Channel items for the other CatalogNo items remain unchanged.

An alternative way to accomplish an ad hoc rearrangement of items is to type over an existing item label. For example, you could also move International above Mail Order in the example just cited, as follows:

1 Select the International heading under CatalogNo 23524.

2 Type **Mail Order**.

When you overtype an existing item label with the name of another item label, Excel interprets your action as a command to swap the two labels. Ad hoc rearrangements are preserved when you pivot the table.

Showing the Top or Bottom Items in a Field

The AutoShow feature lets you display only the top or bottom *n* items in a field, based on values in the data area of your table. To use AutoShow, select the field you're interested in, and then click the Field Settings button on the PivotTable toolbar. (Alternatively, choose PivotTable, Field Settings.) In the PivotTable Field dialog box, click the Advanced button to display the PivotTable Field Advanced Options dialog box, shown in Figure 30-16. Figure 30-17 shows an example of a PivotTable that uses AutoShow. To match this, rearrange the table so that the Quarter field appears on the row axis and the Channel field is on the column axis. Then apply AutoShow to the Quarter field, choosing to display only the top two quarters based on Sum Of Sales.

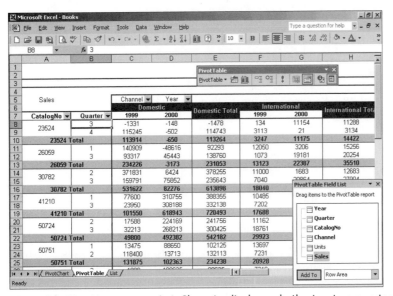

Figure 30-17. You can use AutoShow to display only the top two quarters for each CatalogNo item, based on Sum Of Sales.

Hiding and Showing Inner Field Items

In the PivotTable shown in Figure 30-2, CatalogNo and Year are *outer* fields, and Channel and Quarter are *inner* fields. The PivotTable repeats the items of the inner field for each item in the outer field. You can suppress a set of inner field items by double-clicking the associated outer field item.

For example, to hide the quarterly detail for 1999 in Figure 30-2, you can double-click the 1999 heading. Figure 30-18 on the next page shows the result. To redisplay the inner field detail, double-click the outer field heading a second time. Alternatively, you can hide detail by selecting an outer field heading and clicking the Hide Detail tool on the PivotTable toolbar. To redisplay the detail, select the same heading and click the Show Detail tool.

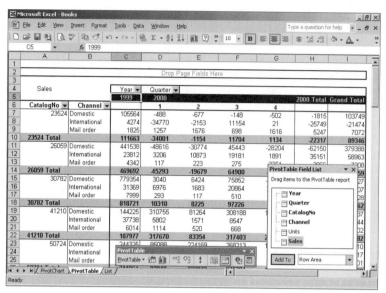

Figure 30-18. You can hide the 1999 quarterly detail by double-clicking the 1999 heading.

Displaying the Details Behind a Data Value

By double-clicking a data value, you "drill down" to the details behind the value. Excel copies the detail figures to a new workbook page.

Figure 30-19 shows an example of this process. When you double-click the 1999 Total cell for CatalogNo 23524 (cell G10 in Figure 30-2), Excel responds by listing all the entries from the data source that contributed to that PivotTable value.

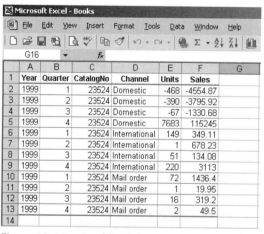

Figure 30-19. Double-clicking a value causes Excel to display the entries summarized by that value.

You can turn off this capability by opening the PivotTable Options dialog box (choose PivotTable, Table Options) and clearing the Enable Drill To Details check box.

Grouping and Ungrouping Data

PivotTables group inner field items under each outer field heading and, if requested, create subtotals for each group of inner field items. You might find it convenient to group items in additional ways—for example, to collect monthly items into quarterly groups or sets of numbers into larger numeric categories. Excel provides several options for grouping items.

Creating Ad Hoc Item Groupings

Suppose that after looking at Figure 30-2 you decide you'd like to see the Domestic and International sales figures grouped into a category called Retail. To create this group, follow these steps:

1 Select the Domestic and International headings anywhere in the table (for example, cells B7 and B8 in Figure 30-2).

2 Choose PivotTable, Group And Show Detail, Group.

Excel responds by creating a new field heading called Channel2 and grouping the selected items into a new item called Group1. Figure 30-20 shows these developments.

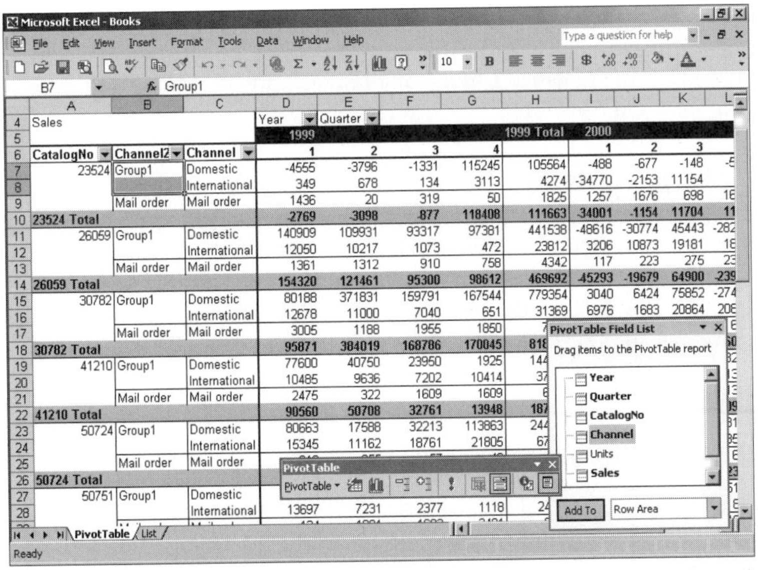

Figure 30-20. In this table, the Domestic and International items have been grouped.

3 Select any cell that says Group1 and type the new name for Group1: **Retail**.

At this point, the group is named appropriately, but the PivotTable still shows both the group and the items that comprise the group. You can suppress the detail behind the group by double-clicking the new group heading anywhere it appears in the table (or by clicking the Hide Detail tool on the PivotTable toolbar). To see the group's component values again, double-click the group heading a second time (or click Show Detail on the toolbar). If you want to eliminate the group's component values—in this case, Channel—from the table entirely, drag the innermost field heading off the table. Excel rebuilds the PivotTable, as shown in Figure 30-21.

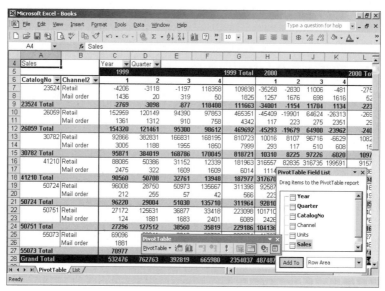

Figure 30-21. We renamed Group1 and removed the original Channel grouping from the PivotTable shown in Figure 30-20.

Grouping Numeric Items

To group numeric items in a field, such as the items in the Quarter field of Figure 30-2, select any item in the field and choose PivotTable, Group And Show Detail, Group. You'll see a dialog box similar to the one shown in Figure 30-22, but tailored for the numeric range of your own data.

Figure 30-22. Use the Grouping dialog box to group items in a numeric field.

Fill in the Starting At, Ending At, and By values as appropriate. For example, to divide the year into two-quarter groups, you would enter 1 and 4 in the Starting At and Ending At edit boxes and enter 2 in the By box.

Grouping Items in Date or Time Ranges

Figure 30-23 shows a PivotTable that summarizes daily transactions by payee. As you can see, the data in this table is extremely sparse. Most intersections between a day item and a payee item are blank.

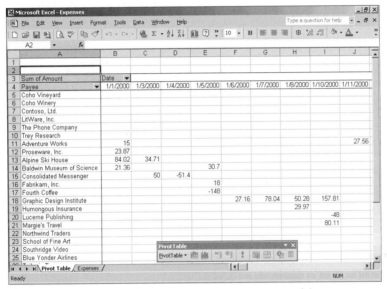

Figure 30-23. To make the data in this table more meaningful, you can group the date field.

To make this kind of table more meaningful, you can group the date field. You do this by selecting an item in that field, choosing PivotTable, Group And Show Detail, Group, and then filling out the Grouping dialog box shown in Figure 30-24.

Figure 30-24. Excel gives you lots of ways to group by date.

Excel gives you a great deal of flexibility in the way your data and time fields are grouped. In the By list, you can choose any common time interval from seconds to years, and if the standard time intervals don't meet your needs, you can select an ad hoc number of days. You can also create two or more groupings at the same time, as shown in Figure 30-25, by selecting more than one entry in the By list. To make a multiple selection—say, of Quarters and Months—hold down the Ctrl key while you click each component of your selection.

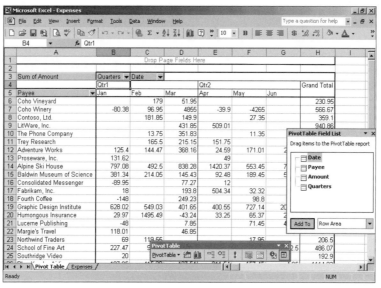

Figure 30-25. Here is the table from Figure 30-23 with the date field grouped by months and quarters.

Removing Groups (Ungrouping)

To remove any group and restore a field to its ungrouped state, select a grouped item and choose PivotTable, Group And Show Detail, Ungroup.

Using Grand Totals and Subtotals

By default, Excel generates grand totals for all outer fields in your table and subtotals for all inner fields except the innermost. You can suppress the default totals and also generate subtotals for the innermost fields.

Grand Totals

If you use more than one data field, the PivotTable And PivotChart Wizard generates separate grand totals for each data field. A grand total always uses the same summary function as the data field it totals. For example, if your PivotTable uses the Sum function, its grand totals are grand sums. If you use Average instead of Sum, you get grand averages, and so on.

> **tip** **Change summary functions**
>
> To switch from one summary function to another, select an item in the data area of your PivotTable, click the Field Settings button on PivotTable toolbar, and then choose the function you want from the list that appears in the PivotTable Field dialog box.

To remove grand totals from a PivotTable, choose PivotTable, Table Options. Then clear the Grand Totals For Columns check box or the Grand Totals For Rows check box.

Subtotals

By default, Excel creates subtotals for each field on the column and row axes of the PivotTable, with the exception of the innermost fields. For example, in Figure 30-2, column G displays subtotals for the items in the Year field, and rows 10, 14, 17, 22, and 26 display subtotals for the items in the CatalogNo field. Excel does not create subtotals for the items in the Channel and Quarter fields because these are the innermost fields on their respective axes.

As with grand totals, Excel generates one subtotal line for each data field in the table, and the subtotals, by default, use the same summary function as the associated data field. The subtotals that appear in Figure 30-2 were calculated using the Sum function because the Sum function was used to calculate the numbers in the data area of the table.

In the case of subtotals, however, you can override the default summary function, and you can use more than one summary function. You can also suppress the generation of subtotals for particular fields. The steps for each of these actions follow.

To override the default summary function or use multiple functions, follow these steps:

1 Double-click the field heading (not an item in the field), and the PivotTable Field dialog box appears. Alternatively, you can select the field heading and then click the Field Settings button on the PivotTable toolbar.

2 Select one function or hold down Ctrl while you click to make multiple selections. When you are finished, click OK.

To remove subtotals for a field, follow these steps:

1 Double-click the field heading (not an item in the field), and the PivotTable Field dialog box appears. Alternatively, you can select the field heading and then click the Field Settings button on the PivotTable toolbar.

2 Select the None option, and then click OK.

If you decide later that you want the subtotals to appear after all, you can redisplay them:

1 Double-click the field heading (not an item in the field), and the PivotTable Field dialog box appears. Alternatively, you can select the field heading and then click the Field Settings button on the PivotTable toolbar.

2 Select the Automatic option, and then click OK.

Subtotals for Innermost Fields

Although Excel does not generate subtotals for innermost fields, you can specify as many as you like, and you can use multiple summary functions. Such subtotals appear at the bottom or right edge of the PivotTable, just above or to the left of the grand totals. Figure 30-26 shows an example of innermost field subtotals (the subtotals appear in rows 35 through 40).

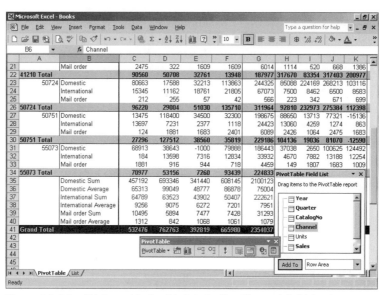

Figure 30-26. We've added subtotals to the Channel field (an innermost field) using the Sum and Average functions.

To add subtotals for an innermost field, follow these steps:

1 Double-click an innermost field heading (not an item in the field) to display the PivotTable Field dialog box. Alternatively, select the field heading and then click the Field Settings button on the PivotTable toolbar.

2 Select one or more functions, and then click OK.

Changing a PivotTable's Calculations

By default, Excel populates the data area of your PivotTable by applying the Sum function to any numeric field you put in the data area or the Count function to any nonnumeric field. But you can choose from many alternative forms of calculation, and you can add your own calculated fields to the table.

Using a Different Summary Function

To switch to a different summary function, select any cell in the data area of your PivotTable. Then click the Field Settings button on the PivotTable toolbar (or choose PivotTable, Field Settings). Excel displays the PivotTable Field dialog box (refer to Figure 30-12). Select the function you want to use, and then click OK.

Applying Multiple Summary Functions to the Same Field

You can apply as many summary functions as you want to a field. To use a second or subsequent function with a field that's already in the data area of your PivotTable, drag another copy of the field from the PivotTable Field List into the data area of the table. Then select a data cell, choose PivotTable, Field Settings, choose the function you want to use, and click OK. The available summary functions are Sum, Count, Average, Max, Min, Product, Count Nums, StdDev, StdDevp, Var, and Varp.

Using Custom Calculations

In addition to the standard summary functions enumerated in the previous paragraph, Excel also offers a set of custom calculations. With these you can do such things as have each item in the data area of your table report its value as a percentage of the total values in the same row or column, create running totals, or show each value as a percentage of some base value.

To apply a custom calculation, select any item in the data area of your table, and then choose PivotTable, Field Settings. In the PivotTable Field dialog box, click Options. The dialog box expands to reveal additional options, as shown in Figure 30-27 on the next page.

The default calculation is Normal (shown in the Show Data As drop-down list). To apply a custom calculation, open this drop-down list, choose the calculation you want, and then select options from the Base Field and Base Item lists as appropriate. Table 30-1 lists the custom calculation choices.

Figure 30-27. Use the Show Data As
drop-down list to apply a custom calculation.

Table 30-1. Custom Calculation Options

Custom Calculation	Does This
Difference From	Displays data as a difference from a specified base field and base item
% Of	Displays data as a percentage of the value of a specified base field and base item
% Difference From	Displays data as a percentage difference from a specified base field and base item
Running Total In	Displays data as a running total
% Of Row	Displays each data item as a percentage of the total of the items in its row
% Of Column	Displays each data item as a percentage of the total of the items in its column
% Of Total	Displays each data item as a percentage of the grand total of all items in its field
Index	Uses this formula: ((value in cell) x (Grand Total of Grand Totals)) / ((Grand Row Total) x (Grand Column Total))

When you select a member of the Base Field list, the items in the selected field appear in the Base Item list. The Base Item list also includes the items (Previous) and (Next). Figure 30-28 shows how you could set up the PivotTable Field dialog box to calculate the percentage of difference between the current item and that of the previous quarter.

Figure 30-29 shows our PivotTable with such a field added to the data area (we've named the field Q/Q % Change).

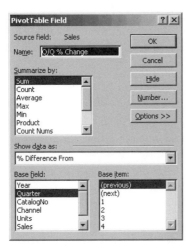

Figure 30-28. These settings will create a field that calculates percentage of change from the previous quarter.

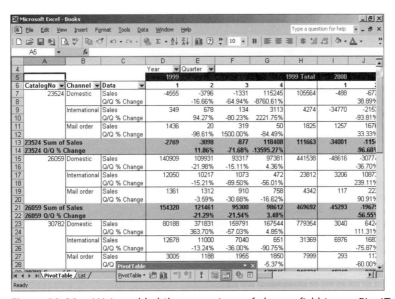

Figure 30-29. We've added the percentage of change field to our PivotTable.

Using Calculated Fields and Items

In case custom calculations don't meet all your analytic needs, Excel allows you to add calculated fields and calculated items to your PivotTables. A *calculated field* is a new field, derived from calculations performed on existing fields in your table. A *calculated item* is a new item in an existing field, derived from calculations performed on other items that are already in the field. After you create a custom field or item, Excel lets you use it in your table, as though it were part of your data source.

Custom fields and items can apply arithmetic operations to any data already in your PivotTable (including data generated by other custom fields or items), but they cannot reference worksheet data outside the PivotTable.

Creating a Calculated Field

To create a calculated field, select any cell in the PivotTable. Then choose PivotTable, Formulas, Calculated Field. The Insert Calculated Field dialog box, shown in Figure 30-30, appears.

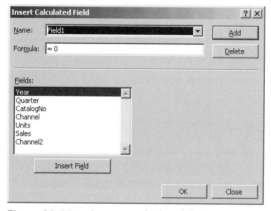

Figure 30-30. Create a calculated field in this dialog box.

Type a name for your calculated field in the Name box. Then type a formula in the Formula box. To enter a field into the formula, select from the Field list and click Insert Field. Figure 30-31 shows an example of a calculated field.

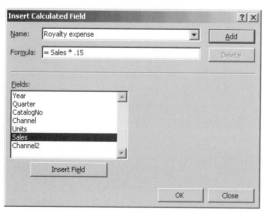

Figure 30-31. This calculated field multiplies an existing field by a constant.

Excel adds a new calculated field to your PivotTable when you click either Add or OK. You can then work with the new field using the same techniques you use to work with existing fields.

Creating a Calculated Item

To create a calculated item for a field, select any existing item in the field or the field heading. Then choose PivotTable, Formulas, Calculated Item. Excel displays the Insert Calculated Item In "*fieldname*" dialog box similar to the one shown in Figure 30-32.

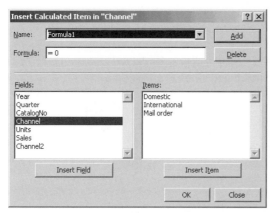

Figure 30-32. Use this dialog box to create a calculated item for a field.

To create a calculated item, type a unique name for the item in the Name box. Then enter its formula in the Formula box. You can select from the Fields and Items lists, and use Insert field and Insert Item, to enter field and item names into the formula.

> **note** You cannot create calculated items in fields that have custom subtotals.

Figure 30-33 on the next page shows an example of a calculated item. In this case the new item represents Domestic sales divided by the sum of International and Mail Order sales.

Displaying a List of Calculated Fields and Items

To display a list of your calculated fields and items, along with their formulas, choose PivotTable, Formulas, List Formulas. Excel displays this information on a new worksheet, as shown in Figure 30-34 on the next page.

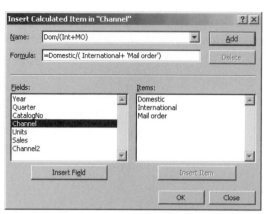

Figure 30-33. This calculated item will appear by default whenever the Channel field is included in the PivotTable.

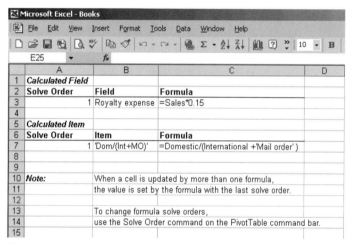

Figure 30-34. Excel displays a list of calculated fields and items on a new worksheet.

As the Note in Figure 30-34 indicates, you need to be careful when a cell in your table is affected by more than one calculated field or item. In such cases, the value is set by the formula that's executed last. The Solve Order information in the list of calculated fields and items tells you which formula that is. If you need to change the solve order, choose PivotTable, Formulas, Solve Order.

Referencing PivotTable Data from Worksheet Cells

Excel's GETPIVOTDATA function lets you reference an item in a PivotTable by its position within the field structure of the table, not by its current worksheet location. With this function, you can perform calculations on PivotTable data without worrying about what will happen to your calculations if the table is rearranged. As long as the referenced data continues to exist somewhere within the PivotTable, the GETPIVOTDATA function will find it. If you reference a table item and subsequently remove that item from the table, the function returns #REF!

The GETPIVOTDATA function itself is not new in this version of Excel. What's new is that Excel supplies the function arguments for you automatically. If you point to a PivotTable cell while building a formula outside the table, Excel creates a GETPIVOTDATA reference to that cell.

Creating a PivotTable from External Data

You can create a PivotTable from selected fields and records of an external data source in either of two ways. If you've already set up a query to an external source using Microsoft Query (or its simplified front-end, the Query Wizard), you will see the dialog box shown in Figure 30-35 before the data appears in Excel. (For information about using Microsoft Query and the Query Wizard, see Chapter 29, "Working with External Data.") Instead of selecting Existing Worksheet or New Worksheet in this dialog box, click the Create A PivotTable Report link. This link takes you to Step 3 of the PivotTable And PivotChart Wizard (refer to Figure 30-6). Tell the wizard where to put the table, lay out your fields, and you're finished.

Figure 30-35. If you've already set up a query, you can turn it into a PivotTable by clicking Create A PivotTable Report.

If you haven't yet created a query to your external data source, you can do so from within the PivotTable And PivotChart Wizard. In the wizard's first dialog box, select External Data Source. When you click Next, the dialog box shown in Figure 30-36 on the next page appears.

Figure 30-36. You can click Get Data in the wizard's second dialog box to create a new query.

Click Get Data. The dialog box shown in Figure 30-37 appears. The Databases tab of this dialog box lists data sources established by means of existing DSN files. You can select one of these and create your query, or you can create a new DSN file by selecting <New Data Source>. Queries already set up for your use are listed on the Queries tab, and available offline OLAP cube files are listed on the OLAP Cubes tab. You can select any of these items and use it to generate a PivotTable.

Figure 30-37. The Choose Data Source dialog box lets you create a new DSN file or select an existing query or OLAP cube.

Note that you cannot create a new ODC file by means of the Choose Data Source dialog box. If your data source must be specified by means of an ODC file, you need to cancel out of the PivotTable And PivotChart Wizard and choose Data, Import External Data, Import Data to create your ODC file. For information about how to do this, see Chapter 29, "Working with External Data."

Refreshing PivotTable Data from an External Source

If the refreshing of your PivotTable is a time-consuming process, you might want to let Excel do the job in the background so that you can continue working while your PivotTable is being updated. To do this, select any cell in the table, choose PivotTable, Table Options, and then select the Background Query check box in the PivotTable Options dialog box. This option is available only for tables created from external data.

If your PivotTable uses page fields, you can choose a querying mode in which Excel fetches only the data needed for the page you're currently looking at. This option uses less memory and might serve you best if you're working with a large external database. You might also prefer to use this option if you switch pages infrequently.

To query your external data source one page at a time, double-click the field heading for any page field in your table. In the PivotTable Field dialog box that appears, click Advanced. In the PivotTable Field Advanced Options dialog box, click the option labeled Query External Data Source As You Select Each Page Field Item.

Refreshing at Regular Time Intervals

To have your table refreshed at periodic intervals, choose PivotTable, Table Options. Select the Refresh Every check box and then specify a time interval in minutes. This option is available only for tables created from external data.

Working with OLAP Data

The following limitations apply to PivotTables created from OLAP data:

- If you rename fields in a PivotTable based on OLAP data, the fields revert to their original names on refresh.
- The detail behind data values is usually not available.
- You cannot change the summary function used for subtotals.
- You cannot change the summary functions for data fields or use multiple summary functions.
- You cannot display subtotals for inner fields.
- You cannot create calculated fields and items.
- If your PivotTable is based on external OLAP data, the PivotTable Field dialog box is not available for page fields.

Using a PivotTable to Consolidate Ranges

In a PivotTable used to consolidate data in separate Excel ranges, each source range can be displayed as an item on the page axis. By using the drop-down list on the page axis, you can see each source range at a glance, as well as the table that consolidates the ranges. For example, Figure 30-38 shows quarterly examination scores. The data is stored in four separate worksheets: Exam 1, Exam 2, Exam 3, and Exam 4.

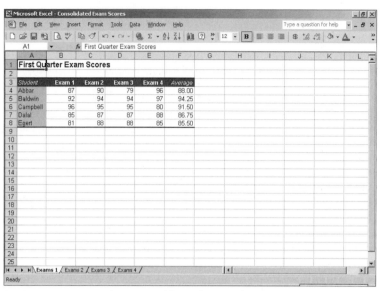

Figure 30-38. Use the PivotTable And PivotChart Report command to consolidate the four worksheets in this workbook.

To generate a consolidation PivotTable from these worksheets, follow these steps:

1 Choose Data, PivotTable And PivotChart Report.

2 When the Step 1 dialog box appears, select the Multiple Consolidation Ranges option, and then click Next.

3 When the Step 2a dialog box appears, accept the Create A Single Page Field For Me option (the default option). Click Next and Excel displays the Step 2b dialog box, shown in Figure 30-39.

Figure 30-39. In the Step 2b dialog box, specify each data range that you want your PivotTable to consolidate.

> **tip**   **Include headings, omit totals**
>
> When specifying ranges to consolidate, include column and row headings, but do not include summary columns and rows. In other words, do not include in the source range columns and rows that calculate totals or averages.

4 Select the first data range that you want the PivotTable to consolidate, and then click the Add button. You might find it easier to use the Collapse Dialog button to select the data. In this example, the first range you'll want to consolidate is 'Exams 1'!A3:E8. You'll also want to consolidate 'Exams 2'!A3:E8, 'Exams 3'!A3:E9, and 'Exams 4'!A3:E7.

5 Repeat step 4 for each additional source range. When you have specified all your source ranges, click Next, tell Excel where you want the new PivotTable, and then click Finish.

Figure 30-40 shows the finished PivotTable. Notice that the current page-axis item is (All). This page shows the consolidated exam scores. Every other item on the page axis displays an unconsolidated source range, in effect duplicating the four source ranges within the PivotTable. If your source ranges are in separated workbook files, you can see these ranges much more easily by stepping through the page axis of the PivotTable than by opening each source file.

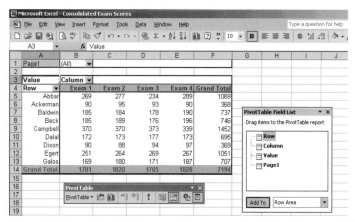

Figure 30-40. The (All) item on the page axis displays the consolidated exam scores.

In this example, we selected the Create A Single Page Field For Me option in the wizard's second dialog box. Let's look now at an example in which you might want to select the I Will Create The Page Fields option.

Figure 30-41 on the next page shows a workbook in which each of eight worksheets displays unit and sales figures for a particular year and quarter, broken out by catalog number. In consolidating these eight worksheets you'll want to have two page-axis fields, Year and Quarter.

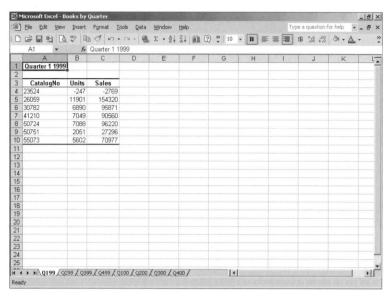

Figure 30-41. Each worksheet in this workbook displays quarterly unit and sales figures for each book in the catalog.

To create this PivotTable, follow these steps:

1 Choose Data, PivotTable And PivotChart Report. When the Step 1 dialog box appears, select the Multiple Consolidation Ranges option and then click Next.

2 When the Step 2a dialog box appears, select the I Will Create The Page Fields option. Click Next.

Excel displays the Step 2b dialog box, shown in Figure 30-42. Because you selected the I Will Create Page Fields option, this version of the Step 2b dialog box is slightly more complex than the one shown in Figure 30-39.

3 In the Step 2b dialog box, select the first data range that you want the PivotTable to consolidate, and then click the Add button.

4 Repeat step 3 for each additional source range.

5 When you have identified all your source ranges, select the 2 Page Fields option.

You select 2 in this case because you want to create two page-axis fields. You are allowed to create as many as four. Figure 30-43 shows the Step 2b dialog box after you have identified your data source and selected the 2 Page Fields option.

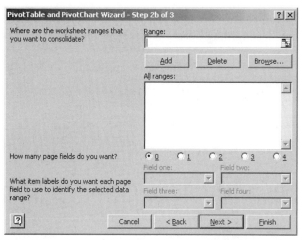

Figure 30-42. When you create your own page fields, the Step 2b dialog box requires some additional information from you.

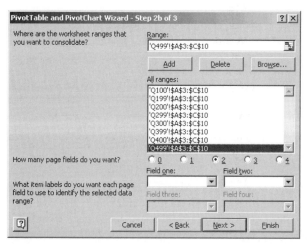

Figure 30-43. After you identify your data sources and specify how many page-axis fields you want, complete the Step 2b dialog box by telling Excel which source ranges should be associated with which page-axis fields.

6 Select the first range in the All Ranges list. Then enter **2000** in the Field One box. Next enter **Q1** in the Field Two box.

7 Select the second range in the All Ranges list. Enter **1999** and **Q1** in the Field One and Field Two boxes. Continue in this manner until you have identified each range specified in the All Ranges list. Click Next, and tell Excel where you want your PivotTable.

Figure 30-44 shows the completed PivotTable. By working with the drop-down lists beside the two page-axis field headings, you can make the table show various perspectives on your data.

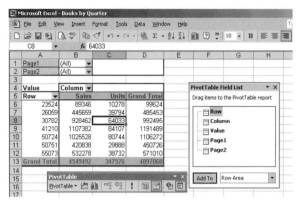

Figure 30-44. This consolidated PivotTable has two page-axis fields.

Building a PivotTable from an Existing PivotTable

The first time you create a PivotTable from any data source, internal or external, Excel creates a copy of the data source, as a *cache*, in memory. When you modify the table, for example, by rearranging column and row fields, Excel refers to the cache, not to the original data source. (When you refresh the table, of course, Excel goes back to the original data source.)

If you're creating a second or subsequent PivotTable based on the same internal data source or the same query of external data, it's most efficient to let Excel use the same cache. Otherwise, the program duplicates memory unnecessarily. To let Excel know that you're planning to reuse data that's already in use for another PivotTable, select Another PivotTable Report Or PivotChart Report on the wizard's first dialog box.

Printing PivotTables

Excel includes some special features to assist with the printing of PivotTables. Each of these features assumes that the PivotTable to be printed is the only one on the current worksheet. If you have more than one PivotTable on the current sheet, be sure to set the PivotTable you want to print as a *print area* before you print.

For information about setting a print area, see " Defining A Default Print Area" on page 349.

Using Row and Column Headings as Print Titles

Print titles are cell contents that appear at the top or left edge of each printed page (see "Specifying Rows and Columns to Print on Every Page" on page 342. You can make a multipage PivotTable printout much easier to read and understand by setting your row and column field headings as print titles. To do this, first make sure you don't have any ordinary print titles set for the current worksheet. (Choose File, Page Setup. On the Sheet tab, clear Rows To Repeat At Top and Columns To Repeat At Left.) Next, select any cell in your PivotTable, and choose PivotTable, Table Options. In the PivotTable Options dialog box, select Set Print Titles.

Repeating Item Labels on Each Printed Page

The option just described uses field headings as print titles. It's also a good idea to have the current row-field item to appear after each horizontal page break and the current column-field item to appear after each vertical page break. To do this, select any cell in the PivotTable, choose PivotTable, Table Options, and, in the PivotTable Options dialog box, select Repeat Item Labels On Each Printed Page.

Printing Each Outer Row Field Item on a New Page

You can have Excel insert a page break every time the outermost row field changes. That way you get separate pages for each item in that outermost field. To do this, double-click the outermost row-field heading. In the PivotTable Field dialog box, click Layout. In the PivotTable Field Layout dialog box, select Insert Page Break After Each Item.

Using the PivotTable Web Component

Figure 30-45 shows the Books PivotTable as published to the Web using the interactive PivotTable Web component. (For information about publishing Excel documents to the Web, see Chapter 20, "Transferring Files to and from Internet Sites.") The user interface for the PivotTable Web component, unfortunately, differs strongly from Excel's own PivotTable user interface.

Part 9: Managing Databases and Lists

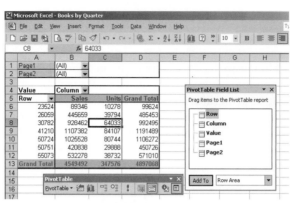

Figure 30-45. The PivotTable Web component's UI differs significantly from Excel's.

Here are some highlights to note:

- To pivot the table, you can drag field headings between axes, as you can in Excel.

- To remove a field from the table, right-click its heading and choose Remove Field from the shortcut menu.

- To add a field to the table, drag it from the PivotTable Field List window. If that window isn't visible, click the Field List button on the toolbar (it's just to the left of the Help button).

- The Web component calls the page axis the *filter area*, but it works exactly like the page axis in Excel.

- Use the plus and minus signs next to outer field items to reveal and hide associated inner field items. (In Figure 30-45, we've expanded the first CatalogNo item and first Year item.)

- Use the plus sign next to an inner field item to show the individual records that contribute to that item. This action is equivalent to double-clicking a data-area element in Excel.

- The Web component has no menu bar of its own. To access the component's menus, right-click the table and choose Commands and Options from the shortcut menu.

- If you're using Microsoft Internet Explorer 4.01 or later, changes you make to a Web component PivotTable are retained if you browse to another Web page and then return during the same session.

- If you don't prefer the Web component's user interface, click Export to Microsoft Excel on the toolbar. Your table will open in Excel, and you can work with it there.

Part 10

Working with Visual Basic and Macros

Recording Macros

A macro is a set of instructions that tells Microsoft Excel (or another application) to perform one or more actions for you. Macros are like computer programs, but they run completely within Excel. You can use them to automate tedious or frequently repeated tasks.

Macros can carry out sequences of actions much more quickly than you could yourself. For example, you can create a macro that enters a series of dates across one row of a worksheet, centers the date in each cell, and then applies a border format to the row. Or you can create a macro that defines special print settings in the Page Setup dialog box and then prints the document. Macros can be very simple or extremely complex. They even can be interactive; that is, you can write macros that request information from the user and then act upon that information.

There are two ways to create a macro: you can record it, or you can build it by entering instructions in a *module*. To enter instructions in a module, you use Microsoft Visual Basic for Applications (VBA).

In this chapter, you'll first learn how to record and execute a simple macro. Then you'll learn how to view the recorded macro and make it more useful by doing some simple editing.

Subsequent chapters in this section explain the use of VBA to create custom worksheet functions and show how you can tie macros and functions together to build a small VBA application. This section covers only the beginnings of what you can do with VBA in Excel, however. For a more detailed treatment of the subject, see *Microsoft Excel 2000/Visual Basic for Applications Fundamentals*, published by Microsoft Press.

Using the Macro Recorder

Rather than type macros character by character, you can have Excel create a macro by recording the menu commands, keystrokes, and other actions needed to accomplish a task.

After you've recorded a series of actions, you can run the macro to perform the task again. As you might expect, this playback capability is most useful with macros that automate long or repetitive processes, such as entering and formatting tables or printing a certain section of a worksheet.

The overall process for recording a macro consists of three steps. First you start the macro recorder and supply a name for the macro. Next you perform the actions you want to record, such as choosing menu commands, selecting cells, and entering data. Finally you stop the macro recorder.

Let's investigate this process by creating a simple macro that inserts a company name and address in a worksheet. Begin by saving and closing all open workbooks, and then open a new workbook. Next follow these steps:

1 Choose Tools, Macro, Record New Macro. Excel displays the Record Macro dialog box shown in Figure 31-1.

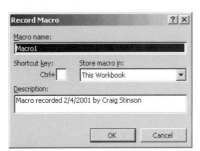

Figure 31-1. Open the Record Macro dialog box to begin recording your own macro.

2 Assign a name to the macro. You can accept Excel's suggestion (Macro1) or enter your own name. Let's use **CompanyAddress**. Note that this name cannot have any spaces.

3 Assign a key combination to the macro by entering a letter—in this case, uppercase **A**—in the Shortcut Key edit box.

4 Store the macro in the currently active workbook by making sure the This Workbook option is selected.

5 Enter a description for the macro in the Description box; in this case, type **Enter company address**.

6 To begin recording, click OK. Excel displays the message Recording in the status bar, and the Stop Recording toolbar, shown in Figure 31-2.

Stop
Recording   Relative
macro | Reference

Figure 31-2. Use the Stop Recording toolbar
if you need to stop the recording process.

7 Select A6, and enter **Coho Winery**. In A7, enter **3012 West Beaujolais St**. In
A8, enter **Walla Walla, WA 98765**

8 Click the Stop Recording Macro button on the Stop Recording toolbar. If the
toolbar isn't visible, choose Tools, Macro, Stop Recording. This step is important; if you don't stop the macro recorder, Excel continues to record your
actions indefinitely.

To test the new macro, clear the worksheet and then press Ctrl+Shift+A. Excel runs the
macro and performs the sequence of actions in the same way you recorded them.

> **note** Keyboard shortcuts in VBA are case-sensitive.

Running a Macro Without Using a Keyboard Shortcut

You don't have to know a macro's key combination to run the macro. (In fact, you
don't have to assign a keyboard shortcut when you record a macro.) Instead, you can
use the Macro dialog box:

1 Choose Tools, Macro, Macros to display the dialog box shown in Figure 31-3.

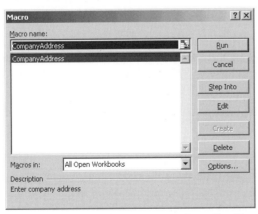

Figure 31-3. You can run macros from the Macro dialog box.

2 Select the name of the macro, and click Run.

You can also use the Macro dialog box to view and edit macros, as you'll see
in the next section.

Behind the Scenes: The VBA Environment

Now that you've recorded your macro, let's find out what Excel did. When you clicked OK in the Record Macro dialog box, Excel created something called a *module* in the active workbook. As you entered the company name and address in the worksheet, Excel recorded your actions and inserted the corresponding VBA code in the module.

The new module doesn't appear with the other sheets in the workbook; to view the module, choose Tools, Macro, Macros. Next, select the CompanyAddress macro, and click the Edit button. The Visual Basic Editor (VBE) starts up, and the module that contains the CompanyAddress macro appears, as shown in Figure 31-4.

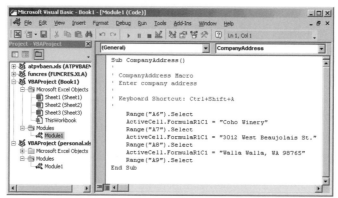

Figure 31-4. After translating each action you performed into VBA code, Excel stores the code in the module.

As you can see, a module looks like a window that you might see in a word processing program. The menu bar above the module includes menus for editing, debugging, and running VBA code. In the module you can review, enter, copy, move, insert, and delete VBA statements and comments using techniques that are similar to those you use in a word processing program. Of course, because the VBE is a separate application, you can switch back and forth between your Excel workbook and the VBE by clicking the appropriate button in the Windows taskbar.

The VBA environment is a big place, full of interesting details, but for now let's focus only on the code we've recorded. On the right side of the VBE is a window displaying the module containing the code.

The first and last lines of the code act as the beginning and endpoints for the macro you've recorded; a Sub statement starts the macro and names it, and an End Sub statement ends the macro. You'll notice that special VBA terms, called *keywords*, are displayed in dark blue. (You can view and change the colors assigned to various elements of a macro by choosing Tools, Options in the VBE and clicking the Editor Format tab.)

Getting Help on VBA Keywords

You can get detailed information about a keyword by clicking the word and pressing F1. In Figure 31-4, if you place the insertion point in the keyword Sub and press F1, Excel presents a Help screen containing an entry for the Sub statement, as shown in Figure 31-5.

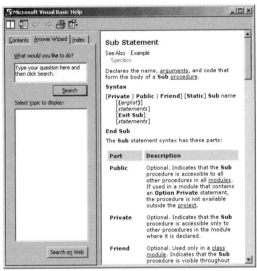

Figure 31-5. You can display detailed Help information about any VBA keyword by selecting the word and pressing F1.

Many Help topics for VBA keywords include a link that, when clicked, displays another Help screen containing one or more examples of the keyword as it might be used in working VBA code. (In Figure 31-5, for example, you can click the word Example just under the Sub Statement title.) You can copy this code, paste it into a module, and edit the resulting text to meet your needs.

Objects, Methods, and Properties

To VBA, every item in the Excel environment is considered an object rather than an abstract set of data structures or an arrangement of pixels on the screen. Objects can contain other objects. At the top of the hierarchy, the largest object within the Excel *object model* is the Excel application itself. Objects contained within this largest container include *workbooks*. Workbooks contain *worksheets* and *chart sheets*, worksheets contain *ranges* (and can also contain *chart objects*), and so on.

The first VBA statement in the CompanyAddress macro after the Sub statement (that is, not including the comments that begin with the single quote character) is the following:

```
Range("A6").Select
```

This illustrates an important characteristic of VBA code: the syntax of many statements specifies first an *object* and then an action. An object can be a range, a worksheet, a graphic object, a workbook, or any of the more than 100 types of objects in Excel. Here, we specify a *range object*—the absolute cell reference A6—and an action—*select*.

The behaviors, or sets of actions, that an object "knows" how to perform are called the *methods* of the object. Methods are like verbs. To understand this concept, imagine that we are programming a robotic dog through VBA. To cause the dog to bark, we might use this statement:

```
Dog.Bark
```

Robotic dogs, however, are (or ought to be) capable of more than just barking. For example, you might want the dog to understand these statements:

```
Dog.Sit
Dog.RollOver
Dog.Fetch
```

The tricks our robodog can perform, such as barking, rolling over, fetching, and so on, are its methods. The list of methods an object can perform depends on the object. A range object, for example, supports almost 80 different methods that you can use to copy and paste cells, sort, add formatting, and so on.

Like objects in the "real" world, objects in VBA also have properties. If you think of objects as the nouns of VBA and methods as the verbs, properties are the adjectives. A *property* is a quality, characteristic, or attribute of an object, such as its color or pattern. Characteristics such as our robodog's color, the number of spots on its back, the length of its tail, and the volume of its bark are among its properties.

You set a property by following the name of the property with an equal sign and a value. Continuing our robotic dog example, we could set the length of the dog's tail with

```
Dog.TailLength = 10
```

where TailLength is a property of the Dog object.

For example, the following executable statement in our CompanyAddress macro:

```
ActiveCell.FormulaR1C1 = "Coho Winery"
```

changes one of the properties, FormulaR1C1, of the active cell, setting that property to the value "Coho Winery".

The remaining statements in the CompanyAddress macro consist of two more cell-selection and text-entry couplets. The macro selects cells A7 and A8 and enters text into each cell.

The Object Browser

You can view the various types of objects, methods, and properties available to Excel by switching to the VBE. To do so, select Tools, Macro, Visual Basic Editor (or press Alt+F11). Then choose View, Object Browser (or press F2). The window displayed on the right of the screen shown in Figure 31-6 appears.

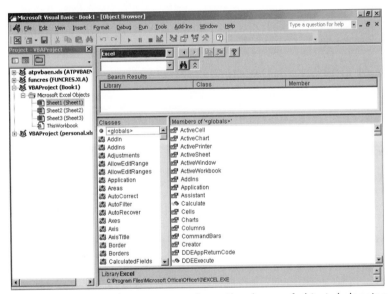

Figure 31-6. The Object Browser shows the classes of objects belonging to the Excel application.

On the left is a list of the various classes of objects available to Excel. You can think of a *class* as a template or description for a type of object; a specific chart, for example, would be an object that is an instance of the Chart class. In VBA, classes belong to a project or library. As shown in Figure 31-6, the Object Browser lists the object classes belonging to the library Excel.

If you scroll down the classes and select a class—the Range class, for example—the right side of the Object Browser lists the properties and methods (called the *members* of the class) that belong to that object. Figure 31-7 on the next page shows the members of the Range class.

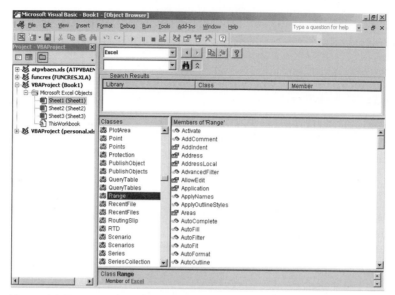

Figure 31-7. Here the Object Browser shows the Range object and some of the Range object's methods and properties.

Collections of Objects

You can have more than one instance of the same VBA object. Together, such instances comprise a *collection*. Each instance in a collection of objects can be identified either by its *index* value (its position within the collection) or by its name. For example, the collection of all sheets in a workbook is

```
Sheets()
```

and a specific instance of a sheet, the third one in the collection, is

```
Sheets(3)
```

If the third sheet were named Summary, it could also be identified as

```
Sheets("Summary")
```

Manipulating Collections with For ... Each In VBA, each item in a collection has its own index, but the index numbers for an entire collection are not necessarily consecutive. If you delete one instance of an object in a collection, the index values of the remaining instances might not be renumbered. For example, if you delete Sheets(3) from a collection of 12 sheets in a workbook, there's no guarantee that Excel will renumber Sheets(4) through Sheets(12) to fill the gap.

In other programming languages, you might use a For … Next construction such as the following to repeat an operation many times:

```
For n = 1 to 12 ' Activate each sheet
    Sheets(n).Activate
Next n
```

If you run this code in a VBA macro after deleting Sheets(3), VBA displays an error message and stops the macro because Sheets(3) no longer exists. To allow for nonconsecutive indexes, VBA offers the For Each … Next statement, a control structure that applies a series of statements to each item in a collection, regardless of the index numbers. For example, suppose you'd like to label each sheet in the active workbook by entering the text **Sheet 1**, **Sheet 2**, and so on, in cell A1 of each sheet. As you won't, in general, know how many sheets there are in any given workbook, you might use the following VBA macro:

```
Sub EnterSheetNum()
    n = 0
    For Each Sheet In Sheets()
        n = n + 1
        Sheet.Activate
        Range("A1").Select
        ActiveCell.FormulaR1C1 = "Sheet" + Str(n)
    Next
End Sub
```

Manipulating an Object's Properties Without Selecting the Object

The code just listed activates each sheet in turn, then selects cell A1 on that sheet, and finally assigns a new value to that cell's FormulaR1C1 property. This sequence of steps mimics the steps that most users would follow if they were working manually. In VBA, everything but the last step in the sequence is unnecessary. That is, you can replace the following instructions:

```
Sheet.Activate
Range("A1").Select
ActiveCell.FormulaR1C1 = "Sheet" + Str(n)
```

with a single instruction:

```
Sheet.Range("A1").FormulaR1C1 = "Sheet" + Str(n)
```

The benefit of this change is that it enables the macro to run faster, because Excel is no longer required to activate sheets and select cells.

Naming Arguments to Methods

Many methods in VBA have arguments that let you specify options for the action to be performed. If the Wag method of the Tail object of our mythical robodog has arguments (for example, *WagRate*, the number of wags per second; *WagTime*, the duration of wagging in seconds; and *WagArc*, the number of degrees of arc in each wag), you can specify them using either of two syntaxes.

In the first syntax, which is often called the *by-name* syntax, you name each argument you use, in any order. For example, this statement wags the tail three times per second for an hour, over an arc of 180 degrees:

```
Robodogs("Fido").Tail.Wag _
    WagRate := 3, _
    WagTime := 3600, _
    WagArc := 180
```

You assign a value to an argument by using a colon and an equal sign, and you separate arguments with commas.

> **note** The underscore character at the end of the first three lines tells VBA that the following line is part of the same statement. Using this symbol makes the list of supplied arguments easier to read. The underscore must always be preceded by a space character.

In the second syntax, which is often called the *by-position* syntax, you enter arguments in a prescribed order. For example, the preceding statement expressed in the by-position syntax looks like this:

```
Robodogs("Fido").Tail.Wag(3,3600,180)
```

Notice that the list of arguments is surrounded by parentheses. The by-position syntax isn't as easy to read as the by-name syntax because you have to remember the order of arguments, and when you review the code at a later date, you won't have the argument names to refresh your memory about their settings.

> **note** Excel's macro recorder records arguments by position rather than by name, which can make it more difficult to understand recorded macros than manually created macros in which you've named the arguments. Similarly, when you select a VBA keyword and press the F1 key, the VBE displays a Help topic describing the by-position syntax for the keyword.

Adding Code to an Existing Macro

Suppose you've recorded a macro that enters a series of labels, sets their font, and then draws a border around them. Then you discover that you forgot a step or that you recorded a step incorrectly—you chose the wrong border format, for example. What do you do?

To add code to an existing macro, you can record actions in a temporary macro and then transfer the code into the macro you want to change. For example, to add to the CompanyAddress macro a step that sets font options for the company's name, follow these steps:

1 Switch to the worksheet containing the address you entered earlier and select cell A6, which contains the name of the company.

2 Choose Tools, Macro, Record New Macro. Excel presents the Record Macro dialog box. In the Macro Name box, enter **MacroTemp** and click OK. Excel displays the Stop Recording toolbar.

3 Choose Format, Cells, and click the Font tab. Select Arial (or any other installed font), 14-point, and Bold Italic. Then click OK to apply the formats.

4 Click the Stop Recording button on the Stop Recording toolbar.

5 Choose Tools, Macro, Macros. In the Macro dialog box, select MacroTemp and click Edit.

6 A window appears that contains the original macro you recorded plus the MacroTemp macro, as shown in Figure 31-8.

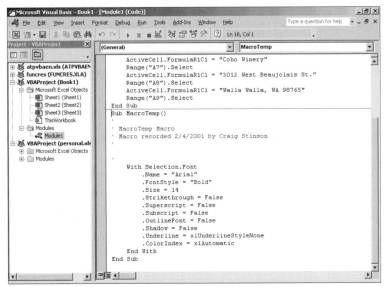

Figure 31-8. The MacroTemp macro now contains the formatting code you recorded.

7 Select all the code inside the macro—from the line beginning With through the line beginning End With—and then choose Edit, Copy.

8 Scroll up to display the CompanyAddress macro.

9 Click at the beginning of the line containing this statement:

```
Range("A7").Select
```

Press Enter to create a blank line. Then position the insertion point at the beginning of the blank line.

10 Choose Edit, Paste.

11 Scroll back down and delete the entire MacroTemp macro, from the Sub statement to the End Sub statement.

The CompanyAddress macro should now look like this (with the comment lines excluded and assuming you've made the company name 14-point Arial Bold):

```
Sub CompanyAddress()
    Range("A6".Select
    ActiveCell.FormulaR1C1 = "Coho Winery"
    With Selection.Font
        .Name = "Arial"
        .FontStyle = "Bold"
        .Size = 14
        .Strikethrough = False
        .Superscript = False
        .OutlineFont = False
        .Shadow = False
        .Underline = xlUnderlineStyleNone
        .ColorIndex = xlAutomatic
    End With
    Range("A7").Select
    ActiveCell.FormulaR1C1 = "3012 West Beaujolais St."
    Range("A8").Select
    ActiveCell.FormulaR1C1 = "Walla Walla, WA 98765"
    Range("A9").Select
End Sub
```

To test the macro, return to Excel (press Alt+F11 or select the Excel button on the taskbar.) Clear the company name and address that you entered earlier when you recorded the macro. Then press Ctrl+Shift+A.

The With and End With statements that the macro recorder created when you recorded MacroTemp (the statements that you subsequently copied into CompanyAddress) specify a group of properties belonging to an object—in this case, the font of the current selection. The With … End With construct provides a kind of shorthand for a series of VBA statements that look like this:

```
Selection.Font.Name = "Arial"

Selection.Font.FontStyle = "Bold Italic"

Selection.Font.Size = 14
```

and so on. In the CompanyAddress macro, the ActiveCell object and the Selection object both refer to the same range on the worksheet, cell A6. Because you can apply a series of font formatting options to an entire range, Excel records the action with Selection, rather than with ActiveCell. Enclosing the property assignments within the With … End With structure simplifies the code and also makes it run faster.

Using Absolute and Relative References

In the CompanyAddress macro, Excel recorded references as absolute references in the A1 format (as opposed to the R1C1 format). As a result, the CompanyAddress macro always enters the company name in A6 and the address in A7 and A8.

In VBA, cell selections are recorded as absolute references unless you click the Relative Reference button on the Stop Recording toolbar. If you click this button, the recorder begins recording relative references. If you click the button again, the recorder records subsequent actions using absolute references—and so on. You can toggle between relative and absolute references at any time while recording.

---

tip   **Check the Relative Reference button before you record**

The Relative Reference button on the Stop Recording toolbar appears pushed in when selected. This is your indication that the recorder is now using relative references. There is no other indication, unfortunately. The button's ScreenTip does not change to say Absolute Reference. Because it's important to know which mode you're in when you record a macro, it's a good idea to check the appearance of the button before you start.

Suppose that instead of inserting the company's name and address in A6:A8 of the active worksheet, you'd like to insert the address beginning at whatever cell happens to be active when you run the macro. To do this, you need to create a new CompanyAddress macro—we'll call it CompanyAddressRel—that uses relative references instead of absolute references:

1 Clear the Coho Winery name and address from A6:A8 of Sheet1.

2 Choose Tools, Macro, Record New Macro. In the Record Macro dialog box, enter **CompanyAddressRel** for the macro's name and lowercase **a** for the shortcut key. Type **Enter company address in any cell** in the Description box, and click OK. Excel displays the Stop Recording toolbar.

3 Click the Relative Reference button on the Stop Recording toolbar.

4 Choose Format, Cells, select 14-point Arial bold, and then click OK.

5 Enter **Coho Winery** in cell A6, **3012 West Beaujolais St.** in A7, and **Walla Walla, WA 98765** in A8.

6 Click the Stop Recording button.

Test this macro by clicking in various cells and pressing Ctrl+a (lowercase this time). If you now choose Tools, Macro, Macros, select CompanyAddressRel, and click Edit, you'll see the following listing:

```
Sub CompanyAddressRel()
With Selection.Font
        .Name = "Arial"
        .FontStyle = "Bold"
        .Size = 12
        .Strikethrough = False
        .Superscript = False
        .Subscript = False
        .OutlineFont = False
        .Shadow = False
        .Underline = xlUnderlineStyleNone
        .ColorIndex = xlAutomatic
    End With
    ActiveCell.FormulaR1C1 = "Coho Winery"
    ActiveCell.Offset(1, 0).Range("A1").Select
    ActiveCell.FormulaR1C1 = "3012 West Beaujolais St."
    ActiveCell.Offset(1, 0).Range("A1").Select
    ActiveCell.FormulaR1C1 = "Walla Walla, WA 98765"
    ActiveCell.Offset(1, 0).Range("A1").Select
End Sub
```

The original macro enters the company name and address in the range A6:A8, regardless of which cell is active when you start the macro. The new macro, on the other hand, enters the address starting in the active cell, no matter where that cell is located.

If you compare the two versions of the macro, you'll see that the only difference between them lies in the statements used to select cells. For example, the new version of the macro does not include a statement for selecting the first cell, because it uses relative references and the first cell is already selected.

In addition to selecting the second cell, the original macro uses the statement

```
Range("A7").Select
```

whereas the new version uses

```
ActiveCell.Offset(1,0).Range("A1").Select
```

To move from the active cell to the cell below it in the new macro, VBA starts with the ActiveCell object, to which it applies the Offset method with two arguments for the number of rows and columns to offset. The Range keyword then returns a range with the same dimensions as its argument. In this case, the argument "A1" specifies that we want a range consisting of a single cell. Finally, the Select method selects the range, as in the original macro.

Which form is better—absolute or relative? It depends. Absolute references are useful when you want to perform the same action in the same spot in several worksheets, or when you want to perform the same action repeatedly in the same part of one worksheet. Relative references are useful when you want to perform an action anywhere in a worksheet.

Macro Subroutines

Suppose you're creating a complex macro and you discover that, among other things, you want the macro to perform a task you've already recorded under a different name. Or suppose you discover that a task you've recorded as part of a macro is something you'd like to use by itself. In our CompanyAddress macro, for example, it might be nice if we could quickly and easily apply the font formats of the company name to other items in a worksheet.

With VBA, you can conveniently divide large macros into a series of smaller macros, and you can easily string together a series of small macros to create one large macro. A macro procedure that is used by another macro is called a *subroutine*. Macro subroutines can simplify your macros because you have to write only one set of instructions rather than repeat the instructions over and over. To use a macro subroutine in another macro, you call the subroutine by using its name in the other macro.

To demonstrate, let's split the CompanyAddressRel macro into two parts:

1 Choose Tools, Macro, Macros. Select CompanyAddressRel and click Edit. Then select the statements that format the font of the company's name:

```
With Selection.Font
            .Name = "Arial"
            .FontStyle = "Bold"
            .Size = 12
            .Strikethrough = False
            .Superscript = False
            .Subscript = False
            .OutlineFont = False
            .Shadow = False
            .Underline = xlUnderlineStyleNone
            .ColorIndex = xlAutomatic
    End With
```

2 Choose Edit, Cut.

3 Click below the End Sub statement at the end of the CompanyAddressRel macro, and type **Sub CompanyFont()**.

4 The VBE types an End Sub statement for you. In the blank line between the Sub and End Sub statements, choose Edit, Paste to insert the font formatting code.

You've created a new CompanyFont macro by moving the font formatting codes from the CompanyAddress macro into the new CompanyFont macro. As mentioned, to run one macro from within another, you must use the name of the second macro in the first. To update the Company Address macro so it uses the CompanyFont macro, follow these steps:

1 Click at the end of this statement:

```
ActiveCell.FormulaR1C1 = "Coho Winery"
```

Press Enter to insert a new line.

2 Type **CompanyFont**.

When you've finished, the two macros should look like the ones in the following listing:

```
Sub CompanyAddressRel()
    ActiveCell.FormulaR1C1 = "Coho Winery"
    CompanyFont
    ActiveCell.Offset(1, 0).Range("A1").Select
    ActiveCell.FormulaR1C1 = "3012 West Beaujolais St."
    ActiveCell.Offset(1, 0).Range("A1").Select
    ActiveCell.FormulaR1C1 = "Walla Walla, WA 98765"
    ActiveCell.Offset(1, 0).Range("A1").Select
End Sub


Sub CompanyFont()
With Selection.Font
        .Name = "Arial"
        .FontStyle = "Bold"
        .Size = 12
        .Strikethrough = False
        .Superscript = False
        .Subscript = False
        .OutlineFont = False
        .Shadow = False
        .Underline = xlUnderlineStyleNone
        .ColorIndex = xlAutomatic
    End With
End Sub
```

When you activate the CompanyAddressRel macro by pressing Ctrl+a , Excel runs the first statement in the macro. When Excel reaches the statement that calls the CompanyFont macro, it switches to the first line of CompanyFont. When Excel reaches the End Sub statement at the end of CompanyFont, it returns to the statement in CompanyAddress immediately after the one that called CompanyFont and continues until it reaches the End Sub statement at the end of CompanyAddress.

Other Ways to Run Macros

Earlier in this chapter we assigned the Ctrl+Shift+A keyboard shortcut to the CompanyAddress macro. Excel offers other ways to run macros: You can assign a macro to a command that appears on one of Excel's menus, to a button on a toolbar, and to a drawing object. You can also assign a macro to a button on a worksheet or chart. See Chapter 33, "A Sample Visual Basic Application," for more about these shortcuts. For more information about customizing menus and commands, see "Customizing Toolbars and Menus" on page 65.

Using the Personal Macro Workbook

When you recorded the CompanyAddress macro earlier in this chapter, you placed the macro in a module that belongs to the active workbook. A macro that has been placed in a module is available only when the workbook containing the module is open.

To make a macro available at all times, store it in the Personal Macro Workbook, which is normally hidden. You can unhide it by choosing Window, Unhide and selecting Personal in the Unhide dialog box. If you don't see the Personal file in the Unhide dialog box, or if the Unhide command is unavailable, you have not yet created a Personal Macro Workbook. To create one, begin recording a macro, as described earlier in this chapter, and select the Personal Macro Workbook option in the Record New Macro dialog box. Excel creates the Personal Macro Workbook and places its file (Personal.xls) in the XLStart folder. Excel opens Personal.xls, as it does any other file in the XLStart folder, each time you start Excel. Because the Personal Macro Workbook is always available when you work in Excel, it's a good place to record macros that you want to be able to use in any workbook.

Going On from Here

In this chapter, you've learned how to create macros with the help of the macro recorder. As you learn more about the VBA programming language (a subject beyond the scope of this book), you'll notice that the macro recorder often creates more code for a task than you really need. In our CompanyFont macro, for example, the following lines that the recorder recorded were unnecessary because all you wanted to do was set the font name, point size, and weight:

```
.Strikethrough = False
.Superscript = False
.Subscript = False
.OutlineFont = False
.Shadow = False
```

```
.Underline = xlUnderlineStyleNone
.ColorIndex = xlAutomatic
```

The recorder added these lines because it didn't (and couldn't) know they weren't necessary. You can edit them out without changing the functionality of the macro in any way.

Earlier in the chapter, you saw that it is possible, using VBA, to change an object's property settings (a cell's font formats, for example) without selecting the cell. Nevertheless, the recorder always selects objects before taking actions that affect those objects. It does so because it must mimic everything you do when you create the recording. As you acquire more proficiency with VBA, you'll learn ways to edit the recorder's code to make it more efficient.

As you move toward expertise in VBA, you will probably find yourself creating most of your code directly in the VBE, bypassing the recorder altogether. Chances are, though, you'll still return to the recorder now and then. The Excel object model includes so many objects, methods, properties, and arguments, that it's difficult—perhaps pointless—to try to remember them all. When you can't remember what property, object, or method is required in a certain programming situation, one of the easiest ways to get the information you need is by turning on the macro recorder, working through by hand the actions that you want to program, and then seeing what code the recorder generates.

Creating Custom Functions

Although Microsoft Excel includes a multitude of built-in worksheet functions, chances are it doesn't have a function for every type of calculation you perform. Excel's designers couldn't possibly anticipate every calculation need of every user. But they did provide you with the ability to create your own custom functions. In the same way that a macro lets you encapsulate a sequence of actions, so that you can execute that sequence with a single command, a custom function lets you encapsulate a sequence of calculations, so that you can perform those calculations with a single formula.

Custom functions, like macros, use Microsoft Excel Version 2002/Visual Basic for Applications Fundamentals. They differ from macros in two significant ways. First, they use *function* procedures instead of *sub* procedures. They start with a Function statement instead of a Sub statement (and end with End Function instead of End Sub). Second, they perform calculations instead of taking actions. Certain kinds of statements (such as statements that select and format ranges) are excluded from custom functions. In this chapter, you learn how to create and use custom functions.

Suppose your company offers a quantity discount of 10 percent on the sale of a product, provided the order is for more than 100 units. In the following paragraphs, you'll build a function to calculate this discount.

The worksheet in Figure 32-1 on the next page shows an order form that lists each item, the quantity, the price, the discount (if any), and the resulting extended price.

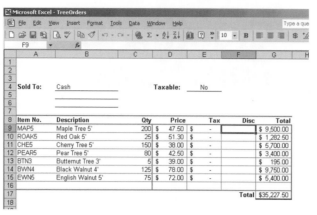

Figure 32-1. In column F, we want to calculate the discount for each item ordered.

To create a custom Discount function in this workbook, follow these steps:

1 Press Alt+F11 to open the Visual Basic Editor, and then choose Insert, Module. A new module appears, as shown in Figure 32-2.

2 In the new module, enter the following code. Use the Tab key to indent lines. After you type an indented line, the VBE assumes that your next line will be similarly indented. To move back out (that is, to the left) one tab character, press Shift+Tab.

```
Function Discount(quantity, price)
    If quantity >=100 then
        Discount = quantity * price * 0.1
    Else
        Discount = 0
    End If
    Discount = Application.Round(Discount, 2)
End Function
```

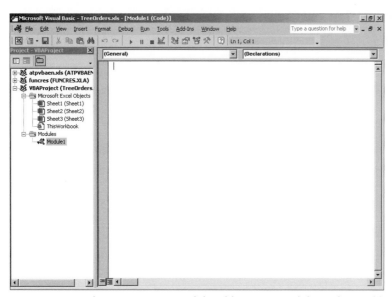

Figure 32-2. Choosing Insert, Module adds a new module to the workbook.

Using Custom Functions

Now you're ready to use the new Discount function. Press Alt+F11 to switch back to the worksheet shown in Figure 32-1. Select cell F9 and enter =**Discount(C9,D9)**. (This workbook, TreeOrders.xls, is included on the CD accompanying this book.) Excel calculates the 10 percent discount on 200 units at $47.50 per unit and returns $950.00.

In the first line of your VBA code, Function Discount(quantity, price), you indicated that the Discount function would require two arguments, *quantity* and *price*. When you call the function in a worksheet cell, you must include those two arguments. In the formula =Discount(C9,D9), C9 is the *quantity* argument, and D9 is the *price* argument. Now you can copy the discount formula into F10:F15 to get the worksheet shown in Figure 32-3 on the next page.

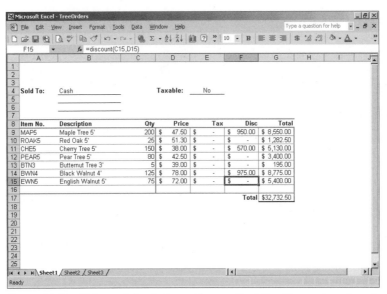

Figure 32-3. This worksheet shows the result of the Discount custom function.

What's Happening

Let's consider how Excel interprets this function procedure. When you press Enter to lock in the formula in the worksheet, Excel looks for the name Discount in the current workbook and finds that it is a procedure in Module1. The argument names enclosed in parentheses—*quantity* and *price*—are placeholders for the values on which the calculation of the discount is based.

The If statement in the following block of code examines the *quantity* argument and determines whether the number of items sold is greater than or equal to 100:

```
If quantity >=100 then
        Discount = quantity * price * 0.1
    Else
        Discount = 0
    End If
```

If the number of items sold is greater than or equal to 100, VBA executes the following statement, which multiplies the *quantity* value by the *price* value and then multiplies the result by 0.1:

```
Discount = quantity * price * 0.1
```

The result is stored as the variable *Discount*. A VBA statement that stores a value in a variable is called an *assignment* statement, because it evaluates the expression on the right side of the equal sign and assigns the result to the variable name on the left. Because the variable *Discount* has the same name as the function procedure itself, the value stored in the variable is returned to the worksheet formula that called the Discount function.

If *quantity* is less than 100, VBA executes the statement

```
Discount = 0
```

Finally, the following statement rounds the value assigned to the *Discount* variable to two decimal places:

```
Discount = Application.Round(Discount, 2)
```

VBA has no Round function, but Excel does. Therefore, to use Round in this statement, you tell VBA to look for the Round method (function) in the Application object (Excel). You do that by adding the word Application before the word Round. Use this syntax whenever you need to access an Excel function from a VBA module.

Understanding Custom Function Rules

A custom function must start with a Function statement and end with an End Function statement. In addition to the function name, the Function statement usually specifies one or more arguments. You may include as many as 29 arguments, using commas to separate them. You can also create a function with no arguments. Excel includes several built-in functions—RAND() and NOW(), for example—that don't use arguments. As you'll see later in this chapter, you can also create functions with optional arguments—arguments that you can omit when you call the function.

Following the Function statement, a function procedure includes one or more statements in VBA to make decisions and perform calculations using the arguments passed to the function. Finally, somewhere in the function procedure, you must include a statement that assigns a value to a variable with the same name as the function. This value is returned to the formula that calls the function.

Using VBA Keywords in Custom Functions

The number of VBA keywords you can use in custom functions is smaller than the number you can use in macros. Custom functions are not allowed to do anything other than return a value to a formula in a worksheet or to an expression used in another VBA macro or function. For example, custom functions cannot resize windows, edit a formula in a cell, or change the font, color, or pattern options for the text in a cell. If you include "action" code of this kind in a function procedure, the function returns the #VALUE! error.

The one action a function procedure can take (apart from performing calculations) is to display a dialog box. You can use an InputBox statement in a custom function as a means of getting input from the user executing the function. You can use a MsgBox statement as a means of conveying information to the user. You also can use custom dialog boxes, or UserForms. In Chapter 33, "A Sample Visual Basic Application," you'll see an example of a UserForm, and in Chapter 34, "Debugging Macros and Custom Functions," you'll see how a MsgBox statement can be a handy debugging tool.

Documenting Macros and Custom Functions

Even simple macros and custom functions can be difficult to read. You can make them easier to understand by entering explanatory text in the form of comments. You add comments by preceding the explanatory text with an apostrophe. For example, Figure 32-4 shows the Discount function with comments. Adding comments like these makes it easier for you or others to maintain your VBA code as time passes. If you need to make a change to the code in the future, you'll have an easier time understanding what you did in the first place.

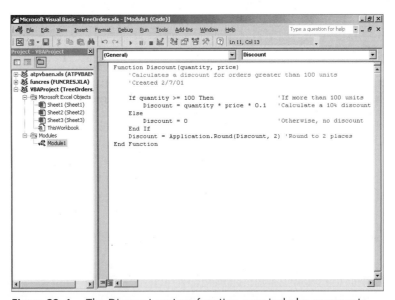

Figure 32-4. The Discount custom function now includes comments.

A apostrophe tells Excel to ignore everything to the right on the same line, so you can place a comment to the right of a VBA statement. You can also insert comments between the statements in a macro or custom function. For example, you might begin a relatively long block of code with a comment that explains its overall purpose and then use inline comments to document individual statements.

Another way to document your macros and custom functions is to give them descriptive names. For example, rather than name a macro *Labels*, you could name it *RelMonthLabels*, where *Rel* indicates that the macro uses relative references and *MonthLabels* describes the type of label the macro creates. Using descriptive names for macros and custom functions is especially helpful when you've created many procedures, particularly if you create procedures that have similar, but not identical, purposes.

How you document your macros and custom functions is a matter of personal preference. It doesn't matter which method you use, as long as you document them. Documentation is most important for long and complex procedures, for procedures that you look at only once in a while, and for procedures that will be maintained by other people.

Creating Custom Functions with Optional Arguments

Some of Excel's built-in functions let you omit certain arguments. For example, if you omit the *type* and *future value* arguments from the PV function, Excel still computes the result, because those arguments are optional. Your custom functions can also make use of optional arguments.

For example, suppose you want to create a custom function called RightTriangle that uses the Pythagorean theorem to compute the length of any side of a right triangle, given the lengths of the other two sides. The equation that expresses the Pythagorean theorem is $a^2 + b^2 = c^2$, where a and b are the short sides and c is the hypotenuse. Given any two sides, you can use this equation to solve for the third side.

In a general-purpose Triangle function, you want to accept three arguments (one for each side of the triangle) but make each argument optional so that the user of the function can omit the argument that the function should solve for. The following code does the trick:

```
Function Triangle(Optional short1, Optional short2, _
    Optional longside)

    If Not(IsMissing(short1)) And Not (IsMissing(short2)) Then
        Triangle = Sqr(short1 ^ 2 + short2 ^ 2)
```

```
    Else
        If Not(IsMissing(short1)) And Not(IsMissing(longside)) Then
            Triangle = Sqr(longside ^ 2 - short1 ^ 2)
    Else
        If Not(IsMissing(short2)) And Not(IsMissing(longside)) Then
            Triangle = Sqr(longside ^ 2 - short2 ^ 2)
        Else
            Triangle = "Please supply two arguments."
        End If
    End If
    End If
End Function
```

The first statement names the custom function and the optional arguments *short1*, *short2*, and *longside*. The following block of code contains a series of If statements that use the VBA IsMissing function to test whether each possible pair of arguments has been supplied and to calculate and return the length of the unknown side:

```
    If Not(IsMissing(short1)) And Not (IsMissing(short2)) Then

        Triangle = Sqr(short1 ^ 2 + short2 ^ 2)
```

This code tests for the presence of *short1* and *short2*. The IsMissing function returns True if the argument has not been supplied. If *short1* is not missing and *short2* is not missing, Excel computes the square root of the sum of the squares of the two short sides and returns the length of the hypotenuse to the worksheet.

If fewer than two arguments are supplied, the following statement returns a text string to the worksheet:

```
Triangle = "Please supply two arguments."
```

Now let's see what happens when we use this custom function in a worksheet formula. The formula =**Triangle(3,4)** returns 5.

The *longside* argument is omitted, so the function returns the square root of $(3^2 + 4^2)$. You could also write the formula =**Triangle(3,4,)**, but the second comma is not necessary. The formula =**Triangle(,4,5)** returns 3, because the *short1* argument is omitted. The formula =**Triangle (4,,5)** also returns 3.

The function as written has at least two flaws. First, if the user supplies all three arguments, the function behaves as though the third argument were omitted. You might prefer to have it return an error message. Second, the function accepts negative and zero arguments, even though triangles cannot have sides of negative or zero length.

You can eliminate the first of these defects by adding the following If … End If block immediately after the Function statement:

```
If Not(IsMissing(short1)) And Not(IsMissing(short2)) And _
    Not(IsMissing(longside)) Then
    Triangle = "Please supply only two arguments."
    Exit Function
End If
```

Note that this block includes an Exit Function statement. This saves the function the trouble of finding the missing argument when it has already discovered that none are missing.

You can use a similar If … End If construction to check for arguments less than or equal to zero, returning an appropriate error message and exiting the function if any are found. Note that other kinds of inappropriate arguments (text, for example) will cause the function to return one of Excel's built-in error constants. If you call the function and offer a text argument, the function returns #VALUE! because it attempts to perform arithmetic operations on a nonarithmetic value.

How much "error trapping" you add to your custom functions depends, of course, on how much work you want to do and how you plan to use the function. If you're writing a function for your personal use, you might not need to deal with every conceivable aberrant use. If you write the function for others, you'll probably want to eliminate all possibility of error—or at least to try to do so.

Making Your Custom Functions Available Anywhere

To use a custom function, the workbook containing the module in which you create the function must be open. If that workbook is not open, you get a #NAME? error when you try to use the function. Even if the workbook is open, if you use the function in a different workbook, you must precede the function name with the name of the workbook in which the function resides. For example, if you create a function called Discount in a workbook called Personal.xls, and you call that function from another workbook, you must write =**personal.xls!Discount**(), not simply =**Discount**().

You can save yourself some keystrokes (and possible typing errors) by selecting your custom functions from the Insert Function dialog box. (Your custom functions appear in the User Defined category.) An easier way to make your custom functions available at all times is to store them in a separate workbook and then save that workbook as an add-in (an XLA file) in your XLSTART folder. (The XLSTART folder is a subfolder of the folder containing your Excel files. When you start Excel, the program opens any documents it finds in XLSTART.) To save a workbook as an add-in, choose File, Save As (or File, Save). Then choose Microsoft Excel Add-in from the Files Of Type list.

If your user-defined functions are stored in an XLA file that is present in memory, you don't have to specify the name of that file when you call a function. If the XLA file is saved in your XLSTART folder, it will be present in memory whenever you run Excel.

A Sample Visual Basic Application

In the preceding two chapters, you learned to record macros and edit them and to create and use custom functions. Those chapters presented enough of the VBA programming language to get a job done. We hope we've demonstrated that working with VBA in Microsoft Excel isn't difficult and that you don't have to belong to the secret society of those fluent in programming esoterica to get started with the language.

Perhaps the best way to begin learning a programming language, or any other kind of language, is to jump in and start reading it. By analyzing VBA code that has already been written or recorded, in the context of a well-defined task, you can more easily understand the correspondence between the code and the task.

In this chapter, you'll take a high-speed reconnaissance flight over the terrain. You'll use a few macros and custom functions as examples that together attempt to solve a problem—transferring data to an Excel worksheet, working with text files, formatting the resulting data, plotting a chart from the data, and finally preparing and printing a report in Microsoft Word. Along the way, the examples will illustrate the range and power of the VBA language for formatting worksheets and charts, modifying the user interface in various ways (you'll create a custom dialog box to gather information from the user), and even operating another application that supports VBA (Microsoft Word).

Creating a VBA Application

Let's say you're measuring the amount of water flowing in the Skagit River in Western Washington, as part of a larger study among people collaborating to develop a model for flood control in the Skagit River Watershed. Others in your group are measuring river depth daily and publishing the data as a file at a Microsoft SharePoint Team Services site. The file, RiverData.txt, contains the dates of the measurements at four sites along the Skagit River. Your Excel application transfers this data from the SharePoint site to your computer, appends it to a list of pre-existing measurements, creates a new chart from the data, and uses Word to prepare and print a report that contains the data and chart. This all happens at a predetermined time, 2:00 A.M., so the printed report is ready for you when you come into the office in the morning.

We'll call this solution the RiverReport project, which is a collection of worksheets, a custom-defined dialog box (in VBA this is called a *userform*), macros, and functions— all contained in one workbook.

Loading a Workbook Automatically

To ensure that the menu command that we'll create for starting the RiverReport Project is always available, you can store the workbook in which the menu command is defined in the XLStart folder. As you know, Excel opens any files in the XLStart folder each time you start Excel.

The XLStart folder needs to be a subfolder of the folder containing your Excel system files. If you're not sure where that is—or if you're not sure that you have an XLStart folder there, follow these steps:

1 Click the Windows Start button and choose Search, For Files Or Folders. Search your local hard drives for the file Excel.exe.

2 When Excel.exe appears in the Search Results window, right-click it and choose Open Containing Folder from the shortcut menu.

3 Now you have a Windows Explorer folder showing the folder that contains your Excel system files. If you do not see an XLStart subfolder listed there, create one. Right-click in the Windows Explorer window and choose New, Folder from the shortcut menu. Name the new folder **XLStart**.

4 Open XLStart in Windows Explorer. Right-click in Windows Explorer, and choose New, Microsoft Excel Worksheet from the shortcut menu. Name the new file **RiverReport.xls**, and double-click its entry in Windows Explorer to open the new file in Excel.

Now that you have your XLStart\RiverReport.xls file, set up the workbook as shown in Figure 33-1.

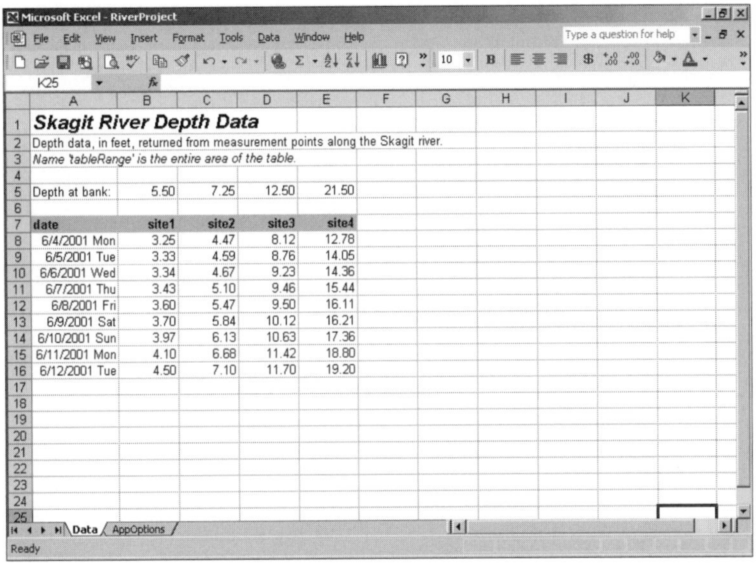

Figure 33-1. The Data worksheet contains information returned from remote measurement sites.

You also need a folder in which to store the finished RiverReport.doc file, the Word document that will contain your formatted data and chart. This application uses C:\RiverReport. You can use a different folder if you want, but you need to specify the location on the AppOptions worksheet, described later in this chapter. Use Windows Explorer to create a RiverReport folder now.

Declaring Public Variables

The RiverReport project uses seven variables that contain information needed by the macros. These variables specify the location of the files used by the project, the URL of the SharePoint site, and so on. You need to declare these variables in a VBA module. *Declaring* a variable reserves memory for that variable. When you declare a variable, you can also specify its data type. Normally, it's a good idea to specify the data type, because doing so can save memory and make your code run more quickly. For the sake of simplicity, we'll omit this step. If you don't specify a data type, VBA uses the *variant* type.

In Excel, press Alt+F11 to open the Visual Basic Editor (VBE). Then choose Insert, Module to create a new module. Your VBE should look similar to the one shown in Figure 33-2 on the next page.

Project Explorer   Properties window   Code window

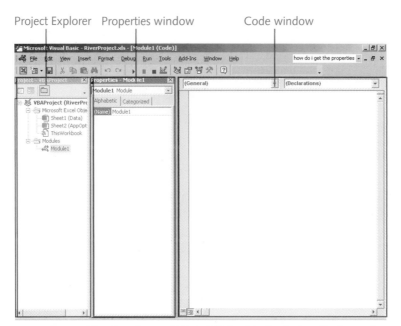

Figure 33-2.   The Visual Basic Editor (VBE) with the Project Explorer, the Properties window, and the Code window.

The Code Window, where you enter VBA code, is the empty window on the right. The window on the left is the Project Explorer. If you don't see this window, press Ctrl+R to display it. The Project Explorer displays the names of open workbooks and modules. If you have other workbooks open, in addition to RiverProject, their names appear here. The window in the center is the Properties window, which displays the names and other properties associated with items you work with in the VBE. If you don't see the Properties window on your system, press F4.

On your screen, the three windows shown in Figure 33-2 might be laid out differently. The layout is not important, and you can rearrange windows with your mouse to suit your needs. On your system, you might see other windows in addition to the ones shown in Figure 33-2. To give yourself more working room, close any others by clicking their Close boxes.

Rename the module you'll be working in before you begin declaring public variables. The Project Explorer lists modules in alphabetical order, and it will be clearer to have your modules listed in the order in which their component macros will be executed. (You can put all your macros in one module if you want to, but we'll put them in separate modules to keep the organization of the project clearer.)

To rename Module1, double-click Module1 in the Properties window (press F4 if the Properties window isn't visible). Then type **AMainCode**. If you want more screen space for the Code window, you can click the Project window's Close button.

Chapter 33

Next enter the following variable declarations in the Code window for the AMainCode module:

```
Public localPath 'Where to store downloaded data
Public docname 'Name of file to download
Public SPpath 'Path to SharePoint site
Public WordDocPath 'Path to Word report
Public startTime 'When to download data
Public MyAppVersion 'RiverReport version number
Public chartSheetName 'Name of chart sheet
```

Using the Public keyword in a VBA variable declaration makes the variable available to all modules in the workbook.

Programming the Main Sequence

The following procedures make up the main tasks in the RiverReport project, in order of execution.

1   Transfer a text file containing a series of recent river depth measurements from a SharePoint site to a folder on your computer. The file will be called RiverData.txt.

2   Open the text file from a macro, select its contents, copy them, and then paste them at the end of an existing series of measurements in the sheet called Data.

3   Format the table containing the data.

4   Create a chart from the table containing the data.

5   Control Word from Excel to create a new report to receive the table and chart.

6   Copy the table and chart in Excel, switch to Word, and then paste them into the new report.

7   Save and print the new report.

To begin programming these tasks, enter the following routine a few lines below the area where you declared the public variables:

```
Sub MainProc()

    LoadVariables 'Load public variables
    GetRemoteData 'Download file from SharePoint site
    ImportData 'Import and convert data
    FormatData 'Format the resulting table
    CreateChart 'Create a new chart
    GenWordReport 'Create a new Word doc for report
End Sub
```

This routine calls procedures to perform the seven tasks. Of course, none of these called procedures exists yet. You'll create them as you go through this chapter.

To allow the user to run these procedures by choosing a command from a menu, you'll add a menu item associated with a procedure that manages the entire project. When you're finished, you'll package the group of routines as an add-in application that can be distributed to others.

Running a Macro Automatically

To run a macro automatically whenever you open the workbook in which it is contained, you need to create an *event procedure*, a procedure (that is, a macro) that runs in response to an event of some kind. Excel provides a long list of event types that can be associated with event procedures. You can create macros that run when a particular cell is changed, when a worksheet is activated, when a worksheet is recalculated, and so on. The event you want to "trap" for this application is the opening of the RiverProject workbook.

In the Project Explorer, double-click VBAProject(RiverProject.xls)\Microsoft Excel Objects\ThisWorkbook. (Use the outline controls to open this heading if it isn't already open.) After you do this, you see two drop-down lists at the top of the Code window. Set the first to Workbook and the second to Open. The VBE responds by displaying

```
Private Sub Workbook_Open()

End Sub
```

Between these two lines, enter

```
StartMyApp
```

Figure 33-3 shows how your VBE should look at this point.

You've created a Workbook_Open event procedure for the ThisWorkbook object. The procedure runs another procedure (which you haven't created yet) called StartMyApp. When you open RiverProject.xls, VBA will run StartMyApp.

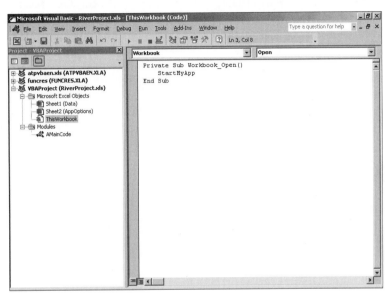

Figure 33-3. The VBE, with a Workbook_Open event procedure associated with the ThisWorkbook object.

(Note that you do need to double-click it. Selecting it isn't sufficient to change the focus of the Code window.) In the Code window, below the End Sub statement that terminates the MainProc procedure, enter the following:

```
Sub StartMyApp()
     'Make sure we want the report
     answer = Notify("Download data tonight?")
     If answer = vbOK Then
          RiverReportOptions 'Dialog box to verify settings
          Application.OnTime _
               EarliestTime:=startTime, _
               Procedure:="MainProc"
     End If
End Sub


Function Notify(msg)
     'Standard message box for RiverReport project
     btns = vbOKCancel + vbQuestion + vbDefaultButton1
     msgboxTitle = "River Depth Data Reporting System"
     Notify = MsgBox(CStr(msg), btns, msgboxTitle)
End Function
```

The StartMyApp procedure calls the Notify function, which in turn uses VBA's MsgBox function to ask the user whether to go ahead with the request. The MsgBox function creates simple dialog boxes. The first argument in the MsgBox function specifies the message to display. The *btns* variable stores a series of VBA constants (each beginning with the letters *vb*) that specify the type of buttons to display, an icon, and which of the buttons to choose if the user presses Enter. The last argument specifies the title to use on the title bar of the dialog box.

For example, the MsgBox statement in the Notify procedure displays the dialog box shown in Figure 33-4. Clicking OK causes the MsgBox function to return TRUE. Clicking Cancel, pressing Escape, or clicking the Close button causes the function to return FALSE. These logical results are then used to branch to different parts of the macro, either ending or continuing the task.

Figure 33-4. The Notify procedure displays this simple dialog box.

The Application.OnTime method runs a macro at a specified date and time—another example of an event procedure. This time the event that triggers the macro is the arrival of a specified moment in time. The *earliestTime* argument supplies a serial date value that represents the date and time at which you want the macro to run. If the value is less than 1, the specified macro runs every day.

Under some circumstances, Excel does not respond to the OnTime method as expected. If the module that contains the macro isn't open when the time arrives, Excel ignores the request. Similarly, if Excel isn't in Ready mode at the specified time or during the tolerance period, it waits until the tolerance period elapses and then cancels the macro's execution. Of course, Excel must be running at the specified time for the event to be trapped.

Using a Custom Dialog Box to Load and Save Options

When the user clicks OK in the dialog box presented by the Notify function, the RiverReport project presents the custom dialog box, titled RiverReport Options, shown in Figure 33-5. This dialog box requests verification of settings for the project. Both the current and default settings are stored on the AppOptions worksheet in the RiverReport workbook, and they are transferred to the custom dialog box. You'll create this custom dialog box in the next section, and you will also develop several VBA routines that manage the process of transferring values between the sheet, the dialog box, and the VBA code.

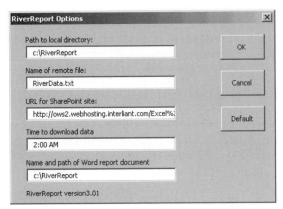

Figure 33-5. The RiverReportProject application uses this custom dialog box.

Creating an Options Sheet

First, create a sheet in the RiverReport workbook to store the current settings. This sheet will also store a set of default settings so that when the user clicks the Default button in the RiverReport Options dialog box, a routine will make the default settings the current settings.

Follow these steps:

1 Switch to the AppOptions worksheet in the RiverReport workbook. If its name is still Sheet2, rename it **AppOptions**.

2 On the sheet, enter the data shown in Figure 33-6.

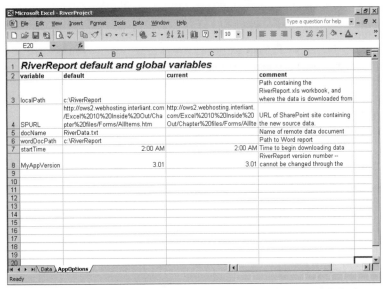

Figure 33-6. The AppOptions sheet, storing the current and default settings.

Chapter 33

3 Next, define range names on the sheet. Select range A3:C8. Then choose Insert, Name, Create. In the Create Names dialog box, make sure only the Left Column check box is selected, and then click OK.

4 Select B2:C8, choose Insert, Name, Create, and, in the Create Names dialog box, make sure only the Top Row check box is selected. Click OK.

You now have a series of names that refer to horizontal two-cell ranges on the AppOptions sheet. The name localPath, for example, is assigned to B3:C3. You also have a pair of names that refer to vertical ranges on the AppOptions sheet. The name default, for example, is assigned to B3:B8.

With these names in place, you can find a current or default setting by using Excel's intersection operator. To find the default start time, for example, you can use the formula =**default startTime**.

Creating a UserForm

Now that you have a place to store RiverReport settings from one session to the next, you need a way to present the settings to the user so they can be checked or changed as needed. To do this, use the VBE to create an object called a *userform*. A userform is a custom dialog box. Follow these steps:

1 If you're in Excel now, press Alt+F11 to switch to the VBE.

2 Choose Insert, UserForm.

A blank form with the default name UserForm1 appears, replacing the Code window. A UserForm1 entry also appears in the Project Explorer. When you click on the new form, a Toolbox window appears. Figure 33-7 illustrates these developments.

If you don't see the blank UserForm (that is, if you still see the Code window), double-click UserForm1 in the Project Explorer. If you don't see the Toolbox window, choose View, Toolbox. You'll soon be needing the Properties window. If that window isn't visible, press F4. The Properties window might arrive in a docked position that reduces the amount of space available for working with the UserForm. You can drag it into a floating position, as shown in Figure 33-7.

A new UserForm is a blank canvas on which you create various kinds of *controls*—such as text boxes, check boxes, option buttons, and command buttons. The Toolbox window is your palette of controls. The custom dialog box used by the RiverProject application employs three kinds of controls: labels, text boxes, and command buttons. To create a control on the UserForm, click the appropriate tool in the Toolbox window, and then drag out a rectangle for the control on the UserForm. The grid of dots on the blank UserForm will help you align your controls.

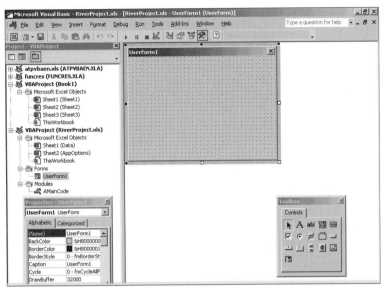

Figure 33-7. When you choose Insert, UserForm, the VBE displays a blank form in which you can create a custom dialog box.

In the next steps, you will add controls to the UserForm to create the dialog box shown in Figure 33-5. You don't have to design your dialog box to look exactly like the one in Figure 33-5, but it needs to have each of the controls shown there.

3 Click the Label tool (the large letter A in the Toolbox window), and for each label shown in Figure 33-5, drag a rectangle, select the text in the rectangle, and then enter the text shown in the figure. You should have six labels when you're finished.

4 Click the TextBox tool (the ab button) and drag a rectangle for each text box shown in Figure 33-5. You should have five text boxes when finished.

5 Click the CommandButton tool and drag a rectangle for each of the three command buttons shown in Figure 33-5. Select the text of each button and replace that text with **OK**, **Cancel**, and **Default**.

Now you need to change the Name property for several of the controls on your UserForm. To change a name property, follow these steps:

1 Select the control on the UserForm.

2 Select the text that appears next to the entry (Name) in the Properties window.

3 Type the new name for the selected control.

Name the controls as shown in Figure 33-8 on the next page. Be careful to match the names in the figure exactly. You'll use these names again in your VBA code, and if the names there don't match the names in the Properties window, your application will not run.

873

SPURL text box
Doc name text box
Local path text box

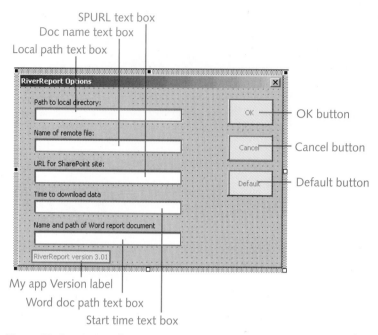

My app Version label
Word doc path text box
Start time text box

Figure 33-8. Assign these names to controls on your new UserForm.

Finally, select the UserForm itself (the title bar, or anywhere outside a control). In the Properties window, scroll down to the Caption property. Change this property to **RiverReport Options.**

Displaying the UserForm

Now that you have a custom dialog box, you need some code to make that dialog box do something useful. The code will display the dialog box and transfer information between it and the AppOptions worksheet. Follow these steps:

1 In the VBE, choose Insert, Module.

2 Press F4 to display the Properties window, if it isn't currently visible.

3 In the Project Explorer, select Module1 (the name of the new module).

4 Using the Properties window, rename the module **BOptionsCode**.

In the code window for the new BOptionsCode module, enter the following:

```
Sub RiverReportOptions
    'Set RiverReport options, stored in sheet AppOptions
    'Code for OK, Cancel, and Default are in UserForm1

    Load UserForm1
    'Get & set public variables, declared in AMainCode
    With Worksheets("AppOptions")
        'Path to directory for downloading data
        LocalPath = .Range("localPath current").Value

        'URL for SharePoint site
        SPURL = .Range("SPURL current").Value

        'Name of remote document
        docName = .Range("docName current").Value

        'Path to Word report
        wordDocPath = .Range("wordDocPath current").Value

        'Time to get data (uses Text property to
        'get the displayed date rather than
        'the underlying date value
        startTime = .Range("startTime current").Text

        'MyApp version number
        MyAppVersion = .Range("MyAppVersion current").Text
    End With

    'Assign variable values to UserForm controls
    With UserForm1
        .localPathTextBox.Value = localPath
        .SPURLTextBox.Value = SPURL
        .docNameTextBox.Value = docName
        .wordDocPathTextBox.Value = wordDocPath
        .startTimeTextBox.Value = startTime
        .MyAppVersionLabel.Caption = "RiverReport version" + _
            CStr(MyAppVersion)
    End With

    'Present the dialog box
    UserForm1.Show
End Sub
```

The first instruction in this routine

```
Load UserForm1
```

loads the UserForm object into memory prior to displaying it to the user. The statement

```
UserForm1.Show
```

displays the UserForm object. The statements between these two lines of code use the With … End construct in VBA to preload the UserForm with values transferred from the AppOptions sheet.

A Minor Problem

As long as you're in the BOptionsCode module, you need to solve one minor problem. When Excel encounters the OnTime statement in the StartMyApp routine and begins waiting for the appointed hour to retrieve the data at the remote site, it "forgets" the values of the public variables you have set. To fix this, you need to add a routine called LoadVariables that reads the current settings from the AppOptions sheet into the public variables you have declared. LoadVariables is called as the first line of executable code in the MainProc routine described on page 869. To implement this routine, place the insertion point at the end of the RiverReportOptions routine and enter the following code:

```
Sub LoadVariables()
     'Get RiverReport options, stored in sheet AppOptions

     With Worksheets("AppOptions")
             LocalPath = .Range("localPath current").Value
             SPURL = .Range("SPURL current").Value
             DocName = .Range("docName current").Value
             WordDocPath = .Range("wordDocPath current").Value
             StartTime = .Range("startTime current").Text
             MyAppVersion = .Range("MyAppVersion current").Text
     EndWith
End Sub
```

Writing UserForm Code

For each of the command buttons on the RiverForm Options dialog box, you need to write a short routine. When the user clicks a button, the associated routine will run. Follow these steps to write the routine:

1 Double-click UserForm1 in the Project Explorer to display the RiverReport Options dialog box.

2 Press F7 to display the code window for the RiverReport Options dialog box.

3 Two drop-down lists appear at the top of the code window. From the one on the left, select OKButton. From the one on the right, select Click.

4 The VBE displays a Sub statement and an End Sub statement for the OKButton_Click event. Between these statements, enter the following:

```
'Transfer info from dialog box to sheet and global
'variables. Get whatever is entered in the text boxes
'and store in worksheet as globals.
'Get and set global variables, declared in AMainCode.
'No validation of user entry in this routine.

With Worksheets("AppOptions")
    'Path to folder for downloading data
    localPath = UserForm1.localPathTextBox.Text
    .Range("localPath current").Formula = localPath

    'URL for SharePoint site
    SPURL = UserForm1.SPURLTextBox.Text
    .Range("SPURL current").Formula = SPURL

    'Name of remote document
    docName = UserForm1.docNameTextBox.Text
    .Range("docName current").Formula = docName

    'Path to Word report
    wordDocPath = UserForm1.wordDocPathTextBox.Text
    .Range("wordDocPath current").Formula = wordDocPath

    'Time to get data. Could add error checking here
    'to see if the text entered can be converted
    'into a date, using IsDate()
    startTime = Cdate(UserForm1.startTimeTextBox.Text)
    .Range("startTime current").Formula = startTime
End With
```

5 From the drop-down list above the Code window, select CancelButton. From the drop-down list on the right, select Click.

6 The VBE displays a Sub statement and an End Sub statement for the CancelButton_Click event. Between these statements, enter this code:

```
'Just hide the UserForm1 dialog without
'updating sheet or global variables.
'Global variables remain as set
UserForm1.Hide
```

7 From the drop-down list above the Code window, select DefaultButton. From the drop-down list on the right, select Click.

8 The VBE displays a Sub statement and an End Sub statement for the DefaultButton_Click event. Between these statements, enter the following code:

```
'Transfer default settings from AppOptions sheet
'to UserForm1 dialog box entries.

'Get and set global variables
'declared in AMainCode
With Worksheets("AppOptions")
        'Path to folder for downloading data
        localPath = .Range("localPath default").Text
        UserForm1.localPathTextBox.Text = localPath

        'set URL for SharePoint site
        SPURL = .Range("SPURL default").Text
        UserForm1.SPURLTextBox.Text = SPURL

        'Name of remote document
        docName = .Range("docName default").Text
        UserForm1.docNameTextBox.Text = docName

        'Path to Word report
        wordDocPath = .Range("wordDocPath default").Text
        UserForm1.wordDocPathTextBox.Text = wordDocPath

        'Time to get data - uses Text property to
        'get the displayed date
        'rather than the underlying date value.
        startTime = .Range("startTime default").Text
        UserForm1.startTimeTextBox.Value = startTime
End With
```

878

As you can see, these three routines are very similar to the RiverReportOptions routine. When the user clicks the OK button, the OKButton_Click routine takes the value entered in the dialog box and transfers it to the cell at the intersection of the range names localPath and current on the AppOptions worksheet. When all values have been transferred to the worksheet, OKButton_Click hides the form.

The CancelButton_Click is much simpler. It hides the form without updating the AppOptions worksheet.

The DefaultButton_Click routine is similar to RiverReportOptions but loads the form with values from the default column, rather than the current column, of the AppOptions worksheet.

Downloading Data from the Internet

So far the project has interrogated the user for the correct settings and waited for the time specified in the *startTime* public variable. When that time has arrived, the MainProc routine begins calling its subroutines, one after another—downloading data, updating the table, creating the chart, and so on.

The first subroutine, GetRemoteData, downloads the file stored in the *docName* variable (that is, RivrData.txt) from the SharePoint site whose URL is stored in SPURL.

> **note** The SharePoint URL listed in this chapter is only an example. It is not the address of a public site. To run this sample application, you need to substitute a site available to you. This application does not include code to make a connection to an Internet service provider. You need to ensure that you are connected to the Internet already at the time the GetRemoteData routine runs.

Choose Insert, Module to create a new module. Rename this module **CDataCode**, and then enter the following in the Code window for CdataCode:

```
Sub GetRemoteData()
    'Open file at SharePoint site
    'and save it in local folder
    Workbooks.Open FileName:=SPURL + docName

    'change to local folder
    ChDir localPath

    'save workbook in local folder
    ActiveWorkbook.SaveAs _
```

```
                          FileName:=localPath + docName, _
                          FileFormat:=xlNormal, _
                          Password:="", _
                          ReadOnlyRecommended:=False, _
                          CreateBackup:=False
    End Sub
```

Working with Text Files

Excel's Text Import Wizard does an admirable job of importing files with formats other than those native to Excel. For example, the text file of river depth measurements downloaded from the SharePoint site looks like this:

```
6/4/01      4.5     7.1     11.7    19.2
```

Each time the RivrData.txt file is accessed, there could be one or more lines of data in the form of text. Each line of text consists of the date and the measurements from each of the four sites along the river. Each item is separated from the next by a tab character.

For the RiverReport project, you need a procedure that can open and read the text for each day of data and transfer each item of data to the correct location at the end of the database that contains previously captured measurements. Figure 33-1 shows the database as it looks when we start recording the macro. Notice that data for a few days has already been entered. After the macro was recorded, it was edited to replace hard-wired file and path names with the public variables and to add comments that describe the actions taken to create the macro.

Now enter the ImportData procedure just after the GetRemoteData procedure in the CDataCode module:

```
Sub ImportData()
    'Import text file downloaded from SharePoint site
    'Go to row below table
    Windows("RiverReport.xls").Activate
    Application.Goto Reference:="tableRange"
    Selection.Offset(Selection.Rows.Count,0).Range("A1").Select

    'Set Text Import Wizard options
    Workbooks.OpenText _
            FileName:=localPath + docName, _
            Origin:=Windows, _
            StartRow:=1, _
            DataType:=xlDelimited, _
            TextQualifier:=xlDoubleQuote, _
```

```
                    ConsecutiveDelimiter:=True, _
                    Tab:=True, _
                    FieldInfo:=Array(Array(1, 3), Array(2, 1), _
                    Array(3, 1), Array(4, 1), Array(5, 1))

            'Copy all the new data in the sheet,
            'switch to RiverReport.xls, and paste it in new row
            Range("A1").CurrentRegion.Select
            Selection.Copy
            Windows("RiverReport.xls").Activate
            ActiveSheet.Paste

            'Redefine tableRange to include new data
            'so that chart code can find it.
            Selection.CurrentRegion.Name = "tableRange"

            'Close source data file
            Windows(docName).Close
    End Sub
```

Formatting a Worksheet

You need a tiny routine to apply the appropriate formats to the table range. Add this below the ImportData procedure in the module CdataCode:

```
Sub FormatData()
Columns("A:A").NumberFormat = "m/d/yyyy ddd"
Columns("B:E").NumberFormat = "0.00"
End Sub
```

Creating a Chart

Next you need to create and format a chart. In the VBE, choose Insert, Module to create a new module. Rename this module **DChartCode**. Then add the following to DChartCode's Code window:

```
Sub CreateChart()
    'Create a chart from tableRange
    Charts.Add
    With ActiveChart
        .ChartType = xlLineMarkers
```

```
        .SetSourceData _
            Source:=Sheets("Data").Range("tableRange"), _
            PlotBy:=xlColumns
        .HasTitle = True
        .ChartTitle.Characters.Text = "Skagit River Depth Data"
        .Axes(xlValue).HasTitle = True
        .Axes(xlValue).AxisTitle.Characters.Text _
            = "Depth, in feet"
            .HasTitle = True
    End With

    'Format the value axis title
    With ActiveChart.Axes(xlValue).AxisTitle.Font
        .Name = "Arial"
        .FontStyle = "Bold"
        .Size = 14
    End With

    'Format the main title
    With ActiveChart.ChartTitle.Font
        .Name = "Arial"
        .FontStyle = "Bold"
        .Size = 16
    End With

    'Format the category axis
    With ActiveChart.Axes(xlCategory)
        .MajorTickMark = xlNone
        .TickLabels.Font.Name = "Arial"
        .TickLabels.Font.Size = 12
    End With

    'Format the legend
    With ActiveChart.Legend.Font
        .Name = "Arial"
        .Size = 12
    End With
End Sub
```

Generating a Report in Word

Finally the application needs to start Word, create a new Word document, copy data and chart into this new document, and then save and print the Word document. In the routine you're about to create, you'll be using a feature of VBA called *automation*. Automation lets you work with applications, other than Excel, that support VBA.

Because you're about to enter code to control Word, you might want to begin by choosing Tools, References and selecting Microsoft Word 10.0 Object Library. This step isn't required to make your code run, but it will make the VBA Help files for Word available to you as you work.

Next choose Insert, Module, rename the module **EWordCode**, and then enter the following into the Code window for the new module:

```
Sub GenWordReport()
    'control Word from Excel, creating new report
    'for Excel table and chart

    Dim wordApp As Object
    Set wordApp = CreateObject("word.application")

    'make Word visible for debugging
    wordApp.Visible = True

    'Create a new Word document
    wordApp.documents.Add

    With wordApp.Selection
        'Enter document title
        .TypeText Text:="Data Collection Report"
        .Style = wordApp.ActiveDocument.Styles("Heading 1")
        .TypeParagraph

        'Enter creation date of document
        .TypeText Text:="Received "
        .InsertDateTime
        .TypeParagraph

        'Enter heading for raw data, in Heading 2 style
        .TypeText Text:="The Data"
        .Style = wordApp.ActiveDocument.Styles("Heading 2")
        .TypeParagraph
    End With
```

883

```
'Create bookmark for raw data table
wordApp.ActiveDocument.Bookmarks.Add _
    Range:=wordApp.Selection.Range, _
    Name:="dataTable"

'Move down two lines and enter heading for charted data
With wordApp.Selection
    .TypeParagraph
    .TypeParagraph
    .TypeText Text:="Charted Data"
    .Style = wordApp.ActiveDocument.Styles("Heading 2")
    .TypeParagraph
End With

'Create bookmark for data chart
wordApp.ActiveDocument.Bookmarks.Add _
    Range:=wordApp.Selection.Range, _
    Name:="dataChart"

'Copy Excel table as picture
Sheets("Data").Select
Range("tableRange").CopyPicture _
    Appearance:=xlScreen, _
    Format:=xlPicture

'Paste into "dataTable" in Word doc
wordApp.Selection.Goto Name:="dataTable"
wordApp.Selection.Paste

'Select chart and copy as picture
Sheets(chartSheetName).Select
ActiveChart.CopyPicture _
    Appearance:=xlScreen, _
    Format:=xlPicture

'Paste into "dataChart" in Word doc
wordApp.Selection.Goto Name:="dataChart"
wordApp.Selection.Paste

'change to localPath directory
wordApp.ChangeFileOpenDirectory localPath
```

```
'save report
wordApp.ActiveDocument.SaveAs _
    Filename:="Data Collection Report.doc"

'print the document
wordApp.ActiveDocument.PrintOut
End Sub
```

Unless you want to modify this application to perform some task that's actually useful to you, you'll probably want to move it out of your XLStart folder. Otherwise, each time you start Excel you'll be asked whether you want to download data tonight. A copy of the application is included in the Author Extras section of the CD that accompanies this book.

Debugging Macros and Custom Functions

If you have made it through the last three chapters, you now have at least a smattering of Microsoft Visual Basic for Applications (VBA) at your command—as well as, we hope, an appetite for learning more. The best ways to acquire more expertise in this versatile programming language are to read a text on the subject (such as *Microsoft Excel 2000/Visual Basic for Applications Fundamentals*, from Microsoft Press) and to experiment. As you do your everyday work in Microsoft Excel, look for chores that are ripe for automating. When you come-across something macro-worthy, record your actions. Then inspect the code generated by the macro recorder. Make sure you understand what the recorder has given you (read the Help text for any statements you don't understand), and see whether you can find ways to make the code more efficient. Eliminate statements that appear unnecessary, and then see whether the code still does what you expect it to do. Look for statements that select ranges or other objects, and see whether you can make your code perform the essential tasks without first selecting those objects.

As you experiment, and as you create larger and more complex macros and functions, you will undoubtedly produce some code that either doesn't run at all or doesn't give you the result you're looking for. Missteps of this kind are an inevitable part of the learning process. (They're also an inherent part of programming, even for experts.) Fortunately, the VBA language and the Visual Basic Editor (VBE) provide tools to help you trap errors and root out bugs. Those tools are the subject of this chapter.

In this chapter, you look at two kinds of error-catching tools: those that help you at *design time*, when you're creating or editing code, and those that work at *run time*, while the code is running.

Using Design-Time Tools

The VBE's design-time error tools let you correct mistakes in VBA syntax and catch misspellings of variable names. They also let you follow the "flow" of a macro or function (seeing each line of code as it is executed) and monitor the values of variables during the course of a procedure's execution.

Catching Syntax Errors

If you enter a worksheet formula incorrectly in Excel, Excel alerts you to the error and refuses to accept the entry. The VBA *compiler* (the system component that converts your English-like VBA code into machine language) normally performs the same service for you if you enter a VBA expression incorrectly. If you omit a required parenthesis, for example, the compiler beeps as soon as you press Enter. It also presents an error message and displays the offending line of code in a contrasting color (red, by default).

Certain kinds of syntax errors don't become apparent to the compiler until you attempt to run your code. For example, if you write the following:

```
With Selection.Border
        .Weight = xlThin
        .LineStyle = xlAutomatic
```

and attempt to run this code without including an End With statement, you will see this error message.

Your procedure will halt, and you will be in *break mode*. (You can tell you're in break mode by the appearance of the word break, in brackets, in the VBE title bar. The line that the compiler was attempting to execute will be highlighted—by default, in yellow.) Break mode lets you fix your code and then continue running it. For example, if you omit an End With statement, you can add that statement while in break mode, and then press F5 (or choose Run, Continue) to go on with the show. If you want to exit from break mode, rather than continue with the execution of your procedure, choose Run, Reset.

If you don't like having the compiler complain about obvious syntax errors the moment you commit them, you can turn that functionality off. Choose Tools, Options, click the Editor tab (shown in Figure 34-1), and clear the Auto Syntax Check check box. With automatic syntax checking turned off, your syntax errors will still be flagged when you try to run your code.

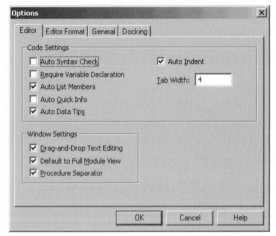

Figure 34-1. Clear Auto Syntax Check if you don't want to know about syntax errors until you run your code.

---

tip   **Change color with the Options dialog box**

You can also use the Options dialog box to change the color that the VBE uses to highlight syntax errors. If you don't like red, click the Editor Format tab, select Syntax Error Text in the code Colors list, and choose a different color.

Auto Syntax Check is on by default. So are three other "auto" options—Auto List Members, Auto Quick Info, and Auto Data Tips. These are all useful, and you should leave them on, especially if you're a relative newcomer to VBA. Auto List Members and Auto Quick Info help you complete a line of VBA code by displaying options available at the current insertion point or the names of arguments required by the function you're currently entering. Auto Data Tips is relevant only in break mode. If you hover your mouse cursor over a variable name in break mode, the Auto Data Tips feature displays the current value of that variable as a ScreenTip.

Catching Misspelled Variable Names

The VBA compiler doesn't care about the capitalization style of your variable names. *MyVar*, *myVar*, and *myvar* are identical names as far as the compiler is concerned. (If you're inconsistent about the capitalization of a variable name, the VBE adjusts all instances of that variable to make them look the same.) If you change the spelling of a variable name in mid-program, however, the compiler creates a new variable—and havoc for your program. An error in programming introduced by a misspelled variable can be especially treacherous because the program might appear to behave normally.

You can virtually eliminate the possibility of inconsistently spelled variable names in a module by adding a single statement at the top of that module (above any Sub or Function statements):

```
Option Explicit
```

The Option Explicit statement forces you to *declare* any variables used in the current module. You declare variables with Dim statements. (For the complete details about Dim, type **Dim** in a module and press F1.) With Option Explicit in place, if you use a variable without first declaring it, you get a Compile Error at run time. If you accidentally misspell a variable name somewhere in your program, the misspelled variable will be flagged by the compiler as an undeclared variable, and you'll be able to fix the problem forthwith.

You can add Option Explicit to every new module you create by choosing Tools, Options, clicking the Editor tab, and selecting Require Variable Declaration. This option is off by default, but it's good programming practice to turn it on. Option Explicit will do more for you than eliminate misspelled variable names. By forcing you to declare your variables, it will also encourage you to think ahead as you work.

Stepping Through Code

The VBE's step commands cause the compiler to execute either a single instruction or a limited set of instructions and then pause in break mode, highlighting the next instruction that will be executed. Execution is suspended until you take another action—such as issuing another step command, resuming normal execution, or terminating execution. By issuing step commands repeatedly, you can follow the procedure's execution path. You can see, for example, which way the program branches when it comes to an If statement, or which of the alternative paths it takes when it encounters a Select Case structure. (A Select Case structure causes the program to execute one of a set of alternative statements, depending on the value of a particular variable. For details, type **case** in a module and press F1.) You can also examine the values of variables at each step along the way.

> **tip**   **Monitor variable value**
>
> You can monitor the value of variables by displaying the Watch window or the Quick Watch dialog box, or by hovering your mouse cursor over particular variables while in break mode. For information about using the Watch window, see "Using the Watch Window to Monitor Variable Values and Object Properties" on page 893.

You have four step commands at your disposal. You'll find these commands—and their keyboard shortcuts—on the Debug menu:

- **Step Into** executes the next instruction only.

- **Step Over** works like Step Into unless the next instruction is a call to another procedure. In that case, Step Into executes the entire called procedure as a unit.

- **Step Out** executes the remaining steps of the current procedure.

- **Run To Cursor** executes everything up to the current cursor position.

You can run an entire procedure one step at a time by pressing F8 (the keyboard shortcut for Debug, Step Into) repeatedly. To begin stepping through a procedure at a particular instruction, move your cursor to that instruction and press Ctrl+F8 (the shortcut for Debug, Run To Cursor). Alternatively, you can force the compiler to enter break mode when it reaches a particular instruction, and then use any of the step commands.

Setting Breakpoints with the Toggle Breakpoint Command

A *breakpoint* is an instruction that causes the compiler to halt execution and enter break mode. The simplest way to set a breakpoint is to put your cursor where you want the breakpoint and choose Debug, Toggle Breakpoint (or press F9). Choose this command a second time to clear a breakpoint. You can set as many breakpoints in a procedure as you like using this method. The Toggle Breakpoint command sets an *unconditional* breakpoint—one that will always occur when execution arrives at the breakpoint. To set a *conditional* breakpoint—one that takes effect only under a specified condition—see the next section.

As Figure 34-2 on the next page shows, the VBE highlights a line where you've set a breakpoint in a contrasting color and displays a large bullet in the left margin of the Code window. To customize the highlighting color, choose Tools, Options, click the Editor Format tab, and select Breakpoint Text.

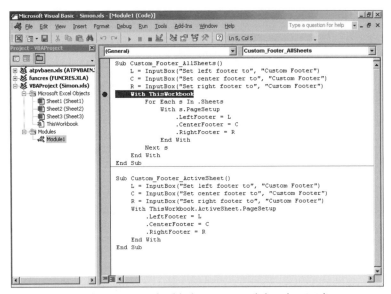

Figure 34-2. The VBE uses highlighting to mark breakpoint lines.

Setting Conditional Breakpoints Using Debug.Assert

With the Assert method of the Debug object, you can cause the VBA compiler to enter break mode only if a particular expression generates a FALSE result. Figure 34-3 provides a simple example.

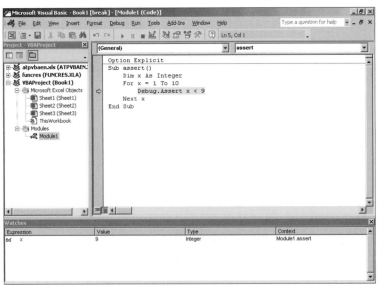

Figure 34-3. This Debug.Assert statement puts the compiler in break mode when the value of *x* becomes 9 or greater.

The Debug.Assert statement in this otherwise useless bit of code asserts that *x* is less than 9. As long as that assertion is true, the procedure runs. When it becomes false, the compiler enters break mode. As the Watch window in Figure 34-3 shows, the compiler enters break mode when *x* is equal to 9. (The Watch window is discussed next.)

You can also use the Watch window to set conditional breakpoints. See "Setting Conditional Breakpoints with the Watch Window" on page 895.

Using the Watch Window to Monitor Variable Values and Object Properties

The Watch window shows the current values of selected variables or expressions and the current property settings for selected objects. You can use the Watch window to monitor the status of variables and objects as you step through a procedure.

In Figure 34-3, the Watch window shows a single variable, *x*. Figure 34-4 shows a Watch window monitoring eight variables. The first four of these are *object variables*—variables set to various worksheet ranges. Because objects have properties, the Watch window displays outline controls beside the names of these variables. Opening an outline control reveals an object's property settings, as Figure 34-5 shows on the next page.

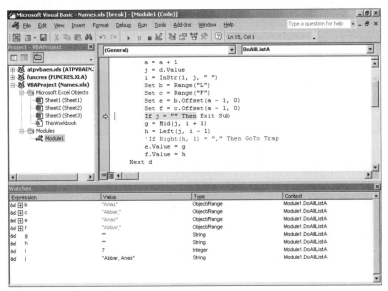

Figure 34-4. You can monitor the status of variables and objects in the Watch window.

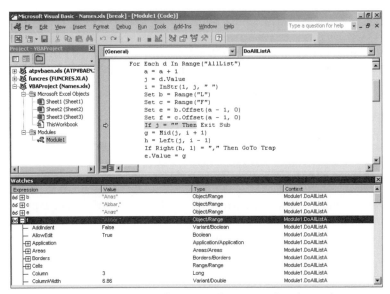

Figure 34-5. Opening an outline control associated with an object or object variable reveals that object's properties.

To display the Watch window, choose View, Watch Window. (To close the window, click its Close button.) To add a variable or object to the Watch window, you can select it in the Code window and drag it into the Watch window. You can add expressions, such as *a + 1*, to the Watch window in this manner. Alternatively, you can add something to the Watch window by choosing Debug, Add Watch. In the Expression box of the Add Watch dialog box (see Figure 34-6), type a variable name or other valid VBA expression.

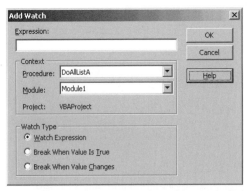

Figure 34-6. You can use the Add Watch dialog box to add a watch variable or set a conditional breakpoint.

Setting Conditional Breakpoints with the Watch Window

As Figure 34-6 shows, you can use the Add Watch dialog box to set a conditional breakpoint. Choose Debug, Add Watch, specify the name of a variable or a VBA expression, and then select either Break When Value Is True or Break When Value Changes. Selecting Break When Value Is True for an expression is comparable to using a Debug.Assert statement to set a conditional breakpoint. The difference is that Debug.Assert causes a break when an expression becomes false, and the Break When Value Is True option does the opposite.

Using Quick Watch to Monitor a Variable or Add a Watch Item

In break mode you can select any variable name or expression in your code and choose Debug, Quick Watch (or press Shift + F9) to see the current value of the selected item. If you decide you want to monitor that item continuously, you can click Add in the Quick Watch dialog box. The VBE then adds the item to the Watch window.

Using the Immediate Window

While in break mode, or before running a procedure, you can execute any VBA statement in the Immediate window. (If the Immediate window isn't visible, choose View, Immediate Window or press Ctrl+G.) For example, you can find out the value of a variable x by typing **Print x** in the Immediate window. (As a shortcut, you can type **?x**. The question-mark character is a synonym for Print in VBA.)

You can also use the Immediate window to monitor action in a procedure while that procedure is running. You do this by inserting Debug.Print statements into the procedure. The statement Debug.Print x, for example, displays the current value of x in the Immediate window.

The Immediate window can be a handy place to test VBA statements while you're still wrestling with the syntax of this programming language. If you're not sure that a particular statement will have the effect that you intend, you can try it out in the Immediate window and see what happens.

Chapter 34

Dealing with Run-Time Errors

In many cases, run-time errors are caused by factors outside your control. For example, suppose you have written the following macro to format the numbers in a selected range using the Indian system of lakhs and crores:

```
Sub LakhsCrores()
    For Each cell In Selection
        If Abs(cell.Value) > 10000000 Then
            cell.NumberFormat = "#"","""##"","""##"","""###"
        ElseIf Abs(cell.Value) > 100000 Then
            cell.NumberFormat = "##"","""##"","""###"
        End If
    Next cell
End Sub
```

This macro works fine if the person who runs it selects a range containing numbers before running the macro. But if the user selects something else—a chart, for example—VBA displays the error message shown here.

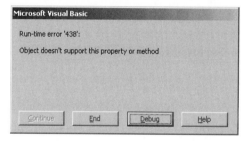

The macro generates run-time error 438 and enters break mode because the For Each statement has to be applied to a collection or an array, and a chart object is neither. (A range is a collection of cells, so For Each does work with a range.) Even though you can figure out easily enough what the error message means and what you have to do about it (try again with a range selected), the message might still be annoying. If you intend for this macro to be used by someone else, it's definitely impolite to let that other user see such a message.

You can "trap" an error like this—that is, shield yourself and others from VBA's run-time error messages—by means of an On Error Goto statement. The statement must appear before the code that might cause a run-time error, and it has the following syntax, where *label* is a name that identifies an error-handling section elsewhere in your program:

```
On Error Goto label
```

If a run-time error occurs, the On Error Goto statement transfers execution to the error-handling code. In the case of your LakhsCrores routine, the macro complete with error handling might look like this:

```
Sub LakhsCrores()
    'Catch run-time error caused by inappropriate selection
    On Error GoTo Errorhandler

    For Each cell In Selection
        If Abs(cell.Value) > 10000000 Then
            cell.NumberFormat = "#"",""##"",""##"",""###"
        ElseIf Abs(cell.Value) > 100000 Then
            cell.NumberFormat = "##"",""##"",""###"
        End If
    Next cell

    'Exit sub statement keeps execution from entering
 'error handler if no error occurs
        Exit Sub

'Error handler
Errorhandler:
    MsgBox "Please select a worksheet range"
End Sub
```

Notice that the error handler goes at the end of the program, introduced by the label that appeared in the On Error statement. The label must be followed by a colon and must appear on a line by itself. An Exit Sub statement appears before the error handler. This statement terminates the macro when no run-time error occurs; without it, execution would "fall into" the error handler regardless of whether an error occurred. Now when the user runs the macro after selecting a chart object, the user sees a polite message box instead of a rude VBA run-time error message.

The macro still has a problem, however. The code works fine when the selected worksheet range includes numbers, text, or blank cells. If it includes a cell containing an Excel error constant, such as #NA, however, a different run-time error occurs—error number 13, Type Mismatch. The message box generated by the error handler shown previously would not be appropriate for this kind of error.

How do you make your code show one message for a non-range selection and another for a range that includes one or more error values? You use the Number property of the Err object. This property is always set to the most recent run-time error number (or 0, if no procedure is running or if no error has occurred). You could handle both run-time errors (438 and 13) with the following code:

```
ErrorHandler:
    If Err.Number=438 Then
    MsgBox "Please select a worksheet range"
    Else
        MsgBox "Please select a range without error values"
    End If
```

In case the code is susceptible to some other run-time error that you haven't antici-pated, you might want to make the handler look like this:

```
ErrorHandler:
    If Err.Number = 438 Then
    MsgBox "Please select a worksheet range"
    ElseIf Err.Number = 13 Then
        MsgBox "Please select a range without error values"
    Else
        MsgBox "Sorry! Unknown error!"
    End If
```

This isn't particularly elegant, but at least you've got all the bases more-or-less covered.

The foregoing error-handler examples assume that your program should terminate when a run-time error occurs. The purpose of the error handler is to prevent the jolt-ing VBA message from showing up—and to provide the user with a simple explanation of what has gone wrong.

In some cases you'll want your procedure to continue running after a run-time error occurs. In such a case, your error handler needs to return VBA to the appropriate instruction so that it can continue executing your program. Use either a Resume or Resume Next statement to do this. A Resume statement causes VBA to re-execute the line that caused the error. A Resume Next statement causes VBA to continue at the line that follows the line that caused the error.

By combining On Error with Resume Next, you can tell VBA to ignore any run-time error that might occur and go to the next statement. If you're sure you've anticipated all the kinds of run-time errors that might occur with your program, On Error Resume Next can often be the simplest and most effective way to deal with potential mishaps. In the LakhsCrores macro, for example, you can write the following:

```
Sub LakhsCrores()
    'Tell VBA to ignore all run-time errors
    On Error Resume Next

    For Each cell In Selection
        If Abs(cell.Value) > 10000000 Then
            cell.NumberFormat = "#"","""##"","""##"",""""###"
        ElseIf Abs(cell.Value) > 100000 Then
            cell.NumberFormat = "##"","""##"",""""###"
        End If
    Next cell
  Exit Sub
```

With this code, if the user selects a chart and runs the macro, the run-time error is ignored, the program moves on to the For Each block, and nothing happens—because nothing can happen. If the user selects a range containing one or more error values, the program skips over those cells that it can't format and formats the ones it can. In all cases, neither error message nor message box appears, and all is well. This solution is ideal for this particular macro.

Of course, when you use On Error Resume Next, you're disabling VBA's run-time checking altogether. You should do this only when you're sure you've thought of everything that could possibly go awry—and the best way to arrive at that serene certainty is to test, test, and then test some more.

Part 11

Appendixes

Installing Microsoft Excel

With every new version of Microsoft Office, the installation process gets easier for Microsoft Excel and all the Office programs. It might not seem that way, however, because every new version usually takes longer to install and eats up more hard-disk space. For most of this appendix, we'll assume that you purchased Excel 2002 as part of a Microsoft Office XP package, which is how most of us get Excel these days, and that you're installing Office from the distribution CD.

> **caution**   You should exercise caution and a bit of healthy pessimism before starting the installation of any new software program. You never know what might happen. To be safe, back up important data files before proceeding.

System Requirements

There are too many different configurations of Office to provide system requirements for each. Instead, we'll list general requirements and provide some specifics for Excel in case you purchased a standalone version. For specifics about your Office package and operating system requirements, see the documentation provided in the Office XP software box.

> **note**   Sometimes it's more helpful to tell you what you *can't* use. None of the new Office XP suites or their component standalone applications will run on the Microsoft Windows 3.x, Microsoft Windows NT 3.5x, or Microsoft Windows 95 operating systems. If your computer is currently running one of these, you must upgrade the operating system before installing.

To install Office XP, your computer must have the following:

- Microsoft Windows 98, Microsoft Windows NT 4.0 with Service Pack 6a, Microsoft Windows 2000, Microsoft Windows Millennium Edition (Me), or any later editions or Service Pack upgrades for these systems.

> **note** The Office Setup program also installs Microsoft Internet Explorer 5.1 (except on Windows 2000 or Windows Me or higher operating system versions, because Internet Explorer 5.1 is already installed with these operating systems). If you prefer to use an earlier version of Internet Explorer, you can turn off the default installation using a customized Setup. Office requires Internet Explorer 4.01 with Service Pack 1 (the version first released with Microsoft Windows 98). Any later version of Internet Explorer will also work correctly.

- A Pentium 133 MHz processor. Speech recognition features require a faster processor, as we discuss later in this appendix.

- The memory requirements specified for your operating system, plus 8 MB per application running simultaneously. Speech recognition features also require more memory. Operating system memory requirements are, for example, 24 MB for Windows 98, 32 MB for Windows Me or Windows NT, 64 MB for Windows 2000 Professional, and 256 MB for Windows 2000 Server.

- Varying hard-disk space, depending on your Office configuration and operating system. For example, space requirements range from 260 MB to 675 MB for the different versions of Office XP running under Windows 2000. To install a standalone version of Excel, you need a maximum of 180 MB, and as little as 140 MB if you are running Windows 2000, Windows Me, or have previously installed Office 2000 Service Release 1.

- At least 4 MB of space available in the registry (Windows NT and Windows 2000 only).

- An additional 50 MB of hard-disk space for each language version of the user interface you install. You should install the same language version of Office as the operating system you have installed.

- 115 MB on the operating system drive for the Office system files, if you install Office on a different drive than the one where your operating system files reside.

- An additional 100 MB of hard-disk space for use by the Windows swap file.

- A CD-ROM drive.

- A VGA or higher-resolution monitor—SVGA recommended.

- A mouse or other pointing device.

Additional Requirements and Recommendations

The following are requirements and recommendations for specific features:

- **Modem/Internet access.** (Required for Web features and sending/routing features.) Minimum 9600 baud modem—14,400 baud recommended.

- **E-mail features.** Microsoft Exchange, Internet SMTP/POP3, IMAP4, or other MAPI-compliant messaging software.

- **Multimedia.** (Required for sounds and other multimedia effects.) An accelerated video card or MMX processor is recommended.

- **Speech recognition.** For all operating systems, the recommended hardware requirements increase to a Pentium 400 MHz (or higher) processor and a minimum of 128 MB of RAM. Any microphone compatible with your computer's sound system is acceptable, but the recommended microphone is a high-quality, close-talk type, preferably a headset where the microphone element can be located within four inches of the speaker's mouth. A USB microphone, with which a sound card is not required, is highly recommended.

- **Handwriting.** Graphics tablet recommended, but not required.

Installing Office

To start the installation process, do the following:

1 Exit all programs that are running on your computer. You must be logged on with administrator privileges. (If you are running Windows Me or Windows 98, you do not need to log on in this manner.)

2 Insert the first CD, and follow the instructions on the screen.

> **note** If the "autorun" program fails to start after inserting the CD (it might take a minute), use Windows Explorer to navigate to the CD and double-click the Setup icon.

3 Before the installation can proceed, you are prompted to enter a Product Key. Look for this key on the CD case, and enter it in the space provided.

> **note** There are two types of Product Key—the Office Product Key, and the Office Subscription Product Key—which indicate the version of Office you purchased. When you are prompted in step 3, you need to enter the appropriate Product Key.

Renewing Office Subscriptions

If you purchased Microsoft Office as a subscription, you will be prompted periodically to renew your subscription. You can update your subscription at any time by choosing Activate Product on the Help menu, which starts the Microsoft Office Activation Wizard. The easiest way to handle renewals is by using the Internet, but you can also call Microsoft to renew your subscription, using the telephone number offered in the Microsoft Office Activation Wizard. If you do not renew your subscription in time, Office will revert to "reduced functionality mode," allowing you to view documents, but not save them.

Uninstalling Office

To remove Office from your computer, do the following:

1 On the Windows Start menu, choose Settings, Control Panel.

2 Double-click the Add/Remove Programs icon.

3 Click the Change Or Remove Programs icon, and then click Microsoft Office (or Microsoft Excel).

4 Click Remove, and follow the instructions on the screen.

---

note If you are running Windows 98 or Windows NT 4, and you installed the Office System Files Update, you should also uninstall this update using the Add/Remove Programs dialog box.

Installing Additional Components

Most Office features are installed with the program. All others should be available as "install-on-demand" (also known as "install on first use"), meaning that when you choose the command for one of these features, you see a dialog box telling you that the feature is not installed and asking whether you want to install it. You'll need to put the CD in your CD-ROM drive to do so.

---

note Before running Setup, check to see whether the feature you want is available as an add-in. In Excel, choose Tools, Add-Ins, and check the list of add-ins available. To install an add-in, click the adjacent check box to select it, and then click OK to install. You'll need to insert the CD to complete the installation.

If you run across a command or feature that is not available in the interface, you might need to rerun the Setup program. To do so, follow these steps:

1 On the Windows Start menu, choose Settings, Control Panel.

2 Double-click the Add/Remove Programs icon.

3 Click the Change Or Remove Programs icon (or the Install/Uninstall tab), and then click Microsoft Office (or Microsoft Excel).

4 Click Change.

5 In the Microsoft Office Setup dialog box, select Add Or Remove Features and click the Next button.

6 In the Features To Install list, click the plus signs to expand each item, and look for items that show an X or a 1 adjacent to the item name.

7 Click the icon adjacent to the item you want to install and select Run From My Computer.

8 Click the Update button.

> **note** Additional discs in the Microsoft Office CD pack contain other items you might want to install that are not part of the regular Office installation.

Installing International Features

Among the optional components available via custom installation are several tools to assist in situations where you need to share documents created using multiple languages. If you need to work with documents created in a language version of Microsoft Office other than the one you use, you need to install the Microsoft Office Multilingual User Interface Pack or the Microsoft Office Proofing Tools for the specific language you need. These optional components might be available in the Office CD package, but they are not included with all Office versions. If these components are not included, check with your system administrator or see the Microsoft Office Web site (*office.microsoft.com*) for information.

Improved international features include the following:

● **Support for multilingual user interface.** Many Office components support a multiple-language user interface (UI). In those that do, the Help system displays UI terms in the selected language, even when Help itself is in another language.

- **Improved support for specific languages.** Improved support for Korean Hangul and Hanja conversions includes over 20,000 new characters and new fonts that allow the characters to be displayed properly. Office also now supports 70,000 new Chinese characters, as well as upgraded Unicode character extensions. All Office programs now support the use of East Asian characters on any system, including computers that are not running East Asian operating systems.

- **Windows parity.** Office now supports all of the same languages supported by Windows 2000.

Using Microsoft Visual Keyboard

When you use the Text Services icon in the Windows Control Panel to specify a keyboard layout that is customized for a specific language, the characters printed on your keyboard might not correspond to the actual characters entered using those keys. You can install Microsoft Visual Keyboard, which provides an on-screen display that includes the correct characters for the selected language. You can use Visual Keyboard as an on-screen reference, and you can also use it to enter text.

Microsoft Visual Keyboard is available on the Microsoft Excel Inside Out companion CD, and on the Office Update Web site (*officeupdate.microsoft.com*).

> **note** If the Text Services icon is not available in your Windows Control Panel, double-click the Keyboard icon, click the Languages (or Input Locales) tab, where you can change or add a language.

Repairing Your Office Installation

Sometimes you have to kick the old washing machine to get it running. And sometimes inexplicable things happen to bits stored on your computer. If you find that something just doesn't seem to be working quite right, you can use one of two repair methods to apply a "kick" to the virtual machine. For either of these scenarios, you will probably need to insert the Office XP CD in your CD-ROM drive.

To repair your Office installation, choose Detect And Repair on the Help menu of any installed Office application. This searches for errors in all Office files and returns them to their original state. When you do so, you can choose to discard any customized settings, which will restore all defaults, including toolbar and menu customizations.

If Detect And Repair doesn't do the job, you can take more drastic measures. To reinstall your Office installation, do the following:

1 On the Windows Start menu, choose Settings, Control Panel.

2 Double-click the Add/Remove Programs icon.

3 Click the Change Or Remove Programs icon (or the Install/Uninstall tab), and then click Microsoft Office (or Microsoft Excel).

4 Click Change.

5 In the Microsoft Office Setup dialog box, select Repair Office and click Next.

6 Select Reinstall Office, and click Install.

Appendix B

Using Speech and Handwriting Recognition

Microsoft Excel 2002 now supports two alternative-input methods—speech input and handwriting. You can use a microphone to dictate text, issue commands, select toolbar buttons, and control items in dialog boxes or the task pane. You can input handwritten text using a drawing pad and stylus, or with a mouse. This appendix covers the basics of using these powerful alternative-input tools.

Speech Recognition System Requirements

For all operating systems, the recommended hardware requirements for Microsoft Office XP are much greater if you want to use speech recognition. You need a Pentium-class computer with a 400 MHz or higher processor and a minimum of 128 MB of RAM. For more about system requirements, see Appendix A, "Installing Microsoft Excel."

In addition, you need a microphone. Any microphone that is compatible with your computer's sound system is acceptable, but a USB headset microphone is recommended. Because it is best if you can locate the microphone element within four inches of your mouth, using a headset is recommended. A headset also helps minimize background noise and the effects of off-axis volume and tone fluctuations.

---

newfeature!
Using the Language Bar

The Language bar is a special toolbar that includes commands and buttons controlling all aspects of the built-in voice recognition and handwriting services. The Language bar appears either in the upper right corner of the screen, or as an icon in the system tray area of the Windows taskbar, as shown in Figure B-1 on the next page. (The system tray is on the opposite end of the taskbar from the Start button.) The taskbar icon displays an abbreviation for the current system language, such as EN for English.

---

note If neither the Language bar nor the EN icon is visible, you may need to choose Windows Start, Settings, Control Panel, double-click the Text Services icon, and then click the Language bar button.

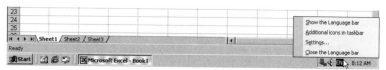

Figure B-1. Right-click the EN icon in the taskbar to display the Language bar.

If it is not already displayed, you display the Language bar by right-clicking the icon in the Taskbar while any Office application is active, and choosing Show The Language Bar on the shortcut menu. To hide the Language bar, click the Minimize button (the dash in the upper right corner). The Language bar disappears and the icon reappears in the system tray.

> **note** You cannot close the Language bar if you have an Input Method Editor (IME) installed. An IME is a program that enters East Asian text into programs by converting keystrokes into complex characters in traditional or simplified Chinese, Japanese, or Korean.

The default configuration of the Language bar includes the following buttons and commands:

- **Microphone.** If you have not yet configured speech recognition, this button displays a dialog box that starts the training process, which is necessary for voice recognition to work. After training has been done, this button activates your microphone and toggles the display of the Dictation and Voice Command buttons, and the Dictation Balloon.

  - **Dictation.** This button is activated only if you have configured your microphone. Click this button (or say **Dictation**) when you want to input text using your microphone.

  - **Voice Command.** This button is activated only if you have configured your microphone. Click this button (or say **Voice Command**) when you want to issue commands using your microphone.

  - **Dictation Balloon.** This display window looks like a cartoon speech balloon. When you are in dictation mode, this balloon displays the word Dictating, indicating that speech recognition is taking place. When you are in voice-command mode, the recognized command name briefly appears in the balloon. The balloon also might display tips such as Too fast, or What was that? if Excel is having difficulty recognizing text in either mode. You can hide the Dictation Balloon by clicking the Tools button on the Language bar and choosing Show Speech Messages. This is a toggle—choose the command again to display the balloon (a check mark appears next to the command when it is activated).

● **Speech Tools.** This menu contains the following commands:

■ **Options** displays the Speech Properties dialog box, where you can change the language recognition engine, add voice profiles, configure your microphone, select an audio input device, and control the voice used for speech playback. (See Figure B-2.)

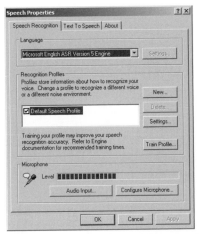

Figure B-2. Use the Speech Properties dialog box to control voice-recognition settings.

■ **Show Speech Messages** toggles the display of the Dictation Balloon.

■ **Training** displays the Voice Training Wizard, shown in Figure B-3, and allows you to further train your computer to recognize your voice.

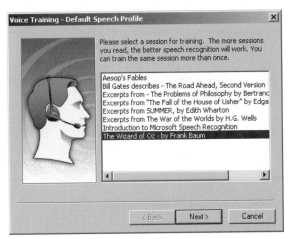

Figure B-3. The more you use the Voice Training Wizard, the better speech recognition will work.

913

- **Add/Delete Word(s)** displays the Add/Delete Word(s) dialog box, shown in Figure B-4, where you can type a unique word you want Excel to recognize. Then click the Record Pronunciation button and speak the word so that Excel can learn how you say it. When you select words in the list, Excel speaks them back to you. If you want to try recording the pronunciation again, click Delete to remove the selected word, type it again, and rerecord the pronunciation.

Figure B-4. Add proper names and unusual words with the Add/Delete Word(s) dialog box.

- **Save Speech Data** saves speech input data in Word documents. Inactive in Excel.

- **Current User** displays a submenu containing all available speech profiles. If more than one person uses your computer, you can use the Options command on the Speech Tools menu to create separate profiles for each user.

- **Handwriting** displays a menu containing commands that display the corresponding item on your screen. Clicking one of these commands also changes the button that appears to the right of the Handwriting button, including the following:

- **Writing Pad** displays the Writing Pad, shown in Figure B-5, and specifies the Writing Pad to accept handwriting input.

Figure B-5. Use the Writing Pad to input handwritten text.

- **Write Anywhere** displays the Write Anywhere toolbar (essentially the same as the control section of the Writing Pad), and allows handwriting input anywhere on the worksheet.

- **Drawing Pad** displays a box similar to the Writing Pad in Word and Outlook only. Inactive in Excel.

- **On-Screen Standard Keyboard** displays a representation of a standard keyboard on-screen. Primarily intended for use with touch-screen computers, but you can use the mouse to click keys and enter the corresponding character.

- **On-Screen Symbol Keyboard** displays a representation of a keyboard on-screen that displays only symbols, similar to the Symbol command on the Insert menu. Primarily intended for use with touch-screen computers, but you can use the mouse to click keys and enter the corresponding symbol.

- **Help** displays a Help file specifically for the Language bar.

Controlling the Language Bar

The Language bar has special features that set it apart from Excel's toolbars. For example, you can choose to have the Language bar be semitransparent when it is not in use, allowing easier viewing of the work area beneath it. This option is not available in Windows 98, Windows Me, or Windows NT 4.0. If you right-click the Language bar, a shortcut menu appears containing the following commands:

- **Minimize** hides the Language bar and displays the Language bar icon in the Taskbar.

- **Transparency** turns on transparency. (Click the button again to turn off transparency.)

- **Text Labels** displays or hides text labels on the Language bar.

- **Additional Icons In Taskbar** allows two additional Language bar buttons to be displayed as separate icons in the system tray area of the Windows taskbar, as shown in Figure B-6. The Microphone icon turns the microphone on and off when clicked. The second icon represents the option that was last selected on the Handwriting menu. Figure B-6 shows the Microphone and Writing Pad icons to the right of the EN Language bar icon.

Figure B-6. Click either of the two icons shown to the right of the EN Language bar icon to activate the corresponding item.

- **Settings** displays the Text Services dialog box shown in Figure B-7 on the next page, which allows you to select any one of the installed languages and to select services and preferences available for that installed language.

Figure B-7. Use the Text Services dialog box
to change the default voice recognition language.

- **Close The Language Bar** closes the Language bar and removes the icon
  from the Taskbar. To redisplay the Language bar, choose the Windows Start
  menu, Settings, Control Panel, double-click the Text Services icon, and
  then click the Language Bar button.

Using Speech Recognition

You can use Excel's built-in speech recognition features to enter text into cells on your
worksheet, making repetitive typing a little easier. You can also use your voice to control menus, toolbars, and dialog boxes in the Excel user interface. Before doing so, you
first need to train the speech recognition software to recognize your voice.

Training Your Computer and Your Voice

The first time you use speech recognition, click the Microphone button on the Language bar to display a dialog box that starts the training process. The Voice Training
Wizard guides you through the process. In the first training session, you'll be asked to
read several paragraphs of prepared text entitled "Introduction to Microsoft Speech
Recognition," while the wizard listens and records data about the characteristics of
your voice. You need to allocate 15 or 20 minutes to this task, and you should wait until
you can proceed undisturbed and when extraneous noise is at a minimum.

As you speak, the Voice Training Wizard highlights the text as it recognizes it, as shown
in Figure B-8. If text stops being highlighted, you need to go back and start reading
again at the next word after the last highlighted word. When speaking to a computer,
consistency is key. After a few minutes, you'll begin to get a feel for the optimum verbal
pace. It will feel unnatural at first, but you'll probably need to speak a little more slowly

and a little more clearly than you usually do. However, you might not need to enunciate as precisely as you think. In fact, it probably won't work as well if you slow down too much or emphasize syllables too distinctly. Watch the highlighted text as you speak. This helps you train your "computer speaking voice" while simultaneously training your computer to recognize it.

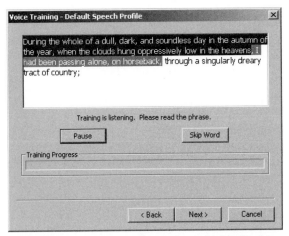

Figure B-8. As you speak, words are highlighted in a light color; as words are recognized, the highlight turns dark.

The more you train, the better speech recognition will work. After the initial session is completed, you can continue to train your system using the additional training sessions available when you click the Speech Tools button and choose the Training command. The Voice Training Wizard offers a number of interesting training exercises you can use, including writings by Edith Wharton, H.G. Wells, Edgar Allan Poe, and even Bill Gates.

Issuing Verbal Commands

When the initial training process is complete, you can begin using the microphone to issue commands. This is not intended as a complete alternative-input method; you'll still need to use the keyboard for certain things. But the voice-command system is quite effective and can save a lot of keystrokes and mouse clicks.

To begin, click the Microphone button on the Language bar, which expands the Language bar to include the Dictation and Voice Command buttons. When you click the Voice Command button, you can begin issuing verbal commands. Simply speak the name of the item you want to select. For example, say **Insert** and the Insert menu appears; then say the name of any command on the Insert menu to issue that command or display that submenu. Any word that appears in the interface is theoretically available for voice control, but expect to spend some time working with it.

Special Voice Commands

There are some special voice commands you can use to issue particular keystrokes or mouse clicks. Table B-1 lists some of these special voice commands.

Table B-1. Special Voice Commands

Say	To
Microphone	Click the Microphone button. Turns off the microphone. (You can't verbally turn on the microphone.)
Enter	Press the Enter key.
Tab	Press the Tab key.
Delete	Press the Delete key.
Last word	Move the cursor to before the previous word.
Space	Press the Spacebar.
Escape or cancel	Press the Esc key or click the Cancel button.
Right-click	Display the shortcut menu for the selected item.
End	Press the End key.
Home	Press the Home key.
Up, down, left, or right	Press the corresponding arrow key.
Page down	Press the Page Down key.
Page up	Press the Page Up key.

Using Your Voice to Input Text

Dictation using voice recognition has always been a challenge for software developers, because, compared to computer memory chips, the human voice is random and unpredictable. Excel's voice recognition is pretty good, and it gets better with training, but you should be prepared to proofread and make corrections. Still, when you and your computer get the hang of each other, you can really cut down the keystrokes and mouse clicks when you have a lot of text to enter.

To begin verbal text input, click the Microphone button on the Language bar, and then click the Dictation button or say **Dictation**. Anything you say thereafter is processed by the voice recognition software and appears in the active cell. It takes a few seconds for Excel to process the verbal input, and you'll first see a line of highlighted dots (periods) appear on the screen while the voice input is being processed; then the recognized text appears, as shown in Figure B-9. You will probably be surprised at how the "translation" appears, as shown in Figure B-9. You will probably be surprised at how the "translation" works at first. For example, we read the previous sentence in dictation mode; voice recognition translated it as "you will probably be surprised at how the ensuing she works in his." After additional training, recognition will be much more accurate.

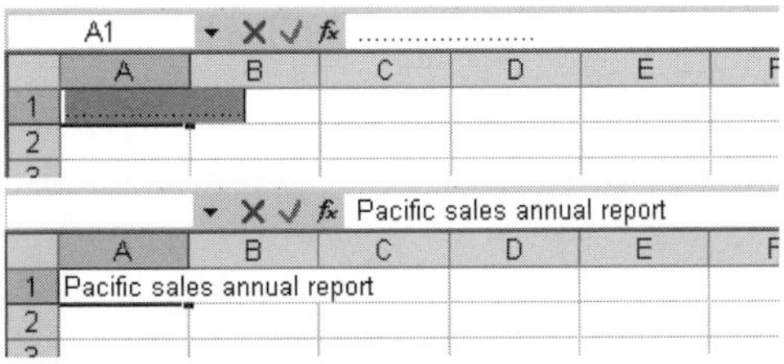

Figure B-9. A line of dots appears in the active cell as you speak; text appears after the words are recognized.

Speaking Punctuation

You can also enter punctuation verbally in dictation mode. Excel recognizes the following words as the equivalent punctuation character: period (or dot), comma, colon, semicolon, question mark, exclamation point, ampersand, asterisk, backslash, slash, vertical bar, hyphen (or dash), equals, plus sign, percent sign, dollar sign, underscore, pound sign, tilde, open quote, close quote, open single quote, close single quote, greater than, less than, caret, at sign, vertical bar, double dash, and ellipsis. Table B-2 lists some additional dictation commands and the resulting entry.

Table B-2. Additional Dictation Commands

Say	To enter
Left bracket	[
Right bracket	]
Left brace	{
Right brace	}
Left paren	(
Right paren	)
One-half (and other simple fractions)	½

Forcing Numeric Recognition

Normally in dictation mode, spoken numbers less than 20 are spelled out, and those greater than 20 are inserted as numerals. Saying **force num** compels Excel to recognize the next thing you say as a numeral rather than spelling it out as text. Pause before saying the number for best results, and pause afterward to return to normal dictation mode.

Spelling Out Words

Normally, Excel "listens" for whole words, and translates anything spoken to the closest word. If you want to spell out something in dictation mode, such as a proper name or any word not being correctly recognized, you can say **spelling mode** and then pause and say the individual characters. Pause after the last character to return to normal dictation mode.

The Talking Spreadsheet

You can make a selection on your worksheet and have Excel recite the contents of that selection using the Speak Cells buttons on the Text to Speech toolbar. This is a handy auditing feature you can use whenever you need to check printed material against what's on your screen after entering it by hand. For details about this feature, see "Having Excel Read Cells to You" on page 271.

Using Handwriting Recognition

Excel's new handwriting recognition feature gives you the option of entering text in Excel using a handwriting input device, such as a graphics tablet and stylus, or using your mouse.

To begin, click the Handwriting button on the Language bar and choose an input method. Choose Writing Pad to display a dialog-box style input area, or choose Write Anywhere to allow handwriting input to occur anywhere on the screen. When you do so, the corresponding button appears to the right of the Handwriting button. You can subsequently click this button to turn on and off the selected handwriting input method. The main advantage of using the Write Anywhere feature is visibility, because the Writing Pad takes up a lot of space on the screen. In general, however, you'll find that using the Writing Pad results in greater input accuracy.

To begin entering handwriting using the Writing Pad, start writing in the pale yellow input area. This input area includes a horizontal blue line, which represents the baseline. The recognition software uses this line to help distinguish characters based on the position of *descenders* in relation to other letters. For example, if you write the word **jet** above the baseline, it might be recognized as the word set. Handwriting recognition works better if you use the baseline. For example, making sure that the descender of the j extends below the baseline improves the chance that the word will be correctly recognized.

If you use the Write Anywhere option instead of the Writing Pad, you can write freely wherever you like on the screen. For maximum accuracy, you should try to keep your handwriting straight and horizontal with consistent location of descenders.

You can write in cursive style or printed letters. Either way, you can write entire words before recognition takes over when you pause, complete an easily recognized word, or run out of space on a line. The recognized text appears in the active cell, as shown in Figure B-10.

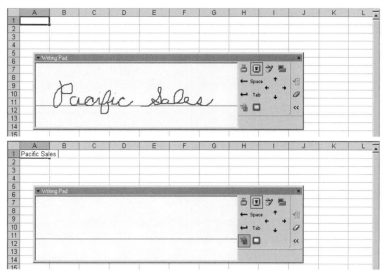

Figure B-10. As text is recognized, it disappears from the Writing Pad and appears in the selected cell.

The Writing Pad includes a group of control buttons that duplicate some of the most often-used keyboard characters: Space, Backspace, Tab, Enter, and the four Arrow keys. (The Arrow keys are not visible unless you click the Expand button.) You can also use buttons on the Writing Pad to display the On-Screen Standard Keyboard, or to switch to Write Anywhere, which effectively hides the input area of the Writing Pad, leaving only the buttons. The name Writing Pad changes to Write Anywhere, and the Write Anywhere button changes to Drawing Pad, allowing you to switch back and forth between the two input modes.

The Recognize Now button allows you to choose when recognition occurs. This button is ineffective unless you turn off the Automatic Recognition option in the Handwriting Options dialog box shown in Figure B-11.

> **note** On the Drawing Pad (or the Write Anywhere toolbar), there are several buttons that don't work in Excel (but they are available in Word and/or Outlook): Ink, Drawing Pad, and Correction.

Setting Handwriting Options

At the left side of the Writing Pad's title bar, click the downward-pointing arrow to display the Options menu, and then click Options to display the Handwriting Options dialog box shown in Figure B-11.

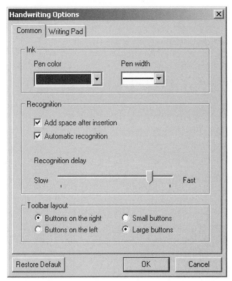

Figure B-11. Use the Handwriting Options dialog box to control handwriting-recognition settings.

The two tabs in the Handwriting Options dialog box (Common and Writing Pad) control the following settings:

- **Pen Color** and **Pen Width** change the color and width of the "ink" used to display handwritten text.

- **Add Space After Insertion** inserts a space character after recognized text.

- **Automatic Recognition** recognizes text on the fly. If you turn off this option, you can input as much handwritten text as you want, and then click the Recognize Now button on the Writing Pad to force recognition.

- **Recognition Delay** controls the length of the pause required before recognition begins (if automatic recognition is turned on).

- **Toolbar Layout** controls the position and size of buttons.

- **Restore Default** returns any changed settings back to their original state.

- **The Writing Pad Tab** controls the background color of the Writing Pad input area, and the number of lines displayed there.

The Automatic Recognition option, which is normally turned on, allows you to enter text on a semicontinuous basis; recognition is applied when you pause or when you reach the end of a line. If you'd prefer to decide for yourself when recognition is applied to your handwritten text, turn off this option and use the Recognize Now button on the Writing Pad (or the Write Anywhere toolbar) to convert your writing to text.

Keyboard Shortcuts

This appendix lists every keyboard-accessible command and control in Excel. Besides being an essential accessibility table, it also provides a glimpse into the depth and breadth of the features available.

Keyboard shortcuts are divided into the following subcategories in this appendix, listed in alphabetical order:

- Charts and Select Chart Elements
- Data Forms
- Dialog Box Edit Boxes
- Dialog Boxes
- Edit Data
- Enter and Calculate Formulas
- Enter Data
- Enter Special Characters
- Extend a Selection
- Filter Lists
- Format, Cells Dialog Box—Border Tab
- Format Data
- Help
- Help—Office Assistant Balloon
- Help—Wizards and Dialog Boxes
- Help Window
- Insert, Delete, and Copy Cells
- Languages
- Macros
- Menus and Toolbars
- Move and Scroll—In End Mode
- Move and Scroll—Scroll Lock Activated
- Move and Scroll—Worksheets

- Move Within a Selected Range
- Open, Save As, and Insert Picture Dialog Boxes
- PivotTable And PivotChart Wizard Layout Dialog Box
- PivotTable Field—Display and Hide Items
- PivotTable Report—Change the Layout
- Print
- Print Preview
- Select Cells, Rows, Columns, and Objects
- Select Cells with Special Characteristics
- Send E-Mail Messages
- Show, Hide, and Outline Data
- Smart Tags
- Speech Recognition and Text-to-Speech
- Task Panes
- Windows and Office Interface
- Worksheets

Charts and Select Chart Elements

Press	To
F11 or Alt+F1	Create a chart of the data in the current range.
Ctrl+Page Down	Select a chart sheet. Selects the next sheet in the work book until the chart sheet you want is selected.
Ctrl+Page Up	Select a chart sheet. Selects the previous sheet in the workbook until the chart sheet you want is selected.
Down Arrow	Select the previous group of elements in a chart.
Up Arrow	Select the next group of elements in a chart.
Right Arrow	Select the next element within a group.
Left Arrow	Select the previous element within a group.

Data Forms

Press	To
Down Arrow	Move to the same field in the next record.
Up Arrow	Move to the same field in the previous record.
Tab or Shift+Tab	Move to each field in the record, and then to each command button.
Enter	Move to the first field in the next record.
Shift+Enter	Move to the first field in the previous record.
Page Down	Move to the same field 10 records forward.
Ctrl+Page Down	Start a new, blank record.
Page Up	Move to the same field 10 records back.
Ctrl+Page Up	Move to the first record.
Home or End	Move to the beginning or end of a field.
Shift+End	Extend the selection to the end of a field.
Shift+Home	Extend the selection to the beginning of a field.
Left Arrow or Right Arrow	Move one character left or right within a field.
Shift+Left Arrow	Select the character to the left within a field.
Shift+Right Arrow	Select the character to the right within a field.

Dialog Box Edit Boxes

Press	To
Home	Move to the beginning of the entry.
End	Move to the end of the entry.
Left Arrow or Right Arrow	Move one character to the left or right.
Ctrl+Left Arrow	Move one word to the left.
Ctrl+Right Arrow	Move one word to the right.
Shift+Left Arrow	Select or deselect one character to the left.
Shift+Right Arrow	Select or deselect one character to the right.
Ctrl+Shift+Left Arrow	Select or deselect one word to the left.

(continued)

Dialog Box Edit Boxes *(continued)*

Press	To
Ctrl+Shift+Right Arrow	Select or deselect one word to the right.
Shift+Home	Select from the insertion point to the beginning of the entry.
Shift+End	Select from the insertion point to the end of the entry.

Dialog Boxes

Press	To
Tab	Move to the next option or option group.
Shift+Tab	Move to the previous option or option group.
Ctrl+Tab or Ctrl+Page Down	Switch to the next tab in a dialog box.
Ctrl+Shift+Tab or Ctrl+Page Up	Switch to the previous tab in a dialog box.
Arrow keys	Move between options in an open drop-down list, or between options in a group of options.
Spacebar	Perform the action for the selected button, or select or clear the selected check box.
First letter of an option	Open the list if it is closed and in a drop-down list move to that option in the list.
Alt+the underlined letter in an option	Select an option, or select or clear a check box.
Alt+Down Arrow	Open the selected drop-down list.
Enter	Perform the action for the default command button in the dialog box (the button with the bold outline, often the OK button).
Esc	Cancel the command and close the dialog box.

Edit Data

Press	To
F2	Edit the active cell and position the insertion point at the end of the cell contents.
Alt+Enter	Start a new line in the same cell.
Backspace	Edit the active cell and then clear it, or delete the preceding character in the active cell as you edit cell contents.
Delete	Delete the character to the right of the insertion point, or delete the selection.
Ctrl+Delete	Delete text to the end of the line.
F7	Start the spelling checker.
Shift+F2	Edit a cell comment.
Enter	Complete a cell entry and select the next cell below.
Ctrl+Z	Undo the last action.
Esc	Cancel a cell entry.
Ctrl+Shift+Z	When the AutoCorrect Smart Tag is displayed, undo or redo the last automatic correction.

Enter and Calculate Formulas

Press	To
= (equal sign)	Start a formula.
F2	Move the insertion point into the formula bar when editing in a cell is turned off.
Backspace	In the formula bar, delete one character to the left.
Enter	Complete a cell entry from the cell or formula bar.
Ctrl+Shift+Enter	Enter a formula as an array formula.
Esc	Cancel an entry in the cell or formula bar.
Shift+F3	In a formula, display the Insert Function dialog box.
Ctrl+A	When the insertion point is to the right of a function name in a formula, display the Function Arguments dialog box.

(continued)

Enter and Calculate Formulas *(continued)*

Press	To
Ctrl+Shift+A	When the insertion point is to the right of a function name in a formula, insert the argument names and parentheses.
F3	Paste a defined name into a formula.
Alt+= (equal sign)	Insert an AutoSum formula with the SUM function.
Ctrl+Shift+" (quotation mark)	Copy the value from the cell above the active cell into the cell or the formula bar.
Ctrl+' (apostrophe)	Copy a formula from the cell above the active cell into the cell or the formula bar.
Ctrl+' (single left quotation mark)	Alternate between displaying cell values and displaying formulas.
F9	Calculate all worksheets in all open workbooks or, when a portion of a formula is selected, calculate the selected portion. Then press Enter or Ctrl+Shift+Enter (for array formulas) to replace the selected portion with the calculated value.
Shift+F9	Calculate the active worksheet.
Ctrl+Alt+F9	Calculate all worksheets in all open workbooks, regardless of whether they have changed since the last calculation.
Ctrl+Alt+Shift+F9	Recheck dependent formulas and then calculate all cells in all open workbooks, including cells not marked as needing to be calculated.

Enter Data

Press	To
Enter	Complete a cell entry and select the cell below.
Alt+Enter	Start a new line in the same cell.
Ctrl+Enter	Fill the selected cell range with the current entry.
Shift+Enter	Complete a cell entry and select the previous cell above.

(continued)

Enter Data *(continued)*

Press	To
Tab	Complete a cell entry and select the next cell to the right.
Shift+Tab	Complete a cell entry and select the previous cell to the left.
Esc	Cancel a cell entry.
Arrow keys	Move one character up, down, left, or right.
Home	Move to the beginning of the line.
F4 or Ctrl+Y	Repeat the last action.
Ctrl+Shift+F3	Create names from row and column labels.
Ctrl+D	Fill down.
Ctrl+R	Fill to the right.
Ctrl+F3	Define a name.
Ctrl+K	Insert a hyperlink.
Enter (in a cell with a hyperlink)	Open a hyperlink.
Ctrl+; (semicolon)	Enter the date.
Ctrl+Shift+: (colon)	Enter the time.
Alt+Down Arrow	Display a drop-down list of the values in the current column of a list.
Ctrl+Z	Undo the last action.

Enter Special Characters

Press F2 to edit the cell, turn on Num Lock, and then press the following keys using the numeric keypad.

Press	To
Alt+0162	Enter the cent character ¢.
Alt+0163	Enter the pound sterling character £.
Alt+0165	Enter the yen symbol ¥.
Alt+0128	Enter the euro symbol ¤.

Extend a Selection

Press	To
F8	Turn on or off extend mode. In extend mode, EXT appears in the status line, and the arrow keys extend the selection.
Shift+F8	Add another range of cells to the selection; or use the arrow keys to move to the start of the range you want to add, and then press F8 and the arrow keys to select the next range.
Shift+arrow key	Extend the selection by one cell.
Ctrl+Shift+arrow key	Extend the selection to the last nonblank cell in the same column or row as the active cell.
Shift+Home	Extend the selection to the beginning of the row.
Ctrl+Shift+Home	Extend the selection to the beginning of the worksheet.
Ctrl+Shift+End	Extend the selection to the last used cell on the worksheet (lower right corner).
Shift+Page Down	Extend the selection down one screen.
Shift+Page Up	Extend the selection up one screen.
End+Shift+arrow key	Extend the selection to the last nonblank cell in the same column or row as the active cell.
End+Shift+Home	Extend the selection to the last used cell on the worksheet (lower right corner).
End+Shift+Enter	Extend the selection to the last cell in the current row. This key sequence does not work if you have turned on transition navigation keys (Tools menu, Options command, Transition tab).
Scroll Lock+Shift +Home	Extend the selection to the cell in the upper left corner of the window.
Scroll Lock+Shift+End	Extend the selection to the cell in the lower right corner of the window.

Filter Lists

Press	To
Alt+Down Arrow	In the cell that contains the drop-down arrow, display the AutoFilter list for the current column.
Down Arrow	Select the next item in the AutoFilter list.

(continued)

Filter Lists *(continued)*

Press	To
Up Arrow	Select the previous item in the AutoFilter list.
Alt+Up Arrow	Close the AutoFilter list for the current column.
Home	Select the first item (All) in the AutoFilter list.
End	Select the last item in the AutoFilter list.
Enter	Filter the list based on the item selected from the AutoFilter list.

Format, Cells Dialog Box—Border Tab

Press	To
Alt+T	Apply or remove the top border.
Alt+B	Apply or remove the bottom border.
Alt+L	Apply or remove the left border.
Alt+R	Apply or remove the right border.
Alt+H	If cells in multiple rows are selected, apply or remove the horizontal divider.
Alt+V	If cells in multiple columns are selected, apply or remove the vertical divider.
Alt+D	Apply or remove the downward diagonal border.
Alt+U	Apply or remove the upward diagonal border.

Format Data

Press	To
Alt+' (apostrophe)	Display the Style dialog box.
Ctrl+1	Display the Cells dialog box. (Note that you must use the 1 key above the keyboard, not the keypad.)
Ctrl+Shift+~ (tilde)	Apply the General number format.
Ctrl+Shift+$	Apply the Currency format with two decimal places (negative numbers in parentheses).
Ctrl+Shift+%	Apply the Percentage format with no decimal places.
Ctrl+Shift+^ (caret)	Apply the Exponential number format with two decimal places.

(continued)

Format Data *(continued)*

Press	To
Ctrl+Shift+# (pound)	Apply the Date format with the day, month, and year.
Ctrl+Shift+@	Apply the Time format with the hour and minute and AM or PM.
Ctrl+Shift+! (exclamation point)	Apply the Number format with two decimal places, thousands separator, and minus sign (–) for negative values.
Ctrl+B	Apply or remove bold formatting.
Ctrl+I	Apply or remove italic formatting.
Ctrl+U	Apply or remove underlining.
Ctrl+5	Apply or remove strikethrough.
Ctrl+9	Hide the selected rows.
Ctrl+Shift+((opening parenthesis)	Unhide any hidden rows within the selection.
Ctrl+0 (zero)	Hide the selected columns.
Ctrl+Shift+) (closing parenthesis)	Unhide any hidden columns within the selection.
Ctrl+Shift+& (ampersand)	Apply the outline border to the selected cells.
Ctrl+Shift+_ (underscore)	Remove the outline border from the selected cells.

Help

Press	To
F1	Display the Assistant balloon. (If the Assistant is turned off, F1 opens the Help window.)

> **note** If you use a screen review utility or other accessibility aid, you'll get the best results with Help if you enter questions using the Answer Wizard tab in the Help window rather than the Office Assistant balloon, or in the Ask A Question box on the menu bar. To turn off the Assistant, press F1 (to display the Assistant), press Alt+O to open the Options tab in the Office Assistant dialog box. Press Alt+U to clear the Use The Office Assistant check box, and then press Enter. The next time you press F1, the Help window appears.

Help—Office Assistant Balloon

Press	To
Alt+*number*	Select a Help topic from the list the Assistant displays. Alt+1 is the first topic, Alt+2 is the second, and so on.
Alt+Down Arrow	Display more Help topics in the Assistant list.
Alt+Up Arrow	Display previous Help topics in the Assistant list.
Esc	Close an Assistant message or a tip.

Help—Wizards and Dialog Boxes

Press	To
Tab	Move to the Help button in the wizard.
Spacebar, with the Help button selected	Show the Assistant in a wizard or dialog box. To hide the Assistant, press Spacebar again. Note that not all wizards or dialog boxes have Help provided by the Assistant.

Help Window

Press	To
Tab or Shift+Tab	Select the next or previous hidden text or hyperlink, or Show All or Hide All at the top of a topic.
Shift+Tab	Select the previous hidden text or hyperlink, or the View button at the top of a Microsoft Office Web article.
Enter	Perform the action for the selected Show All, Hide All, hidden text, or hyperlink.
Alt+O	Display the Options menu to access any Help toolbar command.
Alt+O, and then press T	Hide or show the pane with the Contents, Answer Wizard, and Index tabs.
Alt+O, and then press B	Display the previously viewed topic.
Alt+O, and then press F	Display the next topic in a previously displayed sequence of topics.
Alt+O, and then press H	Return to the specified home page.
Alt+O, and then press S	Stop the Help window from opening a Help topic (useful if you want to stop a Web page from downloading).

(continued)

Help Window *(continued)*

Press	To
Alt+O, and then press I	Open the Internet Options dialog box for Microsoft Internet Explorer, where you can change accessibility settings.
Alt+O, and then press R	Refresh the topic (useful if you have linked to a Web page).
Alt+O, and then press P	Print all topics in a book or a selected topic only.
Alt+F4	Close the Help window.
Ctrl+Tab	Switch to the next tab.
Alt+C	Switch to the Contents tab.
Alt+A	Switch to the Answer Wizard tab.
Alt+I	Switch to the Index tab.
Enter	Open a selected book or Help topic.
Down Arrow	Select the next book or Help topic.
Up Arrow	Select the previous book or Help topic.
Shift+F10	Display a shortcut menu.
Alt+Right Arrow	Go to the next Help topic.
Alt+Left Arrow	Go to the previous Help topic.
Up Arrow or Down Arrow	Scroll toward the beginning or end of a Help topic.
Page Up or Page Down	Scroll toward the beginning or end of a Help topic in large increments.
Home or End	Go to the beginning or end of a Help topic.
Ctrl+P	Print the current Help topic.
Ctrl+A	Select the entire Help topic.
Ctrl+C	Copy the selected items to the Clipboard.

Insert, Delete, and Copy Cells

Press	To
Ctrl+C	Copy the selected items to the Clipboard.
Ctrl+C	Copy the selected cells.
Ctrl+C, immediately followed by another Ctrl+C	Display the Microsoft Office Clipboard (multiple copy and paste).
Ctrl+X	Cut the selected cells.
Ctrl+V	Paste copied cells.
Delete	Clear the contents of the selected cells.
Ctrl+- (hyphen)	Delete the selected cells.
Ctrl+Shift++ (plus sign)	Insert blank cells.

Languages

Press	To
Ctrl+X	Cut the selected cells.
Ctrl+Right Shift	Switch to right-to-left paragraph direction. (The text must contain only neutral characters.)
Ctrl+Left Shift	Switch to left-to-right paragraph direction. (The text must contain only neutral characters.)
Alt+Shift+Up Arrow	In Japanese text for which you've displayed phonetic guides, move the pointer into the phonetic guides.
Alt+Shift+Down Arrow	Move the pointer from the phonetic guides back to the parent string of characters.
Num Lock, Alt+numeric pad number	Enter a unicode character.
Alt+X	Pressed immediately after typing the hexadecimal code for a unicode character, convert the numbers to the character. Pressed immediately following a unicode character, convert the character to its hexadecimal code.

Macros

Press	To
Alt+F8	Display the Macro dialog box.
Alt+F11	Display the Visual Basic Editor.
Ctrl+F11	Insert a Microsoft Excel 4.0 macro sheet.

Menus and Toolbars

Press	To
F10 or Alt	Select the menu bar, or close an open menu and submenu at the same time.
Tab or Shift+Tab	When a toolbar is selected, select the next or previous button or menu on the toolbar.
Ctrl+Tab or Ctrl+Shift+Tab	When a toolbar is selected, select the next or previous toolbar.
Enter	Open the selected menu, or perform the action for the selected button or command.
Shift+F10	Display the shortcut menu for the selected item.
Alt+Spacebar	Display the Control menu for the Excel window.
Down Arrow or Up Arrow	When a menu or submenu is open, select the next or previous command.
Left Arrow or Right Arrow	Select the menu to the left or right. When a submenu is open, switch between the main menu and the submenu. When a toolbar is selected, select the adjacent button.
Home or End	Select the first or last command on the menu or submenu.
Esc	Close an open menu. When a submenu is open, close only the submenu.
Ctrl+Down Arrow	Display the full set of commands on a menu.
Ctrl+7	Show or hide the Standard toolbar.

Move and Scroll—In End Mode

Press	To
End key	Turn on or off End mode. (END appears in the status bar when End mode is activated.)
End+arrow key	Move by one block of data within a row or column.
End+Home	Move to the last cell on the worksheet, in the lowest used row of the rightmost used column.
End+Enter	Move to the rightmost nonblank cell in the current row. This key sequence does not work if you have turned on transition navigation keys (Tools menu, Options command, Transition tab).

Move and Scroll—Scroll Lock Activated

Press	To
Scroll Lock	Turn Scroll Lock on or off.
Home	Move to the cell in the upper left corner of the window.
End	Move to the cell in the lower right corner of the window.
Up Arrow or Down Arrow	Scroll one row up or down.
Left Arrow or Right Arrow	Scroll one column left or right.

Move and Scroll—Worksheets

Press	To
Arrow keys	Move one cell up, down, left, or right.
Ctrl+arrow key	Move to the edge of the current data region.
Home	Move to the beginning of the row.
Ctrl+Home	Move to the beginning of the worksheet.
Ctrl+End	Move to the last cell on the worksheet, in the lowest used row of the rightmost used column.
Page Down	Move down one screen.
Page Up	Move up one screen.
Alt+Page Down	Move one screen to the right.

(continued)

Move and Scroll—Worksheets *(continued)*

Press	To
Alt+Page Up	Move one screen to the left.
F6	Switch to the next pane in a worksheet that has been split.
Shift+F6	Switch to the previous pane in a worksheet that has been split.
Ctrl+Backspace	Scroll to display the active cell.
F5	Display the Go To dialog box.
Shift+F5	Display the Find dialog box.
Shift+F4	Repeat the last Find action (same as Find Next).
Tab	Move between unlocked cells on a protected worksheet.

Move Within a Selected Range

Press	To
Enter	Move from top to bottom within the selected range.
Shift+Enter	Move from bottom to top within the selected range.
Tab	Move from left to right within the selected range. If cells in a single column are selected, move down.
Shift+Tab	Move from right to left within the selected range. If cells in a single column are selected, move up.
Ctrl+. (period)	Move clockwise to the next corner of the selected range.
Ctrl+Alt+Right Arrow	In nonadjacent selections, switch to the next selection to the right.
Ctrl+Alt+Left Arrow	Switch to the next nonadjacent selection to the left.

Open, Save As, and Insert Picture Dialog Boxes

Press	To
Alt+1	Go to the previous folder.
Alt+2	Open the folder up one level above the open folder.
Alt+3	Close the dialog box and open your Web search page.

(continued)

Open, Save As, and Insert Picture Dialog Boxes *(continued)*

Press	To
Alt+4	Delete the selected folder or file.
Alt+5	Create a new folder.
Alt+6	Switch among available folder views.
Alt+7 or Alt+L	Show the Tools menu.
Shift+F10	Display a shortcut menu for a selected item, such as a folder or file.
Tab	Move between options or areas in the dialog box.
F4 or Alt+I	Open the Look In list.
F5	Refresh the file list.

PivotTable and PivotChart Wizard Layout Dialog Box

To display this dialog box, press Tab until Layout is selected in Step 3 of the PivotTable And PivotChart Wizard.

Press	To
Up Arrow or Down Arrow	Select the previous or next field button in the list on the right.
Left Arrow or Right Arrow	With two or more columns of field buttons, select the button to the left or right.
Alt+R	Move the selected field into the Row area.
Alt+C	Move the selected field into the Column area.
Alt+D	Move the selected field into the Data area.
Alt+P	Move the selected field into the Page area.
Alt+L	Display the PivotTable Field dialog box for the selected field.

PivotTable—Display and Hide Items

Press	To
Alt+Down Arrow	Display the drop-down list for a field in a PivotTable or PivotChart report. Use the arrow keys to select the field.
Up Arrow	Select the previous item in the list.
Down Arrow	Select the next item in the list.

(continued)

PivotTable—Display and Hide Items *(continued)*

Press	To
Right Arrow	For an item that has lower level items available, display the lower level items.
Left Arrow	For an item that has lower level items displayed, hide the lower level items.
Home	Select the first visible item in the list.
End	Select the last visible item in the list.
Enter	Close the list and display the selected items.
Spacebar	Check, double-check, or clear a check box in the list. Double-check selects both an item and all of its lower level items.
Tab	Switch among the list, the OK button, and the Cancel button.

PivotTable—Change the Layout

Press	To
Ctrl+Shift+* (asterisk)	Select an entire PivotTable.
Alt+Shift+Right Arrow	Group the selected items in a PivotTable field.
Alt+Shift+Left Arrow	Ungroup grouped items in a PivotTable field.

Print

Press	To
Ctrl+P or Ctrl+Shift+F12	Display the Print dialog box.
Alt+F, and then press V	Open Print Preview.

Print Preview

Press	To
Arrow keys	Move around the page when zoomed in.
Page Up or Page Down	Move by one page when zoomed out.
Ctrl+Up Arrow or Ctrl+Left Arrow	Move to the first page when zoomed out.
Ctrl+Down Arrow or Ctrl+Right Arrow	Move to the last page when zoomed out.

Select Cells, Rows, Columns, and Objects

Press	To
Ctrl+Spacebar	Select the entire column.
Shift+Spacebar	Select the entire row.
Ctrl+A	Select the entire worksheet.
Shift+Backspace	With multiple cells selected, select only the active cell.
Ctrl+Shift+Spacebar	With an object selected, select all objects on a sheet.
Ctrl+6	Alternate among hiding objects, displaying objects, and displaying placeholders for objects.

Select Cells with Special Characteristics

Press	To
Ctrl+Shift+* (asterisk)	Select the current region around the active cell (the data area enclosed by blank rows and blank columns). In a PivotTable, select the entire PivotTable.
Ctrl+/ (slash)	Select the array containing the active cell.
Ctrl+Shift+O (the letter O)	Select all cells that contain comments.
Ctrl+\ (backslash)	In a selected row, select the cells that don't match the value in the active cell.
Ctrl+Shift+I (vertical bar)	In a selected column, select the cells that don't match the value in the active cell.
Ctrl+[(opening bracket)	Select all cells directly referenced by formulas in the selection.
Ctrl+Shift+{ (opening brace)	Select all cells directly or indirectly referenced by formulas in the selection.
Ctrl+] (closing bracket)	Select cells that contain formulas that directly reference the active cell.
Ctrl+Shift+} (closing brace)	Select cells that contain formulas that directly or indirectly reference the active cell.
Alt+; (semicolon)	Select the visible cells in the current selection.

Send E-Mail Messages

To use keys to send e-mail messages, you must configure Microsoft Outlook as your default e-mail program. Most of these keys do not work with Outlook Express.

Press	To
Shift+Tab	Move to the Introduction box in the e-mail message header when cell A1 is selected. In the message header, move to the Subject, Bcc (if displayed), Cc, To, and From (if displayed) boxes, then to the address book for the Bcc, Cc, To, and From boxes, and then to cell A1.
Alt+S	Send the e-mail message.
Ctrl+Shift+B	Open the Address Book.
Alt+P	Open the Outlook Message Options dialog box (Options menu, Options command).
Alt+K	Check the names in the To, Cc, and Bcc boxes against the Address Book.
Alt+. (period)	Open the Address Book for the To box.
Alt+C	Open the Address Book for the Cc box.
Alt+B	If the Bcc box is displayed, open the Address Book for the Bcc box.
Alt+J	Go to the Subject box.
Ctrl+Shift+G	Create a message flag.

Show, Hide, and Outline Data

Press	To
Alt+Shift+Right Arrow	Group rows or columns.
Alt+Shift+Left Arrow	Ungroup rows or columns.
Ctrl+8	Display or hide the outline symbols.
Ctrl+9	Hide the selected rows.
Ctrl+Shift+((opening parenthesis)	Unhide any hidden rows within the selection.
Ctrl+0 (zero)	Hide the selected columns.
Ctrl+Shift+) (closing parenthesis)	Unhide any hidden columns within the selection.

Smart Tags

Press	To
Alt+Shift+F10	Display the menu or message for a smart tag. If more than one smart tag is present, switch to the next smart tag and display its menu or message.
Down Arrow	Select the next item in a smart tag menu.
Up Arrow	Select the previous item in a smart tag menu.
Enter	Perform the action for the selected item in a smart tag menu.
Esc	Close the smart tag menu or message.

Speech Recognition and Text-To-Speech

Press	To
Ctrl	Switch between command mode and dictation mode.
Esc	Stop reading when text is being read aloud.

Task Panes

Press	To
F6	Move to a task pane from another pane in the program window. (You may need to press F6 more than once.) Note: If pressing F6 doesn't display the task pane you want, try pressing Alt to place focus on the menu bar, and then pressing Ctrl+Tab to move to the task pane.
Ctrl+Tab	When a menu or toolbar is active, move to a task pane. (You may need to press Ctrl+Tab more than once.)
Tab or Shift+Tab	When a task pane is active, select the next or previous option in the task pane.
Ctrl+Down Arrow	Display the full set of commands on the task pane menu.
Down Arrow or Up Arrow	Move among choices in a selected submenu, or move among certain options in a group of options.
Spacebar or Enter	Open the selected menu, or perform the action assigned to the selected button.
Shift+F10	Open a shortcut menu, or open a drop-down menu for the selected gallery item.

(continued)

945

Task Panes *(continued)*

Press	To
Home or End	When a menu or submenu is visible, select the first or last command on the menu or submenu.
Page Up or Page Down	Scroll up or down in the selected gallery list.
Ctrl+Home or Ctrl+End	Move to the top or bottom of the selected gallery list.

Windows and Office Interface

Press	To
Alt+Tab	Switch to the next program.
Alt+Shift+Tab	Switch to the previous program.
Ctrl+Esc	Display the Windows Start menu.
Ctrl+W or Ctrl+F4	Close the selected workbook window.
F6	Switch to the next pane in a worksheet that has been split.
Shift+F6	Switch to the previous pane in a worksheet that has been split.
Ctrl+F6	When more than one workbook window is open, switch to the next workbook window.
Ctrl+Shift+F6	Switch to the previous workbook window.
Ctrl+F7	When a workbook window is not maximized, perform the Move command (on the Control menu for the workbook window). Use the arrow keys to move the window, and when finished press Esc.
Ctrl+F8	When a workbook window is not maximized, perform the Size command (on the Control menu for the workbook window). Use the arrow keys to resize the window, and when finished press Esc.
Ctrl+F9	Minimize a workbook window to an icon.
Ctrl+F10	Maximize or restore the selected workbook window.
Print Screen	Copy a picture of the screen to the Clipboard.
Alt+Print Screen	Copy a picture of the selected window to the Clipboard.

Worksheets

Press	To
Shift+F11 or Alt+Shift+F1	Insert a new worksheet.
Ctrl+Page Down	Move to the next sheet in the workbook.
Ctrl+Page Up	Move to the previous sheet in the workbook.
Shift+Ctrl+Page Down	Select the current and next sheet. To cancel selection of multiple sheets, press Ctrl+Page Down, or to select a different sheet, press Ctrl+Page Up.
Shift+Ctrl+Page Up	Select the current and previous sheet.
Alt+O H R	Rename the current sheet (Format menu, Sheet submenu, Rename command).
Alt+E M	Move or copy the current sheet (Edit menu, Move or Copy Sheet command).
Alt+E D	Delete the current sheet (Edit menu, Delete Sheet command).

Function Reference

This Appendix lists all the worksheet functions available in Microsoft Excel 2002 in alphabetical order. The table includes a description, the function syntax, and a description of each argument. Arguments that appear in bold text are required; arguments that do not appear in bold text are optional. Function names that appear in shaded table cells are Analysis ToolPak functions. You must have the Analysis ToolPak installed to access these functions.

For more information, see "Installing the Analysis ToolPak" on page 405.

All function arguments must be entered in the order shown, and you must not add any spaces between or within arguments. If you need to enter spaces in a text argument or a reference, the argument must be enclosed in double quotation marks.

Function	Description
ABS	Returns the absolute value of a number, and takes the form =ABS(**number**). If a number is negative, this function simply removes the sign, making it a positive number.
ACCRINT	Returns the interest accrued by a security that pays interest on a periodic basis, and takes the form =ACCRINT(**issue, first interest, settlement, rate**, par, **frequency**, basis), where *issue* is the issue date of the security; *first interest* is the date of the initial interest payment; *settlement* is the day you pay for the security; *rate* is the interest rate of the security at the issue date; *par* is the par value of the security; *frequency* is the number of coupon payments made per year (1 = annual; 2 = semiannual; 4 = quarterly); and *basis* is the day-count basis of the security (if 0 or omitted = 30/360; if 1 = actual/actual; if 2 = actual/360; if 3 = actual/365; if 4 = European 30/360). See "Analyzing Securities" on page 465.
ACCRINTM	Returns the interest accrued by a maturity security that pays interest at maturity, and takes the form =ACCRINTM(**issue, maturity, rate**, par, basis), where *issue* is the issue date of the security; *maturity* is the security's maturity date; *rate* is the interest rate of the security at the issue date; *par* is the par value of the security; and *basis* is the day-count basis of the security (if 0 or omitted = 30/360; if 1 = actual/actual; if 2 = actual/360; if 3 = actual/365; if 4 = European 30/360). See "Analyzing Securities" on page 465.
ACOS	Returns the arccosine (inverse cosine) of a number in radians, and takes the form =ACOS(**number**), where *number* is the cosine of an angle.
ACOSH	Returns the inverse hyperbolic cosine of a number, and takes the form =ACOSH(**number**), where *number* must be >=1.

Function	Description
ADDRESS	Builds references from numbers, and takes the form =ADDRESS(**row_num, column_num**, abs_num, a1, sheet_text), where *row_num* and *column_num* designate the row and column values for the address; *abs_num* determines whether the resulting address uses absolute references (1), mixed (2-absolute row, relative column or 3-relative row, absolute column), or relative (4); *a1* is a logical value (if TRUE, the resulting address is in A1 format; if FALSE, the resulting address is in R1C1 format); and *sheet_text* specifies the name of the sheet. See "Using Selected Lookup and Reference Functions" on page 411.
AMORDEGRC	Returns the depreciation for each accounting period (French accounting system only), including any partial period, and takes the form =AMORDEGRC(**cost, date_purchased, first_period, salvage, period, rate, basis**), where *cost* is the cost of the asset, *date_purchased* is the date of the purchase, *first_period* is the date of the end of the first period, *salvage* is the salvage value at the end of the life of the asset, *period* is the period for which you want to calculate depreciation, *rate* is the rate of depreciation, and *basis* is the year basis to be used (0 = 360 days; 1 = actual; 3 = 365 days; 4 = European 360 days). This function is similar to AMORLINC, except that a depreciation coefficient is applied, depending on the asset life (1.5 if 3–4years; 2 if 5–6 years; 2.5 if > 6 years).
AMORLINC	Returns the depreciation for each accounting period (French accounting system only), including any partial period. See AMORDEGRC for syntax and arguments.
AND	Helps develop compound conditional test formulas in conjunction with the simple logical operators: =, >, <, >=, <=, and <>. The AND function can have as many as 30 arguments, and takes the form =AND(**logical1**, logical2, ...), where *logicals* can be conditional tests, arrays, or references to cells that contain logical values. See "Using Selected Logical Functions" on page 424.
AREAS	Returns the number of references (a cell or block of cells), and takes the form =AREAS(**reference**), where *reference* can be a cell reference, a range reference, or several range references enclosed in parentheses. See "Using Selected Lookup and Reference Functions" on page 411.
ASIN	Returns the arcsine of a number in radians, and takes the form =ASIN(**number**), where *number* is the sine of the angle you want and must be from −1 to 1.
ASINH	Returns the inverse hyperbolic sine of a number, and takes the form =ASINH(**number**).
ATAN	Returns the arctangent of a number, and takes the form =ATAN(**number**), where *number* is the tangent of an angle.
ATAN2	Returns the arctangent of the specified x- and y-coordinates, in radians, and takes the form =ATAN2(**x_num, y_num**), where *x_num* is the x-coordinate of the point, and *y_num* is the y-coordinate of the point. A positive result represents a counterclockwise angle from the x-axis; a negative result represents a clockwise angle.
ATANH	Returns the inverse hyperbolic tangent of a number, and takes the form =ATANH(**number**), where *number* must be between (not including) −1 and 1.

Function	Description
AVEDEV	Returns the average of the absolute deviations of data points from their mean, takes the form =AVEDEV(**number1**, number2, …), where the numbers can be names, arrays, or references that resolve to numbers, and accepts up to 30 arguments.
AVERAGE	Returns the arithmetic mean of the specified numbers, and takes the form =AVERAGE(**number1**, number2, …), where the numbers can be names, arrays, or references that resolve to numbers. Cells containing text, logical values, or empty cells are ignored, but cells containing a zero value are included. See "Using Built-In Statistical Functions" on page 472.
AVERAGEA	Same as AVERAGE, except that text and logical values are included in the calculation. See "Using Built-In Statistical Functions" on page 472.
BAHTTEXT	Converts a number to Thai text and adds the suffix Baht, using the form =BAHTTEXT(**number**), where *number* can be a reference to a cell containing a number, or a formula that resolves to a number.
BESSELI	Returns the modified Bessel function, which is equivalent to the Bessel function evaluated for imaginary arguments, and takes the form =BESSELI(**x, n**), where *x* is the value at which to evaluate the function and *n* is the order of the Bessel function.
BESSELJ	Returns the Bessel function, using the form =BESSELJ(**x, n**), where *x* is the value at which to evaluate the function and *n* is the order of the Bessel function.
BESSELK	Returns the modified Bessel function, which is equivalent to the Bessel function evaluated for imaginary arguments, and takes the form =BESSELK(**x, n**), where *x* is the value at which to evaluate the function and *n* is the order of the Bessel function.
BESSELY	Returns the Bessel function (also called the Weber or Neumann function), and takes the form =BESSELY(**x, n**), where *x* is the value at which to evaluate the function and *n* is the order of the function.
BETADIST	Returns the cumulative beta probability density function, and takes the form =BETADIST(**x, alpha, beta**, A, B), where *x* is the value between A and B at which to evaluate the function, *alpha* is a parameter to the distribution, *beta* is a parameter to the distribution, A is an optional lower bound to the interval of *x*, and B is an optional upper bound to the interval of *x*.
BETAINV	Returns the inverse of the cumulative beta probability density function, and takes the form =BETAINV(**probability, alpha, beta**, A, B), where *probability* is a probability associated with the beta distribution. For additional argument descriptions, see BETADIST.
BINOMDIST	Returns the individual term binomial distribution probability, and takes the form =BINOMDIST(**number_s, trials, probability_s, cumulative**), where *number_s* is the number of successes in trials; *trials* is the number of independent trials; *probability_s* is the probability of success on each trial; and *cumulative* is a logical value that determines the form of the function. If TRUE, returns the probability that there are at most *number_s* successes; if FALSE, it returns the probability that there are *number_s* successes.
CEILING	Rounds a number up to the nearest given multiple and takes the form =CEILING(**number, multiple**), where *number* and *multiple* must be numeric and have the same sign. If they have different signs, Excel returns the #NUM! error value. See "Using the Rounding Functions" on page 417.

Function	Description
CELL	Returns information about the contents, location, or formatting of a cell, and takes the form =CELL(**info_type**, reference), where *info_type* specifies the type of information you want and *reference* is the cell you want information about. Info_type can be any of the following: *address, col* (column #), *color, contents, filename, format, parentheses, prefix, protect, row, type,* or *width.* See online Help for a table of *format* codes returned.
CHAR	Returns the character that corresponds to an ASCII code number, and takes the form =CHAR(**number**), where *number* accepts ASCII codes with or without leading zeros. See "Using Selected Text Functions" on page 419.
CHIDIST	Returns the one-tailed probability of the chi-squared distribution (used to compare observed vs. expected values), and takes the form =CHIDIST(**x, degrees_freedom**), where *x* is the value at which you want to evaluate the distribution and *degrees_freedom* is the number of degrees of freedom.
CHIINV	Returns the inverse of CHIDIST (one-tailed probability of the chi-squared distribution), and takes the form =CHIINV(**probability, degrees_freedom**), where *probability* is a probability associated with the chi-squared distribution and *degrees_freedom* is the number of degrees of freedom.
CHITEST	Returns the test for independence, and takes the form =CHITEST(**actual_range, expected_range**), where *actual_range* is the range of data that contains observations to test against expected values and *expected_range* is the range of data that contains the ratio of the product of row totals and column totals to the grand total.
CHOOSE	Retrieves an item from a list of values, and takes the form =CHOOSE(**index_num, value1**, value2,...), where *index_num* is the position in the list of the item you want to look up and the *value* arguments are the elements of the list, which can be values or cell references. Returns the value of the element of the list that occupies the position indicated by *index_num*. See "Using Selected Lookup and Reference Functions" on page 429.
CLEAN	Removes nonprintable characters such as tabs and program-specific codes from a string, and takes the form =CLEAN(**text**). See "Using Selected Text Functions" on page 419.
CODE	Returns the ASCII code number for the first character of its argument, and takes the form =CODE(**text**). See "Using Selected Text Functions" on page 419.
COLUMN	Returns the column number of the referenced cell or range, and takes the form =COLUMN(reference). If *reference* is omitted, the result is the column number of the cell containing the function. If *reference* is a range or a name and the function is entered as an array (by pressing Ctrl+Shift+Enter), the result is an array of the numbers of each of the columns in the range. See "Selected Lookup and Reference Functions" on page 429.
COLUMNS	Returns the number of columns in a reference or an array, and takes the form =COLUMNS(**array**), where *array* is an array constant, a range reference, or a range name. See "Selected Lookup and Reference Functions" on page 429.

Function	Description
COMBIN	Determines the number of possible group combinations that can be derived from a pool of items, and takes the form =COMBIN(**number, number_chosen**), where *number* is the total items in the pool, and *number_chosen* is the number of items you want in each group. See "Selected Mathematical Functions" on page 414.
COMPLEX	Converts real and imaginary coefficients into a complex number of the form x + yi or x + yj, and takes the form =COMPLEX(**real_num, i_num**, suffix), where *real_num* is the real coefficient of the complex number; *i_num* is the imaginary coefficient of the complex number; and *suffix* is the suffix for the imaginary component of the complex number. If omitted, suffix is assumed to be *i*.
CONCATENATE	Assembles larger strings from smaller strings, takes the form =CONCATENATE(**text1, text2**, ...), and accepts up to 30 arguments, which can be text, numbers, or cell referneces. See "Using the Substring Text Functions" on page 422.
CONFIDENCE	Returns the confidence interval for a population mean, and takes the form =CONFIDENCE(**alpha, standard_dev, size**), where *alpha* is the significance level used to compute the confidence level (an alpha of 0.1 indicates a 90 percent confidence level); *standard_dev* is the population standard deviation for the data range and is assumed to be known; and *size* is the sample size.
CONVERT	Converts a number from one measurement system to another, and takes the form =CONVERT(**number, from_unit, to_unit**), where *number* is the value to convert; *from_unit* is the units for *number*; and *to_unit* is the units for the result. See online Help for a table of unit codes.
CORREL	Returns the correlation coefficient of the array1 and array2 cell ranges, and takes the form =CORREL(**array1, array2**), where arrays are ranges of cells containing values.
COS	Returns the cosine of an angle. The complement of the SIN function. It takes the form =COS(**number**), where *number* is the angle in radians.
COSH	Returns the hyperbolic cosine of a number, and takes the form =COSH(**number**), where *number* is any real number.
COUNT	Tells you how many cells in a given range contain numbers, including dates and formulas that evaluate to numbers, takes the form =COUNT(**number1**, number2,...), and can accept up to 30 arguments, ignoring text, error values, and logical values. See "Using Built-In Statistical Functions" on page 472.
COUNTA	Same as COUNT, except that text and logical values are included in the calculation. See "Using Built-In Statistical Functions" on page 472.
COUNTBLANK	Counts empty cells in a specified range, and takes the form =COUNTBLANK(**range**). See "Using Selected Lookup and Reference Functions" on page 411.
COUNTIF	Counts only those cells that match specified criteria, and takes the form =COUNTIF(**range, criteria**), where *range* is the range you want to test and *criteria* is the logical test to be performed on each cell. See "Using Built-In Statistical Functions" on page 472.

Function	Description
COUPDAYBS	Calculates the number of days from the beginning of the coupon period to the settlement date, and takes the form =COUPDAYBS(**settlement, maturity, frequency**, basis), where *settlement* is the day you pay for the security; *maturity* is the maturity date of the security; *frequency* is the number of coupon payments made per year (1 = annual; 2 = semiannual; 4 = quarterly); and *basis* is the day-count basis of the security (if 0 or omitted = 30/360; if 1 = actual/actual; if 2 = actual/360; if 3 = actual/365; if 4 = European 30/360). See "Analyzing Securities" on page 465.
COUPDAYS	Calculates the number of days in the coupon period that contains the settlement date, and takes the form =COUPDAYS(**settlement, maturity, frequency**, basis). See COUPDAYBS for argument definitions. See "Analyzing Securities" on page 465.
COUPDAYSNC	Calculates the number of days from the settlement date to the next coupon date, and takes the form =COUPDAYSNC(**settlement, maturity, frequency**, basis). See COUPDAYBS for argument definitions. See "Analyzing Securities" on page 465.
COUPNCD	Calculates the next coupon date after the settlement date, and takes the form =COUPNCD(**settlement, maturity, frequency**, basis). See COUPDAYBS for argument definitions. See "Analyzing Securities" on page 465.
COUPNUM	Calculates the number of coupons payable between the settlement date and the maturity date and rounds the result to the nearest whole coupon, and takes the form =COUPNUM(**settlement, maturity, frequency**, basis). See COUPDAYBS for argument definitions. See "Analyzing Securities" on page 465.
COUPPCD	Calculates the coupon date previous to the settlement date, and takes the form =COUPPCD(**settlement, maturity, frequency**, basis). See COUPDAYBS for argument definitions. See "Analyzing Securities" on page 465.
COVAR	Returns covariance, the average of the products of deviations for each data point pair, and takes the form =COVAR(**array1, array2**), where *arrays* are cell ranges containing integers.
CRITBINOM	Returns the smallest value for which the cumulative binomial distribution is greater than or equal to a criterion value, and takes the form =CRITBINOM(**trials, probability_s, alpha**), where *trials* is the number of Bernoulli trials, *probability_s* is the probability of a success on each trial, and *alpha* is the criterion value.
CUMIPMT	Returns the cumulative interest paid on a loan between *start_period* and *end_period*, and takes the form =CUMIPMT(**rate, nper, pv, start_period, end_period, type**), where *rate* is the interest rate; *nper* is the total number of payment periods; *pv* is the present value; and *start_period* is the first period in the calculation. Payment periods are numbered beginning with 1, *end_period* is the last period in the calculation, and *type* is the timing of the payment.
CUMPRINC	Returns the cumulative principal paid on a loan between *start_period* and *end_period*, and takes the form =CUMPRINC(**rate, nper, pv, start_period, end_period, type**). For argument descriptions, see CUMIPMT.

Function	Description
DATE	Returns the serial number that represents a particular date, and takes the form =DATE(**year, month, day**), where *year* can be one to four digits from 1 to 9999, *month* is a number representing the month of the year, and *day* is a number representing the day of the month.
DATEVALUE	Translates a date into a serial value, and takes the form =DATEVALUE(**date_text**), where *date_text* represents a date entered as text in quotation marks. See "Working with Date and Time Functions" on page 449.
DAVERAGE	Averages the values in a column in a list or database that match conditions you specify, and takes the form =DAVERAGE(**database, field, criteria**), where *database* is the range of cells that make up the list or database and the first row of the list contains labels for each column; *field* indicates which column is used in the function (by label name or by position); and *criteria* is the range of cells that contains the conditions you specify.
DAY	Returns the value of the day portion of a serial date/time value, and takes the form =DAY(**serial_number**), where *serial_number* can be a date value, a reference, or text in date format enclosed in quotation marks. See "Working with Date and Time Functions" on page 449.
DAYS360	Returns the number of days between two dates based on a 360-day year (12 30-day months), which is used in some accounting calculations, and takes the form =DAYS360(**start_date, end_date**, method), where *start_date* and *end_date* are the two dates between which you want to know the number of days and *method* is a logical value that specifies whether to use the U.S. or European method in the calculation If FALSE or omitted, uses U.S. (NASD) method; if TRUE, uses the European method.
DB	Computes fixed declining balance depreciation for a particular period in the asset's life, and takes the form =DB(**cost, salvage, life, period**, month), where *cost* is the initial asset cost; *salvage* is the remaining value after asset is fully depreciated; *life* is the length of depreciation time, *period* is the individual period to be computed; and *month* is the number of months depreciated in the first year. See "Calculating Depreciation" on page 462.
DCOUNT	Counts the cells that contain numbers in a column in a list or database that match conditions you specify, and takes the form =DCOUNT(**database, field, criteria**), where *database* is the range of cells that make up the list or database; *field* indicates which column is used in the function; and *criteria* is the range of cells that contains the conditions you specify.
DCOUNTA	Same as DCOUNT, except that it also includes cells containing text, logical values, and error values. See DCOUNT for arguments.
DDB	Computes double-declining balance depreciation, and takes the form =DDB(**cost, salvage, life**, period, factor), where *cost* is the initial asset cost; *salvage* is the remaining value after asset is fully depreciated; *life* is the length of depreciation time; *period* is the individual period to be computed; and *factor* indicates the method used (2 or omitted indicates double-declining balance; 3 indicates triple-declining balance). See "Calculating Depreciation" on page 462.

Function	Description
DEC2BIN	Converts a decimal number to binary, and takes the form =DEC2BIN(**number**, places), where *number* is the decimal integer you want to convert and *places* is the number of characters to use. *places* is useful for padding the return value with leading 0s (zeros).
DEC2HEX	Converts a decimal number to hexadecimal, and takes the same form and arguments as DEC2BIN.
DEC2OCT	Converts a decimal number to octal, and takes the same form and arguments as DEC2BIN.
DEGREES	Converts radians to degrees, and takes the form =DEGREES(angle), where *angle* represents an angle measured in radians.
DELTA	Tests whether two values are equal, and takes the form =DELTA(number1, number2), where *number1* is the first number, and *number2* is the second number (which, if omitted, is assumed to be zero). Returns 1 if number1 equals number2; otherwise returns 0.
DEVSQ	Returns the sum of squares of deviations of data points from their sample mean, takes the form =DEVSQ(number1, number2,...), where numbers can be names, arrays, or references that resolve to numbers, and accepts up to 30 arguments.
DGET	Extracts a single value from a column in a list or database that matches conditions you specify, and takes the form =DGET(database, field, criteria), where *database* is the range of cells that make up the list or database; *field* indicates which column is used in the function; and *criteria* is the range of cells that contains the conditions you specify.
DISC	Calculates the discount rate for a security, and takes the form =DISC(**settlement, maturity, price, redemption, basis**), where *settlement* is the day you pay for the security; *maturity* is the maturity date of the security; *price* is the security's price per $100 face value; *redemption* is the value of the security at redemption; and *basis* is the day-count basis of the security (if 0 or omitted = 30/360; if 1 = actual/actual; if 2 = actual/360; if 3 = actual/365; if 4 = European 30/360). See "Analyzing Securities" on page 465.
DMAX	Returns the largest number in a column in a list or database that matches conditions you specify, and takes the form =DMAX(**database, field, criteria**), where *database* is a range that makes up the list or database; *field* indicates which column is used in the function; and *criteria* is the range of cells that contains the conditions you specify.
DMIN	Returns the smallest number in a column in a list or database that matches conditions you specify, and takes the same form and arguments as DMAX.
DOLLAR	Converts a number into a string formatted as currency with the specified number of decimal places, and takes the form =DOLLAR(**number**, decimals). If you omit *decimals*, the result is rounded to two decimal places. If you use a negative number for *decimals*, the result is rounded to the left of the decimal point. See "Using Selected Text Functions" on page 419.
DOLLARDE	Converts the familiar fractional pricing of securities to decimals, and takes the form =DOLLARDE(**fractional dollar, fraction**), where *fractional dollar* is the value you want to convert expressed as an integer followed by a decimal point and the numerator of the fraction you want and *fraction* is an integer indicating the denominator to be used. See "Analyzing Securities" on page 465.

Function	Description
DOLLARFR	Converts a security price expressed in decimals to fractions, and takes the form =DOLLARFR(**decimal dollar, fraction**), where *decimal dollar* is the value you want to convert expressed as a decimal and *fraction* is an integer indicating the denominator of the fraction you want. See "Analyzing Securities" on page 465.
DPRODUCT	Multiplies the values in a column in a list or database that match conditions you specify, and takes the form =DPRODUCT(**database, field, criteria**), where *database* is a range that makes up the list or database, *field* indicates which column is used in the function, and *criteria* is the range of cells that contains the conditions you specify.
DSTDEV	Estimates the standard deviation of a population based on a sample, using the numbers in a column in a list or database that match conditions you specify, and takes the same form and arguments as DPRODUCT.
DSTDEVP	Calculates the standard deviation of a population based on the entire population, using the numbers in a column in a list or database that match conditions you specify, and takes the same form and arguments as DPRODUCT.
DSUM	Adds the numbers in a column in a list or database that match conditions you specify, and takes the same form and arguments as DPRODUCT.
DURATION	Calculates the weighted average of the present value of the bond's cash flows for a security whose interest payments are made on a periodic basis, and takes the form =DURATION(**settlement, maturity, coupon, yield, frequency**, basis), where *settlement* is the day you pay for the security; *maturity* is the maturity date of the security; *coupon* is the security's annual coupon rate; *yield* is the annual yield of the security; *frequency* is the number of coupon payments made per year (1 = annual; 2 = semiannual; 4 = quarterly); and *basis* is the day-count basis of the security (if 0 or omitted = 30/360; if 1 = actual/actual; if 2 = actual/360; if 3 = actual/365; if 4 = European 30/360). See "Analyzing Securities" on page 465.
DVAR	Estimates the variance of a population based on a sample, using the numbers in a column in a list or database that match conditions you specify, and takes the form =DVAR(**database, field, criteria**), where *database* is the range of cells that make up the list or database; *field* indicates which column is used in the function; and *criteria* is the range of cells that contains the conditions you specify.
DVARP	Calculates the variance of a population based on the entire population, using the numbers in a column in a list or database that match conditions you specify, and takes the same form and arguments as DVAR.
EDATE	Returns the exact date that falls an indicated number of months before or after a given date, and takes the form =EDATE(**start_date, months**), where *start_date* is the date to calculate from and *months* is the number of months before (negative) or after (positive) the start date. See "Working with Specialized Date Functions" on page 451.
EOMONTH	Returns a date that falls on the last day of the month an indicated number of months before or after a given date, and takes the form =EOMONTH(**start_date, months**), where *start_date* is the date to calculate from and *months* is the number of months before (negative) or after (positive) the start date. See "Working with Specialized Date Functions" on page 451.

Function	Description
ERF	Returns the error function integrated between *lower_limit* and *upper_limit*, and takes the form =ERF(**lower_limit**, upper_limit), where *lower_limit* is the lower bound and *upper_limit* is the upper bound. If omitted, ERF integrates between zero and *lower_limit*.
ERFC	Returns the complementary ERF function integrated between x and infinity, and takes the form =ERFC(**x**), where *x* is the lower bound for integrating ERF.
ERROR.TYPE	Detects the type of error value in a referenced cell, and takes the form =ERROR.TYPE(**error_val**). Returns a code designating the type of error value in the referenced cell: 1 (#NULL!), 2 (#DIV/0!), 3 (#VALUE!), 4 (#REF!), 5 (#NAME!), 6 (#NUM!), and 7 (#N/A). Any other value in the referenced cell returns the error value #N/A. See "Using Selected Lookup and Reference Functions" on page 411.
EUROCONVERT	Converts a number to Euros—or converts any Euro member currency to Euros or any other member currency—and takes the form =EUROCONVERT(**number, source, target**, full_precision, triangulation_precision), where *number* is the value you want to convert; *source* is the ISO country code for the source currency; *target* is the ISO country code for the currency to which you want to convert; *full_precision* is a logical value that if TRUE, displays all significant digits, and if FALSE, uses a currency-specific rounding factor; and *triangulation_precision* is an integer equal to 3 or greater that specifies the number of significant digits to use when converting from one Euro member currency to another. This function is installed with the Euro Currency Tools add-in. See online Help for tables of ISO codes and rounding factors.
EVEN	Rounds a number up to the nearest even integer, and takes the form =EVEN(**number**). Negative numbers are correspondingly rounded down. See "Using the Rounding Functions" on page 417.
EXACT	Determines whether two strings match exactly, including uppercase and lowercase letters, not including formatting differences, and takes the form =EXACT(**text1, text2**), where both arguments must be either literal strings enclosed in double quotation marks or references to cells that contain text. See "Using Selected Text Functions" on page 419.
EXP	Computes the value of the constant *e* (approx. 2.71828183) raised to the power specified by its argument, and takes the form =EXP(number). The EXP function is the inverse of the LN function.
EXPONDIST	Returns exponential distribution, and takes the form =EXPONDIST(**x, lambda, cumulative**), where *x* is the value of the function; *lambda* is the parameter value; and *cumulative* is a logical value that indicates which form of the exponential function to provide (if TRUE, returns the cumulative distribution function; if FALSE, returns the probability density function).
FACT	Returns the factorial of a number, and takes the form =FACT(**number**), where *number* is a positive integer.
FACTDOUBLE	Returns the double factorial of a number, and takes the form =FACT(**number**), where *number* is a positive integer.

Function	Description
FALSE	An alternative representation of the logical condition FALSE, which accepts no arguments, and takes the form =FALSE( ). See "Using Selected Logical Functions" on page 419.
FDIST	Returns the F probability distribution, and takes the form =FDIST(**x, degrees_freedom1, degrees_freedom2**), where *x* is the value at which to evaluate the function, *degrees_freedom1* is the numerator degrees of freedom, and *degrees_freedom2* is the denominator.
FIND	Returns the position of specified text within a string, and takes the form =FIND(**find_text, within_text**, start_num), where *find_text* is the text you want to find (case-sensitive) and *within_text* indicates where to look. Both arguments accept either literal text enclosed in double quotation marks or cell references. Optional *start_num* specifies the character position in *within_text* where you want to begin the search. You get a #VALUE! error value if *find_text* isn't contained in *within_text*, if *start_num* isn't greater than zero, or if *start_num* is greater than the number of characters in *within_text* or greater than the position of the last occurrence of *find_text*. See "Using the Substring Text Functions" on page 422.
FINDB	Returns the position of specified text within a string based on the number of bytes each character uses from the first character of *within_text*, takes the form =FINDB(**find_text, within_text**, start_num), and takes the same arguments as FIND. This function is for use with double-byte characters.
FINV	Returns the inverse of the F probability distribution, and takes the form =FINV(**probability, degrees_freedom1, degrees_freedom2**), where *probability* is a probability associated with the F cumulative distribution; *degrees_freedom1* is the numerator degrees of freedom; and *degrees_freedom2* is the denominator degrees of freedom.
FISHER	Returns the Fisher transformation at x, and takes the form =FISHER(**x**), where *x* is a value between –1 and 1 (not inclusive).
FISHERINV	Returns the inverse of the Fisher transformation, and takes the form =FISHERINV(**y**), where *y* is any numeric value.
FIXED	Rounds a number to the specified number of decimals, formats the number in decimal format using a period and commas, and returns the result as text. This function takes the form =FIXED(**number**, decimals, no_commas), where *number* is the number you want to round and convert to text; *decimals* is the number of digits to the right of the decimal point (assumes 2 if omitted); and *no_commas* is a logical value (if TRUE, prevents commas; if FALSE or omitted, includes commas).
FLOOR	Rounds a number down to the nearest given multiple, and takes the form =FLOOR(**number, multiple**), where *number* and *multiple* must be numeric and have the same sign. If they have different signs, Excel returns the #NUM! error value. See "Using the Rounding Functions" on page 417.
FORECAST	Returns a single point along a trend line, and takes the form =FORECAST(**x, known_y's, known_x's**). For arguments and usage details, see "The FORECAST Function" on page 482.
FREQUENCY	Returns the number of times that values occur within a population, and takes the form =FREQUENCY(**data_array, bins_array**) For usage and argument details, see "Analyzing Distribution with the FREQUENCY Function" on page 488.

Function	Description
FTEST	Returns the result of an F-test, the one-tailed probability that the variances in *array1* and *array2* are not significantly different, and takes the form =FTEST(**array1, array2**).
FV	Computes the value at a future date of an investment that makes payments as a lump sum or as a series of equal periodic payments, and takes the form =FV(**rate, nper, payment**, pv, type), where *rate* is the interest rate; *nper* is the term (periods) of the investment; *payment* is the amount of each periodic payment when individual amounts are the same; *pv* is the investment value today, and *type* indicates when payments are made (0 or omitted = at end of period; 1 = at beginning of period). See "Calculating Investments" on page 455.
FVSCHEDULE	Returns the future value of an initial principal after applying a series of variable compound interest rates, and takes the form =FVSCHEDULE(**principal, schedule**), where *principal* is the present value and *schedule* is an array of interest rates to apply.
GAMMADIST	Returns the gamma distribution, and takes the form =GAMMADIST(**x, alpha, beta, cumulative**), where *x* is the value at which you want to evaluate the distribution; *alpha* is a parameter to the distribution; *beta* is a parameter to the distribution; and *cumulative* is a logical value that determines the form of the function (if TRUE, returns the cumulative distribution function; if FALSE, returns the probability mass function).
GAMMAINV	Returns the inverse of the gamma cumulative distribution, and takes the form =GAMMAINV(**probability, alpha, beta**), where *probability* is the probability associated with the gamma distribution; *alpha* is a parameter to the distribution; and *beta* is a parameter to the distribution.
GAMMALN	Returns the natural logarithm of the gamma function, and takes the form =GAMMALN(**x**), where *x* is a positive value.
GCD	Returns the greatest common divisor of two or more integers (the largest integer that divides both number1 and number2 without a remainder), and takes the form =GCD(**number1**, number2, ...), where *numbers* are 1 to 29 positive integer values.
GEOMEAN	Returns the geometric mean of an array or range of positive data, and takes the form =GEOMEAN(**number1**, number2, ...), where *numbers* are 1 to 29 positive integer values.
GESTEP	Returns 1 if number • step; otherwise returns 0 (zero), and takes the form =GESTEP(**number**, step), where *number* is the value to test against *step* and *step* is the threshold value (zero if omitted).
GETPIVOTDATA	Returns data stored in a PivotTable report, and takes the form =GETPIVOTDATA(**data_field, pivot_table**, field1, item1, field2, item2, ...), where *data_field* is the name, in quotation marks, for the data field that contains the data you want retrieved; *pivot_table* is a reference to a cell in the PivotTable report that contains the data you want to retrieve; and *fieldx* and *itemx* are one to 14 pairs of field names and item names that describe the data you want to retrieve.
GROWTH	Returns values of points that lie along an exponential growth trend line, and takes the form =GROWTH(**known_y's**, known_x's, new_x's, const). For arguments and usage details, see "The GROWTH Function" on page 483.

Function	Description
HARMEAN	Returns the harmonic mean of a data set, and takes the form =HARMEAN(**number1**, number2, ...), where *numbers* are 1 to 30 positive values.
HEX2BIN	Converts a hexadecimal number to binary, and takes the form =HEX2BIN(**number**, places), where *number* is the hexadecimal number you want to convert and *places* is the number of characters to use (useful for padding the return value with leading zeros).
HEX2DEC	Converts a hexadecimal number to decimal, and takes the form =HEX2DEC(**number**), where *number* is the hexadecimal number you want to convert.
HEX2OCT	Converts a hexadecimal number to octal, and takes the form =HEX2OCT(**number**, places), where *number* is the hexadecimal number you want to convert and *places* is the number of characters to use (useful for padding the return value with leading zeros).
HLOOKUP	Looks for a specified value in the top row in a table, returns the value in the same column and a specified row, and takes the form =HLOOKUP(**lookup_value, table_array, row_index_num**, range_lookup), where *lookup_value* is the value to look for; *table_array* is the range containing the lookup and result values sorted in alphabetical order by the top row; *row_index_num* is the row number containing the value you want to find; and *range_lookup* is a logical which, if FALSE, forces an exact match. See "Using Selected Lookup and Reference Functions" on page 411.
HOUR	Returns the hour portion of a serial date/time value, and takes the form =HOUR(**serial_number**), where *serial_number* can be a time/date value, a reference, or text in time/date format enclosed in quotation marks. See "Working with Date and Time Functions" on page 449.
HYPERLINK	Creates a shortcut or jump that opens a document stored on a network server, an intranet, or the Internet. When you click the cell that contains the HYPERLINK function, Excel opens the file stored at *link_location*. This function takes the form =HYPERLINK(**link_location**, friendly_name), where *link_location* is the path and file name to the document to be opened, and *friendly_name* is the jump text or numeric value that is displayed in the cell.
HYPGEOMDIST	Returns the hypergeometric distribution (the probability of a given number of sample successes, given the size of the sample and population, and the number of population successes, and takes the form =HYPGEOMDIST(**sample_s, number_sample, population_s, number_population**), where *sample_s* is the number of successes in the sample; *number_sample* is the size of the sample; *population_s* is the number of successes in the population; and *number_population* is the population size.
IF	Returns values based on supplied conditional tests, and takes the form =IF(**logical_test, value_if_true**, value_if_false). You can nest up to seven additional functions within an IF function. If you use text arguments, the match must be exact, except for case. See "Using Selected Logical Functions" on page 424.

Function	Description
IMABS	Returns the absolute value (modulus) of a complex number in x + yi or x + yj text format, and takes the form =IMABS(**inumber**), where *inumber* is a complex number for which you want the absolute value.
IMAGINARY	Returns the imaginary coefficient of a complex number in x + yi or x + yj text format, and takes the form =IMAGINARY(**inumber**), where *inumber* is a complex number for which you want the imaginary coefficient.
IMARGUMENT	Returns the argument theta, an angle expressed in radians, and takes the form =IMARGUMENT(**inumber**), where *inumber* is a complex number for which you want the argument theta.
IMCONJUGATE	Returns the complex conjugate of a complex number in x + yi or x + yj text format, and takes the form =IMCONJUGATE(**inumber**), where *inumber* is a complex number for which you want the conjugate.
IMCOS	Returns the cosine of a complex number in x + yi or x + yj text format, and takes the form =IMCOS(**inumber**), where *inumber* is a complex number for which you want the cosine.
IMDIV	Returns the quotient of two complex numbers in x + yi or x + yj text format, and takes the form =IMDIV(**inumber1, inumber2**), where *inumber1* is the complex numerator or dividend, and *inumber2* is the complex denominator or divisor.
IMEXP	Returns the exponential of a complex number in x + yi or x + yj text format, and takes the form =IMEXP(**inumber**), where *inumber* is a complex number for which you want the exponential.
IMLN	Returns the natural logarithm of a complex number in x + yi or x + yj text format, and takes the form =IMLN(**inumber**), where *inumber* is a complex number for which you want the natural logarithm.
IMLOG10	Returns the common logarithm (base 10) of a complex number in x + yi or x + yj text format, and takes the form =IMLOG10(**inumber**), where *inumber* is a complex number for which you want the common logarithm.
IMLOG2	Returns the base-2 logarithm of a complex number in x + yi or x + yj text format, and takes the form =IMLOG2(**inumber**), where *inumber* is a complex number for which you want the base-2 logarithm.
IMPOWER	Returns a complex number in x + yi or x + yj text format raised to a power, and takes the form =IMPOWER(**inumber, number**), where *inumber* is a complex number you want to raise to a power, and *number* is the power to which you want to raise the complex number.
IMPRODUCT	Returns the product of 2 to 29 complex numbers in x + yi or x + yj text format, and takes the form =IMPRODUCT(**inumber1**, inumber2,...), where *inumbers* are 1 to 29 complex numbers to multiply.
IMREAL	Returns the real coefficient of a complex number in x + yi or x + yj text format, and takes the form =IMREAL(**inumber**), where *inumber* is a complex number for which you want the real coefficient.
IMSIN	Returns the sine of a complex number in x + yi or x + yj text format, and takes the form =IMSIN(**inumber**), where *inumber* is a complex number for which you want the sine.

Function	Description
IMSQRT	Returns the square root of a complex number in x + yi or x + yj text format, and takes the form =IMSQRT(**inumber**), where *inumber* is a complex number for which you want the square root.
IMSUB	Returns the difference of two complex numbers in x + yi or x + yj text format, and takes the form =IMSUB(**inumber1, inumber2**), where *inumber1* is the complex number from which to subtract *inumber2* and *inumber2* is the complex number to subtract from *inumber1*.
IMSUM	Returns the sum of two or more complex numbers in x + yi or x + yj text format, and takes the form =IMSUM(**inumber1**, inumber2,...), where *inumbers* are 1 to 29 complex numbers to add.
INDEX	Returns a value or values, or a reference to a cell or range, using one of two forms, *array* or *reference*: =INDEX(**array**, row_num, column_num) =INDEX(**reference**, row_num, column_num, area_num) The array form works only with array arguments and returns the resulting values located at the intersection of *row_num* and *column_num*. The reference form returns a cell address using similar arguments, where *reference* can be one or more ranges (areas), and *area_num* is needed only if more than one area is included in *reference*. See "Using Selected Lookup and Reference Functions" on page 411.
INDIRECT	Returns the contents of a cell using its reference, and takes the form =INDIRECT(**ref_text**, a1), where *ref_text* is a reference or a name and *a1* is a logical value indicating the type of reference used in *ref_text* (FALSE indicates R1C1 format; TRUE or omitted indicates A1 format). See "Using Selected Lookup and Reference Functions" on page 411.
INFO	Returns information about the current operating environment, and takes the form =INFO(**type_text**), where *type_text* is text specifying what type of information you want returned. Information types include *directory, memavail, memused, numfile, origin, osversion, recalc, release, system,* and *totmem*. See online Help for more information.
INT	Rounds numbers down to the nearest integer, and takes the form =INT(**number**). When *number* is negative, INT also rounds that number down to the nearest integer. See "Using the Rounding Functions" on page 417.
INTERCEPT	Calculates the point at which a line will intersect the y-axis by using existing x-values and y-values, and takes the form =INTERCEPT(**known_y's, known_x's**), where *known_y's* is the dependent set of observations or data and *known_x's* is the independent set of observations or data.
INTRATE	Calculates the rate of interest (discount rate) for a fully invested security, and takes the form =INTRATE(**settlement, maturity, investment, redemption**, basis), where *settlement* is the day you pay for the security; *maturity* is the maturity date of the security, *investment* is the amount invested in the security; *redemption* is the amount to be received at maturity; and *basis* is the day-count basis of the security (if 0 or omitted = 30/360; if 1 = actual/actual; if 2 = actual/360; if 3 = actual/365; if 4 = European 30/360). See "Analyzing Securities" on page 465.

Function	Description
IPMT	Computes the interest portion of an individual payment made to repay an amount over a specified time period with constant periodic payments and a constant interest rate, and takes the form =IPMT(**rate, period, nper ,pv, fv, type**), where *rate* is the interest rate; *period* is the number of an individual periodic payment; *nper* is the term (periods) of the investment; *pv* is the investment value today; *fv* is the investment value at the end of the term; and *type* indicates when payments are made (0 or omitted = at end of period; 1 = at beginning of period). See "Calculating Investments" on page 455.
IRR	Returns the rate that causes the present value of the inflows from an investment to exactly equal the cost of the investment, and takes the form =IRR(**values**, guess), where *values* is an array or a reference to a range of cells that contain numbers beginning with the cost expressed as a negative value and *guess* is an approximate interest rate (assumes 10% if omitted). See "Calculating Investments" on page 455.
ISBLANK	Returns TRUE if the referenced cell is empty, otherwise returns FALSE, and uses the form =ISBLANK(**value**). See "Using the IS Information Functions" on page 427.
ISERR	Returns TRUE if value contains any error value except #N/A, otherwise returns FALSE, and uses the form =ISERR(**value**). See "Using the IS Information Functions" on page 427.
ISERROR	Returns TRUE if value contains any error value (including #N/A), otherwise returns FALSE, and uses the form =ISERROR(**value**). See "Using the IS Information Functions" on page 427.
ISEVEN	Returns TRUE if value is an even number, otherwise returns FALSE, and uses the form =ISEVEN(**value**). See "Using the IS Information Functions" on page 427.
ISLOGICAL	Returns TRUE if value is a logical value, otherwise returns FALSE, and uses the form =ISLOGICAL(**value**). See "Using the IS Information Functions" on page 427.
ISNA	Returns TRUE if value is the #N/A error value, otherwise returns FALSE, and uses the form =ISNA(**value**). See "Using the IS Information Functions" on page 427.
ISNONTEXT	Returns TRUE if value is not text, otherwise returns FALSE, and uses the form =ISNONTEXT(**value**). See "Using the IS Information Functions" on page 427.
ISNUMBER	Returns TRUE if value is a number, otherwise returns FALSE, and uses the form =ISNUMBER(**value**). See "Using the IS Information Functions" on page 427.
ISODD	Returns TRUE if value is an odd number, otherwise returns FALSE, and uses the form =ISODD(**value**). See "Using the IS Information Functions" on page 427.
ISPMT	Calculates the interest paid during a specific period of an investment. Provided for Lotus 1-2-3 compatibility, and takes the form =ISPMT(**rate, per, nper, pv**), where *rate* is the interest rate for the investment; *per* is the period for which you want to find the interest; *nper* is the total number of payment periods for the investment; and *pv* is the present value of the investment (or the loan amount).

Function	Description
ISREF	Returns TRUE if *value* is a reference—otherwise returns FALSE—and uses the form =ISREF(**value**). See "Using the IS Information Functions" on page 427.
ISTEXT	Returns TRUE if value is text, otherwise returns FALSE, and uses the form =ISTEXT(**value**). See "Using the IS Information Functions" on page 427.
KURT	Returns the kurtosis of a data set (characterizes the relative "peaked-ness" or flatness of a distribution compared with the normal distribution), takes the form =KURT(**number1**, number2, ...), and accepts up to 30 numeric arguments.
LARGE	Returns the *k*th largest value in an input range, and takes the form =LARGE(**array, k**), where *k* is the position from the largest value in *array* you want to find. See "Functions That Analyze Rank and Percentile" on page 473.
LCM	Returns the least common multiple of integers (the smallest positive integer that is a multiple of all arguments), takes the form =LCM(**number1**, number2, ...), and accepts up to 30 numeric integer arguments.
LEFT	Returns the leftmost series of characters from a string, and takes the form =LEFT(**text**, num_chars), where *num_chars* indicates how many characters you want to extract from the string (1, if omitted). See "Using the Substring Text Functions" on page 422.
LEFTB	Returns the leftmost series of characters from a string, based on the specified number of bytes, and takes the form =LEFT(**text**, num_bytes), where *num_bytes* indicates how many characters you want to extract from the string, based on bytes.
LEN	Returns the number of displayed characters in an entry, and takes the form =LEN(**text**), where *text* is a number, a string enclosed in double quotation marks, or a reference to a cell. Trailing zeros are ignored, but spaces are counted. See "Using Selected Text Functions" on page 419.
LENB	Returns the number of characters in an entry, expressed in bytes, and takes the form =LENB(**text**). It is otherwise identical to the LEN function. This function is intended for use with double-byte characters.
LINEST	Calculates the statistics for a line using the least squares method to arrive at a slope that best describes the given data, and takes the form LINEST(**known_y's**, known_x's, const, stats). For arguments and usage details, see "The LINEST Function" on page 478.
LN	Returns the natural (base e) logarithm of the positive number referred to by its argument, and takes the form =LN(**number**). LN is the inverse of the EXP function.
LOG	Returns the logarithm of a positive number using a specified base, and takes the form =LOG(**number**, base). If you don't include the base argument, Excel assumes the base is 10.
LOG10	Returns the base-10 logarithm of a number, and takes the form =LOG10(**number**), where *number* is a positive real number.
LOGEST	Returns statistics describing known data in terms of an exponential curve, and takes the form =LOGEST(**known_y's**, known_x's, const, stats). For arguments and usage details, see "The LOGEST Function" on page 483.

Function	Description
LOGINV	Returns the inverse of the lognormal cumulative distribution function of x, where ln(x) is normally distributed with parameters mean and standard_dev, and takes the form =LOGINV(**probability, mean, standard_dev**), where *probability* is a probability associated with the lognormal distribution; *mean* is the mean of ln(x); and *standard_dev* is the standard deviation of ln(x).
LOGNORMDIST	Returns the cumulative lognormal distribution of x, where ln(x) is normally distributed with parameters *mean* and *standard_dev*. This function takes the form =LOGNORMDIST(x, **mean, standard_dev**), where *x* is the value at which to evaluate the function; *mean* is the mean of ln(x); and *standard_dev* is the standard deviation of ln(x).
LOOKUP	Looks for a specified value in a one- or two-dimensional range, and takes two forms, *vector* or *array*: =LOOKUP(**lookup_value, lookup_vector, result_vector**) =LOOKUP(**lookup_value, array**) where *lookup_value* is the value to look for; *lookup_vector* is a one-row or one-column range containing the lookup values sorted in alphabetical order; *result_vector* is a range that contains the result values and must be identical in size to *lookup_vector;* and *array* is a two-dimensional range containing both lookup and result values. The array form of this function works like HLOOKUP if *array* is wider than it is tall, and works like VLOOKUP if *array* is taller than it is wide. See "Using Selected Lookup and Reference Functions" on page 411.
LOWER	Converts a text string to all lowercase letters, and takes the form =LOWER(**text**). See "Using Selected Text Functions" on page 419.
MATCH	Returns the position in a list of the item that most closely matches a lookup value, and takes the form =MATCH(**lookup_value, lookup_array, match_type**), where *lookup_value* is the value or string to look up; *lookup_array* is the range that contains the sorted values to compare; and *match_type* defines the rules for the search (if 1 or omitted, finds in a range sorted in ascending order, the largest value that is less than or equal to *lookup_value;* if 0, finds the smallest value that is equal to lookup_value; if –1, finds in a range sorted in descending order, the smallest value that is greater than or equal to *lookup_value*). See "Using Selected Lookup and Reference Functions" on page 411.
MAX	Returns the largest value in a range, takes the form =MAX(**number1, number2,...**), and can accept up to 30 arguments, ignoring text, error values, and logical values. See "Using Built-In Statistical Functions" on page 472.
MAXA	Same as MAX, except that text and logical values are included in the calculation. See "Using Built-In Statistical Functions" on page 472.
MDETERM	Returns the matrix determinant of an array, and takes the form =MDETERM(**array**), where *array* is a numeric array with an equal number of rows and columns.

Function	Description
MDURATION	Calculates the annual modified duration for a security with interest payments made on a periodic basis, adjusted for market yield per number of coupon payments per year, and takes the form =MDURATION(**settlement, maturity, coupon, yield, frequency**, basis), where *settlement* is the day you pay for the security; *maturity* is the maturity date of the security; *coupon* is the security's annual coupon rate; *yield* is the annual yield of the security; *frequency* is the number of coupon payments made per year (1 = annual; 2 = semiannual; 4 = quarterly); and *basis* is the day-count basis of the security (if 0 or omitted = 30/360; if 1 = actual/actual; if 2 = actual/360; if 3 = actual/365; if 4 = European 30/360). See "Analyzing Securities" on page 465.
MEDIAN	Computes the median of a set of numbers, takes the form =MEDIAN(**number1**, number2,...), and can accept up to 30 arguments, ignoring text, error values, and logical values. See "Using Built-In Statistical Functions" on page 472.
MID	Extracts a series of characters (substring) from a text string, and takes the form =MID(**text, start_num, num_chars**), where *text* is the string from which you want to extract the substring; *start_num* is the location in the string where the substring begins (counting from the left); and *num_chars* is the number of characters you want to extract. See "Using the Substring Text Functions" on page 422.
MIDB	Extracts a series of characters (substring) from a text string, based on the number of bytes you specify, and takes the form =MID(**text, start_num, num_bytes**), where *text* is the string from which you want to extract the substring; *start_num* is the location in the string where the substring begins (counting from the left); and *num_bytes* is the number of characters you want to extract, in bytes. This function is for use with double-byte characters.
MIN	Returns the smallest value in a range, takes the form =MIN(**number1**, number2,...), and can accept up to 30 arguments, ignoring text, error values, and logical values. See "Using Built-In Statistical Functions" on page 472.
MINA	Same as MIN, except that text and logical values are included in the calculation. See "Using Built-In Statistical Functions" on page 472.
MINUTE	Returns the minute portion of a serial date/time value, and takes the form =MINUTE(**serial_number**), where *serial_number* can be a time/date value, a reference, or text in time/date format enclosed in quotation marks. See "Working with Date and Time Functions" on page 449.
MINVERSE	Returns the inverse matrix for the matrix stored in an array, and takes the form =MINVERSE(**array**), where *array* is a numeric array with an equal number of rows and columns.
MIRR	Calculates the rate of return of an investment, taking into account the cost of borrowed money and assuming resulting cash inflows are reinvested, and takes the form =MIRR(**values, finance rate, reinvestment rate**), where *values* is an array or a reference to a range of cells that contain numbers beginning with the cost expressed as a negative value, *finance rate* is the rate at which you borrow money, and *reinvestment rate* is the rate at which you reinvest the returns. See "Calculating Investments" on page 455.

Function	Description
MMULT	Returns the matrix product of two arrays (resulting in an array with the same number of rows as *array1* and the same number of columns as *array2*), and takes the form =MMULT(**array1, array2**).
MOD	Returns the remainder of a division operation (modulus), and takes the form =MOD(**number, divisor**). If *number* is smaller than *divisor*, the result of the function equals *number*. If *number* is exactly divisible by *divisor*, the function returns 0. If *divisor* is 0, MOD returns the #DIV/0! error value. See "Using Selected Mathematical Functions" on page 414.
MODE	Determines which value occurs most frequently in a set of numbers, takes the form =MODE(**number1**, number2,...), and can accept up to 30 arguments, ignoring text, error values, and logical values. See "Using Built-In Statistical Functions" on page 472.
MONTH	Returns the value of the month portion of a serial date/time value, and takes the form =MONTH(**serial_number**), where *serial_number* can be a date value, a reference, or text in date format enclosed in quotation marks. See "Working with Date and Time Functions" on page 449.
MROUND	Rounds any number to a multiple you specify, and takes the form =MROUND(**number, multiple**), where *number* and *multiple* must both have the same sign. The function rounds up if the remainder after dividing *number* by *multiple* is at least half the value of *multiple*. See the sidebar "Using the Flexible MROUND Function" on page 418.
N	Returns a value converted to a number, and takes the form =N(**value**), where *value* is the value you want converted. This function is included for compatibility with other spreadsheet programs, but is not necessary in Excel.
NA	An alternative representation of the error value #N/A, which accepts no arguments, and takes the form =NA( ).
NEGBINOMDIST	Returns the negative binomial distribution (the probability that there will be *number_f* failures before the *number_s*-th success, when the constant probability of a success is *probability_s*), and takes the form =NEGBINOMDIST(**number_f, number_s, probability_s**), where *number_f* is the number of failures; *number_s* is the threshold number of successes; and *probability_s* is the probability of a success.
NETWORKDAYS	Returns the number of working days between two given dates, and takes the form =NETWORKDAYS(**start_date, days**, holidays), where *start_date* is the date you want to count from; *days* is the number of workdays before or after the start date, excluding weekends and holidays; and *holidays* is an array or reference containing any dates you want to exclude. See "Working with Specialized Date Functions" on page 451.
NOMINAL	Returns the nominal annual interest rate, and takes the form =NOMINAL(**effect_rate, npery**), where *effect_rate* is the effective interest rate and *npery* is the number of compounding periods per year.

Function	Description
NORMDIST	Returns the normal cumulative distribution for the specified mean and standard deviation, and takes the form =NORMDIST(**x, mean, standard_dev, cumulative**), where *x* is the value for which you want the distribution, *mean* is the arithmetic mean of the distribution; *standard_dev* is the standard deviation of the distribution; and *cumulative* is a logical value that determines the form of the function (if TRUE, returns the cumulative distribution function; if FALSE, returns the probability mass function).
NORMINV	Returns the inverse of the normal cumulative distribution for the specified mean and standard deviation, and takes the form =NORMINV(**probability, mean, standard_dev**), where *probability* is a probability corresponding to the normal distribution; *mean* is the arithmetic mean of the distribution; and *standard_dev* is the standard deviation of the distribution.
NORMSDIST	Returns the standard normal cumulative distribution function, and takes the form =NORMSDIST(**z**).
NORMSINV	Returns the inverse of the standard normal cumulative distribution (with a mean of zero and a standard deviation of one), and takes the form =NORMSINV(**probability**), where *probability* is a probability corresponding to the normal distribution.
NOT	Helps develop compound conditional test formulas in conjunction with the simple logical operators: =, >, <, >=, <=, and <>. The NOT function has only one argument, and takes the form =NOT(**logical**), where *logical* can be a conditional test, an array, or a reference to a cell containing a logical value. See "Using Selected Logical Functions" on page 424.
NOW	Returns the serial value of the current date and time, takes the form =NOW( ), and accepts no arguments. See "Working with Date and Time Functions" on page 449.
NPER	Computes the number of periods required to amortize a loan, given a specified periodic payment, and takes the form =NPER(**rate, payment, present value**, future value, type), where *rate* is the interest rate; *payment* is the amount of each periodic payment when individual amounts are the same; *present value* is the investment value today; *future value* is the investment value at the end of the term; and *type* indicates when payments are made (0 or omitted = at end of period; 1 = at beginning of period). See "Calculating Investments" on page 455.
NPV	Determines the profitability of an investment, and takes the form =NPV(**rate, value1**, value2,...), where *rate* is the interest rate and *values* represent up to 29 payments (or any size array) when individual amounts differ. See "Calculating Investments" on page 455.
OCT2BIN	Converts an octal number to binary, and takes the form =OCT2BIN(**number**, places), where *number* is the octal number you want to convert, and *places* is the number of characters to use (if omitted, uses the minimum number of characters necessary).
OCT2DEC	Converts an octal number to decimal, and takes the form =OCT2DEC(**number**), where *number* is the octal number you want to convert.

Function	Description
OCT2HEX	Converts an octal number to hexadecimal, and takes the form =OCT2HEX(**number**, places), where *number* is the octal number you want to convert and *places* is the number of characters to use (if omitted, uses the minimum number of characters necessary).
ODD	Rounds a number up to the nearest odd integer, and takes the form =ODD(**number**). Negative numbers are correspondingly rounded down. See "Using the Rounding Functions" on page 417.
ODDFPRICE	Returns the price per $100 of face value for a security having an odd first period, and takes the form =ODDFPRICE(**settlement, maturity, issue, first coupon, rate, yield, redemption, frequency**, basis), where *settlement* is the day you pay for the security; *maturity* is the maturity date of the security; *issue* is the issue date of the security; *first coupon* is the security's first coupon due date as a serial date value; *rate* is the interest rate of the security at the issue date; *yield* is the annual yield of the security; *redemption* is the value of the security at redemption; *frequency* is the number of coupon payments made per year (1 = annual; 2 = semiannual; 4 = quarterly); and *basis* is the day-count basis of the security (if 0 or omitted = 30/360; if 1 = actual/actual; if 2 = actual/360; if 3 = actual/365; if 4 = European 30/360).
ODDFYIELD	Calculates the yield of a security that has an odd first period, and takes the form =ODDFYIELD(**settlement, maturity, issue, first coupon, rate, price, redemption, frequency**, basis), where *price* is the security's price. See ODDFPRICE for additional argument definitions.
ODDLPRICE	Calculates the price per $100 face value of a security having an odd last coupon period, and takes the form =ODDLPRICE(**settlement, maturity, last interest, rate, yield, redemption, frequency**, basis), where *last interest* is the security's last coupon due date as a serial date value. See ODDFPRICE for additional argument definitions.
ODDLYIELD	Calculates the yield of a security that has an odd last period, and takes the form =ODDLYIELD(**settlement, maturity, last interest, rate, price, redemption, frequency**, basis), where *last interest* is the security's last coupon due date and *price* is the security's price. See ODDFPRICE for additional argument definitions.
OFFSET	Returns a reference of a specified height and width, located at a specified position relative to another specified reference, and takes the form =OFFSET(**reference, rows, cols**, height, width), where *reference* specifies the position from which the offset is calculated; *rows* and *cols* specify the vertical and horizontal distance from *reference*; and *height* and *width* specify the shape of the reference returned by the function. The *rows* and *cols* arguments can be positive or negative: positive values specify offsets below and to the right of *reference*; negative values specify offsets above and to the left of *reference*.
OR	Helps develop compound conditional test formulas in conjunction with logical operators, and takes the form =OR(**logical1**, logical2,...), where *logicals* can be up to 30 conditional tests, arrays, or references to cells that contain logical values. See "Using Selected Logical Functions" on page 424.

970

Function	Description
PEARSON	Returns the Pearson product moment correlation coefficient, *r*, a dimensionless index that ranges from –1 to 1 (inclusive) and reflects the extent of a linear relationship between two data sets. This function takes the form =PEARSON(**array1, array2**), where *array1* is a set of independent values and *array2* is a set of dependent values.
PERCENTILE	Returns the member of an input range that is at a specified percentile ranking, and takes the form =PERCENTILE(**array, k**), where *array* is the input range and *k* is the rank you want to find. See "Using Functions That Analyze Rank and Percentile" on page 473.
PERCENTRANK	Returns a percentile ranking for any member of a data set, and takes the form =PERCENTRANK(**array, x**, significance), where *array* specifies the input range; *x* specifies the value whose rank you want to obtain; and the optional *significance* indicates the number of digits of precision you want. If *significance* is omitted, results are rounded to three digits (0.xxx or xx.x%). See "Using Functions That Analyze Rank and Percentile" on page 473.
PERMUT	Returns the number of permutations for a given number of objects that can be selected from number objects, and takes the form =PERMUT(**number, number_chosen**), where *number* is an integer that describes the number of objects, and *number_chosen* is an integer that describes the number of objects in each permutation.
PI	Returns the value of pi, accurate to 14 decimal places: 3.14159265358979, and takes the form =PI( ). It takes no arguments, but you must still enter empty parentheses after the function name. To calculate the area of a circle, multiply the square of the circle's radius by the PI function.
PMT	Computes the periodic payment required to amortize a loan over a specified number of periods, and takes the form =PMT(**rate, nper, pv**, fv, type), where *rate* is the interest rate, *nper* is the term (periods) of the investment; *pv* is the investment value today; *fv* is the investment value at the end of the term; and *type* indicates when payments are made (0 or omitted = at end of period; 1 = at beginning of period). See "Calculating Investments" on page 455.
POISSON	Returns the Poisson distribution, and takes the form =POISSON(**x, mean, cumulative**), where *x* is the number of events; *mean* is the expected numeric value; and *cumulative* is a logical value that determines the form of the probability distribution returned (if TRUE, returns the cumulative Poisson probability that the number of random events occurring will be between *zero* and *x* inclusive; if FALSE, returns the Poisson probability mass function that the number of events occurring will be exactly *x*).
POWER	Returns the result of a number raised to a power, and takes the form =POWER(**number, power**), where *number* is the base number and *power* is the exponent to which the base number is raised.

Function	Description
PPMT	Computes the principal component of an individual payment made to repay a loan over a specified time period with constant periodic payments and a constant interest rate, and takes the form =PPMT(**rate, period, nper, pv,** fv, type), where *rate* is the interest rate; *period* is the number of an individual periodic payment; *nper* is the term (periods) of the investment; *pv* is the investment value today; *fv* is the investment value at the end of the term; and *type* indicates when payments are made (0 or omitted = at end of period; 1 = at beginning of period). See "Calculating Investments" on page 455.
PRICE	Calculates the price per $100 of a security that pays periodic interest, and takes the form =PRICE(**settlement, maturity, rate, yield, redemption, frequency,** basis), where *settlement* is the day you pay for the security; *maturity* is the maturity date of the security; *rate* is the interest rate of the security at the issue date; *yield* is the annual yield of the security; *redemption* is the value of the security at redemption, *frequency* is the number of coupon payments made per year (1 = annual; 2 = semiannual; 4 = quarterly); and *basis* is the day-count basis of the security (if 0 or omitted = 30/360; if 1 = actual/actual; if 2 = actual/360; if 3 = actual/365; if 4 = European 30/360). See "Analyzing Securities" on page 465.
PRICEDISC	Returns the price per $100 of a discounted security, and takes the form =PRICEDISC(**settlement, maturity, discount, redemption,** basis), where *settlement* is the day you pay for the security; *maturity* is the maturity date of the security; *discount* is the security's discount rate; *redemption* is the value of the security at redemption; and *basis* is the day-count basis of the security (if 0 or omitted = 30/360; if 1 = actual/actual; if 2 = actual/360; if 3 = actual/365; if 4 = European 30/360). See "Analyzing Securities" on page 465.
PRICEMAT	Returns the price per $100 of a security that pays interest at maturity, and takes the form =PRICEMAT(**settlement, maturity, issue, rate, yield,** basis), where *settlement* is the day you pay for the security; *maturity* is the maturity date of the security; *issue* is the issue date of the security; *rate* is the interest rate of the security at the issue date; *yield* is the annual yield of the security; and *basis* is the day-count basis of the security (if 0 or omitted = 30/360; if 1 = actual/actual; if 2 = actual/360; if 3 = actual/365; if 4 = European 30/360). See "Analyzing Securities" on page 465.
PROB	Returns the probability that values in a range are between two limits, and takes the form =PROB(**x_range, prob_range, lower_limit,** upper_limit), where *x_range* is the range of numeric values of x with which there are associated probabilities; *prob_range* is a set of probabilities associated with values in *x_range*; *lower_limit* is the lower bound on the value for which you want a probability; and *upper_limit* is the optional upper bound on the value for which you want a probability.
PRODUCT	Multiplies all the numbers referenced by its arguments, takes the form =PRODUCT(**number1,number2,...**), and can take as many as 30 arguments. Text, logical values, and blank cells are ignored. See "Using Selected Mathematical Functions" on page 414.

Function	Description
PROPER	Capitalizes the first letter in each word and any other letters in a text string that do not follow another letter—all other letters are converted to lowercase—and takes the form =PROPER(**text**). See "Using Selected Text Functions" on page 419.
PV	Computes the present value of a series of equal periodic payments, or a lump-sum payment, and takes the form =PV(**rate, nper, payment**, future value, type), where *rate* is the interest rate; *nper* is the term (periods) of the investment; *payment* is the amount of each periodic payment when individual amounts are the same; *future value* is the investment value at the end of the term; and *type* indicates when payments are made (0 or omitted = at end of period; 1 = at beginning of period). See "Calculating Investments" on page 455.
QUARTILE	Returns the value in an input range that represents a specified quarter-percentile, and takes the form =QUARTILE(**array, quart**). For usage and argument details, see "The PERCENTILE and QUARTILE Functions" on page 474.
QUOTIENT	Returns the integer portion of a division, and takes the form =QUOTIENT(numerator, denominator), where *numerator* is the dividend and *denominator* is the divisor.
RADIANS	Converts degrees to radians, and takes the form =RADIANS(**angle**),where *angle* represents an angle measured in degrees.
RAND	Generates a random number between 0 and 1, and takes the form =RAND() with no arguments, but you must still enter empty parentheses after the function name. The result changes with each sheet recalculation. See "Using Selected Mathematical Functions" on page 414.
RANDBETWEEN	Generates random integer values between a specified range of numbers, and takes the form =RANDBETWEEN(**bottom, top**), where *bottom* is the smallest and *top* is the largest integer you want to use, inclusive. See "Using Selected Mathematical Functions" on page 414.
RANK	Returns the ranked position of a particular number within a set of numbers, and takes the form =RANK(**number, ref**, order). For usage and argument details, see "The RANK Function" on page 475.
RATE	Calculates the rate of return of an investment that generates a series of equal periodic payments or a single lump-sum payment, and takes the form =RATE(**nper, payment, present value**, future value, type, guess), where *nper* is the term (periods) of the investment; *payment* is the amount of each periodic payment when individual amounts are the same; *present value* is the investment value today; *future value* is the investment value at the end of the term; *type* indicates when payments are made (0 or omitted = at end of period; 1 = at beginning of period); and *guess* is an approximate interest rate (assumes 10% if omitted). See "Calculating Investments" on page 455.
RECEIVED	Calculates the amount received at maturity for a fully invested security, and takes the form =RECEIVED(**settlement, maturity, investment, discount**, basis), where *settlement* is the day you pay for the security; *maturity* is the maturity date of the security, *investment* is the amount invested in the security; *discount* is the security's discount rate; and *basis* is the day-count basis of the security (if 0 or omitted = 30/360; if 1 = actual/actual; if 2 = actual/360; if 3 = actual/365; if 4 = European 30/360). See "Analyzing Securities" on page 465.

Function	Description
REPLACE	Substitutes one string of characters with another string, and takes the form =REPLACE(**old_text, start_num, num_chars, new_text**), where *old_text* is the text string in which you want to replace characters; *start_num* specifies the starting character to replace; *num_chars* specifies the number of characters to replace (counting from the left); and *new_text* specifies the text string to insert. See "Using the Substring Text Functions" on page 422.
REPLACEB	Substitutes one string of characters with another string, and takes the form =REPLACEB(**old_text, start_num, num_bytes, new_text**), where *old_text* is the text string in which you want to replace characters; *start_num* specifies the starting character to replace; *num_bytes* specifies the number of bytes to replace; and *new_text* specifies the text string to insert. This function is for use with double-byte characters.
REPT	Fills a cell with a string of characters repeated a specified number of times, and takes the form =REPT(**text,number_times**), where *text* specifies a string in double quotation marks and *number_times* specifies how many times to repeat *text*, up to 255.
RIGHT	Returns the rightmost series of characters from a string, and takes the form =RIGHT(**text**, num_chars), where *num_chars* indicates how many characters you want to extract from the string (1, if omitted). Blank spaces count as characters. See "Using the Substring Text Functions" on page 422.
RIGHTB	Returns the rightmost series of characters from a string, based on the number of bytes you specify, and takes the form =RIGHTB(**text,** num_bytes), where *num_bytes* indicates how many characters you want to extract from the string, based on bytes. This function is for use with double-byte characters.
ROMAN	Converts an Arabic numeral to Roman numerals, as text, and takes the form =ROMAN(**number**, form), where *number* is the Arabic numeral you want converted and *form* is a number specifying the type of Roman numeral you want (1, 2, or 3 = more concise notation; 4 or FALSE = simplified notation; TRUE = classic notation).
ROUND	Rounds numbers to a specified number of decimal places, and takes the form =ROUND(**number, num_digits**), where *number* can be a number, a reference to a cell that contains a number, or a formula that results in a number. *num_digits* can be any positive or negative integer and determines the number of decimal places. Enter a negative *num_digits* to round to the left of the decimal; enter zero to round to the nearest integer. See "Using the Rounding Functions" on page 417.
ROUNDDOWN	Rounds numbers down to a specified number of decimal places and takes the same form and arguments as ROUND. See "Using the Rounding Functions" on page 417.
ROUNDUP	Rounds numbers up to a specified number of decimal places, and takes the same form and arguments as ROUND. See "Using the Rounding Functions" on page 417.

Function	Description
ROW	Returns the row number of the referenced cell or range, and takes the form =ROW(reference). If *reference* is omitted, the result is the row number of the cell containing the function. If *reference* is a range or a name and the function is entered as an array (by pressing Ctrl+Shift+Enter), the result is an array of the numbers of each of the rows or columns in the range. See "Using Selected Lookup and Reference Functions" on page 411.
ROWS	Returns the number of rows in a reference or an array, and takes the form =ROWS(**array**), where *array* is an array constant, a range reference, or a range name. See "Using Selected Lookup and Reference Functions" on page 411.
RSQ	Returns the square of the Pearson product moment correlation coefficient through data points in the arrays *known_y's* and *known_x's*, and takes the form =RSQ(**known_y's, known_x's**).
RTD	Returns real-time data from a program that supports COM automation, and takes the form =RTD(**progID**, server, topic1, topic2...), where *progID* is the program identifier (enclosed in quotation marks) for a registered COM automation add-in that has been installed on the local computer, *server* is the name of the server where the add-in should be run (if other than the local computer), and *topics* are up to 28 parameters describing the real-time data you want.
SEARCH	Returns the position of specified text within a string, and takes the form =SEARCH(**find_text, within_text**, start_num), where *find_text* is the text you want to find, *within_text* indicates where to look, *start_num* specifies the character position in *within_text* where you want to begin the search. See "Using the Substring Text Functions" on page 422.
SEARCHB	Returns the position of specified text within a string, expressed in bytes, and takes the form =SEARCHB(**find_text, within_text**, start_num), and is otherwise identical to SEARCH.
SECOND	Returns the seconds portion of a serial date/time value, and takes the form =SECOND(**serial_number**), where *serial_number* can be a time/date value, a reference, or text in time/date format enclosed in quotation marks. See "Working with Date and Time Functions" on page 449.
SERIESSUM	Returns the sum of a power series, and takes the form =SERIESSUM(**x, n, m, coefficients**), where *x* is the input value to the power series; *n* is the initial power to which you want to raise *x*; *m* is the step by which to increase *n* for each term in the series; and *coefficients* is a set of coefficients by which each successive power of *x* is multiplied. The number of values in coefficients determines the number of terms in the power series.
SIGN	Determines the sign of a number. Returns 1 if the number is positive, zero (0) if the number is 0, and –1 if the number is negative, and takes the form =SIGN(**number**), where *number* is any real number.
SIN	Returns the sine of an angle. The complement of the COS function, it takes the form =SIN(**number**), where *number* is the angle in radians.
SINH	Returns the hyperbolic sine of a number, and takes the form =SINH(**number**), where *number* is any real number.

newfeature!

Function	Description
SKEW	Returns the skew of a distribution (the degree of asymmetry of a distribution around its mean); takes the form =SKEW(**number1**, number2,...); and accepts up to 30 arguments.
SLN	Returns straight-line depreciation for an asset for a single period, and takes the form =SLN(**cost, salvage, life**), where *cost* is the initial asset cost; *salvage* is the remaining value after asset is fully depreciated; and *life* is the length of depreciation time. See "Calculating Depreciation" on page 462.
SLOPE	Returns the slope of a linear regression line, and takes the form =SLOPE(**known_y's, known_x's**). For arguments and usage details, see "The SLOPE Function" on page 482.
SMALL	Returns the *k*th smallest value in an input range, and takes the form =SMALL(**array, k**), where *k* is the position from the smallest value in *array* you want to find. See "Using Functions That Analyze Rank and Percentile" on page 473.
SQRT	Returns the positive square root of a number, and takes the form =SQRT(**number**).
SQRTPI	Returns the square root of (number * pi), and takes the form =SQRTPI(**number**).
STANDARDIZE	Returns a normalized value from a distribution characterized by *mean* and *standard_dev*, and takes the form =STANDARDIZE(**x, mean, standard_dev**), where *x* is the value you want to normalize, *mean* is the arithmetic mean of the distribution, and *standard_dev* is the standard deviation of the distribution.
STDEV	Computes standard deviation, assuming that the arguments represent only a sample of the total population, and takes the form =STDEV(**number1**, number2,...), accepting up to 30 arguments. See "Using Sample and Population Statistical Functions" on page 476.
STDEVA	Same as STDEV, except that text and logical values are included in the calculation. See "Using Sample and Population Statistical Functions" on page 476.
STDEVP	Computes the standard deviation, assuming that the arguments represent the total population, and takes the form =STDEVP(**number1**, number2,...). See "Using Sample and Population Statistical Functions" on page 476.
STDEVPA	Same as STDEVP, except that text and logical values are included in the calculation. See "Using Sample and Population Statistical Functions" on page 476.
STEYX	Calculates the standard error of a regression, and takes the form =STEYX(**known_y's, known_x's**). For arguments and usage details, see "The SLOPE Function" on page 482.
SUBSTITUTE	Replaces specified text with new text within a specified string, and takes the form =SUBSTITUTE(**text,old_text,new_text**,instance_num), where *text* is the string you want to work on; *old_text* is the text to be replaced; *new_text* is the text to substitute; and *instance_num* is optional, indicating a specific occurrence of *old_text* within *text*. See "Using the Substring Text Functions" on page 422.

Function	Description
SUBTOTAL	Returns a subtotal in a list or database, and takes the form =SUBTOTAL(**function_num, ref1**, ref2,...), where *function_num* is a number that specifies which function to use in calculating subtotals (1=AVERAGE, 2=COUNT, 3=COUNTA, 4=MAX, 5=MIN, 6=PRODUCT, 7=STDEV, 8=STDEVP, 9=SUM, 10=VAR, 11=VARP), and *refs* are 1 to 29 ranges or references for which you want the subtotal.
SUM	Totals a series of numbers, and takes the form =SUM(**num1,num2...**), where *nums* (max 30) can be numbers, formulas, ranges, or cell references. Ignores arguments that refer to text values, logical values, or blank cells. See "Using the SUM Function" on page 414.
SUMIF	Tests each cell in a range before adding it to the total, and takes the form =SUMIF(**range, criteria**, sum_range), where *range* is the range you want to test; *criteria* is the logical test to be performed on each cell; and *sum_range* specifies the cells to be totaled. See "Using Built-In Statistical Functions" on page 472.
SUMPRODUCT	Multiplies the value in each cell in a specified range by the corresponding cell in another equal-sized range, and then adds the results. It takes the form =SUMPRODUCT (**array1, array2**, array3, ...) and can include up to 30 arrays. Nonnumeric entries are treated as zero. See "Using Selected Mathematical Functions" on page 414.
SUMSQ	Returns the sum of the squares of each specified value in a specified range, takes the form =**SUMSQ(number1,number2,...)**, and takes up to 30 arguments, or a single array or array reference.
SUMX2MY2	Calculates the sum of the differences of the squares of the corresponding values in *x* and *y*, and takes the form =SUMX2MY2(**array_x, array_y**), where *x* and *y* are arrays that contain the same number of elements.
SUMX2PY2	Calculates the sum of the sum of the squares of the corresponding values in *x* and *y*, and takes the form =SUMX2PY2(**array_x, array_y**), where *x* and *y* are arrays that contain the same number of elements.
SUMXMY2	Calculates the sum of the squares of the differences of the corresponding values in X and Y, and takes the form =SUMXMY2(**array_x, array_y**), where X and Y are arrays that contain the same number of elements.
SYD	Computes depreciation for a specific time period with the sum-of-the-years'-digits method, and takes the form =SYD(**cost, salvage, life, period**), where *cost* is the initial asset cost, *salvage* is the remaining value after asset is fully depreciated, *life* is the length of depreciation time, and *period* is the individual period to be computed. See "Calculating Depreciation" on page 462.
T	Returns the text referred to by value, and takes the form =T(**value**), where *value* is the value you want to test. This function is included for compatibility with other spreadsheet programs, but is not necessary in Excel.
TAN	Returns the tangent of an angle, and takes the form =TAN(**number**), where *number* is the angle in radians.
TANH	Returns the hyperbolic tangent of a number, and takes the form =TANH(**number**), where *number* is any real number.

Function	Description
TBILLEQ	Calculates the bond-equivalent yield for a Treasury bill, and takes the form =TBILLEQ(**settlement, maturity, discount**), where *settlement* is the day you pay for the security, *maturity* is the maturity date of the security, and *discount* is the discount rate of the security. See "Analyzing Securities" on page 465.
TBILLPRICE	Calculates the price per $100 of face value for a Treasury bill, and takes the form =TBILLPRICE(**settlement, maturity, discount**), where *settlement* is the day you pay for the security; *maturity* is the maturity date of the security; and *discount* is the discount rate of the security. See "Analyzing Securities" on page 465.
TBILLYIELD	Calculates a Treasury bill's yield, and takes the form =TBILLYIELD(**settlement, maturity, price**), where *settlement* is the day you pay for the security; *maturity* is the maturity date of the security; and *price* is the security's price. See "Analyzing Securities" on page 465.
TDIST	Returns the percentage points (probability) for the student t-distribution, where a numeric value (x) is a calculated value of *t* for which the percentage points are to be computed. This function takes the form =TDIST(**x, degrees_freedom, tails**), where *x* is the numeric value at which to evaluate the distribution; *degrees_freedom* is an integer indicating the number of degrees of freedom; and *tails* specifies the number of distribution tails to return (if 1, returns the one-tailed distribution; if 2, returns the two-tailed distribution).
TEXT	Converts a number into a text string using a specified format, and takes the form =TEXT(**value, format_text**), where *value* can be any number, formula, or cell reference and *format_text* specifies the format using built-in custom formatting symbols. See "Using Selected Text Functions" on page 419.
TIME	Returns the decimal number for a particular time, and takes the form =TIME(**hour, minute, second**), where *hour* is a number from 0 (zero) to 23 representing the hour; *minute* is a number from 0 to 59 representing the minute; and *second* is a number from 0 to 59 representing the second.
TIMEVALUE	Translates a time into a decimal value, and takes the form =TIMEVALUE(**time_text**), where *time_text* represents a time entered as text in quotation marks. See "Working with Date and Time Functions" on page 449.
TINV	Returns the t-value of the Student's t-distribution as a function of the probability and the degrees of freedom, and takes the form =TINV(**probability, degrees_freedom**), where *probability* is the probability associated with the two-tailed Student's t-distribution and *degrees_freedom* is the number of degrees of freedom to characterize the distribution.
TODAY	Returns the serial value of the current date, takes the form =TODAY( ), and accepts no arguments. See "Working with Date and Time Functions" on page 449.
TRANSPOSE	Changes the horizontal or vertical orientation of an array, and takes the form =TRANSPOSE(**array**). If *array* is vertical, the result is horizontal, and vice versa. Must be entered as an array formula by pressing Ctrl+Shift+Enter, with a range selected with the same proportions as *array*. See "Using Selected Lookup and Reference Functions" on page 411.

Function	Description
TREND	Returns values of points that lie along a linear trend line, and takes the form =TREND(**known_y's**, known_x's, new_x's, const). For arguments and usage details, see "The TREND Function" on page 480.
TRIM	Removes leading, trailing, and extra blank characters from a string, leaving single spaces between words, and takes the form =TRIM(text). See "Using Selected Text Functions" on page 419.
TRIMMEAN	Returns the mean of the interior of a data set (the mean taken by excluding a percentage of data points from the top and bottom tails of a data set). This function takes the form =TRIMMEAN(**array, percent**), where *array* is the array or range of values to trim and average, and *percent* is the fractional number of data points to exclude from the calculation.
TRUE	An alternative representation of the logical condition TRUE, which accepts no arguments, and takes the form =TRUE( ). See "Using Selected Logical Functions" on page 424.
TRUNC	Truncates everything to the right of the decimal point, regardless of its sign, and takes the form =TRUNC(**number**, num_digits). Truncates everything after the specified *num_digits* to the right of the decimal point. See "Using the Rounding Functions" on page 417.
TTEST	Returns the probability associated with a student's t-test, and takes the form =TTEST(**array1, array2, tails, type**), where *array1* is the first data set; *array2* is the second data set; *tails* specifies the number of distribution tails (if 1, uses the one-tailed distribution; if 2, uses the two-tailed distribution); and *type* is the kind of t-Test to perform (1 = paired: 2 = Two-sample equal variance; 3 = Two-sample unequal variance).
TYPE	Determines the type of value a cell contains, and takes the form =TYPE(**value**). The result is one of the following numeric codes: 1 (number), 2 (text), 4 (logical value), 16 (error value), or 64 (array). See "Using Selected Lookup and Reference Functions" on page 411.
UPPER	Converts a text string to all uppercase letters, and takes the form =UPPER(**text**). See "Using Selected Text Functions" on page 419.
VALUE	Converts a text string that represents a number to a number, and takes the form =VALUE(**text**), where *text* is the text enclosed in quotation marks or a reference to a cell containing the text you want to convert. This function is included for compatibility with other spreadsheet programs, but is not necessary in Excel.
VAR	Computes variance, assuming that the arguments represent only a sample of the total population, and takes the form =VAR(**number1**, number2,...), accepting up to 30 arguments. See "Using Sample and Population Statistical Functions" on page 476.
VARA	Same as VAR, except that text and logical values are included in the calculation. See "Using Sample and Population Statistical Functions" on page 476.
VARP	Computes variance, assuming that the arguments represent the total population, and takes the form =VARP(**number1**, number2,...). See "Using Sample and Population Statistical Functions" on page 476.
VARPA	Same as VARP, except that text and logical values are included in the calculation. See "Using Sample and Population Statistical Functions" on page 476.

Function	Description
VDB	Calculates depreciation for any complete or partial period, using either double-declining balance or a specified accelerated-depreciation factor, and takes the form =VDB(**cost, salvage, life, start_period, end_period,** factor, no_switch), where *cost* is the initial asset cost; *salvage* is the remaining value after asset is fully depreciated; *life* is the length of depreciation time; *start_period* is the period number after which depreciation begins; *end_period* is the last period calculated; *factor* is the rate at which the balance declines; and *no_switch* turns off the default switch to straight-line depreciation when it becomes greater than the declining balance. See "Calculating Depreciation" on page 462.
VLOOKUP	Looks for a specified value in the leftmost column in a table, returns the value in the same row and a specified column, and takes the form =VLOOKUP(**lookup_value, table_array, col_index_num**, range_lookup), where *lookup_value* is the value to look for; *table_array* is the range containing the lookup and result values sorted in alphabetical order by the leftmost column; *col_index_num* is the column number containing the value you want to find; and *range_lookup* is a logical which, if FALSE, forces an exact match. See "Using Selected Lookup and Reference Functions" on page 411.
WEEKDAY	Returns a number value representing the day of the week for a specified date, and takes the form =WEEKDAY(**serial_number**, return_type), where *serial_number* is a date value, a reference, or text in date form enclosed in quotation marks; and *return_type* determines the way the result is represented (if 1 or omitted, Sunday is day 1; if 2, Monday is day 1; if 3, Monday is day 0). See "Working with Date and Time Functions" on page 449.
WEEKNUM	Returns a number that indicates where the week falls numerically within a year, and takes the form =WEEKNUM(**serial_num**, return_type), where *serial_num* is a date within the week, and *return_type* is a number that determines the day on which the week begins (1 or omitted = week begins on Sunday; 2 = week begins on Monday).
WEIBULL	Returns the Weibull distribution, and takes the form =WEIBULL(**x, alpha, beta, cumulative**), where *x* is the value at which to evaluate the function; *alpha* is a parameter to the distribution; *beta* is a parameter to the distribution; and *cumulative* determines the form of the function.
WORKDAY	Returns a date that is a specified number of working days before or after a given date, and takes the form =WORKDAY(**start_date, days**, holidays), where *start_date* is the date you want to count from; *days* is the number of workdays before or after the start date, excluding weekends and holidays; and *holidays* is an array or reference containing any dates you want to exclude. See "Working with Specialized Date Functions" on page 451.
XIRR	Returns the internal rate of return for a schedule of cash flows that is not necessarily periodic, and takes the form =XIRR(**values, dates**, guess), where *values* is a series of cash flows that corresponds to a schedule of payments in dates; *dates* is a schedule of payment dates that corresponds to the cash flow payments; and *guess* is a number that you think is close to the result.

Function	Description
XNPV	Returns the net present value for a schedule of cash flows that is not necessarily periodic, and takes the form =XNPV(**rate, values, dates**), where *rate* is the discount rate to apply to the cash flows; *values* is a series of cash flows that corresponds to a schedule of payments in dates; and *dates* is a schedule of payment dates that corresponds to the cash flow payments.
YEAR	Returns the value of the year portion of a serial date/time value, and takes the form =YEAR(**serial_number**), where *serial_number* can be a date value, a reference, or text in date format enclosed in quotation marks. See "Working with Date and Time Functions" on page 449.
YEARFRAC	Returns a decimal number that represents the portion of a year that falls between two given dates, and takes the form =YEARFRAC(**start_date, end_date**, basis), where *start_date* and *end_date* specify the span you want to convert to a decimal; and *basis* is the type of day count (0 or omitted = 30/360; 1 = actual/actual; 2 = actual/360; 3 = actual/365; 4 = European 30/360). See "Working with Specialized Date Functions" on page 451.
YIELD	Determines the annual yield for a security that pays interest on a periodic basis, and takes the form =YIELD(**settlement, maturity, rate, price, redemption, frequency**, basis), where *settlement* is the day you pay for the security; *maturity* is the maturity date of the security; *rate* is the interest rate of the security at the issue date; *price* is the security's price; *redemption* is the value of the security at redemption; *frequency* is the number of coupon payments made per year (1 = annual; 2 = semiannual; 4 = quarterly); and *basis* is the day-count basis of the security (if 0 or omitted = 30/360; if 1 = actual/actual; if 2 = actual/360; if 3 = actual/365; if 4 = European 30/360). See "Analyzing Securities" on page 465.
YIELDDISC	Calculates the annual yield for a discounted security, and takes the form =YIELDDISC(**settlement, maturity, price, redemption**, basis), where *settlement* is the day you pay for the security; *maturity* is the maturity date of the security; *price* is the security's price; *redemption* is the value of the security at redemption; and *basis* is the day-count basis of the security (if 0 or omitted = 30/360; if 1 = actual/actual; if 2 = actual/360; if 3 = actual/365; if 4 = European 30/360). See "Analyzing Securities" on page 465.
YIELDMAT	Calculates the annual yield for a security that pays its interest at maturity, and takes the form =YIELDMAT(**settlement, maturity, issue, rate, price**, basis), where *settlement* is the day you pay for the security; *maturity* is the maturity date of the security, *issue* is the issue date of the security; *rate* is the interest rate of the security at the issue date; *price* is the security's price; and *basis* is the day-count basis of the security (if 0 or omitted = 30/360; if 1 = actual/actual; if 2 = actual/360; if 3 = actual/365; if 4 = European 30/360). See "Analyzing Securities" on page 465.
ZTEST	Returns the two-tailed P-value of a z-test (generates a standard score for *x* with respect to the data set, *array*, and returns the two-tailed probability for the normal distribution). This function takes the form =ZTEST(**array, x**, sigma), where *array* is the array or range of data against which to test *x*; *x* is the value to test; and *sigma* is the known population's standard deviation.

Index to Troubleshooting Topics

L
M
O
P
Q
R
S
T
U
V
W

Index

S

About the Authors

Craig Stinson, an industry journalist since 1981, is a contributing editor of *PC Magazine* and was editor of *Softalk for the IBM Personal Computer*, one of the earliest machine-specific computer magazines. He is author or coauthor of more than fifteen Microsoft Press books on Microsoft Windows and Excel. Craig lives with his wife and kids in Bloomington, Indiana.

Mark Dodge was still a professional musician in 1982 when he bought his first "computer," a tiny Timex-Sinclair ZX-1000. Within two years, he was off the road and using a Compaq luggable on a daily basis running spreadsheets in a corporate accounting office. Three years later, Mark began working for Microsoft Press, and over the past 14 years has coauthored eight editions of Windows and Macintosh books on Microsoft Excel. He was the technical editor for a dozen Microsoft Press titles, served as a staff senior technical writer for the Microsoft Office User Education group, and received five awards from the Society for Technical Communication for writing and editing. Mark and his wife Vicki work out of their combined offices and art/recording studios overlooking beautiful Puget Sound.

The manuscript for this book was prepared and galleyed using Microsoft Word 2000. Pages were composed by Microsoft Press using Adobe PageMaker 6.52, with text in Minion and display type in Syntax. Composed pages were delivered to the printer as electronic prepress files.

interiorgraphicdesigner
James D. Kramer

coverdesigner
Girvin/Strategic Branding & Design

coverillustration
Daman Studio

principalcompositor
ProImage

indexer
Sherry Massey

Get a **Free**
*e-mail newsletter, updates,
special offers, links to related books,
and more when you*

register on line!

Register your Microsoft Press® title on our Web site and you'll get a FREE subscription to our e-mail newsletter, *Microsoft Press Book Connections.* You'll find out about newly released and upcoming books and learning tools, online events, software downloads, special offers and coupons for Microsoft Press customers, and information about major Microsoft® product releases. You can also read useful additional information about all the titles we publish, such as detailed book descriptions, tables of contents and indexes, sample chapters, links to related books and book series, author biographies, and reviews by other customers.

Registration is easy. Just visit this Web page and fill in your information:

http://www.microsoft.com/mspress/register

Microsoft

Work smarter
as you experience
Office XP
inside out!

You know your way around the Office suite. Now dig into Microsoft Office XP applications and *really* put your PC to work! These supremely organized references pack hundreds of timesaving solutions, trouble-shooting tips and tricks, and handy workarounds in concise, fast-answer format. All of this comprehensive information goes deep into the nooks and crannies of each Office application and accessory. Discover the best and fastest ways to perform everyday tasks, and challenge yourself to new levels of Office mastery with INSIDE OUT titles!

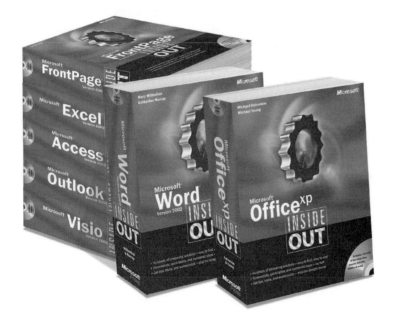

- MICROSOFT® OFFICE XP INSIDE OUT
- MICROSOFT WORD VERSION 2002 INSIDE OUT
- MICROSOFT EXCEL VERSION 2002 INSIDE OUT
- MICROSOFT OUTLOOK® VERSION 2002 INSIDE OUT
- MICROSOFT ACCESS VERSION 2002 INSIDE OUT
- MICROSOFT FRONTPAGE® VERSION 2002 INSIDE OUT
- MICROSOFT VISIO® VERSION 2002 INSIDE OUT

Microsoft®

mspress.microsoft.com

Target your
solution *and fix it*
yourself—fast!

When you're stuck with a computer problem, you need answers right now. *Troubleshooting* books can help. They'll guide you to the source of the problem and show you how to solve it right away. Use easy diagnostic flowcharts to identify problems. Get ready solutions with clear, step-by-step instructions. Go to quick-access charts with *Top 20 Problems* and *Prevention Tips*. Find even more solutions with handy *Tips* and *Quick Fixes*. Walk through the remedy with plenty of screen shots to keep you on track. Find what you need fast with the extensive, easy-reference index. And keep trouble at bay with the Troubleshooting Web site—updated every month with new FREE problem-solving information. Get the answers you need to get back to business fast with *Troubleshooting* books.

Troubleshooting Microsoft® Access Databases
(Covers Access 97 and Access 2000)
ISBN 0-7356-1160-2
U.S.A. $19.99
U.K.   £14.99
Canada $28.99

Troubleshooting Microsoft Excel Spreadsheets
(Covers Excel 97 and Excel 2000)
ISBN 0-7356-1161-0
U.S.A. $19.99
U.K.   £14.99
Canada $28.99

Troubleshooting Microsoft® Outlook®
(Covers Microsoft Outlook 2000 and Outlook Express)
ISBN 0-7356-1162-9
U.S.A. $19.99
U.K.   £14.99
Canada $28.99

Troubleshooting Microsoft Windows®
(Covers Windows Me, Windows 98, and Windows 95)
ISBN 0-7356-1166-1
U.S.A. $19.99
U.K.   £14.99
Canada $28.99

Troubleshooting Microsoft Windows 2000 Professional
ISBN 0-7356-1165-3
U.S.A. $19.99
U.K.   £14.99
Canada $28.99

Troubleshooting Your Web Page
(Covers Microsoft FrontPage® 2000)
ISBN 0-7356-1164-5
U.S.A. $19.99
U.K.   £14.99
Canada $28.99

Troubleshooting Your PC
ISBN 0-7356-1163-7
U.S.A. $19.99
U.K.   £14.99
Canada $28.99

Microsoft Press® products are available worldwide wherever quality computer books are sold. For more information, contact your book or computer retailer, software reseller, or local Microsoft Sales Office, or visit our Web site at mspress.microsoft.com. To locate your nearest source for Microsoft Press products, or to order directly, call 1-800-MSPRESS in the U.S. (in Canada, call 1-800-268-2222).

Prices and availability dates are subject to change.

Microsoft®

mspress.microsoft.com